Exploring Innovative and Successful Applications of Soft Computing

Antonio D. Masegosa
Universidad de Granada, Spain

Pablo J. Villacorta
Universidad de Granada, Spain

Carlos Cruz-Corona
Universidad de Granada, Spain

M. Socorro García-Cascales
Universidad Politécnica de Cartagena, Spain

María T. Lamata
Universidad de Granada, Spain

José L. Verdegay
Universidad de Granada, Spain

A volume in the Advances in
Computational Intelligence and Robotics
(ACIR) Book Series

Managing Director:	Lindsay Johnston
Production Manager:	Jennifer Yoder
Publishing Systems Analyst:	Adrienne Freeland
Development Editor:	Allyson Gard
Acquisitions Editor:	Kayla Wolfe
Typesetter:	John Crodian
Cover Design:	Jason Mull

Published in the United States of America by
Information Science Reference (an imprint of IGI Global)
701 E. Chocolate Avenue
Hershey PA 17033
Tel: 717-533-8845
Fax: 717-533-8661
E-mail: cust@igi-global.com
Web site: http://www.igi-global.com

Library of Congress Cataloging-in-Publication Data

Exploring innovative and successful applications of soft computing / Antonio D. Masegosa, Pablo J. Villacorta, Carlos Cruz-Corona, M.Socorro Garcia-Cascales, Maria T. Lamata and Jose L. Verdegay, editors.
    pages cm
 Includes bibliographical references and index.
 Summary: "This book highlights the applications and conclusions associated with soft computing in different technological environments, providing potential results based on new trends in the development of these services"-- Provided by publisher.
 ISBN 978-1-4666-4785-5 (hardcover) -- ISBN 978-1-4666-4786-2 (ebook) -- ISBN 978-1-4666-4787-9 (print & perpetual access) 1. Soft computing. 2. Soft computing--Technological innovations. 3. Soft computing--Industrial applications. I. Masegosa, Antonio D., 1982- II. Villacorta, Pablo J., 1986- III. Cruz-Corona, Carlos, 1963-
 QA76.9.S63E95 2014
 006.3--dc23
                                      2013027882

This book is published in the IGI Global book series Advances in Computational Intelligence and Robotics (ACIR) (ISSN: 2327-0411; eISSN: 2327-042X)

British Cataloguing in Publication Data
A Cataloguing in Publication record for this book is available from the British Library.

For electronic access to this publication, please contact: eresources@igi-global.com.

Advances in Computational Intelligence and Robotics (ACIR) Book Series

ISSN: 2327-0411
EISSN: 2327-042X

MISSION

While intelligence is traditionally a term applied to humans and human cognition, technology has progressed in such a way to allow for the development of intelligent systems able to simulate many human traits. With this new era of simulated and artificial intelligence, much research is needed in order to continue to advance the field and also to evaluate the ethical and societal concerns of the existence of artificial life and machine learning.

The **Advances in Computational Intelligence and Robotics (ACIR) Book Series** encourages scholarly discourse on all topics pertaining to evolutionary computing, artificial life, computational intelligence, machine learning, and robotics. ACIR presents the latest research being conducted on diverse topics in intelligence technologies with the goal of advancing knowledge and applications in this rapidly evolving field.

COVERAGE

- Adaptive & Complex Systems
- Agent Technologies
- Artificial Intelligence
- Cognitive Informatics
- Computational Intelligence
- Natural Language Processing
- Neural Networks
- Pattern Recognition
- Robotics
- Synthetic Emotions

IGI Global is currently accepting manuscripts for publication within this series. To submit a proposal for a volume in this series, please contact our Acquisition Editors at Acquisitions@igi-global.com or visit: http://www.igi-global.com/publish/.

Titles in this Series

For a list of additional titles in this series, please visit: www.igi-global.com

Exploring Innovative and Successful Applications of Soft Computing
Antonio D. Masegosa (Universidad de Granada, Spain) Pablo J. Villacorta (Universidad de Granada, Spain) Carlos Cruz-Corona (Universidad de Granada, Spain) M.S. Garcia-Cascales (University of Cartagena, Columbia) María T. Lamata (Universidad de Granada, Spain) and José L. Verdegay (Universidad de Granada, Spain)
Information Science Reference • copyright 2014 • 291pp • H/C (ISBN: 9781466647855) • US $190.00 (our price)

Research Developments in Computer Vision and Image Processing Methodologies and Applications
Rajeev Srivastava (Indian Institute of Technology (BHU), India) S. K. Singh (Indian Institute of Technology (BHU), India) and K. K. Shukla (Indian Institute of Technology (BHU), India)
Information Science Reference • copyright 2014 • 388pp • H/C (ISBN: 9781466645585) • US $195.00 (our price)

Handbook of Research on Novel Soft Computing Intelligent Algorithms Theory and Practical Applications
Pandian M. Vasant (Petronas University of Technology)
Information Science Reference • copyright 2014 • 1004pp • H/C (ISBN: 9781466644502) • US $495.00 (our price)

Intelligent Technologies and Techniques for Pervasive Computing
Kostas Kolomvatsos (University of Athens, Greece) Christos Anagnostopoulos (Ionian University, Greece) and Stathes Hadjiefthymiades (University of Athens, Greece)
Information Science Reference • copyright 2013 • 351pp • H/C (ISBN: 9781466640382) • US $195.00 (our price)

Mobile Ad Hoc Robots and Wireless Robotic Systems Design and Implementation
Raul Aquino Santos (University of Colima, Mexico) Omar Lengerke (Universidad Autónoma de Bucaramanga, Colombia) and Arthur Edwards-Block (University of Colima, Mexico)
Information Science Reference • copyright 2013 • 344pp • H/C (ISBN: 9781466626584) • US $190.00 (our price)

Intelligent Planning for Mobile Robotics Algorithmic Approaches
Ritu Tiwari (ABV – Indian Institute of Information, India) Anupam Shukla (ABV – Indian Institute of Information, India) and Rahul Kala (School of Systems Engineering, University of Reading, UK)
Information Science Reference • copyright 2013 • 322pp • H/C (ISBN: 9781466620742) • US $195.00 (our price)

Simultaneous Localization and Mapping for Mobile Robots Introduction and Methods
Juan-Antonio Fernández-Madrigal (Universidad de Málaga, Spain) and José Luis Blanco Claraco (Universidad de Málaga, Spain)
Information Science Reference • copyright 2013 • 499pp • H/C (ISBN: 9781466621046) • US $195.00 (our price)

Prototyping of Robotic Systems Applications of Design and Implementation
Tarek Sobh (University of Bridgeport, USA) and Xingguo Xiong (University of Bridgeport, USA)
Information Science Reference • copyright 2012 • 522pp • H/C (ISBN: 9781466601765) • US $195.00 (our price)

Cross-Disciplinary Applications of Artificial Intelligence and Pattern Recognition Advancing Technologies
Vijay Kumar Mago (Simon Fraser University, Canada) and Nitin Bhatia (DAV College, India)
Information Science Reference • copyright 2012 • 786pp • H/C (ISBN: 9781613504291) • US $195.00 (our price)

www.igi-global.com

701 E. Chocolate Ave., Hershey, PA 17033
Order online at www.igi-global.com or call 717-533-8845 x100
To place a standing order for titles released in this series, contact: cust@igi-global.com
Mon-Fri 8:00 am - 5:00 pm (est) or fax 24 hours a day 717-533-8661

Editorial Advisory Board

Table of Contents

Foreword xv

Preface xvii

Acknowledgment xxiii

Chapter 1
A Problem of Ecological Dynamic Logistics.. 1
José M. Cadenas, Universidad de Murcia, Spain
María del Carmen Garrido, Universidad de Murcia, Spain
Raquel Martínez, Universidad de Murcia, Spain
Enrique Muñoz, European Center for Soft Computing, Spain

Chapter 2
Fuzzy Techniques for Improving Satisfaction in Economic Decisions 19
Clara Calvo, Universidad de Valencia, Spain
Carlos Ivorra, Universidad de Valencia, Spain
Vicente Liern, Universidad de Valencia, Spain

Chapter 3
A Feature Selection Approach in the Study of Azorean Proverbs 38
Luís Cavique, Universidade Aberta, Portugal
Armando B. Mendes, Universidade dos Açores, Portugal
Matthias Funk, Universidade dos Açores, Portugal
Jorge M. A. Santos, Universidade Évora, Portugal

Chapter 4
Hydropower Projects within a Municipal Water Supply System: Optimum Allocation and
Management using Harmony Search 59
Ioannis Kougias, Aristotle University of Thessaloniki, Greece
Thomas Patsialis, Aristotle University of Thessaloniki, Greece
Nicolaos Theodossiou, Aristotle University of Thessaloniki, Greece
Jacques Ganoulis, Aristotle University of Thessaloniki, Greece

Chapter 5

Soft Computing in the Quality of Services Evaluation... 76

 María T. Lamata, Universidad de Granada, Spain

 Daymi Morales Vega, Instituto Superior Politécnico "José Antonio Echeverría", Cuba

Chapter 6

Fuzzy Rules for Risk Assessment and Contingency Estimation within COCOMO Software Project
Planning Model.. 88

 Ekananta Manalif, University of Western Ontario, Canada

 Luiz Fernando Capretz, University of Western Ontario, Canada

 Danny Ho, NFA Estimation Inc., Canada

Chapter 7

Modeling and Prediction of Time-Varying Environmental Data Using Advanced Bayesian
Methods.. 112

 Majdi Mansouri, Université de Liège, Belgium

 Benjamin Dumont, Université de Liège, Belgium

 Marie-France Destain, Université de Liège, Belgium

Chapter 8

Fuzzy Modeling for Manpower Scheduling 138

 Michael Mutingi, University of Johannesburg, South Africa & University of Botswana, Botswana

 Charles Mbohwa, University of Johannesburg, South Africa

Chapter 9

Group Genetic Algorithm for Heterogeneous Vehicle Routing 161

 Michael Mutingi, University of Johannesburg, South Africa & University of Botswana, Botswana

Chapter 10

Fuzzy Nonlinear Optimization Model to Improve Intermittent Demand Forecasting 181

 Raúl Poler, Universitat Politècnica de València, Spain

 Josefa Mula, Universitat Politècnica de València, Spain

 Manuel Díaz-Madroñero, Universitat Politècnica de València, Spain

 Mariano Jiménez, Universidad del País Vasco (UPV/EHU), Spain

Chapter 11

Decision Criteria for Optimal Location of Wind Farms 199

 Juan Miguel Sánchez-Lozano, Universidad Politécnica de Cartagena, Spain

 M. Socorro García-Cascales, Universidad Politécnica de Cartagena, Spain

 María T. Lamata, Universidad de Granada, Spain

 Carlos Sierra, Universitat Politècnica de Catalunya, Spain

Chapter 12

Bipolarity in Decision Analysis: A Way to Cope with Human Judgment 216

 Ayeley P. Tchangani, Université de Toulouse, France

Chapter 13

A Soft Computing-Based Idea Applied to the Truck and Trailer Routing Problem 245

Isis Torres Pérez, Instituto Superior Politécnico "José Antonio Echeverría," Cuba
Alejandro Rosete Suárez, Instituto Superior Politécnico "José Antonio Echeverría," Cuba
Carlos Cruz-Corona, Universidad de Granada, Spain
José L. Verdegay, Universidad de Granada, Spain

Chapter 14

Improving the Performance of Neuro-Fuzzy Function Point Backfiring Model with Additional
Environmental Factors 260

Justin Wong, University of Western Ontario, Canada
Danny Ho, NFA Estimation Inc., Canada
Luiz Fernando Capretz, University of Western Ontario, Canada

Chapter 15

An Integrated Bi-Objective Reverse Logistics Network Design for Remanufacturing 281

Ali Zolghadr Shojai, Amirkabir University of Technology, Islamic Republic of Iran
Jamal Shahrabi, Amirkabir University of Technology, Islamic Republic of Iran
Masoud Jenabi, Amirkabir University of Technology, Islamic Republic of Iran

Compilation of References 317

About the Contributors 339

Index 349

Detailed Table of Contents

Foreword xv

Preface xvii

Acknowledgment xxiii

Chapter 1

A Problem of Ecological Dynamic Logistics 1

    José M. Cadenas, Universidad de Murcia, Spain

    María del Carmen Garrido, Universidad de Murcia, Spain

    Raquel Martínez, Universidad de Murcia, Spain

    Enrique Muñoz, European Center for Soft Computing, Spain

Companies have to be competitive to survive, offering their customers a more customized and complete service. Moreover, society is increasingly more aware of the need to solve problems in an ecological way trying to reduce pollution/environmental impact. Furthermore, when we try to solve management problems in crowded cities, companies expect their solutions not to depend excessively on traffic conditions and not to have an effect on the worsening of these conditions. In this chapter, the authors study how to handle the aforementioned requirements, defining the problem of ecological dynamic logistics in urban environments. In this problem, a fleet of agile environmentally friendly vehicles have to pick-up and deliver items. However, these vehicles have a limited storage capacity, and they need the support of larger environmentally friendly vehicles, mobile warehouses, to increment their range. The problem is solved by planning the routes for both delivery/pick-up vehicles and mobile warehouses in a coordinated manner, allowing the incorporation of new items during execution of the plan. To obtain a solution for this problem the authors propose to use the Ant Colony Optimization metaheuristic.

Chapter 2

Fuzzy Techniques for Improving Satisfaction in Economic Decisions 19

    Clara Calvo, Universidad de Valencia, Spain

    Carlos Ivorra, Universidad de Valencia, Spain

    Vicente Liern, Universidad de Valencia, Spain

The authors use fuzzy set theory to improve classical decision-making problems by incorporating the inherent vagueness in decision-makers' preferences into the model. They specifically study two representative models: the p-median problem and the portfolio selection problem. The first one is a location problem, which on the one hand fits many real world management situations and on the other hand is suitable for a theoretical analysis of the techniques. The version of the portfolio selection problem presented here is a harder problem, which allows the authors to show the scope of their methods. Some numerical examples are provided to illustrate how fuzzy optimal solutions improve classical ones. Finally, the authors present some results about how fuzzy solutions depend on the membership functions of fuzzy parameters.

Chapter 3
A Feature Selection Approach in the Study of Azorean Proverbs 38

> *Luís Cavique, Universidade Aberta, Portugal*
> *Armando B. Mendes, Universidade dos Açores, Portugal*
> *Matthias Funk, Universidade dos Açores, Portugal*
> *Jorge M. A. Santos, Universidade Évora, Portugal*

A paremiologic (study of proverbs) case is presented as part of a wider project based on data collected among the Azorean population. Given the considerable distance between the Azores islands, the authors present the hypothesis that there are significant differences in the proverbs from each island, thus permitting the identification of the native island of the interviewee based on his or her knowledge of proverbs. In this chapter, a feature selection algorithm that combines Rough Sets and the Logical Analysis of Data (LAD) is presented. The algorithm named LAID (Logical Analysis of Inconsistent Data) deals with noisy data, and the authors believe that an important link was established between the two different schools with similar approaches. The algorithm was applied to a real world dataset based on data collected using thousands of interviews of Azoreans, involving an initial set of twenty-two thousand Portuguese proverbs.

Chapter 4
Hydropower Projects within a Municipal Water Supply System: Optimum Allocation and
Management using Harmony Search 59

> *Ioannis Kougias, Aristotle University of Thessaloniki, Greece*
> *Thomas Patsialis, Aristotle University of Thessaloniki, Greece*
> *Nicolaos Theodossiou, Aristotle University of Thessaloniki, Greece*
> *Jacques Ganoulis, Aristotle University of Thessaloniki, Greece*

The interest of those involved in hydroelectricity has been attracted by mini-hydro projects due to their minimal environmental impact and low installation cost. Besides, mini hydros can cooperate with an impressively wide extent of water-related infrastructure, offering a broad potential for investment. In the present chapter, the integrated solution of hydro implementation in water supply systems is presented. Thus, the benefits of a water-supply installation (with constant Q) are extended to energy production. However, defining the optimum operation of such a project is a complicated task, which may involve environmental, hydraulic, technical, and economical parameters. In the present chapter a novel approach is presented, the optimum management of mini hydros in a water supply system with the use of an optimization algorithm (i.e. Harmony Search Algorithm [HAS]). This approach is applied at a site in Northern Greece and is used as a case study of the present chapter.

Chapter 5
Soft Computing in the Quality of Services Evaluation 76

> *María T. Lamata, Universidad de Granada, Spain*
> *Daymi Morales Vega, Instituto Superior Politécnico "José Antonio Echeverría", Cuba*

The evaluation of the Quality of Services (QoS) has been a topic of particular interest to many authors. In the literature, many works have been developed where different models are proposed to assess the QoS in different environments. These models evaluate the QoS from a set of criteria, which may vary from one environment to another, and thus they do not always have the same importance. Considering this, there have been many studies proposing techniques to evaluate the performance of the quality criteria. Techniques have also been developed to obtain the ranking of a given service provider. The purpose of this chapter is to make a literature review of service quality models, methods for determining the weights of the criteria, and the methods used to conduct an overall assessment of service providers.

Chapter 6

Fuzzy Rules for Risk Assessment and Contingency Estimation within COCOMO Software Project Planning Model.. 88

Ekananta Manalif, University of Western Ontario, Canada
Luiz Fernando Capretz, University of Western Ontario, Canada
Danny Ho, NFA Estimation Inc., Canada

Software development can be considered to be a most uncertain project when compared to other projects due to uncertainty in the customer requirements, the complexity of the process, and the intangible nature of the product. In order to increase the chance of success in managing a software project, the project manager(s) must invest more time and effort in the project planning phase, which involves such primary and integrated activities as effort estimation and risk management, because the accuracy of the effort estimation is highly dependent on the size and number of project risks in a particular software project. However, as is common practice, these two activities are often disconnected from each other and project managers have come to consider such steps to be unreliable due to their lack of accuracy. This chapter introduces the Fuzzy-ExCOM Model, which is used for software project planning and is based on fuzzy technique. It has the capability to not only integrate the effort estimation and risk assessment activities but also to provide information about the estimated effort, the project risks, and the effort contingency allowance necessary to accommodate the identified risk. A validation of this model using the project's research data shows that this new approach is capable of improving the existing COCOMO estimation performance.

Chapter 7

Modeling and Prediction of Time-Varying Environmental Data Using Advanced Bayesian Methods.. 112

Majdi Mansouri, Université de Liège, Belgium
Benjamin Dumont, Université de Liège, Belgium
Marie-France Destain, Université de Liège, Belgium

The problem of state/parameter estimation represents a key issue in crop models, which are nonlinear, non-Gaussian, and include a large number of parameters. The prediction errors are often important due to uncertainties in the equations, the input variables, and the parameters. The measurements needed to run the model and to perform calibration and validation are sometimes not numerous or known with some uncertainty. In these cases, estimating the state variables and/or parameters from easily obtained measurements can be extremely useful. In this chapter, the authors address the problem of modeling and prediction of time-varying Leaf area index and Soil Moisture (LSM) to better handle nonlinear and non-Gaussian processes without a priori state information. The performances of various conventional and state-of-the-art estimation techniques are compared when they are utilized to achieve this objective. These techniques include the Extended Kalman Filter (EKF), Unscented Kalman Filter (UKF), Particle Filter (PF), and the more recently developed technique Variational Bayesian Filter (VF). The original data was issued from experiments carried out on silty soil in Belgium with a wheat crop during two consecutive years, the seasons 2008-09 and 2009-10.

Chapter 8

Fuzzy Modeling for Manpower Scheduling 138

    Michael Mutingi, University of Johannesburg, South Africa & University of Botswana, Botswana

    Charles Mbohwa, University of Johannesburg, South Africa

Fuzzy theory is an important phenomenon in manpower scheduling, especially in the context where managerial and employee objectives are imprecise and, worst of all, conflicting. In such fuzzy environments, developing robust tools for addressing the fuzzy nature of the problem is imperative. Decision analysts concerned with staff scheduling need robust decision support tools to construct equitable work schedules spanning over a given planning horizon so as to meet organizational objectives, to meet customer requirements, and to satisfy worker preferences. This chapter presents a framework for fuzzy modeling for manpower scheduling based on fuzzy set-theoretic concepts. First, a background on fuzzy modeling approaches is provided, together with their solution methods. Second, key characteristic dimensions of the manpower scheduling problem are identified, leading to a taxonomic framework for classifying manpower scheduling problems. Third, a framework developing fuzzy models for manpower scheduling is derived from the taxonomy, the fuzzy modeling approaches, and the fuzzy solution approaches. The fuzzy models developed can be solved by any appropriate solvers or meta-heuristic methods.

Chapter 9

Group Genetic Algorithm for Heterogeneous Vehicle Routing 161

    Michael Mutingi, University of Johannesburg, South Africa & University of Botswana, Botswana

Cost-efficient transportation is a central concern in the transportation and logistics industry. In particular, the Heterogeneous Vehicle Routing Problem (HVRP) has become a major optimization problem in supply chains involved with delivery (collection) of goods to (from) customers. In this problem, there are limited vehicles of different types with respect to capacity, fixed cost, and variable cost. The solution to this problem involves assigning customers to existing vehicles and, in relation to each vehicle, defining the order of visiting each customer for the delivery or collection of goods. Hence, the objective is to minimize the total costs, while satisfying customer requirements and visiting each customer exactly once. In this chapter, an enhanced Group Genetic Algorithm (GGA) based on the group structure of the problem is developed and tested on several benchmark problems. Computational results show that the proposed GGA algorithm is able to produce high quality solutions within a reasonable computation time.

Chapter 10

Fuzzy Nonlinear Optimization Model to Improve Intermittent Demand Forecasting 181

    Raúl Poler, Universitat Politècnica de València, Spain

    Josefa Mula, Universitat Politècnica de València, Spain

    Manuel Díaz-Madroñero, Universitat Politècnica de València, Spain

    Mariano Jiménez, Universidad del País Vasco (UPV/EHU), Spain

This chapter proposes a fuzzy nonlinear programming model for intermittent demand forecasting purposes. The authors formulated the Syntetos and Boylan (SB) forecasting method as a crisp nonlinear programming model. They also attempted to improve it with a new fuzzy nonlinear programming formulation. This fuzzy model is based on fuzzy decision variables, which represent fuzzy triangular numbers. The authors applied fuzzy arithmetic operations, such as addition and subtraction of fuzzy numbers, fuzzy decision variables. They carried out the defuzzification of the fuzzy decision variables through the possibilistic mean value of fuzzy numbers. Finally, the authors validated and tested it by comparing it with the deterministic nonlinear programming model that they adopted as the basis of this work. The computational studies show that fuzzy model performance is consistently better than the SB nonlinear programming model, especially when intermittency is high.

Chapter 11
Decision Criteria for Optimal Location of Wind Farms 199
Juan Miguel Sánchez-Lozano, Universidad Politécnica de Cartagena, Spain
M. Socorro García-Cascales, Universidad Politécnica de Cartagena, Spain
María T. Lamata, Universidad de Granada, Spain
Carlos Sierra, Universitat Politècnica de Catalunya, Spain

The objective of the present chapter is to obtain the weights of the criteria that influences a decision problem of vital necessity to the current energy perspectives, which is the optimal localisation of wind farms. The location problem posed presents a hierarchical structure on three levels. The objective or goal to be achieved is in the top level, that is to say the optimal location of wind farms. The second level is constituted by the general criteria that influences the decision and which are the environmental, orographic, location, and climate criteria. These general criteria are then divided into sub-criteria, which constitute the third level of the hierarchy. The information provided by the criteria are of different natures, with qualitative-type criteria coexisting with quantitative-type criteria, and therefore, linguistic labels and numerical values are employed to model, by means of fuzzy triangular numbers, the importance coefficients of the criteria. In order to compare different models for extracting the knowledge, two surveys are prepared based on the Fuzzy AHP methodology, which are submitted to experts in the specific field.

Chapter 12
Bipolarity in Decision Analysis: A Way to Cope with Human Judgment 216
Ayeley P. Tchangani, Université de Toulouse, France

Decision analysis, the mechanism by which a final decision is reached in terms of choice (choosing an alternative or a subset of alternatives from a large set of alternatives), ranking (ranking alternatives of a set from the worst to the best), classification (assigning alternatives to some known classes or categories), or sorting (clustering alternatives to form homogeneous classes or categories) is certainly the most pervasive human activity. Some decisions are made routinely and do not need sophisticated algorithms to support decision analysis process whereas other decisions need more or less complex processes to reach a final decision. Methods and models developed to solve decision analysis problems are in constant evolution going from mechanist models of operational research to more sophisticated and soft computing-oriented models that attempt to integrate human attitude (emotion, affect, fear, egoism, altruism, selfishness, etc.). This complex, soft computing and near human mechanism of problem solving is rendered possible thanks to the overwhelming computational power and data storage possibility of modern computers. The purpose of this chapter is to present new and recent developments in decision analysis that attempt to integrate human judgment through bipolarity notion.

Chapter 13
A Soft Computing-Based Idea Applied to the Truck and Trailer Routing Problem 245
Isis Torres Pérez, Instituto Superior Politécnico "José Antonio Echeverría", Cuba
Alejandro Rosete Suárez, Instituto Superior Politécnico "José Antonio Echeverría", Cuba
Carlos Cruz-Corona, Universidad de Granada, Spain
José L. Verdegay, Universidad de Granada, Spain

Techniques based on Soft Computing are useful to model and solve real-world problems where decision makers use subjective knowledge or linguistic information when making decisions, measuring parameters, objectives, and constraints, and even when modeling the problem. In many problems in transport and logistics, it is necessary to take into account that the available knowledge about some data and parameters of the problem model is imprecise or uncertain. Truck and Trailer Routing Problem, TTRP, is one of most recent and interesting problems in transport routing planning. TTRP is a combinatorial optimization problem, and it is computationally more difficult to solve than the known Vehicle Routing Problem, VRP. Most of models used in the literature assume that the data available is accurate; but this consideration does not correspond with reality. For this reason, it is appropriate to focus research toward defining TTRP models for incorporating the uncertainty present in their data. The aims of the present chapter are: a) to provide a study on the Truck and Trailer Routing Problem that serves as help to researchers interested on this topic and b) to present an approach using techniques of Soft Computing to solve this problem.

Chapter 14

Improving the Performance of Neuro-Fuzzy Function Point Backfiring Model with Additional
Environmental Factors 260

Justin Wong, University of Western Ontario, Canada
Danny Ho, NFA Estimation Inc., Canada
Luiz Fernando Capretz, University of Western Ontario, Canada

Backfiring is a technique used for estimating the size of source code based on function points and programming. In this study, additional software environmental parameters such as Function Point count standard, development environment, problem domain, and size are applied to the Neuro-Fuzzy Function Point Backfiring (NFFPB) model. The neural network and fuzzy logic designs are introduced for both models. Both estimation models are compared against the same data source of software projects. It is found that the original NFFPB model outperforms the extended model. The results are investigated, and it is explained why the extended model performed worse.

Chapter 15

An Integrated Bi-Objective Reverse Logistics Network Design for Remanufacturing 281

Ali Zolghadr Shojai, Amirkabir University of Technology, Islamic Republic of Iran
Jamal Shahrabi, Amirkabir University of Technology, Islamic Republic of Iran
Masoud Jenabi, Amirkabir University of Technology, Islamic Republic of Iran

Growing environmental and economical concern has led to increasing attention towards management of product return flows. An effective and efficient reverse logistics network enables companies to gain more profit and customer satisfaction. Consequently, the reverse logistics network design problem has become a critical issue. After a brief introduction to the basic concepts of reverse logistics, the authors formulate a new integrated multi-stage, multi-period, multi-product reverse logistics model for a remanufacturing system where the inventory is considered. Two objectives, minimization of the costs and maximization of coverage, are addressed. Since such network design problems belong to a class of NP-hard problems, a multi-objective genetic algorithm and a multi-objective evolutionary strategy algorithm are developed in order to find the set of non-dominated solutions. Finally, the model is tested on test problems with different sizes, and the proposed algorithms are compared based on the number, quality, and distribution of non-dominated solutions that belong to the Pareto front.

Compilation of References 317

About the Contributors 339

Index 349

Foreword

When the book editors asked me to write this foreword, it was clear for me that I would need to talk about why a book on exploring innovative applications of soft computing could be of interest.

And the answer needs a bit of context…

If we need to indicate some relevant features about problems emerging today in the current socio-technological context, we may find a general agreement on mentioning these two: firstly, the real world is not static and, secondly, there exist uncertainties, vagueness, unknowns, that pose at least two challenges: how to understand, describe, and model them, and how to solve the problem taking them into account.

In order to deal with those features of such problems, soft computing (or the closer concept of computational intelligence) is the way to go; moreover, if we consider it a step beyond its constituting elements (fuzzy logic, neural networks, metaheuristics, and probabilistic reasoning to cite the usual ones), we observe the potential for hybridization among them.

At the beginning of May 2013, I conducted a quick search on research articles (using Scopus database, www.scopus.com) and patents (through the European Patent Office's Espacenet tool, www.epo.org/searching/free/espacenet.html) where soft computing-based hybrids were applied. As metaheuristics is a quite general term, I have considered either genetic or evolutionary algorithms in the search.

In the case of research articles, the query was searched only in the title of articles or reviews (no conference proceedings) published in English since year 2000 until now in all the research areas covered by Scopus. Regarding the patents, the query was searched in the title and the abstract and no time limits or languages criterion were set. Table 1 collects the results.

These illustrative results allow one to conclude that soft computing-based methods are being widely used and applied, and the experience indicates that its usefulness emerges at two levels: as a way to obtain more appropriated models of the world, and/or to provide *good enough, soon enough* solutions to the problem at hand.

So the relevance of soft computing is clear. Now, why do we need to look at innovative applications or, maybe better said, interesting scenarios for the use of soft computing?

We may agree that the concept of "optimization" appears at the core of many applications as there is a need to obtain the best possible solution to the problem at hand. This idea led to a sort of algorithmic "race" where the focus was more on the methods than on the applications, trying to provide a fine tuning

Table 1. Search results

Query	Results in Scopus	Result in Espacenet
fuzzy AND (genetic OR evolutionary)	742	111
fuzzy AND (neural OR neuro)	3566	1013
(genetic OR evolutionary) AND (neural OR neuro)	935	221
fuzzy AND (genetic OR evolutionary) AND (neural OR neuro)	146	27

xvi

of the former to obtain (many times) a micro-improvement in the solutions for the later. Please note that this is not related with the fact that we need more efficient algorithms to deal with bigger problems or to take more advantage of parallel computers.

Many people, including myself, did research like the previous one, but for several years now, it seems that the focus on "optimization" is varying, mainly due to the mentioned features of the problems that need to be solved. Nowadays, a different perspective and new opportunities emerge if we consider that *it is better to satisfy than to optimize*, and this claim puts the potential user in the cycle of the problem resolution.

In my opinion, there is a need to foster the connection among different areas of research where people are eager to find solutions to their problems, or to explore novel solutions beyond those provided by, let's say, standard techniques. Moreover, from my experience, there is no need to apply the last-ultimate-cool version of method M to produce satisfactory solutions for the problem that, for example, my colleagues in the Chemistry Department have. Many times, being able to deliver a set of solutions (like the ones given by a population-based heuristic) instead of just one, or to have a set of fuzzy rules able to explain certain phenomena may produce an impact from the user's point of view that is hardly achieved just observing from the methods' side.

It is clear that there are still many areas and applications where soft computing techniques can show their potential and some examples are provided in this book. One can find here applications ranging from scheduling, routing problems, software project planning, demand forecasting, to decision making in different contexts, quality of service evaluation, and even the study of Azorean proverbs. Regarding the applied methods, genetic algorithms, fuzzy modeling, fuzzy non-linear optimization, fuzzy rules, neuro-fuzzy methods, rough sets, etc. are used either as a solving or as a modeling tool in the problem at hand.

Of course, I would like to say a few words about the editors. First of all, the reader should be aware that I know them personally. I belong to the same research group, and I work closely with some of them. Nevertheless, from the (not so) oldest to the youngest editors, they are recognized researchers in the field of soft computing, with wide academic experience and internationally renowned. The best I can suggest is to look at their CVs to observe their qualifications to edit a book like this.

Finally, I definitely consider this book useful not only for practitioners and researchers already working in the field, but also for students in their first stages of research as they can observe how soft computing techniques can be applied in novel scenarios.

David A. Pelta
Universidad de Granada, Spain

David A. Pelta is Associate Professor at the Dept. of Computer Science and AI, University of Granada, Spain. He obtained a Computer Science degree (1998) from the National University of La Plata, Argentina and a PhD (2002) from the University of Granada, Spain. He is a member of the Models of Decision and Optimization Research Group, where he conducts research on soft computing techniques, cooperative strategies for optimization, adversarial reasoning and interdisciplinary applications. He is actively involved in research projects funded by different organizations (Spanish Government, European Community, Andalusian Government, etc.). He has published more than 30 journal papers, co-edited 7 books and 5 special issues on relevant journals. He co-advised five PhD and 3 Master's theses. He founded (jointly with Natalio Krasnogor), the Workshop series on Nature Inspired Cooperative Strategies for Optimization (NICSO), serves on the editorial board of the Memetic Computing journal and acts as reviewer for many other journals like Soft Computing, Applied Soft Computing, Swarm Intelligence, etc.

Preface

Soft Computing can be seen as a set of methodologies and techniques that working together can create synergies that facilitate new ways to address problems in practical and real scenarios. Its application has provided highly effective and efficient solutions to a wide number of complex problems in many fields, mainly related with intelligent systems.

However, there exist technological environments in which its applicability has not been studied or its potential has not been exploited enough. This is the case of Renewable Energies, Logistics, Quality of Service, Software Engineering, Environment, Agriculture, etc. They are highly technological areas of great importance for the current society where the right resolution of the problems they present can have direct implications on our way of life. This book aims to gather innovative and successful applications of Soft Computing in these advanced technological environments.

Since the first appearance of the term Soft Computing, the amount of applications and developments directly related to this methodology has amazingly grown, and nowadays, the turnover can be counted in billions of Euro. As it is well known, L.A. Zadeh presented in 1994 the seminal definition of Soft Computing. Since then, the definition, because of the bodies involved in it, has changed to be enhanced. In essence, Soft Computing can be considered as a set of techniques whose synergies allow solving practical problems more efficiently than the classic methods and in a similar way to how humans solve problems in contexts with uncertainty, vagueness, and that are difficult to categorize. In this way, we follow the more recent definition by Verdegay, Yager, and Bonissone:

Soft Computing is the result of the collaboration, association and complementariness of the different techniques that integrate it and that cooperate from their basics. Their main objective is to take advantage of inherent tolerance of the imprecision and uncertainty to obtain tractability, robustness and low solution-cost. Their main components are Fuzzy Logic, Artificial Neural Networks, Probabilistic Reasoning and Metaheuristics. From the different associations that can happen among them, Fuzzy Logic is an essential ingredient, is mainly concerned with imprecision and approximate reasoning; neurocomputing with learning and curve-fitting; probabilistic reasoning with uncertainty and belief propagation; and Metaheuristics with search methods and optimization. The high dimensionality of the addressed problems recommends the use of Data Mining. (Verdegay, Yager, & Bonissone, 2008)

The areas where Soft Computing has been applied are many and diverse. We can find successful applications in logistics, where in classic models such aspects as costs, transportation times, characteristics, and conditions of the environment are assumed as perfectly known. This is not suitable for real scenarios where demands, times, or constraints are usually uncertain and vague. The use of Soft Computing techniques, especially Fuzzy Sets and Metaheuristics, have shown to be very effective to deal with this type of information. Similar problems also appear in Bioinformatics, where Soft Computing is increasingly used to deal with the processing of the huge amount of incomplete or ambiguous biological data. Decision Making Support can be considered another of its greatest application fields. Soft Computing has been employed to model subjective assessments and linguistic information, aggregate data from different experts, guide opinions to reach a consensus, etc., but these are just three of the hundreds of application areas, among which are also:

- Robotics
- Renewable Energies
- ICT Security
- Business
- Economics
- Humanities and Social Sciences
- Prospective technology
- Systems Biology
- Quality of Services
- Health Care
- Planning and Scheduling
- Human Resources
- Medicine
- Aeronautic

Although Soft Computing-based solutions have been successfully applied in a broad range of areas, as we have seen above, its short existence period—less than 20 years—and the fast evolution of the current society suggest the existence and emergence of new problems potentially solvable by these methodologies.

To explore some of these areas, this book has gathered innovative and successful applications of Soft Computing in Renewable Energies, Software Engineering, Agriculture, Manpower Scheduling, Vehicle Routing, Logistics Networks, Economics, Business Management, Decision Making, Quality of Services Evaluation, and Paremiologic (study of proverbs). These applications involve to a greater or lesser extent all the methodologies that comprise Soft Computing (Fuzzy Sets, Approximate Reasoning, Neural Networks, and Metaheuristics). With this book, we hope to provide both researchers and practitioners with a catalogue of some of the most successful Soft Computing-based methodologies that can be applied to the problems arising in these highly technological areas.

From this point of view, the book contains fifteen chapters listed by first author, last name alphabetical order. In the following, each of them is shortly introduced.

In Chapter 1, "A Problem of Ecological Dynamic Logistics", J. M. Cadenas, M.C. Garrido, R. Martínez, and E. Muñoz address one of the most current challenges in logistics: reducing pollution while keeping or increasing benefits and quality of service. Concretely, they introduce a new Pick up/Delivery Vehicle Routing Problem with two types of vehicles, agile environmentally friendly vehicles to pick up and deliver items (e.g. motorbikes) and large vehicles to act as mobile warehouse (e.g. vans or trucks). The results obtained by the ant colony algorithm proposed to solve the problem demonstrate the potential of both the model and the solver to be applied in real urban environments.

C. Calvo, C. Ivorra, and V. Liern point out in Chapter 2, "Fuzzy Techniques for Improving Satisfaction in Economic Decisions", how the handling of the vagueness and uncertainty by fuzzy set theory can lead to better solutions in two classic problems in economics: the p-median problem and the portfolio selection problem. The two fuzzy models developed for these problems provide more stable solutions than their crips counterparts against the variation of problem parameters whose values are not known in a precise way. The authors also show how the fuzzy solutions provided depend on the membership functions of fuzzy parameters.

Chapter 3, "A Feature Selection Approach in the Study of Azorean Proverbs", presents a very interesting and uncommon application field for Soft Computing, Paremiology. L. Cavique, A. B. Mendes, M. Funk, and J. M.A. Santos study the possibility of identifying the native island of the Azorean people by his/her knowledge of proverbs. More specifically, they aim to establish if there exist significant differences among the proverbs of each island. To this end, they develope a feature selection method named Logical Analysis of Inconsistent Data that combines Rough Sets and the Logical Analysis of Data to deal with noisy data. This method allows an important reduction of the number of proverbs (attributes) required to determine the mentioned significance differences. The tests performed establish that it is possible to differentiate the native island group (central or occidental) but not the concrete native island of the people analyzed in the study.

Renewable Energies are the focus of the next chapter, "Hydropower Projects within a Municipal Water Supply System: Optimum Allocation and Management using Harmony Search," written by I. Kougias, T. Patsialis, N. Theodossiou, and J. Ganoulis. The authors discuss the great role of Mini Hydropower Plants within Renewable Energies due to its high efficiency, low cost, and almost null environmental impact. Then, they state how the installation of these Mini Hydropower plants can be addressed as an optimization problem where the decision variables are the type and quantity of turbines to install. Finally, they propose a Harmony Search Algorithm for this optimization problem and apply it to a real case in Greece with satisfactory results.

M. T. Lamata and D. Morales do a review of the literature concerning the application of Soft Computing to Quality of Services evaluation in Chapter 5, "Soft Computing in the Quality of Services Evaluation". They overview the evaluation models, emphasizing the widespread use of SERVQUAL; the methods to obtain the relative importance (weights) of the evaluation criteria, classifying them into heuristics, AHP, DEMANTEL, GRA, and OWA; and the Soft Computing-based multi-criteria decision techniques applied in this field as TOPSIS, PROMETHEE, VIKOR, AHP, etc. Apart from this, the authors point out the need to combine the results of different multi-criteria methods, in order to provide more robust evaluations, and propose a methodology in this direction.

Software Engineering is one of the emergent application areas for Soft Computing as E. Manalif, L. F. Capretz, and D. Ho point out in Chapter 6, "Fuzzy Rules for Risk Assessment and Contingency Estimation within COCOMO Software Project Planning Model". The planning of software development projects is subject to a high uncertainty for many reasons (changing customer requirements, complexity of the process, intangible nature of the product, etc.), especially the activities related to effort estimation and risk management. The contribution of this work, the Fuzzy-ExCOM Model, incorporates fuzzy rules-based systems into Expert-COCOMO to handle linguistic information and uncertainty in risk assessments and Effort Contingency, respectively. The validation done proves the superiority of this method versus the estimations provided by COCOMO-II.

In Chapter 7, "Modeling and Prediction of Time-Varying Environmental Data Using Advanced Bayesian Methods", M. Mansouri, B. Dumont, and M.-F. Destain focus on Agriculture, and more specifically in predictive crop models. The authors extend four advance Bayesian methods for state and parameter estimation (i.e. extended Kalman filter, unscented Kalman filter, particle filter, and Variational Bayesian filter) to better handle nonlinear and non-Gaussian processes without a priori state information, by utilizing a time-varying assumption of statistical parameters. The methods are evaluated over a model that predicts the leaf area index and soil moisture. They conclude that Variational Bayesian filter outperforms the other methods.

M. Mutingi and C. Mbohwa address the manpower-scheduling problem in Chapter 8, "Fuzzy Modeling for Manpower Scheduling". The uncertainty present in information on target values of management objectives or workers' preferences, among other aspects, make appropriate the use of fuzzy techniques as authors maintain in this work. After reviewing the fuzzy modeling approaches available in the literature, they establish a taxonomy that classifies them into flexible demand, fixed demand, and task-oriented demand. From this taxonomy, the authors propose a unified fuzzy modeling framework that provides flexibility and interactivity to the decision maker.

One of the former authors, M. Mutingi, makes another interesting contribution concerning the application of Soft Computing to Logistics in the next Chapter, "Group Genetic Algorithm for Heterogeneous Vehicle Routing". The variability in transportation demand features in the current world, and the long-term use of the acquired vehicles in transport industry propitiate a bigger heterogeneity of vehicle fleets in this sector. For this reason, the problem tackled here has achieved a great importance in recent years. M. Mutingi presents a new Genetic Algorithm whose components are designed according to the structure of this problem to make the most of the information available. The results show a better global performance than state-of-the-art methods in two well-known benchmarks.

Chapter 10, "Fuzzy Nonlinear Optimization Model to Improve Intermittent Demand Forecasting", provides a new Soft Computing application area to this book, business management. The more specific topic of this work, Demand Forecasting, plays a key role in this area for many reasons. For example, at the organization level it is an essential input to planning production or purchases, managing inventories, etc. The authors, R. Poler, J. Mula, M. Díaz-Madroñero, and M. Jiménez center their work on intermittent demand, where periods with positive and null demand alternate. Their proposal consists on a new fuzzy non-linear programming method for intermittent demand forecasting that models the estimated demand, the time between consecutive transactions and the forecasted demand as fuzzy numbers. The experimentation done shows the better robustness of this method versus its crisp counterpart, especially in complex scenarios with high intermittency.

In Chapter 11, "Decision Criteria for Optimal Location of Wind Farms," J. M. Sánchez-Lozano, M. Socorro García-Cascales, M. T. Lamata, and C. Sierra refocus the book on Renewable Energies but in a different generation method, Wind Farms. The right location of the Wind Farms is a key issue to reduce risks in terms of viability and environmental damage. It is a complex problem where the decision maker should take into account a big number of environmental, locational, orographic, and climatological criteria. Furthermore, in these criteria we found both qualitative (linguistic) and quantitative data. The authors use a Soft Computing-based multi-criteria method, Fuzzy AHP, to handle both linguistic and numerical information when determining the importance (weight) for each criterion in the final decision, obtaining satisfactory results.

A. Tchangani brings us a new Soft Computing-based model for Decision Making in Chapter 12, "Bipolarity in Decision Analysis: A Way to Cope with Human Judgment". Human attitude, behavior, and judgment can bias the final decision in many real situations where impartiality and objectivity are essentials. This author claims that dealing with is issues is a must when dealing with decision analysis processes. To this end, he introduces the concept of bipolarity in a new decision support framework to model the possible indecision of a decision maker between two alternatives and to address relationships between objectives and attributes through supporting and rejecting notions. Its application to a social sensitive decision problem, the hypothetical installation of a chemical plant, where environmental and economic interests are confronted, show the ability of this method to consider the agreement and dis-agreement that may exist among decision makers.

I.T. Pérez, A.R. Suárez, C. Cruz-Corona, and J.L. Verdegay introduce in "A Soft Computing-Based Idea Applied to the Truck and Trailer Routing Problem," a new Soft Computing application approach to Logistics with respect to those seen in this book so far. In the two former approaches (Chapters 1 and 9), Soft Computing is used at solver level while in this chapter it is applied to the model. Being more specific, they address one of the most recent problems in this field, the Truck and Trailer Routing Problem, a variant of the Vehicle Routing Problem where vehicles (trucks) are allowed to pull trailers to increase their capacity. The authors stand that all the models proposed in the literature assume the existence of accurate data (number of vehicles, vehicle capacity, etc.), which is far from true in many real scenarios. They propose fuzzy constraints to model the uncertainty in some of these data and a fuzzy parametric approach to provide solutions that collect this uncertainty.

Chapter 14, "Improving the Performance of Neuro-Fuzzy Function Point Backfiring Model with Additional Environmental Factors," presents another application of Soft Computing to Software Engineering. J. Wong, D. Ho, and L. F. Capretz deal with the estimation of the software size, a key issue in software development to determine the necessary time and budget for planning. They focus on Backfiring, a technique used to estimate the size of source code from the functional size of the software by means of predefined conversion ratios. The main concerns about this technique are the low accuracy and specificity of these conversion ratios. To cope with these problems, the authors develop a Neuro-Fuzzy Function Point Backfiring model that combines Neural Networks and Fuzzy sets to provide more accurate conversion rations respect to the programming language as well as the environmental and organizational factors.

A. Zolghadr Shojai, J. Shahrabi, and M. Jenabi close the book with another application of Soft Computing to Logistics in "An Integrated Bi-Objective Reverse Logistics Network Design for Remanu-facturing". Reverse logistics, the process of transporting goods or products from their usual destination to other locations and facilities to obtain value or to manage safe disposal, has gained interest in recent years mainly due to its utility to reduce environmental damage (e.g. recycling, waste disposal, etc.). In this chapter, the authors formulate a new bi-objective mixed integer programming model for integrated reverse logistics in remanufacturing systems with inventory. The objective of the problem is to minimize costs while maximizing coverage and customer satisfaction. Furthermore, they propose two multi-objective evolutionary algorithms for its resolution. The experimentation shows complementary results for these methods depending on the performance measure.

To summarize, along its almost 20-year history, Soft Computing has become a very powerful meth-odology to obtain effective and efficient solutions for real world problems in many fields. However, its short life span and the strong technological evolution of some sectors make probable the existence and the emergence of problems where the application of Soft Computing techniques have not been still explored in depth or has much room for improvement.

This book can be considered an evidence of this fact. The chapters' authors illustrate how Soft Computing can provide successful and competitive solutions for problems that arise in areas as hetero-geneous as Renewable Energies, Software Engineering, Agriculture, Manpower Scheduling, Logistic, Economics, Business Management, Decision Making, Quality of Service evaluation or Paremiology.

These solutions allow, for example, reducing pollution and environmental damage; increasing efficiency of energy generation; improving quality of services; supporting decision making in business, economics, and logistics; or determining the birthplace of a person by his/her use of proverbs.

We hope this book can be used, on the one hand, as a catalog of Soft Computing-based solutions for these areas, and on the other hand, as a starting point for other innovative and successful applications of Soft Computing.

Antonio D. Masegosa
Universidad de Granada, Spain

Pablo J. Villacorta
Universidad de Granada, Spain

Carlos Cruz-Corona
Universidad de Granada, Spain

M. Socorro Garcia-Cascales
Universidad Politécnica de Cartagena, Spain

María T. Lamata
Universidad de Granada, Spain

José L. Verdegay
Universidad de Granada, Spain

REFERENCES

Verdegay, J. L., Yager, R. R., & Bonissone, P. P. (2008). On heuristics as a fundamental constituent of soft computing. *Fuzzy Sets and Systems*, *159*(7), 846–855. doi:10.1016/j.fss.2007.08.014.

Acknowledgment

This work has been partially funded by the projects TIN2011-27696-C02-01 from the Spanish Ministry of Economy and Competitiveness and P11-TIC-08001 from the Andalusian Government (including FEDER funds from the European Union).

Antonio D. Masegosa
Universidad de Granada, Spain

Pablo J. Villacorta
Universidad de Granada, Spain

Carlos Cruz-Corona
Universidad de Granada, Spain

M. Socorro Garcia-Cascales
Universidad Politécnica de Cartagena, Spain

María T. Lamata
Universidad de Granada, Spain

José L. Verdegay
Universidad de Granada, Spain

Chapter 1
A Problem of Ecological Dynamic Logistics

José M. Cadenas
Universidad de Murcia, Spain

María del Carmen Garrido
Universidad de Murcia, Spain

Raquel Martínez
Universidad de Murcia, Spain

Enrique Muñoz
European Center for Soft Computing, Spain

ABSTRACT

Companies have to be competitive to survive, offering their customers a more customized and complete service. Moreover, society is increasingly more aware of the need to solve problems in an ecological way trying to reduce pollution/environmental impact. Furthermore, when we try to solve management problems in crowded cities, companies expect their solutions not to depend excessively on traffic conditions and not to have an effect on the worsening of these conditions. In this chapter, the authors study how to handle the aforementioned requirements, defining the problem of ecological dynamic logistics in urban environments. In this problem, a fleet of agile environmentally friendly vehicles have to pick-up and deliver items. However, these vehicles have a limited storage capacity, and they need the support of larger environmentally friendly vehicles, mobile warehouses, to increment their range. The problem is solved by planning the routes for both delivery/pick-up vehicles and mobile warehouses in a coordinated manner, allowing the incorporation of new items during execution of the plan. To obtain a solution for this problem the authors propose to use the Ant Colony Optimization metaheuristic.

DOI: 10.4018/978-1-4666-4785-5.ch001

INTRODUCTION

In a competitive economic environment, where the number of alternatives for companies and consumers is greater than ever, it is crucial for the companies to effectively organize their logistics activities in order to face the changing needs of the XXI century. Nowadays, companies work in an environment where customer's requirements are very demanding, and in particular, they cannot allow themselves to have problems with the delivery of their goods. Delivery requirements may include, in many occasions, to perform them on the same day in which they are sent. For this reason, courier companies must make sure to provide really efficient services and to offer to the customers a more detailed and specific support.

Additionally, today's concerns about the environment, are encouraging the search of solutions that try to reduce emissions, and consequently, environmental impact to a minimum. In this sense, courier companies can find new business opportunities by adopting more environmentally friendly policies. A good way to adapt to these requirements is to use low or no-emission vehicles to deliver their items, as for example, bicycles or electric vehicles. Along with these ecological requirements, courier companies are interested in finding solutions that can overcome cities' traffic problems, which may include, changing traffic conditions, blocked streets... For this reason it is advisable to use agile vehicles like bicycles or small motorcycles that can move faster on a city, and that are less affected by traffic conditions. However, these vehicles have a limited capacity to carry items, and to improve their range of action it is useful to rely on bigger vehicles that can carry more items. These other vehicles may also be environmentally friendly, as electric vans or cars.

Taking all these requirements into account, a new niche market is appearing, which encourages the appearance of courier companies that focus on the delivery and pick up of items on cities, using a flexible and ecological approach. However this is a complex problem that includes many challenges:

1. It has to permit the traceability of goods, effectively and on time;
2. It needs to ensure a maximum utilization of resources;
3. It has to allow to make decisions on real time, like updating orders while the process has started;
4. It has to avoid as much as possible problems due to cities' traffic conditions, taking into account the availability of online information; and
5. It needs to use ecological vehicles that can reduce environmental impact to a minimum.

Given this idea, this paper focuses on the problem of organizing the fleet of vehicles that carry out the delivery/pick-up activities. We have named this problem "ecological dynamic logistics in urban environments". In order to solve this problem we have to define the routes that must be followed by the vehicles. Additionally, these routes have to reduce the cost for the company and provide an optimum service in terms of time. We propose to perform the delivery/pick-up operations using agile ecological vehicles (called terminal vehicles), which as was previously stated, have a limited storage capacity. For this reason, they must be supported by higher capacity vehicles (called mobile warehouses) that allow them to gather new items which must be delivered and to deposit the items that have already been picked up. This approach allows to reduce both the costs for the company and the environmental impact of their actions. Hence, the problem consists in planning the routes of both kinds of vehicles in a coordinated manner, given a set of delivery and pick-up points, and a set of points were mobile warehouses can wait for terminal vehicles. Additionally, the solution has to allow the adding of new elements of delivery/pick-up during the execution of a plan.

In this paper we analyze this problem and propose to use Ant Colony Optimization to solve it in approximate way. In particular, this paper shows a feasibility study for a company that wants to develop this new type of business in cities. The remainder of the paper is organized as follows: in Section "Background" we study related works, in Section "Understanding the Problem" we detail the problem and explain its different parameters and constraints, in Section "Methodology of Resolution" we describe the proposed algorithm to provide a feasible solution to this problem, in addition we show how to construct the solution of the problem and possible actions to take in case of not finding a feasible solution. In Section "Application Examples" we show examples of application, and finally, in Section "Conclusions" we present the conclusions of this study.

BACKGROUND

Logistics problems have been and continue being an important research topic that has had an important impact in everyday life. In this paper we are interested in a particular kind of logistics problems known as vehicle routing problems. Some examples of these kind of problems are the popular Travelling Salesman Problem (Puris, Bello, Martinez & Nowe, 2007) or the problem of finding optimal paths for the delivery and pick up of items (Montemanni, Lucibello & Gambardella, 2007).

Vehicle routing problems have been applied to a wide variety of real world problems, such as garbage collection in a city, (Nuortioa, Kytöjokib, Niskaa & Bräysyb, 2006), or the distribution of aid after a natural disaster, such as an earthquake, (Tzeng, Cheng & Huang, 2007), considering that aid must first reach the worst affected areas. Among the many application areas we have to emphasize those that paid attention to environmentally friendly solutions, as the works of (Crainic, Ricciardi & Storchi, 2009; Kenworthy, 2006) that

try to solve logistics problems in urban centers using ecological approaches.

The main problem when we try to solve this kind of problems is that most of them belong to the class of NP-complete problems, which means that it cannot be resolved in a polynomial time. Consequently, when the size of the problem is relatively large, its resolution becomes intractable using exact methods. For this reason, many researchers have proposed to solve them using approximation methods. Among these methods we can emphasize metaheuristics. Several studies have shown that metaheuristics are successful tools for providing reasonably good solutions to optimization problems (in some cases excellent) using a moderate number of resources (Donati, Montemanni, Casagrande, Rizzoli & Gambardella, 2008; Silva, Sousa & Runkler, 2008; Cadenas, Garrido & Muñoz, 2009).

In particular, there is a metaheuristic that is especially well suited for the resolution of vehicle routing problems, Ant Colony Optimization (Dorigo & Stützle, 2003; Silva, Sousa & Runkler, 2008). This metaheuristic has been used to solve problems similar to the one proposed in this study. For example, in (Bella & McMullen, 2004), authors employ Ant Colony Optimization to address an established set of vehicle routing problems. In (Fuellerera, Doernera, Hartla & Iorib, 2009) Ant Colony Optimization was used to solve the Vehicle Routing problem with Charge. In (Gajpal & Abad, 2009) an Ant Colony Multisystem is proposed to solve the Vehicle Routing problem with Return Network. As in the problem proposed in this paper, they have end users with certain items to pick-up and/or deliver. To solve this problem, two multipaths of local search using MACS (Ant Colony Multisystem) are used.

We may treat the problem of ecological dynamic logistics in urban environments as a Dynamic Optimization Problem (Branke, 2002), since new pick-ups and/or deliveries may appear after the final solution has been obtained. Ant Colony Optimization has also been successfully applied to dynamic problems, in (Mavrovouniotis & Yang, 2011) a memetic ant colony optimization was used to solve dynamic travelling salesman problem and in (Montemanni, Gambardella, Rizzoli & Donati, 2005) it was used to solve the problem of Dynamic Routing of Vehicles. However, in this paper we do not address the resolution of the problem of ecological dynamic logistics in urban environments as a dynamic optimization problem, and if during the process of delivery/pick up new tasks are received, we restart the resolution of the problem.

For this reason, in this paper we propose to use Ant Colony Optimization to solve the problem of ecological dynamic logistics in urban environments.

UNDERSTANDING THE PROBLEM

Introduction

In this article we face the problem of studying a viability of the ecological dynamic logistics in urban environments that serves as a reference for companies to establish a new standard in the field.

In the problem, we have a set of items that have to be delivered and another set of items that have to be picked up, both types of items are represented by points on a map and are called delivery and pick-up points, respectively. As previously indicated, the problem considers the use of agile ecological terminal vehicles with limited storage capacity. These terminal vehicles start working from the company head office, visiting delivery and pick-up points until they run out of storage capacity. When that occurs they have to regenerate it by visiting the head office or a mobile warehouse, where they can leave picked up items and gather new items for delivery. This process continues until the terminal vehicles have reached their maximum working hours, taking into account that they have to finish their working day in the head office.

On the other hand, mobile warehouses start from the company head office and have a series of appointments with terminal vehicles, in which they gather picked up items and provide new delivery items. These appointments can take place only at certain locations, where vehicles are allowed to stop for a certain period of time to load/unload their cargo. We call these points, service points. Hence, mobile warehouses' routes only include service points and the head office, which can be considered a special type of service point. As in the case of terminal vehicles, mobile warehouses also have a maximum number of working hours and have to finish their working day in the head office.

One aspect to consider is that there may exist many possible service points in a city, however, we assume that before starting the resolution of the problem we know those which are more feasible.

In addition, it is important to note that the distances between all points (service, delivery, pick-up and head office points) are assumed to be known. In a real environment we will use positioning systems and updated maps, capable of indicating the distance between any two points.

Apart from all previous requirements, companies need flexible solutions that allow them to modify the routes obtained in case there appear very valuable new operations. In order to face such challenge we propose to take a snapshot of the current status of the problem and restart the resolution of the problem, considering only the new tasks and those delivery and pick-up points that have not been handled yet, and taking into account current positions of terminal vehicles and mobile warehouses.

Characterization of the Problem

This section defines the problem of ecological dynamic logistics in urban environments and introduces the concepts used in this paper. The formalization is similar to that used for pickup and delivery routing problems with time windows

(Bent & Van Hentenryck, 2006). In contrast to that problem, which only considers one type of vehicle, in the ecological dynamic logistics problem, there are two types of vehicles, terminal vehicles and mobile warehouses. In addition, deliveries and pick-ups do not have an associated time window. Nonetheless, when a terminal vehicle runs out of capacity it has to regenerate it, imposing a time window constraint to mobile warehouses.

Pickup, delivery and service points: The problem is defined in terms of n customer points (including deliveries and pick-ups), a set of s service points, and a head office ($depot$). We use *Customers* to define the set of customer points, *Services* to define the set of service points, and *Sites* to denote the whole set of points. We use $Customer^p$ and $Customer^d$ to designate pick-up and delivery points, respectively. The cost of traveling from any two points is denoted by c_{ij}. Every customer point has a service time z_i. On the other hand, terminal vehicles require a time g to regenerate their capacity at a service point.

Vehicles: The problem is defined in terms of two sets of vehicles. T represents the set of terminal vehicles, each vehicle having a capacity Q_t. On the other hand M represents the set of mobile warehouses, each one having a capacity Q_m

Terminal vehicle routes: A terminal vehicle route starts at the $depot$, visits a set of customers and, possibly, service points and returns to the $depot$. In other words, the route of a terminal vehicle i is a sequence

$$r_t^i = < 0, a_1^i, ..., a_h^i, \quad b_1^i, a_{h+1}^i, ..., a_k^i, b_l^i, a_{k+1}^i, .., a_o^i, 0 >$$

where $a_j^i \in Customers$, $j = 1, ..., o$, and all a_j^i are different, $b_j^i \in Services$, $m = 1, ..., l$, which are not required to be different, and 0 represents the $depot$. We define a subroute as a subset of a route that includes all customer points between two consecutive service points. The customer points of a route r_t^i, denoted by $cust(r_t^i)$, is the set $\{a_1, ..., a_o\}$. The service points of a route, denoted by $serv(r_t^i)$, is the set $\{b_1, ..., b_l\}$. The size of a route, denoted by $|r_t^i|$, is the number of customers $| cust(r_t^i) |$. The travel cost of a route r_t^i, denoted by $c_t(r_t^i)$, is the cost of visiting all its customers (see Box 1) if the route is not empty, and 0 otherwise.

Terminal vehicle routing plan: A terminal vehicle routing plan is a set of routes $\{r_t^1, ..., r_t^u\}$ with $u \le |T|$ visiting every customer exactly once, i.e.,

$$\bigcup_{i=1}^u cust\left(r_t^i\right) = Customers$$

$$cust\left(r_t^i\right) \bigcap cust\left(r_t^j\right) = \varnothing \quad \forall i, j, \ 1 \le i, j \le |T|$$

We define a visited-service-point as a service point j visited by terminal vehicle i and denote it b_j^i. We define the set s_σ, which includes all visited-service-points used in the routing plan σ. In other words, s_σ contains

Box 1.

$$c_t\left(r_t^i\right) = c_{oa_1^i} + c_{a_1^i a_2^i} + ... + c_{a_h^i b_1^i} + c_{b_1^i a_{h+1}^i} + ... + c_{a_k^i b_l^i} + c_{b_l^i a_{k+1}^i} + ... + c_{a_o^i o}$$

$\{b_1^1, ..., b_l^1, b_1^2, ..., b_x^2, ..., b_1^n, ..., b_y^n\}$. To simplify the notation we will consider $s_\sigma = \{v_i, ..., v_d\}$ where d is the total number of visited-service-points. In addition we define the set $x_\sigma = Customers \bigcup s_\sigma$, which includes all the points visited in the terminal vehicle routing plan, and call a point $x_i \in x_\sigma$, $i = 1, ..., (n+d)$ a visited-point. Note that in a terminal vehicle routing plan, every visited-point is visited exactly once.

Observe that a terminal vehicle routing plan assigns a unique successor and predecessor to every visited-point. The successor and predecessor of customer i in routing plan σ are denoted by $succ(i, \sigma)$ and $pred(i, \sigma)$. For simplicity, our definitions assume an underlying routing plan σ and we use i_σ^+ and i_σ^- to denote the successor and predecessor of i in σ. We use the function $presubroute(x)$, which returns the set of customer points that precede a visited-point p in the subroute where it is included, and the function $postsubroute(x)$ which returns the set of customer points that succeed visited-point x in the subroute where it is included. Note that if p is a visited-service-point, it is included in two subroutes, in this case $presubroute(x)$ returns the set of customer points of the subroute that ends in x, and $postsubroute(x)$ returns the set of customer points of the subroute that starts in x.

Mobile warehouse Routes: a mobile warehouse route starts at the *depot*, visits a set of visited-service-points included in a terminal vehicle routing plan σ, and returns to the *depot*. In other words, a mobile warehouse route is a sequence $r_w^i =< 0, v_1, ..., v_e, 0 >$, where all v_i represent visited-service-points, and are required to be different. The service points of a route $r_w^i =< 0, v_1^i, ..., v_e^i, 0 >$ is the set $\{v_1^i, ..., v_e^i\}$, denoted by $serv(r_w^i)$. The function $preroute(v)$

returns the set of visited-service-points that precede the visited-service-point v in the mobile warehouse route in which it is included, without including the *depot*. The function $postroute(v)$ returns the set of visited-service-points that succeed the visited-service-point v in the mobile warehouse route in which it is included, without including the *depot*. The travel cost of a route $r_w^i =< 0, v_1, ..., v_e, 0 >$ denoted by $c_w(r_w^i)$ is the cost of visiting all its service points, i.e., $c_w(r_w^i) = c_{0v_1^i} + c_{v_1^i v_2^i} + ... + c_{v_e^i 0}$, if the route is not empty, and zero otherwise.

Mobile warehouse routing plan: A mobile warehouse routing plan is a set of mobile warehouse routes $\{w_r^1, ..., w_r^m\}$, with $m \le |M|$, visiting every visited-service-point included in the set s_σ of a terminal vehicle routing plan σ exactly once, i.e.,

$$\bigcup_{i=1}^{m} serv\left(r_w^i\right) = s_\sigma$$

$$serv\left(r_w^i\right) \bigcap serv\left(r_w^j\right) = \varnothing \quad \forall \ i,j, \ 1 \le i,j \le |M|$$

Observe that a mobile warehouse routing plan φ assigns a unique successor and predecessor to every service point. These successors and predecessors are sites. The successor and predecessor of customer i in routing plan φ are denoted by $succ(i, \varphi)$ and $pred(i, \varphi)$. For simplicity, our definition assume an underlying routing plan φ and we use i_φ^+ and i_φ^- to denote the successor and predecessor of i.

Full routing plan: A full routing plan is a tuple $< \sigma, \varphi >$, where σ is a terminal vehicle routing plan and φ is a mobile warehouse routing plan.

Time constraints: terminal vehicles that visit a service point impose some time constraints to mobile warehouses. A visited-service-point v_i of a terminal vehicle routing plan σ is visited at time δ_{v_i}. A mobile warehouse that includes v_i in its route must arrive at that point before δ_{v_i}. It may arrive earlier but it has to wait for the terminal vehicle until time δ_{v_i}. In addition, it has to spend a time g regenerating the terminal vehicle capacity. The time at which a visited-point $i \in x_\sigma$ is visited is calculated recursively as

$$\delta_0 = 0$$

$$\delta_i = \delta_{i_\sigma^-} + c_{i_\sigma^- i} + z_i \qquad if \ i \in Customers$$

or

$$\delta_i = \delta_{i_\sigma^-} + c_{i_\sigma^- i} + g \qquad if \ i \in Service$$

On the other hand the earliest time α_j at which a mobile warehouse arrives to a visited-point j, which also is a visited-service-point, is calculated recursively as

$$\alpha_0 = 0$$

$$\alpha_j = \alpha_{j_\varphi^-} + g + c_{j_\varphi^- j}$$

A full routing plan $< \sigma, \varphi >$ satisfies the time constraints if $\alpha_i \leq \delta_i \ \forall i \in s_\varphi$.

Working day constraints: Each terminal vehicle i can deliver and pick up items for a given period of time $[s_i, l_i]$, where s_i and l_i represent its start and the leaving times, which correspond to its working hours. If we define β_i the time of the last visit of terminal vehicle i to the *depot* (which indicates the time when its working day

ends), a full routing plan $< \sigma, \varphi >$ satisfies the working day constraints if $\beta_i \leq l_i$, $\forall i \in T$.

Analogously, each mobile warehouse j can work for a given period of time $[d_j, f_j]$, where d_j and f_j represent the departure and the finish time, which correspond to its working hours. If we define γ_j as the time of the last visit of mobile warehouse j to the *depot* (which indicates the time when its working day ends), a full routing plan $< \sigma, \varphi >$ satisfies the working day constraints of mobile warehouses if $\gamma_j \leq d_j$, $\forall j \in M$.

Capacity constraints: The used capacity of a terminal vehicle at visited-point x includes the number of pick-ups preceding x in the subroute that includes x, the number of deliveries succeeding x in the subroute that includes x, and one more item if x is a pick-up. The used capacity is calculated as

$$q_t(x) = \sum_{i \in presubroute(x)} pickup(i) + \sum_{i \in postsubroute(x)} delivery(i) + pickup(x)$$

where $pickup(i)$ is a function that returns 1 if $i \in Customers^p$ and 0 otherwise. Analogously $delivery(i)$ is a function that returns 1 if $i \in Customers^d$ and 0 otherwise. The constraints on terminal vehicles capacity are satisfied if $q_t(x) \leq Q_t$, $\forall x \in Customers$.

The used capacity of a mobile warehouse at a visited-service-point v includes the number of pick-ups of the terminal vehicles that regenerate their capacity using the mobile warehouse in the service points preceding v, the number of deliveries of the terminal vehicles that will regenerate their capacity using the mobile warehouse in the service points succeeding v, and the pick-ups of the terminal vehicle that regenerates its capacity in service point v. It is calculated in the equation in Box 2.

The constraints on mobile warehouses capacity are satisfied if $q_w(v) \leq Q_w$, $\forall v \in s_\sigma$.

Box 2.

$$q_w(v) = \sum_{i \in preroute(v)} \sum_{j \in presubroute(i)} pickup(j) + \sum_{i \in postroute(x)} \sum_{j \in postsubroute(i)} delivery(j) + \sum_{i \in presubroute(v)} pickup(i)$$

Final formulation: A solution to the proposed problem is a full routing plan $< \sigma, \varphi >$ that satisfies the time constraints, the working day constraints and the capacity constrains, i.e.,

$$\alpha_i \leq \delta_i \qquad \forall i \in s_\varphi$$

$$\beta_j \leq l_j \qquad \forall j \in T$$

$$q_t(v) \leq Q_t \qquad \forall v \in Customers$$

$$q_w(v) \leq Q_w \qquad \forall w \in s_\sigma$$

The size of a terminal vehicle routing plan σ, denoted by $|\sigma|$ is the number of non-empty terminal vehicle routes in σ, i.e., $\{r_t^i \in \sigma \ / cust(r_t^i) \neq \varnothing\}$. The size of a mobile warehouse routing plan φ, denoted by $|\varphi|$ is the number of non-empty mobile warehouses routes in φ, i.e., $\{r_w^i \in \varphi \ / serv(r_w^i) \neq \varnothing\}$. Specifically, these conditions of size allow us to optimize the number of terminal vehicles and mobile warehouses. The cost of a terminal vehicle routing plan is calculated as $\sum_{r_t^i \in \sigma} c_t(r_t^i)$. On the other hand, the cost of a mobile warehouse routing plan is calculated as $\sum_{r_w^i \in \varphi} c_w(r_w^i)$. Therefore, the objectives of the problem are:

$$\min |\sigma| \tag{1.1}$$

$$\min |\varphi| \tag{1.2}$$

$$\min \sum_{r_t^i \in \sigma} c_t(r_t^i) \tag{1.3}$$

$$\min \sum_{r_w^i \in \varphi} c_w(r_w^i) \tag{1.4}$$

METHODOLOGY OF RESOLUTION

To solve the problem, a specific exact method to find the optimal solution could be used. However, the business expectations indicate that the size of the instances of the problem can grow to intractable sizes (distribution in a medium city, as Murcia, or big as Madrid in Spain where the number of nodes that define the problem may be much larger). This fact means the exact method needs a lot of time (of the order of days) to obtain a solution. In cases where it is not possible to obtain an optimal solution in a feasible time, it is necessary to use techniques that are able to obtain high-quality solutions in a reasonable time. Among these techniques, metaheuristics stand out. Metaheuristics are intelligent strategies to design or improve very general heuristic procedures with high performance. Such strategies have been widely used in the resolution of all kinds of optimization problems obtaining excellent results. Among metaheuristics various techniques stand out such as Genetic Algorithms, Tabu Search, the Particle Swarm Optimization, Ant Colony Optimization, ... For the problem to be solved, the metaheuristic that may be more appropriate is the Ant Colony Optimization (ACO) (Dorigo & Stützle, 2003; Silva, Sousa & Runkler, 2008), since it was specifically designed to solve problems of minimization of paths and has been applied with great success to several problems such as the Traveling Salesman problem, Packet Routing problems in Telecommunication Networks, problems of Pick-up and Delivery. For this reason, we propose to use it (Dorigo, Maniezzo & Colorni, 1996; Dorigo & Stützle, 2003).

Ant Colony

Ants are social insects that live in colonies and whose behavior is directed to the development of the colony as a whole rather than to individual development, (Bella & McMullen, 2004). An interesting feature of the behaviour of ant colonies is how they can find the shortest path between the nest and the food, because they are blind. Ants are able to do so because, in their path, they deposit a substance called pheromone that they can smell. This trail allows ants to find the best path from the food back to their nest. In particular, ants move in a random way and choose those paths where the pheromone is stronger with a higher probability. Thus, the most promising paths accumulate greater amounts of pheromone because they are used by more ants, while the less promising paths lose pheromone by evaporation because they are gradually abandoned by ants. Natural ants are able to solve shortest path problems with minimum effort. The algorithms of Ant Colony Optimization (ACO) try to reproduce the behaviour of real ants to solve such problems.

Principles of the Ant Colony

Each ant is a probabilistic mechanism able to construct solutions. To construct a solution each ant uses:

- Artificial pheromone trails which change with time to reflect the experience of the other ants in solving the problem.
- Some heuristic information about the particular instance of the problem.

The basic operating mode of an ACO algorithm is as follows: the ants of the colony move concurrently and asynchronously, through adjacent states of the problem. This movement is performed following a transition rule which is based on local information available to the components (nodes). This local information includes heuristic information and the pheromone trails to guide the search. By moving through the construction graph, ants incrementally build solutions. Once each ant has generated a solution, this is evaluated and the ant can deposit a quantity of pheromone which is a function of the quality of the solution. This information will guide the search for other ants in the colony in the future. In addition, the operating mode of a generic ACO algorithm includes two additional procedures, the evaporation of the pheromone trails and the daemon actions. The pheromone evaporation is performed by the environment and is used as a mechanism to avoid the local optima in the search and allows the ants to find and explore new regions of space. The daemon actions are optional actions, which have no natural counterpoint, able to implement tasks from a global perspective that the ants cannot perform because they offer a local perspective. Some of these actions used in ACO algorithms are: monitoring the quality of the solutions generated and deposit an additional amount of pheromone only in transitions/components associated with some solutions, or apply a local search procedure that improves the obtained solutions before updating the pheromone trail.

The generic structure of an ACO is presented in Algorithm 1.

There are various implementations of the concept of ACO, one of the most competitive being the MAX-MIN ant system (MM-AS) (Stützle Hoos, 1996, 2000). This MM-AS version will be used to solve the problem proposed in this paper. MM-AS provides a good balance between exploration and exploitation and reduces the pos-

Algorithm 1. ACO_metaheuristic

```
ACO(N:integer; F:initial pheromone) = x_best
var
    C /*neighborhood structure of an ant*/
    M /*collective memory structure of ants */
    P /*probability structure for each movement of
an ant */
    pos /*ants positions*/
begin
    repeat
    for i:=1 to N do
            {M}:= UpdateMemory(M);
            while not Solution do
                {C}:= Neighborhood(pos);
                {P}:= EvaluateNeighbours(C,M);
                {pos}:= AntMovement(P);
                {F}:= DepositPheromone(pos);
                {x}:= AddComponent(pos);
        end
        {x}:= UpdateSolutions(x);
    end
    {F}:= EvaporatePheromone(x,F);
    {F}:= DaemonActions(x,F);
    until termination;
    {x_best}:= ChooseBest(x);
end
```

sibility to reach local optima, obtaining very competitive results.

MM-AS has the following particular aspects:

- An update of the pheromone trails is applied offline. That is, after all ants have constructed their solutions, each pheromone trail suffers evaporation and the pheromone is deposited only on the best solution which can be either the best global solution or the best solution of the iteration.

- Possible values for the pheromone trails are limited to the range $[\tau_{min}, \tau_{max}]$, so as to reduce the likelihood of the algorithm stalling. Also, it should be noted that in order to increase the exploration of new solutions, a re-initialization of these trails is sometimes used.

- Pheromone trails are initialized to a high value (the maximum allowed τ_{max}), instead of a lower one as usual. This helps in diversification of the search since the initial differences in the trails will be small.

Applying the Algorithm to the Problem

As we have discussed above, the metaheuristic that will be used to solve the problem is the Ant Colony Optimization in its MAX-MIN version.

Construction of the Solution Using Ants

The process to obtain solutions is constructive, and each ant has to build its own solution in each iteration. This process is supported by the use of a pheromone matrix that links all points of the problem ($Customers \bigcup Services$) between them, regardless of whether they represent points of pick-up, delivery or service. Thus the cell (i, j) of the matrix represents the suitability of moving from points x_i to point x_j.

This pheromone trail matrix associated to connections is initialized to the maximum value of range (as we have mentioned above): $\tau_{ij} = \tau_{max}$, $\forall (i, j)$ links.

The construction of the solution is divided into three subprocesses:

- First the route of a terminal vehicle is built until its capacity is exhausted (both delivery and pick-up). It should be noted that all terminal vehicles start from the head office.
- Second, after exhausting the capacity, we have to decide how to regenerate it (charging items to deliver and downloading the picked-up items) either the terminal vehicle could return to the head office or it could go to a point of service in which a mobile warehouse is waiting for it.
- Third, after regenerating its capacity, we can continue to construct routes in the same way until the maximum allowed hours for terminal vehicles are reached. After that, it is necessary to use a new terminal vehicle, following this process, until all tasks are completed.

In this process, the pheromone matrix is updated every iteration following Equation (2).

$$\tau_{ij}\left(t+1\right) = \begin{cases} \rho\tau_{ij}(t) & if\, the\, link\, \left(i,j\right)\; not\, belongs\, to\, BS \\ \rho\tau_{ij}\left(t\right) + \Delta\tau(t) & if\, the\, link\, \left(i,j\right)\; belongs\, to\, BS \end{cases}$$
(2)

where $0 \le \rho \le 1$ is the pheromone trail evaporation rate, $\Delta\tau\left(t\right)$ is the amount of the added information in the iteration t and BS is the best route obtained.

$\Delta\tau\left(t\right)$ is defined as $\Delta\tau\left(t\right) = \dfrac{1}{A}$ where A is the value obtained when evaluating BS by the objective function (5).

The construction process of the routes uses the pheromone matrix and a simple heuristic, which is the inverse of the distance to be covered. Thus the ant decides which is the next node to visit based on the assessment of the nodes that can be reached considering its constraints of schedule and capacity (transition rule). It should be noted that one of these limitations is that the terminal vehicle has to return to the head office before ending its workday. This transition rule for the k -th ant is shown in Equation (3).

$$\vartheta_{ij}\left(k\right) = \eta_{ij}^{\beta} \cdot \tau_{ij}^{\alpha}$$

$$\forall\; i,j \in T\bigcup M \tag{3}$$

where i represents the location of the mobile vehicle, j is the point of its neighborhood where mobile vehicle would go, α and β are parameters of the algorithm, and heuristic value is $\eta_{ij} = \dfrac{1}{c_{ij}}$ and represents heuristic information not provided by the ants.

Given these evaluations of the transition rule, every possible movement receives a selection probability, and finally the movement is selected from a stochastic mode.

These probabilities of selection are calculated from Equation (3) and are shown in Equation (4) in Box 3.

Having exhausted the capacity of the terminal vehicle, this must be regenerated going to either a service point or head office. This decision is made in a similar way to the decision of the next point of delivery/pick-up. Firstly, the service points which both terminal vehicle and mobile warehouse may reach are calculated. Additionally, the head office is added, which is always available. Finally, each of the points is assessed using the Equation (3) and based on its assessment receives a probability using the Equation (4). Using these probabilities the service point is chosen in a stochastic way. There is one exception to this process, which happens when a mobile warehouse is parked at a service point near the terminal vehicle and the latter is able to reach its position before it leaves. In this case the service point is automatically selected to reduce costs.

To calculate what service points are available for the terminal vehicle we perform the following process. First service points that are closer than the head office are checked. From these points, we analyze if it is possible for some of the mobile warehouse already in circulation to reach the point

Box 3.

$$p_{ij}\left(an\right) = \begin{cases} \dfrac{\eta_{ij}^{\beta} \cdot \tau_{ij}^{\alpha}}{\sum_{h} \eta_{ij}^{\beta} \cdot \tau_{ij}^{\alpha}} & for\, the\, h\; \text{possible movements of the } an - \text{th ant} \\ \\ 0 & otherwise \end{cases} \tag{4}$$

when needed. Otherwise, if there are available mobile warehouses which have not yet begun their workday, they may be used. Once the service points have been decided (where terminal vehicles have to go), the task of supplying a terminal vehicle is assigned to the mobile warehouse which is closer and is able to get there in time. However, if no mobile warehouse is available at that time, then the terminal vehicle has to return to the head office.

As we can see, the construction of the routes of the mobile warehouses depends on the terminal vehicle routes. In order to construct them we use a time table, which stores the location of each mobile warehouse at each moment. At this point, we could include, instead of a time table, time windows as it is specified in works as (Figliozzi, 2009) and (Bent & Van Hentenryck, 2006). In this case, we would first plan the routes of the terminal vehicles, theses routes would define time windows for the mobile warehouses, and using these time windows we could calculate the routes of the mobile warehouses. The main reason why we have not chosen this solution is because we need to find a feasible solution in the shortest possible time.

When a terminal vehicle finishes its workday, it has to return to the head office and, if there are terminal vehicles available, a new one will begin to perform tasks until it exhausts its workday. This process is repeated iteratively until all tasks have been completed or all terminal vehicles have been used.

A notable aspect regarding the terminal vehicle management is that although the solution is constructed sequentially, in the case of requiring more than one terminal vehicle, all start their workday at the same time, but it is possible that one of them finishes delivery/pick-up items before the end of its workday, because there are no more items for that day.

Evaluation of the Solutions

The solution is provided as a sequence of points to which vehicles must go. Each terminal vehicle is assigned a route and each mobile warehouse is also assigned a schedule indicating where it must be found in certain moments.

The cost of the solution provided by the metaheuristic is given by the cost of all terminal vehicle routing plans and the cost of all mobile warehouses routing plans. To minimize the number of terminal vehicles and mobile warehouses, when the cost of each solution is calculated, it is penalized in function of the number of terminal vehicles and mobile warehouses used in the solution at a rate of $\frac{|\sigma|}{|T|}$ and $\frac{|\varphi|}{|M|}$. So, the smaller the number of terminal vehicles and mobile warehouses used in the solution, the lower the cost. Therefore, the four objective functions (1.1), (1.2), (1.3) and (1.4) are replaced by the objective function (5).

$$\min\left[\left(\sum_{r_t^i \in \sigma} c_t(r_t^i) \cdot \sum_{r_w^i \in \varphi} c_w(r_w^i)\right) \cdot \left(\frac{|\sigma|}{|T|} \cdot \frac{|\varphi|}{|M|}\right)\right] \quad (5)$$

But, it is possible that for certain input parameters such as the number of terminal vehicles, the number of mobile warehouses and items to deliver and/or pick up, there will not be a feasible solution. Then the following solutions are adopted:

- Discard items remaining to deliver/pick up when no more terminal vehicles available. In this case we shall take into account the priority of the items. For this, the objective (5) must be modified to include these priorities.

Each item contains a value indicating the priority of delivery or pick-up. This value will range from 1 to 10 where 1 indicates lowest priority and 10 the highest. Value pri_i denote the priority of item i, $\forall i \in Customers$. The objective function that reflects these priorities is as follows

$$\min \left[10 \cdot | Customers | - \sum_{\substack{i \in Customer \\ i \in Sol}} pri_i \right]$$

where

$$Sol = \bigcup_{i=1}^{u} cust\left(r_t^i\right).$$

In this situation, the new objective function is added in (5) as a new factor weighted by K positive constant indicating the weight of this component.

- Increasing the workday of the last terminal vehicle in order to complete the work.

Decision making when there isn't a feasible solution, is carried out by the company, which must determine the most favorable decision based on various input parameters. Because the computation time of metaheuristic is not very high, the company will evaluate the different solutions running the metaheuristic as many times as it is necessary.

Resource Requirements and Scalability

Once we have selected the metaheuristic, which we are going to use, we can make an estimate of resources required for its application. One of the main limiting factors is the size of the distance matrix that links the different delivery, service and pick-up points, in particular the size of the distance

matrix can be estimated. The memory used by today's personal computers, may be between 4 and 8 GB, assuming you could only use 2 GB, a distance matrix of 20000 points can be handled without problems, which could be considered a number of really significant deliveries and pick-ups for a single company of distribution.

Regarding the time necessary to get the solutions, as it is a metaheuristic that is always able to provide an approximate solution (although not the best), it will depend on how much time we want to spend to improve the initial solutions. We expect that the time necessary is in the order of minutes. Tests carried out using the prototype designed show a reasonable time, from a few seconds for small instances (100 points) to about 5 minutes for instances of larger size (1000 points).

If constraints of time were too tight, the ant colony could be parallelized easily, since each ant can build its solution in parallel during the same iteration, which will help to reduce the execution time in an important factor. Therefore, we believe that initially the needs for instances of a significant magnitude (20000 points of delivery, pick-up and service) could be fulfilled with a personal computer of the last generation. In the case that the magnitude of the instances is increased or time constraints could be overflowed, we could choose to configure a cluster composed of several personal computers.

APPLICATION EXAMPLES

The proposal is tested in a network of a simulated urban city. We identify each point, which may represent a delivery, pick-up, or service point, by a number. There is a limited number of vehicles and each vehicle has a limited capacity and speed. The proposed solution obtains an acceptable route for deliver/pick up items. This solution uses the minimum number vehicles required to give sufficient coverage.

Table 1. Parameters to run MM-AS

ρ	τ_{min}	τ_{max}	α	β	# ants	iterations
0.9	1	5	1	2	10	50

We show two test cases. The first shows how to find a solution for a problem of delivery and pick-up of items with different priorities, having a maximum number of vehicles. The second shows how the solution is adapted running the previous case when we introduce new delivery and pick-up items. Note that the procedure penalizes solutions which contain lower priority items. For these test cases, the algorithm MM-AS runs with the parameters shown in Table 1.

Case 1

We are going to suppose we have a graph with the structure of the streets of a city and every possible points of delivery, pick-up and service are described in this structure: each point is denoted by a number. Table 2 shows the input data to configure the problem.

Both the graph and the points of delivery and pick-up of the problem are defined in Table 2, where the speed of vehicles, their capacities, their working time and the maximum available amount of each them are described too. We assume that 30 delivery points, 30 pick-up points and 2 pairs of pick-up/delivery points are known. We also have 30 service points that can be used. These points are randomly generated in a square area of 10 by 10. All points of the area are labeled from 1 to 100. The label 1 is used to designate the Head office and it is located (without loss of generality) in the lower left corner. All labels are associated from bottom to top and from left to right. Moreover, under the delivery and pick-up points, a value indicating the priority of the item appears. This information is shown on Table 3.

Table 4 shows the obtained solution. In this table we use the following nomenclature:

- TV_x: Terminal vehicle x
- MW_x: Mobile warehouse x
- $WTPS$: Waiting time of MW_x at the point of service.
- TM_x: Time of meeting with mobile warehouse or at the head office.
- e_x: Item to pick up at point x
- r_x: Item to deliver at the point x
- s_x: The terminal vehicle is at a service point x
- rr_x: Item to be picked up at the point x and delivered on the same route.
- ee_x: Item picked up over the route of the terminal vehicle to be delivered at the point x
- c_x: Head Office of the company

We briefly analyze the route of TV_1, which is divided in 3 subroutes. After leaving the head of-

Table 2. Configuration file of Model

File of Distances distance.file=Murcia.map
File of Points(services,deliveries,pick-ups) point.file=pointsMurcia.txt
Terminal vehicle features terminal.v.speed=8 terminal.v.capacity=5 terminal.v.hours=8 terminal.v.quantity=10
Warehouse vehicle features warehouse.v.speed=40 warehouse.v.capacity=1000 warehouse.v.hours=8 warehouse.v.quantity=5

Table 3. Configuration of points of delivery, pick-up, service and head office

	21	51	30	36	27	58	80	81	33	13	26	73	76	45	100	17	3	16	54	71	25	94	90	39	78	19	14	15	86	11
Pick-ups	1	1	2	1	1	1	1	2	8	5	4	2	2	2	1	1	1	2	7	1	1	1	3	3	1	1	9	4	1	1
Deliveries	41	4	50	75	32	98	52	22	35	60	87	67	89	66	68	34	47	12	99	69	61	93	48	43	7	2	20	49	92	24
	1	1	3	1	4	1	1	2	3	1	2	6	9	2	1	7	9	7	4	3	2	1	1	1	6	1	3	2	1	2
Pick-ups/ Deliveries	57/55	96/28																												
	9	1																												
Service points	88	97	72	59	40	77	64	82	53	84	95	31	38		6	85	63	18	46	23	29	44	37	9	65	42	62	10	56	5
Head office	1																													

Table 4. Feasible solution for case 1

TV₁	c_1	r_2	r_{12}	e_{11}	e_{13}	c_3	r_{20}	r_7	s_6	e_{16}	c_{17}	c_{27}	c_{26}	r_{24}	r_{22}	r_{32}	c_{33}	r_{43}	r_{34}	c_1	e_{14}	e_{15}	c_{25}	r_{35}	c_{36}	c_{59}	r_{48}	r_{87}	r_{41}	c_1
TMₓ									2:37											4:45	ee_{55}	c_1 7:37								7:55
TV₂ / TMₓ	c_1	r_{21}	e_{19}	e_{30}	r_{50}	r_{60}	e_{49}	e_{58}	r_{69}	s_{59} 3:00	c_{45}	c_{51}	r_{61}	r_{71}	r_{73}	c_{54}	r_{52}	rr_{57}	r_{67}	r_{66}										
TV₃	c_1	r_{75}	c_{76}	e_{86}	c_{94}	e_{92}	e_{81}	r_{87}	e_{89}	s_{79} 3:45	e_{80}	e_{90}	e_{78}	r_{98}	r_{99}	e_{100}	rr_{96}	ee_{28}	c_1 7:37											
TMₓ																														
MW₁	c_1					s_6			s_6	s_{59}			s_{79}			c_1														
WTPS	0:00-0:00					2:26-2:41			2:55-3:10				3:41-3:56			4:25-4:25														

fice, TV_1 can deliver three items and pick up five. Once it has exhausted its capacity it regenerates it at service point 6 where it meets MW_1. On the other hand, after finishing its second subroute, it regenerates its capacity at the head office. We can also outline that MW_1 can also support TV_2 and TV_3.

Case 2

We are going to suppose we introduce in the chain of delivery/pick-up an urgent item. It has to be picked up at point 91 and has to be delivered at the point 74. This request was made when four hours have passed since the beginning of the route. At this moment, the algorithm is executed once again, but we discard all the tasks that have already been treated. Consequently the algorithm only takes into account the remaining tasks and the new one. The proposed solution is shown in Table 5.

In this situation, TV_1 is supported by MW_1 again in point 44, where it can pick up or deliver some items. As we can see in the readjustment of plans, tasks 14, 15, 25, 36 and 39 are discarded.

CONCLUSION

This paper presents the study, analysis and proposed solution for the problem of finding routes for delivery and/or pick-up of items using environmentally friendly vehicles. In the problem the cost of the solution is minimized, along with the number of resources used: the number of mobile warehouses and terminal vehicles.

This study has been performed to show the feasibility of this approach, so that a company, which tries to open a new market from the ecological viewpoint and wants to provide a more customized attention for the end user, can use it. We propose to address this problem using the ant colony metaheuristic, which provides a flexible and scalable system that can fulfill the needs of the company of the future. Tests show that the proposed solution is feasible since it is possible to find good solutions in a few minutes for a medium size problem.

ACKNOWLEDGMENT

Supported by the project TIN2011-27696-C02-02 of the Ministry of Economy and Competitiveness of Spain. Thanks also to "Fundación Séneca – Agencia de Ciencia y Tecnología de la Región de Murcia" (Spain) for the Funding Program for Research Groups of Excellence (04552/GERM/06) and the support given to R. Martínez by FPI scholarship program.

Table 5. Feasible solution for case 2

TV_1	r_{34}	s_{44}	r_{52}	r_{48}	r_{35}	r_{47}	r_{41}	c_1	
TM_x	4:15	4:23							
TV_2	e_{51}	r_{61}	e_{71}	rr_{91}	r_{98}	e_{73}	ee_{74}	e_{54}	c_1
TM_x	4:15								
TV_3	e_{78}	r_{67}	r_{66}	e_{99}	e_{100}	rr_{96}	ee_{28}	c_1	
TM_x	4:15								
MW_1	s_{44}				c_1				
WTPS	4:15 - 4:30				4:40 - 4:40				

REFERENCES

Bella, J. E., & McMullen, P. R. (2004). Ant colony optimization techniques for the vehicle routing problem. *Advanced Engineering Informatics, 18,* 41–48. doi:10.1016/j.aei.2004.07.001.

Bent, R., & Van Hentenryck, P. (2006). A two-stage hybrid algorithm for pickup and delivery vehicle routing problems with time windows. *Computers & Operations Research, 33,* 875–893. doi:10.1016/j.cor.2004.08.001.

Branke, J. (2002). *Evolutionary optimization in dynamic environments.* Boston: Kluwer Academic Publishers. doi:10.1007/978-1-4615-0911-0.

Cadenas, J. M., Garrido, M. C., & Muñoz, E. (2008). Using machine learning in a cooperative hybrid parallel strategy of metaheuristics. *Information Sciences: An International Journal, 179,* 3255–3267. doi:10.1016/j.ins.2009.05.014.

Crainic, T. G., Ricciardi, N., & Storchi, G. (2009). Models for evaluating and planning city logistics systems. *Transportation Science, 43*(4), 432–454. doi:10.1287/trsc.1090.0279.

Donati, A. V., Montemanni, R., Casagrande, N., Rizzoli, A. E., & Gambardella, L. M. (2008). Time dependent vehicle routing problem with a multi ant colony system. *European Journal of Operational Research, 185*(3), 1174–1191. doi:10.1016/j.ejor.2006.06.047.

Dorigo, M., Maniezzo, V., & Colorni, A. (1996). Ant system: Optimization by a colony of cooperating agents. *IEEE Transactions on Systems, Man, and Cybernetics - Part B, 26*(1), 29–41. doi:10.1109/3477.484436 PMID:18263004.

Dorigo, M., & Stützle, T. (2003). Ant colony optimization metaheuristic. In F. Glover, & G. A. Kochenberger (Eds.), *Handbook of Metaheuristics* (pp. 251–286). London: Kluwer Academic Publisher..

Figliozzi, M. A. (2009). Planning approximations to the average length of vehicle routing problems with time window constraints. *Transportation Research Part B: Methodological, 43,* 438–447. doi:10.1016/j.trb.2008.08.004.

Fuellerera, G., Doernera, K. F., Hartla, R. F., & Iorib, M. (2009). Ant colony optimization for the two-dimensional loading vehicle routing problem. *Computers & Operations Research, 36,* 655–673. doi:10.1016/j.cor.2007.10.021.

Gajpal, Y., & Abad, P. L. (2009). Multi-ant colony system (MACS) for a vehicle routing problem with backhauls. *European Journal of Operational Research, 196,* 102–117. doi:10.1016/j.ejor.2008.02.025.

Kenworthy, J. R. (2006). The eco-city: Ten key transport and planning dimensions for sustainable city development. *Environment and Urbanization, 18*(1), 67–85. doi:10.1177/0956247806063947.

Mavrovouniotis, M., & Yang, S. (2011). A memetic ant colony optimization algorithm for the dynamic travelling salesman problem. *Soft Computing, 15*(7), 1405–1425. doi:10.1007/s00500-010-0680-1.

Montemanni, R., Gambardella, L. M., Rizzoli, A. E., & Donati, A. V. (2005). Ant colony system for a dynamic vehicle routing problem. *Journal of Combinatorial Optimization, 10,* 327–343. doi:10.1007/s10878-005-4922-6.

Nuortioa, T., Kytöjokib, J., Niskaa, H., & Bräysyb, O. (2006). Improved route planning and scheduling of waste collection and transport. *Expert Systems with Applications, 30,* 223–232. doi:10.1016/j.eswa.2005.07.009.

Puris, A., Bello, R., Martinez, Y., & Nowe, A. (2007). Twostage ant colony optimization for solving the traveling salesman problem. In J. Mira, & J. R. Álvarez (Eds.), *Nature Inspired Problem-Solving Methods in Knowledge Engineering* (pp. 307–316). Berlin: Springer. doi:10.1007/978-3-540-73055-2_33.

Rizzoli, A. E., Montemanni, R., Lucibello, E., & Gambardella, L. M. (2007). Ant colony optimisation for real world vehicle routing problems: From theory to applications. *Swarm Intelligence*, *1*(2), 135–151. doi:10.1007/s11721-007-0005-x.

Silva, C. A., Sousa, J. M. C., & Runkler, T. A. (2008). Rescheduling and optimization of logistic processes using GA and ACO. *Engineering Applications of Artificial Intelligence*, *21*(3), 343–352. doi:10.1016/j.engappai.2007.08.006.

Stützle, T., & Hoos, H.H. (1996). *Improving the ant system: A detailed report on the max-min ant system* (Technical Report AIDA- 96-12). Darmstadt, Germany: FG Intellektik, FB Informatik, TU Darmstadt.

Stützle, T., & Hoos, H. H. (2000). Max-min ant system. *Future Generation Computer Systems*, *16*(8), 889–914. doi:10.1016/S0167-739X(00)00043-1.

Tzeng, G.-H., Cheng, H.-J., & Huang, T. D. (2007). Multi-objective optimal planning for designing relief delivery systems. *Transportation Research Part E, Logistics and Transportation Review*, *43*, 673–686. doi:10.1016/j.tre.2006.10.012.

KEY TERMS AND DEFINITIONS

Ant Colony: Approach to problem solving that takes inspiration from the foraging behaviour of some ant species. These ants deposit pheromone on the ground in order to mark the best routes that should be followed by other members of the colony.

Dynamic Problem: When a problem, defined in terms of the input data, allows them to change over time.

Ecological Logistics Problem: Supply chain management and of the flow of resources between points of origin/destination in order to meet some requirements for the improvement of company efficiency (of customers and corporations) that reduce the environmental and energy footprint.

Ecological Vehicle: Vehicle (with or without motor) that produces less damage to the environment that the conventional combustion engine.

Logistics Problem: Supply chain management and of the flow of resources between points of origin and points of destination in order to meet some requirements for the improvement of company efficiency (of customers and corporations).

Metaheuristic: A high-level strategy for solving a very general class of computational problems by combining user given black-box procedures — usually heuristics — in a hopefully efficient way.

Pheromone: Number indicating how suitable a route is in the search process of an algorithm. This amount is deposited by local agents and it is decreasing as time passes.

Chapter 2
Fuzzy Techniques for Improving Satisfaction in Economic Decisions

Clara Calvo
Universidad de Valencia, Spain

Carlos Ivorra
Universidad de Valencia, Spain

Vicente Liern
Universidad de Valencia, Spain

ABSTRACT

The authors use fuzzy set theory to improve classical decision-making problems by incorporating the inherent vagueness in decision-makers' preferences into the model. They specifically study two representative models: the p-median problem and the portfolio selection problem. The first one is a location problem, which on the one hand fits many real world management situations and on the other hand is suitable for a theoretical analysis of the techniques. The version of the portfolio selection problem presented here is a harder problem, which allows the authors to show the scope of their methods. Some numerical examples are provided to illustrate how fuzzy optimal solutions improve classical ones. Finally, the authors present some results about how fuzzy solutions depend on the membership functions of fuzzy parameters.

INTRODUCTION

The classical way of handling a real-world problem is to build a mathematical model, taking into account all its relevant aspects and trying to evaluate all its parameters in the most accurate way. However, this approach is clearly naive in most cases, for two main reasons: On the one hand, many real-world characteristics that must be incorporated into a model are subject to a certain degree of uncertainty which must be handled by statistical or fuzzy techniques. On the other hand, some parameters of a decision model are not intended to reflect real-world data, but a decision-maker's preferences, which are not

DOI: 10.4018/978-1-4666-4785-5.ch002

subject to any kind of stochastic uncertainty but rather to inherent vagueness. For example, there is not much sense in saying that an investor wants a portfolio with an expected return not less than 3% with a probability of 0.95. All we can say is that he wants a 3% expected return, more or less.

Whereas there are many appropriate techniques for dealing with stochastic uncertainty when modelling real-world problems, subjective vagueness becomes more problematic and the quality of solutions provided by mathematical models is easily jeopardized by inadequate handling.

The natural way of handling subjective vagueness in those decision-maker related parameters is by means of soft constraints. In fact, since this means extending the preferences of the decision-maker from a single objective function to every vague aspect of the problem, we are led to a multi-objective environment in which even the "constraint" of optimizing the objective function becomes a soft constraint, since a slightly worse value for the objective function can be thought of as more satisfactory if it has any kind of significant counterpart.

The purpose of this chapter is to study the consequences of incorporating in this way the vagueness of the decision-maker's criteria into the mathematical formulation of a decision problem, both from a practical and theoretical point of view. With regard to the practical aspects, we will see that fuzzy solutions, i.e. the solutions of the fuzzy version of the problem, often turn out to be substantially more satisfactory than the crisp ones, but we will also check the theoretical suitability of the fuzzy models. Namely, we will see that whereas optimal solutions are very sensitive to crisp parameters expressing subjective criteria, they show very low sensitivity to reasonably chosen fuzzy tolerances.

We will analyze two classical decision problems: the p-median location problem and a generalized version of the Markowitz portfolio selection problem. Both of them are mixed-integer problems of unquestionable practical interest, but the first

one, being a linear-integer program, provides an opportunity to make an in-depth theoretical sensitivity study. On the other hand, the portfolio selection problem is non-linear and, by extending it with some computationally complex additional constraints, it becomes quite representative of the difficulties we can expect to find when dealing with fuzzy versions of general decision problems.

BACKGROUND

Introduction to Fuzzy Optimization

The concept of fuzzy set was introduced by Zadeh (1965) and has become a powerful tool for introducing vagueness into all kinds of mathematical theories. Its application to fuzzy optimization is particularly noteworthy, mainly because fuzzy set theory perfectly fits the problem of capturing the unavoidable vagueness that affects every subjective criterion imposed by a decision-maker. Decision-makers are human beings and they think and express their preferences with an inherent degree of vagueness. Classical optimization theory ignores this fact by artificially reducing the parameters representing this kind of subjective constraint to mere real numbers, and this almost unconscious fact occurring at the very beginning of the modellization process can be enough to hide possible solutions that the decision-maker could prefer to a solution strictly satisfying the artificially simplified imposed constraints.

As we have indicated, the Soft Computing approach for handling vagueness in this context relies on fuzzy optimization, which has been widely studied in the literature. The seminal paper on the topic is Bellman and Zadeh (1970), but here we will follow those presented by Delgado et al. (1994) and Zimmermann (1997).

A fuzzy optimization problem is determined by a fuzzy constraint set $\tilde{C}$ and a fuzzy goal set $\tilde{G}$. The fuzzy constraint set specifies the degree of feasibility of a given solution, that is, we will not distinguish between feasible and infeasible solutions anymore, but instead we will admit partially feasible solutions that the decision-maker could consider more or less acceptable. On the other hand, the goal set measures how satisfactory a given solution is considered to be by the decision-maker. Hence, the set $\tilde{G}$ classifies the possible solutions into absolutely satisfactory solutions and absolutely inadmissible solutions, but also into partially satisfactory solutions that the decision-maker could approve of in some cases.

More precisely, the constraint set $\tilde{C}$ is determined by a membership function $\mu_{\tilde{C}} : \mathrm{R}^n \rightarrow [0,1]$ so that, for a given solution $x \in \mathrm{R}^n$, the degree of feasibility $\mu_{\tilde{C}}(x)$ indicates how feasible x is: 0 means that the solution is absolutely infeasible (it cannot be accepted in any case), 1 means that the solution is absolutely feasible (it clearly meets all the decision-maker's requirements) and intermediate values correspond to partially feasible solutions (which can be thought of as meeting the decision-maker's criteria, taking into account the vagueness of its limits). Similarly, the satisfaction provided by a solution is measured by the membership function $\mu_{\tilde{G}} : \mathrm{R}^n \rightarrow [0,1]$ of the goal set $\tilde{G}$.

The decision set of a fuzzy optimization problem is defined as the fuzzy intersection $\tilde{D} = \tilde{C} \cap \tilde{G}$ of the constraint and the goal set, i.e. the fuzzy set whose membership function is given by

$$\mu_{\tilde{D}}(x) = \min\left\{\mu_{\tilde{C}}(x),\ \mu_{\tilde{G}}(x)\right\}$$

The optimal solutions of the problem are those maximizing the membership degree of the decision set. We will call this degree the *global satisfaction level* of a given solution.

Although a fuzzy optimization problem does not need to be related to any classical (crisp) opti-mization problem, many of them arise in a natural way by introducing fuzziness into a previous model. The main idea in these cases is to change from considering just crisp feasible solutions to admitting some partially feasible ones which could be acceptable, because in many cases it is unrealistic to interpret the constraints imposed by the decision-maker literally, at least when they express subjective criteria, which is the case we are interested in. By expanding the feasible set in this way, we can find partially feasible solutions improving the goal function of the optimal solution of the original problem in which only totally feasible solutions are allowed. The extent to which a partially feasible solution improves this original optimal goal value can be used as a basis to determine its fuzzy degree of satisfaction.

Next we proceed to describing two particular instances of this general context. In this background section we will present the classical versions of the problems, while the fuzzy versions will be studied in the main body of the chapter.

The P-Median Problem

The *p*-median problem was formulated by S. L. Hakimi (Hakimi, 1964, 1965; Daskin, 1995). It can be applied in many different contexts, but in a typical formulation we have a set of n cities connected by a road network and we wish to select a set of p of them to locate facilities from which a product will be distributed to the other cities. The problem consists in finding the best location for those p facilities to minimize the transport costs. From a mathematical point of view, we have a non-directed connected graph with a set of vertices $V=\{v_1,\ldots,v_n\}$ representing the cities, and a set of edges representing the roads connecting the cities. In the simplest models of the problem, the unit transport cost between vertices v_i and v_j, is assumed to be proportional to the length d_{ij} of the shortest path joining them. Let w_j be the demand for the product that must be delivered at vertex v_j. Although the formulation of the problem allows the facilities to be located at any point, it can be shown that there is at least one optimal solution in which all the facilities are located at p vertices of the network (Hakimi and Maheshwari, 1972; Wendell, and Hurter, 1973). Taking this into account, following ReVelle and Swain (1972), the p-median problem can be formulated as the following mixed-integer linear programming model:

$$\text{Min} \quad \sum_{i=1}^{n}\sum_{j=1}^{n} d_{ij} x_{ij}$$

$$\text{s.t.} \quad \sum_{i=1}^{n} x_{ij} = w_j \qquad 1 \le j \le n$$

$$0 \le x_{ij} \le w_j y_i \qquad 1 \le i,j \le n$$

$$\sum_{i=1}^{n} y_i = p \qquad 1 \le i \le n$$

$$y_i \in \{0,1\}$$

where x_{ij} is the part of the demand of vertex v_j covered by a facility at vertex v_i (if any), y_i takes the value 1 if there is a facility at vertex v_i and 0 otherwise. The constraints ensure that all the demand is covered at each vertex v_j, that only vertices with a facility will supply product, and that exactly p facilities will be located.

The Portfolio Selection Problem

The modern portfolio selection problem was formulated by Markowitz (1952, 1959). In its original formulation it consists in determining the composition of a portfolio from a given set of possible assets in order to obtain at least an expected return r_0 with the minimum possible risk. If we define x_i as the proportion of each asset in the total investment fund, the problem can be formulated as the following quadratic model:

$$\text{Min} \quad R = x^t Q x$$

$$\text{s.t.} \quad \sum_{i=1}^{n} r_i x_i \ge r_0$$

$$\sum_{i=1}^{n} x_i = 1$$

$$x_i \ge 0, \quad 1 \le i \le n$$

Here, r_i is the expected return on the i-th asset, which in practice is calculated as the mean value of a list of historical data, and Q is the variance-covariance matrix of these data so that the quadratic form $x^t Q x$ represents the variance of $r_1 x_1 + \ldots + r_n x_n$ considered as a random variable. From an economic point of view, the square root of $x^t Q x$ can be thought of as the risk in the portfolio determined by the variables x_i. Hence the Markowitz model minimizes the risk in a portfolio subject to the constraints stating that the expected return must be at least a value r_0 according to the investor's preferences, that the sum of the weights of the assets composing the portfolio must be equal to 1, and finally that those weights must be non-negative.

The problem can be simplified by removing the sign constraints, which is interpreted as allowing so-called short sales (Chifu & Litzenberg, 1988). However, we are interested in those variants incorporating new constraints into the original Markowitz model. Portfolio selection models including additional constraints have mainly been considered since powerful computational techniques were developed, allowing dealing with more sophisticated programs than the original model with reasonable CPU times. These new constraints can reflect market constraints or further investor preferences beyond the desired trade-off between risk and return. For instance, the so-called socially responsible investment (Hallerbach et al., 2004) requires adding many constraints reflecting an investor's highly subjective preferences.

In this chapter we are mainly interested in those constraints that are more complicated to handle from a computational point of view since, as we have explained, we wish to use this case to illustrate how the fuzzy techniques we are presenting can be applied in a computationally hard context. Therefore, we have chosen two kinds of such constraints, namely semicontinuous variable and cardinality constraints.

Considering the variables x_i in the portfolio selection problem to be semicontinuous means that the investor fixes a minimum and a maximum possible weight for the i-th asset, so that $l_i \leq x_i \leq u_i$ is required, but only if the i-th asset actually appears in the portfolio, i.e. that the constraint is either $x_i = 0$ or $l_i \leq x_i \leq u_i$. The cardinality constraints impose lower and/or upper bounds on the total number of assets appearing in the whole portfolio, or on the number of assets belonging to certain categories. Those constraints can be incorporated into the basic model by introducing a new set of binary variables y_i taking the value 1 if and only if the i-th asset actually appears in the portfolio. The model with semi-continuous variables then becomes this mixed-integer quadratic program:

$$\text{Min} \quad R = \mathbf{x}^t Q \mathbf{x}$$

$$\text{s.t.} \quad \sum_{i=1}^{n} r_i x_i \geq r_0$$

$$\sum_{i=1}^{n} x_i = 1$$

$$l_i y_i \leq x_i \leq u_i y_i, \quad 1 \leq i \leq n$$

$$y_i \in \{0,1\}$$

Once the auxiliary binary variables are introduced, it is easy to express cardinality constraints in terms of them. For instance, a constraint on the total number of assets appearing in the portfolio can be expressed as

$$m \leq \sum_{i=1}^{n} y_i \leq M,$$

where m and M are a lower and an upper bound for the number of assets.

Even in the presence of additional constraints, we are going to focus our analysis on the trade-off between the risk of the investment and the expected return, and this leads to the study of the efficient frontier of the problem, i.e. the set of risk-return pairs corresponding to efficient portfolios. Recall that a portfolio is said to be efficient if there is no other portfolio possessing a strictly lower risk

and at least the same expected return, or a strictly greater expected return and at most the same risk. In the simplest case of the portfolio selection problem (even with the sign constraints removed), it is well known that the efficient frontier is just a branch of parabola, whereas under the sign constraint the efficient frontier becomes piecewise parabolic (Markowitz, 1959). When semicontinuous variable and cardinality constraints are considered, the efficient frontier becomes more involved (Calvo et al., 2012a).

THE FUZZY MODELS

Formulation of the Fuzzy P-Median Problem

Now let us see how the problems we have described should be modified to introduce into the model the flexibility associated with those parameters depending on the decision-maker's criteria. In the case of the p-median problem, this means that we are not interested in the possible imprecision of the accepted data about distances and costs, but in that of the quantities of product to be delivered at each vertex. Notice that a private firm may prefer to leave a part of the demand uncovered if it finds this possibility advantageous.

This means considering those solutions leaving part of the possible demand uncovered as partially feasible solutions. The more demand left uncovered, the more infeasible the solution is. Hence, we want the membership degree of the fuzzy constraint set $\tilde{C}$ to depend on the actually covered demand which each solution provides, i.e. the degree of feasibility of each solution $(\mathbf{x}, \mathbf{y})$ where $\mathbf{x} = (x_{ij})$ and $\mathbf{y} = (y_i)$ will depend on the difference between the total demand that should be covered and the demand actually covered. Hence, it will be expressed as a function of

$$\sum_{j=1}^{n} w_j - \sum_{i=1}^{n} \sum_{j=1}^{n} x_{ij}.$$

If we choose linear membership functions to remain in the environment of linear programming, we calculate the *degree of feasibility* of each solution $(\mathbf{x}, \mathbf{y})$, i.e. The membership degree to fuzzy set $\tilde{C}$, as

$$\mu_f(\mathbf{x}, \mathbf{y}) = h_f\left(\sum_{j=1}^{n} w_j - \sum_{i=1}^{n}\sum_{j=1}^{n} x_{ij}\right),$$

where $h_f(x)$ is an auxiliary function given by

$$h_f(x) = \begin{cases} 1 & \text{if} & x < 0 \\ 1 - x/p_f & \text{if} & 0 \le x \le p_f \\ 0 & \text{if} & x > p_f \end{cases}$$

Here, p_f represents the maximum tolerance level for a solution to be considered feasible.

Our fuzzy goal $\tilde{G}$ is to reduce the cost. We start with the crisp optimum cost z^* and define, for each solution $(\mathbf{x}, \mathbf{y})$, its *degree of improvement of the goal* (i.e. the membership degree to fuzzy goal $\tilde{G}$) as

$$\mu_g(\mathbf{x}, \mathbf{y}) = h_g\left(z^* - \sum_{i=1}^{n}\sum_{j=1}^{n} d_{ij} x_{ij}\right),$$

where h_g is another auxiliary function (see Figure 1) given by

$$h_g(y) = \begin{cases} 0 & \text{if} & y < 0 \\ y/p_g & \text{if} & 0 \le y \le p_g \\ 1 & \text{if} & y > p_g \end{cases}$$

and p_g indicates how much should the cost be reduced to consider the improvement as completely satisfactory.

The fuzzy sets $\tilde{C}$ and $\tilde{G}$ define a fuzzy version of the *p*-median problem, whose objective is maximizing the degree of global satisfaction $\lambda = \min\left\{\mu_{\tilde{C}}(\mathbf{x}), \mu_{\tilde{G}}(\mathbf{x})\right\}$. This is clearly equivalent to solving the following auxiliary crisp problem:

$$\begin{aligned} \text{Max} \quad & \lambda \\ \text{s.t.} \quad & \lambda \le \mu_g(\mathbf{x}, \mathbf{y}) \\ & \lambda \le \mu_f(\mathbf{x}, \mathbf{y}) \\ & \sum_{j=1}^{n} x_{ij} \le w_j \quad 1 \le j \le n \\ & 0 \le x_{ij} \le w_j y_i \quad 1 \le i, j \le n \\ & \sum_{i=1}^{n} y_i = p \\ & y_i \in \{0,1\} \quad 1 \le i \le n \end{aligned}$$

By replacing μ_f and μ_g by their definitions, we get a linear program:

Figure 1. Auxiliary functions h_f and h_g

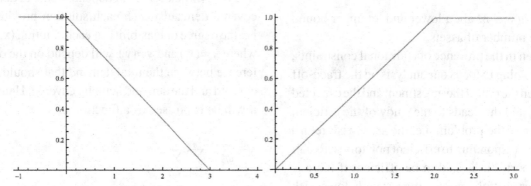

$$\text{Max} \quad \lambda$$

$$\text{s.t.} \quad \lambda + \sum_{i=1}^{n}\sum_{j=1}^{n}\frac{d_{ij}}{p_g}x_{ij} \leq \frac{z*}{p_g}$$

$$\lambda - \sum_{i=1}^{n}\sum_{j=1}^{n}\frac{1}{p_f}x_{ij} \leq 1 - \frac{1}{p_f}\sum_{j=1}^{n}w_j$$

$$0 \leq x_{ij} \leq w_j y_i \qquad\qquad 1 \leq i,j \leq n$$

$$\sum_{i=1}^{n}x_{ij} \leq w_j \qquad\qquad 1 \leq j \leq n$$

$$\sum_{i=1}^{n}y_i = p$$

$$y_i \in \{0,1\} \qquad\qquad 1 \leq i \leq n$$

Notice that, without loss of generality, we do not have considered the values 0 and 1 for the membership functions since the optimal value for λ cannot be either of these extreme cases.

Formulation of the Fuzzy Portfolio Selection Problem

In the literature many fuzzy versions of the portfolio selection problem can be found. Several authors apply possibility distributions to model uncertainty (see for instance Tanaka & Guo (1999), Inuiguchi & Tanino (2000), Tanaka et al. (2000), Zhang et al (2003)). Besides, Bilbao et al. (2006) use fuzzy compromise programming and Watada (1997) introduces vague goals. Further, Lacagnina & Pecorella (2006) combine stochastic and fuzzy techniques. Here we follow a different approach in which the vague subjective parameters are those associated with the investor's preferences about the acceptable risk and the desired expected return. We propose a fuzzy model whose constraint and goal sets will be fuzzy subsets of the (crisp) universe set consisting of portfolios satisfying the hard constraints. The fuzzy constraint set $\tilde{C}$ must be such that, for a given portfolio $x \in X$, the value $\mu_{\tilde{C}}(x)$ is high when the expected return on **x** is not much less than r_0 and the risk is not much greater than the corresponding optimal risk R_0.

This means that $\tilde{C}$ can be defined as the fuzzy intersection of two fuzzy sets $\tilde{C}_r$ and $\tilde{C}_R$, such that the degree of membership of each portfolio $x \in X$ is given by $\mu_{\tilde{C}_r}(x) = f_1(r(x))$ and $\mu_{\tilde{C}_R}(x) = g_1(R(x))$, where $r(\mathbf{x})$ and $R(\mathbf{x})$ are respectively, the expected return and risk of the portfolio **x**, $f_1 : R \to [0,1]$ is a non-decreasing function such that $f_1(r_0) = 1$ and $g_1 : R \to [0,1]$ is a non-increasing function such that $g_1(R_0) = 1$. The specific choice of f_1 and g_1 will depend on the available information about the investor's preferences regarding risk and return. Hence the membership function of the fuzzy feasible set $\tilde{C} = \tilde{C}_r \cap \tilde{C}_R$ is given by

$$\mu_{\tilde{C}}(x) = \min\left\{\mu_{\tilde{C}_r}(x),\ \mu_{\tilde{C}_R}(x)\right\}$$

which is of the form

$$\mu_{\tilde{C}}(x) = h_1\left(r(x),\ R(x)\right),$$

where the function $h_1(r,R) = \min\left\{f_1(r),\ g_1(R)\right\}$ generally has the shape shown in Figure 2(a). On the other hand, the degree of membership of the goal set $\tilde{G}$ of the fuzzy problem must be high for portfolios whose expected return is much greater than r_0 or the risk is much less than R_0. Hence, $\tilde{G}$ is the fuzzy union of the fuzzy sets $\tilde{G}_r$ and $\tilde{G}_R$ whose membership functions are of the form $\mu_{\tilde{G}_r}(\mathbf{x}) = f_2\left(r(\mathbf{x})\right)$ and $\mu_{\tilde{G}_R}(\mathbf{x}) = g_2\left(R(\mathbf{x})\right)$, where $f_2 : R \to [0,1]$ is a non-decreasing function such that $f_2(r_0)=0$ and $g_2 : R \to [0,1]$ is a non-increasing function such that $g_2(R_0)=0$.

Hence, the membership function of the fuzzy goal set $\tilde{G} = \tilde{G}_r \cup \tilde{G}_R$ (which can be called the degree of improvement of the goal) is given by

$$\mu_{\tilde{G}}(\mathbf{x}) = \max\left\{\mu_{\tilde{G}_r}(\mathbf{x}),\ \mu_{\tilde{G}_R}(\mathbf{x})\right\} = h_2\left(r(\mathbf{x}), R(\mathbf{x})\right),$$

Figure 2. Membership functions of $\tilde{C}$ and $\tilde{G}$

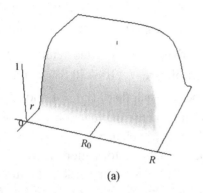

(a)

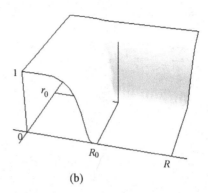

(b)

where $h_2(r, R) = \max\left\{f_2(r), \ g_2(R)\right\}$ has the shape shown in Figure 2 (b), and so the fuzzy decision set, i.e. the fuzzy intersection $\tilde{D} = \tilde{C} \cap \tilde{G}$, has the shape in Figure 3.

As in the *p*-median case, the degree of membership of a portfolio **x** of $\tilde{D}$ is called its *degree of global satisfaction*:

$$\lambda(\mathbf{x}) = \min\left\{\mu_{\tilde{C}}(\mathbf{x}), \ \mu_{\tilde{G}}(\mathbf{x})\right\}.$$

Notice that this symmetric fuzzy approach to portfolio selection emphasizes the bi-objective nature of the problem, since we determine the global satisfaction of a portfolio in terms of both its risk and its expected return. Namely, those portfolios providing less expected return than the crisp optimum improve the risk objective making the return objective worse, whereas, reciprocally, those providing a greater expected return improve the return objective making the risk objective worse. The constraint set controls the return objective for those portfolios with low return and the risk objective for those with high return, whereas the goal set controls the risk objective for those portfolios with low return and the return objective

for those with high return. Notice that if we had started from the dual portfolio selection problem we would have arrived at the same fuzzy problem with the constraint and the goal sets exchanged.

In Figure 3 we have also represented a possible (simplified) efficient frontier of the crisp problem and the pair (r_0, R_0) chosen by the investor as the starting point of the fuzzy model. We see that its degree of feasibility is 1 but its degree of improvement of the goal is 0, and so the degree of global satisfaction is 0. We can also see the lifting of the efficient frontier to the graph of the degree of global satisfaction. In Figure 3 we can see that the degree of global satisfaction has two

Figure 3. Degree of global satisfaction and the efficient frontier (dashed line)

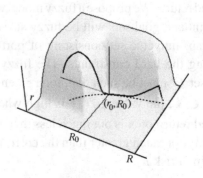

local maxima on the efficient frontier, the best of which is the optimal solution of the fuzzy model we are introducing.

In order to calculate the efficient portfolio providing the best degree of global satisfaction, the efficient frontier is parameterized by expressing the risk as a function $R = R(r)$ of the expected return. Assuming that this function is available, we can express the three degrees of membership of a given efficient portfolio as functions of its expected return. Of course, we also need to choose concrete functions f_1, f_2, g_1, g_2. The problem of choosing membership functions suitable for modelling a real uncertain situation is a very subtle issue in fuzzy set theory. Here, in the absence of specific preferences, we will consider the simplest case which may be considered suitable in this context. Notice that we intend to compare possible variations in the expected return with possible variations in the risk, and what is really comparable with a variation in the expected return is not a variation in its variance but a variation in its standard deviation. The difference between the variance and the standard deviation is just a square root, which is irrelevant when minimizing the risk, but it must be incorporated into our membership functions. In other words, the natural way to express the investor's preferences on the trade-off between variations in the expected return and variations in the risk is in terms of the mean and the standard deviation instead of the mean and the variance. In the absence of more specific criteria, we will assume a piecewise linear dependence on r and $\sqrt{R}$. Namely, we take

$$
f_1(r) = \begin{cases} 0 & \text{if } r < r_0 - p_{f_1}, \\ 1 - \dfrac{r_0 - r}{p_{f_1}} & \text{if } r_0 - p_{f_1} \leq r \leq r_0, \\ 1 & \text{if } r > r_0, \end{cases}
$$

$$
g_1(R) = \begin{cases} 1 & \text{if } \sqrt{R} < \sqrt{R_0}, \\ 1 - \dfrac{\sqrt{R} - \sqrt{R_0}}{p_{g_1}} & \text{if } \sqrt{R_0} \leq \sqrt{R} \leq \sqrt{R_0} + p_{g_1}, \\ 0 & \text{if } \sqrt{R} > \sqrt{R_0} + p_{g_1}, \end{cases}
$$

$$
f_2(r) = \begin{cases} 0 & \text{if } r < r_0, \\ \dfrac{r - r_0}{p_{f_2}} & \text{if } r_0 \leq r \leq r_0 + p_{f_2}, \\ 1 & \text{if } r > r_0 + p_{f_2}, \end{cases}
$$

$$
g_2(R) = \begin{cases} 1 & \text{if } \sqrt{R} < \sqrt{R_0} - p_{g_2}, \\ \dfrac{\sqrt{R_0} - \sqrt{R}}{p_{g_2}} & \text{if } \sqrt{R_0} - p_{g_2} \leq \sqrt{R} \leq \sqrt{R_0}, \\ 0 & \text{if } \sqrt{R} > \sqrt{R_0}. \end{cases}
$$

Notice that with this choice the functions f_1, f_2, g_1, g_2 are completely determined by the tolerance levels $p_{f1}, p_{f2}, p_{g1}, P_{g2}$.

EXPERIMENTAL STUDY

Fuzzy vs. Classical Solutions

In this chapter we will not describe the various computational methods available for solving the stated problems. In the p-median case, an exact algorithm is proposed in Canós et al. (1999) and several heuristic procedures are presented in Canós et al. (2003, 2004) and Cadenas et al. (2011). Cadenas et al. (2012) deal with solving the fuzzy portfolio selection problem obtained from the original Markowitz problem. To solve the mixed integer version stated here, we have adapted those methods by means of the techniques for computing the efficient frontier described in Calvo et al. (2011, 2012a). Further details are given in Calvo et al. (2012b).

Let us now compare the optimal solutions of the classical and fuzzy versions of both problems. For the sake of brevity they will be called the *crisp* and the *fuzzy* optimal solutions, respectively, for each problem.

Consider first a simple instance of the p-median problem, namely the 2-median problem in the six-vertex network given in Figure 4.

The crisp optimal solution happens to be locating the facilities on vertices 4 and 5, with a cost $z^* = 2,640$. Now suppose that we want to study the possibility of reducing this cost by about 100 units. Then we fix $p_g = 200$, in such a way that a

reduction of 100 units will have a degree of satisfaction of 0.5. On the other hand, we would accept a reduction in the covered demand by about 1 unit, and hence we fix $p_f = 2$.

The fuzzy solution with these parameters locates the facilities at vertices 2 and 6, with a degree of satisfaction $\lambda = 72.4\%$, so it provides a good improvement. Table 1 compares both solutions: by reducing the demand at vertex v_4 by just 0.55 units, we get a cost reduction of 144.8 units.

As can be seen in Table 2, the optimal fuzzy location (2, 6) is in fourth place among the best crisp locations, and it provides the very same cost as location (2, 4). However, both locations have very different fuzzy behaviour: one of them is the fuzzy optimum, while the other is in eighth place in Table 3. So we see that a fuzzy algorithm must always be something more sophisticated than a relaxed crisp algorithm.

Let us now consider a simple example of a portfolio selection problem. Table 4 contains the annual returns of American Tobacco, AT&T, United States Steel, General Motors and Atcheson, Topeka & Santa Fe, taken from Markowitz (1952).

Figure 4. A network for a 2-median problem

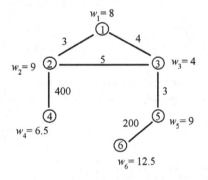

Table 1. Comparison of crisp and fuzzy solutions

	w_1	w_2	w_3	w_4	w_5	w_6	z^*	**Location**	
Crisp	8	9	4	6.50	9	12.5	2640	4 and 5	
Fuzzy	8	9	4	5.95	9	12.5	2495.2	2 and 6	$\lambda = 72.4\%$
Difference	0	0	0	-0.55	0	0	-144.8		

Table 2. Best crisp locations

	Location	**Cost** z	z-z^*
1	4 and 5	2640	0
2	3 and 4	2641.5	1.5
3	1 and 4	2693.5	53.5
4	2 and 4	2716	76
4	2 and 6	2716	76

Table 3. Best fuzzy locations

	Location	λ
1	2 and 6	72.40
2	1 and 6	71.62
3	3 and 6	70.64
4	3 and 4	66.75
5	4 and 5	66.67
6	5 and 6	65.35
7	1 and 4	58.71
8	2 and 4	55.19

We consider the portfolio selection problem with the vectors of bounds

$$l = (0.2, 0.3, 0.2, 0.3, 0.2), u = (0.6, 0.6, 0.6, 0.6, 0.6)$$

and the cardinality constraint with $m = 2$, $M = 5$.

The efficient frontier is shown in Figure 5. It comprises 12 arcs of parabola ranging from an expected return $r_{min} = 0.094$ to $r_{max} = 0.13738$. Table 5 contains the change points together with the corresponding risk levels. The interval within two successive change points corresponds to either an arc of parabola ax^2+bx+c (whose coefficients a, b, c are indicated in the table) or to a vertical line. The last column contains the indexes of the

assets appearing in the optimal portfolio in the corresponding interval.

We can see in Figure 5 that there are three discontinuities in which a small increment in r gives rise to a big increment in R. On the other hand, there are six "vertical lines" (one of them is very small and can hardly be seen in the picture) which are drawn just for the technical reasons explained above, but in fact they do not belong to the efficient frontier. For instance, the first one is on the interval $[0.0981, 0.10242]$, with corresponding risk $R = 0.03226$. This means that if an investor requires a minimum return level r in that interval, the efficient portfolio will in fact provide a return $r = 0.10242$ with risk $R = 0.03226$.

Let us consider an investor that has chosen an expected return $r_0 = 0.125$, whose corresponding risk is $R_0 = 0.0742$. In order to interpret this variance, it is preferable to consider the standard deviation $\sqrt{R_0} = 0.272$. We can see that it is quite a high risk, and so we assume that the investor would be interested in reducing it and a reduction of $p_{g2} = 0.06$ would be considered as totally satisfactory. On the other hand, an increment greater than $p_{g1} = 0.01$ would not be acceptable in any case. We assume that the investor would accept variations in the expected return with tolerances $p_{f1} = p_{f2} = 0.02$. These tolerances determine a fuzzy portfolio selection problem. Figure 6 shows the degrees of membership of the feasible and the

Table 4. Returns on five assets

Year	AmT	ATT	USS	GM	ATS
1937	-0.305	-0.173	-0.318	-0.477	-0.457
1938	0.513	0.098	0.285	0.714	0.107
1940	0.055	0.2	-0.047	0.165	-0.424
1941	-0.126	0.03	0.104	-0.043	-0.189
1942	-0.003	0.067	-0.039	0.476	0.865
1943	0.428	0.3	0.149	0.225	0.313
1944	0.192	0.103	0.26	0.29	0.637
1945	0.446	0.216	0.419	0.216	0.373
1946	-0.088	-0.046	-0.078	-0.272	-0.037

Table 5. Change points, equations of the efficient frontier and composition of the efficient portfolios

	r	R	a	b	c	
1	0.09404	0.02688				
			27.559	3.9691	0.1564	{1,2,3}
2	0.09810	0.03226				
3	0.10242	0.03226				
			27.559	-4.2612	0.1796	{1,2}
4	0.10312	0.03325				
5	0.10411	0.03325				
			27.559	-4.5141	0.2045	{1,2,5}
6	0.10855	0.03923				
7	0.11051	0.03923				
			25.652	-4.1541	0.1850	{2,4}
8	0.11168	0.04103				
9	0.11201	0.04102				
			25.652	-4.2890	0.1996	{1,2,4}
10	0.11583	0.04697				
			21.298	3.2803	0.1412	{1,2,4}
11	0.12159	0.05721				
			122.894	-27.987	1.6433	{1,2,4}
12	0.12310	0.06034				
			25.652	-4.1764	0.1897	{2,4,5}
13	0.12479	0.06798				
			122.894	-28.5593	1.7240	{1,3,4}
14	0.12702	0.07914				
15	0.13131	0.07914				
			122.894	-30.2579	1.9333	{ 1,4,5}
16	0.13146	0.07945				
17	0.13165	0.07945	122.894			
				-30.6675	1.9869	{1,4}
18	0.13569	0.08829				
			122.894	-30.2579	1.9333	{1,4,5}
19	0.13738	0.09590				

goal sets as functions of the expected return on a given efficient portfolio.

There we can see that near r_0 there are two horizontal jumps below and a vertical one above, corresponding to the two vertical jumps appearing in Figure 5 to the left of r_0 and to the horizontal jump on the right, respectively. We see in Figure 6 that the degree of global satisfaction has two local maxima. Specifically, they correspond to the efficient portfolios described in Table 6, which also includes the crisp efficient portfolio. Both in

Figure 5. Efficient frontier of the problem

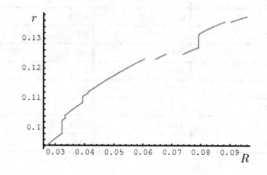

Figure 6. Membership function of the feasible set (thick line) and to the goal set (thin line) as functions of the expected return

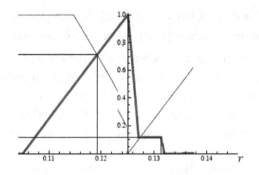

the figure and in the table we can see that the fuzzy optimal solution is the left-hand one with a degree of global satisfaction $\lambda = 0.71$.

Notice that the three portfolios shown in Table 6 have different compositions. In fact, the crisp one corresponds to the interval of the efficient frontier between change points 13 and 14 in Table 5. From this point, the left-hand fuzzy portfolio is three steps up, between change points 10 and 11, whereas the expected return on the right-hand fuzzy portfolio is change point 15.

In Table 6 we can also appreciate the interest of the fuzzy alternative: by changing from the crisp portfolio to the fuzzy one, we reduce the risk of the investment by a bit more than 1% at the cost of reducing the expected return by just 0.0058. The significantly lower degree of global satisfaction of the right-hand fuzzy solution is

reasonable since the increment on the expected return is far less than the increment on the risk.

In Figure 7 we can see a global picture of the relationship between the crisp and the fuzzy portfolio. Notice that the risk and return axes are on the same scale, and so we can appreciate that when moving from the crisp solution *A* to the left-hand fuzzy solution *B,* the reduction in risk is significantly less than the reduction in the expected return.

Marginal Analysis for the Fuzzy P-Median Problem

We have chosen the *p*-median problem because of its relative simplicity, which allows us to obtain simple formulas expressing the satisfaction degrees in terms of the data of the problem. In particular, we can see how they depend on the "subjective" parameter, which in this case is the demand that the decision-maker is accepting to leave uncovered, as well as on the tolerance levels p_f and p_g. In Canós et al. (2008), this fact is used to develop some marginal analysis techniques about the sensitivity of the optimal solution to small variations in the parameters p_f and p_g. We summarize the results here.

The basic fact is that the global satisfaction degree λ is a piecewise linear function of the reduced demand *s*, so that its slope λ'_s is locally constant, and it can be easily computed. From this value we can calculate the partial derivatives of the global satisfaction degree with respect to these parameters, which are given by

Table 6. Comparison between the crisp and the fuzzy solutions

	x_1	x_2	x_3	x_4	x_5	r	$\sqrt{R}$	λ	Δr	ΔR
Crisp	0.31486	0	0.2	0.486	0	0.1250	0.273			
FzL	0.244	0.354	0	0.40	0	0.1192	0.23	0.71	-0.0058	-0.013
FzR	0.5	0	0	0.3	0.2	0.1313	0.281	0.12	0.0063	0.008

Figure 7. 3D-graph of the degree of global satisfaction

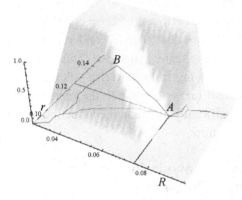

$$\frac{\partial \lambda}{\partial p_f} = \rho \lambda_s'(1 - \lambda), \qquad \frac{\partial \lambda}{\partial p_g} = -\rho \frac{\lambda}{p_g}$$

where $\rho = (1 + p_f \lambda_s')^{-1}$ is locally constant.

However, these derivatives should be corrected since the change in the degree of global satisfaction is partially due to the change of scale determined by the change of the tolerances, and this has no intrinsic meaning. By removing this scale effect two corrected derivatives can be defined, which are given by

$$\lambda_{p_f}^D = -\rho \frac{1 - \lambda}{p_f}, \qquad \lambda_{p_g}^D = (1 - \rho) \frac{\lambda}{p_g}$$

We refer to Canós et al. (2008) for the computations and further explanations, and we content ourselves with mentioning that these expressions can be obtained because of the theoretical simplicity of the p-median problem. Computational results show that λ_{pg}^D usually takes small values and this means that the quality of the fuzzy optimal solution is not very sensitive to changes in the parameter p_g. This is not true for p_f, but it can be shown that λ_{pf}^D admits an expression in the form

$$\lambda_{p_f}^D = -\frac{1}{\lambda_s'(2p_f^2 + Cp_f)}$$

for a certain constant C, and this allows us to determine the range for p_f where λ_{pf}^D is reasonably small. If the decision-maker's preferences are within this range, we have reduced the usually sensitive parameters of the classical problem to less sensitive parameters in the fuzzy model. Let us present an example showing the way these derivatives can be used to analyze a solution:

Example: Here we present the results for a 2-median problem on a 20-vertex network. The crisp demand value is 99 and the optimal crisp cost is 2654. Table 7 shows the result of taking p_f as equal to 5% of the total demand. The low value of λ seems to indicate that the crisp solution is good, so it is not worth reducing the transport cost by reducing the demand covered. However, the value of $\lambda_{pf}^D = 5.6$ is too large, which suggests that greater satisfaction is not attained because the tolerance for the reduction in demand is too restrictive. Solving the problem for several values of p_f, we see a behaviour of λ_{pf}^D that fits the above equation. From this we can get a value of p_f making $\left| \lambda_{pf}^D \right|$ small. For instance, we can take as p_f the 20% of total demand. For this value, the fuzzy solution is also given in Table 7.

Notice that the high value of λ we now obtain is not significant if we think of it as a measure of satisfaction with regard to the reduced demand, as such an increment is just reflecting the variation in our criterion (the variation of p_f). However, it is worth recalling that λ also measures the satisfaction derived from the reduction in cost, and this time the evaluation criterion remains unchanged (p_g is the same). Hence, we can conclude that the new solution is clearly better than the first one. More specifically, the demand reduction changes from 3 to 4, whereas the cost reduction changes from 252 to 415.

Table 7. Marginal analysis of a 2-median problem

Parameters		Location	λ	Reduction		Marginal indicators		
p_f	p_g			Cost	Demand	λ'_s	$\lambda^D_{p_f}$	$\lambda^D_{p_g}$
5	531	v_8, v_{14}	0.475	252	3	**0.18**	-5.589	0.042
20	531	v_8, v_{14}	0.782	415	4	**0.17**	-0.245	0.115

Furthermore, this example illustrates that the intrinsic criterion given by the analysis of λ^D_{pf} can be more operative than consulting the decision-maker, as a decision-maker who considers a reduction in demand of 5% to be reasonable would probably consider a tolerance of 20% to be excessive. However, we have seen that by fixing $p_f = 20\%$ we do not obtain a reduction in demand of this magnitude, but the necessary reduction is about 4%, which remains within the range acceptable to the decision-maker. Even if 4% were considered too large, we could offer the decision-maker a range of intermediate possibilities.

FUTURE RESEARCH DIRECTIONS

Selecting adequate membership functions is a fundamental issue in fuzzy set theory. Hence considerable efforts have been made to study different kinds of membership functions which are suitable to fit the different subtleties and peculiarities that a vague parameter may show. When fuzzy set theory is applied to model any vague situation, it is usual to be careful to select appropriate functions within the computational possibilities, but it is not always possible to verify the impact of a specific choice on the quality of the corresponding solutions. In many cases a systematic study in this direction would require hard computational effort. This is one of the reasons why the marginal analysis described in the previous section for the fuzzy *p*-median problem is of theoretical interest, since it

provides an accurate picture of how the choice of the fuzzy tolerances affects the optimal solution.

Making a similar theoretical study in the portfolio selection case may be impossible because of the higher complexity of the problem, but the authors think that it could be useful to make a parallel empirical study for this problem, which could lead to similar techniques for validating a solution as in the example in the previous section. More generally, these sensitivity techniques studied in relatively simple problems like the *p*-median and the portfolio selection ones (in which just a few fuzzy parameters are considered) could lead to the proposal of more general tests and criteria not based on exact computations but on more capable soft-computing methods. In this way, it would also be useful to gradually extend the kind of analysis developed in this chapter to more complex problems suitable for a soft-computing approach.

CONCLUSION

The main contribution that can be extracted from this chapter is the importance of a good treatment of those data in a problem carrying inherent vagueness. We have seen in several examples that fuzzy versions of well-known crisp problems provide more satisfactory alternative solutions (even over the exact crisp optimum) that would have been ignored by any procedure designed for solving the crisp version of the problem. We have seen that by changing a crisp parameter for an adequately chosen fuzzy one, we transform a problem that can be very unstable (with regard to vague parameters) into a much more stable model in which the parameters can be fixed with greater ease, since a reasonable variation does not affect the optimal solution significantly.

Although we have not emphasized the computational aspects, we have seen that this approach can be used even with computationally hard problems like the mixed integer version of the portfolio selection problem that we have chosen. This leads to extension of our proposals to many other problems as one softer computing tool. Decision making in economics and finance provides a huge field of potential application for these techniques, the two examples dealt with here being just a small sample.

REFERENCES

Bellman, R. E., & Zadeh, L. A. (1970). Decision making in a fuzzy environment. *Management Science*, *17*(4), 141–164. doi:10.1287/mnsc.17.4.B141.

Cadenas, J. M., Canós, M. J., Garrido, M. C., Ivorra, C., & Liern, V. (2011). Soft-computing based heuristics for location on networks: The p-median problem. *Applied Soft Computing*, *11*, 1540–1547. doi:10.1016/j.asoc.2008.03.015.

Cadenas, J. M., Carrillo, J. V., Garrido, M. C., Ivorra, C., & Liern, V. (2012). Exact and heuristic procedures for solving the fuzzy portfolio selection problem. *Fuzzy Optimization and Decision Making*, *11*, 29–46. doi:10.1007/s10700-011-9114-5.

Calvo, C., Ivorra, C., & Liern, V. (2011). The geometry of the efficient frontier of the portfolio selection problem. *Journal of Financial Decision Making*, *7*, 27–36.

Calvo, C., Ivorra, C., & Liern, V. (2012a). On the computation of the efficient frontier of the portfolio selection problem. *Journal of Applied Mathematics*. doi:10.1155/2012/105616.

Calvo, C., Ivorra, C., & Liern, V. (2012b). Fuzzy portfolio selection under integer conditions. *European Journal of Operational Research*.

Canós, M. J., Ivorra, C., & Liern, V. (1999). An exact algorithm for the fuzzy p-median problem. *European Journal of Operational Research*, *116*, 80–86. doi:10.1016/S0377-2217(98)00330-0.

Canós, M. J., Ivorra, C., & Liern, V. (2001). The fuzzy p-median problem: A global analysis of the solutions. *European Journal of Operational Research*, *130*, 430–436. doi:10.1016/S0377-2217(99)00500-7.

Canós, M. J., Ivorra, C., & Liern, V. (2003). Finding satisfactory near-optimal solutions in location problems. In J. L. Verdegay (Ed.), *Fuzzy Sets Based Heuristics for Optimization*. Heidelberg, Germany: Physica-Verlag. doi:10.1007/978-3-540-36461-0_17.

Canós, M. J., Ivorra, C., & Liern, V. (2004). The fuzzy p-median problem. *International Journal of Technology. Policy and Management*, *4*, 365–381.

Canós, M. J., Ivorra, C., & Liern, V. (2008). Marginal analysis for the fuzzy p-median problem. *European Journal of Operational Research*, *191*, 264–271. doi:10.1016/j.ejor.2007.08.011.

Chifu, H., & Litzenberg, R. H. (1988). *Foundations for finalcial economics*. Amsterdam: North Holland..

Daskin, M. S. (1995). *Network and discrete location: Models, algorithms and application*. New York: Wiley & Sons. doi:10.1002/9781118032343.

Delgado, M., Verdegay, J. L., & Vila, M. A. (1994). Fuzzy linear programming: from classical methods to new applications. In M. Delgado, J. Kacprzyk, J. L. Verdegay, & M. A. Vila (Eds.), *Fuzzy optimization: Recent advances.* Heidelberg, Germany: Physica-Verlag..

Hakimi, S. L. (1964). Optimum locations of switching centers and the absolute centers and medians of a graph. *Operations Research, 12*, 450–459. doi:10.1287/opre.12.3.450.

Hakimi, S. L. (1965). Optimum distribution of switching centers in a communication network and some related graph theoretic problems. *Operations Research, 13*, 462–475. doi:10.1287/opre.13.3.462.

Hakimi, S. L., & Maheshwari, S. N. (1972). Optimum locations of centers in networks. *Operations Research, 20*, 967–973. doi:10.1287/opre.20.5.967.

Hallerbach, W., Ning, H., Soppe, A., & Spronk, J. A. (2004). A framework for managing a portfolio of socially responsible investments. *European Journal of Operational Research, 153*, 517–529. doi:10.1016/S0377-2217(03)00172-3.

Inuiguchi, M., & Tanino, T. (2000). Portfolio selection under independent possibilistic information. *Fuzzy Sets and Systems, 115*, 83–92. doi:10.1016/S0165-0114(99)00026-3.

Lacagnina, V., & Pecorella, A. (2006). A stochastic soft constraints fuzzy model for a portfolio selection problem. *Fuzzy Sets and Systems, 157*, 1317–1327. doi:10.1016/j.fss.2005.10.002.

Markowitz, H. M. (1952). Portfolio selection. *The Journal of Finance, 7*, 79–91.

Markowitz, H. M. (1959). *Portfolio selection: Efficient diversification of investments*. New York: John Willey..

ReVelle, C.S., & Swain, R.W. (1972). Central facilities location. *Geographical Analysis, 2*, 30–42.

Tanaka, H., & Guo, P. (1999). Portfolio selection based on upper and lower exponential possibility distributions. *European Journal of Operational Research, 114*, 115–126. doi:10.1016/S0377-2217(98)00033-2.

Tanaka, H., Guo, P., & Türksen, L. B. (2000). Portfolio selection based on fuzzy possibility distributions. *Fuzzy Sets and Systems, 111*, 387–397. doi:10.1016/S0165-0114(98)00041-4.

Watada, J. (1997). Fuzzy portfolio selection and its application to decision making. *Tratra Mountains Mathematical Publication, 13*, 219–248.

Wendell, R. E., & Hurter, A. P. (1973). Location theory, dominance and convexity. *Operations Research, 21*, 314–320. doi:10.1287/opre.21.1.314.

Zadeh, L. A. (1965). Fuzzy sets. *Information and Control, 8*, 338–353. doi:10.1016/S0019-9958(65)90241-X.

Zimmermann, H. J. (1997). Fuzzy mathematical programming. In T. Gal, & H. J. Greenberg (Eds.), *Advances in sensitivity analysis and parametric programming*. Dordrecht, The Netherlands: Kluwer Academic Press. doi:10.1007/978-1-4615-6103-3_15.

ADDITIONAL READING

Arenas Parra, M., Bilbao Terol, A., & Rodríguez Uría, M. V. (2001). A fuzzy goal programming approach to portfolio selection. *European Journal of Operational Research, 113*, 287–297. doi:10.1016/S0377-2217(00)00298-8.

Arenas Parra, M., Bilbao Terol, A., & Rodríguez Uría, M. V. (2006). Fuzzy compromise programming for portfolio selection. *Applied Mathematics and Computation, 173*, 251–264. doi:10.1016/j. amc.2005.04.003.

Cadenas, J. M., Carrillo, J. V., Garrido, M. C., Canós, M. J., Ivorra, C., & Liern, V. (2008). A hybrid algorithm for the fuzzy *p*-median problem. In *IADIS International Conference Intelligent Systems and Agents. Proceedings of Intelligent Systems and Agents, 2008*, 77–84.

Canós Darós, M. J., Martínez Romero, M. L., & Mocholí Arce, M. (2005). Un algoritmo para el cálculo del conjunto dominante finito del problema generalizado de la *p*-centdiana. *Rect, 6*, 87–112.

Cooper, W. W., Lelas, V., & Sueyoshi, T. (1997). Goal programming models and their duality relations for use in evaluating security portfolio and regression relations. *European Journal of Operational Research, 98*, 431–443. doi:10.1016/S0377-2217(96)00358-X.

Delgado, M., Verdegay, J. L., & Vila, A. (1994). *Fuzzy linear programming: from classical methods to new applications,* Heildelberg: Physica-Verlag.

Feinstein, C. D., & Thapa, M. N. (1552–1553). M. N. (1993). Notes: A reformulation of a mean-absolute deviation portfolio optimization model. *Management Science, 39*.

Goddard, J., de los Cobos Silva, S. G., & Gutiérrez Andrade, M. A. (2010). Solving *p*-median problems using bee foraging. *Fuzzy Economic Review, 15*, 53–60.

Huang, X. (2007). A new perspective for optimal portfolio selection with random fuzzy returns. *Information Sciences, 177*, 5404–5414. doi:10.1016/j.ins.2007.06.003.

Inuiguchi, M., & Ramik, J. (2000). Possibilistic linear programming: A brief review of fuzzy mathematical programming and a comparison with stochastic programming in portfolio selection problem. *Fuzzy Sets and Systems, 111*, 3–28. doi:10.1016/S0165-0114(98)00449-7.

Konno, H., & Wijayanayake, A. (2001). Portfolio optimization problem under concave transaction costs and minimal transactions unit constraints. *Mathematical Programming, 89*, 233–250. doi:10.1007/PL00011397.

Konno, H., & Yamazaki, H. (1991). Mean-absolute deviation portfolio optimization model and its applications to Tokyo stock market. *Management Science, 37*, 519–531. doi:10.1287/mnsc.37.5.519.

Kutangila-Mayoya, D., & Verdegay, J. L. (2005). *p*-median problems in a fuzzy environment. *Mathware & Soft Computing, 12*, 97–106.

Lai, Y. J., & Hwang, C. L. (1992). *Fuzzy Mathematical Programming: Theory and Applications*. Berlin: Springer. doi:10.1007/978-3-642-48753-8.

León, T., Liern, V., & Vercher, E. (2002). Two fuzzy approaches for solving multiobjective decision problems. *Computational Economics, 19*, 273–286. doi:10.1023/A:1015540718447.

Location problems. The Fuzzy p-median. Retrieved February 11, 2013, from http://heurimind. inf.um.es/fuzzy-pmedian/marcos_Location.htm

Moreno-Pérez, J. A., Moreno-Vega, J. M., & Verdegay, J. L. (2004). Fuzzy location problems on networks. *Fuzzy Sets and Systems, 142*, 393–405. doi:10.1016/S0165-0114(03)00091-5.

Nayeem, S. M. A., & Pal, M. (2008). The *p*-center problem on fuzzy networks and reduction of costs. *Iranian Journal of Fuzzy Systems*, *5*, 1–26.

Sharpe, W. F. (1963). A simplified model for portfolio analysis. *Management Science*, *9*, 277–293. doi:10.1287/mnsc.9.2.277.

Sharpe, W. F. (1970). *Portfolio theory and capital market*. New York: McGraw Hill..

Speranza, M. G. (1993). Linear programming model for portfolio optimization. *Finance*, *14*, 107–123.

Tanaka, H., & Guo, P. (1999). Portfolio selection based on upper and lower exponential possibility distributions. *European Journal of Operational Research*, *114*, 115–126. doi:10.1016/S0377-2217(98)00033-2.

Watada, J. (1997). Fuzzy portfolio selection and its applications to decision making. *Tatra Mountains Mathematical Publication*, *13*, 219–248.

Zenios, S. A., & Kang, K. (1993). Mean-absolute deviation portfolio optimization for mortgage-backed securities. *Annals of Operations Research*, *45*, 433–450. doi:10.1007/BF02282062.

Zhang, W. G., Wang, Y. L., Chen, Z. P., & Nie, Z. K. (2007). Possibilistic mean-variance models and efficient frontiers for portfolio selection problem. *Information Sciences*, *177*, 2787–2801. doi:10.1016/j.ins.2007.01.030.

Zimmermann, H. J. (1991). *Fuzzy sets theory and its applications* (2nd ed.). Boston: Kluwer Academic, Publishers. doi:10.1007/978-94-015-7949-0.

KEY TERMS AND DEFINITIONS

Decision Support: Mathematical techniques for data analysis intended to provide the necessary information to make a good decision by understanding the effects of all the alternatives.

Efficient Frontier: For a given portfolio selection problem, the set of all return-risk pairs corresponding to all efficient portfolios of the problem.

Efficient Portfolio: A portfolio such that there exists no other portfolio providing a greater or equal expected return and lower risk, or a lower or equal risk and greater expected return.

Fuzzy Optimization: Techniques for solving optimization problems whose objective function and constraint set are fuzzy.

Mixed-Integer Programming: Optimization techniques for solving problems containing continuous as well as integer variables.

***P*-Median Problem:** Location problem consisting in determining where one or more facilities should be placed in the plane or in a network to deliver certain quantities of a certain product to several points. In fact, this particular interpretation corresponds to a general mathematical model that fits many other problems of a very different nature.

Portfolio Selection Problem: Optimization problem for minimizing the risk of a portfolio composed from a given set of assets satisfying certain requirements, mainly to provide at least a minimum expected return.

Chapter 3
A Feature Selection Approach in the Study of Azorean Proverbs

Luís Cavique
Universidade Aberta, Portugal

Armando B. Mendes
Universidade dos Açores, Portugal

Matthias Funk
Universidade dos Açores, Portugal

Jorge M. A. Santos
Universidade Évora, Portugal

ABSTRACT

A paremiologic (study of proverbs) case is presented as part of a wider project based on data collected among the Azorean population. Given the considerable distance between the Azores islands, the authors present the hypothesis that there are significant differences in the proverbs from each island, thus permitting the identification of the native island of the interviewee based on his or her knowledge of proverbs. In this chapter, a feature selection algorithm that combines Rough Sets and the Logical Analysis of Data (LAD) is presented. The algorithm named LAID (Logical Analysis of Inconsistent Data) deals with noisy data, and the authors believe that an important link was established between the two different schools with similar approaches. The algorithm was applied to a real world dataset based on data collected using thousands of interviews of Azoreans, involving an initial set of twenty-two thousand Portuguese proverbs.

1. INTRODUCTION

Proverb, "proverbium" in Latin, can be defined as a condensed saying with popular roots, recorded by an anonymous author and expressed by a minimal text, which is generally known and is based on

oral tradition of a particular region, such as: "an apple a day keeps the doctor away".

This study is based on several paremiologic works. Paremiology is the science that deals with the description, classification, etymology and pragmatics of proverbs. One of these works is the relevant collection of three books about the "Pearls

DOI: 10.4018/978-1-4666-4785-5.ch003

of the Portuguese Popular Wisdom" (Funk, Funk 2001a), (Funk, Funk 2001b), (Funk, Funk 2003).

In a series of interviews, several million records were collected from thousands of people denoting whether or not they recognized Portuguese proverbs, based on an initial set of twenty-two thousand proverbs. This constitutes a unique source for a socio-cultural analysis of the transmission mechanisms involved in oral culture in geographically separated places.

Two forms of knowledge validation were used: passive and active. In passive recognition, the interviewer read the proverb and the interviewee stated whether he recognized it. In active recognition, the interviewer read only the initial part of the proverb and the interviewee completed it. For example, the interviewer began by reading "An apple a day…" and the interviewee completed it with "…keeps the doctor away".

This case study is based on data collected in eleven geographically separated areas inside the Azorean community cultural space. This community lives in the Portuguese Azorean archipelago located in the mid-Atlantic rift. In this particular case, it is interesting to analyze the relationship between local and overall knowledge within a common linguistic and cultural space. On the one hand, there is the geographical distance and isolation brought about by the natural sea barrier of this archipelago composed of nine inhabited islands. On the other hand, this archipelago not only extends over 2,330 km2, but it also spreads over a 630 km rectangle in a west-east direction and a 130 km in a north-south direction. The original groups can be seen in three main geographical clusters composed of the occidental, central and oriental groups as can be seen in Figure 1.

We can find some geographical continuity in the Central group, which is composed of 5 islands that are relatively close to each other: Faial (15,063 inhabitants), Pico (14,806), São Jorge (9,674), Terceira (55,823) and Graciosa (4,780). The same

Figure 1. The Azores Archipelago showing the geographical distribution of the nine islands

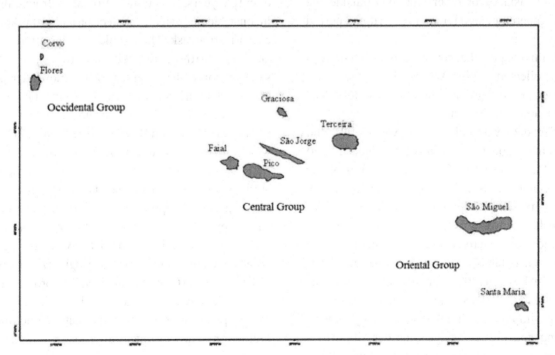

is true of the two Occidental islands, Corvo (425) and Flores (3,995). However, the Oriental group composed of Santa Maria (5,578) and São Miguel (131,609) is separated by 80 km.

Due to the significant waves of emigrants from the Azorean archipelago entering the United States, from the end of the 19th century until the end of the 20th century, twice as many emigrants left the archipelago as those who remained there, about 250,000 inhabitants. The population flux also includes the Azorean migration, mainly characterized by the attraction to urban centers, namely the former administrative capitals: Ponta Delgada in São Miguel, Angra in Terceira and Horta in Faial.

On small islands like Corvo, Santa Maria, Graciosa, Flores and São Jorge, the population shows low mobility as the large majority lived their entire life on only one island. On the other hand, the islands with local capitals are characterized by higher mobility rates, probably because they are deemed more attractive by the population of the surrounding islands. By "mobile" we are referring to the persons that lived on at least two different islands or other locations outside the Azorean archipelago for an uninterrupted period of five years.

In this chapter, the proverb recognition surveys were collected on nine Azores islands and in two regions of emigration to the United States: California and New England.

The data was collected between 1997 and 2000 and published in (Funk and Funk, 2001a) and (Funk and Funk, 2001b) the studies of the Azorean proverbs in the USA and in São Miguel. The same authors (Funk and Funk, 2003) also published proverbs of the Azores central group. All these data were collected and recorded in a relational database, named "Knowledge of the Azorean Proverbs 2000". Finally, the database was restructured, cleaned and statistically analyzed, using simple description statistics, hypothesis testing and cluster analysis, as described in a previous publication (Mendes, Funk, Funk 2009).

This work is part of a larger project based on the oral tradition of proverbs published in (Mendes, Funk, Cavique 2010).

Given the widely scattered Azores islands, in this chapter we aim to highlight the following hypothesis.

Hypothesis 1: There are significant differences in the sayings from each island, thus it is possible to identify the native island of an interviewee based on his/her knowledge of proverbs.

The purpose of this chapter is to find the minimum number of proverbs that allows the identification of the native island of an interviewee, based on the assumption of H1 which states that there are significant differences in the proverbs from each island. This is clearly a Feature Selection problem, where the classes are islands, the attributes are proverbs and the observations are interviewees.

The concept of native island was extended to locations where the interviewees lived for more than five years, thus unintentionally introducing inconsistencies in feature selection and in the data classification task. The mobile persons introduce an obstacle to the feature selection process, *i.e.* the same person with the same proverb knowledge is classified in different classes as they lived in different places. To overcome this handicap, we use an approach based on Rough Sets (Pawlak 1991), which are tolerant of these types of inconsistencies.

Rough Sets differ from classical sets in their ability to deal with inconsistent data. Rough Sets have a particular application in feature selection since they filter the attributes while keeping the underlying semantics of the data. A parallel approach of feature selection is the Logical Analysis of Data, LAD, (Crama et al. 1988), (Boros et al. 2000). The LAD procedure can be divided into two steps: first, transform the data reduction problem into an optimization problem, and then solve the transformed problem as a minimum set covering problem.

In this chapter, we combine both techniques, by using the flexibility of Rough Sets and the straightforwardness of LAD. The known LAD handicaps, like the inability to cope with the contradictions and the limited number of classification classes, will be overcome using this new approach we have called Logical Analysis of Inconsistent Data (LAID).

The main contribution of this work is the development of a Feature Selection algorithm which combines Rough Sets and LAD characteristics, named LAID because it deals with noisy data. We believe that an important link was established between the two different schools with similar approaches. The algorithm was applied to a real world dataset with data collected from the Azorean population and involving a large set of proverbs.

The chapter is organized in six sections. In section 2, two parallel ways of feature selection are compared, the Rough Sets and LAD. In section 3, we present LAID algorithm, which combines the flexibility of Rough Sets and the efficiency of LAD. Section 4 is dedicated to LAID validation techniques and the method results are presented in section 5. Finally, in section 6 we draw some conclusions.

2. FEATURE SELECTION

Given that every 20 months, the amount of information in the world doubles, the motivation for feature selection is to reduce the dimension of the feature space. The reason is associated with Occam's razor principle and aims to obtain the simplest model. There are two basic models in feature selection, Filter model and Wrapper model.

Filter Model is divided into two sequential steps. The feature selection step is executed before the prediction model and there is no interaction between the selection and the prediction model. The best-known algorithms are FOCUS (Al-

muallim, Dietterich 1991) and RELIEF (Kira, Rendell 1992). FOCUS algorithm uses the concept of conflict, that is, two examples with the same feature values but different class values. The algorithm searches subsets with a minimum number of conflicts. RELIEF algorithm evaluates a feature subset based on the difference between the distance from the nearest example of the same class and the nearest example of a different class.

Wrapper model (John, Kohavi, Pfleger 1994) is also divided into two steps, but there is a strong interaction between the feature selection and the prediction model, where the results of the prediction are used as a criterion of choice of the features.

Filter models present a faster performance since they only build one solution and are more intuitive. On the other hand, they present the disadvantages of ignoring the model, i.e. most of the relevant features might not be optimal in the prediction model and the selection criterion is hard to estimate.

In the Wrapper models, the selection criterion is easy to estimate since the features are chosen by the prediction model and for the same reason they are classified as model-aware, i.e. they incorporate the knowledge of the predictor. They also present the opposite disadvantages of the Filter models, which are computationally too expensive and are not intuitive. In other words, the Wrapper models do not identify statistical dependency, so the features might not be the most explanatory variables and therefore the model lacks some theoretical basis.

To sum up, in the Filter models, the selection criterion is hard to estimate, whereas the Wrapper models tend to destroy the underlying semantics of the features after reduction.

It would be highly desirable to find a theory that could not only reduce the number of features, but also preserve the data semantics. In this context, Rough Set theory emerges as the desired tool by discovering the data dependencies and reducing the dimension (Pawlak 1991). In parallel, Peter Hammer's group (Crama et al. 1988), (Boros et al. 2000), with works in discrete optimization, developed the LAD approach. The key features of LAD are the discovery of the minimum number of attributes that are necessary for explaining all observations and the detection of hidden patterns in a dataset with two classes.

Rough Sets and LAD approaches are a subset of Filter models that aim to reduce the number of attributes of datasets using the same two phases. Their specificity is to keep the semantics of the data by removing only the redundant data based on a combinatorial optimization problem.

Although the methods have many similarities, the works that compare the two approaches are scarce. A very recent book (Chikalov et al. 2013) presents three similar approaches to data analysis: Test Theory, Rough Sets and Logical Analysis of Data.

2.1. Rough Sets

Rough Sets theory was initially proposed as a tool to reason about vagueness and uncertainty in information systems by Pawlak (1982) and later it was also proposed for attribute selection by Pawlak (1991). The applications of the Rough Sets method are wide; it leads to significant results in many fields, such as conflict analysis, finance, industry, multimedia, medicine, and most recently bioinformatics (Polkowski 2002) (Peters, Skowron 2010). Below we review the basics of Rough Sets.

A dataset $D=\{O, X \cup C\}$ where the observations $O=\{o_1, o_2, \ldots, o_n\}$ is a non-empty set of objects (observations, cases or lines), $X=\{x_1, x_2, \ldots, x_m\}$ is a non-empty set of attributes and C is the class attribute. The following equation will serve as a running example in this section.

$$D = \begin{vmatrix} O & x_1 & x_2 & x_3 & x_4 & C \\ o_1 & 1 & 1 & 0 & 1 & 1 \\ o_2 & 1 & 0 & 1 & 0 & 0 \\ o_3 & 1 & 0 & 1 & 1 & 1 \\ o_4 & 1 & 0 & 1 & 0 & 1 \\ o_5 & 0 & 1 & 1 & 1 & 2 \\ o_6 & 0 & 1 & 1 & 1 & 2 \end{vmatrix}$$

In a Rough Set table values other than the binary values are allowed. Note also that the table has redundant values (o_5 and o_6) and inconsistent values (o_2 and o_4). By inconsistencies we mean, two cases having the same values for all attributes, but belonging to different decision classes D. A practical example is two sick people that have the same symptoms but different diseases. With real data this is possible, because the table might have a missing attribute that could discriminate between them.

Rough Sets do not correct or exclude the inconsistencies, but rather for each class they determine a lower and an upper approximation. Given $D=\{O, X \cup C\}$, the subset of objects $Y \subseteq O$ and the subset of attributes $B \subseteq X$, Pawlak's Rough Sets theory defines two approximation spaces: the lower and upper rough approximation. The lower approximation $B_L(Y)$ is the least composed set that is contained in Y, and the upper approximation $B^U(Y)$ is the greatest composed set that contains Y. Example, for $B=X=\{x_1, x_2, x_3, x_4\}$ and $Y=\{o_1, o_3, o_4\}$ with C=1, the lower and upper approximations are, $B_L(Y)=\{o_1, o_3\}$ and $B^U(Y)=\{o_1, o_2, o_4, o_3\}$.

As a consequence of the approximation space $B_L(Y) \subseteq Y \subseteq B^U(Y)$. Also, the lower and upper approximations of a subset $Y \subseteq O$ can be seen as operators in the universe of objects *O* that divides it into three disjoint regions, the positive region POS(Y), the negative region NEG(Y) and the boundary region BR(Y):

- $POS(Y) = B_L(Y)$
- $NEG(Y) = O - B^U(Y)$
- $BR(Y) = B^U(Y) - B_L(Y)$

In the example, the decision class is rough since the boundary region is not empty, $BR(Y) = \{(o_2, o_4)\}$.

In Figure 2 the lower and upper bound of subset Y with C=1 are shown, where the grey area represents the Rough Set. The observations of lower bound $B_L(Y) = \{o_1, o_3\}$ are entirely covered by the grey area and they are associated with only one class. The observations of boundary region $BR(Y) = \{o_2, o_4\}$ has two colors, white and grey and they belong to different classes. And the upper bound $B^U(Y) = \{o_1, o_2, o_4, o_3\}$ is the union of the described subsets. The negative region $NEG(Y) = \{o_5, o_6\}$ is also shown in the figure.

When the lower and upper approximations are equal, $B_L(Y) = B^U(Y)$, there are no inconsistencies and the rough set is called crispy rough set.

Another way to identify the roughness of the set is using measures. The accuracy approximation measure is given by:

$$\alpha(Y) = \frac{\left| B_L(Y) \right|}{\left| B^U(Y) \right|}$$

where |Y| denotes the cardinality of Y≠0 and $0 \le \alpha(Y) \le 1$. If $\alpha(Y)=1$, X is crisp; otherwise, it is a rough set.

The goal of Rough Sets is to discover decision rules from dataset D. The minimum number of attributes needed to explain all the classes need to be found. In other words, the number of attributes must be reduced in order to find the core ones. Discovering the minimum number of attributes is an NP-hard problem. One of the following techniques is normally used: Reduction by Heuristics or Discernibility Matrix.

In Reduction by Heuristics, the search for a core is given by the following procedure: for each iteration, one attribute is removed and the augmentation of inconsistency is verified. As already referred, inconsistency occurs when two or more observations have the same values in all attributes, but belong to different decision classes. If the inconsistency does not increase, the attribute can be removed. When no further attributes can be removed, the remaining ones are considered indispensable and thus the core is found.

Using a discernibility matrix of T, denoted by M; an (n×n) matrix is defined as follows, where $M(i,j) = \varnothing$ denotes that this case does not need to be considered.

$$M(i,j) = \begin{cases} \{x \in X : x(o_i) \ne x(o_j)\} & if \quad c(o_i) \ne c(o_j) \\ \varnothing & otherwise \end{cases}$$

Figure 2. Lower and upper bound

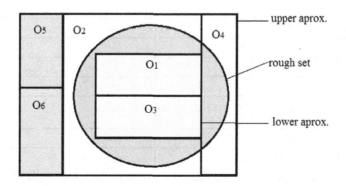

A Feature Selection Approach in the Study of Azorean Proverbs

The discernibility matrix keeps the distinct attributes for each pair of observations belonging to different classes. In our example, the discernibility matrix M is depicted in Table 1.

Note that for the pair (x_2, x_4) the result of the matrix is empty due to the inconsistency of the data. On the other hand, the pair (x_5, x_6) is an empty-set due to the redundancy of the data.

Discernibility function F(B) is a Boolean function, written in the disjunctive normal form (DNF), that is a normalization of a logical formula which is a conjunction of disjunction clauses. F(B) determines the minimum subset of attributes that allows the differentiation of classes: $F(B) = \wedge\{\vee M(i, j): i, j = 1, 2, \ldots, n; M(i,j) \neq \varnothing\}$.

The F(B) decision problem is equivalent to the Satisfiability problem (SAT), which was the first known example of an NP-complete problem.

In our running example: $F = (x_2 \vee x_3 \vee x_4) \wedge (x_1 \vee x_3) \wedge (x_4) \wedge (x_1 \vee x_2 \vee x_4) \wedge (x_1 \vee x_4)$. The solution for the reduction of the attributes is, $x_1=1$, $x_2=0$, $x_3=0$ and $x_4=1$, where the core= $\{x_1, x_4\}$ and the attributes x_2 and x_3 are redundant. Consequently, the decision rules are:

- If $(x_1=1)$ and $(x_4=1)$ then C=1;
- If $(x_1=1)$ and $(x_4=0)$ then C=0;
- If $(x_1=1)$ and $(x_4=0)$ then C=1;
- If $(x_1=0)$ and $(x_4=1)$ then C=2;

Rough Sets do not exclude or correct the inconsistencies of the data, permitting discordant output decision rules. For instance (if $(x_1=1)$ and $(x_4=0)$ then C=0) and (if $(x_1=1)$ and $(x_4=0)$ then C=1), making it difficult for the final user to interpret the results.

2.2. Logical Analysis of Data (LAD)

The LAD method developed by P. Hammer´s group refers to the discovery of the minimum number of attributes that are necessary for explaining all observations and the detection of hidden patterns in a dataset with two classes.

The method works on binary data. Let D be the dataset of all observations, then each observation is described using several attributes, and each observation belongs to a class.

An extension of the Boolean approach is needed when nominal non-binary attributes are used. The binarization (or discretization) of these attributes is performed by associating to attribute x, the value v_s, a Boolean variable $b(x, v_s)$ such that:

$$b(x, v_s) = \begin{cases} 1 & if \ x = v_s \\ 0 & otherwise \end{cases}$$

Dataset D is given as a D^+ set for "positive" observations and as a set D^- set for "negative" observations, where $D = D^+ \cup D^-$ and the sets are disjoint $D^+ \cap D^- = \varnothing$. Observations are classified as positive or negative based on a hidden function,

Table 1. Discernibility matrix

	o_1	o_2	o_3	o_4	o_5	o_6
o_1	-					
o_2	x_2,x_3,x_4	-				
o_3	$\varnothing$	x_4	-			
o_4	$\varnothing$	$\varnothing$ (inconsistency)	$\varnothing$	-		
o_5	x_1,x_3	x_1,x_2,x_4	x_1,x_2	x_1,x_2,x_4	-	
o_6	x_1,x_3	x_1,x_2,x_4	x_1,x_2	x_1,x_2,x_4	$\varnothing$ (redundancy)	-

44

and the goal of the LAD method is to approximate this hidden function with a union of intervals.

The following dataset will serve as a running example in this section, where $D^+=\{o_1,o_2\}$ and $D^-=\{o_3, o_4, o_5\}$.

$$D = \begin{vmatrix} O & x_1 & x_2 & x_3 & x_4 & C \\ o_1 & 1 & 1 & 0 & 1 & 1 \\ o_2 & 1 & 0 & 1 & 1 & 1 \\ o_3 & 0 & 1 & 1 & 1 & 0 \\ o_4 & 1 & 0 & 1 & 0 & 0 \\ o_5 & 0 & 0 & 1 & 0 & 0 \end{vmatrix}$$

To guarantee disjointness of D^+ and D^-, let us compare $o_2=(1,0,1,1)\in D^+$ and $o_3=(0,1,1,1)\in D^-$.

In order to identify the redundant attributes we are going to transform the variables x. In the transformation problem, the variable x will be transformed into a new variable y. To keep the differences between o_2 and o_3, $y_1=1$ or $y_2=1$, because $x_1(o_2) \neq x_1(o_3)$ and $x_2(o_2) \neq x_2(o_3)$, so the constraint is expressed by $y_1+y_2 \geq 1$. Similarly, $y_1+y_3 \geq 1$, $y_2+y_3+y_4 \geq 1$, $y_1+y_2+y_3+y_4 \geq 1$, $y_4 \geq 1$ and $y_1+y_6 \geq 1$.

Keeping the reduction of attributes in mind and with this set of constraints, a combinatorial optimization problem can be applied. The minimal support set corresponds to the linear programming formulation in Box 1.

In order to systematize the process, a disjoint matrix $[a(i,j)]$ will be defined and applied in a well-established optimization problem.

By a disjoint matrix $[a(i,j)]$, we mean a matrix with at most $(n.(n-1))/2$ constraints and with m attributes, defined in Box 2.

The dimension of index i in matrix $[a(i,j)]$ depends on the constraint structure of data set D. However, the upper bound of variable i is $(n.(n-1))/2$ constraints, due to the comparison of pairs of observations (o_a,o_b). Each constraint results from the comparison of two different arbitrary observations o_a and o_b that belong to distinct classes. If one attribute j is different in the observations o_a and o_b the value of $a(i,j)$ is assigned with 1, denoting that at least one column (attribute) j must be maintained in order to differentiate the rows (constraint) i. The optimization problem that finds the minimum number of columns that covers all the rows is the Set Covering problem.

In experimental research where each experiment is represented by an attribute, the expense of each experiment can be included in the optimization model. So, for each attribute y, an expense can be associated by using a vector e_j, allowing a cost differentiation among attributes.

The disjoint matrix and the expense vector are then used in the set covering problem, defined as:

$$minimize\, z = \sum e_j y_j$$

$$subject\, to \sum a_{i,j} y_j \geq 1$$

$$and\, y_j \in \{0,1\} \qquad j=1,\ldots,m$$

The Set Covering problem is a very well-studied problem in Combinatorial Optimization, with many computational resources which implement quasi-exact algorithms and heuristic approaches.

For the given example, the minimal support set is $\{y_1, y_4\}$, so the columns 1 and 4 will be chosen, and the new dataset D* is as follows:

Box 1.

minimize	y1+y2+y3+y4	
subject to	y1+y3 ≥1	(comparing o1 with o3)
	y2+y3+y4 ≥1	(comparing o1 with o4)
	y1+y2+y3+y4 ≥1	(comparing o1 with o5)
	y1+y2 ≥1	(comparing o2 with o3)
	y4 ≥1	(comparing o2 with o4)
	y1+y6 ≥1	(comparing o2 with o5)
and	yi∈{0,1}, i=1,...,4	

Box 2.

$$a\left(i,j\right)=\begin{cases}1 & \forall i: x_j\left(o_a\right)\neq x_j\left(o_b\right),C\left(o_a\right)\neq C\left(o_b\right),\left(o_a,o_b\right)\in O\times O\\0 & otherwise\end{cases}$$

$$D^*=\begin{vmatrix}O & x_1 & x_4 & C\\o_{1,2} & 1 & 1 & 1\\o_3 & 0 & 1 & 0\\o_4 & 1 & 0 & 0\\o_5 & 0 & 0 & 0\end{vmatrix}$$

3. LOGICAL ANALYSIS OF INCONSISTENT DATA (LAID)

3.1. Motivation

The goal of Rough Sets and LAD is to reduce the number of attributes and subsequent generation of rules in order to classify the given dataset. Both procedures can be divided into two steps: first, the transformation step and second, the reduction of the number of attributes.

The classic LAD approach uses two non-intersected classes and binary values for the attributes. This method has the drawback of only working with dichotomous attributes, which can be overcome with the discretization of the attribute values. In contrast, the Rough Sets support inconsistency, many classes and different nominal attribute values.

An advantage of LAD over Rough Sets is the possibility of using expenses associated to the attributes by minimizing not only the number of attributes but also the global cost.

Since Rough Sets do not exclude inconsistencies from real data, a large number of rules are generated, thus the interpretation of the results may become difficult. On the other hand, LAD presents a systematic, accurate, robust and flexible approach that avoids ambiguities and is easy to interpret by its users.

To summarize, Rough Sets are more flexible and diffuse and LAD more basic and straightforward. By combining the two approaches, we propose LAID, developed in the next section, which blends the best features of the presented methods. The LAID method should deal with integer attributes associated with costs such as LAD, and is tolerant to inconsistency and deals with more than two classes like Rough Sets.

In the following sub-sections, the inconsistency tolerance and the capacity to deal with many classes will be reported for the LAID algorithm.

3.2. "Deroughfication"

The driving idea of this work is to solve an inconsistency, created by the way the sample was developed, allowing an interviewee to belong to more than one class.

In a medical diagnosis, it is possible for two sick people to have the same symptoms but different diseases. To overcome this situation, medical doctors run one more test to identify the disease. In our approach, the solution will be similar, where the new test corresponds to a new attribute in the dataset. For each inconsistency, a dummy binary variable will be added to explain "je ne sais quoi" that should be tested, in such a way that the LAD procedure could be used without the need for any change. This approach values the simplicity principle over complexity in understanding the contradictory rules of Rough Sets.

If two observations are repeated, but belong to different classes, then a new dummy binary variable is needed. If three or four observations belonging to distinct classes are repeated, then two new dummy binary variables must be added. So, this number of unexplained variables is equal to the logarithm, base 2, of the number of repeated observations within a diverse class. This basic approach, besides the removal of the inconsistencies, avoids the upper and lower approximation approach, which is a very relevant research field in Rough Sets theory (Yao, 2007). In the following lines the link between lower and upper rough approximations and the dummy binary variable will be established.

Figure 3, on the left, shows the data present in subsection 2.1, using orthogonal areas o_1 to o_6, where the grey area represents the boundary of the Rough Set. For class C=1, $Y=\{o_1,o_3,o_4\}$, the lower approximation $B_L(Y)=\{o_1,o_3\}$ is completely shaded in grey, the upper approximation $B^U(Y)=\{o_1,o_2,o_3,o_4\}$ combines grey and white colors and the boundary region $BR(Y)= B^U(Y)- B_L(Y) =\{o_2,o_4\}$.

As already defined, the boundary region BR, is given by the upper approximation minus the lower approximation. The process to remove the roughness, or "deroughfication", is implemented by adding the dummy binary variable "je ne sais quoi" which is given by the intersection of BR and class D=1. For the given example, the dummy binary variable can be established as follows:

$$jnsq_i= \begin{cases} 1 \; if \; (o_i \in BR) and \; (class = 1) \\ 0 \qquad\qquad\qquad\quad otherwise \end{cases}$$

Figure 3 shows the Deroughficated Set, where for observation 4, the $jnsp_4$ was set equal to 1. In the Deroughficated Set, the grey area belongs to class D=1 and the white area to class D≠1.

As with Rough Sets, the LAID method is tolerant with inconsistencies. We believe that a hidden property causes the inconsistency of the classification. This issue is overcome by introducing the dummy binary variable. At this stage the problem is no longer inexact (or rough) and a straightforward method, like LAD, can be applied.

3.3. Two Phase Algorithm

In order to implement the reduction of the dataset, a two-phase algorithm is presented. First, the problem is transformed by generating a matrix with a disjoint constraint. Second, a minimal subset of attributes is chosen using an algorithm for the Set Covering Problem.

Figure 3. Rough set (left) and deroughficated set (right)

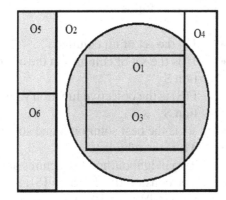 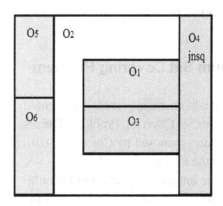

- **Procedure 1:** A Two-Phase Algorithm
- **Input:** dataset D with dummy binary variables
- **Output:** minimal subset of attributes S
  - Disjoint Constraints Matrix Generation
  - Algorithm for the Set-Covering Problem

The reduced dataset is obtained by the projection of the minimal subset of attributes. The number of lines in the dataset is also reduced by removing the repeated observations in the new reduced set of attributes.

3.4. Disjoint Matrix Generation

Dataset D={O, X∪C} has a relational database table format, with a key-column observation O and remaining columns attributes X_i and class C. Each class has a set of observations and each observation is measured by a set of attributes.

LAD only deals with two classes. The proposed disjoint [a(i,j)] matrix generation works with an unlimited number of classes. The procedure is described in Box 3.

Given that *n* is the number of observations, the upper bound for the number of constraints is (n.(n-1))/2, resulting from the comparison of all pairs of observations.

A disjoint matrix [a(i,j)] will be used as input in the Minimum Set Covering problem, where all constraints must be covered, at least once by some attributes.

3.5. Minimum Set Covering Problem

In this section, a heuristic approach is presented for the Minimum Set Covering Problem. The set covering heuristic, proposed by Chvatal (1979), is described in the following pseudo-code.

In the Linear Integer Programming formulation we can identify the matrix [a(i,j)] and the vector [c(j)]. We consider the following notation: [a(constraint, attribute)] for the input constraint

Box 3. Procedure 2: Disjoint matrix generation

```
Input: Dataset D={O, X∪C}
Output: Matrix [a(constraint, attribute)]
1.  For all observations oᵢ: i=1,...,n
2.     class=cᵢ;
3.     For all observations oⱼ: j=i+1,...,n, with cⱼ≠class
4.        constraint = succ(constraint);
5.        For all attributes xₖ: k=1,...,m
6.           if (xₖ(oᵢ) ≠ xₖ(oⱼ)) a(constraint, k)=1
7.           else a(constraint, k)=0;
8.        End for
9.     End for
10. End for
```

matrix, [e(attribute)] for the expense of each attribute, and S for the set covering solution (see Box 4).

In this constructive heuristic, for each iteration, a line is chosen to be covered. Next, the best column that covers the line and finally, solution S is built and the remaining matrix R updated. The chosen line is usually the line that is more difficult to cover, i.e. the line that corresponds to fewer columns. After reaching the cover set, the second step is to remove redundancy, by sorting the cover in descending order of cost and checking if each attribute is really essential.

This constructive heuristic is improved by using a Tabu Search heuristic that removes the most redundant columns and re-builds a new solution as presented in (Cavique, Rego, Themido 1999) and (Gomes, Cavique, Themido 2006) (see Box 5).

The Tabu Search procedure used for improving the Set Covering Problem solutions can be described as follows:

- J is the set of all columns
- J* is the set of columns in the current solution S
- F(S) is the objective function value of solution S
- S* is the best solution found so far
- TL is the tabu list
- Two neighbourhood structures are used:
- The constructive $N^+(S) = \{S': S' = S \cup \{j\}$ with $j \in J \backslash J^*$ and $j \notin TL\}$
- and the obliterate $N^-(S) = \{S': S' = S \backslash \{j\}$ with $j \in J^*\}$

Box 4. Procedure 3: Heuristic for the set-covering problem

```
Input: [a(constraint, attribute)], [e(attribute)]
Output: the minimum set cover S
1. Initialize R=[a(i,j)], S=∅
2. While R ≠ ∅ do
3.     Choose the best line i*∈R such that |a(i*,j)|=min
       |a(i,j)|, ∀j
4.     Choose the best column j* that covers line i*,
       considering f(e,j)
5.     Update R and S, R=R\a(i,j*), ∀i, S=S∪{j*}
6. End while
7. Sort cover S by descending order of costs
8. For each Si do if (S\Si is still a cover) then S=S\Si
9. Return S
```

Box 5. Procedure 4: Tabu search for the set-covering problem

```
Input: J, J*
Output: the minimum set cover S*
1. Set TL = ∅;
2. Construct initial solution S; (Proc.3)
3. Set S* = S;
4. Repeat for k iterations:
5.     Set S''=S;
6.     Repeat S'∈N⁻(S''), S''=S', TL=TL∪ {j} until end
       condition;
7.     Repeat S'∈N⁺(S''), S''=S' until S' is a cover;
8.     If F(S') > F(S*) then set S* = S';
9.     Set S=S';
10.    Update J and J*;
11. End repeat
```

3.6. Numeric Example

In this LAID numeric example, dataset D will be used as a running example in this section.

$$D = \begin{array}{c|ccccc|c} O & x_1 & x_2 & x_3 & x_4 & C \\ \hline o_1 & 1 & 0 & 1 & 0 & 0 \\ o_2 & 1 & 1 & 0 & 1 & 1 \\ o_3 & 1 & 0 & 1 & 1 & 1 \\ o_4 & 1 & 0 & 1 & 0 & 1 \\ o_5 & 0 & 1 & 1 & 1 & 2 \\ o_6 & 0 & 1 & 1 & 1 & 2 \end{array}$$

As already noted, dataset D has redundancy in observations o_5 and o_6, and inconsistencies in observations o_1 and o_4. As proposed in the previous section, the "deroughfication" is obtained by adding a dummy binary attribute to allow the differentiation of observations o_1 and o_4. With these adaptations, dataset D' is as follows:

$$D' = \begin{array}{c|cccccc|c} O & x_1 & x_2 & x_3 & x_4 & jnsq & C \\ \hline o_1 & 1 & 0 & 1 & 0 & 0 & 0 \\ o_2 & 1 & 1 & 0 & 1 & 0 & 1 \\ o_3 & 1 & 0 & 1 & 1 & 0 & 1 \\ o_4 & 1 & 0 & 1 & 0 & 1 & 1 \\ o_{5,6} & 0 & 1 & 1 & 1 & 0 & 2 \end{array}$$

As stated in 2.2., with the LAD Disjoint Matrix procedure, matrix [a(i,j)] is obtained, by comparing each pair of observations from different classes, such as:

$$\begin{bmatrix} a_{i,j} \end{bmatrix} = \begin{bmatrix} 0 & 1 & 1 & 1 & 0 \\ 0 & 0 & 0 & 1 & 0 \\ 0 & 0 & 0 & 0 & 1 \\ 1 & 1 & 0 & 1 & 0 \\ 1 & 0 & 1 & 0 & 0 \\ 1 & 1 & 0 & 0 & 0 \\ 1 & 1 & 0 & 1 & 1 \end{bmatrix} \begin{array}{l} comparing\ o_1\ with\ o_2 \\ o_1\ with\ o_3 \\ o_1\ with\ o_4 \\ o_1\ with\ o_{5,6} \\ o_2\ with\ o_{5,6} \\ o_3\ with\ o_{5,6} \\ o_4\ with\ o_{5,6} \end{array}$$

In the original problem x variables are used while in the transformed problem y variables are used. When a(i,j)=1 it means that column y(j) is relevant to discriminate between the two observations reported in line i. In order to reduce the problem while maintaining the discrimination of the pairs of observations, for each line i at least one column with a(i,j)=1 must be chosen. Accordingly, by applying the set covering problem, variables y_1, y_4 and jnsq ensure the cover of all lines. The solution obtained is $S=\{y_1, y_4, jnsq\}$.

The reduced dataset D* is given by the projection of variables x_1, x_4 and jnsq, as follows:

$$D^* = \begin{vmatrix} O & x_1 & x_4 & jnsq & C \\ o_1 & 1 & 0 & 0 & 0 \\ o_{2,3} & 1 & 1 & 0 & 1 \\ o_4 & 1 & 0 & 1 & 1 \\ o_{5,6} & 0 & 1 & 0 & 2 \\ - & 0 & 0 & 0 & ? \end{vmatrix}$$

One last line was added to the dataset to show that entries x1=0 and x4=0 are not presented in the set of observations and therefore this entry is not explained.

Given the limited size of the example consisting of only two variables, all possible variable entries are presented except the unexplained area represented by symbol "?", as in Table 2.

We must refer that unexplained areas are different from inconsistent areas. Unexplained areas are a result of no observations, while inconsistent areas result from contradictory observations.

The validation of the feature selection method presented in the following sections, is a means used to measure the quality of the data reduction, and is based on the prediction of the unexplained areas.

4. LAID VALIDATION

The performance of a feature selection algorithm is usually measured by the computational results of a classification problem after the data reduction.

Suppose dataset D={O, X∪C} where O={$o_1,o_2,...,o_n$} is a non-empty set of observations (or instances), X={$x_1,x_2,...,x_m$} is a non-empty set of attributes and C is the decision attribute (or class), exemplified as follows:

$$D = \begin{vmatrix} O & x_1 & x_2 & x_3 & x_4 & C \\ o_1 & 1 & 0 & 0 & 0 & 0 \\ o_2 & 1 & 1 & 0 & 0 & 0 \\ o_3 & 1 & 0 & 1 & 1 & 0 \\ o_4 & 0 & 1 & 0 & 0 & 1 \\ o_5 & 0 & 1 & 1 & 0 & 1 \\ o_6 & 1 & 1 & 0 & 1 & 1 \end{vmatrix}$$

The general approach for solving classification problems split D into two datasets: the Training Set and the Test Set. The classification task is to identify which class a new Test Set observation belongs to, based on a Training Set which contains observations whose class is known.

In the predicting process, the original LAD algorithm used to distinguish between observations belonging to two disjoint classes uses the so-called *discriminant function*, which is similar to the k-nearest neighbor classification algorithm. To classify an unknown observation x, let P(x) and N(x) be associated with the positive and negative pattern, where Pos(x): x⊆D⁺ and Neg(x): x⊆D⁻, as follows: $\Delta(x) = \left| Pos(x) \right| - \left| Neg(x) \right|$. If Δ(x)>0 then x is classified as 1, and 0 otherwise.

In the prediction class process, the discriminant function for *p* classes is expressed in Box 6.

Observation *x* contains binary values of the *m* proverbs, showing knowledge of the proverb or lack of it. The function H_i(x) returns a value that is an average of the Hamming Distance between *x* and the known *i* observations. The function predicted_class(x) returns the class of the k-nearest neighbors of *x*. The function used to find and measure the nearest neighbors takes into consideration the Hamming Distance.

Table 2. Classes of the attribute x_1 and x_4

	x_1=0	x_1=1
x_4=0	?	0,1
x_4=1	2	1

Using dataset D, defined in this section, the process to predict the class of x=(1,0,1,0), for k=3 is the following:

- The Hamming distance between the known observation o_1=(1,0,0,0) and x=(1,0,1,0) is 1, since there is a difference in the third element. This process is repeated for all observations.
- The value of function $H_0(x)$=(1+2+1)/3 and the value of $H_1(x)$=(3+2+3)/3.
- The predicted class is class 0, since it has the lowest average Hamming distance.

The method presented initially, that splits the dataset into two sets, has the drawback of not using all available samples. The major method for supervised learning models validation is the cross-validation, which uses all samples available. This is a very useful technique, involving the partition of the sample dataset into *n* subsamples, using *(n-1)* for repeated training and the remaining for testing. In this work, we adopt the special case of Leave-One-Out cross-validation, which consists in removing one observation from the original sample, training the algorithm and then, testing the observation using the resulting model.

The performance of a classification model is based on the total counts of correct and incorrect predictions. These counts are tabulated in a table known as Confusion Matrix. The Confusion Matrix is a specific square table, actual class versus predicted class, which allows for the visualization of the performance of an algorithm, see Table 3.

Given dataset D with *n* observations, and vector of classes C, the procedure to generate the Confusion Matrix is described in Box 7.

Based on the Confusion Matrix many performance measures can be extracted. In this work the accuracy or hit-rate measure will be used, expressed in Box 8.

Another way to evaluate a classifier consists in the use of Receiver Operating Characteristic, ROC curve (Fawcett 2006), which shows the performance of a two-class classifier. The overall performance of a classifier can be measured by Area Under the Curve, AUC. A scale for classifying the accuracy of AUC of the ROC curve is: excellent (0.91-1.00), good (0.81-0.90), fair (0.71-0.80), poor (0.61-0.70) and fail (0.51-0.60).

For a number of classes greater than two, a multi-class ROC analysis will be needed, using a multi-objective optimization function in order to find the Pareto front in the convex hull. In our approach we will use the Hit-rate comparison and Cohen's Kappa-statistic (Cohen 1960). When hit-rate is greater than the modal class assure that the classifier is better than a random classifier;

Box 6.

$$predicted\_class(x) = arg\_min\left(H_0(x), H_1(x), H_2(x), ..., H_p(x)\right)$$

Table 3. Confusion Matrix for a 2-class problem

		Predicted Class	
		Class=1	Class=0
Actual Class	Class=1	f_{11}	f_{10}
	Class=0	f_{01}	f_{00}

Box 7. Procedure 5: Confusion matrix

```
Input: Confusion-Matrix=∅, dataset D;
Output: Confusion-Matrix;
1. for i=1 to n-observations
2.    for j=1 to n-observations
3.       if i≠j // leave this out
4.          update every H_p(i);
5.       end if
6.    end for
7.    predicted-class = arg_min(H_1(i), H_2(i), ...,H_n(i));
8.    update Confusion-Matrix with predicted-class;
9.    update Confusion-Matrix with real-class;
10. end for
```

by modal class we mean the most frequent class. Kappa-statistic measures the agreement using the input data of the Confusion Matrices for a number of classes larger than two, with the following scale: 0–0.20 as slight, 0.21–0.40 as fair, 0.41–0.60 as moderate, 0.61–0.80 as substantial, and 0.81–1 as perfect agreement.

5. LAID RESULTS

In this section the computational results of the data reduction and the chosen proverbs are presented. After setting the study datasets extracted from the "Knowledge of the Azorean Proverbs 2000" database, the computational performance of the algorithms and the test of the hypotheses are discussed. Finally, the chosen proverbs are shown.

5.1. The Study Datasets

The survey data was organized in a relational database called "Knowledge of the Azorean Proverbs 2000", which centralizes all information about the recognition of proverbs. This exhaustive survey was taken to clarify the relevance of over 22,000 Portuguese proverbs in the Azorean society and to calculate the percentage of recognition of these proverbs within the cultural community as a whole or within a single location.

The initial set includes different linguistic forms for the same proverb. For practical reasons, it was impossible to submit the 22,000 proverbs to a single person. Therefore, the corpus was reduced to 1,500 proverbs and divided into 14 packages. The database included 900 respondents and a group of 1,500 proverbs recognized in different locations.

The following relational database exemplified in Figure 4, supports two large volume tables respondents-proverbs and respondents-locations. For the respondents a sampling procedure was used that controls the following factors: gender, three classes for age and two classes for education.

The relational joint operation of the respondents table with the respondents-location table produces a duplication of the responses for the respondents with more than one location. In the classification table, the same respondent, with the same knowledge of proverbs, will be classified in different classes, which is a clear inconsistency. For each inconsistency a dummy binary variable was added.

This study uses the number 9 package from the "Knowledge of the Azorean Proverbs 2000" database, as the test dataset, with 240 respondents, 180 proverbs and 15,300 records in the table of person-proverb. In this dataset, the percentage of proverb recognition is 35%, i.e. 15300/(240x180).

Due to the poor results obtained in previous studies, we decided to enhance the persons with greater knowledge of proverbs by removing the

Box 8.

$$hit\_rate = \frac{number\,of\,correct\,predictions}{total\,number\,of\,predictions} = \frac{f_{11} + f_{00}}{f_{11} + f_{10} + f_{01} + f_{00}}$$

Figure 4. Example of "Knowledge of the Azorean Proverbs 2000"

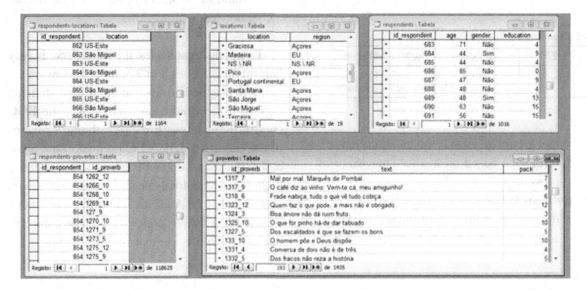

respondent from the database who recognized less than 50% of the proverbs.

By applying these successive filters, only seven of the locations were selected from the Occidental and Central Group: Corvo, Flores, Faial, Graciosa, Pico, São Jorge and Terceira.

Two datasets were prepared to run the algorithms, the first with two classes, which corresponds to the two chosen groups and a second with 7 classes, which relates to the seven referred islands. See Table 4.

5.2. LAID Computational Results

To implement the computational results of the Two-Phase Algorithm, some choices had to be made, such as the computational environment and the performance measures. The computer programs were written in C language and the Dev-C++ compiler was used. The computational results were obtained using a 2.53GHz Intel Core-2Duo processor with 4.00 GB of main memory running under the Windows Vista operating system.

The performance measures for the first phase of the algorithm, the Disjoint Constraint Matrix (DCM), are the number of constraints and the time in seconds. For the second phase, the Set Covering Heuristic (SCH), the number of attributes and also the time in seconds were taken into account. In Table 5, the computational results are presented, from class 2 to 7.

The number of constraints tends to grow exponentially with the number of classes (or birthplaces), while the growth of the number of attributes (or proverbs) and computational times remain linear, showing the good scalability of the algorithm, see Figure 5.

5.3. Testing the Hypotheses

Hypothesis H1, stated in the introduction, where «there are significant differences in the sayings of each island, so that it is possible to identify the native island of an interviewee based on his/her knowledge of proverbs», will be checked in this section for each dataset. So, H1 will be split into H2 and H3, as follows:

Hypothesis 2: There are significant differences in the sayings from the Occidental and Central group, so that it is possible to identify

Table 4. Datasets used in the study

Number of Classes	Description
2	1- Ocidental group, 2- Central group
7	1- Corvo, 2- Flores, 3- Faial, 4- Graciosa, 5- Pico, 6 - São Jorge and 7 - Terceira

the group of islands of an interviewee's birthplace based on his/her knowledge of proverbs;

Hypothesis 3: There are significant differences in the sayings from each of the seven islands, so that it is possible to identify the native

island of an interviewee based on his/her knowledge of proverbs;

To test the hypotheses, the ROC curve is very helpful for 2 classes. For 3 or more classes we are going to use the Hit-rate and the Kappa-statistic.

Given the Confusion Matrix 2x2, the ROC curve is the usual way to measure the performance of the classifiers. The AUC is equal to the probability that a classifier will rank a positive instance higher than a randomly negative one, so a random classifier has an AUC=0.5, and the ideal value is AUC=1.0. In the dataset for 2 classes, the Hit-rate of the Confusion matrix, the area under the

Table 5. Number of constraints and computing time

Num Class	Disjoint Constraint Matrix (DCM)		Set Covering Heuristic (SCH)	
	Num constraints	Time in seconds	Num attributes	Time in seconds
2	703	<1	6	<1
3	1,711	<1	9	<1
4	3,043	<1	11	<1
5	5,803	<1	12	<1
6	8,731	<1	14	1
7	12,965	<1	15	1

Figure 5. Growth of the number of constraints (DCM)

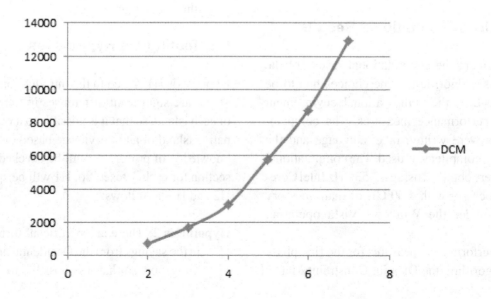

ROC curve are the following: Hit-rate=89% and AUC=80%.

The values with a Hit-rate close to 90% and an AUC greater than 80% take us to an accepted H2, in that there are significant differences in the sayings from the Occidental and Central group.

Hit-rate and modal class classification are calculated in Table 6, where we can see that the algorithm performs better with 2 classes than with 7 classes and where the hit-rate values overcome modal class classification in the first case. For the second case, with 7 classes the condition (hit rate > modal class) is false. It is clear that, as the number of classes increases, the classification procedure tends to degenerate its performance.

Cohen's Kappa measures the agreement between the classification performances of two algorithms when both are rating the same object. A value of 1 indicates perfect agreement while a value of 0 indicates that the agreement is no better than a random value. Also in Table 6, the Kappa-statistic shows a substantial agreement for the dataset with 2 classes and a weak agreement for the dataset with 7 classes.

Finally, the four measures, Hit-rate, AUC, Hit-rate comparison and Kappa-statistic show that there are significant differences in the sayings from the Occidental and Central group, allowing us to conclude that H2 should be accepted. On the other hand, the three measures, Hit-rate, Hit-rate comparison with modal class and Kappa-statistic, show that the identification of the native island of an interviewee cannot be proved, as stated in H3.

5.4. The Chosen Proverbs

Given that hypothesis H3 is plausible, the results for the selected 2 locations (or classes), returned 6 proverbs as the minimum information needed to identify the birthplace of the interviewees, which are presented in Table 7.

Analyzing the meaning of the 6 proverbs sounds bittersweet, because the chosen proverbs are not the best known, nor the most beautiful, but they are surely those that best differentiated the two groups.

In conclusion, the LAID algorithm reduces the number of attributes from 180 to a mere 6 proverbs in a few seconds.

6. CONCLUSION

To sum up, we would like to clarify the major motivations and contributions in this chapter. The motivation was the paremiologic study, which aims to discover the native island of the interviewees. The major contribution of LAID was a new hybrid feature selection algorithm for inconsistent data that dealt successfully with the paremiologic challenge.

This work was part of a wider paremiologic project, based on data collected from thousands of interviews with people from the Azores, asking for the recognition of thousands of Portuguese proverbs, with the purpose of discovering the minimum information needed to guess the native island of an interviewee.

Table 6. Performance measures

Number of Classes	AUC ROC	Hit Rate	Modal Class	Hit rate > Modal Class	Kappa-Statistic	Agreement
2	80%	89%	64%	True	67%	substantial
7	---	33%	48%	False	19%	slight

Table 7. The six proverbs needed to differentiate the groups

Proverb ID	Proverb Text
010_9	In foreign land the ox is cow. (O boi em terra alheia é vaca.)
011_9	Do not let the rightful be the doubtful. (Não se deixa o certo pelo duvidoso.)
115_9	The expensive is cheap, cheap is expensive. (O caro é barato, o barato sai caro.)
121_9	The devil sets the trap. (O diabo tece-as.)
122_9	The devil has a blanket to cover him and another to uncover him. (O diabo tem uma manta com que cobre e outra com que se descobre.)
148_9	Nobody knows his dawn nor his dusk. (Ninguém sabe para que amanhece, nem para que anoitece.)
999_9	dummy binary variable « je ne sais quoi »

In this chapter we tried to highlight the hypothesis that, given the fact that the islands are widely scattered, there are significant differences in the sayings from each island, so that it is possible to identify the native island of an interviewee based on his/her knowledge of proverbs.

In the sample that included mobile persons, i.e. persons that lived in several locations for at least five years in each, there was some inconsistency (or class noise) introduced by the mobile persons, that made the problem more difficult to solve.

In this study, many unreported attempts were carried out using several feature selection and classification techniques but without success. The approach of combining Rough Sets and LAD was the most successful.

Although Rough Sets and LAD have many similarities, their comparison in the literature is scarce or nonexistent. A brief review of Rough Sets and LAD is presented and combined in the proposed LAID. This new technique includes the inconsistency tolerance and multiplicity of classes of Rough Sets, and the efficiency and attributes cost optimization of the LAD. Although Rough Sets do not exclude or correct the inconsistencies of the data, LAID does not exclude but correct the inconsistencies by adding dummy binary variables. The integration of both approaches is so tight that LAID can be seen as a Rough Set extension.

The paremiologic case study used a dataset with 240 interviewees (observations) and 180 proverbs (attributes), classified into 2 and 7 locations (or classes). The LAID algorithm reduces the number of attributes from 180 to a mere 6 proverbs in a few seconds.

The computational results showed that there are significant differences in the sayings from the Occidental and Central group, which allow us to conclude that H2 should be accepted, therefore it is possible to identify the group of islands of an interviewee's birthplace based on his/her knowledge of proverbs. On the other hand, a more detailed approach to identify the native island of an interviewee cannot be proved, as stated in H3.

Finally, we believe that an important link was established between Rough Sets and Logical Analysis of Data with the LAID method. In future work, we also intend to associate these techniques with the instance selection method, and explore the potential of these three strategies, of including, excluding or adding discerning variables to inconsistent data.

REFERENCES

Almuallim, H., & Dietterich, T. G. (1991). Learning with many irrelevant features. In *Proceedings of the 9th National Conference on Artificial Intelligence* (pp. 547-552). Cambridge, MA: MIT Press.

Beasley, J. E., & Jörnsten, K. (1992). Enhancing an algorithm for set covering problems. *European Journal of Operational Research*, *58*, 293–300. doi:10.1016/0377-2217(92)90215-U.

Boros, E., Hammer, P. L., Ibaraki, T., Kogan, A., Mayoraz, E., & Muchnik, I. (2000). An implementation of logical analysis of data. *IEEE Transactions on Knowledge and Data Engineering*, *12*(2), 292–306. doi:10.1109/69.842268.

Cavique, L., Rego, C., & Themido, I. (1999). Subgraph ejection chains and tabu search for the crew scheduling problem. *The Journal of the Operational Research Society*, *50*(6), 608–616.

Chikalov, I., Lozin, V., Lozina, I., Moshkov, M., Nguyen, H. S., Skowron, A., & Zielosko, B. (2013). *Three approaches to data analysis: Test theory, rough sets and logical analysis of data*. Berlin: Springer. doi:10.1007/978-3-642-28667-4.

Chvatal, V. (1979). A greedy heuristic for the set-covering problem. *Mathematics of Operations Research*, *4*, 233–235. doi:10.1287/moor.4.3.233.

Cohen, J. (1960). A coefficient of agreement for nominal scales. *Educational and Psychological Measurement*, *20*, 37–46. doi:10.1177/001316446002000104.

Crama, Y., Hammer, P. L., & Ibaraki, T. (1988). Cause-effect relationships and partially defined boolean functions. *Annals of Operations Research*, *16*, 299–326. doi:10.1007/BF02283750.

Fawcett, T. (2006). An introduction to ROC analysis. *Pattern Recognition Letters*, *27*, 861–874. doi:10.1016/j.patrec.2005.10.010.

Funk, G., & Funk, M. (2001a). *Pérolas da sabedoria popular: Os provérbios Açoreanos nos EUA*. Lisboa: Salamandra..

Funk, G., & Funk, M. (2001b). *Pérolas da sabedoria popular: Os provérbios de S. Miguel*. Lisboa: Salamandra..

Funk, G., & Funk, M. (2003). *Pérolas da sabedoria popular: Provérbios das Ilhas do Grupo Central dos Açores (Faial, Graciosa, Pico, São Jorge e Terceira)*. Lisboa: Salamandra..

Gomes, M., Cavique, L., & Themido, I. (2006). The crew time tabling problem: An extension of the crew scheduling problem. *Annals of Operations Research. Optimization in Transportation*, *144*(1), 111–132.

John, G. H., Kohavi, R., & Pfleger, K. (1994). Irrelevant features and the subset selection problem. In *Proceedings of the 11th International Conference on Machine Learning*, (pp. 121-129). ICML.

Kira, K., & Rendell, L. A. (1992). The feature selection problem: Traditional methods and a new algorithm. In *Proceedings of Ninth National Conference on Artificial Intelligence* (pp. 129-134). NCAI.

Mendes, A., Funk, G., & Funk, M. (2009). Extrair conhecimento de provérbios. In M. F. Salgueiro (Ed.), *Temas em Métodos Quantitativos* (pp. 89–107). Lisboa: Sílabo..

Mendes, A. B., Funk, M., & Cavique, L. (2010). Knowledge discovery in the virtual social network due to common knowledge of proverbs. In *Proceedings of DMIN' 10, the 6th International Conference on Data Mining,* (pp. 213-219). DMIN.

Pawlak, Z. (1982). Rough sets. *International Journal of Computer and Information Science, 11,* 341–356. doi:10.1007/BF01001956.

Pawlak, Z. (1991). *Rough sets: Theoretical aspects of reasoning about data.* Boston: Kluwer Academic Publishers..

Peters, J. F., & Skowron, A. (2010). *Transactions on rough sets XI.* Berlin: Springer. doi:10.1007/978-3-642-11479-3.

Polkowski, L. (2002). *Rough sets, mathematical foundations.* Berlin: Physica-Verlag Heidelberg. doi:10.1007/978-3-7908-1776-8.

Yao, Y. Y. (2007). Neighborhood systems and approximate retrieval. *Information Sciences, 176,* 3431–3452. doi:10.1016/j.ins.2006.02.002.

Chapter 4
Hydropower Projects within a Municipal Water Supply System:
Optimum Allocation and Management using Harmony Search

Ioannis Kougias
Aristotle University of Thessaloniki, Greece

Thomas Patsialis
Aristotle University of Thessaloniki, Greece

Nicolaos Theodossiou
Aristotle University of Thessaloniki, Greece

Jacques Ganoulis
Aristotle University of Thessaloniki, Greece

ABSTRACT

The interest of those involved in hydroelectricity has been attracted by mini-hydro projects due to their minimal environmental impact and low installation cost. Besides, mini hydros can cooperate with an impressively wide extent of water-related infrastructure, offering a broad potential for investment. In the present chapter, the integrated solution of hydro implementation in water supply systems is presented. Thus, the benefits of a water-supply installation (with constant Q) are extended to energy production. However, defining the optimum operation of such a project is a complicated task, which may involve environmental, hydraulic, technical, and economical parameters. In the present chapter a novel approach is presented, the optimum management of mini hydros in a water supply system with the use of an optimization algorithm (i.e. Harmony Search Algorithm [HAS]). This approach is applied at a site in Northern Greece and is used as a case study of the present chapter.

DOI: 10.4018/978-1-4666-4785-5.ch004

INTRODUCTION

Increasing the non-polluting, renewable energy production is an important aim, for most of the countries, worldwide. European Union (Green Paper, 2001) policy is further emphasized in the "Green Paper" towards a European strategy for sustainable, secure energy supply. The "Green Paper" underlines the potential of hydroelectricity to play a much larger role in both the economy and the energy balance.

Fluctuations in hydroelectricity have a considerable impact on some countries, since they lead to increased coal consumption. The most susceptible to these fluctuations countries in EU are Austria, Sweden, Portugal, Finland, Italy, France and Spain. Large and medium – scale hydroelectric projects rely on hydrological regimes, depending on the seasonal fluctuation. The proposed method, the installation of mini – scale hydros in water networks with a constant flow, answers to the need for stabilization of the energy supply. Besides, recent studies have shown that small scale projects (mini, micro) are the only sector with any prospect in European Union. Furthermore, small hydro established in water systems, has the advantage to exploit the presence of an existing project, reducing construction costs, environmental costs and adds a new environmental and friendly use at the original project, which is the water supply system.

In the present chapter the definition of the optimum capacity and location of mini-scale hydroelectric projects in the presented area, is calculated with the use of Harmony Search Algorithm (HSA). At first glance placing the projects in the existing Break Pressure Tanks (BPT's), as showed in Figure 1, reduces significantly the construction cost. Hydro units, as a rule, are installed where pressure is released from water lines. However, the created HSA algorithm will investigate the

possibility of other alternatives as well. All the technical, economic and environmental data have been included in the created HSA-model in detail.

BACKGROUND

Hydroelectricity as a Renewable Energy Source

Large – scale hydroelectric plants have as a rule enormous size, having a generating capacity up to several hundreds of MW and supply 20% of

Figure 1. Hydropower generation in the break pressure tank (BPT)

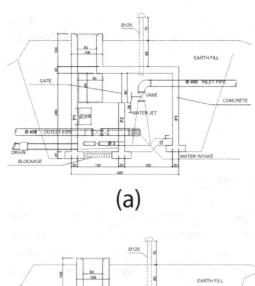

(a)

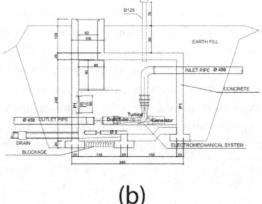

(b)

global electricity in World. There is still a potential of large hydropower installations in developing countries, but these projects may face financial, environmental, and social constraints. According to Demirbas (2002), the global potential of large-scale hydro which is technically exploitable is estimated to be more than 2200 GW, of which only about 25% is currently exploited.

The term "small-scale hydroelectric projects" usually includes plants with a generating capacity lower than 10MW. Small – scale hydros can be further subdivided into Mini, Micro and Pico hydroelectric projects. Micro hydros usually have a very small generating capacity (<100KW), whereas mini hydros, which are surveyed in the present chapter, have a generating capacity smaller than 1000KW.

Pico hydroelectricity usually is used in rural, isolated communities, in order to cover basic needs. According to a report of the World Bank (2007), Pico hydro is potentially the lowest cost technology for off-grid electrification (see Table 1).

Mini Hydroelectric Projects: Advantages

Mini hydro includes projects with a capacity between 100KW and 1000KW. Typically these projects are constructed in the run of the stream without the need of water storage. In some cases a very small reservoir might be constructed as a wooden structure, in order to optimize the energy production. Even in that case, the construction

Table 1. Subdivision of hydroelectric plants

Types of hydroelectric plants	Generating capacity
Large	>100 MW
Small	<10 MW
Mini	**<1000 KW**
Micro	<100 KW
Pico	<5KW

cost is relatively low and the environmental impact minimal. Besides, the quantity of the stored water is small and causes no significant changes to the stream flow. Moreover, the small-scale wooden structure fits harmonically in the natural environment.

Mini hydro electric plants have many advantages and the number of installations has considerably increased during the recent years. Their minimal environmental impact and their relatively low installation cost along with the uninterrupted energy production, has attracted the scientific interest. In particular, they comprise one of the most cost-effective and reliable energy technologies for providing clean electricity generation.

The advantages that mini hydro has over other renewable energy sources (British Hydropower Association, 2005) are:

- *A high efficiency (70 – 90%),* is by far the highest of all energy technologies.
- *A high capacity factor (typically >45%),* compared with 10 – 30% for solar panels and 20 – 30% for wind turbines.
- *A high level of predictability* of the energy production. Energy production follows the annual rainfall – runoff patterns.
- *Gradual change of energy production.* The output power varies only gradually from day to day.
- Hydroelectric generators *respond quickly to changing conditions.*
- Mini hydro systems in streams have a *good correlation with demand* i.e. the output is maximum during winter.
- *It is a long-lasting technology.* Relative to other forms of energy generation, systems can be engineered to last for more than 50 years, with a low maintenance cost.

The minimal environmental impact of small hydroelectric projects is justified by the following (Celso Penche, 1997):

- *Water is not consumed.* It is returned to the stream/pipes and its quality is not deteriorated.
- *Little or no water is stored.* Mini hydro is in most cases "run-of-river" and any dam or barrage is quite small. In the proposed scheme, Mini hydro is inducted in a water supply system.

Therefore mini hydro installations do not have the same kinds of adverse effect on the local environment as large-scale hydro (www.esha.be).

Mini Hydropower Plants within a Drinking Water Network

Very often a drinking water network transfers water from a mountainous spring to the neighbor inhabited area. A typical drinking water network consists of a spring in altitude, a fore bay, a penstock, a reservoir and a water supply network.

Typically the elevation of the spring is high. Since the pressure inside the network and at the consumers cannot exceed certain limits, there has to be an excess of pressure in the networks to recover. The presented approach in this chapter suggests replacement of the pressure breakers, used traditionally to waste the excess pressure, by turbines so as to generate electricity. In this way, the potential for energy recovery that exists at Break Pressure Tanks (BPTs) is exploited. The required modification of the pressure reduction bank is illustrated in Figure 1 (S. Kucukali, 2011).

Other energy recovery possibilities are also possible by altering the turbine positions e.g. the installation on the storage reservoir. This variation is very similar with the installation in pressure breakers. In that case, water passes through the turbine before being accumulated in the reservoir which is located in the edge of the inhabited area. Both variations are most flexible, as it is possible at any time to disconnect the turbine operation from the water supply network.

Installation of such mini hydropower plants in water supply networks has an increased usage. For example, in Austria integrated hydropower in the drinking water supply system is in function in Vienna Mauer, Nasswald, Mühlau and Shreyerbach. Italy has also followed the same method (Poggio Cuculo), while Switzerland has 90 small hydropower plants installed on the municipal water supply network of the country (Byns et al., 2011).

The optimum management of the proposed approach is important in order to ensure the economical viability of the system and the maximum environmental, social and economical benefits. Research in the specific field is still in progress. One such large-scale research project is "*Hydro-BPT*", which is partially funded by the European Regional Development Fund and "will advance the sustainability of the process of water supply in Ireland and Wales by exploiting the potential for energy recovery that exists at Break Pressure Tanks" (Web site: http://hydro-bpt.eu/).

In the present chapter, the use of metaheuristic algorithms towards the optimal operation and management of the proposed scheme is presented. A Harmony Search optimization Algorithm is designed and implemented towards the maximization of the benefits of the presented problem.

INSTALLATION OF MINI HYDROELECTRIC PROJECTS IN A WATER SUPPLY SYSTEM IN NORTHERN GREECE

The case study that will be presented concerns the installation of mini hydroelectric projects in the water supply system of Figure 2, in an optimum way. The selected area belongs to Aliakmonas river basin, Aliakmonas being the longest river in Greece.

The supply system transfers the water from a spring at an elevation of 400m to a small city with a population of 10.000 people, near the city of Thessaloniki. Three Break Pressure Tanks (BPT

Figure 2. The under-study water supply system in northern Greece

1-3) enable the control of the head and pressure, due to the high elevation differences along the pipeline. The elevation difference between consecutive BPT's is 100m.

The city is located 22km far from the third break pressure tank (BPT 3) at an elevation of 7-10m (Figure 3).

The total technically usable hydraulic head is 300m, which equals to a substantial energy potential. The remainder hydraulic head (90m) occurs due to the elevation difference between BPT-3 and the storage tank in the edge of the city. However, this pressure is not exploitable for various reasons. The distance between BPT-3 and the storage tank is 22km. Also the slope of the pipe

is very small (0.4%) and the losses of the friction will be large enough. Thus, in the present study the potential of this pressure is not examined for energy production.

The pipe diameter of the existing network is D=0.55m and its material is steel. The constant water flow is Q=200 lt/sec, unvaried throughout the year. The simplified profile of the existing water supply system is illustrated in Figure 3.

The characteristics of the water supply network are briefly:

- Total Length of the underground water supply system: L= 30 km
- Total Hydraulic Head: H'≈ 390m
- Usable Hydraulic Head: H= 300m

Figure 3. Simplified profile of the water supply network

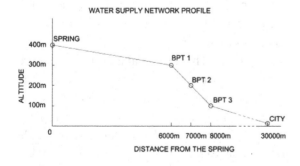

In the present chapter the definition of the optimum capacity and location of mini-scale hydroelectric projects in the presented area, is calculated with the use of HSA. At first glance placing the projects in the existing BPT's, as showed in Figure 1, reduces significantly the construction cost. Hydro units, as a rule, are installed where pressure is released from water lines. However, the created HSA algorithm will investigate the possibility of other alternatives as well. All the technical, economical and environmental data have been included in the created HSA-model in detail.

Defining the type and number of hydro works that will lead to the maximum benefits is the central point of the Harmony Search Algorithm. Obviously, scenarios that include interventions in the existing supply network (e.g. pipe replacement) are regarded as non-realistic and unprofitable.

Another question HSA needs to answer is if it is profitable to create a by-pass and hydroelectric projects in all three Break Pressure Tanks. In other words, we need to know not only if there are other spots offering a potential for energy production, but also if all the obvious spots (BPTs) are economically viable.

Taking a decision between the numerous alternative options for turbine capacity and style is almost impossible without the use of an optimization technique. For example, it is hard to say whether it is better to construct one larger hydro instead of two or three smaller. Thus, HSA has been used for the determination of the number and capacity of the hydros that lead to the optimum management.

DESIGN AND CREATION OF THE OPTIMIZATION MODEL

In order to optimize the presented problem, a model is created. This model will lead to the optimal choice regarding the installation of small hydroelectric projects in the area under consideration.

The concept of the optimization model is quite simple. We need to define the number, the type and the location of the hydroelectric stations in order to maximize the benefits of the system, as expressed by the relation between the income from producing energy and the installation and maintenance cost. The whole system is subjected to the constrain of not exceeding the pipe's pressure tolerance.

This model, following the exact definition of the decision variables, is comprised by the math-

ematical expression of the objective function and the constraints. The technical and environmental constraints are expressed in equations. The basic constraint, presented in detail in the latter, concerns the available hydraulic head, on which both the energy production and safety of the infrastructure depend.

The central point of the modeling process includes the definition of the objective function. The objective function is the mathematical expression that estimates in what extent proposed solutions are optimal. In other words, the objective function surveys in a quantitive, mathematical manner each possible solution. The objective function includes technical, economical and environmental characteristics of the problem. Thus, the maximization of the objective function equals to the maximization of all the goals set, delivering at the same time the constraints of the problem.

Decision Variables

The choice of the decision variables is connected with the information we want HSA to export. In the presented application the needed information include information of the number, the type and the location of hydroelectric stations in a way that leads to maximum benefits.

Regarding the location of the stations, we decided to use an indirect method of defining their position. Defining the exact coordinates (E, N) of the hydroelectric stations leads to an unnecessary increase of the complexity of the model. For this reason, instead of the coordinates, the authors suggest the use of the required hydraulic head of each project. Defining the hydraulic head that each project requires towards the maximum benefit concludes to one or very few applicable, alternative solutions. Then, if the alternatives are more than one, the decision maker can easily choose the best solution that fits to the local conditions, the existing infrastructure and to the local property situation. In that way, the model is kept simple and flexible. At the same time, the decision maker is provided with the ability to adapt the optimum solution according to the real situation and needs.

This strategy leads to a flexible formation of the decision variables. The number of variables is equal to the number of different types of turbines, available for installation. In the studied case the different, available types are ten. The number of each turbine's installations is expressed by the corresponding value of each variable. Example of this encoding is:

$X1= 1, X2= 2$ and $X3= X4=…= X10= 0$

Corresponds to an installation of:

one turbine of type 1, two turbines of type 2 and none of the rest

The selected types of turbines were chosen in the basis of suitability to the requirements and on technical characteristics. Generally, the type of turbine used depends on the flow rate and hydraulic head (pressure) of the water (http://www.canyon-hydro.com/). The conventional Francis turbine is used mainly by small hydropower plants with low head heights and medium flow rates. Kaplan turbines are unsuitable for the studied case, since they are used in plants with low head heights and high-volume flow rates and are suitable for fluctuating amounts of water. The Pelton turbine is used in plants with high head heights and small amounts of water. Cross flow turbines are used in plants with low head heights and small amounts of water that generally have small outputs (http://www.cink-hydro-energy.com/).

Calculating the Amount of Available Power

Another general guide to the turbine selection is the available power. The Power potential of the source is calculated as a function of the hydraulic head and the rate of the water flow. In the present application the total available power is calculated for the technically exploitable hydraulic head of 300m.

$$P= n \bullet \rho \bullet g \bullet Q \bullet H$$

where:

- **P** is the power in kW.
- **n** is the dimensionless efficiency of the installation, which takes typical values between 0.55 and 0.85.
- **ρ** is the density of water in t/m^3.
- **Q** is the flow in m^3/s.
- **g** is the gravity acceleration m/s^2.
- **H** is the head difference between spring and the last tank

In the present application the available power for n= 0.8 is:

$$P= 470 \text{ kW}$$

In Table 2, the available types of turbines are presented along with their technical and economical characteristics.

Constraints

The basic constraint of the model includes limitation of the hydraulic pressure in the water supply system. This constraint protects the pipes from failure and guarantees the constant and continuous function of the system.

Pipe's Pressure $\leq$ Pipe's Tolerance

The following method is followed in order to determine the boundaries of the hydraulic head of the turbines. As already mentioned, the technically available hydraulic head in the studied area is 300m. The hydraulic losses have been calculated with the use of common equations

Table 2. Characteristics of the available turbines

Turbine	Capacity (KW)	Annually Produced Energy (MWh)	Required Hydraulic Head (m)	Cost of Turbine (€)	Annual maintenance cost (€)
1	152	1278	100	97000	5287
2	163	1371	100	99000	5396
3	230	374	30	154000	8393
4	406	374	45	248000	13516
5	80	605	100	45000	2453
6	125	967	100	80000	4360
7	180	1388	100	123000	6704
8	200	1430	100	135000	7358
9	270	1219	80	215000	11718
10	300	1093	70	240000	13080

(e.g. Darcy–Weisbach, Manning) and are equal to 12m for the total distance of 8000m, between the spring and BPT – 3. Thus, the final available hydraulic head is equal to 288m.

If the chosen turbines have a total hydraulic head requirement that is much lower than 288m, then a substantial energy potential will not be utilized. Moreover, it is possible that the extra head will cause major damage and wear to the turbines, because the turbines will not be able to stand the extra pressure.

On the other hand, installing turbines that operate best in a total hydraulic head of much more than 288m should also be avoided. In that case the wrong type of turbines will have probably been selected (e.g. Kaplan instead of Cross-flow). In any case, the power-plants should not operate in such a low efficiency. Thus:

Total Hydraulic Head ≈288m

This constraint is delivered by adding a penalty to those solutions that do not comply with the limits. The penalty is corresponds to an additional cost, which is included to the objective function and corresponds to the additional cost of the redundant hydraulic head.

Objective Function

The objective function expresses the benefits that proposed solutions offer. It includes the installation cost, the maintenance cost and the income of the produced energy.

The investment time horizon is specified at 30 years, assuming that the installed hydroelectric projects will function for at least 30 years, without any further modification except from the annual maintenance. This assumption is realistic, considering that hydroelectric technology is long-lasting and hydro-projects usually operate without any problem for more than 50 years.

Installation Cost

The cost of the plants includes the cost of the turbine and its annual maintenance cost. These expenditures are obviously different for each of the 10 different turbines (Table 2).

Costs that are common for all turbine-installations include:

- Turbine house and its fencing (50.000€/hydroelectric project)
- Studies and license (20.000€/hydroelectric project)

- Installation, cables (15.000€/hydroelectric project)
- Connection to the National Grid (6.000€/ hydroelectric project)
- Electrical installation – ground (3.500€/ hydroelectric project)

The cost of the connection to the National Grid may vary between different plants. However, in the present case the piping system runs in small distance and parallel to the electrical network and the connection to the Grid is in all cases low-cost, since the distance is less than 200m.

The total installation cost is considered to be funded by a 10-year loan with an annual interest rate of 8%.

The annual maintenance cost varies among turbines and is typically calculated as the 5.45% of the purchase cost of each turbine (Table 2).

Annual Profit

Each hydroelectric installation produces electric energy constantly throughout the year according to its technical characteristics and the hydraulic head, since the flow rate is constant and equal to 200l/s.

Each power plant produces energy without any interruption (24hours/day, 365 days/year). However, a factor of safety is introduced in order to cover non-predictable interruption of the flow. Thus, the annual operation is:

Operation duration= (24×365)×0.96= 8409.6 hours

The produced energy is connected and sold to the National Supplier for 0.105 €/kWh. It is assumed that produced energy is sold as a whole at the end of the year. Annual profits are subject to 25% tax, which is also taken into account in the calculations.

Definition of the Objective Function

Finally, the objective function is:

Balance(X) = Sum of Annual Profits(30 years) –

Annual maintenance Cost(30 years) – Installation Cost(10-year loan)

The aim for the created Harmony Search optimization algorithm is to find the decision variables Xi that maximize the objective function Balance(X).

HARMONY SEARCH ALGORITHM (HSA)

Even in ancient civilizations, the relation between music and mathematics was considered to be essential, but only recently scientists found an interesting connection between optimization techniques and music. This technique, the music-inspired harmony search optimization algorithm, is based on the observation that the aim of music creation is the quest of the perfect state of harmony. Just as the musicians try to improve their music (based on aesthetic and acoustic criteria), the algorithm seeks for certain values that optimize the objective function and at the same time satisfy the problem's constraints. And in the same way a music band improves rehearsal after rehearsal, HSA improves iteration after iteration.

Dr. Zong Woo Geem presented the new optimization technique in a Water Resources Conference in 2000. In the following year Geem et al published HSA's structure (Geem, Kim and Loganathan 2001). At that point he believed that a new meta-heuristic algorithm could still be developed and would be an attractive alternative among the already established methods. Moreover, this new technique would be a robust tool, with even better performance, that provides improved results after less iteration.

Many optimization techniques imitate a natural or artificial procedure. Harmony Search Algorithm was inspired from music and imitates the way musicians perform. As a result its elements borrow their names from music:

- **Harmony:** A possible solution to the examined problem.
- **Harmony Memory (HM):** The places where harmonies are stored.
- **Harmony Memory Size (HMsize):** The number of places that HM has.
- **Maximum number of Iterations (MaxIter):** Defines the termination criterion.

Every member of a music band has different options during a performance or a rehearsal. Firstly, the musician can play the famous melody, the well-known theme of the song. Obviously all members of the music band know this theme and can play it from memory. The second option is to play a variation of this theme. In this way the theme is enriched with new music material. Finally, the musician can always start an improvisation creating new -sometimes random- melodies. Harmony Search Algorithm consists of 3 basic mechanisms that imitate the above options:

1. Use of one of the solutions stored in the Harmony Memory (HM). The Harmony Memory Consideration is very important since it ensures that good harmonies, solutions that provide good results, will be considered during the optimization process and will form the basis for the production of even better solutions. For the effective application of this procedure the Harmony Memory Consideration Rate (HMCR) is used. If this index is assigned small values then only a few of the good solutions stored in the HM will be taken into consideration in the evaluation of new solutions resulting to a very slow convergence. On the other hand, large values of HMCR will impose restrictions in the ability of the procedure to investigate a large field of possible solutions. Technically HMCR takes values larger than 70%, sometimes even exceeding 95%.

2. A usually smaller percentage of the solutions selected with the application of the previous mechanism are allowed to be slightly altered. This is the second mechanism of the algorithm where the Pitch Adjusting Rate (PAR) is used. In that concept the algorithm choses to slightly alter the variable xi from a randomly selected solution, stored in the harmonic memory. This will be performed by selecting a neighboring value of x_i:

$$x_i^{new} = x_i \pm Random\ (bw)$$

where Random(bw) is a random number expressing the bandwidth of the adjustment. This procedure is similar to the mutation in Genetic Algorithms. It is worth noting that although PAR usually takes small values, it is considered to play an important role in the convergence.

3. The third procedure is improvisation, which means to introduce completely random values for variables of the created Harmonies – solutions. The probability of introducing random values is (100-HMCR)%. In this way the variability of solutions is enriched. Contrary to the PAR parameter through which the algorithm investigates the area around the values of the Harmony Memory, randomization aims in widening the field of solutions, thus ensuring the determination of global optimal solutions of the objective function.

In Figure 4, a detailed flow-chart of Harmony Search Algorithm, including all the steps, is illustrated.

All information relating to Parameter Settings, Pitch Adjusting Rate and Randomization are included in the reference: [Geem Z., Kim J. and Loganathan G. (2001); Theodossiou N., Kougias

Figure 4. Flowchart of harmony search algorithm

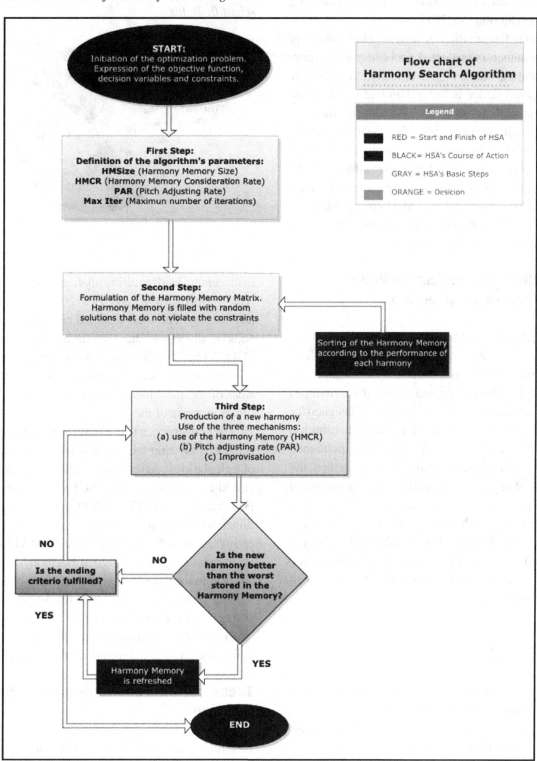

I., Kakoudakis K., & Doikos K. (2011); Kougias, I., Theodossiou, N. (2012)]

After the creation of a new "Harmony", its performance is evaluated according to the corresponding value of the objective function. If this performance is better than that of the worst "Harmony" stored in the Harmony Memory, it replaces it. This procedure is repeated until the ending criterion, usually a maximum number of iterations, is reached. Choosing values for the parameters mentioned above has always been an issue. Moreover, the size of Harmony Memory is one more parameter that needs calibration (Kougias and Theodossiou, 2010).

Applications of HSA on Water Resources Engineering

The HSA method is a new optimization method which can be applied in many cases to great effect, depending on the user's wishes. The method was applied to this project and the results were more than satisfactory. HSA was originally designed for the optimum design of urban water distribution networks and until 2005 most of the published HSA studies were devoted to that. Since then, the range of applications has significantly expanded (Kougias and Theodossiou, 2010).

In Figure 5 the results of a recent study are presented. The percentage of published studies per scientific field, are illustrated. Water engineering applications are still a main research activity, with a percentage of 15%.

RESULTS

The designed model converged to a management that leads to 30-year profits of 7.86 millions €, which is the value of the objective function for best solution found by HSA.

The best solution suggests the installation of three turbines, one turbine of Type-2 and two turbines of Type-8. In other words, the best found

Figure 5. Implementation of HSA in different scientific fields

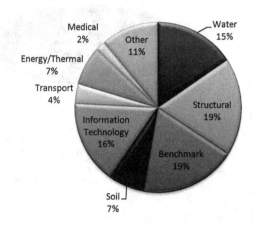

management leads to an installation of one 163kW (H= 100m) turbine and two 200kW turbines (H= 100m). The total installed capacity will be 563kW, which is higher than the available power (470kW) by 20%. This increase is desired, since it results to a better operation and lower rate of wear of the machinery. Moreover, it may cover future increase of the Q.

The convergence to the best solution has been achieved only after few seconds and few hundreds of calculations. After several test – runs it occurred that this solution is the best solution that HSA can detect. In Figure 6 this convergence is illustrated in a graph. This graph pops-out at the end of each run of the created model, in MATLAB. It is obvious that the designed Harmony Search Algorithm locates solutions that are very close to the maximum profit (7.8 million Euros) only after 200 iterations. Then, after only 210 calculations it converges to the best management of the system, which leads to the maximum investment profit.

Technical Characteristics of the Best Solution

As already mentioned, the best found installation consists of two similar turbines with a capacity of 200kW and one with a smaller capacity of 163kW.

Figure 6. Convergence to the optimum solution in MATLAB

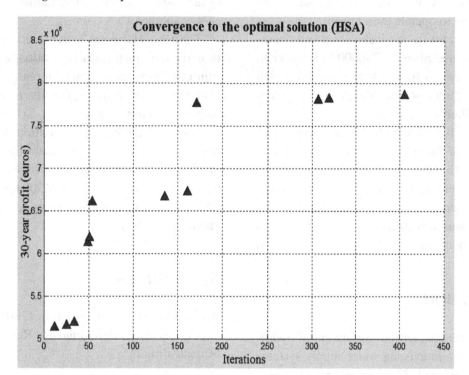

All three turbines have been manufactured to function under a hydraulic pressure of 100m and the total required head is 300m. However, since the available hydraulic head is 300m minus the hydraulic losses (12m), the turbines will not perform in their maximum efficiency.

Placement of the Turbines

Naturally the decision maker has decided to place the three turbines in the existing BPT's. The smaller turbine (163kW) will be placed in the position of the first break pressure tank (BPT-1). BPT-1 is located 6km far from the spring while BPT-2 and BPT-3 are only 1km from each other. This distances result to a proportional distribution of the hydraulic loss, Table 3.

Thus, the smaller turbine will be connected to BPT-1 and will operate under a hydraulic head of 91m. The two, larger turbines will be connected to positions with a hydraulic head of 98.5m (BPT-2 and BPT-3), that results to their operation

at almost maximum efficiency. In that way, the group of hydroelectric projects will offer maximum benefits.

Economical Characteristics of the Best Solution

The optimal installation, detected by HSA, results to a 30-year profit of 7.86 million € and the investment, after 30 years of continuous operation, will result to a positive income of almost 8 million €. Considering that hydropower technology is a long-lasting and reliable renewable energy tech-

Table 3. Hydraulic loss along the water supply network

Route	Distance (km)	Hydraulic Loss (m)
Spring – BPT 1	6	9
BPT 1 – BPT 2	1	1.5
BPT 2 – BPT 3	1	1.5
Total:	8	12

nology, it is very likely that the installed plants will continue to operate even longer.

The total cost for the installation and operation of the three plants is 730000 €. In order to finance this cost, a 10-year loan is needed, which including the interest concludes to a total payment of 1.58 million €.

It results that after the fifth year of operation, redemption of the investment will be completed. This proves that the proposed scheme of hydropower in water supply network is a really profitable investment.

The economical data of the investment that leads to the maximum benefits are given in Table 4.

CONCLUSION

In the present chapter the installation of hydroelectric plants in existing water supply systems has been presented. This technique has already been used in some countries, providing renewable energy in an economically efficient way. The existence of the main particles of the system (pipes and in most cases reservoirs) decreases significantly the cost of the investment. Furthermore the nature of the drinking water networks guarantees that the plants will work continuously throughout the year. For this reason hydropower plants connected to water supply systems have one

of the highest capacity factors among renewable energy sources.

The use of Harmony Search Algorithm, which is a modern metaheuristic optimization algorithm, led to the detection of a reasonably good installation, which maximizes the technical and economical characteristics.

The environmental contribution of the proposed scheme is also important. The optimum installation presented in the present chapter results to an annual saving of almost 4500 tons of CO_2, which is an important contribution against the greenhouse effect.

REFERENCES

British Hydropower Association. (2005). *A guide to UK mini-hydro developments*. Retrieved from britishhydro.org

Byns, N., Leunis, K., Peeters, K., & Tonnet, L. (2011). *The use of hydropower in water supply*. K.U. Leuven..

Celso Penche. (1997). *Layman's guide on how to develop a small hydro site. Directorate-General for Energy by European Small Hydropower Association*. ESHA..

Demirbas, A. (2005). Potential applications of renewable energy sources, biomass combustion problems in boiler power systems and combustion related environmental issues. *Progress in Energy and Combustion Science, 31*(2), 171–192. doi:10.1016/j.pecs.2005.02.002.

Ganoulis, J., & Skoulikaris, C. (2011). Impact of climate change on hydropower generation and irrigation: A case study from Greece. In *Climate Change and its Effects on Water Resources* (pp. 87–95). Berlin: Springer. doi:10.1007/978-94-007-1143-3_10.

Table 4. Economical data of the optimum solution

Description	Amount (€)
Turbine Cost:	448,723.00
Installation Cost:	283,500.00
Total Cost:	732,223.00
Total Cost (10-year loan):	1,580,814.54
Annual maintenance cost:	24,455.40
Annual Income:	444,153.02
Annual net income:	314,773.22
30 – year income:	9,443,196.46
30 – year Balance:	**7,862,381.92**

Geem, Z., Kim, J., & Loganathan, G. (2001). A new heuristic optimization algorithm: Harmony search. *Simulation, 76*(2), 60–68. doi:10.1177/003754970107600201.

Green Paper. (2001). *Opinion of the economic and social committee on the green paper: Towards a European strategy for the security of energy supply*. European Economic and Social Committee, Office for Official Publications of the European Communities..

Kaldellis, J. K. (2007). The contribution of small hydro power stations to the electricity generation in Greece: Technical and economic considerations. *Energy Policy, 35*(4), 2187–2196. doi:10.1016/j.enpol.2006.06.021.

Kougias, I., & Theodossiou, N. (2010). A new music-inspired, harmony based optimization algorithm: Theory and applications. In *Proceedings of 10th International Conference on Protection and Restoration of the Environment*. Athens, Greece: Academic Press.

Kougias, I., & Theodossiou, N. (2012). Application of the harmony search optimization algorithm for the solution of the multiple dam system scheduling. *Optimization and Engineering*.

Kucukali, S. (2010a). Municipal water supply dams as a source of small hydropower in Turkey. *Renewable Energy, 35*, 2001–2007. doi:10.1016/j.renene.2010.01.032.

Kucukali, S. (2010b). Hydropower potential of municipal water supply dams in Turkey: A case study in Ulutan Dam. *Energy Policy, 38*, 6534–6539. doi:10.1016/j.enpol.2010.06.021.

Kucukali, S. (2011). Water supply lines as a source of small hydropower in Turkey: A case study in Edremit. In *Proceedings of World Renewable Energy Congress 2011*. Stockholm: Academic Press.

Report of Shapes FP6 Project. (2010). *Energy recovery in existing infrastructures with small hydropower plants: Multipurpose schemes – Overview and examples*. Retrieved from www.esha.be

Soffia, C., Miotto, F., Poggi, D., & Claps, P. (2010). Hydropower potential from the drinking water systems of the Piemonte region (Italy). In *Proceedings of SEEP 2010 Conference*. SEEP.

World Bank. (2007). *Technical and economic assessment of off-grid, mini-grid and grid electrification technologies*. Washington, DC: World Bank..

ADDITIONAL READING

Byrne, J., Zhou, A., Shen, B., & Hughes, K. (2007). Evaluating the potential of small-scale renewable energy options to meet rural livelihoods needs: A GIS-and lifecycle cost-based assessment of Western China's options. *Energy Policy, 35*(8), 4391–4401. doi:10.1016/j.enpol.2007.02.022.

Castronuovo, E. D., & Lopes, J. A. P. (2004). On the optimization of the daily operation of a wind-hydro power plant. *IEEE Transactions on Power Systems, 19*(3), 1599–1606. doi:10.1109/TPWRS.2004.831707.

Cheng, C. T., Wang, W. C., Xu, D. M., & Chau, K. W. (2008). Optimizing hydropower reservoir operation using hybrid genetic algorithm and chaos. *Water Resources Management, 22*(7), 895–909. doi:10.1007/s11269-007-9200-1.

Doolla, S., & Bhatti, T. S. (2006). Automatic generation control of an isolated small-hydro power plant. *Electric Power Systems Research, 76*(9), 889–896. doi:10.1016/j.epsr.2005.11.002.

Dragu, C., Sels, T., & Belmans, R. (2001). *Small Hydro Power--State of the art and Applications, KU Leuven, ESAT-ELEN*. Leuvan, Belgium: Energy Institute..

Frey, G. W., & Linke, D. M. (2002). Hydropower as a renewable and sustainable energy resource meeting global energy challenges in a reasonable way. *Energy Policy Journal*, *30*, 1261–1265. doi:10.1016/S0301-4215(02)00086-1.

Fritz (1984). *Small and mini hydropower systems: resource assessment and project feasibility.* McGraw-Hill Book Company, New York, NY

Gaius-Obaseki, T. (2010). Hydropower opportunities in the water industry. *International Journal of Environmental Sciences*, *1*(3), 392–402.

Jianxia C., Qiang H., & Yimin W. (2001). Optimal Operation of Hydropower Station Reservoir by Using an Improved Genetic Algorithm. *Journal of hydroelectric engineering*, Vol.3, 85-90.

Kaldellis, J. K. (2008). Critical evaluation of the hydropower applications in Greece. *Renewable & Sustainable Energy Reviews*, *12*(1), 218–234. doi:10.1016/j.rser.2006.05.003.

Kaldellis, J. K., Vlachou, D. S., & Korbakis, G. (2005). Techno-economic evaluation of small hydro power plants in Greece: a complete sensitivity analysis. *Energy Policy*, *33*(5), 1969–1985. doi:10.1016/j.enpol.2004.03.018.

Karlis, A. D., & Papadopoulos, D. P. (2000). A systematic assessment of the technical feasibility and economic viability of small hydroelectric system installations. *Renewable Energy*, *20*(2), 253–262. doi:10.1016/S0960-1481(99)00113-5.

Kenfack, J., Neirac, F. P., Tatietse, T. T., Mayer, D., Fogue, M., & Lejeune, A. (2009). Microhydro-PV-hybrid system: sizing a small hydro-PV-hybrid system for rural electrification in developing countries. *Renewable Energy*, *34*(10), 2259–2263. doi:10.1016/j.renene.2008.12.038.

Kougias, I., Katsifarakis, L., & Theodossiou, N. (2012). *Medley Multiobjective Harmony Search Algorithm. Application on a water resources management problem.* European Water..

Kougias, I., & Theodosiou, N. (2010b). A new music-inspired harmony based optimization algorithm. Theory and applications. *International Conference on Protection and Restoration of the Environment X. Corfu, Greece.*

Kougias, I., & Theodossiou, N. (2010a). A new music-inspired harmony based optimization algorithm. Application in water resources management problems. *International Conference on Protection and Restoration of the Environment X. Corfu, Greece.*

Kougias, I., & Theodossiou, N. (2011). Optimization of multi-reservoir management using harmony search algorithm (hsa). *CEMEPE 2011 // SECOTOX Conference. Skiathos, Greece.*

Meier, T. (2001). *Mini hydropower for rural development: a new market-oriented approach to maximize electrification benefits with special focus on Indonesia* (Vol. 4). Lit Verlag..

Montes, G. M., del Mar Serrano López, M., del Carmen Rubio Gámez, M., & Ondina, A. M. (2005). An overview of renewable energy in Spain. The small hydro-power case. *Renewable & Sustainable Energy Reviews*, *9*(5), 521–534. doi:10.1016/j.rser.2004.05.008.

Ogayar, B., & Vidal, P. G. (2009). Cost determination of the electro-mechanical equipment of a small hydro-power plant. *Renewable Energy*, *34*(1), 6–13. doi:10.1016/j.renene.2008.04.039.

Paish, O. (2002). Small hydro power: technology and current status. *Renewable & Sustainable Energy Reviews*, *6*(6), 537–556. doi:10.1016/S1364-0321(02)00006-0.

Purohit, P. (2008). Small hydro power projects under clean development mechanism in India: A preliminary assessment. *Energy Policy*, *36*(6), 2000–2015. doi:10.1016/j.enpol.2008.02.008.

Richard J. Campbell (2010). Small Hydro and Low-Head Hydro Power Technologies and Prospects. *CRS Report for Congress*, 1-19.

Theodossiou, N., Kougias, I., Kakoudakis, K., & Doikos, K. (2011). Harmony search algorithm, a novel optimization technique. parameter calibration and applications on water resources management problems. *CEMEPE 2011/SECOTOX Conference. Skiathos, Greece.*

Theodossiou, N., & Kougias, K. (2012). *Harmony Search Algorithm. Heuristic Optimization in Hydrology, Hydraulics and Water Resources* (p. 24). W.I.T. Press..

Vieira, F., & Ramos, H. M. (2009). Optimization of operational planning for wind/hydro hybrid water supply systems. *Renewable Energy*, *34*(3), 928–936. doi:10.1016/j.renene.2008.05.031.

KEY TERMS AND DEFINITIONS

Break Pressure Tank: An open container that breaks the hydraulic pressure in a distribution system, typically located between the fluid reservoir and the fluid supply points. A typical break pressure tank allows the flow to discharge into the atmosphere, thereby reducing its hydrostatic pressure to zero.

Harmony Search Algorithm: Harmony Search is a metaheuristic algorithm inspired by the improvisation process of musicians.

Head: This height difference is called the hydraulic head. The amount of potential energy in water is proportional to the head.

Hydroelectricity: The production of electric energy through the gravitational force of falling or flowing water.

Metaheuristics: This term designates a computational method that optimizes a problem by iteratively trying to improve a candidate solution with regard to a given measure of quality. Metaheuristics are a branch of optimization algorithms.

Mini Hydroelectric Plants: Hydropower plants of a smaller scale, having a capacity between 100 – 1000kW. These projects usually don't require the construction of a dam/reservoir and have minimal environmental impact. Additionally they can easily be adapted in existing hydraulic, irrigation or wastewater networks.

Types of Turbines: Selecting the proper Turbine is based mostly on the available water head and less so on the available flow rate, Q. In general, two different types of turbines exist: reaction and impulse turbines. The most common reaction turbines are Kaplan and Francis, while common impulse turbines include Pelton and Crossflow types.

Water Turbine: A large pipe (penstock) delivers water to the turbine. Hydroelectric power comes from the potential energy of water driving a water turbine and generator. The power extracted from the water depends on the volume and on the difference in height between the source and the water's outflow.

Chapter 5
Soft Computing in the Quality of Services Evaluation

María T. Lamata
Universidad de Granada, Spain

Daymi Morales Vega
Instituto Superior Politécnico "José Antonio Echeverría," Cuba

ABSTRACT

The evaluation of the Quality of Services (QoS) has been a topic of particular interest to many authors. In the literature, many works have been developed where different models are proposed to assess the QoS in different environments. These models evaluate the QoS from a set of criteria, which may vary from one environment to another, and thus they do not always have the same importance. Considering this, there have been many studies proposing techniques to evaluate the performance of the quality criteria. Techniques have also been developed to obtain the ranking of a given service provider. The purpose of this chapter is to make a literature review of service quality models, methods for determining the weights of the criteria, and the methods used to conduct an overall assessment of service providers.

INTRODUCTION

The evaluation of the QoS is an issue attracting worldwide debate and interest. An example of this is the creation in 1987 of the ISO 9000 quality standards which specify requirements for a good system of quality management and which have certified more than 50,000 small, medium and international companies in 70 countries. This

shows that the quality control of services is an essential element for the success of service providers, which must ensure that their services are provided in accordance with the standards and also in line with customer expectations.

On the other hand, every day customers are more aware of what they want and become buyers who require their suppliers to meet the highest quality standards, in both their service as well as their products. Therefore, developing models to assess the quality of the services being offered

DOI: 10.4018/978-1-4666-4785-5.ch005

has been of particular interest in the research community.

Moreover, today there are many services (education, hospitality, transportation, banking, government, healthcare, restaurants, insurance companies, etc) and in each of them there are many suppliers, so it would be important to customers to evaluate providers of a given service. One way of doing this could be to determine a ranking of suppliers by assessing the quality of the service provider and thus customers could decide which to choose in the order obtained in the ranking.

Quality of Service is often evaluated from multiple component items, which in turn can have multiple criteria that describe them. This problem can then be structured as a multi-criteria decision problem and often multi-criteria decision methods are used to solve it.

To carry out the evaluation of the alternatives, it will be necessary to deal with linguistic variables. Therefore, in the majority of these problems the solution should be supported by Soft Computing techniques.

We can therefore say that there are two variants associated with the evaluation of the QoS: one is to use a model for evaluating the QoS so that customers can make their assessments of the quality with which providers give a service and the other variant is to obtain rankings of suppliers from the assessment that they receive on the execution of the service they provide.

For the first alternative a model of quality assessment should be chosen to be used to evaluate a service. For the second variant, before obtaining a ranking of suppliers the criteria by which to evaluate; the importance or weight of each criterion; and determine the method of multi-criteria decision to apply should be determined. In each of these variants a large number of papers have been published in different areas.

The main purpose of this chapter is to conduct a literature review of the main items that make proposals under these variants and which take Soft Computing techniques into account. Section

2 will be a summary of the service quality models, furthering the SERVQUAL to be a reference model in the literature. The structure of a decision problem is described in section 3 and there will also be a summary of the work developed for determining the weight of the criteria. Section 4 will offer a summary of multi-criteria decision methods applied to the evaluation of the quality of service, as well as the different environments in which they have been applied. Finally, conclusions are made about the study.

MODELS OF SERVICES QUALITY

The first step before assessing the QoS is to determine under what criteria it will be measured and how to perform the assessment of these criteria. In this sense, many conceptual models have been developed to measure the QoS, which are useful because they allow managers to identify quality problems and improve them to obtain adequate planning, achieve efficiency, effectiveness, profitability and good execution.

Seth & Deshmukh, 2005 conducted a literature review which reflected 19 different models. These models were compared taking into account different aspects. Due to the rise of information technology, there has been an evolution of conventional models to those that include information technology to assess the QoS (Berkley & Gupta, 1994; Broderick & Vachirapornpuk, 2002; Parasuraman, Zeithaml, & Malhotra, 2005; Santos, 2003; Zhu, Wymer, & Chen, 2002). It was also observed that the criteria depend directly on the type of service, the situation in which it develops, the time duration, the needs and other factors.

In the classical literature to collect customers' assessments, it is usual to apply surveys or personal interviews. In these surveys it is normal for the users to answer the different questions in linguistic terms. The most used values are: "strongly disagree", "disagree", "neither agree nor disagree", "agree", "strongly agree". These assessments, to be processed subsequently, could be made using different scales like five value or seven value Likert scales, as well as particular scales.

The study conducted by Seth & Deshumkh in 2005 identified the most widespread and most used models, which are known as "service quality gap" and are defined from the difference between expectations and the perception of customers regarding the QoS. If clients' expectations are greater than the service that the client perceives, then the perception of quality is less than the satisfaction and therefore the client is not satisfied. In this type of model, most work in literature has been developed by Parasuraman (Parasuraman, Zeithaml, & Berry, 1985) who present a general model for assessing the QoS.

SERVQUAL Model

In 1985, the first work of Parasuraman was published in which a proposal was made of a conceptual model for the QoS (Parasuraman, et al., 1985). This model was then formalized under the name of SERVQUAL (Parasuraman, Zeithaml, &

Berry, 1988). SERVQUAL has been implemented in many environments; it was created with the aim of providing a generic instrument to measure the quality of services in such a way that it could be applied to different types of services. This method is based on identifying the differences between five fundamental elements in the development of a service (Figure 1). These differences can be summarized in the following:

1. Difference between customer expectations and what the executives believe that they expect. That is to say, the executives have no knowledge of what the customers expect.
2. Difference between what executives believe that customers expect and the quality standards set for the service. That is to say, the specifications of the service do not correspond with what the executives believe that customers expect, which means that the established quality standards are inadequate.
3. Difference between service quality specifications and the service provided, this

Figure 1. Elements of the services quality according to Parasuraman

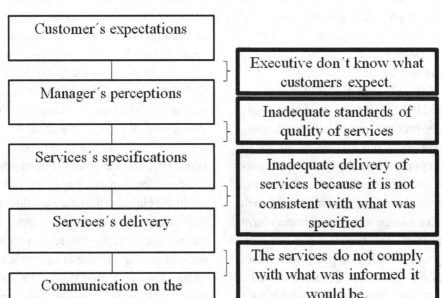

means that there are differences in service performance.

4. Difference between service delivery and what was reported to customers that service would be, this means that promises were not fulfilled with respect to what the service was reported to be before being provided.

5. Difference between the expectations of customers and the perceived service. This difference is the summary of the remaining four, so it depends on the magnitudes that they have.

According to this theory, for determining the quality of a service it is possible to use the following model:

$$SQ = \sum_{j=1}^{k} \left(P_{ij} - E_{ij} \right) (1)$$

where:

- SQ represents the total performance of the service according to the k attributes that describe it.
- P_{ij} represents the perception of customer i with respect to attribute j.
- E_{ij} represents the expectation of customer i with respect to attribute j.

Initially, 10 criteria were proposed for evaluating the above differences (tangibles, reliability, responsiveness, communication, credibility, security, competence, understanding/knowing customers, courtesy, and access), each of which could be described from a subset of criteria or attributes. Later, in (Parasuraman, et al., 1988) the ten criteria were reduced to the following five:

- **Tangibles:** The physical facilities that will be provided, the equipment, and staff.
- **Reliability:** The ability to perform the promised service safely and accurately.
- **Responsiveness:** The willingness to help customers and always provide prompt service.
- **Empathy:** Be aware of the needs of customers and have an individual care of customers
- **Assurance:** The knowledge and courtesy of employees and their ability to inspire trust and confidence.

Thus, the assessment of quality of service according to this model can be determined from the differences found between the perceived service and the expected service by each of the above criteria (Figure 2).

As has already been stated, to collect the information needed for evaluating the above differ-

Figure 2. SERVQUAL Model based on the perceived service and the expected service

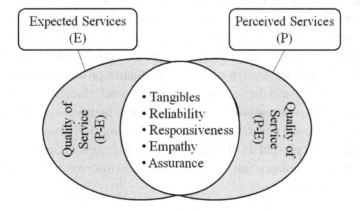

ences, Parasuraman et al proposed the use of surveys.

Depending on the amount of attributes and criteria that are most commonly employed, it can also be used to identify different trends, which can vary from a minimum of two criteria up to a maximum of ten (Ladhari, 2008). This varies directly according to the context and even the country where the service is developed, but in spite of this diversity, it can identify that the criteria proposed in SERVQUAL are applied in the majority of the models (especially the tangible criteria and empathy) although variations can be made by adding or deleting any particular criterion.

Despite the generality provided by the SERVQUAL model there is some disagreement. For example in (Ladhari, 2008), it is argued that the concept of subtraction present in the SERVQUAL model has no theoretical basis from the psychological point of view. The argument also exists that evaluating in terms of expectations can be very versatile with regard to the interpretation that may be made of it, which can lead to a problem in assessing the service.

Structure of the Decision Problem: Criteria and Weights

Generally speaking, a decision problem is a situation where an individual has alternative courses of possible actions, and has to select one of them without previous knowledge of which one is the best (Pavan & Todeschini, 2008). In addition, the current complex organizations do not try to maximize or minimize a determined utility function, but instead different objectives come into question at the same time, the majority of which are incompatible with each other. Finally, what they seek is to obtain a determined level in each objective. Therefore, the objective of the decision process is to generate effective solutions from the available data and supply a good understanding of the structure of the decision problem. These decision problems involve six components:

- The objective or objectives, that the decision maker or the institution wishes to fit
- A set of criteria
- The set of decision alternatives
- The set of weights associated with the criteria
- The set of outcomes or consequences associated with each pair alternative /criteria
- The decision-maker or group of decision-makers involved in the decision-making process with their preferences

One important question in this case is which alternative to choose when multiple alternatives from multiple criteria are being evaluated. To solve this question, Multi-Criteria Decision Methods (MCDM) were created. Applying multi-criteria analysis, a global value can be obtained for each alternative. This value is composed of the values (V_{ij}) of the alternatives (A_i) with respect to each criterion (C_j) and of the weights (W_j) of the criteria (Figure 3). The alternatives are finally ranked according to global values. In general, the alternative with the highest value should be selected as the best one. But, this of course, depends of the type of problem that is being dealt with. If the alternatives are related to cost issues, then the best alternatives will be ones with smaller values.

Given this, an important issue in evaluating the QoS is to determine the importance of the criteria that influence customer perception, which may or may not be the same. If they do not have the same importance the weights associated with each of the criteria must be found. To do so, there are several methods that perform certain tests to finally obtain a vector with the weights of the criteria involved in the assessment. The establishment of the criteria weight is a key part in the evaluation process since the outcome of the ranking depends directly on this.

In the literature several studies have been found addressing this issue. They can be divided into several groups according to the technique they use: heuristics methods, AHP method, DEMATEL

Figure 3. Component of MCDM

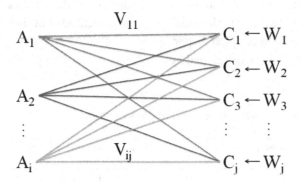

method (Decision Making Trial and Evaluation Laboratory), GRA method (Grey Relational Analysis), OWAs operators (Ordered Weighted Average) etc,…and those which directly assign weights determined by the executive to the criteria.

w refers to some articles where the mentioned methods are applied:

There are studies in the literature that combine these methods, as in the case of (Tseng, 2009) which combines the DEMATEL method with GRA. From the literature, one can observe that the AHP method has been widely used. But in recent years there has been a tendency to use heuristics and OWA operators.

Applying Multicriteria Decision Techniques for Evaluating Quality of Services

There are many jobs where multi-criteria analysis techniques have been combined to evaluate the performance of services in terms of quality. These evaluations, as seen above, are often made from applying customer surveys where linguistic labels can be used to express their evaluations as well as using numeric expressions for the assessments. In the case of using linguistic labels, these are usually represented by triangular fuzzy numbers.

Equally numerous are the environments in which multiple criteria decision methods have been applied to assess the QoS and obtain the ranking of services. Table 2 shows some of these environments and the methods used for the papers where

Table 1. Articles related with weight determination methods

Method	Articles
HEURISTICS	(Bana e Costa & Oliveira, 2012; Bellabas, Lahoud, & Molnár, 2012; Guérin & Orda, 1999; Y.-C. Hu & Liao, 2011; Y. C. Hu, 2009; Van Mieghem & Kuipers, 2004; Wu, Shih, Wang, Liu, & Wang, 2012)
AHP	(Alkahtani, Woodward, & Al-Begain, 2006; Bilsel, Buyukozkan, & Ruan, 2006; Gülin Büyüközkan & Çifçi, 2012; C. W. Chang, Wu, & Lin, 2008, 2009; Tsai, Chou, & Leu, 2011; Tsai, Hsu, & Chou, 2011; Tsaur, Chang, & Yen, 2002)
DEMATEL	(Tsai, Chou, et al., 2011; Tseng, 2011; R. Wang, Shu, Hsu, Lin, & Tseng, 2011)
GRA	(M.-S. Kuo & Liang, 2011; M.-S. Kuo, Wu, & Pei, 2007; M. S. Kuo, 2011)
OWA	(Lamata, & Cables, 2012; Cabrerizo, Martínez, López–Gijón, Esteban, & Herrera–Viedma, 2011; C.-H. Cheng & Chang, 2006; C. H. Cheng, Chang, Ho, & Chen, 2005; Cables, & Lamata, 2009; Okur, Nasibov, Kiliç, & Yavuz, 2009.

the representation of the information is made using linguistic labels (represented by fuzzy numbers)

In Table 2, the methods called "Other Methods" refer to methods that have been adapted to particular environments and have been developed by the same authors. This means that to obtain the ranking of the alternatives they do not use classical methods but their own methods.

Table 2. Multicriteria decision methods applied to QoS evaluation

Multicriteria Decision Methods	Environments	Type of Information Used	Articles
TOPSIS	Airlines	Using matrix values with triangular fuzzy numbers and applying a modification of TOPSIS for working with fuzzy numbers.	(Nejati & Shafaei, 2009)
		Using linguistic labels to evaluate, these linguistic labels are represented by triangular fuzzy numbers. Apply defuzzification and after that the classical TOPSIS method.	(Tsaur, et al., 2002)
	Health care assistance	They start from the valuation matrix with triangular fuzzy numbers and apply a fuzzy variant of TOPSIS.	(Gülin Büyüközkan & Çifçi, 2012)
	Hotels	Describe the weights of the criteria with linguistic labels represented as triangular fuzzy numbers.	(Tseng, 2011)
		They use linguistic labels represented by triangular fuzzy numbers for the weights of the criteria and for the valuation matrix. They later apply a fuzzy variant of TOPSIS to obtain the final ranking.	(Benitez, Martin, & Roman, 2007)
	Web sites	They use linguistic evaluations with respect to each criterion and to obtain weights of criteria. A modified AHP (fuzzy AHP) method is used for obtaining weights and a modified TOPSIS method for the final ranking	(Kaya, 2010)
	Universities	Linguistic labels are used for the valuation matrix and to represent the weight of the criteria. A variant fuzzy TOPSIS is used.	(Socorro García-Cásales & Lamata Jiménez, 2010)
PROMETHEE	Hospitals web sites	Linguistic labels represented by triangular fuzzy numbers are used to perform valuations of the criteria. Then a fuzzy variant Promethee is applied.	(Bilsel, et al., 2006)
VIKOR	Aeronautics (Airlines, Airports, Airlines web sites)	Using linguistic labels represented as triangular fuzzy numbers to pick up the weight of the criteria and their ratings.	(M.-S. Kuo & Liang, 2011)
AHP	Catering service	Apply a variant of the fuzzy AHP method using linguistic labels associated with triangular fuzzy numbers for successive comparisons.	(Kahraman, Cebeci, & Ruan, 2004)
Other Methods	Airports	The assessments of the criteria are performed using linguistic labels represented by fuzzy triangular numbers. For the final ranking, two factors are taken into account: interval "α-cut" and "γ" defining it as the degree of optimality and reflecting how optimistic the customer ratings are.	(Yeh & Kuo, 2003)
	Web Sites	Perform assessments of the criteria using linguistic labels represented by fuzzy triangular numbers. Perform an operation similar to that proposed (Yeh & Kuo, 2003) to obtain the final ranking.	(P. Wang, Chao, Lo, Huang, & Li, 2006)
		The assessments are made using fuzzy numbers and then they aggregate this information to obtain a final ranking. AHP for obtain weight is used.	(Gülçin Büyüközkan, Arsenyan, & Ertek, 2010)
	Airlines	Fuzzy representation of the valuation matrix, as well as for weight criteria representation.	(Y.-H. Chang & Yeh, 2002)
	General	Fuzzy numbers are used to evaluate the criteria and to determine their weights. A linguistic output is obtained.	(Chen, 2001)

Combining MCDM Methods

As is known, to obtain a ranking of alternatives several multi-criteria methods (such as: TOPSIS, VIKOR, PROMETHEE, and so on) can be applied, which do not always obtain the same result, ie alternatives (providers in the case of QoS evaluation) do not always have the same order. By applying various methods and obtaining various rankings, it could happen that an alternative has one position in one method and another different position in another method. Thus, an alternative A could be "better" than an alternative B according to one method, yet applying another method the opposite may occur.

The question would then be how to achieve a consensus among the rankings obtained by various methods so as to obtain an overall assessment for an alternative considering the evaluations obtained by various methods and to determine the best alternative. One idea to solve this would be to perform a similar analysis to the method of "Pareto Optimality" which compares the rank obtained by each alternative in each method applied. It can be said that an alternative A "dominates" an alternative B if it holds that:

- $f_{Ai} \geq f_{Bi}$ for all methods $(1<i<n)$ with at least one inequality.

   where

- f_{Ai} is the evaluation of alternative A in method i
- f_{Bi} is the evaluation of alternative B in method i
- n is the number of methods used.

Those alternatives which are not "dominated" by any other will be called "Pareto optimal points", and collectively constitute the so-called "Pareto front". The set of alternatives in the Pareto front will then represent all the better alternatives (Figure 4)

Figure 4. Pareto front representation

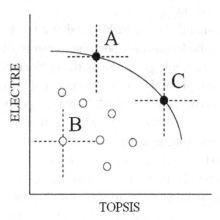

In this figure, points represent alternatives evaluated by two methods (as an example we use the methods ELECTRE and TOPSIS). The location on the graph is given by the values obtained in the evaluation according to each method.

In this case all the alternatives represented by the white points were "dominated" by some other point because worse evaluations were obtained in all methods over any alternative. Conversely, points A and C have been dominated in some cases but not in others, so we can say that they are unmatched among themselves (alternative A is better than alternative C in the assessment by ELECTRE method, but alternative C has a better evaluation than A in the TOPSIS method) therefore these points have not been completely dominated and then make the Pareto front.

With this it is possible to have a method that will allow us not only to obtain a ranking of alternatives, but will also allow us to know what the set of better alternatives is.

CONCLUSION

After analyzing the available information on the subject of service quality and its evaluation with multi-criteria techniques, a number of conclusions can be reached. Clearly, the most widespread model is the SERVQUAL, but nevertheless it is necessary to make adjustments for each particular environment.

It should also be highlighted that the service quality models are incorporating elements of information technology as criteria to consider for QoS; one example of this is the evaluation of web sites where criteria like "security" are incorporated. It is also noteworthy that there has been an increase in conducting assessments of the criteria using linguistic variables and fuzzy theory.

Similarly there are several studies that use linguistic information to represent the weights of the criteria. Regarding the methods for obtaining the weights of the criteria, this highlights the use of AHP; although in recent years there have been several studies which have used heuristics and OWA operators.

Finally, it can be seen that there are different environments where work has been carried out to assess the QoS (aeronautics (airports, airlines), hotels, banks, medical, web sites). In these environments, TOPSIS is the most commonly-used multi-criteria decision method with linguistic information but it should also be highlighted that there is a broad representation of methods developed for a customized environment with their own implementations of multi-criteria decision.

This paper also presents a model to obtain a consensus of ranking using Pareto analysis. It also proposes a solution for achieving a consensus among the rankings obtained by various methods of multi-criteria decision making. Normally these methods of multi-criteria decision making give good results, although it is important to note that the result of a ranking method only indicates which alternatives are the best, and which are the worst, but does not specify whether the results of the evaluation are good or bad.

ACKNOWLEDGMENT

This work is partially supported by FEDER funds, the DGICYT and Junta de Andalucía under projects (TIN2008-06872-C04-04, TIN2011-27696-C02-01) and (P07-TIC02970, P11-TIC-8001), respectively.

REFERENCES

Alkahtani, A. M. S., Woodward, M. E., & Al-Begain, K. (2006). Prioritised best effort routing with four quality of service metrics applying the concept of the analytic hierarchy process. *Computers & Operations Research*, *33*(3), 559–580. doi:10.1016/j.cor.2004.07.008.

Bana e Costa, C. A., & Oliveira, M. D. (2012). A multicriteria decision analysis model for faculty evaluation. *Omega*, *40*, 424–436. doi:10.1016/j.omega.2011.08.006.

Bellabas, A., Lahoud, S., & Molnár, M. (2012). Performance evaluation of efficient solutions for the QoS unicast routing. *Journal of Networks*, *7*(1), 73–80. doi:10.4304/jnw.7.1.73-80.

Benitez, J. M., Martin, J. C., & Roman, C. (2007). Using fuzzy number for measuring quality of service in the hotel industry. *Tourism Management*, *28*(2), 544–555. doi:10.1016/j.tourman.2006.04.018.

Berkley, B. J., & Gupta, A. (1994). Improving service quality with information technology. *International Journal of Information Management*, *14*(1), 109–121. doi:10.1016/0268-4012(94)90030-2.

Bilsel, R. U., Buyukozkan, G., & Ruan, D. (2006). A fuzzy preference-ranking model for a quality evaluation of hospital web sites. *International Journal of Intelligent Systems, 21*(11), 1181–1197. doi:10.1002/int.20177.

Broderick, A. J., & Vachirapornpuk, S. (2002). Service quality in internet banking: The importance of customer role. *Marketing Intelligence & Planning, 20*(6), 327–335. doi:10.1108/02634500210445383.

Büyüközkan, G., Arsenyan, J., & Ertek, G. (2010). Evaluation of e-learning web sites using fuzzy axiomatic design based approach. *International Journal of Computational Intelligence Systems, 3*(1), 28–42.

Büyüközkan, G., & Çifçi, G. (2012). A combined fuzzy AHP and fuzzy TOPSIS based strategic analysis of electronic service quality in healthcare industry. *Expert Systems with Applications, 39*(3), 2341–2354. doi:10.1016/j.eswa.2011.08.061.

Cables, E. H., & Lamata, M. T. (2009). OWA weights determination by means of linear functions. *Mathware & Soft Computing, 16*(2), 107–122.

Cabrerizo, F. J., Martínez, M. A., López–Gijón, J., Esteban, B., & Herrera–Viedma, E. (2011). A new quality evaluation model generating recommendations to improve the digital services provided by the academic digital libraries. In *Proceedings of International Fuzzy Systems Association World Congress & Asian Fuzzy Systems Society* (IFSA 2011). IFSA.

Chang, C. W., Wu, C. R., & Lin, H. L. (2008). Integrating fuzzy theory and hierarchy concepts to evaluate software quality. *Software Quality Journal, 16*(2), 263–276. doi:10.1007/s11219-007-9035-2.

Chang, C. W., Wu, C. R., & Lin, H. L. (2009). Applying fuzzy hierarchy multiple attributes to construct an expert decision making process. *Expert Systems with Applications, 36*(4), 7363–7368. doi:10.1016/j.eswa.2008.09.026.

Chang, Y.-H., & Yeh, C.-H. (2002). A survey analysis of service quality for domestic airlines. *European Journal of Operational Research, 139*(1), 166–177. doi:10.1016/S0377-2217(01)00148-5.

Chen, C. T. (2001). Applying linguistic decision-making method to deal with service quality evaluation problems. *International Journal of Uncertainty Fuzziness and Knowledge-Based Systems, 9*, 103–114. doi:10.1142/S0218488501001022.

Cheng, C.-H., & Chang, J.-R. (2006). MCDM aggregation model using situational ME-OWA and ME-OWGA operators. *International Journal of Uncertainty Fuzziness and Knowledge-Based Systems, 14*(4), 421–443. doi:10.1142/S0218488506004102.

Cheng, C. H., Chang, J. R., Ho, T. H., & Chen, A. P. (2005). Evaluating the airline service quality by fuzzy OWA operators. In V. N. Y. M. S. Torra (Ed.), *Modeling Decisions for Artificial Intelligence* (Vol. 3558, pp. 77–88). Berlin: Springer. doi:10.1007/11526018_9.

García-Cáscales, M. S., & Lamata, M. T. (2010). ¿Cómo clasificar titulaciones de ingeniería por su calidad?. *Dyna, 85*(8).

Guérin, R. A., & Orda, A. (1999). QoS routing in networks with inaccurate information: Theory and algorithms. *IEEE/ACM Transactions on Networking, 7*(3), 350–364. doi:10.1109/90.779203.

Hu, Y. C. (2009). Fuzzy multiple-criteria decision making in the determination of critical criteria for assessing service quality of travel websites. *Expert Systems with Applications, 36*(3), 6439–6445. doi:10.1016/j.eswa.2008.07.046.

Hu, Y.-C., & Liao, P.-C. (2011). Finding critical criteria of evaluating electronic service quality of internet banking using fuzzy multiple-criteria decision making. *Applied Soft Computing*, *11*(4), 3764–3770. doi:10.1016/j.asoc.2011.02.008.

Kahraman, C., Cebeci, U., & Ruan, D. (2004). Multi-attribute comparison of catering service companies using fuzzy AHP: The case of Turkey. *International Journal of Production Economics*, *87*(2), 171–184. doi:10.1016/S0925-5273(03)00099-9.

Kaya, T. (2010). Multi-attribute evaluation of website quality in e-business using an integrated fuzzy AHP TOPSIS methodology. *International Journal of Computational Intelligence Systems*, *3*(3), 301–314.

Kuo, M. S. (2011). A novel interval-valued fuzzy MCDM method for improving airlines' service quality in Chinese cross-strait airlines. *Transportation Research Part E, Logistics and Transportation Review*, *47*(6), 1177–1193. doi:10.1016/j.tre.2011.05.007.

Kuo, M.-S., & Liang, G.-S. (2011). Combining VIKOR with GRA techniques to evaluate service quality of airports under fuzzy environment. *Expert Systems with Applications*, *38*(3), 1304–1312. doi:10.1016/j.eswa.2010.07.003.

Kuo, M.-S., Wu, J.-W., & Pei, L. (2007). A soft computing method for selecting evaluation criteria of service quality. *Applied Mathematics and Computation*, *189*(1), 241–254. doi:10.1016/j.amc.2006.11.084.

Ladhari, R. (2008). Alternative measures of service quality: A review. *Managing Service Quality*, *18*(1), 65–86. doi:10.1108/09604520810842849.

Lamata, M. T., & Cables, E. (2012). Obtaining OWA operators starting from a linear order and preference quantifiers. *International Journal of Intelligent Systems*, *27*, 242–258. doi:10.1002/int.21520.

Nejati, M., & Shafaei, A. (2009). Ranking airlines' service quality factors using a fuzzy approach: Study of the Iranian society. *International Journal of Quality & Reliability Management*, *26*(3), 247–260. doi:10.1108/02656710910936726.

Okur, A., Nasibov, E. N., Kiliç, M., & Yavuz, M. (2009). Using OWA aggregation technique in QFD: A case study in education in a textile engineering department. *Quality & Quantity*, *43*(6), 999–1009. doi:10.1007/s11135-008-9170-2.

Parasuraman, A., Zeithaml, V. A., & Berry, L. L. (1985). A conceptual models of service quality and its implications for future research. *Journal of Marketing*, *29*(4), 41–50. doi:10.2307/1251430.

Parasuraman, A., Zeithaml, V. A., & Berry, L. L. (1988). SERVQUAL: A multiple-item scale for measuring consumers perceptions of service quality. *Journal of Retailing*, *64*(1), 12–40.

Parasuraman, A., Zeithaml, V. A., & Malhotra, A. (2005). E-S-QUAL: A multiple-item scale for assessing electronic service quality. *Journal of Service Research*, *7*(3), 213–233. doi:10.1177/1094670504271156.

Pavan, M., & Todeschini, R. (2008). Total-order ranking methods. *Data Handling in Science and Technology*, *27*, 51–70. doi:10.1016/S0922-3487(08)10002-8.

Santos, J. (2003). E-service quality: A model of virtual service quality dimensions. *Managing Service Quality*, *13*(3), 233–246. doi:10.1108/09604520310476490.

Seth, N., & Deshmukh, S. G. (2005). Service quality models: A review. *International Journal of Quality & Reliability Management*, *22*(9), 913–949. doi:10.1108/02656710510625211.

Tsai, W.-H., Chou, W.-C., & Leu, J.-D. (2011). An effectiveness evaluation model for the web-based marketing of the airline industry. *Expert Systems with Applications*, *38*(12), 15499–15516.

Tsai, W.-H., Hsu, W., & Chou, W.-C. (2011). A gap analysis model for improving airport service quality. *Total Quality Management & Business Excellence, 22*(10), 1025–1040. doi:10.1080/14783363.2011.611326.

Tsaur, S. H., Chang, T. Y., & Yen, C. H. (2002). The evaluation of airline service quality by fuzzy MCDM. *Tourism Management, 23*(2), 107–115. doi:10.1016/S0261-5177(01)00050-4.

Tseng, M.-L. (2009). A causal and effect decision making model of service quality expectation using grey-fuzzy DEMATEL approach. *Expert Systems with Applications, 36*(4), 7738–7748. doi:10.1016/j.eswa.2008.09.011.

Tseng, M.-L. (2011). Using hybrid MCDM to evaluate the service quality expectation in linguistic preference. *Applied Soft Computing, 11*(8), 4551–4562. doi:10.1016/j.asoc.2011.08.011.

Van Mieghem, P., & Kuipers, F. A. (2004). Concepts of exact QoS routing algorithms. *IEEE/ACM Transactions on Networking, 12*(5), 851–864. doi:10.1109/TNET.2004.836112.

Wang, P., Chao, K. M., Lo, C. C., Huang, C. L., & Li, Y. (2006). A fuzzy model for selection of QoS-aware web services. In *Proceedings - IEEE International Conference on e-Business Engineering,* (pp. 585-592). IEEE.

Wang, R., Shu, L., Hsu, Lin, Y. H., & Tseng, M.-L. (2011). Evaluation of customer perceptions on airline service quality in uncertainty. *Procedia - Social and Behavioral Sciences, 25*, 419-437.

Wu, J. J., Shih, S. F., Wang, H., Liu, P., & Wang, C. M. (2012). QoS-aware replica placement for grid computing. *Concurrency and Computation, 24*(3), 193–213. doi:10.1002/cpe.1817.

Yeh, C.-H., & Kuo, Y.-L. (2003). Evaluating passenger services of Asia-Pacific international airports. *Transportation Research Part E, Logistics and Transportation Review, 39*(1), 35–48. doi:10.1016/S1366-5545(02)00017-0.

Zhu, F. X., Wymer, W. J., & Chen, I. (2002). IT-based services and service quality in consumer banking. *International Journal of Service Industry Management, 13*(1), 69–90. doi:10.1108/09564230210421164.

Chapter 6
Fuzzy Rules for Risk Assessment and Contingency Estimation within COCOMO Software Project Planning Model

Ekananta Manalif
University of Western Ontario, Canada

Luiz Fernando Capretz
University of Western Ontario, Canada

Danny Ho
NFA Estimation Inc., Canada

ABSTRACT

Software development can be considered to be a most uncertain project when compared to other projects due to uncertainty in the customer requirements, the complexity of the process, and the intangible nature of the product. In order to increase the chance of success in managing a software project, the project manager(s) must invest more time and effort in the project planning phase, which involves such primary and integrated activities as effort estimation and risk management, because the accuracy of the effort estimation is highly dependent on the size and number of project risks in a particular software project. However, as is common practice, these two activities are often disconnected from each other and project managers have come to consider such steps to be unreliable due to their lack of accuracy. This chapter introduces the Fuzzy-ExCOM Model, which is used for software project planning and is based on fuzzy technique. It has the capability to not only integrate the effort estimation and risk assessment activities but also to provide information about the estimated effort, the project risks, and the effort contingency allowance necessary to accommodate the identified risk. A validation of this model using the project's research data shows that this new approach is capable of improving the existing COCOMO estimation performance.

DOI: 10.4018/978-1-4666-4785-5.ch006

INTRODUCTION

Software development can be considered to be a most uncertain and complex project when compared to other types of projects, because it involves the creation of an intangible product, which is continually changing in response to customers' requirements and the development of new technology. The 2009 Standish Group Chaos report (The Standish Group, 2009) indicated that only 32% of such projects had succeeded. That is, they were delivered on time, were within budget, and had the required features and functions. 44% of the projects did not meet these three requirements, and 24% failed, i.e., they were cancelled prior to completion or were delivered and never used. The results of a study conducted by TATA Consultancy Services in 2007 of 800 senior IT managers from the UK, the US, France, Germany, India, Japan, and Singapore were similar to those of the Standish Group report. In that study, 62% of the projects failed to meet their schedule, 49% experienced budget overruns, 47% experienced higher-than expected maintenance costs, and 41% failed to deliver the expected Return on Investment (ROI) (Marchewka, 2009).

Based on the results of several investigations of software development projects, the main areas responsible for project failure were: project goal setting, project scheduling, project staffing (availability and capabilities), customer requirements, unmanaged risks, improper project execution, stakeholder politics, and commercial pressures (Humprey, 2002; Charette, 2005). Hence, the success of a software project could be described as being highly dependent on the Project Planning Phase, which involves those activities that determine a project's scope, scheduling, cost, resources, and risks. Therefore, while this phase is critical for all types of project management (Heldman and Heldman, 2010), it is especially so for a software development project.

The main activities in the software project planning phase are effort estimation and risk

management which become the major issues in the success of software development project. and the accuracy of the results will provide the great support in project execution phase (Pressman, 2005; Huang, et al, 2004). Software effort estimation calculates the effort necessary to complete the project, in term of scheduling, acquiring resources, and meeting cost objectives. Risk management includes identifying, addressing, and eliminating software project risks before undesirable outcomes occur. Software effort estimation is an essential activity in the planning phase due to its role in guiding project managers with respect to budgeting, scheduling, and the allocation of resources. Risk management also plays a vital role here, considering the fact that a software project will be used in an environment where the results are intangible and subject to a higher level of uncertainty than is typical of other types of projects. In the project planning phase, risk management activities focus mostly on risk assessment, which is a discovery process of identifying the potential risks, analyzing or evaluating their risk effects, and prioritizing the risks.

On the one hand, cost is the most important factor in managing software projects. On the other hand, project risk affect the accuracy of software effort estimation and consequently affected cost, delivery, and the quality of products (Du, et al, 2010). Hence, effort estimation and risk management must be executed as integral parts of the project planning phase. However, in most software development projects, the effort estimation and risk management steps are executed separately. Therefore, the true impact of an identified risk on the accuracy of effort estimation is difficult to identify.

This chapter proposes the use of a Fuzzy-ExCOM (Fuzzy Expert-COCOMO) Model; the COCOMO Software Project Planning based on a fuzzy technique that is capable of integrating effort estimation and risk assessment in the project planning phase and improves the effort estimation result by providing an effort contingency allowance that can be used to compensate for the identified project risks. The information generated from this model can then be used as a decision support system for an individual project manager in conducting a more detailed risk assessment and developing more effective risk mitigation approaches.

BACKGROUND

Software Project Management is the art and science of planning and directing software projects (Stellman and Greene, 2006). It is the software engineering study area that governs the implementation of Project Management principles for a planned, monitored, and controlled software project. Software Project Management involves: system configuration, resource management, and risk management as well as the development and implementation of a software development plan, and a software development strategy. In line with the increasing importance of a software system for a modern organization to service its customer's needs, Software Project Management becomes even more important in managing the development of a large software product consisting of millions of lines of code (LOC).

Based on the project management definition, project failure can be understood as being the failure to meet the project goals, which relate to a project's scope, time constraints (schedule), and budget. As the most risky type of project, a software project can be considered to be the most difficult to manage and subsequently achieve project goals. Several investigations of software development projects indicated that most of the activities responsible for project failure took place during the project planning phase. Hence, in order to ensure that a software development project meets the established requirements of scope, time and budget, a project manager must invest more effort in the project planning phase, which involves

such primary elements as effort estimation and risk management (Pressman, 2005).

Software Project Effort Estimation

Software effort estimation determines the amount of effort necessary to complete a software project, this is an essential activity in the software project planning phase because major problems usually surface in the first three months of a software development project and are related to the hasty scheduling, irrational commitments, and unprofessional estimating techniques (Marchewka, 2009).

In the early stages of a software development life cycle, effort estimation plays a critical role in helping project managers identify the demands of resources in executing the project. The most significant effort estimation models that have been used in software development projects are: SLIM (Software Life Cycle Management) model (Putnam, 1992), SEER-SEM (System Evaluation and Estimation of Resource Software Evaluation Model) (Galorath and Evans, 2006), and the COCOMO (Constructive Cost Model) (Boehm, 1981).

SLIM is an empirical software effort estimation model developed by Lawrence Putnam in the 1970s. This model was developed based on a collection of software project data (size and effort); it calculates the associated effort using an equation that fits the original data. SEER-SEM, which was developed by Galorath and Evans in 1990, is a powerful and sophisticated model that includes a variety tools for several kinds of estimation activities in software development projects as well as effort estimation. SEER-SEM accommodates several knowledge bases (KBs) as inputs to set baselines for over 50 parameters that will impact the estimation output.

COCOMO, which was developed by Barry Boehm in the 1980s, is the most popular and most widely used estimation model for software projects. The COCOMO model is based on scale factors, cost factors, and software size for estimating the cost, effort requirements, and scheduling of a software development project. The Post Architecture Model is the most detailed version of the COCOMO II models and is expressed in the Formula (1).

$$Effort = A \times (Size)^{B+C} \times \prod_{i=1}^{17} EM_i \quad (1)$$
$$C = 0.01 \times \sum_{i=1}^{5} SFi$$

Where, *Effort* is the estimated software development effort in staff-months; *A* and *B* are the baseline calibration constants; *Size* is the size of the software project measured in terms of KSLOC (thousands of Source Lines of Code). The five Scale Factors are identified as SF_i, and the seventeen Effort Multipliers are identified as EM_i. The five scale factors and the seventeen effort multipliers are called by cost drivers of the COCOMO-II Post Architecture model. Table 1 shows the list of COCOMO-II Scale Factors, and the list of Effort Multipliers are shown in Table 2.

The twenty-two cost drivers are measured qualitatively by selecting a rating from the following well-defined rating levels, i.e. Very Low (VL), Low (L), Nominal (N), High (H), Very High (VH) and Extra High (XH). Each cost driver has four to six rating levels and each rating level of every cost driver is associated with a number that is identified with a parameter value, which is used in the COCOMO formula. Table 3 shows parameter values for COCOMO cost drivers (scale factors and effort multipliers).

Software Project Risk Management

Risk always brings uncertainty and is inherent in every project that has the potential for substantial loss. Two intrinsic properties of risk are uncertainty and loss (Iranmanesh, et al., 2009). Uncertainty relates to something with which we are not totally familiar and loss can be understood as an unfavourable outcome or lost opportunity. In project management, risk can be understood as a possible event that would have a negative impact on the outcome of a project if it were to occur. Risk management, which is based on the creation and implementation of an effective plan to either prevent losses or reduce their impact if they should occur, provides a clear and structured approach to identifying and managing such risks. Effective risk management practice, however, does not eliminate risks. It merely provides management with a clear understanding of all the potential risks, which ultimately allows the project managers to measure and prioritize risks and to make well

Table 1. COCOMO-II scale factors (Boehm, et al., 2000)

Scale Factor	Symbol	Explanation
PREC	SF1	**Precedentedness**. Reflects the previous experience of the organization with this type of project. Very Low means no previous experience; Extra high means that the organization is completely familiar with this application domain.
FLEX	SF2	**Development Flexibility**. Reflects the degree of the flexibility in the development process. Very low means a prescribed process is used; Extra high means that the client sets only general goals
RESL	SF3	**Architecture/Risk Resolution**. Reflects the extent of risk analysis carried out. Very low means little analysis; Extra high means a complete ad thorough risk analysis.
TEAM	SF4	**Team Cohesion**. Reflects how well the development team members know each other and work together. Very low means very difficult interactions; Extra high means an integrated and effective team with no communication problems.
PMAT	SF5	**Process Maturity**. Reflects the process maturity of the organization. The computation of this value depends on the CMM Maturity Questionnaire, but an estimate can be achieved by subtracting the CMM process maturity level from 5.

Table 2. COCOMO-II effort multipliers (Boehm, et al.,2000)

Effort Multipliers	Symbol	Explanation
		Product Factors
RELY	EM1	Required Software reliability
DATA	EM2	Size of Database used
CPLX	EM3	Complexity of system modules
RUSE	EM4	Required Reusability
DOCU	EM5	Extent of Documentation required
		Platform Factors
TIME	EM6	Execution-time constraints
STOR	EM7	Main storage constraints
PVOL	EM8	Volatility of development platform
		Personnel Factors
ACAP	EM9	Capability of project analyst
PCAP	EM10	Programmer Capability
PCON	EM11	Personnel Continuity
APEX	EM12	Application Experience
PLEX	EM13	Platform Experience
LTEX	EM14	Language and Tool Experience
		Project Factors
TOOL	EM15	Use of software tools
SITE	EM16	Extent of multisite working and quality of inter-site communications
SCED	EM17	Development schedule compression

informed decisions with respect to the appropriate actions to reduce losses.

Risk in a software development project is also known as "software risk" and is defined as "a measure of likelihood of an unsatisfactory outcome affecting the software project, process, or product" (Pressman, 2005). Risk management in software development has been recognized as an important activity for software projects and has become necessary for managing and developing software systems since the introduction of the risk concept in software development by Barry Boehm in the 1990s (Boehm, 1991).

The two main phases of risk-management are *Risk-Assessment* and *Risk-Control*. Risk-Assessment is a discovery process of identifying the sources of risks, analyzing or evaluating the potential risk effects, and prioritizing such risks. Risk-Control is the process of developing software risk resolution plans, monitoring the risk status, implementing a risk resolution plan, and resolving the risk issues by correcting any potential deviations from the plan. The scope of software risk management activities is shown in Figure 1.

Risk assessment, which is the main activity in the project planning phase, plays a vital role in determining the likely success of a software development project (Heldman and Heldman, 2010). Most risk management in software development is currently based on three popular frameworks, which are: the Top Ten Risks Management methods (Williams, 1997), CMM/CMMI (Capability Maturity Model Integration) (Carr, et al., 1993; Ahern, et al., 2008), and COCOMO.

Table 3. COCOMO-II scale factors and effort multipliers values (Boehm, et al., 2000)

Drivers	Symbol	Scale Factors					
		Very Low	**Low**	**Nominal**	**High**	**Very High**	**Extra High**
PREC	SF1	6.20	4.96	3.72	2.48	1.24	0.00
FLEX	SF2	5.07	4.05	3.04	2.03	1.01	0.00
RESL	SF3	7.07	5.65	4.24	2.83	1.41	0.00
TEAM	SF4	5.48	4.38	3.29	2.19	1.10	0.00
PMAT	SF5	7.80	6.24	4.68	3.12	1.56	0.00
Drivers	**Symbol**	**Effort Multiplier**					
		Very Low	**Low**	**Nominal**	**High**	**Very High**	**Extra High**
Product Factors							
RELY	EM1	0.82	0.92	1.00	1.10	1.26	-
DATA	EM2	-	0.90	1.00	1.14	1.28	-
CPLX	EM3	0.73	0.87	1.00	1.17	1.34	1.74
RUSE	EM4	-	0.95	1.00	1.07	1.15	1.24
DOCU	EM5	0.81	0.91	1.00	1.11	1.23	-
Platform Factors							
TIME	EM6	-	-	1.00	1.11	1.29	1.63
STOR	EM7	-	-	1.00	1.05	1.17	1.46
PVOL	EM8	-	0.87	1.00	1.15	1.30	-
Personnel Factors							
ACAP	EM9	1.42	1.22	1.00	0.85	0.71	-
PCAP	EM10	1.34	1.16	1.00	0.88	0.76	-
PCON	EM11	1.29	1.10	1.00	0.90	0.81	-
APEX	EM12	1.22	1.10	1.00	0.88	0.81	-
PLEX	EM13	1.19	1.12	1.00	0.91	0.85	-
LTEX	EM14	1.20	1.10	1.00	0.91	0.84	-
Project Factors							
TOOL	EM15	1.17	1.09	1.00	090	0.78	-
SITE	EM16	1.22	1.09	1.00	0.93	0.86	0.80
SCED	EM17	1.43	1.14	1.00	1.00	1.00	-

Figure 1. Risk management activities (Boehm, 1991)

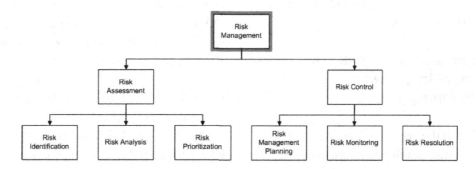

The Top Ten Risk Management method is based on the subjective judgment of a project manager and lacks objective data support. The CMM/CMMI framework, which was developed by the Software Engineering Institute (SEI), provides yet another model for the software development process and can be used for regulating software risk assessments and control. CMM/CMMI is based on the assumption that a good quality software product is the result of a good quality software development process (Hall, 1998).

The COCOMO framework focuses on risk assessment and risk control by estimating the software development cost and the software development effort. COCOMO-II, as the latest version of COCOMO, provides a more detailed estimation of project costs and has the ability to support a spiral model in software development, which is known as the process approach to reducing the risk in a software development process (Sommerville, 2007).

The most important advantage of using risk management in software development projects is that it "helps project managers to focus on many aspects of a problematic situation, emphasizes potential causes of failure, helps link potential threats to possible actions, and facilitates a shared perception of the project among project stakeholders" (Iversen, et al., 2004). However, as compared to an effort estimation activity, risk management—especially risk assessment in software project planning—is rarely practised because it is often difficult to implement due to the scarcity of experts, the unique project characteristics, the lack of sufficient time to do a thorough analysis, and the perception that it is too effort intensive and costly (Odzaly and Sage, 2009).

Effort Estimation and Risk Management in Software Project Planning

As described in the previous paragraph, the success of a software development project depends largely on the ability of a project manager to integrate the estimation and risk assessment activities in the project planning phase and to provide the most accurate effort estimates for scheduling and budget setting purposes, because inaccuracy in effort estimation will be costly and may result in loss of business (Xia, et al, 2008).

To address this problem, some attempts have already been made to improve the accuracy of effort estimation using several techniques (Huang et al., 2007; Attarzadeh and Ow, 2010), and to integrate cost estimation with risk management (Kansala, 1997; Gupta and Sadiq, 2008; Huang et al., 2006) in the project planning phase. However, these approaches have not very successful in helping project manager in project planning because they do not explain the effect of identified risk on the estimated effort. Another factor to be considered here is that the popular risk management methods are highly dependent on human judgment and experience and are, therefore, perceived as being too effort intensive and costly.

Expert-COCOMO Model

Expert-COCOMO is an extension of COCOMO-II that is used to aid in project planning by identifying, categorizing, and prioritizing project risks. This method was introduced by Ray Madachy and was designed to detect and analyze the input anomalies for project effort estimation. Expert-COCOMO utilizes the information taken from effort estimation activities to establish the risk assessment of particular software project (Madachy, 1997).The risk taxonomy in Expert-COCOMO establishes that software risks are related to a variety of COCOMO cost factors, such as: *Schedule Risk, Product Risk, Platform Risk, Personnel Risk, Process Risk,* and *Reuse Risk.* Figure 2 shows the risk taxonomy used in Expert-COCOMO and the related COCOMO cost factors that are responsible for each of these risks.

As discussed below all risks in Expert-CO-COMO are defined as being the result of a com-

Figure 2. Expert-COCOMO risk taxonomy (Madachy, 1997)

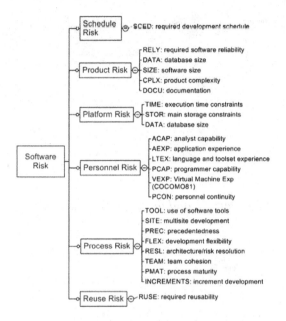

bination of several cost factors. And certain risk rules determine the level of every risk by mapping 2 cost factors (attributes) according to a risk level assignment matrix as shown in Figure 3.

Sample of risk level assignment matrix for SCED_CPLX risk rule is shown in Figure. 4. SCED_CPLX risk rules is combination of the SCED and the CPLX cost factors. Based on this rule, the software development project for a product with a *extra-high* complexity (CPLX) level

has a very-high risk related to scheduling and product risk if it is to be executed under a very-tight (*very-low*) project schedule (SCED).

There are 31 risk rules implemented in Expert-COCOMO which consist of divides in 6 categories of project risk and 15 risk categories related to cost factors. The relationship between risk rules, Risk Categories, Project Risk Categories is shown in Figure 5.

Schedule Risk will emerge if a project with a tight schedule is being developed by a developer(s) with low technical capability. Schedule risk is also considered to be high for a project within which the manager attempts to develop a complex product within a tight schedule.

Product Risk is related to the process deliverable, which is affected by such product related parameters as: the required reliability of the software product, the product size, and product complexity as well as the database and documentation requirements.

Platform Risk is related to the volatility of the development platform that could introduce many problems in the future and the necessity to rework certain project steps.

Personnel Risk is the primary source of project risks and affects the overall productivity of a software project. Personnel risk is related to the analysts' overall capabilities and experience as well as to their experience with the particular

Figure 3. Risk assignment matrix (Madachy, 1997)

		Attribute-1			
	Very Low	Low	Nominal	High	Very High
Very Low					
Low	Very Low				
Nominal	Low	Very Low			
High	Moderate	Low	Very Low		
Very High	High	Moderate	Low	Very Low	
Extra High	Very High	High	Moderate	Low	Very Low

Figure 4. SCED_CPLX risk level assignment matrix

	SCED				
CPLX	**Very Low**	**Low**	**Nominal**	**High**	**Very High**
Very Low					
Low	Very Low				
Nominal	Low	Very Low			
High	Moderate	Low	Very Low		
Very High	High	Moderate	Low	Very Low	
Extra High	Very High	High	Moderate	Low	Very Low

Figure 5. The relationship between risk rules, risk type, risk category, and project risk

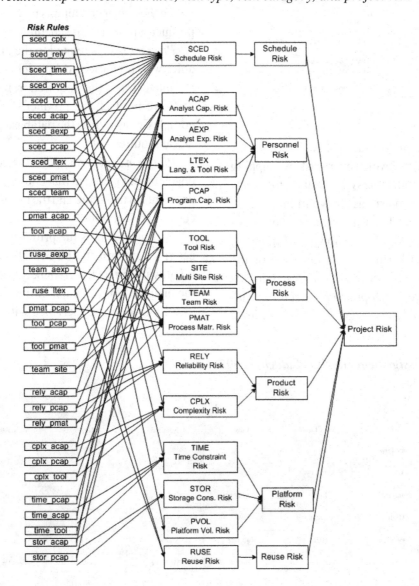

programming language and tools being used. It also depends on the capabilities of the programmer involved in the project. The combination of a low level of programmer capability and a tight project schedule will create a significant risk for the project.

Process Risk is that aspect of risk related to that project attribute in COCOMO known as software tools, multisite development, precedentedness, development flexibility, architecture resolution, team cohesion, and process maturity.

Reuse Risk is related to the impact of a reuse application in software development. Reuse risk will depend on the reuse strategy that requires reliability, experience, appropriate tools, and other elements to ensure the success of a product

In the Expert-COCOMO Model, Software Project Risk is the result of combination of six categories of project risk and quantities based on Formula (2) in Box 1.

Where, *i* is categories risks (related to cost factors), *j* is categories of project risks, and risk level$_{ij}$ are the risk for each category. The effort multiplier product is defined as being the result of (driver #1 effort multiplier) x (driver #2 effort multiplier) x . . . x (driver #*n* effort multiplier) (Madachy, 1997).

The project risk categorization based on Expert-COCOMO is shown in Table 4.

The most recent Expert-COCOMO application was developed using a C program and an HTML interface and is posted at the Center for Systems and Software Engineering (CCSE) website of the University of Southern California[1]. The main advantage of Expert-COCOMO is its capability to use the existing knowledge from a previous effort estimation activity to perform an early stage project risk assessment. The Expert-COCOMO approach reduces the requirement for risk man-

Table 4. Project risk categorization

Value	Risk
0-5	Low
5 - 15	Moderate
15- 50	High
50 -100	Very High

agement expertise and integrates the risk assessment with effort estimation.

However, this approach has a limitation when it deals with cost factors as inputs that are described in such linguistic terms as: Very Low (VL), Low (L), Nominal (N), High (H), Very High (VH) and Extra High (XH). This limitation affects the accuracy and sensitivity of Expert-COCOMO in identifying and determining the size of project risks. Another limitation of Expert-COCOMO is its inability to calculate the effect of identified project risks on the accuracy of an effort estimate.

Fuzzy Rule-Based In Software Effort Estimation

The fuzzy rule-based system is one of three main components of soft computing the field in computer science that deals with imprecision, uncertainty, and approximation to achieve practicability, robustness and low cost solutions. The soft computing components - Neural Network, Probabilistic Reasoning, and Fuzzy Logic - mimic the ability of the human mind to deal with reasoning and approximation problems rather than those that are more exact (Zadeh, 1994).

If a Neural Network deals primarily with learning ability and Probabilistic Reasoning deals with uncertainty, then the Fuzzy rule-based methodology introduced by Professor Lofti Zadeh in 1965

Box 1.

$$\text{Project Risk} = \sum_{j=1}^{\text{\# categories}} \sum_{i=1}^{\text{\# category risks}} \text{risk level} ij \times \text{effort multiplier product} ij \qquad (2)$$

provides a useful tool for dealing with imprecision, uncertainty, and complexity in problems that are difficult to solve quantitatively (Zadeh, 1965).

The soft computing technique in effort estimation has been recently used to either complement or improve on the software effort estimation approach, which includes: the utilization of the neuro-fuzzy technique for SEER-SEM (Du, et al, 2010); the application of the neuro-fuzzy technique for COCOMO (Huang, et al., 2007), and the implementation of an artificial neural network for effort estimation (Attarzadeh and Ow, 2010).

This chapter describes the utilization of fuzzy rule-based in the Fuzzy-ExCOM Model, the novel software project planning model based on COCOMO cost factors that integrates the effort estimation and risk assessment activities within one model.

FUZZY-EXCOM MODEL FOR SOFTWARE PROJECT PLANNING

Fuzzy-ExCOM consists of 2 sub-models, the Risk sub-model and the Effort Contingency sub-model.

Fuzzy rule-based improves the sensitivity of risk identification using the Expert-COCOMO method in the Risk sub-model and is applied to the cost factor parameters as the input that usually describes the qualitative measurements such as very low, low, nominal, high, and very high. In the Effort Contingency sub-model, fuzzy technique is utilized in the calculation of a contingency allowance for the COCOMO effort estimation value based on identified software project risk and software size. The overall diagram of Fuzzy-ExCOM Model is shown in Figure 6.

Fuzzy-ExCOM Risk Model

The Fuzzy-ExCOM Risk model addresses the issue of software project risk assessment based on fuzzy rule-based and Expert-COCOMO methodology. This model is an improvement on the Expert-COCOMO risk assessment methodology, which calculates software project risks based on the inputs from the effort estimation cost factors. There are 22 inputs for the model (5 scale factors and 17 cost drivers) and 7 outputs, namely schedule risk, personnel risk, process risk, product

Figure 6. Fuzzy-ExCOM model

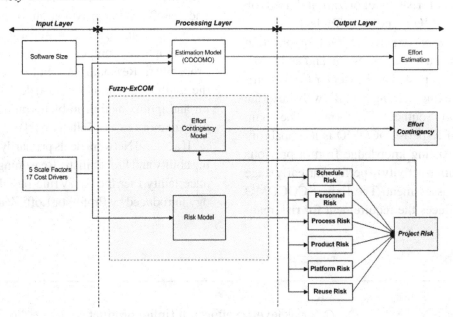

risk, platform risk, reuse risk, and project risk. Fuzzy rule-based calculates the software risks in a Fuzzy-ExCOM Risk Model through the following processes: cost factor fuzzification, fuzzy inference process based the risk rules; risk level defuzzification, and risk quantification. Figure 7 provides an overview of the Fuzzy-ExCOM Risk Sub-Model.

Fuzzy-ExCOM Effort Contingency Model

The Fuzzy-ExCOM Effort Contingency Model calculates the contingency allowance for the CO-COMO effort estimation based on project risk and software size. In a software development project, higher risk can be understood as a project having a high probability of unintended events that can affect the project cost, time, and quality. This means that the project manager should make a higher contingency allowance for a project with a higher risk because the size of the contingency allowance is proportional to that of the project risk (Coombs, 2003). Another parameter that should also be considered in the contingency allowance calculation is software size. A larger software development project will have will have a higher uncertainty level (risk) compared to a smaller project (Jones, 2012).

The Fuzzy-ExCOM Effort Contingency model calculates the contingency allowance based on project risk and software size as well as the ef-

fort estimation value. The model provides an integrated approach to software project planning starting from effort estimation, risk assessment, and contingency allowance calculation. Fuzzy rule-based is implemented in the model by accommodating the effort contingency calculation, which involves such uncertain values as risk and consists of 3 fuzzy processes. These include: the fuzzification process, the fuzzy inference process, and the defuzzification process. Figure 8 is an illustration of the Fuzzy-ExCOM Contingency model.

A contingency allowance provides a range value for the COCOMO Effort Estimation instead of a fixed value. When using a contingency allowance, the effort estimation value will be in the form of a Base Value, a Minimum Value, and a Maximum Value. Software projects with an effort estimation based on 100 staff-months and a contingency allowance of 25% can be described as having a 100 person-months as a base value with a minimum value of 75 person-months and a maximum value of 125 person-months.

The contingency allowance provides a more meaningful estimation of value for project planning purposes, because the allowance value accommodates the project risks and estimation assumptions, which are not covered in the original estimation methodology.

Figure 7. Fuzzy-ExCOM risk model

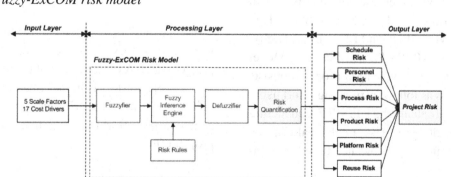

Figure 8. Fuzzy-ExCOM effort contingency model

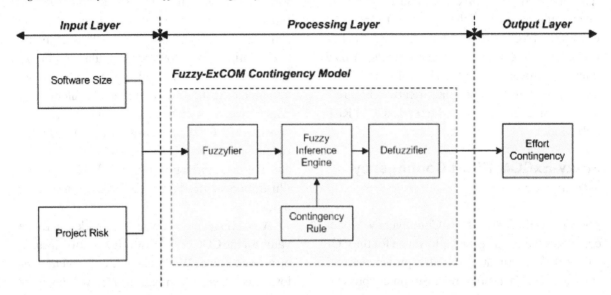

Model Implementation and Evaluation

To understand the effectiveness of a Fuzzy-ExCOM Project Planning Model, the proposed model has been tested with 2 data sets. The first data set is the COCOMO public data set taken from the Turkish Software Industry (12 project data points) posted at PROMISE (Predictor Models in Software Engineering), which is the Repository of Empirical Software Engineering Data website; the second data set is the Industry data set (6 project data points) (Du, 2009).

Table 5 shows the overall 18 project data with the information about project size (in KLOC), actual effort for each project (in staff-month), and 22 cost factors which represent in linguistic term (VL = Very Low, L = Low, N = Nominal, H = High, VH = Very High, and EH = Extra High).

The Fuzzy-ExCOM Project Planning Model implementation and evaluation process consists of 4 main steps as follow: estimating effort using COCOMO and calculating RE/MRE, conducting risk assessment based risk model calculation, calculate contingency allowance based on con-

tingency model calculation, and result analysis. The overall model implementation and evaluation process activity is shown in Figure 9.

In the first step activities, RE (relative error) is calculated to gain an understanding of the accuracy of the estimates reached by comparing the actual to the estimated value and expressing the result as a percentage. In the effort estimation stage of project planning, a higher RE figure suggests that more or less effort than was predicted will be required. The RE formula can be described as follows:

$$RE = \left(\frac{actual - estimated}{actual} \right) \times 100\% \qquad (3)$$

where "actual" is the actual software project effort and "estimated" is the estimated software project effort. A positive RE value means that the actual project effort is higher than the estimated effort, and a negative RE value means that the actual project effort is smaller than the estimated project effort.

Table 5. Project data set

Proj. Id	KLOC	Act Effort (staff-mo)	PREC	FLEX	RESL	TEAM	PMAT	RELY	DATA	CPLX	RUSE	DOCU	TIME	STOR	PVOL	ACAP	PCAP	PCON	AEXP	PEXP	LTEX	TOOL	SITE	SCED
I01	96.60	638.00	H	H	H	VH	L	N	L	H	H	H	H	H	N	H	H	N	N	H	H	H	N	L
I02	51.80	185.00	H	H	H	VH	L	N	L	H	H	H	N	H	N	H	H	N	H	H	H	H	N	L
I03	64.10	332.00	H	H	H	VH	L	N	L	H	H	H	N	H	N	N	N	N	N	H	N	H	N	N
I04	31.00	619.90	H	H	H	VH	L	H	N	N	H	H	N	H	N	N	N	N	N	L	L	N	N	N
I05	3.30	64.80	H	H	H	VH	VL	H	N	H	H	H	N	H	N	N	N	N	N	H	N	N	N	N
I06	9.90	76.60	H	H	H	VH	L	N	L	H	H	H	N	N	N	N	N	N	L	L	L	H	N	N
T01	3.00	1.20	VH	N	L	H	VL	N	N	L	L	L	VH	H	N	H	VH	VH	VH	H	H	H	L	N
T02	2.00	2.00	VH	N	L	VH	VL	H	N	L	N	L	VH	H	N	H	H	VH	VH	VH	VH	H	VL	H
T03	4.25	4.50	EH	N	L	H	VL	H	VH	L	N	L	VH	VH	N	H	H	VH	VH	VH	VH	H	VL	H
T04	10.00	3.00	EH	H	H	H	N	H	H	VH	L	N	N	N	H	H	H	VL	VH	VH	H	N	H	H
T05	15.00	4.00	N	H	L	H	N	L	N	VH	N	H	H	N	N	H	H	H	N	N	N	N	H	L
T06	40.53	22.00	VH	L	EH	EH	H	L	L	N	L	VL	N	N	L	VH	VH	H	N	H	H	VL	EH	L
T07	4.05	2.00	EH	VH	EH	N	H	L	L	VL	N	VL	VH	VH	L	VH	VH	VH	N	VH	VH	VL	H	L
T08	31.85	5.00	VL	VL	VH	N	L	L	VH	L	H	VH	N	N	L	L	H	VH	N	N	N	N	VH	N
T09	114.28	18.00	N	VL	N	VL	L	VL	N	N	VH	L	VH	VH	L	L	H	VH	H	H	H	N	H	N
T10	23.11	4.00	N	VL	VH	L	L	VL	H	N	VH	VL	N	N	L	L	VH	VH	H	VH	H	N	N	L
T11	1.37	1.00	H	N	VH	H	L	L	N	N	N	L	N	N	L	VH	H	VH	N	N	H	VH	VH	H
T12	1.61	2.10	L	N	N	H	N	L	L	H	H	N	N	N	L	L	H	VH	H	N	H	VH	VH	H

Note: **VL** = Very Low; **L** = Low; **N** = Nominal; **H** = High; **VH** = Very High; **EH** = Extra High

Figure 9. Fuzzy-ExCOM model implementation and evaluation steps

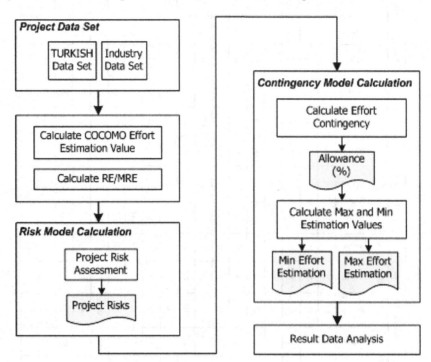

The MRE is the absolute value of the relative error and can be described according to the following formula:

$$MRE = \frac{|actual - estimated|}{actual} \qquad (4)$$

The MRE is used to measure the error contained in the estimated value regardless of whether the error is positive or negative.

The main activity in the first step is calculated the estimate effort based on COCOMO approach as describe in the Equation (1) and on an online COCOMO-II application posted at the CCSE (Center for Systems and Software Engineering) website of University of Southern California.

Table 6 shows the overall result of activity as a list of the estimated Effort values and the actual Effort values for the 18 project data points. Relative Error and Magnitude Relative Error (RE/MRE) are used as an indication of the accuracy of the estimated effort values as compared to those of the actual effort values. The other information presented in the table includes Software Size (in KSLOC = Kilo Source Line of Code) and Size Category.

The second step of implementation is the risk model calculation that provides information about the project risk based on the Fuzzy-ExCOM Risk Model. For model evaluation purposes, MATLAB R2009b is used as the primary tool in the implementation of the risk assessment model that consist of fuzzification process, fuzzy inference process based on risk rules, defuzzification process, and risk quantification.

The fuzzification process converts the input of 5 scale factors and 12 cost drivers to a fuzzy value based on the cost factor values listed in Table 2. The Gaussian membership function is used in the fuzzification process due to the characteristic of this membership function as the most adequate approach to represent uncertainty parameters (Kreinovich, 1992). Figure 10 illustrates the

Table 6. Effort estimate value

Project ID.	Size (KSLOC)	Size Category	ACTUAL Effort (staff-mo)	Effort Estimate (staff-mo)	RE	MRE
I01	196.60	Large	638.00	722.70	-13%	13%
I02	51.80	Medium	185.00	140.00	24%	24%
I03	64.10	Medium	332.00	256.70	23%	23%
I04	131.00	Large	619.90	745.20	-20%	20%
I05	13.30	Small	64.80	68.90	-6%	6%
I06	19.90	Small	76.60	92.70	-21%	21%
T01	3.00	Small	1.20	3.60	-200%	200%
T02	2.00	Small	2.00	2.90	-45%	45%
T03	4.25	Small	4.50	9.30	-107%	107%
T04	10.00	Small	3.00	36.20	-1107%	1107%
T05	15.00	Small	4.00	63.20	-1480%	1480%
T06	40.53	Small	22.00	28.60	-30%	30%
T07	4.05	Small	2.00	2.30	-15%	15%
T08	31.85	Small	5.00	147.10	-2842%	2842%
T09	114.28	Medium	18.00	294.00	-1533%	1533%
T10	23.11	Small	4.00	63.20	-1480%	1480%
T11	1.37	Small	1.00	0.90	10%	10%
T12	1.61	Small	2.10	2.00	5%	5%

Figure 10. Gaussian MF for CPLX cost factor

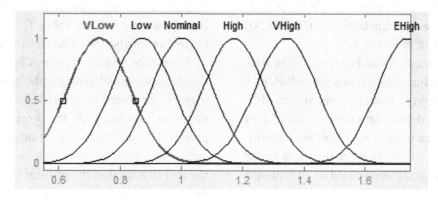

implementation of membership function of the CPLX cost factor using MATLAB application.

The Fuzzy Inference process determines the level of every risk based on the input from 2 cost factors and the related risk rules according to a risk level assignment matrix as described in previous section and shown in Figure 3. The sample of fuzzy inference process implementation within MATLAB application for SCED parameter and CPLX parameter is shown in Figure 11.

The fuzzy inference engine for the Fuzzy-ExCOM Risk Model together with all the risk rules is also implemented using MATLAB. The 31 risk rules in Expert COCOMO are imple-

Figure 11. SCED_CPLX risk implementation

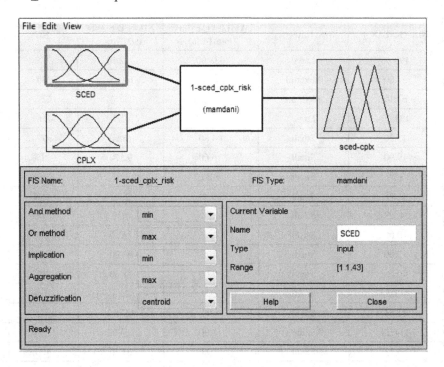

mented as fuzzy-rule type (IF...AND...THEN..) based on the risk-level-assignment matrix as describe in Figure 3. Each risk rule implement by 12 fuzzy-rules type and the sample of SCED_CPLX risk rule implementation on MATLAB R2009b is shown in Figure 12.

The last process in the Fuzzy-ExCOM Risk Model is the defuzzification process, which provides a translation of a fuzzy output to a quantifiable result. The defuzzifier converts every fuzzy risk level from an inference process to a quantifiable value that will be used as the input to the project risks quantification based on an Equation (1).

The implementation of fuzzy rule-based in the Fuzzy-ExCOM Risk model provides a higher level of accuracy and sensitivity in the risk assessment results for a software project compared to that produces by the existing Expert-COCOMO model (Manalif, 2012).

The output of risk identification based on Fuzzy-ExCOM Risk Model for every project

in the data sets is shown in Table 7. There are 4 projects with id. I04, I05, T09, and T10, can be considered having moderate risk while the other projects are considered as a low risk projects. Based on the result on Table 7, we could track the main contribution to the risk in every project.

If we take a look on project I05, the process risk and personnel risk are the two main contributors for overall project risk. In order to reduce the overall project risk, the project manager of project I05 could take the actions to the parameters that related to these risks such as, risk on the tool that used in the project(TOOL), risk on multi site development (SITE), risk on project team member (TEAM), risk on software development process (PMAT), risk on analyst capability (ACAP), risk on analyst experience (AEXP), risk on the utilization of programming language and tool (LTEX), and risk with programmer capability (PCAP). The result of risk model can also be used to prioritize the risk and to prepare the mitigation action for every risks.

Figure 12. The SCED_CPLX rule implementation

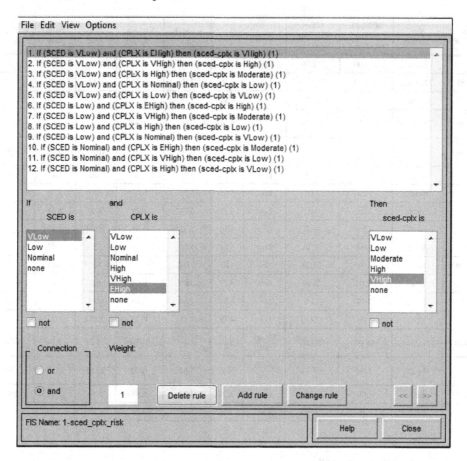

The third step in model implementation is calculate the contingency allowance based on Fuzzy-ExCOM Contingency model which consist of 3 fuzzy processes: the fuzzification process, the fuzzy inference process, and the defuzzification process.

The fuzzifier in the fuzzification process transforms the inputs with respect to software size and software project risk into a fuzzy set value. Since there is no formal guideline or standard for software size, the size categorization used in this paper refers to the Capers Jones and Boehm statement regarding software size. Hence, a large system software project is taken to be about 10,000 function points or greater (Jones, 2012) According to another categorization, a large system software project is taken to be about 128 KLOC and a Super Large System is taken to be 512 KLOC or more (Boehm, 1981). The software size categorization is shown in Table 8.

The contingency rule in the inference process calculates the contingency value based on the combination matrix between the Software Project Size and Software Project Risk. According to this rule, a low risk project, which develops software of a small size, will require a relatively small contingency allowance. While a high risk project, which develops software of a large size, will require a large contingency allowance. The overall rules, which apply to the contingency model, are shown in Table 9.

The implementation of contingency rule in the Fuzzy-ExCOM Model in the MATLAB application is shown in Figure 13.

Table 7. Project risks

Project ID.	Size (KSLOC)	Size Category	ACTUAL Effort (staff-mo)	Effort Estimate (staff-mo)	Project Risk		Schedule Risk	Personnel Risk	Process Risk	Product Risk	Platform Risk	Reuse Risk
I01	196.60	Large	638.00	722.70	Low	4.49	7.25	7.78	9.20	4.48	3.65	1.17
I02	51.80	Medium	185.00	140.00	Low	4.40	7.60	6.81	8.83	4.42	4.31	0.83
I03	64.10	Medium	332.00	256.70	Low	4.58	5.48	9.71	8.20	4.46	4.83	1.50
I04	131.00	Large	619.90	745.20	Moderate	5.24	5.80	10.67	10.43	4.63	5.56	2.03
I05	13.30	Small	64.80	68.90	Moderate	6.32	6.40	11.16	16.04	6.49	5.56	1.50
I06	19.90	Small	76.60	92.70	Low	4.97	5.95	11.21	8.23	4.41	4.80	2.44
T01	3.00	Small	1.20	3.60	Low	3.68	5.21	6.06	8.61	3.95	2.82	0.78
T02	2.00	Small	2.00	2.90	Low	4.01	5.24	6.20	9.60	5.42	2.91	0.54
T03	4.25	Small	4.50	9.30	Low	4.16	5.32	6.34	10.34	5.53	2.97	0.54
T04	10.00	Small	3.00	36.20	Low	3.94	5.51	6.67	7.56	4.47	4.26	0.90
T05	15.00	Small	4.00	63.20	Low	4.58	7.04	8.60	7.87	4.65	4.05	1.95
T06	40.53	Small	22.00	28.60	Low	4.70	7.66	6.64	10.01	2.67	6.58	1.51
T07	4.05	Small	2.00	2.30	Low	4.94	7.88	6.56	12.05	2.50	6.58	1.25
T08	31.85	Small	5.00	147.10	Low	4.79	4.78	11.22	10.94	3.13	4.19	1.50
T09	114.28	Medium	18.00	294.00	Moderate	5.18	5.91	10.94	12.21	2.78	6.14	0.66
T10	23.11	Small	4.00	63.20	Moderate	5.10	7.63	10.75	12.65	2.56	3.80	0.66
T11	1.37	Small	1.00	0.90	Low	3.38	4.87	6.88	5.86	3.14	2.92	1.54
T12	1.61	Small	2.10	2.00	Low	3.95	5.05	9.04	5.67	3.68	5.16	0.83

Table 8. Software size categorization

Size	Value (KLOC)
Small	0 – 50.0
Medium	50.1 – 128.0
Large	128.1 – 512.0
Extra Large	512.1 – up

In the defuzzification process, the fuzzy value of the contingency allowance as an output of the inference process will be transformed to a crisp value. A contingency value describes the percentage amount that should be added to the original effort estimation base-value. As Barry Boehm suggested, software estimation will be accurate to within 20% of the cost and 70% of the time estimates (Boehm, 1981). Based on the above range, the contingency allowance value in the Fuzzy ExCOM Contingency Model was defined as being between the values of 0% and over 75%.

The contingency allowance is categorized as being Low, Medium, High, or Very High. The overall categorization of the Effort Contingency Value is shown in Table 10.

The Fuzzy-ExCOM Contingency model calculates a contingency allowance based on the project risk and software size. The output of this calculation is a contingency allowance value in percent that can be used to calculate the maximum (MAX) and the minimum (MIN) estimation values, which represent the upper and lower levels of the estimated values.

The result of the effort contingency allowance calculation based on the Fuzzy-ExCOM Contingency Model for 18 project data is shown in Table 11.

The second column and fourth column describes the information about the size of software that will be built and also the actual effort that recorded after the project finish. The fifth column

Table 9. Contingency rule matrix

Project Risk		Software Size			
		Small	Medium	Large	X-Large
	Low	Low	Low	Medium	Medium
	Moderate	Low	Medium	High	High
	High	Medium	High	High	Very High
	Very High	Medium	High	Very High	Very High

Figure 13. Fuzzy-ExCOM contingency rule implementation

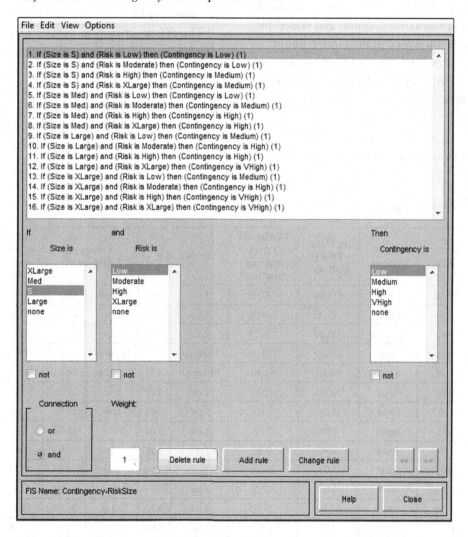

describes the result of effort estimation using COCOMO approach based on software size in the second column and projects cost factors as describe in Table 5. Sixth and seventh column are the project risk value as the result from Fuzzy-ExCOM Risk Model. The result of Fuzzy-ExCOM Contingency model is listed on eighth and ninth.

The last two columns are the list of MIN effort estimation value and MAX effort estimation value. The MIN effort estimate value is calculated based on Effort Estimate (fifth column) and minus the

Table 10. Effort contingency value

Contingency	Value
Low	0% - 25.0%
Medium	25.1% –50.0%
High	50.1% – 75.0%
Very High	75.1% – 100%

percentage allowance in the ninth column. The MAX effort estimate value is calculated based on Effort Estimate (fifth column) and added by the percentage allowance in the ninth column.

Figure 14 shows the chart of Effort Estimation value, Actual Effort value, MIN Effort Estimation value, and MAX Effort Estimation value for all 18 projects.

The Fuzzy-ExCOM Project Planning Model provides the project manager with the necessary

information concerning the Estimated Effort Value, the Project Risk, and the Effort Contingency Allowance used to compensate for the identified project risks. Of these three types of effort estimation values, the most important value for project planning purposes is the MAX Effort Estimation value, which represents the estimated value along with the additional resources (contingency value) that should be allocated by the project manager to compensate for the project risks.

The effort estimation in the software development project can be consider successful if the ACTUAL project effort is lower than the MAX value, because the estimated value will be able to compensate the project risk.

In the performance comparison between the COCOMO-II Model and the Fuzzy-ExCOM mod-

Table 11. Effort contingency allowance results

Project ID.	Size (KSLOC)	Size Category	ACTUAL Effort (staff-mo)	COCOMO Effort Estimate (staff-mo)	Project Risk		Contingency Allowance		MIN Effort Est. Value	MAX Effort Est. Value
I01	196.60	Large	638.00	722.70	Low	4.49	Medium	40.3%	431.45	1013.95
I02	51.80	Medium	185.00	140.00	Low	4.40	Low	25.0%	105.00	175.00
I03	64.10	Medium	332.00	256.70	Low	4.58	Low	25.0%	192.53	320.88
I04	131.00	Large	619.90	745.20	Moderate	5.24	Medium	26.3%	549.21	941.19
I05	13.30	Small	64.80	68.90	Moderate	6.32	Medium	28.6%	49.19	88.61
I06	19.90	Small	76.60	92.70	Low	4.97	Low	25.0%	69.53	115.88
T01	3.00	Small	1.20	3.60	Low	3.68	Low	25.0%	2.70	4.50
T02	2.00	Small	2.00	2.90	Low	4.01	Low	25.0%	2.18	3.63
T03	4.25	Small	4.50	9.30	Low	4.16	Low	25.0%	6.98	11.63
T04	10.00	Small	3.00	36.20	Low	3.94	Low	25.0%	27.15	45.25
T05	15.00	Small	4.00	63.20	Low	4.58	Low	25.0%	47.40	79.00
T06	40.53	Small	22.00	28.60	Low	4.70	Low	25.0%	21.45	35.75
T07	4.05	Small	2.00	2.30	Low	4.94	Low	25.0%	1.73	2.88
T08	31.85	Small	5.00	147.10	Low	4.79	Low	25.0%	110.33	183.88
T09	114.28	Medium	18.00	294.00	Moderate	5.18	Medium	25.7%	218.44	369.56
T10	23.11	Small	4.00	63.20	Moderate	5.10	Medium	25.4%	47.15	79.25
T11	1.37	Small	1.00	0.90	Low	3.38	Low	25.0%	0.68	1.13
T12	1.61	Small	2.10	2.00	Low	3.95	Low	25.0%	1.50	2.50

Figure 14. Effort contingency allowance for project data set

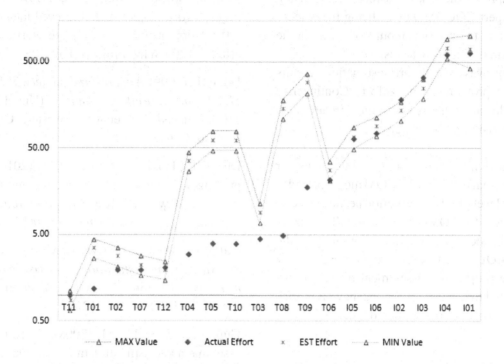

el, the number of project which has the ACTUAL value lower than Estimate value in COCOMO Model is compared with the the number of project which has the ACTUAL value lower than MAX value in Fuzzy-ExCOM Model.

From a total of 18 projects, there are 16 projects (89%) having a MAX value (effort based value + contingency value) that is higher than the actual effort value in Fuzzy-ExCOM Model. This performance level is higher compared to the original COCOMO-II effort estimation figure obtained without a contingency allowance, which could only be reached in 14 projects (78%).

CONCLUSION

As the most uncertain of projects, software project development requires sophisticated methods to help a project manager manage uncertainty in project execution. Some researchers conclude

that the most critical phase in a software development project is the project planning phase which includes goal setting, scheduling, staffing, and risk management. Because most of the software project failures occur in this phase. Software project effort estimation and project risk assessment, the two main activities in software project planning, are integral and interrelated parts of the software project planning phase.

The research that is described in this paper introduces the implementation of fuzzy rule-based, which has the main capability of dealing with uncertain data in the Fuzzy-ExCOM Model. This model has the following characteristics and capabilities:

- Improves the project planning process by integrating the Effort Estimation activity and Risk Assessment activity in software development project.

- Improves the risk assessment results using Expert-COCOMO by utilizing fuzzy techniques to overcome input that comes in the form of linguistic terms.
- Improves the effort estimation results by providing an Effort Contingency Allowance that is based on software project risks and software size.

Validation of the data set used in this chapter indicated that the Fuzzy-ExCOM model provides a higher level of effort prediction performance as compared to COCOMO-II estimation. The Fuzzy-ExCOM Model can be used to complement the COCOMO effort estimate to provide a preliminary software project risk assessment based on cost factors and to calculate a contingency allowance to compensate for the predicted risks.

REFERENCES

Ahern, D. M., Clouse, A., & Turner, R. (2008). *CMMI distilled: A practical introduction to integrated process improvement* (3rd ed.). Boston, MA: Pearson Education Inc.

Attarzadeh, I., & Ow, S. H. (2010). Proposing a new software cost estimation model based on artificial neural networks.In *Proceedings of 2nd International Conference on Computer Engineering and Technology* (ICCET). Chengdu, China: ICCET.

Boehm, B. W. (1981). *Software engineering economics*. Englewood Cliffs, NJ: Prentice Hall..

Boehm, B. W. (1991). Software risk management: Principles and practices. *IEEE Software*, 8(1), 32–41. doi:10.1109/52.62930.

Carr, M., et al. (1993). *Taxonomy–based risk identification* (Report SEI-93-TR-006). Pittsburgh, PA: Software Engineering Institute.

Computerworld. (2002, May 20). *Five reasons why software projects fail*. Retrieved January 20, 2012 from http://www.computerworld.com/s/article/71209/Why_Projects_Fail

Du, W. L. (2009). *A neuro-fuzzy model with SEER-SEM for software effort estimation*. (Unpublished MESc Thesis). University of Western Ontario, Ontario, Canada.

Du, W. L., Ho, D., & Capretz, L. F. (2010). Improving software effort estimation using neuro-fuzzy model with SEER-SEM. *Global Journal of Computer Science and Technology*, 10(12), 52–64.

Galorath, D. D., & Evans, M. W. (2006). *Software sizing, estimation, and risk management*. Boca Raton, FL: Auerbach Publication. doi:10.1201/9781420013122.

Gupta, D., & Sadiq, M. (2008). Software risk assessment and estimation model. In *Proceeding International Conference on Computer Science and Information Technology* (pp. 963-967). Singapore: IEEE.

Hall, E. M. (1998). *Managing risk: Methods for software systems development*. Reading, MA: Addison Wesley Longman, Inc.

Heldman, K., & Heldman, W. (2010). *CompTIA project+: Study guide*. Indianapolis, IN: Wiley Publishing Inc.

Huang, S. J., Lin, C. Y., & Chiu, N. H. (2006). Fuzzy decision tree approach for embedding risk assessment information into software estimation model. *Journal of Information Science and Engineering*, 22, 297–313.

Huang, X., Ho, D., Ren, J., & Capretz, L. F. (2004). A neuro-fuzzy tool for software estimation. In *Proceedings of 20th IEEE International Conference on Software Maintenance*. Chicago: IEEE.

Huang, X., Ho, D., Ren, J., & Capretz, L. F. (2007). Improving the COCOMO model using a neuro fuzzy approach. *Applied Soft Computing Journal*, 7, 29–40. doi:10.1016/j.asoc.2005.06.007.

IEEE Spectrum. (2005, September). *Why software fails*. Retrieved January 20, 2012 from http://spectrum.ieee.org/computing/software/why-software-fails/3

Iranmanesh, S. H., et al. (2009). Risk assessment of software project using fuzzy inference system. In *Proceeding International Conference on Computers & Industrial Engineering* (pp.1149-1154). IEEE.

Iversen, J. H., Mathiassen, L., & Nielsen, P. A. (2004). Managing risk in software process improvement: An action research approach. *Management Information Systems Quarterly*, *28*(3), 395–433.

Jones, C. (2012). *Early sizing and early risk analysis of software project*. New York: Jones & Associates, LLC..

Kansala, K. (1997). Integrating risk assessment with cost estimation. *IEEE Software*, *14*(3), 61–67. doi:10.1109/52.589236.

Kreinovich, V., Quintana, C., & Reznik, L. (1992). Gaussian membership functions are most adequate in representing uncertainty in measurements. In *Proceeding NAFIPS: North America Fuzzy Information Processing Society Conference*, (pp.618–624). NAFIPS.

Madachy, R. (1997). Heuristic risk assessment using cost factors. *IEEE Software*, *14*(3), 51–59. doi:10.1109/52.589234.

Manalif, E., Capretz, L. F., & Ho, D. (2012). Fuzzy-ExCOM software project risk assessment. In *Proceedings of 11th IEEE Conference on Machine Learning and Application*. Boca Raton, FL: IEEE.

Marchewka, J. T. (2009). *Information technology project management* (3rd ed.). Hoboken, NJ: John Wiley & Sons, Inc.

Odzaly, E. E., Greer, D., & Sage, P. (2009). Software risk management barriers: En empirical study. In *Proceeding 3rd International Symposium on Empirical Software Engineering and Measurement* (pp.418-421). IEEE.

Pressman, R. S. (2005). *Software engineering - Practitioner's Approach* (6th ed.). New York: McGraw Hill..

Putnam, L. H., & Myers, W. (1992). *Measures for excellence*. Englewood Cliffs, NJ: Prentice Hall..

Sommerville, I. (2007). *Software engineering* (8th ed.). Essex, UK: Addison-Wesley Published Ltd.

Standish Group. (n.d.). *Chaos report 2009*. Retrieved January 16, 2012, from http://www1.standishgroup.com/newsroom/chaos_2009.php

Stellman, A., & Greene, J. (2006). *Applied software project management*. Sebastopol, CA: O'Reilly Media, Inc.

Williams, R. et al. (1997). Putting risk management into practice. *IEEE Software*, *14*(3), 75–82. doi:10.1109/52.589240.

Xia, W., Ho, D., & Capretz, L. F. (2008). A neuro-fuzzy model for function point calibration. *WSEAS Transactions on Information Science and Applications*, *5*(1), 22–30.

Zadeh, L. A. (1965). Fuzzy sets. *Information and Control*, *8*, 338–353. doi:10.1016/S0019-9958(65)90241-X.

Zadeh, L. A. (1994). Fuzzy logic, neural networks, and soft computing. *Communications of the ACM*, *37*(3), 77–84. doi:10.1145/175247.175255.

ENDNOTES

[1] http://sunset.usc.edu/research/COCOMOII/expert_cocomo/expert_cocomo2000.html

Chapter 7
Modeling and Prediction of Time–Varying Environmental Data Using Advanced Bayesian Methods

Majdi Mansouri
Université de Liège, Belgium

Benjamin Dumont
Université de Liège, Belgium

Marie-France Destain
Université de Liège, Belgium

ABSTRACT

The problem of state/parameter estimation represents a key issue in crop models, which are nonlinear, non-Gaussian, and include a large number of parameters. The prediction errors are often important due to uncertainties in the equations, the input variables, and the parameters. The measurements needed to run the model and to perform calibration and validation are sometimes not numerous or known with some uncertainty. In these cases, estimating the state variables and/or parameters from easily obtained measurements can be extremely useful. In this chapter, the authors address the problem of modeling and prediction of time-varying Leaf area index and Soil Moisture (LSM) to better handle nonlinear and non-Gaussian processes without a priori state information. The performances of various conventional and state-of-the-art estimation techniques are compared when they are utilized to achieve this objective. These techniques include the Extended Kalman Filter (EKF), Unscented Kalman Filter (UKF), Particle Filter (PF), and the more recently developed technique Variational Bayesian Filter (VF). The original data was issued from experiments carried out on silty soil in Belgium with a wheat crop during two consecutive years, the seasons 2008-09 and 2009-10.

DOI: 10.4018/978-1-4666-4785-5.ch007

1. INTRODUCTION

Parameter and states estimation in nonlinear environmental systems is an important issue in diagnosis, measurement and modeling. However, due to the difficulty of, or cost associated with, obtaining these measurements, state and/or parameter estimators are often used to overcome this problem. Crop models such as EPIC (Williams et al., 1989), WOFOST (Diepen et al., 1989), DAISY (Hansen et al., 1990), STICS (Brisson et al., 1998), and SALUS (Basso and Ritchie, 2005) are dynamic non-linear models that describe the growth and development of a crop interacting with environmental factors (soil and climate) and agricultural practices (crop species, tillage type, fertilizer amount, etc.). They are developed to predict crop yield and quality or to optimize the farming practices in order to satisfy environmental objectives, as the reduction of nitrogen lixiviation. More recently, crop models are used to simulate the effects of climate changes on the agricultural production. Nevertheless, the prediction errors of these models may be important due to uncertainties in the estimates of initial values of the states, in input data, in the parameters, and in the equations. The measurements needed to run the model are sometimes not numerous, whereas the field spatial variability and the climatic temporal fluctuations over the field may be high. The degree of accuracy is therefore difficult to estimate, apart from numerous repetitions of measurements. For these reasons, the problem of state/parameter estimation represents a key issue in such nonlinear and non-Gaussian crop models including a large number of parameters, while measurement noise exists in the data.

Several state estimation techniques have been developed and used in practice. These techniques include the extended Kalman filter (EKF), unscented Kalman filter (UKF), particle filter (PF), and more recently the variational Bayesian filter (VF). The classical Kalman Filter (KF) was developed in the 1960s (Kalman, 1960), and has been widely used in various engineering and science applications, including communications, control, machine learning, neuroscience, and many others. In the case where the model describing the system is assumed to be linear and Gaussian, the KF provides an optimal solution (Simon, 2006; Grewal & Andrews, 2008). The KF has also been formulated in the context of Takagi-Sugeno fuzzy systems to handle nonlinear models, which can be described as a convex set of multiple linear models (Chen et al., 1998; Simon, 2003). It is known that KF is computationally efficient; however, it is limited by the non-universal linear and Gaussian modeling assumptions. To relax such assumptions, the Extended Kalman Filter (Simon, 2006; Grewal & Andrews, 2008; Julier et al., 1997; Ljung et al., 1979; Kim et al., 1994) and the Unscented Kalman Filter (Simon, 2006; Grewal & Andrews, 2008; Wan et al., 2000; Wan et al., 2001; Sarkka et al., 2007) have been developed. In extended Kalman filtering, the model describing the system is linearized at every time sample (which means that the model is assumed to be differentiable). Therefore, for highly nonlinear models, EKF does not usually provide a satisfactory performance. The UKF, on the other hand, instead of linearizing the model to approximate the mean and covariance matrix of the state vector, uses the unscented transformation to approximate these moments. In the unscented transformation, a set of samples (called sigma points) are selected and propagated through the nonlinear model to improve the approximation of these moments and thus the accuracy of state estimation. Other state estimation techniques use a Bayesian framework to estimate the state and/or parameter vector (Beal et al. 2003). The Bayesian framework relies on computing the probability distribution of the unobserved state given a sequence of the observed data in addition to the state evolution model. Consider an observed data set y, which is generated from a model defined by a set of unknown parameters z (Smidl et al., 2005). The beliefs about the data are completely expressed via the parametric probabilistic observation model $P(y|z)$. The learning on uncertainty or randomness of a process is solved by constructing a distribution $P(z|y)$, called the posterior distribution, which quantifies our belief about the system after obtaining the measurements. According to Bayes theorem, the posterior can be expresses as

$$P(z|y) = \frac{P(y|z)P(z)}{P(y)}$$

where $P(y|z)$ is the conditional distribution of the data given the vector z, which is called the likelihood function, $P(z)$ is the prior distribution which quantifies our belief about z before obtaining the measurements, and $P(y)$ is the distribution of the data. Unfortunately, for most nonlinear systems and non-Gaussian noise observations, closed-form analytic expressions of the posterior distribution of the state vector are untractable (Kotecha & Djuric, 2003). To overcome this drawback, a nonparametric Monte Carlo sampling based method called Sequential Monte Carlo method (SMC) (also known as particle filtering (PF)) (Doucet & Tadic, 2003; Poyiadjis et al., 2005) has recently gained popularity. The latter method presents several advantages since:

1. It can account for the constraint of small number of data samples,
2. The online update of the filtering distribution and its compression are simultaneously performed, and
3. It yields an optimal choice of the sampling distribution over the state variable by minimizing the Kullback-Leibler (KL) divergence.

Recently, a variational filtering (VF) has been proposed for solving the nonlinear parameter estimation problem encountered in crop models. The authors in (Mansouri et al., 2011; Mansouri et al., 2013) used a Bayesian sampling method for modeling and prediction of nonlinear environmental system, where the nonlinear observed system was assumed to progress according to a probabilistic state space model. In this investigation, the state vector to be estimated (at any time instant) was assumed to follow a Gaussian model, where the expectation and the covariance matrix are constants.

Each of the above state estimation techniques has its advantages and disadvantages. For example, the variational filter can be applied to large parameter spaces, has better convergence properties, and is easier to implement than the particle filter. Both of them can provide improved accuracy over the EKF.

The general objective of this chapter is compare the performances of the EKF, UKF, PF, and VF when used to monitor and model an environmental process called LMS, which represents the temporal evolution of three state variables implied in the wheat crop growth and development: the leaf-area index (LAI), the soil moisture of the topsoil layer (0-30 cm) (HUR1), and the soil moisture of the subsoil layer (30-50 cm) (HUR2). This comparative study will assess the accuracy and convergence of the proposed techniques, as well as the effect of the size of the parameter space (i.e., number of estimated parameters) on the performances of the estimation techniques. Some practical challenges, however, can affect the accuracy of estimated states and/or parameters. Beside the existence of many parameters, it is necessary to consider the presence of noise in the measured data, and the restricted availability of some measured data samples. Consequently, the objectives of this chapter is two-fold: i) we study the accuracy and convergence of EKF, UKF, PF, and VF techniques, ii) we investigate the effect of the above challenges on the performances of these techniques.

The rest of the chapter is organized as follows. In Section 2, a statement of the problem addressed in this chapter is presented, followed by description of variational Bayesian filtering. Then, in Section 3, the performances of the various state estimation techniques are compared through their application to estimate the state variables and model parameters of the LSM process. Finally, some concluding remarks are presented in Section 4.

2. MATERIAL AND METHODS

A. Problem Formulation

Here, the estimation problem of interest is formulated for a general system model. Let a nonlinear state space model be described as follows:

$$\begin{cases} \dot{x} = g\left(x, u, \theta, w\right) \\ y = l\left(x, u, \theta, v\right) \end{cases} \quad (1)$$

where, $x \in R^n$ is a vector of the state variables, $u \in R^p$ is a vector of the input variables (which can be changed as desired), $\, \in R^q$ is an unknown parameter vector, $y \in R^m$ is a vector of the measured variables, g and l are nonlinear differentiable functions, and $w \in R^n$ and $v \in R^m$ are process and measurement noise, which quantify randomness in the process and errors in the measurements, respectively.

Discretizing the state space model (1), the discrete model can be written as follows:

$$\begin{cases} x_k = f\left(x_{k-1}, u_{k-1}, \theta_{k-1}, w_{k-1}\right) \\ y_k = h\left(x_k, u_k, \theta_k, v_k\right) \end{cases} \quad (2)$$

which describes the state variables at some time step (k) in terms of their values at a previous time step ($k-1$). Note that in Equation (2). The process and measurement noise vectors have the following properties:

$$E\left[w_k\right] = 0, \ E\left[w_k w_k^T\right] = Q_k, \ E\left[v_k\right] = 0,$$
$$E\left[v_k v_k^T\right] = R_k.$$

The function f is used to predict the value of the state vector at some time step (k) given its value at the previous time step $(k-1)$, and the function h relates the measured vector (y_k) to the state vector (x_k) at the same time step. Also, defining the augmented vector, u_k is the vector of input variables, θ_k is a parameter vector (assumed to be known), y_k is the vector of the measured variables, w_k and v_k are respectively model and measurement noise vectors, and the matrices, Q_k and R_k, represent the covariance matrices of the process and measurement noise vectors, respectively. We assume that the error terms w_k and v_k have normal distributions with zero expectation, and that they are mutually independent.

Since we are interested to estimate the state vector x_k, as well as the parameter vector θ_k, let's assume that the parameter vector is described by the following model:

$$\theta_k = \theta_{k-1} + \gamma_{k-1} \quad (3)$$

where γ_{k-1} is white noise. In other words, the parameter vector model (3) corresponds to a stationary process, with an identity transition matrix, driven by white noise. We can define a new state vector that augments the two vectors together as follows:

$$z_k = \begin{bmatrix} x_k \\ \theta_k \end{bmatrix} = \begin{bmatrix} f\left(x_{k-1}, u_{k-1}, \theta_{k-1}, w_{k-1}\right) \\ \theta_{k-1} + \gamma_{k-1} \end{bmatrix} \quad (4)$$

where z_k is assumed to follow a Gaussian model as $z_k \sim N(\mu_k, \lambda_k)$, and where at any time k the expectation μ_k and the covariance matrix λ_k are both random. Also, defining the augmented vector,

$$\varepsilon_{k-1} = \begin{bmatrix} w_{k-1} \\ \gamma_{k-1} \end{bmatrix} \quad (5)$$

the model (2) can be written as:

$$\begin{aligned} z_k &= \Im\left(z_{k-1}, u_{k-1}, \varepsilon_{k-1}\right) \\ y_k &= \Re\left(z_k, u_k, v_k\right) \end{aligned} \quad (6)$$

B. Time-Variant Evolution Systems

Instead of the kinematic parametric model (Kotecha and Djuric, 2003) which is usually used in estimation problems, we employ a time-variant evolution systems (Vermaak et al., 2003). This model is more appropriate to practical non-linear and non-Gaussian situations where no *a priori* information on the state value is available. The state variable z_k at instant k is assumed to follow a Gaussian model, where the expectation μ_k and the precision matrix λ_k are both random. Gaussian distribution for the expectation and Whishart distribution for the precision matrix form a practical choice for the filtering implementation. The hidden state z_k is extended to an augmented state $\alpha_k = \left(z_k, \mu_k, \lambda_k\right)$, yielding a hierarchical model as follows,

$$\begin{cases} \mu_k \sim N\left(\mu_k \,|\, \mu_{k-1}, \overline{\lambda}\right) \\ \lambda_k \sim W_n\left(\overline{S} \,|\, \overline{n}\right) \\ z_k \sim N\left(\mu_k, \lambda_k\right) \end{cases} \quad (7)$$

where the fixed hyperparameters $\overline{\lambda}, \overline{S}, and\ \overline{n}$ are respectively the random walk precision matrix, the degrees of freedom and the precision of the Wishart distribution. Note that assuming random mean and covariance for the state z_k leads to a prior probability distribution covering a wide range of tail behaviors allowing discrete jumps in the state variable.

In fact, the marginal state distribution is obtained by integrating over the mean and precision matrix:

$$p(z_k \,|\, z_{k-1}) = \int p(z_k \,|\, \mu_k, \lambda_k) p(\mu_k, \lambda_k \,|\, x_{k-1}) d\mu_k \lambda_k \quad (8)$$

where the integration with respect to the precision matrix leads to the known class of scale mixture distributions introduced by Barndorff-Nielsen (Barndorff-Nielsen, 1977). Low values of the degrees of freedom $\overline{n}$ reflects the heavy tails of the marginal distribution $p(z_k \,|\, z_{k-1})$.

Particle filtering methods offer a number of significant advantages over other conventional methods. However, since they use the prior distribution as the importance distribution (Doucet & Johansen, 2009), the latest data observation is not considered and not taken into account when evaluating the weights of the particles. Even this choice of the importance sampling distribution has computational advantages, it can cause filtering divergence. In cases where the likelihood distribution is too small compared to the prior distribution, very few particles will have significant weights. Hence, a better proposal distribution that takes the latest observation data into account is needed. The VF yields an optimal choice of the sampling distribution over the state variable by minimizing the Kullback-Leibler (KL) divergence. In addition, compared to the particle filtering method, the computational cost and the memory requirements are dramatically reduced by the variational approximation in the prediction phase. In fact, the expectations involved in the computation of the predictive distribution have closed forms, avoiding the use of Monte Carlo integration. Next, we present the variational Bayesian filter algorithm.

C. Variational Bayesian Filter

The variational approach consists in approximating $p(\alpha_k \mid z_{1:k})$ by a separable distribution $q(\alpha_k) = q(x_k)q(\mu_k)q(\lambda_k)$ that minimizes the Kullback-Leibler divergence (KLD) between the true filtering distribution and the approximate distribution,

$$D_{KL}\left(q\|p\right) = \int q\left(\alpha_k\right)\log\frac{q\left(\alpha_k\right)}{p\left(\alpha_k\middle|\alpha_{1:k}\right)}d\alpha_k \quad (9)$$

The minimization is subject to constraint $\int q(\alpha_k)d\alpha_k = 1$. The Lagrange multiplier method used in (Vermaak et al., 2003; Corduneanu and Bishop, 2001) shows that the updated separable approximating distribution $q(\alpha_k)$ has the following form:

$$
\begin{aligned}
q(z_k) &\propto p(y_k \mid z_k)N(z_k \mid \langle\mu_k\rangle,\langle\lambda_k\rangle)\\
q(\mu_k) &\propto N(\mu_k \mid \mu_k^*,\lambda_k^*)\\
q(\lambda_k) &\propto W_n(\lambda_k \mid S_k^*)\\
q(\mu_k \mid \mu_{k-1}) &\propto N(\langle\mu_k^p\rangle,\langle\lambda_k^p\rangle)
\end{aligned}
\quad (10)
$$

where $\langle.\rangle$ denotes the expectation operator relative to the distribution q. The parameters are iteratively updated according to the following scheme:

$$
\begin{aligned}
\mu_k^* &= \lambda_k^{*-1}(\langle\lambda_k\rangle\langle z_k\rangle + \mu_k^p\lambda_k^p)\\
\lambda_k^* &= \langle\lambda_k\rangle + \lambda_k^p\\
n^* &= \bar{n} + 1\\
S_k^* &= (\langle z_k z_k^T\rangle - \langle z_k\rangle\langle\mu_k\rangle^T + \langle\mu_k\rangle\langle z_k\rangle^T + \langle\mu_k\mu_k^T\rangle + \bar{S}^{-1})^{-1}\\
\mu_k^p &= \mu_{k-1}^*\\
\lambda_k^p &= (\lambda_{k-1}^{*-1} + \bar{\lambda}^{-1})
\end{aligned}
$$

$$(11)$$

In fact, taking into account the separable approximate distribution at time $k-1$, the predictive distribution is written,

$$
\begin{aligned}
p(\alpha_{k-1} \mid z_{1:k-1}) &\propto \int p(\alpha_k \mid \alpha_{k-1})q(\alpha_{k-1})d\alpha_{k-1}\\
&\propto p(z_k,\lambda_k \mid \mu_k)q_p(\mu_k)
\end{aligned}
\quad (12)
$$

The exponential form solution, which minimizes the Kullback-Leibler divergence between the predictive distribution $p(\alpha_k \mid z_{1:k-1})$ and the separable approximate distribution $q_{k|k-1}(\alpha)$, yields Gaussian distributions for the state and its mean and Wishart distribution for the precision matrix:

$$
\begin{aligned}
q_{k|k-1}(z_k) &\propto N(\langle\mu_k\rangle_{q_{k|k-1}},\langle\lambda_k\rangle_{q_{k|k-1}})\\
q_{k|k-1}(\mu_k) &\propto N(\mu_{k|k-1}^*,\lambda_{k|k-1}^*)\\
q_{k|k-1}(\lambda_k) &\propto N_n(V_{k|k-1}^*,n_{k|k-1}^*)
\end{aligned}
\quad (13)
$$

where the parameters are updated according to the same iterative scheme as and the expectations are exactly computed in Box 1.and the predictive expectations of the target state are now evaluated by the following expressions:

$$
\begin{aligned}
\langle z_k\rangle_{q_{k|k-1}} &= \langle\mu_k\rangle_{q_{k|k-1}}\\
\langle z_k z_k^T\rangle_{q_{k|k-1}} &= \langle\lambda_k\rangle_{q_{k|k-1}}^{-1} + \langle\mu_k\rangle_{q_{k|k-1}}\langle\mu_k\rangle_{q_{k|k-1}}^T
\end{aligned}
\quad (15)
$$

Box 1.

$$
\mu_k^p = \mu_{k-1}^*
$$
$$
\lambda_k^p = (\lambda_{k-1}^{*}{}^{-1} + \bar{\lambda}^{-1})
$$
$$
\mu_{k|k-1}^* = \lambda_{k|k-1}^{*}{}^{-1}(\langle \lambda_k \rangle_{k|k-1} \langle z_k \rangle_{k|k-1} + \mu_k^p \lambda_k^p)
$$
$$
\lambda_{k|k-1}^* = \langle \lambda_k \rangle_{k|k-1} + \lambda_k^p
$$
$$
n_{k|k-1}^* = \bar{n} + 1 \tag{14}
$$
$$
S_k^* = (\langle z_k z_k^T \rangle_{q_{k|k-1}} - \langle z_k \rangle_{q_{k|k-1}} \langle \mu_k \rangle_{q_{k|k-1}}^T + \langle \mu_k \rangle_{q_{k|k-1}} \langle z_k \rangle_{q_{k|k-1}}^T + \langle \mu_k \mu_k^T \rangle_{q_{k|k-1}} + \bar{S}^{-1})^{-1}
$$

In the next Section, these state estimation techniques (EKF, UKF, PF, and VF) are used to estimate the states variables (the leaf-area index LAI, the volumetric water content of the layer 1, HUR1 and the volumetric water content of the layer 2, HUR2) as well as the model parameters of a LSM process.

3. SIMULATIONS RESULTS ANALYSIS

A. Crop Model

The original data were issued from experiments carried out on a silty soil in Belgium, with a wheat crop (Triticum aestivum L., cultivar Julius), during 2 consecutive years, the crop seasons 2008-09 and 2009-10. The experimental blocks were prepared on two soil types (loamy and sandy loam), corresponding to the agro-environmental conditions of the Hesbaye region in Belgium. The measurements were the results of four repetitions by date, nitrogen level, soil type and crop season. Each repetition was performed on a small block (2 m × 6 m) within the original experiment as a complete randomised block distribution, spread over the field within each soil type, to ensure measurement independence. A wireless microsensor network (eKo pro series system, Crossbow) was used to continuously characterize the soil (water content,

suction, temperature at two depths: 20 and 40 cm) and the atmosphere (radiation, temperature, relative humidity, wind speed) within the vegetation. Pluviometry data were also acquired in the experimental field. The plant characteristics (LAI and biomass) were also measured using reference techniques at regular intervals (2 weeks) along the crop seasons. The measurements were performed since the middle of February (around Julian day 410) till harvest. During the season 2008-2009, yields were quite high and close to the optimum of the cultivar. This was mainly explained by the good weather conditions and a sufficient nitrogen nutrition level. The season 2009-2010 was known to induce deep water stresses, and thus characterized by yield losses.

The model for which the methods were tested is Mini-STICS model. The equations are presented in (Makowski et al., 2004), and the parameters given at Table 1. The dynamic equations indicate how each state variable evolves from one day to the next as a function of the current values of the state variables, of the explanatory variables, and of the parameters value. Encoding these equations over time allows one to eliminate the intermediate values of the state variables and relate the state variables at any time to the explanatory variables on each day.

In the first step we are interested to compare the estimation performances of EKF, UKF, PF and VF in estimating three state variables of the

Table 1. Model parameters (Tremblay and Wallach, 2004)

Parameter name	Meaning	True value
ADENS (-)	Parameter of compensation between stem number and plant density	−0.8
BDENS (plants m^{-2})	Maximum density above which there is competition between plants	1.25
CROIRAC (cm degree − day^{-1})	Growth rate of the root front	0.25
DLAIMAX (m^2 leaves m^{-2} soil degreedays^{-1})	Maximum rate of the setting up of LAI	0.0078
EXTIN (-)	Extinction coefficient of photosynthetic active radiation in the canopy	0.9
KMAX (-)	Maximum crop coefficient for water requirements	1.2
LVOPT (cm root cm^{-3} s)	Optimum root density	0.5
PSISTO (bars)	Absolute value of the potential of stomatal closing	10
PSISTURG (bars)	Absolute value of the potential of the beginning of decrease in the cellular extension	4
RAY ON (cm)	Average radius of roots	0.02
TCMIN (°C)	Minimum temperature of growth	6
TCOPT (°C)	Optimum temperature of growth	32
ZPENTE (cm)	Depth where the root density is 1/2 of the surface root density for the reference profile	120
ZPRLIM (cm)	Maximum depth of the root profile for the reference profile	150

mini-STICS model: the leaf-area index LAI, the volumetric water content of the layer 1, HUR1 and the volumetric water content of the layer 2, HUR2. Based on the model equations described in (Makowski et al., 2004), the mathematical model of the LAI and soil moisture (called in the rest of the document LSM model) is given by:

$$LAI(t) = f_1\left(LAI(t-1) + \theta\right)$$
$$HUR1(t) = f_2(HUR1(t-1) + \theta) \quad (16)$$
$$HUR2(t) = f_3(HUR2(t-1) + \theta)$$

where t is the time, $f_{1:3}$ are the corresponding model functions, and θ is the vector of parameters driving the simulations (Table 1). LAI is the leaf area index and HUR1 (resp. HUR2) is the volumetric water content of the layer 1 (resp. the layer 2). Discretizing the model (15) using a sampling interval of "t (one day), it can be written as,

$$LAI_k = \left[f_1(\theta)\right]\Delta t + LAI_{k-1} + w^1_{k-1}$$
$$HUR1_k = [f_2(\theta)]\Delta t + HUR1_{k-1} + w^2_{k-1} \quad (17)$$
$$HUR2_k = [f_3(\theta)]\Delta t + HUR2_{k-1} + w^3_{k-1}$$

where $w^j_{j\in\{1,...,3\}}$ is a process Gaussian noise with zero mean and known variance $\sigma^2_{\gamma^j}$.

B. Sampling Data Generation

To obtain original dynamic data, the model was first used to simulate the temporal responses LAI_k, $HUR1_k$, $HUR2_k$ on basis of the recorded climatic variables of the crop season "2008-2009". The sampling time used for discretization was 1 day.

Moreover, to characterize the ability of the different approaches to estimate both the states and the parameters at same time, "true" parameter values were chosen (Table 1). The advantage of working by simulation rather than on real data is that the true parameter values are known. It is thus possible to calculate the quality of the estimated parameters and the predictive quality of the adjusted model for each method. The drawback is that the generality of the results is hard to know. The results may depend on the details of the model, on the way the data are generated and on the specific data that are used. The simulated values, assumed to be noise free, are shown in Figure 1. The evolution of LAI during the wheat's lifecycle presents the three expected phases, growth, stability, and senescence. Daily variations of shallow ground water show fluctuations that were damped in the subsoil layer $30 - 50$ cm.

These simulated states were then contaminated with zero mean Gaussian errors, i.e., the measurement noise $v_{k-1} \sim N(0, \sigma_v^2)$, where $\sigma_v^2 = 0.1$.

C. Comparative Study 1: Estimation of State Variables from Noisy Measurements

In the first scenario, it is assumed that the model parameters are known and the objective is to estimate only the state variables, LAI, HUR1, and HUR2. Therefore, we consider the state vector that we wish to estimate as:

$$z_k = x_k = [LAI_k \, HUR1_k \, HUR2_k] \qquad (18)$$

Eventually, to perform comparison between the techniques, the estimation root mean square errors (*RMSE*) criteria are used and calculated on the states (with respect to the noise free data)

$$RMSE = \sqrt{E((x - \hat{x})^2)} \qquad (19)$$

where x (resp. $\hat{x}$) is the true parameter/state (resp. the estimated parameter/state).

*Figure 1. Simulated LSM data used in estimation: state variables (**LAI** leaf area index, **HUR**1 volumetric water content of the layer 1; **HUR**2 volumetric water content of the layer 2)*

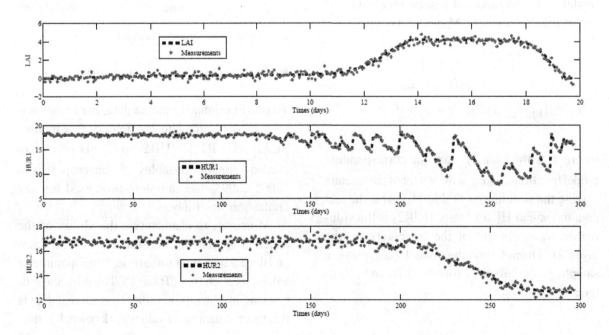

The simulation results of estimating the three states LAI_k, $HUR1_k$ and $HUR2_k$ using EKF, UKF, PF, and VF are shown in Figures 2(a,b,c), Figures 2(d,e,f), Figures 2(g,h,i), Figures 2(j,k,l) respectively. Also, the estimation root mean square errors (*RMSE*) for the estimated states are presented in Table 2. It can be observed from Figure 3 and Table 2 that EKF resulted in the worst performance of all estimation techniques, which is expected due to the limited ability of EKF to accurately estimate the mean and covariance matrix of the estimated states through lineralization of the nonlinear process model. The results also show that the PF provides a significant improvement over the UKF. This is because the covariance is propagated through linearization of the underlying non-linear model, when the state transition and observation models are highly non-linear. VF provides a significant improvement over the PF, which is due to the fact that the VF yields an optimal choice of the sampling distribution, $p(\alpha_k|\alpha_{k-1}, y_k)$, by minimizing a KL divergence criterion that also utilizes the observed data y_k.

D. Comparative Study 2: Simultaneous Estimation of State Variables and Model Parameters

The model (17) assumes that the parameters are fixed and/or have been determined previously. However, the model involves several parameters that are usually not exactly known, or that have to be estimated. Estimating these parameters, to completely define the model, usually requires several experiment setups, which can be expensive and challenging in practice. In a second step, in this work, we propose to use a Bayesian approach that can considerably simplify the task of modeling compared to the conventional experimentally intensive methods. Let's thus consider that some of the parameters have to be estimated to improve the simulations, by example the *ADENS*, *DLAIMAX*,

PSISTURG, *EXTIN*, and *LVOPT* parameters. *ADENS* is the parameter of compensation between stem number and plant density, *DLAIMAX* is the maximum rate of the setting up of LAI, *PSISTURG* is the absolute value of the potential of the beginning of decrease in the cellular extension, *EXTIN* is the extinction coefficient of photosynthetic active radiation in the canopy, and *LVOPT* is the optimum root density. To estimate these parameters, the following equations that describe their evolution are also needed:

$$ADENS_k = ADENS_{k-1} + \gamma_{k-1}^1$$

$$DLAIMAX_k = DLAIMAX_{k-1} + \gamma_{k-1}^2$$

$$PSISTURG_k = PSISTURG_{k-1} + \gamma_{k-1}^3$$

$$EXTIN_k = EXTIN_{k-1} + \gamma_{k-1}^4$$

$$LVOPT_k = LVOPT_{k-1} + \gamma_{k-1}^5 \tag{20}$$

where $\gamma_{j\in\{1,\dots,5\}}^j$ is a process Gaussian noise with zero mean and known variance σ_γ^2. Combining (19) and (20), one obtains:

$$
\begin{aligned}
f_1 &: LAI_k = [g_1(\theta_{k-1})]\Delta t + LAI_{k-1} + w_{k-1}^1 \\
f_2 &: HUR1_k = [g_2(\theta_{k-1})]\Delta t + HUR1_{k-1} + w_{k-1}^2 \\
f_3 &: HUR2_k = [g_3(\theta_{k-1})]\Delta t + HUR2_{k-1} + w_{k-1}^3 \\
f_4 &: ADENS_k = ADENS_{k-1} + \gamma_{k-1}^1 \\
f_5 &: DLAIMAX_k = DLAIMAX_{k-1} + \gamma_{k-1}^2 \\
f_6 &: PSISTURG_k = PSISTURG_{k-1} + \gamma_{k-1}^3 \\
f_7 &: EXTIN_k = EXTIN_{k-1} + \gamma_{k-1}^4 \\
f_8 &: LVOPT_k = LVOPT_{k-1} + \gamma_{k-1}^5
\end{aligned}
\tag{21}
$$

Figure 2. Estimation of state variables using various state estimation techniques (comparative study 1)

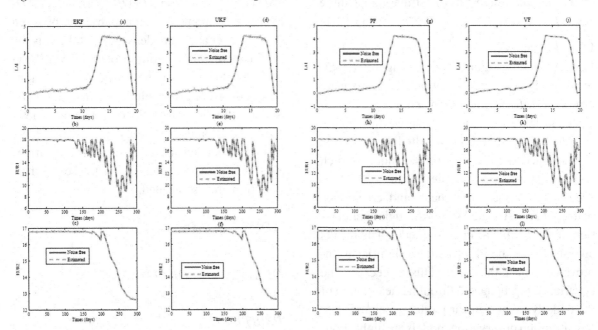

Table 2. Root mean square errors (RMSE) of estimated states

Technique		RMSE		Means at Steady State
	m2leavesm- 2soil	(%)	(%)	(-)
EKF	0. 0634	0. 0598	0. 0297	−0.8
UKF	0. 0612	0. 0517	0. 0201	−0.8
PF	0. 0358	0. 0347	0. 0251	−0.8
VF	0. 0190	0. 0187	0. 0122	−0.8

where $f_{k \in \{1,...,8\}}$ are some nonlinear functions and where $w = \left(w_1, w_2, w_3 \right)^T$ and $\gamma = \left(\gamma_1, \gamma_2, \gamma_3 \right)^T$ are respectively the measurement and process noise vector, which quantify randomness at both levels. In other words, we are forming the augmented state: $z_k = \left(x_k, \theta_k \right)^T$ which is the vector that we wish to estimate. It can be given by a 8 by 1 matrix:

$$
\begin{aligned}
x_k(1,:) &\rightarrow LAI_k \\
x_k(2,:) &\rightarrow HUR1_k \\
x_k(3,:) &\rightarrow HUR2_k \\
\theta_k(1,:) &\rightarrow ADENS_k \\
\theta_k(2,:) &\rightarrow DLAIMAX_k \\
\theta_k(3,:) &\rightarrow PSISTURG_k \\
\theta_k(4,:) &\rightarrow EXTIN_k \\
\theta_k(5,:) &\rightarrow LVOPT_k
\end{aligned}
\tag{22}
$$

Figure 3. Histogram showing the RMSE of estimated states using EKF, UKF, PF and VF

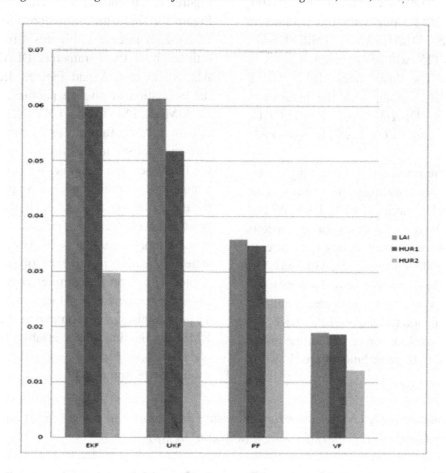

In the following, we denote $w = (w_1 w_2 w_3)^T$, and $\gamma = (\gamma_1 \gamma_2 \gamma_3 \gamma_4 \gamma_5)^T$, respectively the measurement and process noise vectors, which quantify (i) errors in the measurements and (ii) randomness in the process. The idea here is that, if a dynamic model structure is available, the model parameters can be estimated using one of state estimation technique, namely EKF, UKF, PF, and VF. To characterize the ability of the different approaches to estimate both at same time, the states and the parameters, we have chosen true parameter values and then tested each technique to see how well it could retrieve these true parameter values given the data. It was thus possible to calculate the quality of the estimated parameters and the predictive quality of the adjusted model for each method.

To go further in the analysis, the effect of the number estimated parameters on the estimation performances are investigated. Five cases summarized below are considered. In all cases, it is assumed that three states ((LAI, HUR1, and HUR2)) are measured.

- **Case 1:** The three states (LAI, HUR1 and HUR2) along with the parameter ADENS be estimated.
- **Case 2:** The three states (LAI, HUR1 and HUR2) along with the parameters ADENS, and DLAIMAX will be estimated.
- **Case 3:** The three states (LAI, HUR1 and HUR2) along with the parameters ADENS, DLAIMAX and PSISTURG will be estimated.

- **Case 4:** The three states (LAI, HUR1 and HUR2) along with the parameters ADENS, DLAIMAX, PSISTURG, and EXTIN will be estimated.
- **Case 5:** The three states (LAI, HUR1 and HUR2) along with the parameters ADENS, DLAIMAX, PSISTURG, EXTIN and LVOPT will be estimated.

Here, we are interested in examining the effect of the number of estimated parameters on the estimation performances of EKF, UKF, PF and VF and in estimating the states and parameters of the LSM process model, during the first crop season 2008-2009 (unstressed growth data). The estimation of the state variables and parameter(s) for these five cases were performed using the four state estimation techniques, EKF, UKF, PF, and VF, and the estimation results for the model parameters using these techniques are shown in

Figures 4, 5, 6, and 7, respectively. For example, Figure 3(a) shows the estimation of the parameter DLAIMAX in case 1, Figures 4(b,c) show the estimation of the parameters DLAIMAX and ADENS in case 2, and Figures 4(d,e,f) show the estimation of all five parameters ADENS, DLAIMAX, PSISTURG, EXT IN, and LV OPT in case 5. Also, Tables 3 to 7 compare the performances of the four estimation techniques for the five cases. For example, for case 1, Table 3 compares the estimation mean square errors for the three state variables LAI, HUR1 and HUR2 (with respect to the noise-free data) and the mean of the estimated parameter DLAIMAX at steady state (i.e., after convergence of parameter(s)). Tables 4 to 7 present similar comparisons for cases 2-5, respectively. Moreover, Figures 8 to 12 present histograms comparing the estimation RMSE for the three state variables (LAI, HUR1 and HUR2), respectively, using the various state estimation techniques.

Figure 4. Estimation of the LSM model parameters using EKF for all cases - case 1: (a), case 2: (b),(c), case 3: (d),(e),(f), case 4: (g),(h),(i),(j), case 5: (k),(l),(m),(n,),(p)

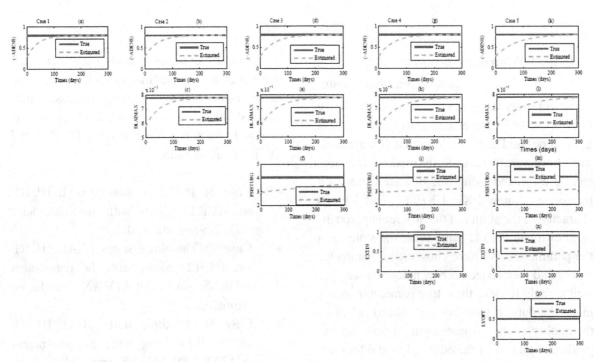

Figure 5. Estimation of the LSM model parameters using UKF for all cases - case 1: (a), case 2: (b),(c), case 3: (d),(e),(f), case 4: (g),(h),(i),(j), case 5: (k),(l),(m),(n,),(p)

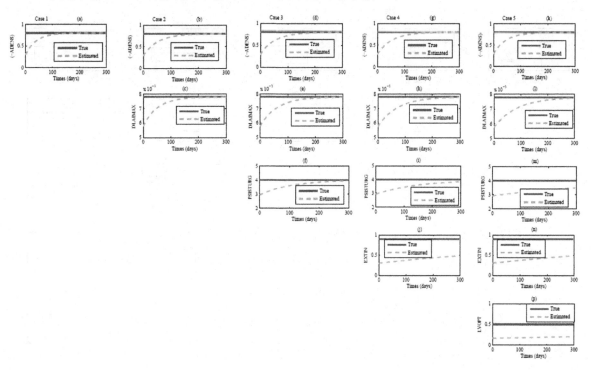

Figure 6. Estimation of the LSM model parameters using PF for all cases - case 1: (a), case 2: (b),(c), case 3: (d),(e),(f), case 4: (g),(h),(i),(j), case 5: (k),(l),(m),(n,),(p)

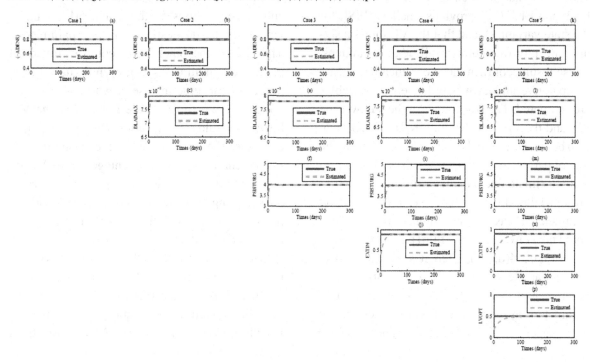

Figure 7. Estimation of the LSM model parameters using VF for all cases - case 1: (a), case 2: (b),(c), case 3: (d),(e),(f), case 4: (g),(h),(i),(j), case 5: (k),(l),(m),(n,),(p)

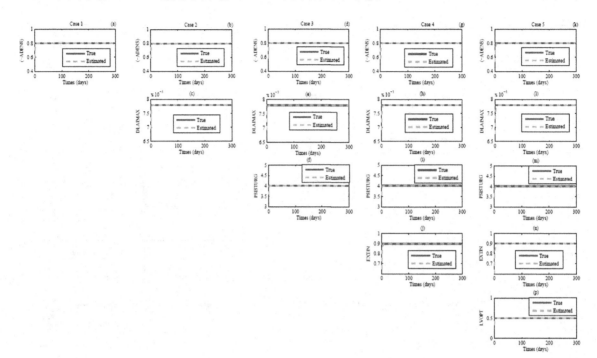

It can be seen from the results presented in Tables 3-7 that in all cases, the PF outperforms UKF and EKF (i.e., provides smaller RMSE for the state variables), and that the VF shows a significant improvement over all other techniques. These results confirm those obtained in the first comparative study, where only the state variables are estimated. The advantages of the VF over the PF (and the PF over the the UKF and EKF) can also be seen through their abilities to estimate the model parameters. For example, EKF could perfectly estimate one parameter in case 1 (see Figure 4(a)), but it took longer to estimate a second parameter in case 2 (see Figures 4(b,c)), and it could not converge for the third parameter in case 3 (see Figure 4(d,e,f)), where it is used to estimate three parameters. While, UKF could estimate one parameter in case 1 (see Figure 5(a)) and two parameters in case 2 (see Figure 5(b,c)), but it took longer to estimate a third parameter in case

3 (see Figures 5(d,e,f)), and it could not converge for the fourth and the fifth parameters in cases 4 and 5 (see Figures 5(g,h,i,j) and 5(k,l,m,n,p)), where it is used to estimate all five parameters. The PF, on the other hand, could estimate all parameters in all cases 1-5, even though it took longer to converge in case 5, where all five parameters are estimated (see Figure 6). The VF, however, could estimate all parameters in all five cases (see Figure 7), and converged faster than all other techniques. These advantages of the VF are due to the fact it provides an optimum choice of the sampling distribution used to approximate the posterior density function, which also accounts for the observed data.

The results also show that the number of estimated parameters affect the estimation accuracy of the estimated state variables. In other words, for all estimation techniques, the estimation RMSE of LAI, HUR1 and HUR2 increases from

Table 3. Root mean square errors (RMSE) of estimated states and mean of estimated parameter - case 1

Technique		RMSE		Mean at Steady State
	m2leaves m-2 soil	(%)	(%)	(-)
EKF	0. 0814	0. 0841	0. 0411	−0.8
UKF	0. 0758	0. 0798	0. 0358	−0.8
PF	0. 0511	0. 0581	0. 0315	−0.8
VF	0. 0315	0. 0317	0. 0278	−0.8

Table 4. Root mean square errors of estimated states and mean of estimated parameters - case 2

Technique		RMSE		Mean at steady state	
	m2 leaves m-2 soil	(%)	(%)	(-)	(m2leavesm−2 soilde-greedays−1)
EKF	0. 105	0. 119	0. 0493	−0.8	0.0078
UKF	0. 0944	0. 104	0. 0423	−0.8	0.0078
PF	0. 0798	0. 091	0. 0412	−0.8	0.0078
VF	0. 0548	0. 0651	0. 0298	−0.8	0.0078

Table 5. Root mean square errors (RMSE) of estimated states and mean of estimated parameters - case 3

Technique		RMSE		Mean at steady state		
	m2leavesm-2soil	(%)	(%)	(-)	(m2 leaves m−2 soil degree days−1)	(bars)
EKF	0. 131	0. 142	0. 061	−0.8	0.0078	Did not converge (DNC)
UKF	0. 125	0. 134	0. 054	−0.8	0.0078	4
PF	0. 117	0. 1023	0. 045	−0.8	0.0078	4
VF	0. 094	0. 0758	0. 0354	−0.8	0.0078	4

Table 6. Root mean square errors (RMSE) of estimated states and mean of estimated parameters - case 4

Technique		RMSE		Mean at Steady State			
	m2leavesm-2soil	(%)	(%)	(-)	(m2 leaves m−2 soil degree days−1)	(bars)	(bars)
EKF	0. 187	0. 202	0. 112	−0.8	0.0078	DNC	DNC
UKF	0. 165	0. 189	0. 092	−0.8	0.0078	DNC	DNC
PF	0. 141	0. 149	0. 085	−0.8	0.0078	4	0.9
VF	0. 113	0. 093	0. 0614	−0.8	0.0078	4	0.9

Table 7. Root mean square errors (RMSE) of estimated states and mean of estimated parameters - case 5

Technique	RMSE				Mean at steady state			
	m2leavesm-2soil	(%)	(%)	(-)	(m2 leaves m−2 soil degree days−1)	(bars)	(bars)	(-)
EKF	0. 221	0. 235	0. 178	−0.8	0.0078	DNC	DNC	DNC
UKF	0. 204	0. 214	0. 196	−0.8	0.0078	DNC	DNC	DNC
PF	0. 149	0. 158	0. 103	−0.8	0.0078	4	0.9	0.5
VF	0. 125	0. 102	0. 096	−0.8	0.0078	4	0.9	0.5

the first comparative study (where only the state variables are estimated) to case 1 (where only one parameter, DLAIMAX, is estimated) to case 5 (where all five parameters, ADENS, DLAIMAX, PSISTURG, EXT IN, and LV OPT, are estimated). For example, the RMSEs obtained using EKF for LAI in the first comparative study and cases 1-5 of the second comparative study are 0.0634, 0.0814, 0.105, 0.131, 0.187 and 0.221, respectively, which increase as the number of estimated parameters increases (refer to Tables 3-7). This observation is valid for the other state variables HUR1 and HUR2 and for all other estimation techniques, UKF, PF and VF.

Figure 8. Histogram showing the RMSE of estimated states for case 1 using EKF, UKF, PF and VF

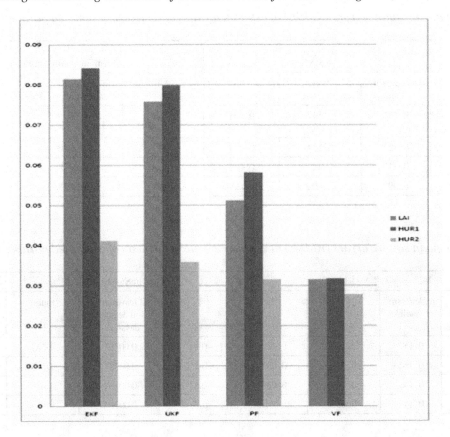

Figure 9. Histogram showing the RMSE of estimated states for case 2 using EKF, UKF, PF and VF

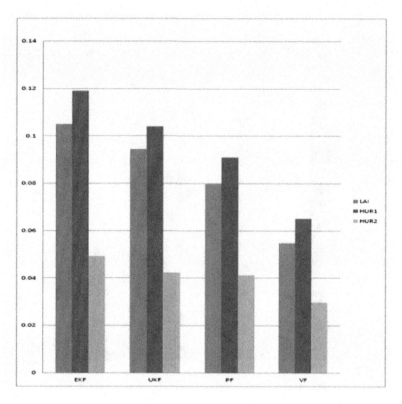

Figure 10. Histogram showing the RMSE of estimated states for case 3 using EKF, UKF, PF and VF

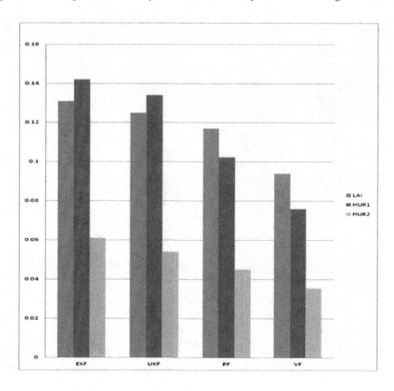

Figure 11. Histogram showing the RMSE of estimated states for case 4 using EKF, UKF, PF and VF

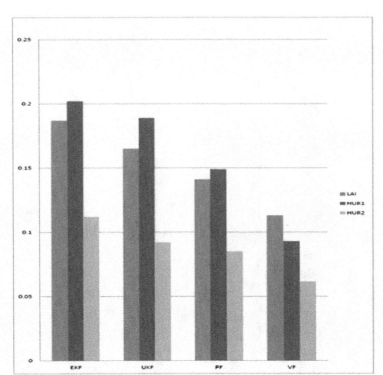

Figure 12 Histogram showing the RMSE of estimated states for case 5 using EKF, UKF, PF and VF

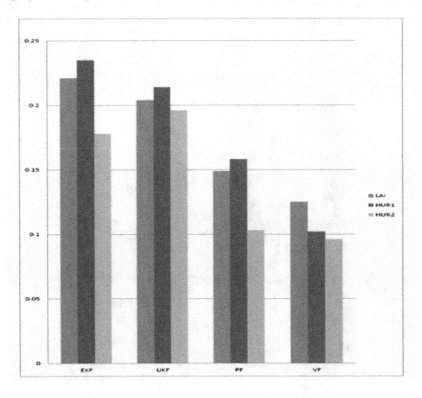

E. The Effect of Driving Variables

Eventually, to achieve the research, the effect of the driving variables are determined. The five studied cases presented at step 2 are applied on the climatic weather database of the crop season 2009- 2010. This procedure was furthermore developed since the PSISTURG parameter was optimised at cases 2 and 3, while the climatic season 2008-2009 was known not to induce stresses. We applied the different algorithms described above, EKF, UKF, PF and VF to simulate the responses of LAI, HUR1 and HUR2 as functions of time, in the second crop season 2009-2010 (season with deep water stresses). And respectively the above techniques are used for estimating the five model parameters, ADENS, DLAIMAX, PSISTURG, EXTIN, and LVOPT. From Tables 8 to 12, we can show that variational Bayesian filtering algorithm outperforms the classical algorithms, and demonstrate the performance and the good behavior of the proposed algorithm when the growing season is varied. Moreover, Figures 13 to 17 present histograms comparing the estimation RMSE for the three state variables (LAI, HUR1 and HUR2), respectively, using the four state estimation techniques EKF, UKF, PF and VF.

4. CONCLUSION

In this chapter, state estimation techniques are used to predict simultaneously three state variates (Leaf area index (LAI) and soil moisture of two soil layers, HUR1 and HUR2) for a winter wheat crop model and several parameters. Various state estimation techniques, which include the extended Kalman filter (EKF), unscented Kalman filter (UKF), particle filter (PF), and variational Bayesian filter (VF) are compared as they are used to achieve this objective.

These techniques (i.e., EKF, UKF, PF and VF) have been extended to better handle nonlinear and non-Gaussian processes with no a priori information on the state, by utilizing a time-varying assumption of statistical parameters. The time-varying assumption of statistical parameters is assumed here to further capture the uncertainty of the state distribution.

Two comparative studies have been conducted to compare the estimation performances of these four estimation techniques. In the first comparative study, EKF, UKF, PF and VF are used to estimate the three state variables, LAI, HUR1, and HUR2. In the second comparative study, the state variables and the model parameters are simultaneously estimated, and the effect of number of estimated parameters on the performances of the four estimation techniques is investigated.

The simulation results of both comparative studies show that the PF provides a higher accuracy than the EKF and the UKF due to the limited ability of the EKF and the UKF to deal with highly nonlinear process models. The results also show that the VF provides a significant improvement over the PF. This is because, unlike the PF which

Table 8. Root mean square errors (RMSE) of estimated states and mean of estimated parameter - case 1

Technique	RMSE			Mean at steady state
	m2leavesm- 2soil	(%)	(%)	(-)
EKF	0. 0939	0. 0901	0. 0461	−0.8
UKF	0. 0714	0. 0745	0. 0387	−0.8
PF	0. 0542	0. 0531	0. 0342	−0.8
VF	0. 0341	0. 0357	0. 0232	−0.8

Table 9. Root mean square errors of estimated states and mean of estimated parameters - case 2

	m2leavesm-2soil	(%)	(%)	(-)	(m2 leaves m−2 soil degree days−1)
EKF	0. 1502	0. 1589	0. 0723	−0.8	0.0078
UKF	0. 122	0. 1325	0. 0618	−0.8	0.0078
PF	0. 0988	0. 0957	0. 0592	−0.8	0.0078
VF	0. 0638	0. 0557	0. 0364	−0.8	0.0078

Table 10. Root mean square errors (RMSE) of estimated states and mean of estimated parameters - case 3

Technique	RMSE			Mean at steady state		
	m2leavesm-2soil	(%)	(%)	(-)	(m2 leaves m−2 soil degree days−1)	(bars)
EKF	0. 213	0. 204	0. 141	−0.8	0.0078	DNC
UKF	0. 183	0. 175	0. 115	−0.8	0.0078	4
PF	0. 1431	0. 1433	0. 0945	−0.8	0.0078	4
VF	0. 0847	0. 0859	0. 0594	−0.8	0.0078	4

Table 11. Root mean square errors (RMSE) of estimated states and mean of estimated parameters - case 4

Technique	RMSE			Mean at steady state			
	m2leavesm-2soil	(%)	(%)	(-)	(m2 leaves m−2 soil degree days−1)	(bars)	(bars)
EKF	0. 2161	0. 235	0. 155	−0.8	0.0078	DNC	DNC
UKF	0. 191	0. 195	0. 124	−0.8	0.0078	DNC	DNC
PF	0. 1435	0. 1454	0. 096	−0.8	0.0078	4	0.9
VF	0. 0853	0. 087	0. 070	−0.8	0.0078	4	0.9

Table 12. Root mean square errors (RMSE) of estimated states and mean of estimated parameters - case 5

Technique	RMSE				Mean at steady state			
	m2 leaves m- 2soil	(%)	(%)	(-)	(m2 leaves m−2 soil degree days−1)	(bars)	(bars)	(-)
EKF	0. 226	0. 255	0. 168	−0.8	0.0078	DNC	DNC	DNC
UKF	0. 196	0. 212	0. 135	−0.8	0.0078	DNC	DNC	DNC
PF	0. 145	0. 1464	0. 0975	−0.8	0.0078	4	0.9	0.5
VF	0.085	0. 0902	0. 0814	−0.8	0.0078	4	0.9	0.5

Figure 13. Histogram showing the RMSE of estimated states for case 1 using EKF, UKF, PF and VF

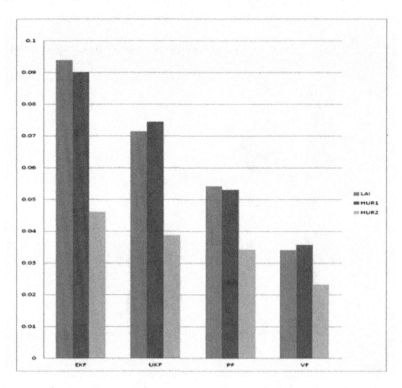

Figure 14. Histogram showing the RMSE of estimated states for case 2 using EKF, UKF, PF and VF

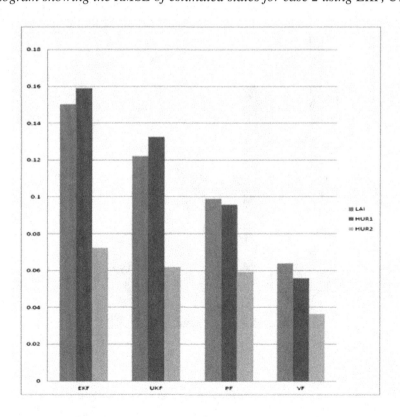

Figure 15. Histogram showing the RMSE of estimated states for case 3 using EKF, UKF, PF and VF

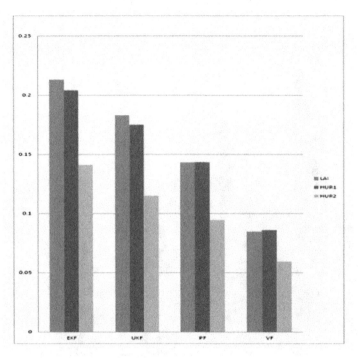

Figure 16. Histogram showing the RMSE of estimated states for case 4 using EKF, UKF, PF and VF

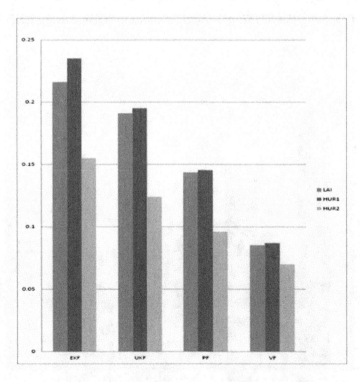

Figure 17 Histogram showing the RMSE of estimated states for case 5 using EKF, UKF, PF and VF

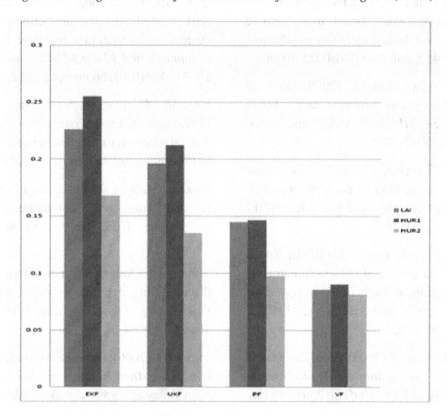

depends on the choice of sampling distribution used to estimate the posterior distribution, the VF yields an optimum choice of the sampling distribution, which also utilizes the observed data. The results of the second comparative study show that, for all techniques, estimating more model parameters affects the estimation accuracy as well as the convergence of the estimated states and parameters. The VF, however, still provides advantages over other methods with respect to estimation accuracy as well convergence.

REFERENCES

Barndorff-Nielsen, O. (1977). Exponentially decreasing distributions for the logarithm of particle size. *Proc. Roy. Soc.*, 401–419.

Beal, M. (2003). *Variational algorithms for approximate bayesian inference*. (Unpublished doctoral dissertation). Gatsby Computational Neuroscience Unit, University College London, London, UK.

Chen, G., Xie, Q., & Shieh, L. (1998). Fuzzy Kalman filtering. *Journal of Information Science*, 197–209.

Corduneanu, A., & Bishop, C. (2001). *Variational Bayesian model selection for mixture distribution*. Artificial Intelligence and Statistics..

Doucet, A., & Johansen, A. (2009). A tutorial on particle filtering and smoothing: Fifteen years later. In *Handbook of Nonlinear Filtering* (pp. 656–704). Academic Press..

Doucet, A., & Tadic, V. (2003). Parameter estimation in general state-space models using particle methods. *Annals of the Institute of Statistical Mathematics*, 409–422. doi:10.1007/BF02530508.

Grewal, M., & Andrews, A. (2008). *Kalman filtering: Theory and practice using MATLAB*. Hoboken, NJ: John Wiley and Sons. doi:10.1002/9780470377819.

Julier, S., & Uhlmann, J. (1997). New extension of the Kalman filter to nonlinear systems. In *Proceedings of SPIE* (pp. 182–193). SPIE. doi:10.1117/12.280797.

Kim, Y., Sul, S., & Park, M. (1994). Speed sensorless vector control of induction motor using extended kalman filter. *IEEE Transactions on Industry Applications*, *30*(5), 1225–1233. doi:10.1109/28.315233.

Kotecha, J., & Djuric, P. (2003). Gaussian particle filtering. *IEEE Transactions on Signal Processing*, 2592–2601. doi:10.1109/TSP.2003.816758.

Kotecha, J., & Djuric, P. (2003). Gaussian particle filtering. *IEEE Transactions on Signal Processing*, *51*(10), 2592–2601. doi:10.1109/TSP.2003.816758.

Ljung, L. (1979). Asymptotic behavior of the extended Kalman filter as a parameter estimator for linear systems. *IEEE Trans. on Automatic Control*, 36–50.

Makowski, D., Hillier, D., Wallach, D., Andrieu, B., & Jeuffroy, M.-H. (2006). Parameter estimation for crop models. In *Working with Dynamic Crop Models*. London: Elsevier..

Mansouri, M., Dumont, B., & Destain, M.-F. (2011). Bayesian methods for predicting LAI and soil Moisture. In *Proceedings of the 12th International Conference on Precision Agriculture (ICPA)*. Indianapolis, IN: ICPA.

Mansouri, M., Dumont, B., & Destain, M.-F. (2013). Modeling and prediction of nonlinear environmental system using bayesian methods. *Computers and Electronics in Agriculture*, *92*, 16–31. doi:10.1016/j.compag.2012.12.013.

Poyiadjis, G., Doucet, A., & Singh, S. (2005). Maximum likelihood parameter estimation in general state-space models using particle methods. In *Proceedings of the American Stat. Assoc.* ASA.

Sarkka, S. (2007). On unscented kalman filtering for state estimation of continuous-time nonlinear systems. *IEEE Trans. Automatic Control*, 1631–1641.

Simon, D. (2003). Kalman filtering of fuzzy discrete time dynamic systems. *Applied Soft Computing*, 191–207. doi:10.1016/S1568-4946(03)00034-6.

Simon, D. (2006). *Optimal state estimation: Kalman, H1, and nonlinear approaches*. Hoboken, NJ: John Wiley and Sons. doi:10.1002/0470045345.

Smidl, V., & Quinn, A. (2005). *The variational Bayes method in signal processing*. New York: Springer-Verlag..

Tremblay, M., & Wallach, D. (2004). Comparison of parameter estimation methods for crop models. *Agronomie*, *24*(6-7), 351–365. doi:10.1051/agro:2004033.

Van Der Merwe, R., & Wan, E. (2001). The square-root unscented kalman filter for state and parameter-estimation. In *Proceedings of IEEE International Conference on Acoustics, Speech, and Signal Processing*, (pp. 3461–3464). IEEE.

Vermaak, J., Lawrence, N., & Perez, P. (2003). Variational inference for visual tracking. In *Proceedings of Computer Vision and Pattern Recognition*. IEEE..

Wan, E., & Van Der Merwe, R. (2000). The unscented Kalman filter for nonlinear estimation. In *Adaptive Systems for Signal Processing, Communications, and Control Symposium*, (pp. 153–158). Academic Press.

KEY TERMS AND DEFINITIONS

Environmental Data: Environmental data is that which is based on the measurement of environmental pressures, the state of the environment and the impacts on ecosystems.

Extended Kalman Filter (EKF): EKF is an estimation technique that is applicable to nonlinear and non-Gaussian models. As the Kalman filter is applicable to linear systems, the EKF can be viewed as an extension of the Kalman filter that is applied to a linearized version of the nonlinear model.

Leaf Area Index: Leaf Area Index is a method of measurement of leaf area in a given section of ground area expressed in terms of half the square meters of leaf per square meter of ground.

Particle Filter (PF): PF, which is based on Bayesian estimation, is a sequential Monte Carlo state estimation method for nonlinear and non-Gaussian systems. The EKF and UKF algorithms do not always provide a satisfactory performance, especially for highly nonlinear processes as model linearization does not necessarily provide good estimates of the mean of the state vector and the covariance matrix of the estimation error, which are used in state estimation. These issues are addressed by the PF.

Soil Moisture: Soil moisture is the volumetric water content in the soil.

States and Parameters Estimation: State and parameter estimation is the process of obtaining the estimators of state variables and model parameters based on a dataset.

Unscented Kalman Filter (UKF): UKF is an estimation technique that uses a deterministic sampling technique known as the unscented transform to approximate the mean and the covariance of the state and parameter vector.

Variational Filter (VF): VF, which is based on Bayesian estimation, is state estimation method for nonlinear and non-Gaussian systems. It has been proposed recently to enhance state estimation because VF yields an optimal choice of the sampling distribution by minimizing a Kullback-Leibler (KL) divergence criterion. In fact, variational calculus leads to a simple Gaussian sampling distribution whose parameters (which are estimated iteratively) also utilize the observed data, which provides more accurate and computationally efficient computation of the posterior distribution.

Chapter 8
Fuzzy Modeling for Manpower Scheduling

Michael Mutingi
University of Johannesburg, South Africa & University of Botswana, Botswana

Charles Mbohwa
University of Johannesburg, South Africa

ABSTRACT

Fuzzy theory is an important phenomenon in manpower scheduling, especially in the context where managerial and employee objectives are imprecise and, worst of all, conflicting. In such fuzzy environments, developing robust tools for addressing the fuzzy nature of the problem is imperative. Decision analysts concerned with staff scheduling need robust decision support tools to construct equitable work schedules spanning over a given planning horizon so as to meet organizational objectives, to meet customer requirements, and to satisfy worker preferences. This chapter presents a framework for fuzzy modeling for manpower scheduling based on fuzzy set-theoretic concepts. First, a background on fuzzy modeling approaches is provided, together with their solution methods. Second, key characteristic dimensions of the manpower scheduling problem are identified, leading to a taxonomic framework for classifying manpower scheduling problems. Third, a framework developing fuzzy models for manpower scheduling is derived from the taxonomy, the fuzzy modeling approaches, and the fuzzy solution approaches. The fuzzy models developed can be solved by any appropriate solvers or meta-heuristic methods.

DOI: 10.4018/978-1-4666-4785-5.ch008

INTRODUCTION

Fuzziness, imprecision, or uncertainties in management objectives and employee preferences are an important area of concern in most organizations, particularly in healthcare institutions (Burke et al. 2004). For instance, fuzzy management goals and objectives, as well as employee preferences, are a common cause for concern when allocating work schedules to employees (Topaloglu and Ozkarahan, 2004). Oftentimes, the management objectives are not expressed precisely but rather in linguistic terms such as "about 8 employees for the morning shift", or "at most 40 working hours per week", or "preferably 2 night shifts per week for each employee" and other related vague expressions. Likewise, employee preferences are frequently expressed in natural language terms, such as "preferably 8 working hours per day", "at least 2 off days", and other examples. As a result, vagueness of information on management objectives as well as individual preferences leads to uncertainties that need to be addressed when constructing manpower schedules. Under such circumstances, conventional crisp models cannot capture fuzziness inherent in most real-world manpower scheduling problems. In the same vein, Burke et al. (2004) emphasized the need to utilize fuzzy modeling concepts to tackle uncertainties in practical manpower scheduling problems in healthcare institutions. Fuzzy modeling approach is a potential tool in addressing imprecise and conflicting management goals and employee preferences in the area of manpower scheduling.

In a fuzzy environment, manpower scheduling involves construction of effective work schedules spanning over a given planning horizon so as to meet organizational goals, satisfy customer requirements at an acceptable level of service quality, and satisfy worker preferences as much as possible (Ernst et al., 2004b). In this connection, suitable combinations of shifts should be selected from a number of possible shifts, subject to three types of constraints:

1. Demand coverage constraints,
2. Time related constraints, as well as
3. Employee preference constraints (Topaloglu and Ozkarahan, 2004).

Demand coverage constraints refer to the number of workers needed in each period over the course of day, throughout the planning horizon. Time related constraints express the time restrictions on personal schedules such as allowable work duration and shift times. These are influenced by national legislation, union regulations, and workplace regulations. As a result, time constraints tend to be problem specific. Preference constraints refer to the workers' requests and wishes that should be satisfied as much as possible, if high quality schedules are to be achieved. In most cases, preference constraints usually consider individual staff choices on working time allocation involving daily shift types, work patterns, or days-off assignments.

The practice of manpower scheduling is a complex undertaking that essential seeks to balance individual workloads and satisfy individual preferences leading to high quality schedules, higher worker morale, hence a more effective workforce. However, organizational objectives and individual worker preferences are usually conflicting; workers prefer individualized schedules that consider their preferences while organizations will always try to fulfill demand coverage. Perceived fairness in schedule assignments is an important measure of the quality of work schedules, without which low morale, poor performance, absenteeism and high job turnover are inevitable. Therefore, it is crucial to satisfy workers' preferences as evenly as possible. On the other hand, the manpower scheduling problem has several possible objectives including

1. Minimizing workforce size,
2. Maximizing worker preferences
3. Minimizing personnel cost,
4. Minimizing violation of demand coverage and time-related constraints.

While hard constraints must be satisfied at all times, soft constraints such as worker preferences may be violated, at a cost, in order to provide a feasible solution. In the real world, manpower scheduling is associated with inherent uncertainties that have to be addressed to come up with a higher quality schedule. Uncertainties usually arise from vagueness of information on target management objectives and individual personnel preferences. Burke et al. (2004) emphasizes the need to consider fuzzy modeling in nurse scheduling in order to deal with inherent uncertainties in the problem. The motivation behind the use of fuzzy set-theoretic approach is three-fold:

1. Decision makers often sacrifice the aspiration levels for organizational goals so as to reflect workers' preferences, hence the need to define goals using fuzzy rather than crisp conventional sets.
2. Given the real-world vagueness and uncertainties of information on management goals and workers' preferences, crisp conventional modeling methods fail to adequately represent such complexity.
3. Real-world manpower scheduling problems are often complex and multi-objective with incommensurable goals. Fuzzy modeling uses a normalization constant to treat the problem in a more realistic way.

In view of the above issues, the main purpose of this chapter is to develop fuzzy set-theoretic models, based on a taxonomy, to address uncertainties prevalent in target management objectives and individual employee preferences.

The remainder of the chapter is organized as follows: a background to fuzzy modeling approaches is presented, covering a basic introduction to fuzzy sets and fuzzy solution approaches. Thereafter, a framework of fuzzy models for manpower scheduling is presented, with new fuzzy-based multi-objective integer programming formula-

tions. Finally, the chapter ends with concluding remarks and further research directions.

FUZZY MODELING

Fuzzy Modeling Approaches

Zadeh (1965) extended the possibility theory into a formal mathematical logic tool known as *fuzzy set theory* or *fuzzy logic*, and introduced the concept for applying natural language terms, providing a means of computing with natural words. Contrary to the two-valued conventional Boolean logic, fuzzy logic is multi-valued, and it deals with degrees of membership and degrees of truth. Fuzzy logic accepts that things can be partly true and partly false at the same time. Thus, fuzzy logic is a superset of Boolean logic that has been extended to handle the concept of partial truth-values between completely true and completely false (Bezdek, 1993). From a mathematical point of view, fuzzy sets are a generalization of classical notions of sets. A fuzzy set A can be defined in terms of its characteristic function $\mu_A(x)$. Classically, a point x belongs to set A if and only if $\mu_A = 1$ and does not belong to the set if $\mu_A(x) = 0$. On the contrary, fuzzy set theory permits gradual assessment of membership (see Figure 1), defined in terms of a membership function that maps to the unit interval $[0, 1]$.

A number of membership functions such as Generalized Bell, Gaussian, Triangular and Trapezoidal can be used to represent the fuzzy membership. However, it has been shown that linear membership functions can provide equally good quality solutions with much ease (Sakawa, 1993). The triangular and trapezoidal membership functions have widely been recommended (Delgado et al., 1993). Figure 1 illustrates a typical triangular membership function. A fuzzy number A is a triangular fuzzy number if its membership function is $\mu_A : X \to [0,1]$ as given in (1);

Figure 1. Triangular fuzzy set

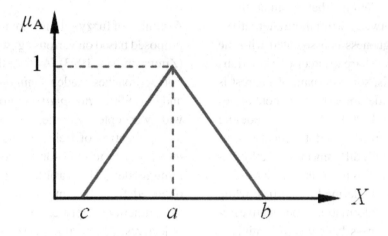

$$\mu_A(x) = \begin{cases} (x-c)/(a-c) & \text{if } c \leq x \leq a \\ (x-b)/(a-b) & \text{if } a \leq x \leq b \\ 0 & \text{if otherwise} \end{cases}$$

(1)

where, $c \leq a \leq b$, and A is the triangular fuzzy number denoted by $A = (c, a, b)$.

In a similar manner, a trapezoidal fuzzy number B is defined by its membership function $\mu_B : X \to [0,1]$ as illustrated in Figure 2. In a more mathematical form, the trapezoidal fuzzy number is defined by the expression in (2).

$$\mu_B(x) = \begin{cases} 1 & \text{if } x \leq a \\ (x-b)/(a-b) & \text{if } a \leq x \leq b \\ 0 & \text{if otherwise} \end{cases}$$ (2)

Here, a is the most preferred value, while c and b are the lower and upper bounds, respectively.

Ambiguity and vagueness are two major kinds of real world uncertainties that can be addressed

Figure 2. Trapezoidal fuzzy set

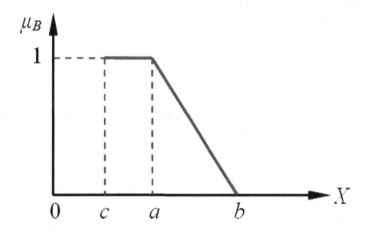

by fuzzy logic. While ambiguity is associated with one-to-many relations, that is, situations in which the choice between two or more alternatives is unspecified, vagueness is associated with the difficulty of making sharp or precise distinctions in the world; that is, some domain of interest is vague if it cannot be delimited by sharp boundaries (Inuiguchi and Ramik, 2000). From the modeling point of view, fuzzy models and statistical models possess philosophically different kinds of information: fuzzy memberships represent similarities of objects to imprecisely defined properties, while probabilities convey information about relative frequencies. Thus, fuzziness deals with deterministic plausibility and not non-deterministic probability. Linguistic variables take on linguistic values which are linguistic terms with associated degrees of membership in the set. The importance of fuzzy logic derives from the fact that most modes of human reasoning, and especially common sense reasoning, are approximate in nature. In such cases, crisp set theory can be somewhat limiting if we wish to describe a humanistic problem in a more mathematical form.

In this study, fuzzy goal programming models are developed based on fuzzy solution approaches. The advantage of the application of fuzzy set theory in goal programming is that it allows for the vague aspirations of the decision maker, which can then be qualified by humanistic language terms. In this context, each fuzzy goal needs an aspiration level determined by the decision maker, as well as the maximum and minimum bounds.

Fuzzy Solution Approaches

A number of fuzzy solution approaches have been proposed based on various aggregation operators (Zimmermann, 1993). Among these fuzzy solution approaches, Zadeh's *min operator* approach and Li (1990)'s *two-phase* approach are the most widely accepted. Zimmermann (1978) proposed the application of Bellman and Zadeh (1970)'s *min operator* to multi-objective linear programming models. The feasible fuzzy solution can be obtained from the intersection of all membership functions representing the fuzzy goals or objectives. The solution set is characterized by its membership function $\mu_F(x)$, according to the expression in Box 1.

The optimum decision is obtained from the maximum degree of membership for the fuzzy decision given by the expression,

$$\max_{x \in F} \mu_F\left(x\right) = \max_{x \in F} \min[\mu_1(x), \mu_2(x), ..., \mu_k(x)] \tag{4}$$

In order to solve model (3), Zimmermann (1978) proposed the conversion of the model into a conventional linear program by introducing an auxiliary variable λ that represents the overall satisfaction level of compromise. In this manner, a linear program can be developed according to the following expression;

Box 1.

$$\mu_F\left(x\right) = \mu_1(x) \wedge \mu_2(x) \wedge ... \wedge \mu_k(x) = \min[\mu_1(x), \mu_2(x), ..., \mu_k(x)] \tag{3}$$

Maximize λ

subject to

$$\left.\begin{array}{ll} \lambda \leq \mu_k\left(x\right), & k = 1,\ldots,q \\[6pt] g_j(x_i) \leq b_j, & i = 1,\ldots,m, \ j = 1,\ldots,n \\[6pt] x_i \geq 0, & i = 1,\ldots,m \\[6pt] \lambda \in [0,1] \end{array}\right\}$$

(5)

where, q denotes the total number of objectives under consideration, and $\mu_k(x)$ is the membership function of objective k.

Li (1990) proposed a *two-phase approach* where the first phase uses the *min operator*, and the second phase maximizes the arithmetic mean value of all memberships restricted by the original constraints and those from phase one (Tiryaki, 2006). Thus, the two-phase approach guarantees that every membership function is at least as large as the *min operator* can offer. This approach yields an efficient solution due to full compensation of the averaging operator. The following program is formulated to find an efficient solution;

$$\left.\begin{array}{l} \text{Maximize } \sum_k \lambda_k \big/ q \\[6pt] \text{subject to} \\[6pt] \lambda' \leq \lambda_k \leq \mu_k\left(x\right), \qquad \forall k \in q, \ \forall x \in X \\[6pt] \lambda', \lambda_k \in [0,1] \\[6pt] \text{Other system constraints} \end{array}\right\}$$

(6)

where, λ' is the solution obtained using the *min operator* approach.

Usually, the decision on which approach to apply is usually based on the nature and characteristics of the specific conditions of the manpower scheduling problem in question. To that effect, we propose a unified approach based on a taxonomy.

TAXONOMIC FRAMEWORK

Our taxonomic framework is based on the recognition that the general scheduling problem can conveniently be classified according to two dimensions: (i) manpower demand type and (ii) shift type. The taxonomy classifies and delineates the manpower scheduling problem based on two identified dimensions: (i) manpower demand type, and (ii) shift type. In this respect, demand is classified into three categories, that is, *task-based*, *flexible/fluctuating*, and *shift-based* demand. Furthermore, shifts are classified into two categories, that is, *flexible* and *fixed* shifts. Fixed shifts are defined by non-overlapping working time blocks and flexible shifts are characterized by overlapping or flexible time blocks. Furthermore, our framework is based on the view that the manpower scheduling problem can be synthesized from a set of three interrelated sub-problems:

1. Manpower demand modeling,
2. Tour scheduling, and
3. Schedule assignment.

Manpower Demand Modeling

This sub-problem analyses manpower requirements in terms of the number of workers required during each period. Workers are needed to carry out duties that arise from customer needs that occur over the scheduling horizon. For instance, customer needs may be specified in terms of call centre enquiries, a list of tasks, or a fixed number of workers. These customer needs are converted into work requirements in order to determine the manpower requirements for each shift time over the scheduling horizon. In practice, forecasts of customer needs are converted into manpower requirements using customer either service standards, economic standards, or productivity standards.

Tour Scheduling

Tour scheduling is a process of generating a working set of schedules covering the entire planning horizon. Logically, the process comprises (i) days-off scheduling, (ii) shift scheduling and (iii) work schedule construction.

- **Days off scheduling**: This determines how recreation or rest days are to be spread across work days for each worker; it seeks to define the sequence of days off and days on for each worker's schedule over the planning horizon. Days-off scheduling is particularly common with *flexible* and *fixed* demand patterns. This stage closely interacts with the shift scheduling sub-problem.
- **Shift scheduling:** The ultimate goal of the shift scheduling stage is to find the optimal or near-optimal number of workers to be assigned to each shift in order to meet demand, considering the days off determined in stage 2. This involves three closely related components: construction of the basic building blocks such as shifts or duties, selection, from a large pool of potential shifts, of best shifts to be worked on, and assignment of a suitable number of workers to each shift so as to meet the service demand. The basic time blocks reflect specific work regulations and rules. Shift scheduling closely interacts with work schedule construction.
- **Work schedule construction:** This stage deals with construction of tours or work schedules covering the entire planning horizon. The work schedule construction process is largely influenced by the set of time blocks or shifts selected in the shift scheduling stage. The process considers constraints related to shift sequences and demand pattern so as to ensure feasibility of the work schedules and to satisfy

the manpower requirements at all times, respectively.

Schedule Assignment

Schedule assignment entails the allocation of work schedules, developed in the work schedule construction stage, to individual workers. In most cases, schedules are assigned based on preferential bidding systems so as to satisfy worker preferences wherever possible. Work schedules may need to be allocated to workers with specific skills, particularly when specific tasks are involved. Schedule assignment and work schedule construction are closely related; hence they are often done interactively. Schedule control involves utilization of feedback obtained from the implementation of the schedules. The following section presents typical formulations for each category of the staff scheduling problem.

In order to provide a more general approach to the manpower scheduling problem, our formulations follow the taxonomy as outlined in the unified framework, delineating the problem formulations into three categories: *task-based demand*, *flexible demand* and *shift-based demand*.

SCHEDULING FOR TASK-BASED DEMAND

The process of scheduling for the task-based demand involves two major activities, that is, task-based demand modeling or task modeling, and task assignment (scheduling). In this category, demand modeling is a task planning problem that is defined as follows: for a given list of individual tasks, obtain a manpower demand pattern that satisfies all work requirements and regulations in the best possible way. In this context, the first step is to combine individual tasks into a large set of feasible duties or task sequences that can be performed by a worker (or a team of workers). The second step involves selecting, from these duties, a good working set that can cover the entire work requirements. The task scheduling process entails allocation of duties or planned tasks to individual workers (Krishnamoorthy et al., 2001). Duties should be allocated to workers with specific skills, while considering worker preferences as much as possible. Thus, schedules must be assigned based on fairness, where planning systems seek to assign workload as fairly as possible, considering planned vacations, requested free days, sick leave, among others factors.

A task or a duty is the smallest building block that can be obtained by decomposing a project, a trip, or a flight into distinct consecutive segments that can be assigned to a worker or a group of workers (Ernst et al., 2004a, Ernst et al., 2004b). There are three notable common characteristics of task-based demand scheduling:

1. In most practical cases, each task is defined by its starting time and location and its finishing time and location, and,
2. Each is determined from a given timetable, a flight, a route or trip, a project task with a start time and end time.
3. Each task requires a specific skill or a set of specific skills to be performed efficiently and effectively.

Examples of application areas in this category include transportation industry where flight legs, railway and road trips are to be assigned to workers (Ernst et al., 2004b; Teodorovic and Lucic, 1998). Of interest, is the home healthcare staff scheduling problem where home healthcare institutions decompose their activities into specific tasks to be assigned to specific healthcare workers with relevant skills (Mutingi and Mbohwa, 2013). Similar empirical cases can be found in the literature (Bachouch et al., 2009; Bachouch et al., 2010).

Crisp Model for Task-Based Demand

In this section, we present a multi-objective integer program for the task-based manpower scheduling problem. For clarity of deliberation, we make use of the following indices, parameters, and decision variables;

- **Indices:**
  - m: Number of workers available
  - n: Number of duties or task pairings
  - q: Number of individual tasks
  - i: Index for workers, $i = 1,\ldots, m$
  - j: Index for duties to be assigned, $j = 1,\ldots,n$
  - k: Index for individual tasks, $k = 1,\ldots,q$
- **Parameters:**
  - a_{jk}: 1 if duty type j includes task k, and 0 otherwise
  - r_k: Manpower demand requirements for task k
  - d_j: Duration or length of duty type j
  - p_{ij}: Preference score of worker i for duty type j to be assigned
  - *pmin*: Preference score if the most undesirable duty is assigned to a worker
  - *pmax*: Preference score if the most desirable duty is assigned to a worker
  - *cmin*: Minimum allowance for each worker for the scheduling horizon
  - *cmax*: Maximum allowance for each worker for the scheduling period
  - c: Preferred ideal allowance for each worker for the scheduling horizon
  - w: Preferred number of workers to staff for the scheduling horizon
  - c_j: Share of allowance for duty type j
  - *lh, uh*: Lower, upper bounds on working hours of each worker for the scheduling horizon
  - h_i: Preferred number of working hours of worker i

- **Decision variables:**
  - X_{ij}: 1 if worker i is assigned to duty j, and 0 otherwise
  - dp_i: Negative deviation from the maximum preference score of worker i for duty type
  - dc_i^-, dc_i^+: Negative, positive deviation from the ideal allowance for worker i
  - dh_i^-, dh_i^+: Negative, positive deviation from the preferred working hours for worker i
  - dw L: positive deviation from the preferred number of workers assigned

Objective Functions

$$\text{Minimise } z_1 = dw \tag{7}$$

$$\text{Minimise } z_2 = \sum_i^m \left(dh_i^- + dh_i^+ \right) \tag{8}$$

$$\text{Minimise } z_3 = \sum_i^m \left(dc_i^- + dc_i^+ \right) \tag{9}$$

$$\text{Minimise } z_4 = \sum_i^m dp_i \tag{10}$$

Here, objective function z_1 seeks to minimize the deviation of the number of workers assigned from the preferred number of workers. Objective z_2 is aimed at minimizing the sum of positive and negative deviations of individual working hours from the respective preferred working hours of all the assigned workers. Similarly, objective z_3 minimizes the sum of the positive and negative deviations from the ideal allowance of each worker. Finally, objective z_4 minimizes the sum of the negative deviations from the maximum preference score of each worker for duty type. The objectives are optimized subject to a number of constraints.

Constraints

$$\sum_i^m \sum_j^n a_{jk} X_{ij} = r_k \qquad \text{for all } k = 1, ..., K \tag{11}$$

$$\sum_j^n X_{ij} \leq 1 \qquad \text{for all } i = 1, ..., m \tag{12}$$

$$lh \geq \sum_j^n d_j X_{ij} \leq uh \qquad \text{for all } i = 1, ..., m \tag{13}$$

$$\sum_j^n d_j X_{ij} + dh_i^- - dh_i^+ = h_i \qquad \text{for all } i = 1, ..., m \tag{14}$$

$$\sum_j^n p_{ij} X_{ij} + dp_i \geq pmax \qquad \text{for all } i = 1, ..., m \tag{15}$$

$$\sum_j^n c_j X_{ij} + dc_i^- - dc_i^+ = c \qquad \text{for all } i = 1, ..., m \tag{16}$$

$$\sum_i^m \sum_j^n X_{ij} - dw \leq w \tag{17}$$

Constraint set (11) ensures that demand requirements for each task are satisfied at all times, while (12) ensures that each worker is assigned at most one task. Constraint set (13) takes care of the restrictions imposed on the upper and lower bounds on the total working hours assigned to each worker. Constraint set (14) limits the working hours of each worker to the respective preferred hours. Expression (15) ensures that each worker is assigned the most desirable duty type. Expression (16) ensures that each worker obtains an allowance that is as close to the most ideal allowance as possible. Finally, constraint set (17) restricts the total number of assigned workers to be as close as possible to the most preferred number of workers.

Fuzzy Model for Task-based Demand

In our fuzzy modeling framework, we consider uncertainty of the management objectives in fulfilling the desired workforce size as well as the satisfaction of the workers' preferences. Therefore it is essential to define the relevant membership functions so as to capture the uncertainties in management targets and workers' preferences.

Membership Functions

- μ_W: Membership function for the desired workforce size objective

- μ_{Hi}: Membership function for the total working hour preference for worker i

- μ_{Ti}: Membership function for duty type preference for worker i

- μ_{Ai}: Membership function for the preferred ideal share of allowance for each worker i

Membership functions such as Generalized Bell, Gaussian, Triangular and Trapezoidal can be used to represent the fuzzy membership for the management targets and individual worker's preferences, with reasonable success (Sakawa, 1993). Assuming linear membership functions for this problem category, we use the trapezoidal membership for the workforce size objective, and the triangular membership functions for the worker preference objectives. In the short term, management often sets a target workforce size to be assigned over the planning period. Denoting the preferred workforce size by w, and its lower and upper bounds by lw and uw, respectively, the membership function for the workforce size objective is presented in Box 2 (see also Figure 3).

Box 2.

$$\mu_W\left(x\right) = \begin{cases} 1 & \text{if } lw \leq \sum_{i}^{m}\sum_{j}^{n}X_{ij} \leq w \\ \left(\sum_{i}^{m}\sum_{j}^{n}X_{ij} - uw\right)\Big/\left(w - uw\right) & \text{if } w \leq \sum_{i}^{m}\sum_{j}^{n}X_{ij} \leq uw \\ 0 & \text{if otherwise} \end{cases} \tag{18}$$

Figure 3. Membership function for the workforce size objective

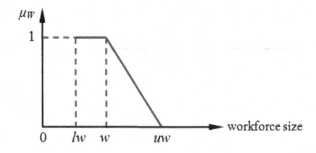

In addition to the membership function of the workforce size, individual preferences on working hours should be taken into account, such that the total working hours are close to the ideal working hours as much as possible. In this respect, the membership functions for the total working hours of each worker can be represented by a linear function. As such, assume that the membership function follows the triangular function as illustrated by the expression in Box 3 and in Figure 4.

Assuming the satisfaction for the membership of the preference score follows a linear function in the interval [*pmax*, *pmin*], the membership functions for duty type preference $\mu_{Ti}(x)$ can be represented in Box 4 (see also Figure 5).

A satisfactory schedule should enable workers to have fairly equal allowances. In real world, an ideal allowance value c, usually known in advance, is used as a target value to achieve high schedule fairness. Thus, the membership functions for the allowance (Figure 6) can be represented by fuzzy triangular functions according to the expression in Box 5.

Additional problem-specific preference membership functions can be defined for different problem scenarios in a similar manner. The fuzzy solution approach for the task-based staff scheduling problem follows.

Box 3.

$$\mu_{Hi}\left(x\right) = \begin{cases} \left(\sum_{j}^{n} d_j X_{ij} - lh\right) \Big/ \left(h_i - lh\right) & \text{if } lh \leq \sum_{j}^{n} d_j X_{ij} \leq h_i \\ \left(\sum_{j}^{n} d_j X_{ij} - uh\right) \Big/ \left(h_i - uh\right) & \text{if } h_i \leq \sum_{j}^{n} d_j X_{ij} \leq uh \\ 0 & \text{if otherwise} \end{cases} \tag{19}$$

Figure 4. Membership function for worker preferences on total working hours

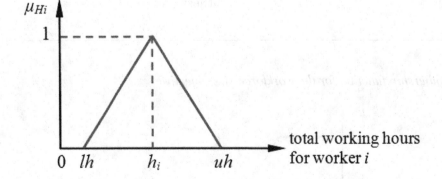

Box 4.

$$
\mu_{Ti}(x) = \begin{cases} 1 & \text{if } \sum_j^n p_{ij}X_{ij} \geq pmax \\[3mm] \left(\sum_j^n p_{ij}X_{ij} - pmin\right)\Big/(pmax - pmin) & \text{if } pmin \leq \sum_j^n p_{ij}X_{ij} \leq pmax \\[3mm] 0 & \text{if otherwise} \end{cases} \quad (20)
$$

Figure 5. Membership function for worker preference on duty type

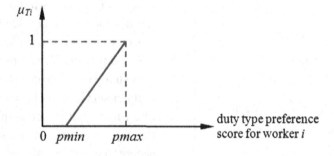

Box 5.

$$
\mu_{Ai}(x) = \begin{cases} \left(\sum_j^n c_j X_{ij} - cmin\right)\Big/(c - cmin) & \text{if } cmin \leq \sum_j^n c_j X_{ij} \leq c \\[3mm] \left(\sum_j^n c_j X_{ij} - cmax\right)\Big/(c - cmax) & \text{if } c \leq \sum_j^n c_j X_{ij} \leq cmax \\[3mm] 0 & \text{if otherwise} \end{cases} \quad (21)
$$

Figure 6. Membership function for schedule fairness on allowances

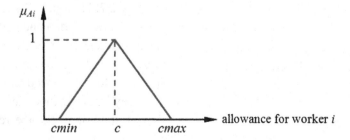

Fuzzy Solution Approach

The fuzzy solution approach for the task-based demand scheduling can be obtained by applying the Bellman and Zadeh's *min operator*. By introducing the auxiliary variable λ, the fuzzy model is then transformed into a mixed-integer programming problem. In this connection, the solution approach consists of two steps.

Step 1: Obtain λ' by solving the following mixed integer program.

$$
\left.
\begin{aligned}
&\text{Maximize } \lambda \\
&\text{subject to} \\
&\qquad \lambda \le \mu_W(x) \\
&\qquad \lambda \le \mu_{Hi}(x) \qquad i = 1,\dots m \\
&\qquad \lambda \le \mu_{Ti}(x) \qquad i = 1,\dots m \\
&\qquad \lambda \le \mu_{Ai}(x) \qquad i = 1,\dots m \\
&\qquad \mu_W(x),\ \mu_{Hi}(x),\ \mu_{Ti}(x),\ \mu_{Ai}(x),\ \lambda \in [0,1] \\
&\qquad \text{Other constraints (11) to (13)}
\end{aligned}
\right\}
$$

(22)

Step 2: Apply the *two-stage approach* to obtain a more efficient solution as shown in following model;

$$
\left.
\begin{aligned}
&\text{Maximize } \left(\lambda_W + \lambda_{Hi} + \lambda_{Ti} + \lambda_{Ai}\right)/q \\
&\text{Subject to} \\
&\qquad \lambda' \le \lambda_W \le \mu_W(x) \\
&\qquad \lambda' \le \lambda_{Hi} \le \mu_{Hi}(x) \qquad i = 1,\dots m \\
&\qquad \lambda' \le \lambda_{Ti} \le \mu_{Ti}(x) \qquad i = 1,\dots m \\
&\qquad \lambda' \le \lambda_{Ai} \le \mu_{Ai}(x) \qquad i = 1,\dots m \\
&\qquad \mu_W(x),\ \mu_{Hi}(x),\ \mu_{Ti}(x),\ \mu_{Ai}(x),\ \lambda \in [0,1] \\
&\qquad \text{Other constraints (11) to (13)}
\end{aligned}
\right\}
$$

(23)

where, q is the number of objective functions under consideration.

In this way, the mixed integer programming model can now be solved by any appropriate solvers, such as CPLEX.

SCHEDULING FOR FLEXIBLE DEMAND

Scheduling for a flexible demand follows through demand modeling, tour construction, and schedule assignment. First demand modeling, provides a time-varying or flexible manpower requirements pattern so as to satisfy customer needs over all time intervals of each day in the scheduling horizon. Since customer needs fluctuate, forecasting methods are often used to estimate flexible demand pattern. Hence, manpower requirements are usually linked to customer needs according to a given service standard and a queuing analysis of a forecast of the customer needs. In practice, the object of using service standards is to provide acceptable and consistent customer service on a period-by-period basis. Service level can be measured in terms of average waiting time before service, or average number of customers waiting for service, or other suitable criteria. Second, scheduling entails the allocation of flexible shifts to individual workers in order to satisfy uncertain demand. For modeling efficiency and convenience, we divide the working time of the day into a set of contiguous periods of uneven length such that each shift consists of a single period or a combination of periods. Each period is assumed to have uniform demand characteristics so that a suitable manpower requirement can be assigned to that particular period with an acceptable level of accuracy.

Figure 7, 12-hour shifts can be represented by a combination of demand periods (1,2) and (3,4), while different 8-hour shifts can be represented by (1), (2,3), and (4). In this context, the demand is stipulated for each period rather than for each shift.

A key feature in this category is the determination of staff or workforce requirements pattern

Figure 7. Example of contiguous demand periods

Period: hrs   1:8 hrs   2:4 hrs   3:4 hrs   4:8 hrs

over the entire planning horizon, which further complicates the scheduling process. Notably, the staff requirements in flexible demand situations vary over time over the course of day, from day to day, and from week to week. Consequently, shift start times and shift lengths have to vary so as to obtain good schedules that adequately cover the staffing requirements. The management objective is to ensure that overstaffing and under-staffing costs are minimized to a satisfactory level, considering the preset target service levels. Examples of application areas in this category are healthcare institutions (Topaloglu and Selim, 2010; Bard and Purnomo, 2005), call centres (Grossman et al., 1999), police and security services, postal services, banking systems, and other civic services (Mould, 1996; Awad and Chinneck, 1998; Bard et al., 2003).

Crisp Model for Flexible Demand

We present a multi-objective integer program for the flexible demand scheduling problem. In this development, the following set of indices, parameters and decision variables are further defined;

- **Indices:**
  - *n:* Number of allowable schedule patterns
  - *t:* Number of time periods over a day
  - *d:* Number of days in the planning horizon
  - *i:* Index for workers, $i = 1,...,m$
  - *j:* Index for schedules, $j = 1,...,n$
  - *d:* Index for days, $d = 1,...,D$
  - *t:* Index for time periods, $t = 1,...,T$
- **Parameters:**

- a_{jdt}: 1 if schedule type j contains period t, on day d, and 0 otherwise
- d_j: Duration of schedule type j
- p_{ij}: Preference score of worker i for schedule type j to be assigned
- **pmin:** Preference score if the most undesirable schedule is assigned to a worker
- **pmax:** Preference score if the most desirable schedule is assigned to a worker
- **cmin:** Minimum allowance for each worker for the scheduling horizon
- **cmax:** Maximum allowance for each worker for the scheduling period
- c_j: Share of allowance for schedule type j
- r_{dt}: Preferred number of workers for period t on day d
- lr_{dt}, ur_{dt}: Lower, upper bounds on demand for workers for period t on day d

- **Decision variables:**
  - X_{ij}: 1 if worker i is assigned to schedule j, and 0 otherwise
  - dr_{dt}: Positive deviation from the preferred number of workers on day j, period t
  - dp_i: Negative deviation from the maximum preference score of worker i for schedule type

Objective Functions

Minimise $z_1 = dw$ (24)

$$\text{Minimise } z_2 = \sum_i^m \left(dh_i^- + dh_i^+ \right) \qquad (25)$$

$$\text{Minimise } z_3 = \sum_i^m \left(dc_i^- + dc_i^+ \right) \qquad (26)$$

$$\text{Minimise } z_4 = \sum_i^m dp_i \qquad (27)$$

Constraints

$$\sum_i^m \sum_j^n a_{jdt} X_{ij} \geq lr_{dt} \qquad \text{for all } d = 1,...,D \text{ and } t = 1,...,T$$
$$(28)$$

$$\sum_j^n X_{ij} \leq 1 \qquad \text{for all } i = 1,...,m$$
$$(29)$$

$$lh \geq \sum_j^n d_j X_{ij} \leq uh \qquad \text{for all } i = 1,...,m$$
$$(30)$$

$$\sum_i^m \sum_j^n a_{jdt} X_{ij} - dr_{dt} \leq r_{dt} \qquad \text{for all } d = 1,...,D \text{ and } t = 1,...,T$$
$$(31)$$

Other Constraints (14) to (17)

According to constraint set (28), all the demand requirements in each period should be satisfied. Constraint set (29) ensures that each worker is assigned at most one schedule. Expression (30) restricts the total working hours assigned to each worker to within the lower and upper bounds, while constraint set (31) ensures that the most preferred number of workers is assigned in each period. Other constraints (14) to (17) are as explained in the previous sections.

Fuzzy Model for Flexible Demand

In this instance we take into account the uncertainty of the management objectives in meeting the flexible demand coverage and the workforce size, as well as the satisfaction of the workers' preferences. In this respect, the following membership functions are defined.

Membership Functions

- μ_{Cdt}: Membership function for demand coverage objective for period t, day d
- μ_W: Membership function for workforce size objective
- μ_{Hi}: Membership function for total working hour preference for worker i
- μ_{Ti}: Membership function for schedule type preference for worker i
- μ_{Ai}: Membership function for preferred ideal share of allowance

Assuming constant rate of increased/decreased membership satisfaction, we employ linear membership functions; triangular and trapezoidal membership functions (Figure 8). The trapezoidal membership function is used for the demand coverage and workforce size objective, while the triangular membership functions are used for the worker preference objectives. The membership function for the demand coverage objective is defined in Box 6.

Here, the expression $\sum_i^m \sum_j^n a_{jdt} X_{ij}$ represents the left-hand side of the fuzzy coverage constraints; r_{dt} represents the right-hand side of the fuzzy constraints, and the expression $(ur_{dt} - r_{dt})$ represents the maximum tolerance interval of violation of the constraint. The rest of the membership functions can be expressed as in the case of the task-based demand. The membership func-

Box 6.

$$\mu_{Cdt}(x) = \begin{cases} 1 & \text{if } lr_{dt} \leq \sum_i^m \sum_j^n X_{ij} \leq r_{dt} \\ \left(\sum_i^m \sum_j^n a_{jdt} X_{ij} - ur_{dt}\right) \Big/ \left(r_{dt} - ur_{dt}\right) & \text{if } r_{dt} \leq \sum_i^m \sum_j^n a_{jdt} X_{ij} \leq ur_{dt} \\ 0 & \text{if otherwise} \end{cases} \tag{32}$$

Figure 8. Membership function for the demand coverage objective

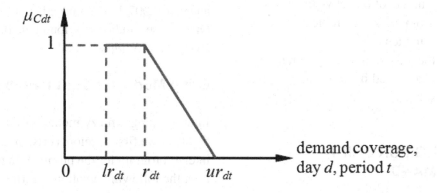

tion for workforce size objective $\mu_W(x)$ can be represented as in expression (18). As for the worker preference objectives, $\mu_{Hi}(x)$, $\mu_{Ti}(x)$ and $\mu_{Ai}(x)$ are represented by the expressions (19), (20) and (21), respectively. In a similar manner, any other preference membership functions can be defined for different scenarios. The fuzzy solution approach for this problem can now be presented as shown in the next section.

Fuzzy Solution Approach

The proposed fuzzy models can be formulated using the fuzzy solution approach by applying the Bellman and Zadeh's fuzzy *min operator* approach. By introducing the auxiliary variable λ, representing the overall satisfactory level, the fuzzy model is transformed into mixed-integer programming models as follows;

Step 1: Obtain a solution λ' by solving the following mixed integer program.

Maximize λ
subject to
$\quad \lambda \leq \mu_{Cdt}(x) \qquad d = 1,...,D, \ t = 1,...,T$
$\quad \lambda \leq \mu_W(x)$
$\quad \lambda \leq \mu_{Hi}(x) \qquad i = 1,...m$
$\quad \lambda \leq \mu_{Ti}(x) \qquad i = 1,...m$
$\quad \lambda \leq \mu_{Ai}(x) \qquad i = 1,...m$
$\quad \mu_{Cdt}(x), \ \mu_W(x), \ \mu_{Hi}(x), \ \mu_{Ti}(x), \ \mu_{Ai}(x), \ \lambda \in [0,1]$
other constraints (28) to (30)

$$\tag{33}$$

Step 2: Apply the following model, formulated based on the two-phase approach, in order to find an efficient solution;

Maximize $\left(\lambda_{Cdt} + \lambda_W + \lambda_{Hi} + \lambda_{Ti} + \lambda_{Ai}\right)/q$
subject to

$$\lambda' \leq \lambda_{Cdt} \leq \mu_{Cdt}(x) \quad d = 1, ..., D, \ t = 1, ..., T$$
$$\lambda' \leq \lambda_W \leq \mu_W(x)$$
$$\lambda' \leq \lambda_{Hi} \leq \mu_{Hi}(x) \qquad i = 1, ...m$$
$$\lambda' \leq \lambda_{Ti} \leq \mu_{Ti}(x) \qquad i = 1, ...m$$
$$\lambda' \leq \lambda_{Ai} \leq \mu_{Ai}(x) \qquad i = 1, ...m$$
$$\mu_{Cdt}(x), \ \mu_W(x), \ \mu_{Hi}(x), \ \mu_{Ti}(x), \ \mu_{Ai}(x), \ \lambda \in [0,1]$$
Other constraints (28) to (30)

(34)

where, q is the number of objective functions; λ' is the solution from the same problem using the *min operator* as in Step 2.

Similarly, the mixed integer programming model can now be solved by any suitable linear programming solvers.

SCHEDULING FOR SHIFT-BASED DEMAND

Like flexible demand, scheduling for a fixed demand begins with the demand modeling stage which specifies the minimum number of workers required in each shift. Hence, the aim is to determine a fixed demand pattern that can satisfy either a time-invariant work requirement pattern, or the maximum work requirement in a time-variant pattern. For instance, in a high-risk ambulance services, the aim is to satisfy all the anticipated demand. Fixed demand pattern is linked to work requirements through productivity standards; preset standard rates of performing duties used to convert workloads to manpower requirements. Scheduling for a shift-based demand entails assigning standard shifts to workers when demand is static over the working time of day. In other words, the manpower requirement is expressed per shift, since it is assumed static over the shift. Table 1 presents an example of a set of shifts

Table 1. An example of shift types

Shift type	Shift Description	Time Allocation
1	D: Day shift	08:00 to 1600 hrs
2	E: Night shift	1600 to 0000 hrs
3	N: Midnight shift	0000 to 0800 hrs

common in healthcare systems, where shifts are defined as day, night and midnight shift with non-overlapping time slots.

A number of empirical instances on shift-based demand scheduling are found in the literature (Kawanaka et al., 2001; Cheang et al., 2003; Moz and Pato, 2007; Maenhout and Vanhoucke, 2011). Other case studies are found in the literature (Azmat and Widmer, 2004).

Crisp Model for Shift-Based Demand

In developing a fuzzy model for the shift-based demand, we first develop a crisp multi-objective integer program for the problem. In this connection, the following notation is further defined;

- **Parameters:**
  - a_{jds}: 1 if schedule type j contains shift s on day d, and 0 otherwise

Objective Functions

$$\text{Minimise } z_1 = dw \qquad (35)$$

$$\text{Minimise } z_2 = \sum_i^m \left(dh_i^- + dh_i^+\right) \qquad (36)$$

$$\text{Minimise } z_3 = \sum_i^m \left(dc_i^- + dc_i^+\right) \qquad (37)$$

$$\text{Minimise } z_4 = \sum_i^m dp_i \qquad (38)$$

Constraints

$$\sum_{i}^{m}\sum_{j}^{n}a_{jds}X_{ij} = r_{ds} \qquad \text{for all } d = 1,...,D \text{ and } s = 1,...,S$$

$$(39)$$

$$\sum_{j}^{n}X_{ij} \leq 1 \qquad \text{for all } i = 1,...,m$$

$$(40)$$

$$lh \geq \sum_{j}^{n}d_{j}X_{ij} \leq uh \qquad \text{for all } i = 1,...,m$$

$$(41)$$

Other Constraints (14) to (17)

In this context, constraint set (39) ensures that the demand requirements in each period is satisfied, while constraint set (40) ensures that at most one single schedule is assigned to each worker. As in the previous models, expression (41) ensures that the assigned working hours for each worker is restricted to the pre-specified upper and lower limits.

Fuzzy Model for Shift-Based Demand

Uncertainty of the management objectives and satisfaction of the workers' preferences should be considered when scheduling for the shift-based demand. In this connection, the following membership functions are defined.

Membership Functions

- μ_W: Membership function for the workforce size objective

- μ_{Hi}: Membership function for the total working hour preference for worker i

- μ_{Ti}: Membership function for schedule type preference for worker i

- μ_{Ai}: Membership function for the preferred ideal share of allowance for worker i

For this problem category, we assume triangular and trapezoidal membership functions. The trapezoidal type is used to model the workforce size objective, while the triangular membership functions are used for the worker preference objectives. Therefore, the membership functions, $\mu_W(x)$, $\mu_{Hi}(x)$, $\mu_{Ti}(x)$ and $\mu_{Ai}(x)$ are represented by expressions (18) to (21), respectively. Additional pertinent membership functions can be defined in a similar manner.

Fuzzy Solution Approach

The proposed model can also be reformulated by applying the Bellman and Zadeh's *min operator* approach. Similar to the previous section, the fuzzy model can be transformed into a mixed-integer programming problem by introducing the variable λ. The solution approach follows through two steps as outlined.

Step 1: Obtain λ' by solving the following mixed integer program.

$$
\begin{aligned}
& \text{Maximize } \lambda \\
& \text{subject to} \\
& \qquad \lambda \leq \mu_W(x) \\
& \qquad \lambda \leq \mu_{Hi}(x) \qquad i = 1,...m \\
& \qquad \lambda \leq \mu_{Ti}(x) \qquad i = 1,...m \\
& \qquad \lambda \leq \mu_{Ai}(x) \qquad i = 1,...m \\
& \qquad \mu_W(x), \ \mu_{Hi}(x), \ \mu_{Ti}(x), \ \mu_{Ai}(x), \ \lambda \in [0,1] \\
& \qquad \text{Other constraints (39) to (41)}
\end{aligned}
$$

$$(42)$$

Step 2: Apply the *two-stage approach* in order to obtain a more efficient solution using the following model;

$$\text{Maximize } \left(\lambda_W + \lambda_{Hi} + \lambda_{Ti} + \lambda_{Ai}\right)\big/K$$
$$\text{subject to}$$
$$\lambda' \le \lambda_W \le \mu_W(x)$$
$$\lambda' \le \lambda_{Hi} \le \mu_{Hi}(x) \qquad i=1,...m$$
$$\lambda' \le \lambda_{Ti} \le \mu_{Ti}(x) \qquad i=1,...m$$
$$\lambda' \le \lambda_{Ai} \le \mu_{Ai}(x) \qquad i=1,...m$$
$$\mu_W(x),\ \mu_{Hi}(x),\ \mu_{Ti}(x),\ \mu_{Ai}(x),\ \lambda \in [0,1]$$
$$\text{Other constraints (39) to (41)}$$

$$(43)$$

In the same way, the mixed integer programming models can be solved by any appropriate existing solvers.

CONCLUSION AND FURTHER RESEARCH

In order to provide higher quality schedules, multiple sources of uncertainties should be considered in real world manpower scheduling problems. Among these sources of uncertainties, vagueness of information on target values of management objectives and workers' preferences are considered in this study. In this respect, this study provides a unified framework based on fuzzy set theory and taxonomy to address these uncertainties common in manpower scheduling problems across disciplines.

Unlike in conventional crisp mathematical programming frameworks, the new framework can provide the decision maker with a platform for flexible and interactive decision making in a fuzzy environment. As a result, worker preferences can be treated using fuzzy modeling approach, which may not be feasible with crisp mathematical methods.

The framework proposed in this study provides a unified fuzzy modeling framework by which manpower scheduling problems can be synthesized based on a taxonomy that delineates man-

power scheduling problems into three independent categories: flexible demand, fixed demand and task-oriented demand problems. The framework provides a platform for constructing interactive decision support systems for manpower policy makers. Hence, the framework can serve as a basis for future research on the development of robust decision support systems for manpower scheduling in a fuzzy environment. Apart from potential practical contribution, the framework gives a real-world multi-objective and interactive paradigm, adding further knowledge to academic research community in the area of manpower scheduling. Retrospectively, the fuzzy modeling framework is potential tool for the practicing decision maker, the academician, and the researcher.

REFERENCES

Awad, R., & Chinneck, J. (1998). Proctor assignment at Carleton University. *Interfaces*, 28(2), 58–71. doi:10.1287/inte.28.2.58.

Azmat, C. S., & Widmer, T. M. (2004). A case study of single shift planning and scheduling under annualized hours: A simple three-step approach. *European Journal of Operational Research, 153*, 148–175. doi:10.1016/S0377-2217(03)00105-X.

Bachou, R. B., Guinet, A., & Hjri-Gabouj, S. (2009). A model for scheduling drug deliveries in a French homecare. In *Proceedings of International Conference on Industrial Engineering and Systems Management*. Montreal, Canada: IEEE.

Bachou, R. B., Guinet, A., & Hjri-Gabouj, S. (2010). An optimization model for task assignment in home health care. In *Proceedings of IEEE Conference on Health Care Management*. IEEE.

Bellman, R. E., & Zadeh, L. A. (1970). Decision making in a fuzzy environment. *Management Science, 17*, 141–164. doi:10.1287/mnsc.17.4.B141.

Bezdek, J. C. (1993). Editorial: Fuzzy models-what are they and why? *IEEE Transactions on Fuzzy Systems*, *1*(1), 1–6. doi:10.1109/TFUZZ.1993.6027269.

Burke, E., Causmaecker, P., Berghe, V. G., & Landeghem, H. (2004). The state of the art of nurse rostering. *Journal of Scheduling*, *7*, 441–499. doi:10.1023/B:JOSH.0000046076.75950.0b.

Ernst, A. T., Jiang, H., Krishnamoorthy, M., Owens, B., & Sier, D. (2004a). An annotated bibliography of personnel scheduling and rostering. *Annals of Operations Research*, *127*, 21–144. doi:10.1023/B:ANOR.0000019087.46656.e2.

Ernst, A. T., Jiang, H., Krishnamoorthy, M., & Sier, D. (2004b). Staff scheduling and rostering: A review of applications, methods and models. *European Journal of Operational Research*, *153*, 3–27. doi:10.1016/S0377-2217(03)00095-X.

Grossman, T., Samuelson, D., Oh, S., & Rohleder, T. (1999). *Call centres*. Calgary, Canada: University of Calgary..

Inuiguchi, M., & Ramik, J. (2000). Possibilistic linear programming: A brief review of fuzzy mathematical programming and a comparison with stochastic programming in portfolio selection problem. *Fuzzy Sets and Systems*, *111*(1), 3–28. doi:10.1016/S0165-0114(98)00449-7.

Inuiguchi, M., Sakawa, M., & Kume, Y. (1994). The usefulness of possibilistic programming in production planning problems. *International Journal of Production Economics*, *33*, 45–52. doi:10.1016/0925-5273(94)90117-1.

Inuiguchi, M., Sakawa, M., & Kume, Y. (1994). The usefulness of possibilistic programming in production planning problems. *International Journal of Production Economics*, *33*(1-3), 45–52. doi:10.1016/0925-5273(94)90117-1.

Kawanaka, H., Yamamoto, K., Yoshikawa, T., Shinogi, T., & Tsuruoka, S. (2001). Genetic algorithm with the constraints for nurse scheduling problem. *IEEE Conference on Evolutionary Computation*, *2*, 1123-1130.

Krishnamoorthy, M., & Ernst, A. T. (2001). The personnel task scheduling problem. In *Optimisation Methods and Applications*. Dordrecht, The Netherlands: Kluwer Academic Publishers. doi:10.1007/978-1-4757-3333-4_20.

Li, R. J. (1990). *Multiple objective decision-making in a fuzzy environment*. (Ph.D. Thesis). Department of Industrial Engineering, Kansas State University, Manhattan, KS.

Maenhout, B., & Vanhoucke, M. (2011). An evolutionary approach for the nurse re-rostering problem. *Computers & Operations Research*, *38*, 1400–1411. doi:10.1016/j.cor.2010.12.012.

Mould, G. (1996). Case study of manpower planning for clerical operations. *The Journal of the Operational Research Society*, *47*(3), 358–368.

Moz, M., & Pato, M. V. (2007). A genetic algorithm approach to a nurse rerostering problem. *Computers & Operations Research*, *34*, 667–691. doi:10.1016/j.cor.2005.03.019.

Mutingi, M., & Mbohwa, C. (2013). A satisficing approach to home healthcare worker scheduling. In *Proceedings of International Conference on Law, Entrepreneurship and Industrial Engineering* (ICLEIE'2013). Johannesburg, South Africa: ICLEIE.

Sakawa, M. (1993). *Fuzzy sets and interactive multi-objective optimization*. New York: Plenum Press. doi:10.1007/978-1-4899-1633-4.

Teodorovic, D., & Lucic, P. (1998). A fuzzy set theory approach to the aircrew rostering problem. *Fuzzy Sets and Systems*, *95*, 261–271. doi:10.1016/S0165-0114(96)00277-1.

Tiryaki, F. (2006). Interactive compensatory fuzzy programming for decentralized multi-level linear programming (DMLLP) problems. *Fuzzy Sets and Systems*, *157*, 3072–3090. doi:10.1016/j.fss.2006.04.001.

Topaloglu, S., & Ozkarahan, I. (2004). An implicit goal programming model for the tour scheduling problem considering the employee work preferences. *Annals of Operations Research*, *128*, 135–158. doi:10.1023/B:ANOR.0000019102.68222.df.

Topaloglu, S., & Selim, H. (2010). Nurse scheduling using fuzzy modelling approach. *Fuzzy Sets and Systems*, *161*(11), 1543–1563. doi:10.1016/j.fss.2009.10.003.

Zadeh, L. A. (1965). Fuzzy sets. *Information and Control*, *8*, 338–353. doi:10.1016/S0019-9958(65)90241-X.

Zadeh, L. A. (1978). Fuzzy sets as a basis for a theory of possibility. *Fuzzy Sets and Systems*, *1*, 3–28. doi:10.1016/0165-0114(78)90029-5.

Zimmerman, H. J. (1993). *Fuzzy set theory and its applications* (2nd ed.). Boston: Kluwer Academic Publishers..

Zimmermann, H. J. (1978). Fuzzy programming and linear programming with several objective functions. *Fuzzy Sets and Systems*, *1*, 45–55. doi:10.1016/0165-0114(78)90031-3.

ADDITIONAL READING

Alfares, H. K. (2004). Survey, categorisation, and comparison of recent tour scheduling literature. *Annals of Operations Research*, *127*, 145–175. doi:10.1023/B:ANOR.0000019088.98647.e2.

Anbil, R., Tanga, R., & Johnson, E. L. (1992). A global approach to crew-pairing optimization. *IBM Systems Journal*, *31*(1), 71–78. doi:10.1147/sj.311.0071.

Baker, K. (1976). Workforce allocation in cyclical scheduling problems: A survey. *Operational Research Quarterly*, *27*(1), 155–167.

Bard, J., Binici, C., & Silva, A. (2003). Staff scheduling at the United States Postal Service. *Computers & Operations Research*, *30*(5), 745–771. doi:10.1016/S0305-0548(02)00048-5.

Bard, J. F., & Purnomo, H. W. (2005). Preference scheduling for nurses using column generation. *European Journal of Operational Research*, *164*, 510–534. doi:10.1016/j.ejor.2003.06.046.

Begur, V. S., Miller, D. M., & Weaver, J. R. (1997). An integrated spatial DSS for scheduling and routing home-health-care nurses. Institute of operations research and management sciences. *Interfaces*, *27*, 35–48. doi:10.1287/inte.27.4.35.

Brusco, M. J., & Jacobs, L. W. (1998). Personnel tour scheduling when starting-time restrictions are present. *Management Science*, *44*(4), 534–547. doi:10.1287/mnsc.44.4.534.

Brusco, M. J., & Johns, T. R. (1995). The effect of demand characteristics on labour scheduling methods. *International Journal of Operations & Production Management*, *15*(1), 74–88. doi:10.1108/01443579510077232.

Buffa, E. S., Cosgrove, M. J., & Luce, B. J. (1976). An integrated work shift scheduling system. *Decision Sciences*, *7*(4), 620–630. doi:10.1111/j.1540-5915.1976.tb00706.x.

Butchers, E., Day, P., Goldie, A., Miller, S., Meyer, J., & Ryan, D. et al. (2001). Optimized crew scheduling at Air New Zealand. *Interfaces*, *31*(1), 30–56. doi:10.1287/inte.31.1.30.9688.

Castillo, I., Joro, T., & Li, Y. Y. (2009). Workforce scheduling with multiple objectives. *European Journal of Operational Research*, *196*(1), 62–170. doi:10.1016/j.ejor.2008.02.038.

Cheang, B., Li, H., Lim, A., & Rodrigues, B. (2003). Nurse rostering problems-a bibliographic survey. *European Journal of Operational Research, 151*, 447–460. doi:10.1016/S0377-2217(03)00021-3.

Delgado, M., Herrera, F., Verdegay, J. L., & Vila, M. A. (1993). Post optimality analysis on the membership functions of a fuzzy linear problem. *Fuzzy Sets and Systems, 53*, 289–297. doi:10.1016/0165-0114(93)90400-C.

Green, V. L., Kolesar, P. J., & Whitt, W. (2007). Coping with time-varying demand when setting staffing requirements for a service system. *Production and Operations Management, 16*(1), 13–39. doi:10.1111/j.1937-5956.2007.tb00164.x.

Guerry, M. A. (1999). Using fuzzy sets in manpower planning. *Journal of Applied Probability, 36*, 155–162. doi:10.1239/jap/1032374238.

Howick, R., & Pidd, M. (1990). Sales force deployment models. *European Journal of Operational Research, 48*(3), 295–310. doi:10.1016/0377-2217(90)90413-6.

Ingolfsson, A., Haque, A., & Umnikov, A. (2002). Accounting for time-varying queueing effects in workforce scheduling. *European Journal of Operational Research, 139*, 585–597. doi:10.1016/S0377-2217(01)00169-2.

Jacobs, L. W., & Brusco, M. J. (1996). Overlapping start-time bands in implicit tour scheduling. *Management Science, 42*(9), 1247–1259. doi:10.1287/mnsc.42.9.1247.

Martel, A., & Price, W. (1981). Stochastic programming applied to human resource planning. *The Journal of the Operational Research Society, 32*(1), 187–196.

Mason, A. J., Ryan, D. M., & Panton, D. M. (1998). Integrated simulation, heuristic, and optimization approaches to staff scheduling. *Operations Research, 46*(2), 161–175. doi:10.1287/opre.46.2.161.

Ozkarahan, I. (1991). A disaggregation model of a flexible nurse scheduling support system. *Socio-Economic Planning Sciences, 25*(1), 9–26. doi:10.1016/0038-0121(91)90025-M PMID:10111677.

Panton, D. (1991). On the creation of multiple shift continuous operation cyclic rosters under general workforce conditions. *Asia–Pacific Journal of Operational Research, 8*(2), 189–201.

Siferd, S., & Benton, W. (1992). Workforce staffing and scheduling: hospital nursing specific models. *European Journal of Operational Research, 60*(3), 233–246. doi:10.1016/0377-2217(92)90075-K.

Silvestro, R., & Silvestro, C. (2000). An evaluation of nurse rostering practices in the National Health Service. *Journal of Advanced Nursing, 32*(3), 525–535. doi:10.1046/j.1365-2648.2000.01512.x PMID:11012793.

Thornthwaite, L., & Sheldon, P. (2004). Employee self-rostering for work-family balance: Leading examples in Austria. *Employee Relations, 26*(3), 238–254. doi:10.1108/01425450410530637.

Warner, D. M. (1976). Scheduling nursing personnel according to nursing preference: a mathematical programming approach. *Operations Research, 24*(5), 842–856. doi:10.1287/opre.24.5.842.

Willis, R., & Huxford, S. (1991). Staffing rosters with breaks: A case study. *The Journal of the Operational Research Society, 42*(9), 727–731.

KEY TERMS AND DEFINITIONS

Crisp Set: A conventional set for which an element is either fully a member of the set or not.

Days-Off: Rest days or off days, where an employee is not assigned any duty, as opposed to days-on.

Fuzzy Logic: A form of many-valued logic that deals with approximate rather fixed or exact reasoning.

Fuzzy Set: A set whose elements have degrees of membership of a set, rather than full membership or no membership as conventional set theory.

Linguistic Variables: A natural language represented as non-numeric variables to facilitate the expression of rules and facts.

Manpower Scheduling: Staff scheduling or rostering; the process of allocating time slots or shifts and duties to a set of available employees in order to meet organizational and customer requirements.

Membership Function: An indicator function representing the degree of truth as an extension of valuation.

Shift: A time slot or time block allocated to an employee in order to execute his/her duties or tasks.

Tour: A defined sequence of days off and days on allocated to an employee spanning over a given planning horizon, e.g., 7 days, or 14 days.

Chapter 9
Group Genetic Algorithm for Heterogeneous Vehicle Routing

Michael Mutingi
University of Johannesburg, South Africa & University of Botswana, Botswana

ABSTRACT

Cost-efficient transportation is a central concern in the transportation and logistics industry. In particular, the Heterogeneous Vehicle Routing Problem (HVRP) has become a major optimization problem in supply chains involved with delivery (collection) of goods to (from) customers. In this problem, there are limited vehicles of different types with respect to capacity, fixed cost, and variable cost. The solution to this problem involves assigning customers to existing vehicles and, in relation to each vehicle, defining the order of visiting each customer for the delivery or collection of goods. Hence, the objective is to minimize the total costs, while satisfying customer requirements and visiting each customer exactly once. In this chapter, an enhanced Group Genetic Algorithm (GGA) based on the group structure of the problem is developed and tested on several benchmark problems. Computational results show that the proposed GGA algorithm is able to produce high quality solutions within a reasonable computation time.

INTRODUCTION

Cost efficient transportation is imperative in logistics and supply chain management. Logistics and transportation costs account for about 20% of the total cost of a product (Hoff et al., 2010).

DOI: 10.4018/978-1-4666-4785-5.ch009

Moreover, increasing globalization, economic growth, and consumption continue to increase the need for efficient transportation. Global completion among logistics service providers lead to higher demand for cost efficiency, better customer services, responsiveness, and agility. Recently, the ever-growing environmental concerns and the ensuing legislation have become one of the major drivers of eco-efficient transportation. As such, logistics and transportation industry is often faced with the problem of fleet composition at almost all decision levels. Decision makers have to strike a balance between vehicle fleet ownership and fleet subcontracting, considering external market variables such as expected demand and transportation costs. This is further complicated by the fact that, in the real-world, vehicle fleets are inherently heterogeneous rather than homogeneous (Mutingi and Mbohwa, 2012). The goal of fleet composition is to determine the optimal fleet, considering all costs, revenues and other relevant constraints.

In an industrial set up, vehicle fleets are seldom homogeneous (Mutingi and Mbohwa, 2012). More often than not, vehicles are acquired over long planning horizons, such that the cumulative fleet will have different features due to technological changes (Hoff et al., 2010). Consequently, vehicle operating costs will vary across vehicles over their lifetimes. In addition, most managers would prefer to keep vehicles of different types as a way of improving their operations agility. Transportation demand features, in terms of volume, time and terrain, may also contribute to the overall need for keeping a heterogeneous fleet. Basically, vehicles differ in their capacity or physical dimensions and operating costs. These factors should be accounted for at all levels of decision making. Overall, fleet composition and routing occurs at strategic, tactical and operational levels.

In the long term, heterogeneous fleet composition and routing involves capacity adjustment (that is, fleet resizing, composition and allocation). This usually entails huge capital involvement, as the organization may wish to acquire capacity to cover a planning horizon of say 15 years. In such cases, uncertainty is high; it is difficult to anticipate transportation demand, costs and revenues in the long term. Consequently, careful risk management practices are crucial; risk can be reduced by establishing long term and short term contracts, which calls for effective usage of heterogeneous fleets.

Over a few years, heterogeneous fleet composition is concerned with capacity resizing, subject to the existing fleet. As such, uncertainty in transportation demand and operational costs will be much less than at the strategic level. Routing aspects are often included at a more detailed level. Decisions at this level involve contract negotiations, optimal vehicles to be acquired or to be chartered in or out, which vehicles should be sold, and vehicle route assignment (Hoff et al., 2010). At operational level, vehicle fleet composition usually consists of the integrative task of selecting the set of vehicles (selected from an existing fleet) to satisfy customer orders, and simultaneously determine the best routing patterns. Over a short term, certainty is relatively higher than in strategic and tactical transportation planning. Oftentimes, the fleet of vehicles to be used is usually fixed over the short term. As a result, flexibility in terms of fleet size adjustment is limited.

The HVRP problem is an NP-hard combinatorial problem, yet it is a very common problem in the logistics and transportation industry. In cases where the ratio of total demand of the customers and the total capacity of the vehicle is close to one, finding a feasible solution can be quite difficult. Also, proving that a given homogeneous fleet can satisfy customer demand requires solving a bin packing problem, which is NP-hard. With a heterogeneous fleet, the problem is an extension of the NP-hard bin-packing problem with different bin sizes. Therefore, the HVRP is an NP-hard combinatorial problem. Because of the inherent complexities associated with the problem, the use of exact methods on large-scale instances is not possible. As a result, most researchers rely on heuristic approaches to obtain near-optimal solutions. Various heuristic approaches have been developed for the problem, such as tabu search (Taillard, 1999; Gendreau et al., 1999; Brandao, 2011), adaptive memory programming (Tutuncu, 2010), and other problem-specific heuristics (Tarantilis and Kiranoudis, 2003; Tarantilis and Kiranoudis, 2004). Group genetic algorithm, a modification of conventional genetic algorithms originally developed by Falkenauer (1992) for addressing grouping problems, is a potential solution approach for solving the HVRP problem. In view of these issues, the aim of this research is to develop and implement a group genetic algorithm (GGA) for addressing the HVRP problem in which existing vehicles are to be assigned to known customers.

The remainder of this chapter is as follows: The next section discusses the heterogeneous fleet composition and routing problem. This is followed by a description of the group genetic algorithm approach. Illustrative computational tests, results and the relevant discussions are then presented. Finally, concluding remarks are then provided, pointing out the contributions of the chapter to theory and to the practicing managers. Further research prospects are also highlighted.

HETEROGENEOUS FLEET VEHICLE ROUTING

The heterogeneous vehicle routing problem (HVRP) is a common operational problem in transportation and logistics; most companies own a heterogeneous fleet of vehicles. Though in recent years, solution methods for the homogeneous vehicle routing problem (VRP) have progressed substantially in the literature (Potvin and Bengio, 1996; Rochat and Taillard, 1995; Badeau et al., 1997; Moghadam and Seyedhosseini, 2010), the HVRP problem has attracted much less attention. As conjectured by Taillard (1999), this may be attributed to the fact that the problem is much harder to solve than the well known classical VRP problem.

Formally, the HVRP can be described in terms of an undirected connected graph $G = (V, E)$, where $V = \{0, 1, ..., n\}$ is a vertex set and $E\{(i, j): i, j \in V\}$ is an edge set, where vertex 0 represents the depot and each other vertex $i \in V\backslash\{0\}$ is a customer with a demand q_i. A distance $d_{ij}(d_{ii}=0, \forall i \in V)$ is associated to each edge $(i, j) \in V$. A fixed

fleet comprising T different types of vehicles is located at the depot (0), and the number of vehicles of each type is denoted by n_k ($k = 1, ..., T$). Each type of vehicle k ($k = 1, ..., T$) is associated with capacity Q_k and a variable cost v_k. Assume that $Q_1 < Q_2... < Q_T$ and $v_1 < v_2... < v_T$. The travelling cost of each edge $(i, j) \in V$ by a vehicle of type k is $c_{ij} = v_k d_{ij}$. The HVRP consists of defining the best set of routes and the vehicles assigned to each route so that the following constraints are satisfied: (i) use no more vehicles than those available; (ii) satisfy customer demand; (iii) visit each customer exactly once; (iv) a vehicle route starts and finishes at the depot; (v) do not exceed the capacity of the vehicle, and (v) each route is assigned to one vehicle. The objective of the HVRP is to minimize the sum of the costs of all the routes subject to the constraints outlined above. In view of the fact that the number of vehicles of each type is limited, there is no guarantee that a feasible solution can be found. In practice, this would mean that other vehicles have to be hired if all customers are to be served, with a reasonable customer satisfaction.

The HVRP problem reduces to the capacitated vehicle routing problem (CVRP) when all vehicles are homogeneous, and the number of vehicles is unlimited. On the other hand, when the number of vehicles is unlimited, we obtain the fleet size and mix vehicle routing problem (FSMVRP), which, in real-world practice, addresses strategic fleet composition decisions. The HVRP is rather more difficult to solve than the FSMVRP (Brandao, 2011).

THE GROUP GENETIC ALGORITHM APPROACH

In this section, we explain the group genetic algorithm (GGA) and its elements, which include objective or fitness function, chromosome representation, population generation, and the genetic operators: selection, crossover, mutation, inversion, diversification, together with their genetic control parameter values.

Objective Function

To evaluate a candidate solution s, customer orders in s are partitioned into groups so that the cumulative load for each group does not exceed the assigned vehicle capacity, and the cumulative cost incurred in delivering all orders is minimized. The target of a candidate solution (chromosome) in GGA is to minimize travel cost as well as loading excess above vehicle capacity. For any candidate solution s, let the objective function be represented by $g(s)$. Therefore, the objective function to be minimized is given by the expression,

$$g(s) = \sum_{i=1}^{r} \left(c_i + p l_i \right). \qquad (1)$$

where, r is the total number of routes or trips in s; c_i is the variable cost of route i, l_i is the loading excess in route i; and p is the penalty for loading excess.

The objective function in expression (1) enables GGA to accept slightly inferior candidate solutions, which may yield better solutions as iterations progress. This enhances exploration of unvisited regions of the solution space during GGA iterations, thereby increasing the search power of GGA optimization process.

Chromosome Coding Scheme

The GGA approach takes advantage of the group structure of a problem situation in order to solve the problem. Therefore, the structure of the problem determines the chromosome coding scheme upon which the efficiency of the GGA strongly depends. An efficient chromosome coding improves the search efficiency of the algorithm. Most of the existing chromosome coding schemes in the literature used integer numbers where the number identifies the vehicle and the position of the number represents the customer node. For instance, a chromosome [1 1 1 2 2 3] may be used to represent a distribution system with 3 vehicles and 6 retailers; this implies that retailers 1, 2 and 3 are assigned to vehicle 1, retailers 4 and 5 are assigned to vehicle 2, and retailer 6 is assigned to vehicle 3:Customer position : 1 2 3 4 5 6Chromosome coding : 1 1 1 2 2 3

The proposed GGA algorithm has an improved coding scheme, deriving from the coding proposed by Filho and Tibert (2006). The coding scheme improves the efficiency of the operation of the algorithm. For illustration purposes, consider the distribution system in Figure 1 with two vehicles of type 1 and one of type 2. There are 6 customers in all ($n = 6$). The capacities of vehicle types 1 and 2 are $Q_1 = 450$ and $Q_2 = 500$, respectively. Additionally, their variable costs are $v_1 = 1.1$ and $v_2 = 1.2$, respectively. The cost per unit of excess

Figure 1. Data for chromosome coding

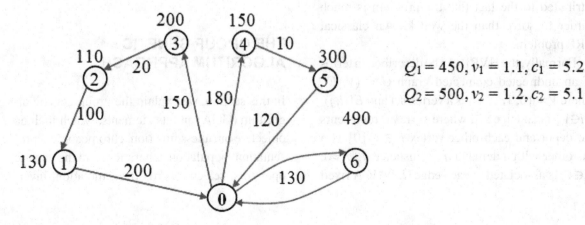

$Q_1 = 450, v_1 = 1.1, c_1 = 5.2$
$Q_2 = 500, v_2 = 1.2, c_2 = 5.1$

loading is set at $c_1 = 5.2$ and $c_2 = 5.1$ for vehicle types 1 and 2, respectively. The numbers on arc(i,j) and node j represent $d_{i,j}$ and q_j, respectively.

In this study, we make all the available vehicles identifiable by assuming that there are three available vehicles, denoted by w_1, w_2, w_3 of types 1, 1 and 2, respectively. For each feasible chromosome, we use a group structure consisting of three coding schemes as illustrated in Figure 2. The first code, code 1 is a chromosome of size n, where n is the total number of customers. This code is used for the generation of initial population. The strength of this code is that it ensures that each customer is assigned to one vehicle, which makes the population generation process more efficient. The second code, code 2 is derived from code 1 by clustering customers served by each vehicle in a single group. The sequence of the customers in each group depicts the order in which the customers are visited. Code 2 is the actual group structure upon which the genetic operators act. The third code, code 3 merely keeps a record of

the position of the last node (frontier) of each trip (group).

From the example given above, the chromosome to be evaluated is represented as [3 2 1 | 4 5 | 6]. With reference to code 2, vehicle type 1 with variable costs 1.1 is assigned trip (0-1-2-3-0). In this connection, the total cost for this trip is 1.1 × (150 + 20 + 100 + 200) + 5.2(0) = 517. The rest of the segments of the code, that is, trips (0-4-5-0) and (0-6-0), are evaluated in a similar manner. Table 1 presents a complete summary of the cost evaluations for all the trips according to their respective vehicle assignments.

Population Initialization

Initial populations of the desired size, popsize, is randomly generated at the beginning of the algorithm by assigning vehicle, identified by IDs, to customer positions as demonstrated in section 3.2. This enhances the population generation process. In addition, the assignment is done

Figure 2. Chromosome coding example

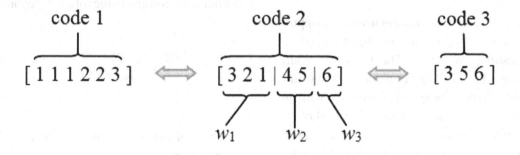

Table 1. GGA coding solution example

Trip or Group	Vehicle Type	Vehicle ID	Variable Cost	Excess Load Cost	Trip Cost
0-3-2-1-0	1	$w_1 = 1$	1.1	5.2	517
0-4-5-0	1	$w_2 = 2$	1.1	5.2	341
0-6-0	2	$w_3 = 3$	1.2	5.1	312
Total Cost:					1170

probabilistically with a bias towards vehicles with the least utilization, a phenomenon called *utilization bias*. In this development, utilization bias, p, is determined as;

$$p = \max\left[\left(1 - l_w/Q_w\right), 0\right] \tag{2}$$

where, l_w is the current total load assigned to vehicle w; and Q_w is the capacity of the vehicle.

As an illustration of the population initialization process, consider a typical HVRP problem consisting of n customers and W vehicles. The initial population is generated according to Algorithm 1.

GENETIC OPERATORS

In this section, unique design features and strategies relating to genetic operators are described, including selection, crossover, mutation, and inversion strategies.

Selection Strategy

The selection strategy concept involves mapping a cost function $g(s)$ to a score function $f(s)$ for chromosome evaluation. The GGA procedure computes the score function for each chromosome so as to determine the chromosome with the maximum score function value. The goal of the optimization problem is to maximize a score function $f(s)$ which is derived from the cost function $g(s)$ according to the mapping procedure. In the proposed GGA approach, a mapping procedure, originally suggested Goldberg (1989), is applied to obtain the fitness function according to the following expression;

$$f(s) = \begin{cases} f_{\max} - g(s) & \text{if } g(s) < f_{\max} \\ 0 & \text{if otherwise} \end{cases} \tag{3}$$

where, $g(s)$ is the objective function of the chromosome; and $f_{\max}$ is the largest objective function in the current population. Hence, it follows that the goal is to maximize the score function of each chromosome, which is the fitness function.

A number of selection strategies have been suggested in the literature, including deterministic sampling, remainder stochastic sampling with replacement, remainder stochastic sampling without replacement, and stochastic tournament (Goldberg, 1989). In this research, remainder stochastic sampling without replacement was applied. Each chromosome s is selected and stored in the mating pool according to its expected count e_s, calculated according to the following expression,

$$e_s = \frac{f_s}{\left(1/popsize\right)\sum_{s=1}^{popsize} f_s} \tag{4}$$

where, f_s is the score function value of the sth chromosome.

Algorithm 1. Initialization

BEGIN
REPEAT
   1: For each vehicle w ($w = 1,...,W$), randomly select and assign a customer;
   2: For the remaining (n-W) unassigned customers, randomly assign a customer to a vehicle, with bias towards the least utilized vehicles, until all customers are assigned.
   3: Encode the chromosome using code 1 and add to the initial population.
UNTIL (population size = *popsize*).
END

Each chromosome receives copies equal to the integer part of e_s, that is, $[e_s]$. The fractional part of e_s, *fract*(e_s), is treated as success probability of obtaining additional copies of the same chromosome into the mating pool or temporal population, called *temppop*. Thus, chromosomes with higher fitness will have higher expected count, and higher chances of surviving into the next generation.

Crossover Operator

Crossover is a stochastic evolutionary mechanism through which selected chromosomes mate to produce a pool of new offspring, called selection pool (*spool*). The new solutions in the selection pool allow exploration of unvisited regions in the solution space. The proposed group crossover operator exchanges groups of genes of selected chromosomes, with probability p_c until the desired pool size *poolsize = popsize×p_c*, is obtained. The procedure for group crossover occurs according to the Algorithm 2.

Figure 3 shows an example of crossover operation, assuming the crossover point is 1. After the crossover process, some customers in the offspring may appear in more than one trip, while some may be missing. To repair the offspring, identify any duplicated customers (genes), and then eliminate those duplicated customers to the left of the crossover point. Missing customers are inserted into the trip (s) with the least load. Hence, the group coding scheme enhances the crossover operator by taking advantage of the group structure. Figure 4 shows an example of repair mechanism using offspring [1 2 | 3 1 | 5 6].

After crossover operation, local search is applied via two mutation operators.

Algorithm 2. Crossover

```
BEGIN
REPEAT
   1: Generate a random integer x = (1, r-1), where r is the number of trips.
   2: Let x define the crossover point.
   3: Swap the groups to the right of the crossover point x to generate two offspring.
   4: Repair the offspring;
      (i) eliminate duplicated genes (customers),
      (ii) introduce missing genes using utilization bias;
UNTIL (poolsize is achieved).
END
```

Figure 3. Crossover operation example

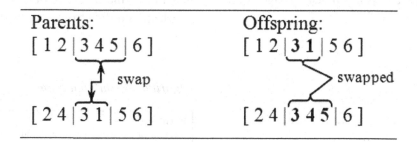

Figure 4. Chromosome repair example

Before repair	:	[1 2 | 3 1 | 5 6]
Eliminate 1	:	⇩
		[2 | 3 1 | 5 6]
Introduce 4	:	⇩
After repair	:	[2 4 | 3 1 | 5 6]

Mutation and Local Search

In order to intensify local search and to maintain population diversity, two types of mutation operators are applied to every new chromosome, that is, *swap mutation* and *shift mutation*. The swap mutation exchanges genes between two randomly chosen groups in a chromosome. The general procedure of the swap mutation is outlined in Algorithm 3.

Figure 5 demonstrates the swap mutation using offspring [2 4 \| 3 1 \| 5 6] an example. Genes 2 and 3 are randomly chosen from trips 1 and 2, and swapped.

The *shift mutation operator* randomly selects a frontier between two adjacent groups and shifts it by one step either to the right or to the left as illustrated in Figure 6. This implies that the number of nodes is increased in one group and decreased in the adjacent group. The procedure for the mutation operator is illustrated by Algorithm 4.

Inversion Strategy

In order to prevent premature convergence, inversion is applied (at a very low probability) on those chromosomes that were selected in the selection stage; the operator is applied prior to crossover operation. In the inversion process, groups of chosen chromosome are rearranged in reverse order. An illustration of the inversion operator is provided in Figure 7 using chromosome [2 4 \| 3 1 \| 5 6] as an example.

Diversification

As the generations proceed, the population tends to converge to a particular solution. However, the population may converge prematurely (genetic drift) before obtaining an acceptable or optimal solution. As such, population diversity should be checked at every generation. There, at every generation, the diversity of the chromosome is checked according to code 2. To check diversity,

Algorithm 3. Swap mutation

```
BEGIN
  1: Randomly select two numbers from the set {1,2,...,r};
  2: Randomly choose a gene from each group;
  3: Swap the selected genes.
END
```

Algorithm 4. Shift mutation

```
BEGIN
  1: Generate a random integer z = rand (1, r-1), and assign it
to frontier f,
  2: Select the shift direction randomly: right or left,
  3: Shift the frontier f in the selected direction.
    END
```

Figure 5. Swap mutation example

Offspring chromosome	:	[2 4 | 3 1 | 5 6]
Select groups or trips	:	2 and 3
Select and swap genes	:	3 and 5
Mutated offspring	:	[2 4 | 5 1 | 3 6]

Figure 6. Shift mutation example

offspring	:	[2 4 | 3 1 | 5 6]
select frontier, rand (1,2)	:	2 shift frontier
select direction	:	right
mutated offspring	:	[2 4 | 3 1 5 | 6]

we define an entropic measure H_i in a population for each customer i, as follows;

$$H_i = \sum_{j=1}^{m} [(n_{ij}/p) \cdot \log (n_{ij}/p)/\log(m)] \qquad (5)$$

where, n_{ij} denotes the number of chromosomes in which location i is assigned position j in the current population; p denotes the population size; and m denotes the number of locations.

Therefore, we can define population divergence or diversity H in accordance with the following expression;

$$H = \sum_{i=1}^{m} H_i/m \qquad (6)$$

The divergence parameter H approaches zero as the iterations progress. Therefore, the diversity of the population can be checked and improved, based on H, by applying the inversion operator till diversity attains the desired preset value. To prevent loss of good solutions, a fraction (e.g., 0.125) of the best chromosomes in the population is always preserved from generation to generation. The rest of the chromosomes are obtained by comparing corresponding candidate solutions in the diversified and undiversified population, preferring those that fare better. This ensures that the fittest chromosomes will always survive, that is, the best performing candidates are always preserved and taken into the next generation.

GGA APPLICATION

The overall GGA structure for solving the HVRP problem includes all the elements and the genetic operators described in the previous section, that is, selection, crossover, mutation, inversion, replacement, and diversification. Figure 8 provides an outline of the pseudo-code for the implementa-

Figure 7. Inversion strategy example

Before inversion	:	[2 4 | 3 1 | 5 6]
After inversion	:	[5 6 | 3 1 | 2 4]

tion of the GGA algorithm. The algorithm begins with data input for genetic parameters such as the maximum number of generations (*maxgen*), the crossover probability (p_c), the mutation probability (p_m), and the inversion probability (p_i).

The GGA pseudo-code, which is *Algorithm* 5, is explained in eight steps as follows: Step 1 involves data input consisting of the initial GGA parameters such as *maxgen*, p_c, p_m, and p_i. Step 2 is concerned with the random generation of chromosomes for the initial population *oldpop* using *Algorithm* 1. Here, the allocation of customers to vehicles is done probabilistically with a bias towards those vehicles with the least capacity utilization, which encourages load balancing. After the initialization process, the algorithms enters into an iterative loop which runs until a termination criteria is reached, that is, until the maximum number of generations *maxgen* is achieved. In Step 3, the best performing chromosomes are selected according to their fitness function values. This is implemented by use of a temporal population *temppop*, which comprises best performing chromosomes that are duplicated according to their relative performance, or fitness. In this manner, best performing candidates are duplicated more than the less performing candidates. Step 4 applies the group crossover operator with a probability p_c to obtain a population of new offspring, that is, selection pool. The inversion operator is applied to every successful crossover. Following the crossover operator, the mutation operator is applied to each offspring at a probability p_m in

Step 5. Each of the offspring is then moved to the new population, that is, *newpop*. In Step 6, the replacement strategy compares the corresponding chromosomes, for instance, *newpop*[1] and *spool*[1] and retains the best performing chromosome. Since the size of *spool* is less than that of *newpop*, the rest of the rest of the chromosomes are selected at a probability (0.55) into the new population. Step 7 performs diversification at a probability p_i whenever the current population diversity H falls below the desired minimum value H_{min}. Following the diversification process, the whole population is re-evaluated to obtain the new fitness values. Finally, step 8 checks the termination criterion; whether the current generation count *gen* has exceeded the maximum count *maxgen*. A summary of the main elements and genetic operators is represented in terms of a flowchart in Figure 9.

The appropriate selection of the GGA parameters is crucial for the efficient and effective operation of the algorithm. In this study, the parameters were adopted from typical values found in the literature, with little fine-tuning (Filho and Tiberti, 2006). Based on numerous experimental runs and past values of the parameters, suitable parameter values were estimated. The selected parameters and their ranges are as listed in Table 2.

The next section presents the test problems, computational results and the relevant discussions for the HVRP problem.

Figure 8. The GGA pseudo-code

Algorithm 5. GGA algorithm
BEGIN
   1:   *Input*: initial data input for GGA parameters, that is, *maxgen, p_c, p_m, p_i*
   2:   *Initialization*: create *oldpop*:
      (i)   Create chromosomes by random generation;
      (ii)   Use utilization bias.
REPEAT
   3:   *Selection*: use stochastic sampling without replacement:
      (i)   evaluate chromosomes by fitness function;
      (ii)   create temporal population, *temppop*: use int [e_i], and fraction(e_i) as success probabilities
   4:   *Crossover* and *recombination*: Apply group crossover to *temppop* to create a selection pool, *spool*.
      (i)   select 2 chromosomes by remainder selection without replacement.
      (ii)   apply crossover operator;
      (iii)   if successful then inversion operator, else go to 5;
      (iv)   apply repair mechanism, with utilization bias, as necessary;
   5:   *Mutation*: apply mutation (swap and shift mutation) and move offspring to new population, *newpop*;
   6:   *Replacement strategy*: replace *oldpop* with corresponding *newpop*;
      (i)   compare *spool* and *oldpop* chromosomes, successively;
      (ii)   take the one that fares better in each comparison;
      (iii)   select the rest of the chromosomes with probability 0.55;
   7:   *Diversification*: diversify by mutation operator;
      (i)   calculate population diversity H;
      (ii)   if ($H < H_{min}$) then diversify till $H \geq H_{min}$;
      (iii)   re-evaluate chromosomes by fitness function;
   8:   *New population*:
      (i)   check generation count, *gen*, against *maxgen*.
      (ii)   return the best solutions;
      (iii)   advance population, *gen = gen + 1*;
UNTIL (*gen $\geq$ maxgen*)
END

COMPUTATIONAL TESTS, RESULTS AND DISCUSSIONS

The proposed GGA approach was implemented in Java and executed on a Pentium 4, at 3GHz. In order to test the efficiency and effectiveness of the approach, illustrative computational tests and comparative analysis were carried out based on well known HVRP benchmark problems found in the literature (Taillard, 1999; Li et al., 2007; Brandao, 2011).

Illustrative Computational Experiments

The performance of our GGA algorithm was tested on 8 benchmark problem instances originally coined by Taillard (1999). Table 3 provides the

Figure 9. Framework for group genetic algorithm

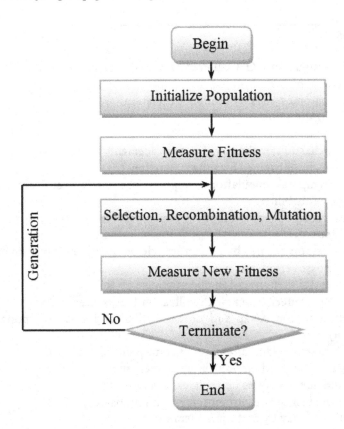

Table 2. GGA parameters and their values

No.	Parameter	Value
1	Number of generations (iterations)	Variable
2	Population size	20-40
3	Crossover probability	0.4 – 0.7
4	Mutation probability	0.01 – 0.1
5	Inversion probability	0.05 – 0.1
6	Chromosome size	Customers

specifications for the first set (set 1) of benchmark problems, numbered from 13 to 20 according to the notation used in Taillard (1999). According to the notation, Q_t represents the capacity of vehicle type t, $(t = A, B,…, F)$; v_t denotes the variable cost of vehicle type t; and n_t defines the available number of vehicle of type t. The percentage ratio defines the ratio between the total demand of the customers and the total capacity of the vehicles, which signifies the 'tightness' of the problem. Thus, when the ratio is close to one, finding a feasible solution can be very difficult. Problem sets 13 to 16 have 50 customers, while problem sets 17 and 18 have 75 customers. Furthermore, problem sets 19 and 20 have 100 customers.

Table 3. Data for benchmark problem set 1

No.	n	Type of Vehicle																		Ratio
		A			B			C			D			E			F			(%)
		Q_A	v_A	n_A	Q_B	v_B	n_B	Q_C	v_C	n_C	Q_D	v_D	n_D	Q_E	v_E	n_E	Q_F	v_F	n_F	
13	50	20	1.0	4	30	1.1	2	40	1.2	4	70	1.7	4	120	2.5	2	200	3.2	1	95.39
14	50	120	1.0	4	160	1.1	2	300	1.4	1										88.45
15	50	50	1.0	4	100	1.6	3	160	2.0	2										94.76
16	50	40	1.0	2	80	1.6	4	140	2.1	3										94.76
17	75	50	1.0	4	120	1.2	4	200	1.5	2	350	1.8	1							95.38
18	75	20	1.0	4	50	1.3	4	100	1.9	2	150	2.4	2	250	2.9	1	400	3.2	1	95.38
19	100	100	1.0	4	200	1.4	3	300	1.7	3										76.74
20	100	60	1.0	6	140	1.7	4	200	2.0	3										95.92

Ratio = 100×(total demand/total capacity)

Table 4 provides a second set of benchmark problems (set 2), identified as H1 to H5. The problems were originally created by Li et al.(2007) and adopted by Brandao (2011). The set has 200 to 360 customers. The computational results obtained in this study are compared with those obtained by the best-performing heuristics in the literature, obtained from Taillard (1999), Tarantilis et al. (2004), Li et al. (2007), and Brandao (2011).

The next section presents the results of the computational experiments together with the relevant discussions.

COMPUTATIONAL RESULTS AND DISCUSSIONS

Table 5 and 6 present the results of the computational tests of the 8 HVRP benchmark problems in set 1, and for the 5 benchmark problems in set 2, respectively. The following information is provided: the number of customers n, the best known solution cost *Best known*, the solution costs obtained by different algorithms in the literature, the GGA best solution *GGA Best* which is the best solution obtained from 10 runs, the computation time (in seconds) corresponding to the best solution obtained from 10 runs, the average deviation *AvDev* in relation to the average of the best known solutions, the number *NBest* of solutions found

Table 4. Data for benchmark problem set 2

No.	n	Type of Vehicle																		Ratio
		A			B			C			D			E			F			(%)
		Q_A	v_A	n_A	Q_B	v_B	n_B	Q_C	v_C	n_C	Q_D	v_D	n_D	Q_E	v_E	n_E	Q_F	v_F	n_F	
H1	200	50	1.0	8	100	**1.1**	6	200	1.2	4	500	**1.7**	3	1000	2.5	1				93.02
H2	240	50	1.0	10	100	**1.1**	5	200	1.2	5	500	**1.7**	4	1000	2.5	1				96.00
H3	280	50	1.0	10	100	**1.1**	5	200	1.2	5	500	**1.7**	4	1000	2.5	2				93.33
H4	320	50	1.0	10	100	**1.1**	8	200	1.2	5	500	**1.7**	2	1000	2.5	2	1500	**3**	1	94.12
H5	360	50	1.0	10	100	**1.2**	8	200	1.5	5	500	**1.8**	1	1000	2.5	2	2000	**3**	1	92.31

Ratio = 100×(total demand/total capacity)

by each algorithm that are identical to or better than the best known.

As shown by the results in Table 5, it can be seen that the GGA approach was able to obtain high quality results in terms of the average solution over the 10 runs on each of the benchmark problem. It is worth mentioning that the approach was able to obtain all the best known solutions within reasonable computation times; the algorithm was able to produce 8 best known solutions. Therefore the GGA performed better when compared to other competitive heuristics, that is, 1 best known solution was obtained in Tarantilis et al. (2004), 7 best known solutions in Li et al. (2007), and 7 in Brandao (2011). Considering the computation time, GGA performance was quite comparable to the Tabu search algorithm developed by Brandao (2011). Based on the average percentage deviation from the best known, all algorithms were capable of producing high quality solutions, with an average percent deviation less than 3%. However, our GGA performed the best in terms of average percentage deviation.

As can be seen from Table 6, computational results show that GGA was able to obtain 4 best solutions, including 1 new solution. Moreover, the average deviation of GGA solutions, 0.0208%, was much lower than the deviations produced by other algorithms; 0.218% from Li et al.(2007) and 1.692% from Brandao (2011). Overall, the GGA heuristic developed in this research is capable of producing high quality solutions within a reasonable computing time.

To further substantiate the robustness of the GGA approach, comparative analysis was carried out in terms of the average fitness of the best solutions obtained over 20 runs. The results of the comparative analysis are shown in Table 7 and Table 8, both for the 8 HVRP benchmark problems in set 1, and for the 5 benchmark problems in set 2, respectively. The important information is provided in terms of the following parameters: the number of customers n, the best known solution cost *Best known*, the solution costs obtained by various algorithms in the literature, the GGA average solution *GGA Ave* which corresponds to

Table 5. Comparative results for benchmark problem set 1

No	n	Best Known	Taillard	Tarantilis et al.	Li et al.	Brandao	GGA Best[a]	CPU Time Best[b] (sec)
13	50	1517.84	1536.55	1519.96	*1517.84*	*1517.84*	*1571.84*	56
14	50	607.53	623.05	611.39	*607.53*	*607.53*	*607.53*	52
15	50	1015.29	1022.05	*1015.29*	*1015.29*	*1015.29*	*1015.29*	48
16	50	1144.94	1159.14	1145.52	*1144.94*	*1144.94*	*1144.94*	92
17	75	1061.96	1095.01	1071.01	*1061.96*	*1061.96*	*1061.96*	205
18	75	1823.58	1894.73	1846.35	*1823.58*	*1823.58*	*1823.58*	198
19	100	1117.51	1156.93	1123.83	1120.34	1120.33	*1117.51*	242
20	100	1534.17	1592.16	1556.35	*1534.17*	*1534.17*	*1534.17*	301
Average		1227.85	1259.95	1236.21	1228.21	1228.21	1227.85	
AvDev (%)			2.05	0.13	0.52	0.029	0	
NBest			0	1	7	7	8	

[a]GGA (Best): Our best solution after 10 runs [b]CPU Time (Best): Computation time for our best solution Italics indicates best solution

Table 6. Comparative results for the benchmark problem set 2

No	n	Best Known	Li et al	Brandao	GGA Best[c]	CPU Time Best[d](sec)
H1	200	12050.08	12067.65	*12050.08*	*12050.08*	988
H2	240	10208.32	10234.40	*10208.32*	*10208.32*	1450
H3	280	16223.39	16231.80	*16223.39*	*16223.39*	2267
H4	320	17458.65	17576.10	17458.65	*16158.65*	7882
H5	360	21850.40	*21850.40*	23166.56	23166.56	11043
Average		15558.17	15592.07	15821.40	15561.40	
AvDev (%)			0.218	1.692	0.0208	
NBest			1	3	4	

[a]GGA (Best): our best solution after 10 runs [b]CPU Time (Best): Computation time for our best solution Italics indicates best solution

the mean of the best solutions obtained from the 20 runs, the mean computation time (in seconds) corresponding to the average CPU times obtained from the 20 runs. The comparative results indicate that the GGA method is will able to provide high quality solutions over the 20 runs, within reasonable computation times. Moreover, the approach is able to consistently produce good results over the trial runs. It was observed during experimental computations that the consistency increases with increasing number of generations, such that the same best solutions were obtained with generations as high as 500. However, increasing the number of generations would imply increasing the cor-

responding computation time. Therefore, overall, GGA is a robust algorithm that can effectively provide high quality solutions within a sensible computation time. The approach can be developed into a useful decision support tool for the practicing decision makers in logistics management.

CONCLUSION AND FURTHER RESEARCH

The heterogeneous vehicle routing problem is a common real-world problem where the decision maker has to assign customers to an existing fleet

Table 7. Comparative results for benchmark problem set 1

No.	N	Best Known	Taillar d	Tarantili s et al.	Lie et al	Brandao	GGA Ave[a]	CPU Time Ave[b (sec)]
13	50	1517.84	1536.55	1519.96	*1517.84*	*1517.84*	1518.37	58
14	50	607.53	623.05	611.39	*607.53*	*607.53*	608.11	57
15	50	1015.29	1022.05	*1015.29*	*1015.29*	*1015.29*	1015.29	49
16	50	1144.94	1159.14	1145.52	*1144.94*	*1144.94*	1144.94	98
17	75	1061.96	1095.01	1071.01	*1061.96*	*1061.96*	1061.96	208
18	75	1823.58	1894.73	1846.35	*1823.58*	*1823.58*	1823.58	218
19	100	1117.51	*1117.51*	1123.83	1120.34	1120.33	1118.14	239
20	100	1534.17	1592.16	1556.35	1534.17	*1534.17*	1534.17	311
Average		1227.85	1259.95	1236.21	1228.21	1228.21	1228.07	

[a]GGA Ave: Average solution for 20 runs [b]CPU Time Ave: Average computation time for 20 runs Italics indicates best solution

Table 8. Comparative results for the benchmark problem set 2

No.	n	Best Known	Li et al	Brandao	GGA Ave[c]	CPU Time Ave[d](sec)
H1	200	12050.08	12067.65	*12050.08*	12050.08	998
H2	240	10208.32	10234.40	*10208.32*	10209.62	1458
H3	280	16223.39	16231.80	*16223.39*	16224.23	2263
H4	320	17458.65	17576.10	17458.65	16158.65	7894
H5	360	21850.40	*21850.40*	23166.56	21850.40	11012
Average		15558.17	15592.07	15821.40	15561.83	

[a]GGA Ave: Average solution for 20 runs [b]CPU Time Ave: Average computation time for 20 runs Italics indicates best solution

of heterogeneous vehicles. The problem assumes that the available number of vehicles of each type is limited. In this chapter, an improved group genetic algorithm is proposed for addressing the HVRP problem.

Contribution to Theory

This research offers useful contribution to the theory of logistics and transportation, and to the area of heuristic optimization. It identifies and elaborates on the practical significance of the heterogeneous vehicle routing problem at strategic, tactical and operational levels. The improved GGA proposed in this research contributes to the advancement of metaheuristic optimization. Among other enhanced features of the GGA, the algorithm uses

1. A group structure in chromosome coding, which takes advantage of the problem structure;
2. The group genetic operators;
3. Vehicle capacity utilization bias, and
4. Improved chromosome generation and repair mechanisms.

Results from comparative analysis using benchmark problems have proven that the GGA metaheuristic is an efficient and effective approach for addressing the HVRP problem. It is capable of finding high quality solutions within a reasonable

computation time. Therefore, the proposed GGA is an effective tool for decision support in logistics and transportation management.

Implications for Decision Makers

This research provides a significant contribution to the field of logistics and transportation, specifically to heterogeneous fleet vehicle routing. The GGA approach is a viable decision support tool that can assist decision makers to make cost efficient decisions in regards to vehicle routing and scheduling, within a reasonable computation time. As a population-based algorithm, GGA provides a population of alternative solutions from which the decision maker can evaluate and select the most appropriate solution, while considering other practical concerns that could not be included in the model. Furthermore, transportation planning, routing decisions, as well as contract negotiations can be done within a reasonable time, with the decision support from the GGA.

Further Research

In the current GGA approach, enhanced group genetic operators are developed and applied on the heterogeneous vehicle routing problem with reasonable success. The GGA approach and its improvements can be extended to other related grouping or clustering problems. An interesting feature of the problem is when the vehicle routing problem is characterized with uncertainty and imprecision in demand, or distance travelled. This may involve the inclusion of fuzzy set theoretic approaches, in the case of imprecision or fuzziness. Furthermore, it will also be interesting to include time window constraints in the vehicle routing problem. The same approach can also be extended to scheduling problems such as home healthcare scheduling where healthcare personnel are scheduled to visit a group of patients at their homes for healthcare services. Another typical extension of the GGA approach is its application in the area of group technology and cell formation problems which involve clustering of machines into cells that can work on a group of parts with similar design features and other manufacturing characteristics.

REFERENCES

Badeau, P., Gendreau, M., Guertin, F., Potvin, J. Y., & Taillard, E. D. (1997). A parallel tabu search heuristic for the vehicle routing problem with time windows. *Transportation Research Part C, Emerging Technologies*, *5*, 109–122. doi:10.1016/S0968-090X(97)00005-3.

Brandao, J. (2011). A tabu search algorithm for the heterogeneous fixed fleet vehicle routing problem. *Computers & Operations Research*, *38*(1), 140–151. doi:10.1016/j.cor.2010.04.008.

Falkenauer, E. (1992). The grouping genetic algorithms - Widening the scope of the GAs. *Belgian Journal of Operations Research. Statistics and Computer Science*, *33*, 79–102.

Filho, E. V. G., & Tiberti, A. J. (2006). A group genetic algorithm for the machine cell formation problem. *International Journal of Production Economics*, *102*, 1–21. doi:10.1016/j.ijpe.2004.12.029.

Gendreau, M., Laporte, G., Musaraganyi, C., & Taillard, E. D. (1999). A tabu search heuristic for the heterogeneous fleet vehicle routing problem. *Computers & Operations Research*, *26*, 1153–1173. doi:10.1016/S0305-0548(98)00100-2.

Goldberg, D. E. (1989). *Genetic algorithm in search, optimization, and machine learning*. Reading, MA: Addison-Wesley..

Hoff, A., Anderson, H., Christiansen, M., Hasle, G., & Lokketangen, A. (2010). Industrial aspects and literature survey: Fleet composition and routing. *Computers & Operations Research*, *37*, 2041–2061. doi:10.1016/j.cor.2010.03.015.

Li, F., Golden, B., & Wasil, E. (2007). A record-to-record travel algorithm for solving the heterogeneous fleet vehicle routing problem. *Computers & Operations Research*, *34*, 2734–2742. doi:10.1016/j.cor.2005.10.015.

Moghadam, B. F., & Seyedhosseini, S. M. (2010). A particle swarm approach to solve vehicle routing problem with uncertain demand: A drug distribution case study. *International Journal of Industrial Engineering Computations*, *1*, 55–66. doi:10.5267/j.ijiec.2010.01.005.

Mutingi, M., & Mbohwa, C. (2012). Enhanced group genetic algorithm for the heterogeneous fixed fleet vehicle routing problem. In *Proceedings of IEEE Conference on Industrial Engineering and Engineering Management*. Hong Kong: IEEE.

Paraskevopoulos, D., Repoussis, P., Tarantilis, C., Ioannou, G., & Prastacos, G. (2008). A reactive variable neighbourhood tabu search for the heterogeneous fleet vehicle routing problem with time windows. *Journal of Heuristics*, *14*, 425–455. doi:10.1007/s10732-007-9045-z.

Potvin, J., & Bengio, S. (1996). The vehicle routing problem with time windows –Part II: Genetic search. *INFORMS Journal on Computing*, *8*, 165–172. doi:10.1287/ijoc.8.2.165.

Rochat, Y., & Taillard, E. D. (1995). Probabilistic diversification and intensification in local search for vehicle routing. *Journal of Heuristics, 1,* 147–167. doi:10.1007/BF02430370.

Taillard, E. D. (1999). A heuristic column generation method for the heterogeneous fleet VRP. *RAIRO, 33,* 1–34. doi:10.1051/ro:1999101.

Tarantilis, C. D., Kiranoudis, C. T., & Vassiliadis, V. S. A. (2003). A list based threshold accepting metaheuristic for the heterogeneous fixes fleet vehicle routing problem. *The Journal of the Operational Research Society, 54*(1), 65–71. doi:10.1057/palgrave.jors.2601443.

Tarantilis, C. D., Kiranoudis, C. T., & Vassiliadis, V. S. A. (2004). A threshold accepting metaheuristic for the heterogeneous fixed fleet vehicle routing problem. *European Journal of Operational Research, 152,* 148–158. doi:10.1016/S0377-2217(02)00669-0.

Tutuncu, G. Y. (2010). An interactive algorithm for the heterogeneous fixed fleet vehicle routing problem with and without backhauls. *European Journal of Operational Research, 201*(2), 593–600. doi:10.1016/j.ejor.2009.03.044.

ADDITIONAL READING

Ai, J., & Kachitvichyanukul, V. (2009). Particle swarm optimization and two solution representations for solving the capacitated vehicle routing problem. *Computers & Industrial Engineering, 56,* 380–387. doi:10.1016/j.cie.2008.06.012.

Brandao, J. (2008). A deterministic tabu search algorithm for the fleet size and mix vehicle routing problem. *European Journal of Operational Research, 195*(3), 716–728. doi:10.1016/j.ejor.2007.05.059.

Braysey, O., & Gendreau, M. (2005). Vehicle routing problems with time windows, part I: Route Construction and Local Search Algorithms. *Transportation Science, 39*(1), 104–118. doi:10.1287/trsc.1030.0056.

Choi, E., & Tcha, D. W. (2007). A column generation approach to the heterogeneous fleet vehicle routing problem. *Computers & Operations Research, 34,* 2080–2095. doi:10.1016/j.cor.2005.08.002.

Clarke, G., & Wright, J. W. (1964). Scheduling of vehicles from a central depot to a number of delivery points. *Operations Research, 12,* 568–581. doi:10.1287/opre.12.4.568.

Dantzig, G. B., & Ramser, J. H. (1959). The truck dispatching problem. *Management Science, 6,* 80–91. doi:10.1287/mnsc.6.1.80.

Desrochers, M., & Verhoog, T. W. (1991). A new heuristic for the fleet size and mix vehicle routing problem. *Computers & Operations Research, 18,* 263–274. doi:10.1016/0305-0548(91)90028-P.

Eksioglu, B., Vural, A. V., & Resiman, A. (2009). The vehicle routing problem: A taxonomic review. *Computers & Industrial Engineering, 57,* 1472–1483. doi:10.1016/j.cie.2009.05.009.

Filho, E. V., & Tiberti, G. A. J. (2006). A group genetic algorithm for the machine cell formation problem. *International Journal of Production Economics, 102,* 1–21. doi:10.1016/j.ijpe.2004.12.029.

García, S., & Molina, D., Lozano, & Herrera, M. F. (2009). A Study on the use of non-parametric tests for analyzing the evolutionary algorithms' behaviour: A case study on the CEC'2005 special session on real parameter optimization. *Journal of Heuristics, 15,* 617–644. doi:10.1007/s10732-008-9080-4.

Gendreau, M., Laporte, G., Musaraganyi, C., & Taillard, E. D. (1999). A tabu search heuristic for the heterogeneous fleet vehicle routing problem. *Computers & Operations Research, 26*, 1153–1173. doi:10.1016/S0305-0548(98)00100-2.

Gillett, B., & Miller, L. (1974). A heuristic for the vehicle dispatching problem. *Operations Research, 22*, 340–349. doi:10.1287/opre.22.2.340.

Goldberg, D. E. (1989). *Genetic Algorithm in Search, Optimization, and Machine Learning*. Reading, MA: Addison-Wesley..

Golden, B., Assad, A., Levy, L., & Gheysens, F. (1984). The fleet size and mix vehicle routing problem. *Computers & Operations Research, 11*, 49–66. doi:10.1016/0305-0548(84)90007-8.

Grefenstette, J. J. (1987). Incorporating problem specific knowledge into genetic algorithms. In L. Davis (Ed.), *Genetic and Simulated Annealing*. London: Pitman..

Holland, J. H. (1975). *Adaptation in Natural and Artificial System*. Ann Arbor, MI: University of Michigan Press..

Lima, C. M. R. R., Goldbarg, M. C., & Goldbarg, E. F. G. (2004). A memetic algorithm for the heterogeneous fleet vehicle routing problem. *Electronic Notes in Discrete Mathematics, 18*, 171–176. doi:10.1016/j.endm.2004.06.027.

Lima, C. M. R. R., Goldbarg, M. C., & Goldbarg, E. F. G. (2004). A memetic algorithm for the heterogeneous fleet vehicle routing problem. *Electronic Notes in Discrete Mathematics, 18*, 171–176. doi:10.1016/j.endm.2004.06.027.

Liu, S., Huang, W., & Ma, H. (2009). An effective genetic algorithm for the fleet size and mix vehicle routing problems. *Transportation Research Part E, Logistics and Transportation Review, l*(45), 434–445. doi:10.1016/j.tre.2008.10.003.

Moghadam, B. F., & Seyedhosseini, S. M. (2010). A particle swarm approach to solve vehicle routing problem with uncertain demand: A drug distribution case study. *International Journal of Industrial Engineering Computations, 1*, 55–66. doi:10.5267/j.ijiec.2010.01.005.

Ochi, L. S., Vianna, D. S., Drummond, L. M., & Victor, A. O. (1998). A parallel evolutionary algorithm for the vehicle routing problem with heterogeneous fleet. *Future Generation Computer Systems, 14*, 285–292. doi:10.1016/S0167-739X(98)00034-X.

Osman, I., & Salhi, S. (1996). Local search strategies for the vehicle fleet mix problem. In V. J. Rayward-Smith, I. H. Osman, C. R. Reeves, & G. D. Smith (Eds.), *Modern Heuristic Search Methods* (pp. 131–153). New York: Wiley. doi:10.1007/978-1-4613-1361-8.

Prins, C. (2004). A simple and effective evolutionary algorithm for the vehicle routing problem. *Computers & Operations Research, 31*, 1985–2002. doi:10.1016/S0305-0548(03)00158-8.

Renaud, J., & Boctor, F. F. (2002). A sweep-based algorithm for the fleet size and mix vehicle routing problem. *European Journal of Operational Research, 140*, 618–628. doi:10.1016/S0377-2217(01)00237-5.

Salhi, S., & Rand, G. K. (1993). Incorporating vehicle routing into the vehicle fleet composition problem. *European Journal of Operational Research, 66*, 313–330. doi:10.1016/0377-2217(93)90220-H.

Taillard, E. D. (1999). A heuristic column generation method for the heterogeneous fleet VRP. *RAIRO, 33*, 1–34. doi:10.1051/ro:1999101.

Tarantilis, C. D., Kiranoudis, C. T., & Vassiliadis, V. S. (2004). A threshold accepting metaheuristic for the heterogeneous fixed fleet vehicle routing problem. *European Journal of Operational Research, 152*, 148–158. doi:10.1016/S0377-2217(02)00669-0.

Toth, P., & Vigo, D. (2002). *The vehicle routing problem. SIAM Monograph on Discrete Mathematics and Applications.* Philadelphia, PA: SIAM. doi:10.1137/1.9780898718515.

Wassan, N. A., & Osman, I. H. (2002). Tabu search variants for the mix fleet vehicle routing problem. *The Journal of the Operational Research Society, 53,* 768–782. doi:10.1057/palgrave.jors.2601344.

Yaman, H. (2006). Formulations and valid inequalities for the heterogeneous vehicle routing problem. *Mathematical Programming, 106,* 365–390. doi:10.1007/s10107-005-0611-6.

KEY TERMS AND DEFINITIONS

Fleet Composition: The determination of the right size and mix of a fleet of vehicles.

Genetic Algorithm: A stochastic metaheuristic algorithm based on the theory of genetics, evolution and natural selection.

Group Genetic Algorithm: A modified genetic algorithm designed to cater for grouping or clustering problems.

Heterogeneous Fleet: A fleet of vehicles of different types in terms of capacity, running costs, and other operational characteristics.

Homogeneous Fleet: A fleet of vehicles of the same type in terms of capacity, running costs, and other operational characteristics.

Metaheuristic: A higher level iterative computational algorithm for optimization through improvement of candidate solution(s).

Optimization: The search for the best solution from among multiple possible solutions in the solution space.

Vehicle Routing: Planning and scheduling of vehicle routes, subject to a set of given operational constraints.

Chapter 10
Fuzzy Nonlinear Optimization Model to Improve Intermittent Demand Forecasting

Raúl Poler
Universitat Politècnica de València, Spain

Josefa Mula
Universitat Politècnica de València, Spain

Manuel Díaz-Madroñero
Universitat Politècnica de València, Spain

Mariano Jiménez
Universidad del País Vasco (UPV/EHU), Spain

ABSTRACT

This chapter proposes a fuzzy nonlinear programming model for intermittent demand forecasting purposes. The authors formulated the Syntetos and Boylan (SB) forecasting method as a crisp nonlinear programming model. They also attempted to improve it with a new fuzzy nonlinear programming formulation. This fuzzy model is based on fuzzy decision variables, which represent fuzzy triangular numbers. The authors applied fuzzy arithmetic operations, such as addition and subtraction of fuzzy numbers, fuzzy decision variables. They carried out the defuzzification of the fuzzy decision variables through the possibilistic mean value of fuzzy numbers. Finally, the authors validated and tested it by comparing it with the deterministic nonlinear programming model that they adopted as the basis of this work. The computational studies show that fuzzy model performance is consistently better than the SB nonlinear programming model, especially when intermittency is high.

DOI: 10.4018/978-1-4666-4785-5.ch010

INTRODUCTION

Forecasting is an estimation of future demand (Blackstone, 2010). Forecasting demand plays a key role in decision-making processes within the business management activities framework. Due to the relation among the various business areas, an incorrect forecast could have substantially adverse effects on the firm as a whole. Forecasting future demand is central for planning and executing business processes in industrial firms at both the macro and micro levels. At the organizational level, forecasting sales are required as essential inputs for many decision activities in several functional areas; e.g., marketing, sales, production, purchases, accountancy and finances (Mentzer & Bienstock, 1998). Demand forecasting is also relevant for managing inventories (Buffa & Miller, 1979; Hax & Candea, 1984; Silver, Pyke, & Peterson, 1998).

Various forecasting methods exist, but a vast variety of problems in this field also abound which require all type of treatments. Selecting a model depends on a wide range of considerations; e.g., time horizons, objectives, data properties, and many other aspects (Poler & Mula, 2011). Furthermore, the forecasting model must be manageable and should produce reliable results that are easy to interpret.

Demand forecasting methods can be classified into three main categories: qualitative methods, causal methods and quantitative methods (Makridakis, Wheelwright, & Hyndman, 1998). On the one hand, qualitative methods are helpful when there is little or no quantitative information available, but there is enough qualitative information or knowledge. Essentially, they are based on expert opinions (the Delphi Method), on studies into customer opinions, etc. The objective of causal or econometric methods is to develop models that relate demand with a set of independent variables. Selecting independent variables depends on the availability of the data and their relation with the demand to be forecasted. Building these

forecast models implies employing trial-and-error techniques. For this purpose, we select explanatory variables, which logically influence demand requirements, and we carry out regression and, finally, we do statistical verifications. While developing the model, we test alternative equation forms to see which better fits the historical data and/or fulfills some statistical standards and scenarios. The model that best fits the historical data may provide more reliable forecasts. Thus, we can deal with the problem by developing several models, followed by a careful analysis before reaching a forecast. On the other hand, quantitative methods require sufficient quantitative information. These methods have two main classes: a) time series, which forecast the continuation of historical data patterns; b) explanatory series, which attempt to explain how certain variables affect the forecast (simple regression, multiple regression, regression with ARIMA (autoregressive-integrated-moving-average), dynamic regression, an analysis of intervention, multivariate autoregressive models, etc-). The traditional quantitative analysis approaches of available time series include heuristic methods, such as decomposition of time series, exponential smoothing, and the regression of time series and ARIMA models with formal statistical bases. A set of advanced methods also exists, which attempt to face certain constraints that are inherent to traditional models. This chapter analyzes quantitative forecasting methods based on the use of time series in an intermittent demand context.

Demand data, which have many time periods with zero demands, characterize intermittent demand (Varghese & Rossetti, 2008). We can find other definitions in Croston (1972) and in Ghobbar & Friend (2003). Many research works exist on forecasting for the intermittent demand of spare parts by (Callegaro, 2010; Willemain, Smart, & Schwarz, 2004) in the automotive industry and in the aviation industry (Ghobbar & Friend, 2003), among others. Callegaro (2010) provides an overview on demand forecasting methods for spare parts. Here, we highlight Croston's method, whose main innovation used many zero values to adapt to demand. Then, the Syntetos-Boylan (SB) method extended that of Croston to diminish the error of the expected estimate of demand per time period. The paper aims to introduce a new intermittent demand forecasting method based on the SB method in order to achieve better performance. The reason for using a fuzzy SB model is to deal with the great uncertainty inherent to intermittent series (that related to if there would, or would not, be demand during a given time period). The main motivation of this proposal is to improve accuracy when applied to the same crisp data as the original SB model. In this sense, Rommelfanger (1995) recommends using fuzzy models to find a better adjustment of a real problem in order to reduce information costs.

Firstly, we formulate the SB method as a nonlinear programming model. Then, we transform it into a fuzzy nonlinear programming model by considering the two main variables of the Croston and SB methods as fuzzy variables; i.e., the time between consecutive transactions and the magnitude of individual transactions. We represent these two fuzzy decision variables as triangular fuzzy numbers and we also contemplate fuzzy arithmetic operations (addition and subtraction). We next provide crisp forecasting through the defuzzification of fuzzy decision variables using the possibilistic mean value of fuzzy numbers. We computed 5 million forecasts of time series with different degrees of intermittency and randomness to evaluate the performance of the fuzzy model.

The rest of the paper is as follows: firstly, we detail with the main characteristics of the quantitative methods, based on time series, for demand forecasting, this being the main study objective. Then, we formulate a nonlinear programming model based on the SB method for intermittent demand forecasting. Next, we propose a fuzzy nonlinear programming model to improve its performance. We carry out computational experiments to validate and test the deterministic and fuzzy models. Finally, we provide further research and conclusions.

BACKGROUND

We detail the main characteristics of the quantitative methods, based on time series, for demand forecasting, this being the main study objective.

Decomposition methods in time series attempt to identify three patterns of the time series considered: trends, seasonality and cyclicity. The main characteristic of these models is to consider that all the information required to produce a forecast remains stable within these series. Nevertheless, the exactness of the forecast critically depends on the stability of the record trends and their patterns. Furthermore, simply extrapolating past trends can generate incorrect results whenever an event perturbs the record pattern of the series. Kandil, El-Debeiky, & Hasanien (2001) demonstrate that those models which adapt the series to a straight line or to a polymonial perform relatively better if compared with other models for a rapidly developed electric system. Moreover, most of the models applied are valid for a normally developed system. Armstrong (1984) discusses univariate models based on time series, also known as extrapolation methods, by comparing them to other more sophisticated approaches.

When a time series includes a trend or a seasonal effect, or both, the simple average may not suffice to capture the data pattern. The intention of exponential smoothing is to improve the average as a forecast for forthcoming periods. We can classify exponential smoothing methods as (Makridakis et al., 1998):

1. Simple exponential smoothing (a parameter/adaptive parameter),
2. A Holt linear method (appropriate for trends),
3. The Holt-Winters method (appropriate for trends and seasonality) and
4. Pegels' classification.

The exponential smoothing concept (Holt, 1957; Winters, 1960) proved an important development for forecast demand when controlling inventories. Segura & Vercher (2001) determine optimum forecasting by the Holt-Winters exponential smoothing model using a Microsoft Excel spreadsheet and a nonlinear programming model. Ghobbar & Friend (2003) examine the results of 13 forecasting methods based on statistical models in an intermittent demand setting; e.g., producing spare parts for the aeronautics industry. The results show that the better methods are the moving weighted average method and the Holt and Croston method for intermittent demand, characterized for their randomness and for having many zero values. Willemain et al. (2004) also deal with the intermittent or irregular demand forecast problem. The authors developed not only a patented algorithm to forecast the accumulated distribution of intermittent demand in a fixed delivery time, but also a new method to evaluate the exactness of these forecasts. These authors demonstrate that this method provides more exact forecasts than those obtained by the Croston exponential smoothing method (1972). Exponential smoothing methods are suitable for immediate or short-term forecasts, while decomposition methods of time series require more calculations; therefore, the user who must predict the time series' cyclic factor has to pay more attention (Makridakis et al., 1998).

The Box-Jenkins approach is the name of the general methodology that Box and Jenkins (1976) suggested to apply ARIMA models in order to analyze time series, forecasting and control. The systematic use of this approach helps identify time series characteristics, like stability, seasonality and eventuality. This method provides a class of stable stochastic processes models. Therefore, it is an iterative approach which identifies a possible useful model from a general class of models. The data record verifies the selected model to check if it describes them accurately. If the specified model proves insatisfactory, we repeat the process using a different model designed to improve the original one. We repeat this process until we identify a satisfactory model. The seasonal ARIMA model is the most advanced model for short-term forecasting and many practical applications have successfully tested it (Chu & Zhang, 2003). In addition, equivalent ARIMA models can implement Winter's additive and multiplicative exponential smoothing models (Bowerman & O'Connell, 1993; McKenzie, 1984).

Nearly all the models considered to date are linear, although there are some characteristics that arise in real data which linear models cannot capture; for instance, modeling asymmetric cycles. One of the important characteristics of nonlinear models is that they can perform chaotically. Chaos is a characteristic of time series in which values can be random and not periodical, despite resulting from a completely deterministic process. Tong (1983), Casdagli & Eubank (1992) and Granger & Terasvita (1993) developed nonlinear models to forecast demand. Thus, one of the main limitations of traditional methods is that they are basically linear methods. To employ them, users must specify the model form without having the true knowledge required on the complex data relation. Evidently, if linear models can well approach the contemplated data generation process, then we must consider them preferred models to other more complex ones. Linear models offer the advantage of being easy to interpret and to implement. Nevertheless, if linear models do not adapt well, then we should contemplate nonlinear models. One nonlinear forecasting model which has recently attracted considerable attention is the model based on artificial neuronal networks. The inspiration behind these models is the structure of the human brain and how it processes information. They are able to learn from data and experiences, identify the pattern or trend, and make generalizations for the future. Wu & Lu (1993) design and implement an artificial neuronal network to forecast stock market trends. The authors also implement a statistical system based on the ARIMA time series model (p, d, q) (Box & Jenkins, 1976). Since neuronal networks-based forecasting occasionally presents inflection values, the authors developed a transfer function model based on indices and forecasts. With the results obtained with both systems, the neuronal networks-based model comes closer to forecasts, but the time series-based model better forecasts market trends. Thus, the neuronal networks-based model performs better for stable markets with a smaller number of historical data available. Meanwhile, the ARIMA model offers better forecasting market trends when many historical data are available. Ijumba & Hunsley (1999) present the results of an artificial neuronal networks-based model to forecast peaks in demand of charges in a recently electrified area on an hourly basis. These authors obtain demand forecasting errors of below 10% by employing only the limited historical data of the charges patterns of that area. Chu and Zhang (2003) compare the Box-Jenkins ARIMA modeling approach with the nonlinear artificial neuronal networks-based approach to forecast a retailer's aggregated sales. Sales data severely fluctuate seasonally. These results of these authors suggest that the nonlinear method is the best approach to model a given retailer's sales movements.

The fuzzy set theory has helped define systems that are difficult to define accurately. Bellman and Zadeh (1970) distinguish between randomness and fuzziness. Randomness relates with uncertainty as to an object belonging, or not, to a nonfuzzy set. Fuzziness, however, considers classes in which there are degrees of belonging between completely belonging and not. An association between fuzziness and fuzzy sets exists. Numerous works have extensively studied the fuzzy set theory over the last 40 years. The vast majority of the initial interest of the fuzzy set theory lay in representing uncertainty in human cognitive processes (Zadeh, 1965). Later, applying the fuzzy set theory proved successful in many different areas like Engineering (Blockley, 1979), Meteorology (Cao & Chen, 1983), Medicine (Vila & Delgado, 1983) and, in general, in all those areas where decision variables are ambiguous and difficult to define accurately, although human experts can optimally manage them by linguistic terms. These areas include decision making, reasoning, learning, etc. Guiffrida and Nagi (1998) conducted a thorough study into applying the fuzzy set theory in the production management area. These authors describe fuzzy set applications in the areas of project scheduling, distribution in the plant, demand forecasting, quality management, production planning and sequencing. Later, Mula, Poler, García-Sabater, and Lario (2006) and Peidro, Mula, Poler, and Lario (2009) provide reviews about models for production planning and supply chain planning under uncertainty. As a methodology, the fuzzy set theory incorporates imprecision and subjectivity into the formulation and model-solving process. This theory is an appealing help tool to investigate demand forecasting in highly dynamic manufacturing settings. Interpolation, calculation of moving averages, exponential smoothing and regression techniques are four common forecasting techniques. In traditional forecasting methods, calculations and results are deterministic. Nonetheless, because information is unavailable or uncertain, or a forecasting model is inappropriate, it is extremely hard to forecast time series data exactly in a highly dynamic setting. Chen and Wang (1999) apply fuzzy concepts in a forecasting model in the electronic semiconductors industry, characterized by a highly dynamic setting. These authors developed two fuzzy forecasting models: Fuzzy Interpolation (FI) (Kaleva, 1994) and Fuzzy Linear Regression (FLR) (Makridakis et al., 1998). They used FI to forecast the future price of a product and FLR to forecast the sales of another product. The forecasts that these methods generate are fuzzy values obtained with fuzzy mathematical programming by means of fuzzy linear and fuzzy nonlinear programming models. Tseng, Tzeng, Yu, and Yuan (2001) developed a fuzzy ARIMA model (FARIMA) and applied it to forecast the change rate from NT (New Taiwan) dollars to US (United States) dollars. The model includes interval models with interval parameters and FARIMA provides the distribution of the possibility of future values. Tseng and Tzeng (2002) propose a fuzzy ARIMA seasonal forecasting model, known as FSARIMA, which combines the advantages of the SARIMA model (ARIMA with seasonality) and the fuzzy linear regression FLR model. The FSARIMA model offers two main advantages: a) it is suitable for the best and worst possible situations; b) it requires a smaller number of observations than that of the SARIMA model. Frantti and Mähönen (2001) present a software tool based on fuzzy logic, called the Fuzzy Logic Advisory Tool (FLAT), to forecast the demand of around 1000 different products to help the process of purchasing the materials of some 14000 different components in the manufacturing processes of Nokia's Haukipudas factory. We can find other fuzzy approaches for forecasting purposes in Bermúdez, Segura, and Vercher (2006) and Azadeh, Moghaddam, Khakzad, and Ebrahimipour (2012).

The work by Chen & Wang (1999) comes close to this chapter, although there are important differences as to the type of demand signal to foresee (in this case, intermittent demand) and the forecasting method adopted as the basis of the fuzzy forecasting model (in this case, the SB method). Thus, we propose for the first time a fuzzy nonlinear programming model based on the use of fuzzy numbers to define the forecasting formulation of the SB method to improve forecasts in a manufacturing context of intermittent demand. The fuzzy model uses the same conventional crisp data, but attempts to improve better performance.

MODEL FORMULATION

Nonlinear Programming Model

Croston (1972) proposes a method to forecast intermittent demands which takes into account both demand size, Z_t, and the inter-arrival time between

demands, X_t. Croston's method separately forecasts the time between consecutive transactions, X_t, and the magnitude of the individual transactions, Z_t. During review period t, if no demand occurs, d_t, during a review period, then the estimates of the demand size, Z_t, and the inter-arrival time at the end of time period t, X_t, remain unchanged. If demand occurs so that $d_t > 0$, then we update estimates as so:

$$Z_t = \alpha \cdot d_{t-1} + (1 - \alpha) \cdot Z_{t-1} \qquad (1)$$

$$X_t = \alpha \cdot q_{t-1} + (1 - \alpha) \cdot X_{t-1} \qquad (2)$$

where $\alpha \in [0, 1]$ is a smoothing constant, d_t is the demand value during period t and q_t is the number of time periods between the consecutive transactions during period t. The forecast of demand per period at time t is as follows:

$$F_t = \frac{Z_t}{X_t} \qquad (3)$$

Next, there are several variations applied to Croston's method (Johnston & Boylan, 1996; Rao, 1973; Snyder, 2002; Willemain, Smart, Shockor, & DeSautels, 1994), but the proposal of Syntetos and Boylan (2001) is one of the most performed by several authors (Callegaro, 2010; Teunter, Syntetos, and Babai (2010)). Syntetos and Boylan (2001) demonstrate the bias of that Croston's estimator we can formulate (3) it as follows:

$$F_t = \left(1 - \frac{\alpha}{2}\right) \cdot \frac{Z_t}{X_t} \qquad (4)$$

Figure 1 shows a fragment of demand data as a function of time and indicates the meaning of parameters X_t and q_t in the plot.

Now, we propose a nonlinear programming model to optimize the SB method. This crisp formulation is, in itself, a new solving approach

Figure 1. Demand data and SB forecasting

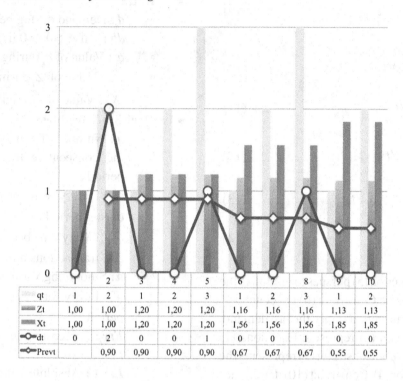

	1	2	3	4	5	6	7	8	9	10
qt	1	2	1	2	3	1	2	3	1	2
Zt	1,00	1,00	1,20	1,20	1,20	1,16	1,16	1,16	1,13	1,13
Xt	1,00	1,00	1,20	1,20	1,20	1,56	1,56	1,56	1,85	1,85
dt	0	2	0	0	1	0	0	1	0	0
Prevt		0,90	0,90	0,90	0,90	0,67	0,67	0,67	0,55	0,55

because the application of Formulas (1), (2) and (4) without optimization solves the original SB.

- **Sets:**
  - T Set of periods of the forecasting horizon ($t=1...T$)
- **Data:**
  - d_t: Demand during period t
  - db_t: 1 if $d_t > 0$ or 0 if d_t is zero
  - q_0: Value of q_t during period 0
  - Z_0: Value of Z_t during period 0
  - X_0: Value of X_t during period 0
- **Decision Variables:**
  - q_t: Number of time periods between the consecutive transactions during period t
  - Z_t: Estimated demand size during period t
  - X_t: Time between the consecutive transactions during period t
  - A: Smoothing variable

  - F_t: Forecasted demand during period t
  - Err_t: Forecasting error during period t
  - $ErrA_t$: Absolute value of forecasting error during period t
- **Objective function:**

$$Minz = \sum_{t=2}^{T-1} ErrA_t \qquad (5)$$

Subject to

$$q_t = q_{t-1} \cdot \left(1 - db_{t-1}\right) + 1 \ \forall t \qquad (6)$$

$$Z_t = Z_{t-1} \cdot \left(1 - \alpha \cdot db_{t-1}\right) + \alpha \cdot d_{t-1} \ \forall t \qquad (7)$$

$$X_t = X_{t-1} \cdot \left(1 - \alpha \cdot db_{t-1}\right) + \alpha \cdot q_{t-1} \cdot db_{t-1} \ \forall t \ (8)$$

$$F_t = \frac{Z_t}{X_t}\left(1 - \frac{\alpha}{2}\right) \forall t \tag{9}$$

$$Errt = Ft - dt \; \forall t \tag{10}$$

$$Err_t \leq ErrA_t \; \forall t \tag{11}$$

$$-Err_t \leq ErrA_t \; \forall t \tag{12}$$

$$q_t, Z_t, X_t, F_t, ErrA_t \geq 0 \; \forall t \tag{13}$$

$$0.1 \leq \alpha \leq 0.9 \; \forall t \tag{14}$$

Objective function (5) pursues to minimize the mean absolute error. Constraint (6) is a counter of the number of time periods since the last demand. Constraints (7) and (8) represent Equations (1) and (2), respectively. Constraint (9) represents the demand estimator (4). Constraint (10) determines the forecasting error, while a linear form of absolute value expresses this deviation in Constraints (11) and (12). Constraint (13) guarantees the non negativity of the decision variables. Finally, constraint (14) binds the values of decision variable α from 0.1 to 0.9 to avoid the use of only one part of Formulas (7) and (8).

Fuzzy Nonlinear Programming Model

Here we propose the following fuzzy nonlinear programming model for forecasting purposes in intermittent demand contexts based on the deterministic SB optimization method. In this model, fuzzy numbers model the estimated demand size during period t, $\tilde{Z}_t$, and the time between the consecutive transactions during period t, $\tilde{X}_t$.

- **Sets:**
  - T: Set of periods of the forecasting horizon ($t=1...T$)

- **Data:**
  - d_t: Demand during period t
  - db_t: 1 if $d_t > 0$ or 0 if d_t is zero
  - q_0: Value of q_t during period 0
  - $\tilde{Z}_0$: Value of $\tilde{Z}_t$ during period 0
  - $\tilde{X}_0$: Value of $\tilde{X}_t$ during period 0

- **Decision Variables:**
  - q_t: Number of time periods between the consecutive transactions during period t
  - $\tilde{Z}_t$: Fuzzy estimated demand size during period t
  - $\tilde{X}_t$: Fuzzy time between the consecutive transactions during period t
  - α: Smoothing variable
  - $\tilde{F}_t$: Fuzzy forecasted demand during period t
  - Err_t: Forecasting error during period t
  - $ErrA_t$: Absolute value of forecasting error during period t

- **Objective function:**

$$Min \cdot z = \sum_{t=2}^{T-1} ErrA_t \tag{15}$$

Subject to

$$q_t = q_{t-1} \cdot \left(1 - db_{t-1}\right) + 1 \; \forall t \tag{16}$$

$$\tilde{Z}_t = \tilde{Z}_{t-1} \cdot \left(1 - \alpha \cdot db_{t-1}\right) + \alpha \cdot d_{t-1} \; \forall t \tag{17}$$

$$\tilde{X}_t = \tilde{X}_{t-1} \cdot \left(1 - \alpha \cdot db_{t-1}\right) + \alpha \cdot q_{t-1} \cdot db_{t-1} \quad \forall t \tag{18}$$

$$\tilde{F}_t = \frac{\tilde{Z}_t}{\tilde{X}_t}\left(1 - \frac{\alpha}{2}\right) \; \forall t \tag{19}$$

$$Err_t = \tilde{F}_t - d_t \ \forall t \tag{20}$$

$$Err_t \leq ErrA_t \ \forall t \tag{21}$$

$$-Err_t \leq ErrA_t \ \forall t \tag{22}$$

$$q_t, \tilde{Z}_t, \tilde{X}_t, \tilde{F}_t, ErrA_t \geq 0 \ ErrA \geq 0 \ \forall t \tag{23}$$

$$0.1 \leq \alpha \leq 0.9 \ \forall t \tag{24}$$

We consider the triangular fuzzy numbers defined by $\tilde{A} = \left(A_l, A_c, A_u \right)$, where A_c is the peak or center, A_l is the left value and A_u is the right value, according to Dubois & Prade (1980). A triangular fuzzy number with center A_c represents a fuzzy quantity "x is approximately equal to A_c". All the fuzzy numbers in the model must fulfill the following conditions: $A_l \geq 0$, $A_c \geq A_l$ and $A_u \geq A_c$. We consider fuzzy arithmetic operations, such as scalar multiplication of a fuzzy number, for Constraints (17) and (18), and the division of two fuzzy numbers for Constraint (19), i.e., given that $\tilde{A} = \left(A_l, A_c, A_u \right)$ and $\tilde{B} = \left(B_l, B_c, B_u \right)$:

$$\frac{\tilde{A}}{\tilde{B}} = \left(\frac{A_l}{B_u}, \frac{A_c}{B_c}, \frac{A_u}{B_l} \right) \tag{25}$$

We use the expected mean value of a fuzzy number as a defuzzification method. Dubois and Prade (1980) define $E(\tilde{A})$, the mean or expected value of a triangular fuzzy number $\tilde{A} = \left(A_l, A_c, A_u \right)$ by

$$E\left(\tilde{A} \right) = \frac{A_l + 4A_c + A_u}{6} \tag{26}$$

The readers can find other properties of fuzzy numbers in Dubois and Prade (1980) and Carlsson and Fullér (2001). By taking into account these properties and the arithmetic operations on triangular fuzzy numbers, we can obtain the following equivalent model:

- **Sets:**
  - T: Set of periods of the forecasting horizon ($t=1...T$)
- **Data:**
  - d_t: Demand during period t
  - db_t: 1 if $d_t > 0$ or 0 if d_t is zero
  - q_0: Value of q_t during period 0
  - $\tilde{Z}_0$: Value of $\tilde{Z}_t$ during period 0 where $\tilde{Z}_0 = (Z_{c0}, Z_{l0}, Z_{u0})$
    - $\tilde{X}_0$: Value of $\tilde{X}_t$ during period 0 where $\tilde{X}_0 = (X_{c0}, X_{l0}, X_{u0})$
  - M: A large number
- **Decision Variables:**
  - q_t: Number of time periods between the consecutive transactions during period t
  - Z_{ct}: Estimated demand size during period t – center value of the fuzzy number
  - Z_{lt}: Estimated demand size during period t – left-width value of the fuzzy number
  - Z_{ut}: Estimated demand size during period t – right-width value of the fuzzy number
  - X_{ct}: Time between consecutive transactions during period t - center value of the fuzzy number
  - X_{lt}: Time between consecutive transactions during period t – left-width value of the fuzzy number
  - X_{ut}: Time between consecutive transactions during period t – right-width value of the fuzzy number
  - A: Smoothing variable
  - F_t: Crisp forecasted demand during period t
  - Err_t: Forecasting error during period t

○ *ErrA_t*: Absolute value of forecasting error during period t

- **Objective function:**

$$Minz = \sum_{t=2}^{T-1} ErrA_t \qquad (27)$$

Subject to

$$q_t = q_{t-1} \cdot \left(1 - db_{t-1}\right) + 1 \ \forall t \qquad (28)$$

$$Z_{ct} = Z_{ct-1} \cdot \left(1 - \alpha \cdot db_{t-1}\right) + \alpha \cdot d_{t-1} \ \forall t \qquad (29)$$

$$Z_{lt} = Z_{lt-1} \cdot \left(1 - \alpha \cdot db_{t-1}\right) + \alpha \cdot d_{t-1} \ \forall t \qquad (30)$$

$$Z_{ut} = Z_{ut-1} \cdot \left(1 - \alpha \cdot db_{t-1}\right) + \alpha \cdot d_{t-1} \ \forall t \qquad (31)$$

$$Z_{ct} \geq Z_{lt} \ \forall t \qquad (32)$$

$$Z_{ut} \geq Z_{ct} \ \forall t \qquad (33)$$

$$X_{ct} = X_{ct-1} \cdot \left(1 - \alpha \cdot db_{t-1}\right) + \alpha \cdot q_{t-1} \cdot db_{t-1} \ \forall t \qquad (34)$$

$$X_{lt} = X_{lt-1} \cdot \left(1 - \alpha \cdot db_{t-1}\right) + \alpha \cdot q_{t-1} \cdot db_{t-1} \ \forall t \qquad (35)$$

$$X_{ut} = X_{ut-1} \cdot \left(1 - \alpha \cdot db_{t-1}\right) + \alpha \cdot q_{t-1} \cdot db_{t-1} \ \forall t \qquad (36)$$

$$X_{ct} \geq X_{lt} \ \forall t \qquad (37)$$

$$X_{ut} \geq X_{ct} \ \forall t \qquad (38)$$

$$Ft = \frac{\dfrac{Z_{lt}}{X_{ut}} + 4\dfrac{Z_{ct}}{X_{ct}} + \dfrac{Z_{ut}}{X_{lt}}}{6}\left(1 - \frac{\alpha}{2}\right) \ \forall t \qquad (39)$$

$$Errt = F_t - d_t \ \forall t \qquad (40)$$

$$Err_t \leq ErrA_t \ \forall t \qquad (41)$$

$$-Err_t \leq ErrA_t \ \forall t \qquad (42)$$

$$q_t, Z_{ct}, Z_{lt}, Z_{ut}, X_{ct}, X_{lt}, X_{ut}, F_t, ErrA_t \geq 0 \ \forall t \qquad (43)$$

$$0.1 \leq \alpha \leq 0.9 \ \forall t \qquad (44)$$

Objective function (27) pursues to minimize the mean absolute error. Constraint (28) is a counter of the number of time periods since the last demand. Constraints from (29) to (31) relate to Constraint (7), but when considering $\tilde{Z}_t$ a fuzzy triangular number. Thus, constraint (29) denotes the center value of $\tilde{Z}_t$, constraint (30) represents the left value of $\tilde{Z}_t$ and constraint (31) denotes the right value of $\tilde{Z}_t$. These constraints consider the scalar multiplication of a fuzzy triangular number (Dubois & Prade, 1980). Constraint (32) guarantees that the center, Z_{ct}, of fuzzy number $\tilde{Z}_t$ is higher than the left value Z_{lt}. Constraint (33) also ensures that the upper value, Z_{ut}, of fuzzy number $\tilde{Z}_t$ is higher than the center, Z_{ct}. Constraints (34) to (36) relate to Constraint (8) by considering $\tilde{X}_t$ as a fuzzy triangular number. Constraints (37) and (38) are similar to Constraints (32) and (33), but for $\tilde{X}_t$. Constraint (39) applies Equations (25) and (26) to Constraint (19) to defuzzify the forecasting value, $\tilde{F}_t$. The rest of the constraints are similar to those in deterministic nonlinear programming.

COMPUTATIONAL STUDY

This work has carried out a computational study to compare the performance of the proposed fuzzy nonlinear programming model against the SB optimization method (crisp nonlinear programming model), both of which take the SB approach as a basis. Forecasts have been calculated over time series to randomly generate by using uniform distributions for demand intermittence and scale. The number of periods generated was $T=30$. We used the demand data from $t=1$ to $t=29$ to calculate F_{30}, because we do not employ d_{30} to calculate the forecast, but to test the model. We can summarize the experiment characteristics as follows:

Time Series Generation: Intermittency simulated using a standard continuous uniform distribution to randomly generate p values (between 0 and 1) to determine the existence of demand during a given period t is as follows: if $p \leq x$ then demand exists ($i_t = 1$), otherwise it does not ($i_t = 0$). We established a set of five values for $x = \{0.1, 0.15, 0.2, 0.25, 0.3\}$.

The scale simulated using a standard continuous uniform distribution to randomly generate q values to determine the amount of demand as follows: $d_t = q \cdot y$. We established a set of five values for $y = \{2, 4, 8, 16, 32\}$.

Thus we obtain the demand value for a given period t as $d_t = q \cdot y \cdot i_t$. We rounded the values in order to work with integer demand.

The number of periods generated was $T = 30$. Nevertheless, we did not employ d_T to solve the crisp nonlinear programming and fuzzy nonlinear programming models.

For each pair of (x, y) values, we generated 100 sets of demand data (time series). As there were 5 values for x and 5 values for y, we generated 2500 time series.

In order to eliminate the influence of the model values initialization, all the generated models use the same initialization values: $Z_{c0} = 0$; $Z_{l0} = 0$; $Z_{u0} = 0$; $X_{c0} = 2$; $X_{l0} = 1$; $X_{u0} = 3$

Models resolution: We employed the 2500 time series to obtain one-step forecasts with both the crisp and fuzzy models, solved using the CONOPT solver (Drud, 1994) to obtain F_T (with $T = 30$).

New demand generation and forecast error calculation: For the 2500 time series, we randomly generated 1000 d_T values (with $T = 30$) using the same uniform distributions described, which means 2.5 million values of new demand.

We calculated one-step forecasting errors for each generated demand as: $e_T = d_T - F_T$, obtained by both crisp and fuzzy models, and we estimated the weighted absolute percentage error (WAPE), as shown in (45). One-step forecasting error suffices to evaluate forecasting models performance because, in the same way as the SB forecasting method, they provide only one level to forecast future demand points. Thus the forecasts beyond T have the same value and we compare them with simulated demand to obtain the same result as done with 1000 d_T values. We computed 5 million errors (1000 demand values for each 2500 time series for both the crisp and fuzzy models).

$$WAPE_T = \frac{|e_T|}{\dfrac{1}{T-1} \cdot \sum_{t=1}^{T-1} d_t} \qquad (45)$$

Figure 2 shows the demand average and the standard deviation of the 1000 values of random demand generated per pair of (x, y) values. We can observe that the demand average increases not only when scale increases (y values increase), but when intermittency decreases (x values increase). Moreover, the demand standard deviation exhibits the same behavior, but with high scales.

We can employ the square coefficient of variation of demand (CV^2) and the average inter-demand interval (ADI) parameters to evaluate randomness and intermittence, respectively. According to its values, we can classify a time series into four categories (Syntetos, 2001) based on the Williams (1984) criteria (Figure 3).

Table 1 shows the characterization of the generated time series regarding CV^2 and ADI. All the time series are clearly below the 0.49 value for CV^2, and are over the 1.32 value of ADI, which means that they are all "intermittent no erratic".

Figure 4 shows the graphical representation of the CV^2 and ADI values. Intermittence grows when x decreases (the ADI values are similar for any y). Randomness grows when both x and y grow.

After solving the 2500 generated time series using the crisp nonlinear programming model and the proposed fuzzy model, and having calculated the forecasting error for 1000 d_T values, we compared the performance of both models. Table 2 shows the differences between the fuzzy model and the crisp nonlinear programming model WAPE per pair of intermittency and scale values.

The values represent the percentage of reduction of WAPE by the fuzzy model in relation to the crisp nonlinear programming model. Figure 5 is a graphical representation of the values, where the gray and black circles sizes respectively represent the positive and negative differences for the fuzzy model.

From the results obtained with the computational study, we summarize that:

Figure 3. Erratic and intermittent time series. Source: (Ghobbar & Friend, 2002)

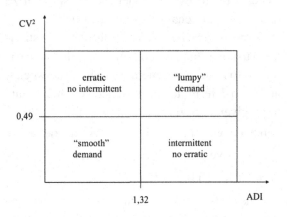

Figure 2. Demand average and the standard deviation of generated demand

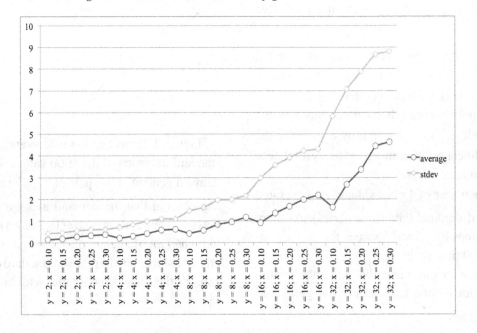

Table 1. The CV² and ADI values of the generated time series

ADI	x=0.10	x=0.15	x=0.20	x=0.25	x=0.30
y=2	8.18	5.84	4.93	4.14	3.21
y=4	8.14	6.46	4.83	3.62	3.17
y=8	8.85	6.20	5.38	3.93	3.31
y=16	7.38	6.08	4.96	3.91	3.37
y=32	8.71	5.84	4.89	3.80	3.29

CV²	x=0.10	x=0.15	x=0.20	x=0.25	x=0.30
y=2	0.06	0.09	0.09	0.10	0.10
y=4	0.14	0.20	0.21	0.21	0.21
y=8	0.19	0.25	0.28	0.29	0.29
y=16	0.23	0.25	0.26	0.30	0.34
y=32	0.26	0.32	0.33	0.35	0.29

Figure 4. The CV² and ADI chart of the generated time series

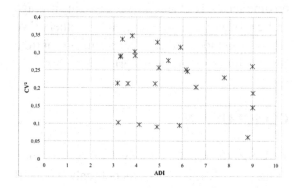

The fuzzy nonlinear programming model is consistently better than the SB optimization method in almost all the combinations of intermittency (x) and scale (y). The average WAPE reduction is 3.1%.

When intermittency is high $(x \leq 0.15)$, the fuzzy nonlinear programming model performs much better than the SB optimization method.

The performance of the fuzzy nonlinear programming model in comparison with the SB optimization method does not vary significantly with the scale (y). WAPE reduction is higher for values $y \geq 4$.

There are two cells in which the fuzzy nonlinear programming model performs slightly worse than the SB optimization method: $(x = 0.1 ; y = 2)$ and $(x = 0.15 ; y = 4)$.

In additional to the descriptive statistics, we ran a two sample t-test or Student's t-test in order to determine any statistically significant difference between the means of the forecasting errors obtained by the crisp nonlinear programming model and the proposed fuzzy model. We employed the SPSS software to perform the test of the two groups of 2.5 million errors, and we obtained these results:

Table 2. Differences between the fuzzy model and the crisp nonlinear programming model

	$x = 0.10$	$x = 0.15$	$x = 0.20$	$x = 0.25$	$x = 0.30$
$y = 2$	-0.15%	5.39%	0.58%	2.13%	0.71%
$y = 4$	8.27%	-0.80%	3.47%	0.56%	4.01%
$y = 8$	3.54%	2.95%	0.76%	5.28%	2.27%
$y = 16$	4.23%	6.25%	6.56%	3.71%	4.54%
$y = 32$	4.19%	4.63%	2.09%	2.94%	2.70%

Figure 5. Chart with differences in performance between models

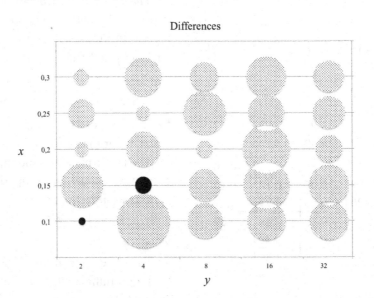

- The Levene's test for equality of variances obtained $F = 105.795$ and $p = 0.000$, which means that the two samples have unequal variances, which means that we cannot assume equal variances for the t-test.
- The t-test for the equality of means obtained $t = 20.598$; $df = 4999854.845$; $p = 0.000$; Mean difference = 0.0644424; Std. error difference = 0.0031286; 95% confidence interval of the difference Lower = 0.0583104 Upper = 0.0705743. Therefore, we conclude that there is a statistically significant difference between the forecasting errors provided by both models.

FUTURE RESEARCH DIRECTIONS

In the experiments preparation phase, we identified that the initialization of the model values during period 0 is highly relevant. Thus, we will conduct further research in order to determine the best way to initialize the model. Moreover, we will conduct forthcoming works to extend our fuzzy approach to other forecasting methods, such as decomposition on time series, Holt and Winters, moving average and exponential smoothing, among others. We will also include a battery of experiments for time series with different characteristics.

CONCLUSION

This chapter provides a novel fuzzy extension of an existing time series model (called the SB method) for demand forecasting under intermittency conditions (i.e., when periods with positive demand alternate with another one without demand). We transform the fuzzy optimization model into a new crisp one, and we compare both models' performance with the synthetic generated data. Thus, we apply soft computing techniques based on fuzzy nonlinear programming to the well-known SB approach in order to forecast in intermittent demand contexts. The main reason for our fuzzy method is to improve accuracy when applied to the same crisp data as the original SB model. We modeled the SB method as a nonlinear programming model, and then we transformed it into a fuzzy nonlinear programming model. The two main variables of the method are fuzzy variables, which we represent as triangular fuzzy numbers. We contemplated the fuzzy addition and subtraction arithmetic operations of fuzzy values. We used the mean value of these fuzzy values as a defuzzification method and as a previous calculus of the forecasts. WE conducted an ample, exhaustive experimental study to test fuzzy model performance. These computational experiments based on different levels of intermittency and randomness demonstrate that our fuzzy approach provides consistent results that are better than the SB optimization method, especially when intermittency is high, which represent the more complex situation in terms of forecasting. Finally, we did statistical tests to check the comparisons made between both models. Improvement was 3.1% and the average of errors was statistically significant.

ACKNOWLEDGMENT

Mariano Jiménez wishes to gratefully acknowledge financial support from the Spanish Ministry of Education, project ECO 2011-26499

REFERENCES

Armstrong, J. S. (1984). Forecasting by extrapolation: Conclusions from 25 years of research. *Interfaces*, *14*(6), 52–66. doi:10.1287/inte.14.6.52.

Azadeh, A., Moghaddam, M., Khakzad, M., & Ebrahimipour, V. (2012). A flexible neural network-fuzzy mathematical programming algorithm for improvement of oil price estimation and forecasting. *Computers & Industrial Engineering*, *62*(2), 421–430. doi:10.1016/j.cie.2011.06.019.

Bellman, R. E., & Zadeh, L. A. (1970). Decision-making in a fuzzy environment. *Management Science*, *17*(4), B-141–B-164. doi:10.1287/mnsc.17.4.B141.

Bermúdez, J. D., Segura, J. V., & Vercher, E. (2006). A decision support system methodology for forecasting of time series based on soft computing. *Computational Statistics & Data Analysis*, *51*(1), 177–191. doi:10.1016/j.csda.2006.02.010.

Blackstone, J. H. (Ed.). (2010). *APICS dictionary* (13th ed.). APICS The Association for Operations Management..

Blockley, D. I. (1979). The role of fuzzy sets in civil engineering. *Fuzzy Sets and Systems*, *2*(4), 267–278. doi:10.1016/0165-0114(79)90001-0.

Bowerman, B. L., & O'Connell, R. T. (1993). Forecasting and time series: An applied approach. Belmont.

Box, G. E. P., & Jenkins, G. M. (1976). *Time series analysis: Forecasting and control*. San Francisco: Holden-Day..

Buffa, E. S., & Miller, J. G. (1979). *Production-inventory systems: Planning and control*. Richard D. Irwin..

Callegaro, A. (2010). Forecasting methods for spare parts demand. Universita' Degli Studi Di Padova, Italy..

Cao, H., & Chen, G. (1983). Some applications of fuzzy sets to meteorological forecasting. *Fuzzy Sets and Systems*, *9*(1–3), 1–12. doi:10.1016/S0165-0114(83)80001-3.

Carlsson, C., & Fuller, R. (2000). Soft computing and the bullwhip effect. *Ecological Complexity*, *2*, 1–26.

Carlsson, C., & Fuller, R. (2001). On possibilistic mean value and variance of fuzzy numbers. *Fuzzy Sets and Systems*, 22, 315–326. doi:10.1016/S0165-0114(00)00043-9.

Casdagli, M., & Eubank, S. (1992). *Nonlinear modeling and forecasting*. Westview Press..

Chen, T., & Wang, M. J. J. (1999). Forecasting methods using fuzzy concepts. *Fuzzy Sets and Systems*, 105(3), 339–352. doi:10.1016/S0165-0114(97)00265-0.

Chu, C. W., & Zhang, G. P. (2003). A comparative study of linear and nonlinear models for aggregate retail sales forecasting. *International Journal of Production Economics*, 86(3), 217–231. doi:10.1016/S0925-5273(03)00068-9.

Croston, J. D. (1972). Forecasting and stock control for intermittent demands. *Operational Research Quarterly*, 23(3), 289.

Drud, A. S. (1994). CONOPT: A large scale GRG code. *ORSA Journal on Computing*, 6, 207–216. doi:10.1287/ijoc.6.2.207.

Dubois, D., & Prade, H. M. (1980). *Fuzzy sets and systems: Theory and applications*. Academic Press..

Frantti, T., & Mähönen, P. (2001). Fuzzy logic-based forecasting model. *Engineering Applications of Artificial Intelligence*, 14(2), 189–201. doi:10.1016/S0952-1976(00)00076-2.

Ghobbar, A. A., & Friend, C. H. (2002). Sources of intermittent demand for aircraft spare parts within airline operations. *Journal of Air Transport Management*, 8, 221–231. doi:10.1016/S0969-6997(01)00054-0.

Ghobbar, A. A., & Friend, C. H. (2003). Evaluation of forecasting methods for intermittent parts demand in the field of aviation: A predictive model. *Computers & Operations Research*, 30(14), 2097–2114. doi:10.1016/S0305-0548(02)00125-9.

Granger, C. W. J., Clive, W. J., & Terasvita, T. (1993). *Modelling nonlinear economic relationships*. Oxford, UK: Oxford University Press..

Guiffrida, A. L., & Nagi, R. (1998). Fuzzy set theory applications in production management research: A literature survey. *Journal of Intelligent Manufacturing*, 9(1), 39–56. doi:10.1023/A:1008847308326.

Hax, A. C., & Candea, D. (1984). *Production and inventory management*. Upper Saddle River, NJ: Prentice-Hall..

Holt, C. (1957). *Forecasting trends and seasonals by exponentially weighted averages*. Pittsburgh, PA: Carnegie Institute of Technology..

Ijumba, N. M., & Hunsley, J. P. (1999). Improved load forecasting techniques for the newly electrified areas. In Proceedings of 1999 IEEE Africon, (Vol. 2, pp. 989 -994). IEEE..

Johnston, F. R., & Boylan, J. E. (1996). Forecasting for items with intermittent demand. *The Journal of the Operational Research Society*, 47(1), 113.

Kaleva, O. (1994). Interpolation of fuzzy data. *Fuzzy Sets and Systems*, 61(1), 63–70. doi:10.1016/0165-0114(94)90285-2.

Kandil, M., El-Debeiky, S., & Hasanien, N. (2001). Overview and comparison of long-term forecasting techniques for a fast developing utility: Part I. *Electric Power Systems Research*, 58(1), 11–17. doi:10.1016/S0378-7796(01)00097-9.

Makridakis, S. G., Wheelwright, S. C., & Hyndman, R. J. (1998). *Forecasting: Methods and applications*. Hoboken, NJ: Wiley..

McKenzie, E. (1984). General exponential smoothing and the equivalent ARMA process. *Journal of Forecasting*, 3(3), 333–344. doi:10.1002/for.3980030312.

Mentzer, J. T., & Bienstock, C. C. (1998). *Sales forecasting management*. Thousand Oaks, CA: SAGE..

Mula, J., Poler, R., García-Sabater, J. P., & Lario, F. C. (2006). Models for production planning under uncertainty: A review. *International Journal of Production Economics, 103*(1), 271–285. doi:10.1016/j.ijpe.2005.09.001.

Peidro, D., Mula, J., Poler, R., & Lario, F. C. (2009). Quantitative models for supply chain planning under uncertainty: A review. *International Journal of Advanced Manufacturing Technology, 43*(3-4), 400–420. doi:10.1007/s00170-008-1715-y.

Poler, R., & Mula, J. (2011). Forecasting model selection through out-of-sample rolling horizon weighted errors. *Expert Systems with Applications, 38*(12), 14778–14785. doi:10.1016/j.eswa.2011.05.072.

Segura, J. V., & Vercher, E. (2001). A spreadsheet modeling approach to the Holt–Winters optimal forecasting. *European Journal of Operational Research, 131*(2), 375–388. doi:10.1016/S0377-2217(00)00062-X.

Silver, E. A., Pyke, D. F., & Peterson, R. (1998). *Inventory management and production planning and scheduling*. Hoboken, NJ: John Wiley & Sons..

Snyder, R. (2002). Forecasting sales of slow and fast moving inventories. *European Journal of Operational Research, 140*(3), 684–699. doi:10.1016/S0377-2217(01)00231-4.

Syntetos, A. A. (2001). *Forecasting of intermittent demand*. (Ph.D. thesis). Buckinghamshire Business School, Brunel University, UK.

Teunter, R. H., Syntetos, A. A., & Babai, M. Z. (2010). Determining order-up-to levels under periodic review for compound binomial (intermittent) demand. *European Journal of Operational Research, 16*, 619–624. doi:10.1016/j.ejor.2009.09.013.

Tong, H. (1983). *Threshold models in non-linear time series analysis*. Berlin: Springer-Verlag. doi:10.1007/978-1-4684-7888-4.

Tseng, F. M., & Tzeng, G.-H. (2002). A fuzzy seasonal ARIMA model for forecasting. *Fuzzy Sets and Systems, 126*(3), 367–376. doi:10.1016/S0165-0114(01)00047-1.

Tseng, F. M., Tzeng, G.-H., Yu, H.-C., & Yuan, B. J. C. (2001). Fuzzy ARIMA model for forecasting the foreign exchange market. *Fuzzy Sets and Systems, 118*(1), 9–19. doi:10.1016/S0165-0114(98)00286-3.

Varghese, V., & Rossetti, M. (2008). A classification approach for selecting forecasting techniques for intermittent demand. In *Proceedings of the 2008 Industrial Engineering Research Conference*. IEEE.

Vila, M. A., & Delgado, M. (1983). On medical diagnosis using possibility measures. *Fuzzy Sets and Systems, 10*(1–3), 211–222. doi:10.1016/S0165-0114(83)80116-X.

Willemain, T. R., Smart, C. N., & Schwarz, H. F. (2004). A new approach to forecasting intermittent demand for service parts inventories. *International Journal of Forecasting, 20*(3), 375–387. doi:10.1016/S0169-2070(03)00013-X.

Willemain, T. R., Smart, C. N., Shockor, J. H., & DeSautels, P. A. (1994). Forecasting intermittent demand in manufacturing: A comparative evaluation of Croston's method. *International Journal of Forecasting, 10*(4), 529–538. doi:10.1016/0169-2070(94)90021-3.

Williams, T. M. (1984). Stock control with sporadic and slow-moving demand. *The Journal of the Operational Research Society*, *35*(10), 939–948.

Winters, P. R. (1960). Forecasting sales by exponentially weighted moving averages. *Management Science*, *6*(3), 324–342. doi:10.1287/mnsc.6.3.324.

Wu, S. I., & Lu, R. P. (1993). Combining artificial neural networks and statistics for stock-market forecasting. In *Proceedings of the 1993 ACM conference on Computer Science* (pp. 257–264). New York, NY: ACM.

Zadeh, L. (1965). Fuzzy sets. *Information and Control*, *8*(3), 338–353. doi:10.1016/S0019-9958(65)90241-X.

KEY TERMS AND DEFINITIONS

Forecasting: Estimation of future demand.

Fuzzy Arithmetic Operations: Arithmetic operations carried out on fuzzy numbers.

Fuzzy Triangular Numbers: Set of numbers associated with a membership function defined by three components; e.g., the center, the left and the right values.

Intermittent Demand: Random demand with many zero values per period.

Mean Value of Fuzzy Values: A defuzzification method for a fuzzy number.

Nonlinear Programming: Mathematical programming with a nonlinear objective function and/or constraints.

Time Series: Historical data per period in a time horizon.

Chapter 11
Decision Criteria for Optimal Location of Wind Farms

Juan Miguel Sánchez-Lozano
Universidad Politécnica de Cartagena, Spain

M. Socorro García-Cascales
Universidad Politécnica de Cartagena, Spain

María T. Lamata
Universidad de Granada, Spain

Carlos Sierra
Universitat Politècnica de Catalunya, Spain

ABSTRACT

The objective of the present chapter is to obtain the weights of the criteria that influences a decision problem of vital necessity to the current energy perspectives, which is the optimal localisation of wind farms. The location problem posed presents a hierarchical structure on three levels. The objective or goal to be achieved is in the top level, that is to say the optimal location of wind farms. The second level is constituted by the general criteria that influences the decision and which are the environmental, orographic, location, and climate criteria. These general criteria are then divided into sub-criteria, which constitute the third level of the hierarchy. The information provided by the criteria are of different natures, with qualitative-type criteria coexisting with quantitative-type criteria, and therefore, linguistic labels and numerical values are employed to model, by means of fuzzy triangular numbers, the importance coefficients of the criteria. In order to compare different models for extracting the knowledge, two surveys are prepared based on the Fuzzy AHP methodology, which are submitted to experts in the specific field.

DOI: 10.4018/978-1-4666-4785-5.ch011

1. INTRODUCTION

Although Arrhenius (1896) first identified the greenhouse effect in the late 19th century, it was not until the late 20th century when through the United Nations Environment Programme (PNUMA) and the World Meteorological Organization (OMM) that the Intergovernmental Panel on Change Climate (IPCC) was developed. The IPCC developed an initial report (Working Group I-II-III, 1990) which indicated the veracity of global warming and as a result thereof, the international community became aware of the impact that the high emission levels of greenhouse gases was having on the atmosphere (United Nations & World Meteorological Organization, 1992).

With the aim of stabilizing the concentrations of greenhouse gases in the atmosphere at a level that would prevent dangerous anthropogenic interference with the climate system the famous Earth Summit was held in Rio de Janeiro (United Nations, 1992). However, it was not until the development of the Kyoto Protocol (United Nations, 1997) when limits were set for net greenhouse emissions for the major developed countries and with economies in transition, with reference to the emissions in 1990

and defining a first commitment period (from 2008 to 2012). Before the end of the period of validity agreed in Kyoto, at the summit held in Doha in late 2012 (United Nations Framework Convention on Climate Change, 2013), attempts were made to reach new commitments among countries and, although the agreements were not very positive given the global economic situation, a small number of countries agreed to extend the time signed in the Kyoto Protocol until the year 2020.

From the Kyoto protocol, a favorable legislative framework was developed which set out a series of policies and measures, including most notably the increased use of renewable energy sources. The European Union had recognized the need for effective management of all available resources through a balanced fuel mix, in which each of the energy sources performed its role in order to support sustainable economic growth. Therefore in the Commission of the European Communities held in Brussels in 1996, the so-called Green Paper was introduced, which marked an ambitious target consisting of achieving a contribution of RES close to 12% of gross inland energy consumption by 2010. The Green Paper was the first stage in establishing a strategy for

Figure 1. Chronological evolution of the major advances in the fight against climate change

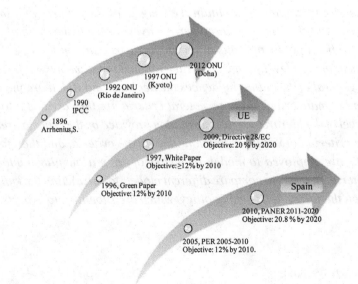

energy sources with renewable sources. It was intended to open a debate on the most urgent and necessary measures that could be undertaken by the European Community and Member States, as well as on the nature of these measures.

Based on feedback and observations of consultations with Member States and other EU institutions, the European Commission published the so-called White Paper in mid-1997 which set out a common approach to energy sources from renewable sources, accompanied by an action plan. Strategic plans and actions of the White Paper were headed towards the goal of achieving greater penetration of these energy sources in the European Union, reaching more than 12% by 2010. That meant that the overall objective of the European Union States should encourage the increased sources of energy from renewable sources according to their potential. Before the end of 2010, a new European regulatory framework (Directive 2009/28/EC) was defined, in which national mandatory targets were established which involved reaching a 20% share of energy from renewable sources in European Community energy consumption in 2020.

In Spain, the necessary containment of growth in emissions of greenhouse gases set by the Kyoto Protocol, and the fulfillment of the objective set out in the White Paper of the European Union, were the main reasons why the Institute for Diversification and Saving of Energy (IDAE) in 2005 developed the Renewable Energy Plan in Spain (PER) 2005-2010. The PER maintained the commitment that renewable energy should cover at least 12% of total energy consumption in 2010.

Before the end of the term of the PER 2005-2010, a new plan called the National Action Plan for Renewable Energy (PANER) was defined for the period 2011-2020, (IDAE,2010). After preparing the PANER 2010-2020, and in the context of a very negative evolution of the Spanish and global economy, in December 2010 the Congress of Deputies approved a document, in which it was recommended that the participation of RES should be 20.8% in 2020. This is the overall objective set out in the PANER 2011-2020, which sets the same goals as the Directive 2009/28/EC.

The energy crisis suffered in the 1970s and the energy needs of industrialized countries were the starting point of the first studies of wind farms, in order to take advantage of the inexhaustible energy source, which wind power generation represents (Skikos & Machias, 1992; Beccali et al, 1998, Kaminaris et al, 2006).

When implementing this type of renewable energy facilities, the promoter must find and select the best location in order to obtain a better use of energy and reduce the risks that, in facilities of this size, can cause serious economic and environmental damage (Kahraman et al, 2009). It is, however, not unusual that in choosing the right site among various sites, there is a degree of uncertainty. If the knowledge and experience of the decision group are combined with methodologies or tools to assist in decision making (Ramirez-Rosado et al, 2008), this uncertainty could be avoided.

Seeking optimal locations for wind farms, firstly restrictive criteria (Dominguez-Bravo et al, 2007; Van Haaren and Fthenakis, 2011) which allow any area of study to be reduced by discarding those areas which, due to existing regulations, are not suitable for implementing any such facility, are determined with criteria for selecting the best fit from among these areas (Aydin, 2010). The latter criteria not only depend directly on the type of renewable technology to implement but also may be of a different nature; so that, for the problem of locating wind farms, quantitative criteria (for example, the sub-criterion called distance to cities from the location as a general criterion) will coexist with qualitative criteria (for example, the sub-criterion called agrological capacity from the environment general criterion).

Therefore, when selecting an optimum location to build a wind farm, the decision group must choose from among the different tools of decision support currently available the one which will allow to accurately assess all the criteria that influence the decision. To that end, in this paper, the use of the widespread variant of a multi criteria decision method, Fuzzy AHP methodology (Saaty, T., 1980) is proposed.

The article will be structured as follows: in the second part the particular case study will be defined, in the third part the methodology applied to the two alternatives proposed will be described, and finally the results and conclusions of the study will be shown.

2. DECISION CRITERIA FOR THE OPTIMAL LOCATION OF WIND FARMS

Once the objective has been achieved, it is necessary to know which criteria influence (and to what extent), the decision making problem proposed. Although previous studies have been conducted indicating the features that these criteria should meet (Janke, 2010, Al-Yahyai et al, 2012), the fact of using one or the other will depend mainly on the study area. However, it is possible to establish common generic criteria that subsequently may be decomposed into specific criteria of sub-criteria, which will depend on the characteristics, and nature of the area to be analysed.

Therefore, following the guidelines established in Aran Carrión et al (2008), four groups of main criteria will be established.

- C_1: Environment criterion
- C_2: Location criteria
- C_3: Orography criteria
- C_4: Climatology criteria

For the proposed location problem, it is necessary to decompose each of these criteria into a certain number of sub-criteria, which will constitute the set of factors that influence the decision. The resulting hierarchical structure is represented by a criteria tree in Figure 2.

Each of the sub-criteria mentioned are then described briefly.

- C_{11}: Agrological capacity (Classes). Suitability of land for agricultural development, if the land presents excellent agrological capacity it will not be suitable to implement the renewable facility and vice versa.
- C_{21}: Slope (%). Inclination of the land, the higher the percentage of surface inclination, the worse fitness it will have to implement a wind farm.
- C_{22}: Area (m^2). Surface contained within a perimeter of land that can accommodate a renewable energy facility.
- C_{31}: Distance to main airports (m). Space of interval between the nearest airport and the different possible sites.
- C_{32}: Distance to main roads (m). Space of interval between the nearest main road and the different possible sites.
- C_{33}: Distance to power lines (m). Space of interval between the nearest power line and the different possible sites.
- C_{34}: Distance to cities (m). Space of interval between the population centers (cities and towns) and the different possible sites.
- C_{35}: Distance to electricity transformer substations (m). Space of interval between the nearest electricity transformer substation and the different possible sites.
- C_{36}: Distance to mast (m). Space of interval between the nearest mast and the different possible sites.
- C_{41}: Wind speed (m/s). It corresponds to the wind speed at an elevation of 80 meters in the different possible sites.

Figure 2. Criteria tree for optimizing the location of wind farms

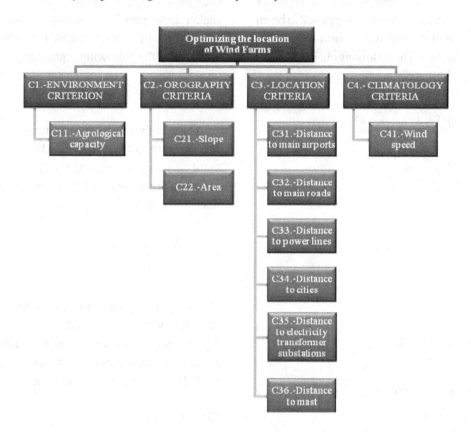

3. METHODOLOGY

3.1 Analytic Hierarchy Process

The AHP methodology (Saaty 1980, 1989) has been accepted by the international scientific community as a robust and flexible multi-criteria decision making (MCDM) tool for dealing with complex decision problems. AHP has been applied to numerous decision problems, such as energy policy (Kablan 2004); project selection (Cheng et al 1999); measuring business performance (Al Harbi 2001); and the evaluation of advanced manufacturing technology (Chan et al. 2000a,b).

Basically, AHP has three underlying concepts: structuring the complex decision problem as a hierarchy of goal, criteria and alternatives, pairwise comparison of elements at each level of the hierarchy with respect to each criterion on the preceding level, and finally vertically synthesizing the judgments over the different levels of the hierarchy. AHP attempts to estimate the impact of each alternative on the overall objective of the hierarchy. In this case, we only apply the method in order to obtain the criteria's weights.

We assume that the quantified judgments provided by the decision-maker on pairs of criteria (C_i, C_j) are represented in an nxn matrix as in the following:

$$C = \begin{array}{c} \\ C_1 \\ C_2 \\ \vdots \\ C_n \end{array} \begin{array}{cccc} C_1 & C_2 & \cdots & C_n \\ \begin{bmatrix} c_{11} & c_{12} & \cdots & c_{1n} \\ c_{21} & c_{22} & \cdots & c_{2n} \\ \vdots & \ddots & \cdots & \vdots \\ c_{n1} & c_{n2} & \ddots & c_{nn} \end{bmatrix} \end{array} \quad (1)$$

If $w = \{w_1, w_2, ..., w_n\}$ represents the weights of the criteria, then, the c_{12} value is supposed to be an approximation of the relative importance of C_1 to C_2, i.e., $c_{12} \approx (w_1/w_2)$. The following characteristics will be taken into account:

$$c_{ij} \approx \left(w_i/w_j\right) \ \forall i, j = 1, 2, ..., n$$

$$c_{ii} = 1, \forall i = 1, 2, ..., n$$

If

$$c_{ij} = \alpha, \ \alpha \neq 0,$$

then

$$a_{ji} = 1/\alpha, \ \forall i, j = 1, 2, ..., n$$

If C_i is more important than C_j then $c_{ij} \cong \left(w_i/w_j\right) > 1$

This implies that matrix C should be a positive and reciprocal matrix with 1's in the main diagonal and hence the decision maker needs only to provide value judgments in the upper triangle of the matrix. It can be shown that the number of judgments (L) needed in the upper triangle of the matrix is:

$$L = n\left(n - 1\right)/2 \tag{2}$$

where n is the size of the matrix C.

The usual method for computing the ranking and weight of alternatives in the AHP is the eigenvector, but it is also possible to obtain the weight by means of another estimator such as the geometric mean. In the eigenvector method, the weight vector is the eigenvector corresponding to the maximum eigenvalue λmax of the matrix C. According to the Perron-Frobenius Theorem,

(Perron 1907), the eigenvalue λ_{max} is positive and real. Furthermore, the vector w can be chosen with all positive coordinates. It is a normalized solution of the following equation:

$$C\,w = \lambda_{max}\,w \tag{3}$$

The traditional eigenvector method for estimating weights in the Analytic Hierarchy Process yields a way of measuring the consistency of the referee's preferences arranged in the comparison matrix. The consistency index *(CI)* is given by

$$CI = \frac{\lambda_{max} - n}{n - 1} \tag{4}$$

(Saaty 1980) has shown that if the referee is completely consistent then $c_{ij} \cdot c_{jk} = c_{ik}$ ($\forall \ i,j,k$), $\lambda_{max} = n$ and *CI = 0*. However, if the referee is not absolutely consistent $\lambda_{max} > n$ and Saaty proposes the following index of consistency measure:

$$CR = CI / RI \tag{5}$$

where *RI* is the average value of *CI* obtained by Alonso and Lamata, 2006.

In the ideal case of total consistence $\lambda_{max} = n$. Saaty suggests that a consistency index less than or equal to CR≤0.10 indicates that the decision maker has structured the problem in question well.

The values assigned to c_{ij} according to the Saaty scale are usually in the interval of 1-9 or their reciprocals. In our case, Table 2 presents the linguistic decision-maker's preferences in the pair-wise comparison process, which are similar to Saaty's values but with references to linguistic labels, that is to say the information provided by the experts.

In many cases the expert is not sure whether to choose a particular label or its adjacent, so that it is also possible to find evaluations in the form $(+I, S + I) = (5,6,7)$ which would indicate that the value is somewhat larger than "strongly more

Table 1. Table of the random index for different matrix dimension

n	3	4	5	6	7	8	9	10
RI	0.5245	0.8815	1.1086	1.2479	1.3417	1.4056	1.4499	1.4854

Table 2. Decision-maker's linguistic preferences in the pair-wise comparison process

Labels	Verbal judgments of preferences between criterion *i* and criterion *j*	Triangular fuzzy scale and reciprocals
(*EI*)	C_i and C_j is equally important	(1, 1, 1) /(1,1,1)
(*s+I*)/(*s-I*)	C_i is slightly more/less important than C_j	(2, 3, 4)/(1/4,1/3,1/2)
(*+I*)/(*-I*)	C_i is strongly more/less important than C_j	(4, 5, 6)/ (1/6,1/5,1/4)
(*S+I*)/(*S-I*)	C_i is very strongly more/less important than C_j	(6, 7, 8)/ (1/8,1/7,1/6)
(*Ex+I*)/(*Ex-I*)	C_i is extremely more/less important than C_j	(8, 9, 9)/ (1/9,1/9,1/8)

important than" but without being "very strongly more important than".

In AHP problems, where the values are fuzzy, we will use the geometric normalized average, expressed by the following expression:

$$w_i = \frac{\prod_{j=1}^{n}\left(a_{ij},b_{ij},c_{ij}\right)}{\sum_{i=1}^{m}\prod_{j=1}^{n}\left(a_{ij},b_{ij},c_{ij}\right)} \quad (6)$$

where, $\left(a_{ij},b_{ij},c_{ij}\right)$ is a fuzzy number.

4. OBTAINING THE WEIGHT

It is well known that in multi-criteria decision problems, not all criteria are of equal importance. Therefore, the most important criteria will also have a higher weight or a higher score.

As mentioned, one of the possible methods to obtain the weights is the AHP model. In this case, we consider that there are two ways to obtain the weighted criteria using the AHP method:

1. **Top to Bottom:** The weights of the main criteria can be obtained by comparing the first level matrices. After that the weight from every criterion can be rescaled to the sub-criteria from the second level.
2. **Bottom to Top:** This is to calculate all the weights of the sub-criteria at the second level by comparing all the sub-criteria with each other. Subsequently, the sub-criteria are aggregated to their main criterion.

4.1 Method 1: Fuzzy AHP Survey

Its development corresponds to the first of these cases. In the first case, the information requested on the upper triangular matrix of these paired arrays is such that for each array $n\left(n-1\right)/2$ questions must be asked. The lower triangular matrix is calculated in terms of the property of reciprocity. For this case we need to ask the expert 22 questions.

The questions are distributed as follows: 6 for the first level corresponding to Figure 3, Table 3 and Figure 4; and for the second level there will be (0+1+15+0)=16, which correspond to Figures 5, 6, 7 and 8 and Tables 3, 4, 5, 6 and 7.

The solution of the corresponding matrices, after applying the expression (6), and explained below.

We note that the importance of the climatology criterion C_4 is one to which the expert gives more importance while the environmental criteria C_1 is given minor importance. Upon looking at Figure 2 it can be deduced that these criteria are not subdivided into sub-criteria, therefore the agricultural capacity weight will be given by the triple (0.045, 0.050, 0.085) and the wind speed criterion (0.453, 0.601, 0.795), as shown in Tables 4 and 5, respectively.

When comparing the 2 sub-criteria hanging from C_2, slopes and areas, we can see that the value is the same for both as shown in Table 6, and therefore their weights are equal.

With respect to the third criteria, "location", its importance (0.199, 0.266, 0.363) will be dis-

tributed it among the 6 sub-criteria. In this case the results are detailed in Table 7.

Once all the data have been collected and the weights have been obtained, the last phase will consist in rescaling Tables 5 and 6 in the weights of the criteria in Figure 3.

The data are contained in Table 8.

According to these results, the order of the criteria is shown in Figures 7 and 8.

4.2 Method 2: Modified AHP Survey

In this case we have 10 criteria to compare. This implies that the number of comparisons will be $n(n-1)/2 = 45$. We know that as the value of n increases, it is also easier for consistency problems to appear. Therefore we propose an alternative

Figure 3. Compared matrix for the main criteria

$$C = \begin{array}{c} \\ C_1 \\ C_2 \\ C_3 \\ C_4 \end{array} \begin{array}{cccc} C_1 & C_2 & C_3 & C_4 \\ \left[\begin{array}{cccc} EI & s+I & +I & S+I \\ s-I & EI & -I,S-I & S-I \\ -I & +I,S+I & EI & S-I,-I \\ S-I & S+I & S+I,+I & EI \end{array} \right] \end{array}$$

Figure 4. Main weighted criteria

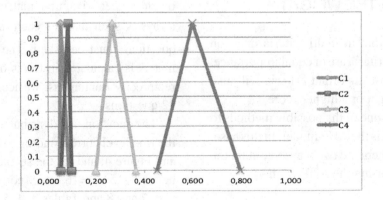

Figure 5. Compared matrix for the sub-criteria C_{2j}

$$
\begin{array}{c}
 & \begin{array}{cc} C_{21} & C_{22} \end{array} \\
\begin{array}{c} C_{21} \\ C_{22} \end{array} & \left(\begin{array}{cc} EI & EI \\ EI & EI \end{array} \right)
\end{array}
$$

Figure 6. Compared matrix for the sub-criteria C_{3j}

$$
\begin{array}{c}
 & \begin{array}{cccccc} C_{31} & C_{32} & C_{33} & C_{34} & C_{35} & C_{36} \end{array} \\
\begin{array}{c} C_{31} \\ C_{32} \\ C_{33} \\ C_{34} \\ C_{35} \\ C_{36} \end{array} & \left[\begin{array}{cccccc}
EI & S+I & +I & +I & EI & +I \\
S-I & EI & -I & EI & S-I & S-I \\
-I & +I & EI & S+I & -I & +I \\
-I & EI & S-I & EI & S-I & S-I \\
EI & S+I & -I & S+I & EI & +I \\
-I & S+I & -I & S+I & -I & EI
\end{array} \right]
\end{array}
$$

method, which only requires making $(n-1)$ comparisons.

For that purpose, a questionnaire similar to that made by Garcia-Cascales et al (2011) was developed, which was given to experts with the aim of reducing the uncertainly and imprecision of the proposed problem.

The survey is divided into two parts:

1. The decision problem is explained indicating what the goal to achieve is (optimal location of sites of wind farms), the methodology used as well as the criteria that influence the decision making process. Thus, the basic elements of the decision problem are

Figure 7. Order of the 10 sub-criteria

$$
C_{41} \succ C_{35} \succ C_{31} \succ C_{11} \succ C_{21} = C_{22} \succ C_{33} \succ C_{36} \succ C_{34} \succ C_{32}
$$

Figure 8. Weights of all Sub-criteria

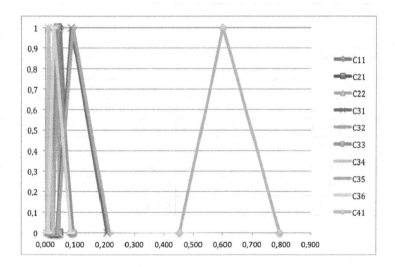

Table 3. Main weighted criteria

Criteria	Weight Vector		
C_1	**0.045**	**0.050**	**0.085**
C_2	0.051	0.083	0.095
C_3	0.199	0.266	0.363
C_4	0.453	0.601	0.795

Table 4. Weight of sub-criteria C_{1j}

Criteria	Weight Vector		
$C_1=C_{11}$	0.045	0.050	0.085

Table 5. Weight of sub-criteria C_{4j}

Criteria	Weight Vector		
$C_4=C_{41}$	0.453	0.601	0.795

Table 6. Weight of sub-criteria C_{2j}

Criteria	Weight Vector		
C_{21}	0.500	0.500	0.500
C_{22}	0.500	0.500	0.500

Table 7. Weight of sub-criteria C_{3j}

Criteria	Weight Vector		
C_{31}	0.192	0.332	0.568
C_{32}	0.021	0.036	0.071
C_{33}	0.071	0.145	0.258
C_{34}	0.023	0.038	0.072
C_{35}	0.202	0.346	0.593
C_{36}	0.049	0.104	0.236

Table 8. Weights of all sub-criteria

Criteria	Weight Vector		
C_{11}	0.045	0.050	0.085
C_{21}	0.026	0.042	0.048
C_{22}	0.026	0.042	0.048
C_{31}	0.038	0.088	0.206
C_{32}	0.004	0.009	0.026
C_{33}	0.014	0.039	0.094
C_{34}	0.005	0.010	0.026
C_{35}	0.040	0.092	0.215
C_{36}	0.010	0.028	0.086
C_{41}	0.453	0.601	0.795
Sum	0.659	1.000	1.628

described through a hierarchical structure, as shown in the criteria tree (Figure 2).

2. It is based on the hierarchical structure described and its purpose is to gather data to obtain the weight or coefficient of importance of criteria. The survey consists of a block of 3 questions:

a. $\mathbf{Q_1}$: Do you believe that the ten criteria considered have the same weight?

   i. If the answer is yes, $w_i = w_j = 1/n \, \forall i,j$ it will not be necessary to apply any MCDM to obtain the weights of the criteria as these will all have the same value. Otherwise, i.e., if an expert considers that not all the criteria have equal importance, the second question in the survey will be posed:

b. $\mathbf{Q_2}$: List the criteria in descending importance.

c. $\mathbf{Q_3}$: Compare the approach to be considered first with respect to that considered secondly and successively, using the following tags{(EI), (s+)/(s-I), (+I)/(-I), (S+I)/(S-I), (Ex+I)/(Ex-I)} according to the meanings in Table 2 (see also Figure 9).

According to Garcia-Cascales and Lamata (2011) and by expression (6) the weights for the example shown will be obtained (Figure 10, Figure 11).

Once the weights have been derived from the sub-criteria we will pass to determine the weights of the criteria C_1, C_2, C_3 and C_4. So for example, $C_2 = C_{21} + C_{22}$ according to the sum of fuzzy numbers, we obtain the related solution in Table 9 and Figure 12.

In the comparative for the two sub-criteria (Table 10) we can see that the order of the sub-

Figure 9. Values given by expert for location of wind farms

$$C_{41} \quad \begin{bmatrix} C_{41} & C_{33} & C_{21} & C_{35} & C_{32} & C_{34} & C_{31} & C_{22} & C_{36} & C_{11} \\ (EI) & (S+I) & (S+I) & (S+I) & (S+I) & (S+I) & (Ex+I) & (Ex+I) & (Ex+I) & (Ex+I) \end{bmatrix}$$

Figure 10. Weight sub-criteria expert for the location of wind farms

$$
\begin{array}{c}
\\
C_{41} \\
C_{33} \\
C_{21} \\
C_{35} \\
C_{32} \\
C_{34} \\
C_{31} \\
C_{22} \\
C_{36} \\
C_{11}
\end{array}
\begin{bmatrix}
\quad C_{41} \quad \\
(1,1,1) \\
(1/8,1/7,1/6) \\
(1/8,1/7,1/6) \\
(1/8,1/7,1/6) \\
(1/8,1/7,1/6) \\
(1/8,1/7,1/6) \\
(1/9,1/9,1/8) \\
(1/9,1/9,1/8) \\
(1/9,1/9,1/8) \\
(1/9,1/9,1/8)
\end{bmatrix}
=
\begin{bmatrix}
(0.429,0.463,0.483) \\
(0.054,0.066,0.081) \\
(0.054,0.066,0.081) \\
(0.054,0.066,0.081) \\
(0.054,0.066,0.081) \\
(0.054,0.066,0.081) \\
(0.048,0.051,0.060) \\
(0.048,0.051,0.060) \\
(0.048,0.051,0.060) \\
(0.048,0.051,0.060)
\end{bmatrix}
$$

$$(2.069,2.159,2.333)$$

Figure 11. Weight sub-criteria expert for the location of wind farms

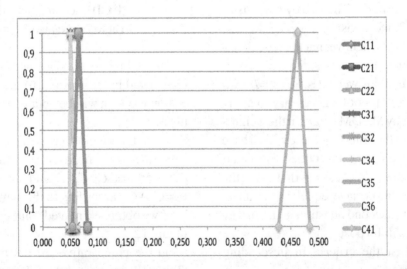

criteria with higher weight C_{41}, C_{35}, and C_{31} is the same in both methods, while it can be seen that the weights of the criteria are not as relevant, since the order of the sub-criteria differs from one method to another.

We can also see that the first method gives a higher weight value to the sub-criteria with more weight than the second method.

In the case of the main criteria, we can see that both methods give the same ranking of criteria, but that their weights differ. For the most

Table 9. Weight main criteria expert for the location of wind farms

Criteria	Weight Vector		
C_1	0.048	0.051	0.060
C_2	0.101	0.118	0.141
C_3	0.310	0.368	0.443
C_4	0.429	0.463	0.483

Figure 12. Weight main criteria expert for the location of wind farms

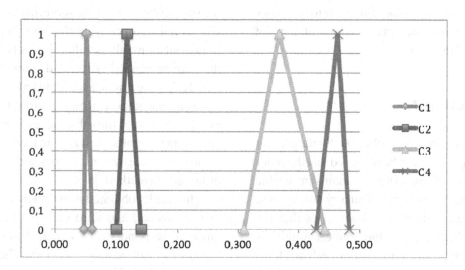

Table 10. Weights ratio obtained by all sub-criteria for both methods

	Method 1				Method 2			
Criteria	Weight vector			Order	Weight vector			Order
C_{11}	0.045	0.050	0.085	4th	0.048	0.051	0.060	3rd
C_{21}	0.026	0.042	0.048	5th	0.054	0.066	0.081	2nd
C_{22}	0.026	0.042	0.048	6th	0.048	0.051	0.060	3rd
C_{31}	0.038	0.088	0.206	3rd	0.048	0.051	0.060	3rd
C_{32}	0.004	0.009	0.026	10th	0.054	0.066	0.081	2nd
C_{33}	0.014	0.039	0.094	7th	0.054	0.066	0.081	2nd
C_{34}	0.005	0.010	0.026	9th	0.054	0.066	0.081	2nd
C_{35}	0.040	0.092	0.215	2nd	0.054	0.066	0.081	2nd
C_{36}	0.010	0.028	0.086	8th	0.048	0.051	0.060	3rd
C_{41}	0.453	0.601	0.795	1st	0.429	0.463	0.483	1st
Sum	0.659	1.000	1.628		0.891	0.997	1.128	

Table 11. Weights ratio obtained by main criteria for both methods

Criteria	Weight Vector			Order	Weight Vector			Order
C_1	0.045	0.050	0.085	4th	0.048	0.051	0.060	4th
C_2	0.051	0.083	0.095	3rd	0.101	0.118	0.141	3rd
C_3	0.199	0.266	0.363	2nd	0.310	0.368	0.443	2nd
C_4	0.453	0.601	0.795	1st	0.429	0.463	0.483	1st

important criterion the first method gives greater weight than the second method, while for the other criteria the first method give less weight than the second one. Table 11.

5. CONCLUSION

Upon analyzing the values obtained for the general criteria (Table 11) it can be observed that the order of importance of said criteria remains invariable independently of the type of survey carried out. It should be highlighted in both cases that the criterion, which presents the greatest weight, is the climate (C_4). This is to a certain extent a logical result since it is the only criterion in which humankind cannot intervene to improve it, that is to say that although a site may offer excellent conditions to implant a wind farm, if there is hardly any wind or the wind is very slight, then it cannot be an optimal site for such an installation.

The second criterion in terms of importance corresponds to the general criterion of location (C_3). The fact that this criterion is in said position is principally due to the fact that the proximity to or distance from population nuclei or infrastructures which influence the decision, are of great importance when deciding if a zone is optimal for establishing a wind farm.

The remaining general criteria present similar importance coefficients, with the criterion of orography (C_2) being the third most important, while the environmental criterion (C_1) occupied

the fourth position. Proceeding analogously with the values obtained for the sub-criteria (Table 9) it is observed that once again, the sub-criterion which stands out above all the others is that belonging to the climate general criterion denominated wind speed (C_{41}), the importance of this sub-criterion is unchanged whatever survey is carried out. However for the rest of the sub-criteria, certain differences can be appreciated among them depending if the survey carried out is complete (method 1) or bounded (method 2).

The results obtained using method 1 indicate that the second and third sub-criteria in importance correspond to the distance to electricity transformer sub-stations (C_{35}) and the distance to airports (C_{31}). However, excessive differences are not observed for the rest of the sub-criteria – their values are very close. Observing the results obtained from method 2, scant differences can be seen in the rest of the sub-criteria, so it cannot be clearly stated that one sub-criterion is superior to another

Therefore with this analysis it can be concluded that, starting from a modified AHP survey, a high level of accuracy is not achieved in the results, yet the difference observed between these results and those obtained using a complete fuzzy AHP survey reflecting all the questions according to the AHP methodology, is not significant. This means that it can be stated that the complexity in answering a questionnaire with a large number of questions does not clearly reflect an improvement in the results obtained.

ACKNOWLEDGMENT

This work is partially supported by FEDER funds, the DGICYT and Junta de Andalucía under projects TIN2011-27696-C02-01 and P11-TIC-8001, respectively.

REFERENCES

Al Harbi, K. M. A. (2001). Application of the AHP in project management. *International Journal of Project Management, 19*(1), 19–27. doi:10.1016/S0263-7863(99)00038-1.

Al-Yahyai, S., Charabi, Y., Gastli, A., & Al-Badi, A. (2012). Wind farm land suitability indexing using multi-criteria analysis. *Renewable Energy, 44*, 80–87. doi:10.1016/j.renene.2012.01.004.

Alonso, J. A., & Lamata, M. T. (2006). Consistency in the analytic hierarchy process: New approach. *International Journal of Uncertainty. Fuzziness and Knowledge-Based Systems, 14*(4), 445–459. doi:10.1142/S0218488506004114.

Arán-Carrión, J., Espín-Estrella, A., Aznar-Dols, F., Zamorano-Toro, M., Rodríguez, M., & Ramos-Ridao, A. (2008). Environmental decision-support systems for evaluating the carrying capacity of land areas: Optimal site selection for grid-connected photovoltaic power plants. *Renewable & Sustainable Energy Reviews, 12*, 2358–2380. doi:10.1016/j.rser.2007.06.011.

Arrhenius, S. (1896). On the influence of carbonic acid in the air upon the temperature of the ground. *Philosophical Magazine and Journal of Science, 5*(41), 237–276. doi:10.1080/14786449608620846.

Aydin, N. Y., Kentel, E., & Duzgun, S. (2010). GIS-based environmental assessment of wind energy systems for spatial planning: A case study from Western Turkey. *Renewable & Sustainable Energy Reviews, 14*, 364–373. doi:10.1016/j.rser.2009.07.023.

Beccali, M., Cellura, M., & Ardente, D. (1998). Decision making in energy planning: The ELECTRE multicriteria analysis approach compared to a fuzzy-sets methodology. *Energy Conversion and Management, 39*(16-18), 1869–1881. doi:10.1016/S0196-8904(98)00053-3.

Chan, F. T. S., Chan, M. H., & Tang, N. K. H. (2000a). Evaluation methodologies for technology selection. *Journal of Materials Processing Technology, 107*, 330–337. doi:10.1016/S0924-0136(00)00679-8.

Chan, F. T. S., Jiang, B., & Tang, N. K. H. (2000b). The development of intelligent decision support tools to aid the design flexible manufacturing systems. *International Journal of Production Economics, 65*(1), 73–84. doi:10.1016/S0925-5273(99)00091-2.

Cheng, C.-H., Yang, K.-L., & Hwang, C.-L. (1999). Evaluating attack helicopters by AHP based on linguistic variable weight. *European Journal of Operational Research, 116*(2), 423–435. doi:10.1016/S0377-2217(98)00156-8.

Comisión de las Comunidades Europeas. (1996). *Energía para el futuro: Fuentes de energía renovables: Libro verde para una estrategia comunitaria. Bruselas*. Author..

Comisión Europea. (1997). *Energía para el futuro: Fuentes de energía renovables: Libro blanco para una estrategia y un plan de acción comunitarios. Bruselas*. Author..

Domínguez-Bravo, J., García-Casals, X., & Pinedo Pascua, I. (2007). GIS approach to the definition of capacity and generation ceilings of renewable energy technologies. *Energy Policy*, *35*, 4879–4892. doi:10.1016/j.enpol.2007.04.025.

García-Cascales, M. S., Lamata, M. T., & Sánchez-Lozano, J. M. (2012). Evaluation of photovoltaic cells in a multi-criteria decision making process. *Annals of Operations Research*, *199*, 373–391. doi:10.1007/s10479-011-1009-x.

Instituto para la Diversificación y Ahorro de la Energía IDAE. (2005). *Plan de energías renovables en españa (PER) 2005-2010*. Madrid: Ministerio de Industria, Turismo y Comercio..

Instituto para la Diversificación y Ahorro de la Energía IDAE. (2010). *Plan de acción nacional de energías renovables de españa (PANER) 2011 – 2020*. Madrid: Ministerio de Industria, Turismo y Comercio..

Janke, J. R. (2010). Multicriteria GIS modeling of wind and solar farms in Colorado. *Renewable Energy*, *35*, 2228–2234. doi:10.1016/j.renene.2010.03.014.

Kablan, M. M. (2004). Decision support for energy conservation promotion: An analytic hierarchy process approach. *Energy Policy*, *32*(10), 1151–1158. doi:10.1016/S0301-4215(03)00078-8.

Kahraman, C., Kaya, I., & Cebi, S. (2009). A comparative analysis for multiattribute selection among renewable energy alternatives using fuzzy axiomatic design and fuzzy analytic hierarchy process. *Energy*, *34*, 1603–1616. doi:10.1016/j.energy.2009.07.008.

Kaminaris, S. D., Tsoutsos, T. D., Agoris, D., & Machias, A. V. (2006). Assessing renewables-to-electricity systems: A fuzzy expert system model. *Energy Policy*, *34*, 1357–1366. doi:10.1016/j.enpol.2004.08.054.

Parlamento Europeo. (2009). *Directiva 2009/28/ EC del parlamento europeo y del consejo relativa al fomento del uso de energía procedente de fuentes renovables. Bruselas*. Author..

Perron, O. (1907). Zur theorie der matrizen. *Math. Ann., 64*.

Ramírez-Rosado, I. J., García-Garrido, E. G., Fernández-Jiménez, L. A., Zorzano-Santamaría, P. J., Monteiro, C., & Miranda, V. (2008). Promotion of new wind farms based on a decision support system. *Renewable Energy*, *33*, 558–566. doi:10.1016/j.renene.2007.03.028.

Saaty, T. L. (1980). *The analytic hierarchy process*. New York: McGraw-Hill..

Saaty, T. L. (1989). *Group decision making and the AHP*. New York: Springer Verlag..

Skikos, G. D., & Machias, A. V. (1992). Fuzzy multi criteria decision making for evaluation of wind sites. *Wind Energy (Chichester, England)*, *6*(4), 213–228.

United Nations. (1992). *Conference on environment and development: Rio declaration on environment and development*. Rio de Janeiro, Brazil: UN.

United Nations. (1997). *Framework convention on climatic change: Report of the conference of the parties on its third session*. Kyoto, Japan: UN.

United Nations Environment Programme/ World Meteorological Organization. (1992). *Climate change: The IPCC 1990 and 1992 assessments*. Intergovernmental Panel on Climate Change..

United Nations Framework Convention on Climate Change. (2013). *Message to parties: Early submission of information and views*. United Nations Climate Change Secretariat..

Van Haaren, R., & Fthenakis, V. (2011). GIS-based wind farm site selection using spatial multi-criteria analysis (SMCA): Evaluating the case for New York State. *Renewable & Sustainable Energy Reviews*, *15*, 3332–3340. doi:10.1016/j.rser.2011.04.010.

Working Group I. (1990). *Climate change: The IPCC scientific assessment*. Cambridge, UK: Cambridge University Press..

Working Group II. (1990). *Climate change: The IPCC impacts assessment*. Canberra, Australia: Australian Government Publishing Service..

Working Group III. (1990). *Climate change: The IPCC response strategies*. World Meteorological Organization/United Nations Environment Program.

Chapter 12

Bipolarity in Decision Analysis:
A Way to Cope with Human Judgment

Ayeley P. Tchangani
Université de Toulouse, France

ABSTRACT

Decision analysis, the mechanism by which a final decision is reached in terms of choice (choosing an alternative or a subset of alternatives from a large set of alternatives), ranking (ranking alternatives of a set from the worst to the best), classification (assigning alternatives to some known classes or categories), or sorting (clustering alternatives to form homogeneous classes or categories) is certainly the most pervasive human activity. Some decisions are made routinely and do not need sophisticated algorithms to support decision analysis process whereas other decisions need more or less complex processes to reach a final decision. Methods and models developed to solve decision analysis problems are in constant evolution going from mechanist models of operational research to more sophisticated and soft computing-oriented models that attempt to integrate human attitude (emotion, affect, fear, egoism, altruism, selfishness, etc.). This complex, soft computing and near human mechanism of problem solving is rendered possible thanks to the overwhelming computational power and data storage possibility of modern computers. The purpose of this chapter is to present new and recent developments in decision analysis that attempt to integrate human judgment through bipolarity notion.

DOI: 10.4018/978-1-4666-4785-5.ch012

INTRODUCTION

Decision making is certainly the most pervasive human activity; indeed we spend a great proportion of our working day, hour, minute and even second, making decisions. Some decisions are made routinely and do not need models to support them whereas other decisions are so complex or important that sound decision support models are needed in order to avoid failure that may lead to very damageable or catastrophic consequences. These complex decisions share some features such as: multiplicity of objectives, multiplicity of attributes or criteria that characterize alternatives, uncertainty, multiplicity of actors, and so on. For these decision situations there is a need to have procedures or models that permit to capture all interactions and relationships between different elements of decision making process in order to reach an effective and efficient decision. Thus, a decision analysis problem is structured around the following important elements: *decision makers, players, actors* or *stakeholders* that are entities (persons, group of persons, organizations, etc.) that do have some interest or are engaged in decision analysis process; *objectives* (an objective in a decision analysis problem is something a decision maker cares about, wants to achieve, wants to optimize, wants to reach, etc.); *alternatives* (an alternative is a possibility opened to a decision maker that may permit him or her to realize his objectives); *attributes* or *criteria* (an attribute is a feature of an alternative that is used by a decision maker to evaluate this alternative with regard to pursued objectives).

The existence of many decision makers necessitate to have a *coordination* mechanism; the coordination scheme depends on the nature of the problem to solve and mainly the structure of alternatives: does each decision maker have his/her own decision alternatives set or all decision makers have to express their preferences over a common alternatives set ? The case where all decision makers have to pronounce themselves on a same set of alternatives is known in the literature as social choice or collective decision problems, see for instance Arrow (1951), whereas the case where each decision maker dispose of his/her own decisions set is referred to as game theory problems (von Neumann and Morgenstern, 1964). These two problems are considered in this chapter. Formerly these problems are presented in the following definition.

Definition 1: A collective decision problem is a decision problem where a certain number (possibly reduced to one) of agents, stakeholders or decision makers must select, rank, classify, or sort alternatives from a large set or universe $U = \left\{ u_1, u_2, \ldots, u_n \right\}$ of alternatives in order to satisfy some collective and/or individual objectives. The choice problem is the main concern of this chapter.

A game problem is a decision problem where a certain number of agents, stakeholders, decision makers or players, each one having his/her own decision set $D_i = \left\{ d_1, d_2, \ldots, d_{n_i} \right\}$ where n_i is the number of alternative decisions for player i and where the outcome (impact on one's objectives) of a given player decision is conditioned by other players decisions.

Decision analysis is, in general, a process with many steps such as formulating decision goal or objectives, identifying attributes that characterize potential alternatives that can respond to the decision goal and making recommendation regarding these alternatives given the decision goal. The final recommendation step in a decision process can be reduced to following main processes: choosing (this is a relative evaluation that search for a subset, possibly reduced to a singleton, of alternatives that satisfy the decision goal), ranking (relative evaluation that ranks alternatives from the best to the worst with regard to the decision goal), classifying (assigning objects to pre-defined classes or categories), or sorting (an absolute evaluation that sorts alternatives according to a prescribed norm regarding the decision goal). The construction of an evaluation model, often carried up by an expert known in the literature as the analyst (Bouyssou *et al.*, 2000) is an important step in the decision process; this step is the main purpose of this chapter. Indeed, we consider that the upstream processes have been considered and we are in possession of the set of alternatives, the consequences tree, attributes measures and our duty is to construct an evaluation model, thus we act as an analyst for the final recommendation.

In the next section how these problems or slightly different versions of these problems are treated in the literature will be presented with a highlight on the limitations of models used to solve them.

BACKGROUND

Collective decision making problem as defined previously can represent practical situations in many domains such as management, engineering, economics, politics etc., see for instance (Bouyssou *et al.*, 2000), (Brauers *et al.*, 2008), (Hokkanen and Salminen, 1997) Steuer (1986), Vincke (1989), and references therein for some real world applications. Classically, three main approaches have dominated evaluation process in decision analysis: value type approach (a value function or an utility measure is derived for each alternative to represent its adequacy with decision goal); outranking methods (a pair comparison of alternatives are carried up under each attribute or criteria to derive a pre-order on the alternatives set); and decision rules approach (a set of decision rules are derived from a decision table with possible missing data). All these approaches suppose to have a single objective to satisfy and a common attributes set for alternatives. These approaches are briefly described below.

- **Value Type Approach:** Roughly speaking these techniques consider a numerical function A known as value or utility function defined on the alternatives set U such that:

$$\pi\left(u\right) \geq \pi\left(v\right) \Leftrightarrow u \succsim v \qquad (1)$$

where "$u \succsim v$" stands for "u is at least as good, with regard to decision goal, as v" leading to an order on U. The evaluation modeling process then consists in building such a function based on attributes measures and decision makers preference (obtained in general by answering some particular questions of the analyst); there are many techniques employed in the literature for constructing such a function where a number of them suppose a particular form for A such as an expected utility form or an additive value function (interested reader may consult (Bouyssou *et al.*, 2000), Steuer (1986) and references therein.

- **Outranking methods**: A pair comparison of alternatives is carried up under each attribute or criteria to derive a pre-order on the alternatives set U allowing incomparability and/or intransitivity; methods such as ELECTRE procedures and PROMETHEE techniques (Bouyssou *et al.*, 2000), (Brans *et al.*, 1986, 1986a), Vincke (1989) belong to this category.
- **Decision rules approach**: A set of decision rules are derived by a learning process from a known decision table with possibly incomplete data, see (Greco *et al.*, 2001).

The approach that will be developed in this chapter brings together aspects of value type methods and outranking approaches as it will evaluate each alternative by two numerical measures. Indeed, when evaluation and selection process is considered using an indicator that is a function of these measures, this method is purely a value type method whereas when all these two measures are used for evaluation and selection, this method is more closed to outranking methods as it will lead to a pre-order over alternatives set instead of a total order. Though, the possible incomparability of two alternatives induced by using two numerical measures for evaluation make this method closed to outranking methods, there are some novelties in this method such as taking into account social relationships between many stakeholders engaged in the decision process which is almost absent from outranking approaches.

In many situations, mainly in democratic context, collective decision making is made through a voting process. But voting process does not capture in our opinion all the attitudes such as ambiguity, indecision, social values consideration, etc. that are often observed in human behavior. Indeed, decision makers often face some issues that cannot allow them to express their opinion or preferences by just voting. Decision makers often face uncertainties and interactions: uncertainties are related to the impossibility of decision makers to clearly express their objectives, to elicit and assess attributes that should be used to evaluate the adequacy between an alternative and their objectives, and the relationships between attributes and objectives; this situation leads to the fact that a decision maker can be in a situation where he is not able to pronounce himself about some issues; interactions come from the fact that a decision maker may be influenced by other decision makers when expressing his or her judgment.

In this chapter we adopt an approach that highlights *bipolarity notion*, be it between attributes and objectives, between a decision maker and an alternative in terms of evaluation, or between decision makers in terms of social influence that we consider to be inherent to any decision analysis problem. We are motivated by the fact that cognitive psychologists have observed for long time that human evaluate alternatives by considering separately their positive aspects and their negative aspects; that is on a bipolar basis, see for instance

(Caciopo and Berntson, 1994) and (Osgood *et al.*, 1957); this view is also common in computer science for information representation, see (Dubois and Fargier, 2006). To this end, we introduce supporting and rejecting notions (Tchangani, 2010; Tchangani and Pérès, 2010; Tchangani et al., 2012) that relate attributes to objectives leading to an evaluation model in terms of two measures or indices (selectability and rejectability) for each alternative in the framework of satisficing game theory (Stirling, 2003) that lead to an evaluation of an alternative by two measures so that a decision maker can be in position of not being able to discriminate between two alternatives. These notions permit to partition criteria or attributes set into three subsets given an objective: attributes that support this objective, attributes that reject this objective and attributes that are neutral with regard to this objective; of course only supporting and rejecting attributes are interesting for evaluation process. Selecting and rejecting degrees of an attribute with regard to an objective may be assessed using known techniques such as analytic hierarchy process (AHP), see (Saaty, 2005) or any method that could assign a measure to an attribute with regard to a pair of objective and alternative; the advantage of using AHP approach reside in its ability to deal with hierarchy (which allows to decompose attributes from more general statements to more measurable or comparable attributes) and intangible variables. This model allows alternatives to be characterized by heterogeneous attributes and incomparability between alternatives in terms of Pareto-equilibrium. Indeed, collective decision making situations where alternatives are characterized by attributes of different nature are pervasive in real world applications. One may think about a government evaluating projects that belong to different domains such as health, infrastructures, social, economics, etc. with the main objective to enhance a country developing process or an enterprise planning to invest in projects of different nature. In these situations, though attributes characterizing projects may be completely different, the important thing is their adequacy with regards to the pursued objectives, so that alternative projects can be ultimately compared on the same basis (decision maker desires). The social influence between decision makers will be taken into account through concordance and discordance measures to capture the extent to which a given decision maker may agree or disagree with his counterparts respectively.

Coordination mechanism in what concern game theory problems is mainly dominated by the concept of cooperative (the case where decision makers or players are disposed to form coalitions in order to increase their revenue) and non cooperative (a non-cooperative game is one in which players make decisions independently; thus, while they may be able to cooperate, any cooperation must be self-enforcing) games models. Classical treatment of game theory is mainly based on utility theory (von Neumann and Morgenstern, 1964) that requires each player to assign preferences to rank various outcomes as a function of the possible strategy vectors. Solution concepts here are essentially dominance, Nash equilibrium, Pareto equilibrium and coordination equilibrium. But in practice, players are not always either cooperating or non cooperating agents and they may exhibit an intermediate attitude; they may for instance cooperate with some players and not cooperate with other, etc. The approach considered in this chapter through bipolarity concept will permit to allow a decision maker to modulate his attitude according to context.

MAIN FOCUS OF THE CHAPTER

When making decision in complex situation, it is rather rare that a human reach a final decision without hesitation. Indeed, most of the time there exist some dubitative attitude, some indecision between several possible alternative decisions. In order to dispose of an intelligent and sound decision support model, this attitude must be correctly

modeled. This modeling process is carried up in this chapter through satisficing game (Stirling, 2003); an approach that evaluates alternatives on a bipolar basis by two degrees: a goal achievement degree and a degree that acts in the opposite side or the "cost" associated with each alternative.

Furthermore, most of decisions are made within a group of decision makers so that a particular decision maker will be inevitably influenced by some other decision makers; this *social influence* should be correctly addressed in order to reach a near human way of decision making by artificial entities. This issue is addressed here by defining an influence degree that result from the combination of a positive view one may have toward a counterpart that we refer to as *concordance* degree and a negative view that we refer to as *discordance* degree.

On the other hand, human often evaluate alternatives by listing their positive aspect and their negative aspect in order to balance these aspects for final decision. In this chapter we propose *supporting* and *rejecting* notions that together with uncertainty lead to BOCR (Benefit, Opportunity, Cost, and Risk) analysis framework that represents a good framework to address such issue, see (Tchangani and Pérès, 2010; Tchangani *et al.*, 2012).

Finally, all materials gathered from social influence and BOCR analysis must be aggregated; given the synergy resulting from the homogeneity obtained from clustering attributes by BOCR analysis, Choquet integral is used as the appropriate aggregation operator as it permits to take into account interactions between elements to aggregate.

The four concepts outlined here, namely, possibly *indecision* when a decision maker is confronted to many alternatives, the inherent *social influence* when decisions are made within a group, the bipolar relationships between attributes and objectives in terms of *supporting* and *rejecting* notions as well as the aggregation process taking into account interactions through *Choquet integral* are developed in the subsequent subsections.

BIPOLARITY TO COPE WITH INDECISION: SATISFICING GAMES

To evaluate alternatives, humans, often make a list of positive aspects and a list of negative aspects of each alternative and then make a list of alternatives for which positive aspects "exceed" negative aspects in some sense. This way of evaluation is theorized by satisficing game theory (Stirling, 2003). Let us consider a universe X of alternatives (X may be U in collective decision problem, D_i for decision maker i or the joint decisions set as defined below in game theory); then for each alternative $x \in X$, a *selectability function* $\mu_S(x)$ and a *rejectability function* $\mu_R(x)$ are defined to measure the degree to which x works towards success in achieving the decision maker's goal and costs associated with this alternative respectively. This pair of measures called *satisfiability functions or measures* are mass functions (they have mathematical structure of probabilities, see Stirling (2003)): they are non negative and sum to one over X. The set of alternatives arguable to be "good enough or satisficing" are those for which the "benefit" expressed by the function μ_S exceeds the cost expressed by the function μ_R up to a possible caution or boldness index q.

By so doing there may be indecision between two alternatives, mainly for those known as satisficing equilibrium (in the sense of Pareto).

Thus, a satisficing game theory in the case of social choice or collective decision is given by the following definition.

Definition 2: A satisficing game consists in the triplet $\langle U, \mu_S, \mu_R \rangle$ where:

- U is the set (discrete) of units, alternatives, decisions or options,
- μ_S and μ_R represent mass functions or measures defined from U onto the interval [0, 1] where μ_S measures the selectability degree and μ_R that of rejectability; a function p is said to be a mass function on a discrete set U if it possesses a probability structure that is it verifies $p(u) \geq 0$ for any element u of U and the sum of p(u) over U is one.

In the case of collective decision making, the problem can be formulated as a single satisficing game problem by aggregating individual selectability and rejectability measures or as n single decision making problems where each decision maker comes with his own selectability and rejectability and then some procedures are used to reach the final collective decision.

The case of game theory is bit different as each decision maker dispose of his own alternative decisions set; in this case, the corresponding satisficing game is defined as in the following.

Definition 3: A n persons satisficing game consists in the triplet $\left\langle D_1 \times D_2 \times \dots \times D_n, \mu_{S_1 S_2 \dots S_n}, \mu_{R_1 R_2 \dots R_n} \right\rangle$ where:

$$D = D_1 \times D_2 \times \dots D_n$$

is the set of joint decisions;

$$\mu_S = \mu_{S_1 S_2 \dots S_n}$$

and

$$\mu_R = \mu_{R_1 R_2 \dots R_n}$$

are joint selectability and joint rejectability measures respectively.

Applying the satisficing game theory to collective decision and game theory problems defined previously return then to determining satisfiability measures for each alternative *x* in the case of collective decision problem be it at local level or at global level and individual as well as collective measures in the case of game problem when taking into account possible relationships between actors; these measures will be obtained by aggregating information about attributes-objectives relationships and actors relationships.

SOCIALITY IN DECISION ANALYSIS: MODELING SOCIAL INFLUENCE

In multi-actors decision analysis situation, there is always some *conditionality* in the sense that the preferences of a given actor may be conditioned to that of other ones (Stirling, 2012). When making decision, an actor may be influenced by its social vicinity; the influence one actor may have on another actor result of a sort of combination of positive and negative perception of later one. Particularly, influence does not always means positive perception (altruism, deference) of the influenced actor toward actors that influence him; it may represent repulsion, aggresivity of the influenced actor with regard to those influencing him; even for the same influencing actor, the influenced one may have a sort of combination of positive and negative perception. Given a decision analysis situation and two decision makers *i* and *j*, there will be some decision aspects for which *j* will be in concordance with *i* and other aspects for which he will be in discordance. So, the global influence an actor *j* may have on another actor *i* will result from a combination of positive perception measured through a *concordance degree* and a negative perception measured through a *discordance degree*, highlighting once again the bipolarity.

Let define by $V(i)$ the social vicinity of actor *i* that is the set of actors whose opinion matter for *i* or that do have some influence on *i*, be it negative, positive or both; for each actor $j \in V(i)$, let us define the relative concordance degree ω_{ij}^c to measure the extent to which the opinion of actor *i* is in concordance with actor *j* compared to other actors of its vicinity $V(i)$ and the relative discordance degree ω_{ij}^d defined similarly to ω_{ij}^c and denote by $\omega_i^c = \begin{bmatrix} \omega_{i1}^c & \omega_{i2}^c, \dots & \omega_{i|V(i)|}^c \end{bmatrix}$ and $\omega_i^d = \begin{bmatrix} \omega_{i1}^d & \omega_{i2}^d, \dots & \omega_{i|V(i)|}^d \end{bmatrix}$ the normalized concordance and discordance vectors for actor *i* respectively where notation $|\mathcal{M}|$ stands for the cardinality or number of elements of the discrete set $\mathcal{M}$; these measures can be obtained by actor *i* using AHP analysis or any other procedure. Let us denote by $\theta = \begin{bmatrix} \theta_1 & \theta_2, \dots & \theta_{|V(i)|} \end{bmatrix}$ the relative importance weights vector between decision makers where θ_i is the importance degree of decision maker *i* within the group; it may be not easy to determine this degree; nevertheless it seems fair to consider that the importance of a decision maker is commensurate to the margin between concordance and discordance degrees so that this measure (for a particular decision maker *i*) can be obtained (among other possibilities) by the following Equation (2)

$$\theta_i = \frac{\sum_{k=1}^n \left\{ \frac{1}{1 + exp\left(-\alpha\left(\omega_{ki}^c - \omega_{ki}^d\right)\right)} \right\}}{\sum_{j=1}^n \left\{ \sum_{k=1}^n \left\{ \frac{1}{1 + exp\left(-\alpha\left(\omega_{kj}^c - \omega_{kj}^d\right)\right)} \right\} \right\}}$$

(2)

where α is a turning parameter.

ATTRIBUTES – OBJECTIVES RELATIONSHIPS: BOCR ANALYSIS

Cognitive psychologists noticed for long time that humans generally evaluate alternatives in decision process by comparing pros and cons of each alternative with regard to decision goal, see (Caciopo and Berntson, 1994) and (Osgood *et al.*, 1957). Building on this observation, we introduce *supporting/rejecting* notions to characterize relationships between attributes and objectives: an objective *o* is said to be supported (respect. rejected) by an attribute *a* if and only if its variation is positively (respect. negatively) correlated with the variation of that attribute. Otherwise this attribute is said to be neutral with regard to that objective. In order to dispose with a structured framework for the elicitation process of such bipolar relationships, we propose to use BOCR analysis, see (Tchangani, 2010; Tchangani and Pérès, 2010; Tchangani *et al.*, 2012), that comes from the convergence of these supporting and rejecting notions and uncertainty consideration to give a framework where the set of attributes *A(x,o)* characterizing an alternative *x* with regards to an objective *o* is divided into the following subsets:

- **Benefit (B) attributes, $A_B(x,o)$:** Certain attributes that support objective *o*;
- **Opportunity (O) attributes, $A_O(x,o)$:** Uncertain attributes that support objective *o*;
- **Cost (C) attributes, $A_C(x,o)$:** Certain attributes that reject objective *o*, and;
- **Risk (R) attributes, $A_R(x,o)$:** Uncertain attributes that reject objective *o*.

This consideration has the advantage to allow alternatives to be characterized by different attributes, the important things being the relationships (positive or negative) between these attributes and the pursued objectives. Final evaluation of alternative decision *x* with regards to objective *o* will be obtained by aggregating separately positive aspects in terms of benefit and opportunity and negative aspects in terms of cost and risk to measure how well this alternative with regard to that objective and opposite forces in the realization of that objective.

AGGREGATION TO SYNTHESIZE GATHERED INFORMATION

As it is mentioned in previous section, aggregation is used in each step to obtain global and sound measures of some parameters that will be used in final step of decision process. Many aggregation procedures do exist in literature, going from the basic arithmetic mean to more sophisticated ones that take into account the interaction of elements to aggregate, see Grabisch (1996). One such sophisticated operator that take into account interaction behavior such as synergy, redundancy or independency between elements to aggregate is the so called Choquet integral (Grabisch, 1996) which utilization in practice is sometime compromised by the difficulty to define a tractable associated capacity or fuzzy measure. Let $X = \left\{ x_1 \quad \ldots \quad x_n \right\}$ be a set of numerically valued elements to aggregate by Choquet integral, the following definition gives the necessary materials for this purpose.

Definition 4: Let 2^x be the power set of X, a function $\mu : 2^X \rightarrow \begin{bmatrix} 0 & 1 \end{bmatrix}$ is a capacity or a fuzzy measure over X if it verifies:

$$\mu\left(\varnothing\right) = 0$$

$$\mu(X) = 1$$

$$\mu\left(A\right) \leq \mu\left(B\right), \forall A \subseteq B \subseteq X$$

The Choquet integral of vector x of elements of the set X associated to the capacity or fuzzy measure μ is given by Equation (3)

$$C_\mu(x) = \sum_{i=1}^{n} \left(x_{\sigma(i)} - x_{\sigma(i-1)} \right) \mu\left(A_i\right) \qquad (3)$$

where is a permutation over the set X verifying relations of Equation (4)

$$x_{\sigma(1)} \leq x_{\sigma(2)} \leq \ldots \leq x_{\sigma(n)} \; with \; by \, convention \; x_{\sigma(0)} = 0 \qquad (4)$$

and the subset $A_i \subseteq X$ is given by Equation (5)

$$A_i = \left\{ \sigma(i), \sigma(i+1), \ldots, \sigma(n) \right\} \qquad (5)$$

The difficulty of computing Choquet integral is to define a fuzzy measure over the set X that necessitates obtaining coefficients that represent the measure of subsets of X other than σ and X itself. In the case where elements to aggregate behave in synergy as it is the case here because of the bipolarity, and if it is possible to rank these elements by assigning them relative importance normalized weights, one can use a weighted cardinal fuzzy measure (WCFM) that leads to a straightforward formula for the corresponding Choquet integral, see (Tchangani, 2013).

Definition 5: A weighted cardinal fuzzy measure (WCFM) over X associated to a relative normalized weights vector $\omega = \left[\omega_1, \omega_2, \ldots, \omega_n \right]$ is given by Equation (6)

$$\mu(\Omega) = \frac{|\Omega|}{|X|} \left(\sum_{j \in \Omega} \omega_j \right) \qquad (6)$$

where $\Omega \subseteq X$ is a subset of X.

It is straightforward to verify that this function fulfils conditions of a capacity or fuzzy measure, see for instance Tchangani (2013).

Let us denote by $C_w^{wcfm}(x)$ the Choquet integral of numerical n dimension vector x associated to a WCFM with relative vector , then this integral, is given by Equation (7)

$$C_\sigma^{wcfm}(x) = \sum_{k=1}^{n} \left\{ \left[\left(\frac{n-(k-1)}{n} \right) \left(\sum_{j \in A_k} \omega_j \right) \right] \left(x_{\sigma(k)} - x_{\sigma(k-1)} \right) \right\}$$

$$(7)$$

where A_k is defined as in the Equation (5). There is no difficulty to verify this straightforward formula.

Now that the main approaches, models and tools to construct a framework of decision analysis based on the notion of bipolarity are outlined, we will consider modeling and solving the two main problems of decision analysis considered in this chapter, namely collective decision and game problems, in the subsequent sections.

MODELING COLLECTIVE DECISION PROBLEM

Model

Locally each actor i may wish to satisfy a certain set of own objectives; to this end he or she will use a set of features, criteria or attributes to evaluate the adequacy of an alternative with regard to his or her objectives; these sets may be common to all actors. We propose to elicit satisfiability measures in two steps: firstly, each agent i will derive its categorical satisfiability measures $\mu_{S_i}^0(u)$ and $\mu_{R_i}^0(u)$ for each alternative $u \in U$. In this work we adopt an approach that highlights the bipolarity of attributes with regards to objectives that we consider to be inherent to any decision analysis problem. We are motivated by the fact that cognitive psychologists have observed for long time that human, often, evaluate alternatives by considering separately their positive aspects and their negative aspects; that is on a bipolar basis, see for instance (Caciopo and Osgood, 1994), (Osgood *et al.*, 1957); this view is also common in computer science for information representation, see (Dubois and Fargier, 2006). To this end, we introduce supporting and rejecting notions (Tchangani, 2009a, 2010) that relate attributes to objectives leading to an evaluation model in terms of two measures or indices (selectability and rejectability) for each alternative in the framework of satisficing game theory (Stirling, 2003). These notions permit to partition criteria or attributes set into three subsets given an objective: attributes that support this objective, attributes that reject this objective and attributes that are neutral with regard to this objective; of course only supporting and rejecting attributes are interesting for evaluation process. The basis of this approach has been laid in (Tchangani, 2006, 2006a) where input-output assessments of a system were used to derive satisfiability measures to evaluate this system; in (Tchangani, 2009) where "positive" and "negative" attributes notions where introduced; and in (Tchangani and Pérès, 2010) where authors suggest to elicit and assess attributes in a decision analysis by partitioning them into benefit (B): certain attributes that support decision objective; opportunity (O): uncertain attributes that support decision objective; cost (C): certain attributes that reject decision objective; and risk (R): uncertain attributes that reject decision objective; leading to a framework known as BOCR analysis. Let us denote by $b_k^o(u), o_k^o(u), c_k^o(u)$, and $r_k^o(u)$ the normalized values of benefit, opportunity, cost and risk for attribute k of alternative u with regard to objective o; and by $\boldsymbol{b}^o(u)$, $\boldsymbol{o}^o(u)$, $c^o(u)$ and $r^o(u)$ vectors gathering normalized benefit, opportunity, cost and risk measures respectively. Let us suppose now that decision maker is able to supply for benefit, opportunity,

cost and risk attributes normalized relative degrees vectors in terms of w_b, w_o, w_c, and w_r then the overall benefit ($B^o(u)$), opportunity ($O^o(u)$) cost ($C^o(u)$) and risk ($R^o(u)$ measures of alternative u for objective o are given by Equations (8) and (9)

$$B^o(u) = C_{\omega_b}^{wcfm}\left(b^o(u)\right), \qquad O^o(u) = C_{\omega_o}^{wcfm}\left(o^o(u)\right) \tag{8}$$

$$C^o(u) = C_{\omega_c}^{wcfm}\left(c^o(u)\right), \qquad R^o(u) = C_{\omega_r}^{wcfm}\left(r^o(u)\right) \tag{9}$$

Let us now denote by $b(u), o(u), c(u)$ and $\boldsymbol{r}(u)$ vectors gathering benefit, opportunity, cost and risk measures with regard to all objectives and by, w^o the relative importance vector of objectives of the corresponding decision maker, then the overall opinion of this decision maker regarding the alternative u is captured by the benefit measure $B(u)$, opportunity measure $O(u)$ cost measure $C(u)$ and risk measure $R(u)$ that are given by Equations (10) and (11)

$$B(u) = C_{\omega^o}^{wcfm}\left(b(u)\right), \quad O(u) = C_{\omega^o}^{wcfm}\left(o(u)\right) \tag{10}$$

$$C(u) = C_{\omega^o}^{wcfm}\left(c(u)\right), \quad R(u) = C_{\omega^o}^{wcfm}\left(r(u)\right) \tag{11}$$

The categorical selectability measure measures $\mu_{S_i}^0(u)$ and the categorical rejectability measure $\mu_{R_i}^0(u)$ of alternative u in the point of view of decision maker i can finally be obtained by Equations (12) and (13)

$$\mu_{S_i}^0(u) = \frac{\phi_i B(u) + \left(1 - \phi_i\right)O(u)}{\sum_{v \in U}\left\{\phi_i B(v) + \left(1 - \phi_i\right)O(v)\right\}} \tag{12}$$

$$\mu_{R_i}^0(u) = \frac{(1-\phi_i)C(u) + \phi_i R(u)}{\sum_{v \in U}\{(1-\phi_i)C(v) + \phi_i R(v)\}} \quad (13)$$

where $0 \le \phi_i \le 1$ is the risk averse index of actor i; this index permits to adjust the attitude of a decision maker toward uncertainty; for instance a risk averse decision maker, for who $\phi_i \to 1$, will balance immediate benefit (B) with potential harm (R) regardless of potential benefit (O) and immediate cost to pay (C).

Considering the influence of his/her vicinity, one can admit that if two actors are in discordance then the conditioned selectability of one should be proportional to the categorical rejectability of the other and in the case they are in concordance it must be proportional to the categorical selectability of the other actor; a similar observation holds for the rejectability. So let us denote by $\mu_{S_i/V(i)}$ and $\mu_{R_i/V(i)}$ the conditional selectability and rejectability of agent i given his position with regard to his social vicinity and by $\mu_{S_{V(i)}}^0(u) = \left[\mu_{S_1}^0(u), \mu_{S_2}^0(u), ..., \mu_{S_{|V(i)|}}^0(u)\right]$ and $\mu_{R_{V(i)}}^0 = \left[\mu_{R_1}^0 \quad \mu_{R_2}^0, ... \quad \mu_{R_{|V(i)|}}^0\right]$ the vectors of categorical selectability measures and rejectability measures of all member of social vicinity of actor i. The measures $\mu_{S/V(i)}$ and $\mu_{R_i/V(i)}$ are therefore given by Equations (14) and (15)

$$\mu_{S_i/V(i)}(u) = $$
$$\frac{\gamma_i C_{\omega_i^c}^{wcfm}\left(\mu_{S_{V(i)}}^0(u)\right) + (1-\gamma_i)C_{\omega_i^d}^{wcfm}\left(\mu_{R_{V(i)}}^0(u)\right)}{\sum_{v \in U}\left\{\gamma_i C_{\omega_i^c}^{wcfm}\left(\mu_{S_{V(i)}}^0(v)\right) + (1-\gamma_i)C_{\omega_i^d}^{wcfm}\left(\mu_{R_{V(i)}}^0(v)\right)\right\}}$$
$$(14)$$

$$\mu_{R_i/V(i)}(u) = $$
$$\frac{\gamma_i C_{\omega_i^c}^{wcfm}\left(\mu_{R_{V(i)}}^0(u)\right) + (1-\gamma_i)C_{\omega_i^d}^{wcfm}\left(\mu_{S_{V(i)}}^0(u)\right)}{\sum_{v \in U}\left\{\gamma_i C_{\omega_i^c}^{wcfm}\left(\mu_{R_{V(i)}}^0(v)\right) + (1-\gamma_i)C_{\omega_i^d}^{wcfm}\left(\mu_{S_{V(i)}}^0(v)\right)\right\}}$$
$$(15)$$

where $0 \le \gamma_i \le 1$ is a degree that measures the altruist attitude of actor i.

The ultimate selectability measure $\mu_{S_i}(u)$ and the rejectability measure $\mu_{R_i}(u)$ of the alternative u in the opinion of decision maker i are corrected as shown by Equations (16) and (17)

$$\mu_{S_i}(u) = \delta_i \mu_{S_i}^0(u) + (1-\delta_i)\mu_{S_i/V(i)}(u) \quad (16)$$

$$\mu_{R_i}(u) = \delta_i \mu_{R_i}^0(u) + (1-\delta_i)\mu_{R_i/V(i)}(u) \quad (17)$$

where $0 \le \delta_i \le 1$ is the selfishness degree of decision maker i.

Solution Procedures

Given the developed approach, to reach a community level solution one can consider two possibilities: obtaining an aggregated satisfiability measures and then analyzing the selection problem as a single decision maker problem, or obtaining short lists of local satisficing sets and then try to converge to a community satisficing alternative.

Aggregated Satisfiability Measures Approach

Here let us denote by $\mu_S(u)$ and $\mu_R(u)$ the aggregated selectability measure and aggregated rejectability measure of alternative u respectively which are obtained from individual measures of all decision makers. Selected or rejected alternative by two decision makers is more sound than that selected or rejected by one decision maker; this means therefore that, one should consider synergy relationship when aggregating these measures so Choquet integral with a weighted cardinal fuzzy measure is a good candidate as an aggregation operator.

Let θ be the relative weights vector of decision makers with dimension corresponding to the number of decision makers as defined in previous sections and $\mu_S(u)$ and $\mu_R(u)$ be vectors which i^{th} entry is occupied by $\mu_{S_i}(u)$ and $\mu_{S_i}(u)$ respectively; then $\mu_S(u)$ and $\mu_R(u)$ are given by the following Equations (18) and (19)

$$\mu_S(u) = \frac{C_\theta^{wcfm}\left(\mu_S(u)\right)}{\sum_{v \in U}\left(C_\theta^{wcfm}\left(\mu_S(v)\right)\right)} \tag{18}$$

$$\mu_R(u) = \frac{C_\theta^{wcfm}\left(\mu_R(u)\right)}{\sum_{v \in U}\left(C_\theta^{wcfm}\left(\mu_R(v)\right)\right)} \tag{19}$$

Once these measures are obtained, the analysis process in order to reach a final decision can begin; here are some materials that participate to this purpose.

At a boldness or caution index q, the alternatives arguable to be good enough for the community and known as satisficing alternatives are given by the following definition.

Definition 6. *The set $\sum_q$ of community satisficing alternatives at boldness index q is given by Equation (20)*

$$\Sigma_q = \left\{u \in U : \mu_S(u) \geq q\mu_R(u)\right\} \tag{20}$$

But for a satisficing alternative u there can exist other satisficing alternatives that are better (having more selectability and at most the same rejectability or having less rejectability and at least the same selectability) than u; it is obvious that in this case any rational decision maker will prefer the later alternatives. So the interesting set is that containing satisficing alternatives for which there are no better alternatives: this is the satisficing equilibrium set . To define this set, let us define first, for any alternative u, the set $D(u)$

of alternatives that are strictly better than u; $D(u)$ is given by Equation (21)

$$D(u) = D_S(u) \bigcup D_R(u) \tag{21}$$

where $D_S(u)$ and $D_R(u)$ are defined by Equations (22) and (23)

$$D_S(u) = \left\{v \in U : \mu_R(v) < \mu_R(u) \quad and \quad \mu_S(v) \geq \mu_S(u)\right\} \tag{22}$$

$$D_R(u) = \left\{v \in U : \mu_R(v) \leq \mu_R(u) \quad and \quad \mu_S(v) > \mu_S(u)\right\} \tag{23}$$

The equilibrium set $\mathcal{E}$ that is, alternatives for which there are no strictly better alternatives, which cannot be empty by construction, is defined by Equation (24)

$$\mathcal{E} = \left\{u \in U : D(u) = \varnothing\right\} \tag{24}$$

and the satisficing equilibrium set $\sum_q^e$ is given by Equation (25)

$$\Sigma_q^e = E \bigcap \Sigma_q \tag{25}$$

Notice that the set $\sum_q^e$ constitutes a Pareto-equilibria set so that there is incomparability between a pair of alternatives in this set, so a trade-off process is necessary for final choice purpose for instance; which means possible indecision; these alternatives are those laying on the portion of the curve (above which there is no alternatives meaning the Pareto equilibrium) that is above the straight line (separating satisficing and not satisficing alternatives) of Figure 1.

From this analysis, if the satisficing equilibrium set is a singleton, then the choice is obvious whereas in other cases there is necessity to find a way to reach a final decision. In this case, the

Figure 1. Social choice results using aggregated satisfiability measures in the plan $\left(\mu_R,\ \mu_S\right)$

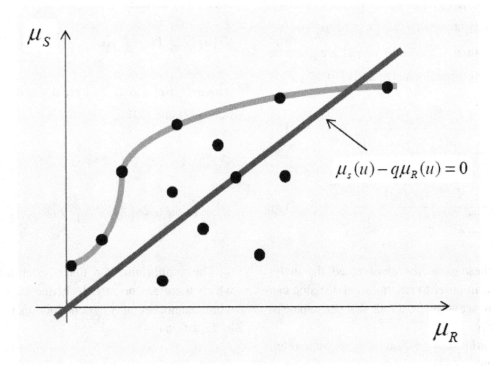

final choice will be operated in this satisficing equilibrium set when optimizing some additional desires or optimizing some performances indices. Let us designate by the ultimate selected alternative then some indices that may be used to choose this alternative are as the following.

- **Maximum discriminant**: If a boldness or caution index q is accepted by all decision makers, the ultimate alternative u^* will be selected using the following Equation (26)

$$u^* = \arg\left\{\max_{u\in\Sigma_q^e}\left\{\mu_S\left(u\right) - q\mu_R\left(u\right)\right\}\right\} \qquad (26)$$

- **Maximum boldness index**: This is well suited for the case where there is no consensus around a boldness index; u^* will be selected using the following Equation (27)

$$u^* = \arg\left\{\max_{u\in\Sigma_q^e}\left[\frac{\mu_S\left(u\right)}{\mu_R\left(u\right)}\right]\right\} \qquad (27)$$

- **Maximum selectability index**: u^* is given by Equation (28)

$$u^* = \arg\left\{\max_{u\in\Sigma_q^e}\left\{\mu_S\left(u\right)\right\}\right\} \qquad (28)$$

- **Minimum rejectability index**: u^* is given by Equation (29)

$$u^* = \arg\left\{\min_{u\in\Sigma_q^e}\left\{\mu_S\left(u\right)\right\}\right\} \qquad (29)$$

Convergence from Local Analysis Approach

Here, instead of aggregating individual satisfiability measures to reason on a single decision maker basis, we consider that each decision maker i comes with his own satisficing equilibrium set $\sum_i^q$ his caution or boldness index q_i and possibly his "best" alternative u_i^* that may be obtained as done in the previous section. From these materials, some procedures may be used to reach the final decision; here are some of those possible procedures that can be used for this purpose.

Convergence from Local "Best" Alternative u_i^*

If it happens that a same alternative is the local best alternative for all decisions makers then final selection is resolved and this common alternative is implemented. But this will constitute an exceptional situation and in most cases, local best alternatives will differ from one decision maker to another so that an adequate mechanism is needed to reach a final decision. One possibility is to use a voting process by implementing the alternative that is best for the majority of decision makers; but this approach may not allow reaching a final consensus decision. One way to not create problem within the community is to select the closest alternative to all local best alternatives when integrating the importance of each decision maker; this approach return to select the alternative that minimize the sum of weighted distance between it and the best alternatives in the plan of satisfiability measures. Let us define by d a distance in the plan μ_R, μ_S, then the ultimate consensual alternative u^* selected by this approach will minimized a weighted sum of distance, therefore u^* is given by the following Equation (30)

$$u^* = arg\left\{\min_{u \in U}\left[\sum_{i=1}^{n}\theta_i d\left(u_i^*, u\right)\right]\right\} \qquad (30)$$

The distance d is generally given by Equation (31)

$$d\left(u_i^*, u\right) = \left(\left|\mu_R\left(u_i^*\right) - \mu_R\left(u\right)\right|^p + \left|\mu_S\left(u_i^*\right) - \mu_S\left(u\right)\right|^p\right)^{\frac{1}{p}} \qquad (31)$$

where p is an integer; values of p often used are $p = 1, p = 2$ that corresponds to Euclidian distance, and $p = \infty$, in which case the distance is given by Equation (32)

$$d\left(u_i^*, u\right) = max\left\{\left|\mu_R\left(u_i^*\right) - \mu_R\left(u\right)\right|, \left|\mu_S\left(u_i^*\right) - \mu_S\left(u\right)\right|\right\} \qquad (32)$$

Consensus Seeking from Individual Satisficing Sets

The purpose here is to go from the local satisficing equilibrium sets $\sum_i^{eq}$ for $i = 1, 2, ..., n$, thus we consider that each decision maker i will formulate his own satisficing set and then some procedures are used to reach a final decision that maximize as much as possible community satisfaction. If the intersection of all local satisficing equilibrium sets is not empty, then it is natural to select the final alternative in this set using some criteria; thus if relation of Equation (33) is verified

$$\bigcap_i^n \left\{\Sigma_{q_i}^e\right\} \neq \varnothing \qquad (33)$$

then select the alternative to implement u^* using for instance Equation (34)

$$u^* = arg\left\{\max_{u \in \bigcap_i^n\left\{\Sigma_{q_i}^e\right\}}\left\{\prod_{i=1}^{n}\left[\frac{\mu_{S_i}\left(u\right)}{\mu_{R_i}\left(u\right)}\right]\right\}\right\} \qquad (34)$$

In the case where the intersection set is empty, that is $\bigcap_{i=1}^{n}\left\{\sum \frac{e}{q_i}\right\} = \varnothing$ and in order to treat all decision makers on the same basis, the alternative to implement u^* may be selected from the set of all satisficing equilibrium alternatives when optimizing an index such as that given by Equation (35)

$$u^* = \arg\left\{\max_{u\in\bigcup_{i}^{n}\left\{\Sigma_{q_i}^{e}\right\}}\left\{\prod_{i=1}^{n}\left\{\frac{\mu_{S_i}(u)}{\mu_{R_i}(u)}\right\}\right\}\right\} \quad (35)$$

Another possibility, in the case of emptiness of the intersection set, is to use a vote oriented procedure to obtain the alternative to implement as given by the following Equation (36)

$$u^* = \arg\left\{\max_{u\in\bigcup_{i}^{n}\left\{\Sigma_{q_i}^{e}\right\}}\left\{\sum_{i=1}^{n}\left\{1_{\Sigma_{q_i}^{e}}(u)\right\}\right\}\right\} \quad (36)$$

where is the indicator function of the set and given by (37)

$$1_{\Omega}(x) = \begin{cases} 1 & if\, x\in\Omega \\ 0 & if\,not \end{cases} \quad (37)$$

ILLUSTRATIVE EXAMPLE FOR COLLECTIVE DECISION MAKING

The illustrative problem considered here is adapted from a real word application studied in (Brauers *et al.*, 2008).

Problem and Data

Let us consider a problem where 3 decision makers with different sensitivity regarding the three pillars (economic issues, social issues and environmental issues) of sustainable development concept must select a design for a high way infrastructure with the ultimate goal to have the best sustainable design. There is the economist (decision maker 1) that considers that economical objective (*objective 1*) is 80% more important than the two other objectives that he considers to be equally important; there is the socialist (decision maker 2) that considers the social objective (*objective 2*) to be 75% more important than the two other objectives that he weights as 15% for economical objective and 10% for environmental objective; there is the environmentalist (decision maker 3) who considers that environmental objective (*objective 3*) has a weight of 60%, social objective is weighted 30% and economical objective, 10%; this means that the objectives weighting vectors according to decision makers are given by Equation (38)

$$\omega_1 = \begin{bmatrix} 0.80 & 0.10 & 0.10 \end{bmatrix}; \quad \omega_2 = \begin{bmatrix} 0.15 & 0.75 & 0.10 \end{bmatrix};$$
$$\omega_3 = \begin{bmatrix} 0.10 & 0.30 & 0.60 \end{bmatrix}$$

$$(38)$$

Six alternatives design are identified by experts and five attributes are used to evaluate alternatives. These attributes, along with their relationships with the 3 main sustainable development objectives, are as the following:

- **Attribute a_1 ; Longevity [In Years]:** This is an important attribute and we consider it to support the three objectives because a high way with long life duration will not necessitate renovations expenditures, a frequent negative impact on environment due to renovation process, will permit stable relationships between users, etc.;

- **Attribute a_2 ; Construction Price [In 10^6 €]:** This attribute is very important because generally most decision makers want a lower construction price when seeking high quality so we consider this attribute to reject economical objective (o_1) but to support social objective (o_2) and environmental objective (o_3) because high construction price may mean shortest duration, smaller number of detours or changes of direction, low number of accidents during construction and maintenance;

- **Attribute** a_3 ; **Environment Protection [In 10 Db(A)]:** This attribute supports environmental objective (o_3);

- **Attribute** a_4 ; **Economic Validity [100 M]:** This attribute depends on average distance for soil transportation; consequently, we consider it to reject economical objective (o_1) and environment objective (o_3);

- **Attribute** a_5 ; **Construction Duration [In 100 Days]:** Duration will impact negatively economical, social and environmental objectives so we consider this attribute to reject the three objectives.

Data, that is the assessment of each attribute for each of six alternatives, extracted from (Brauers *et al.*, 2008), are given on the following Table 1.

According to the description of attributes given above, the supporting/rejecting relationships between attributes and the three objectives and hierarchies scheme is given by Figure 2 below.

Results

Let us consider the attributes to have the same importance in their respective category and let us denote by $S^{o_i}(u_j) / R^{o_i}(u_j)$ the aggregated (obtained from Choquet integral) supporting measure (respectively rejecting measure) of the alternative u_j with regard to objective o_i ; notice that we are directly talking here about supporting / rejecting measures because we are not distinguishing certain and uncertain attributes. These data are summarized on the following Table 2.

Thus let us denote by
$$S(u_i) = \left[S^{o_1}(u_i), S^{o_2}(u_i), S^{o_3}(u_i) \right] \quad \text{and}$$
$$R(u_i) = \left[R^{o_1}(u_i), R^{o_2}(u_i), R^{o_3}(u_i) \right] \text{ the vectors}$$
of supporting and rejecting measures of the alternative u_i toward the three objectives. Categorical satisfiability measures using Choquet integral as

Table 1. Raw and normalized data of the illustrative application

	Raw Data					Normalized Data				
	a_1	a_2	a_3	a_4	a_5	a_1	a_2	a_3	a_4	a_5
u_1	30	12.49	6.26	10.88	7.61	0.2222	0.1814	0.1706	0.1767	0.1805
u_2	20	12.37	5.96	10.88	7.46	0.1481	0.1796	0.1624	0.1767	0.1770
u_3	27	11.10	6.26	09.92	6.69	0.2000	0.1612	0.1706	0.1611	0.1587
u_4	18	10.98	5.96	09.92	6.54	0.1333	0.1595	0.1624	0.1611	0.1552
u_5	24	11.02	6.28	09.98	7.00	0.1778	0.1600	0.1711	0.1621	0.1661
u_6	16	10.90	5.98	09.98	6.85	0.1185	0.1583	0.1629	0.1621	0.1625

Figure 2. Hierarchy and supporting/rejecting relationships between attributes and objectives

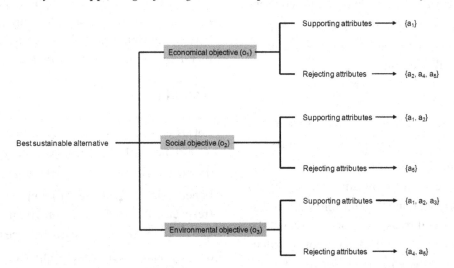

Table 2. Aggregated supporting and rejecting measures for each objective with equal importance assumptions for each category of attributes

Economical objective (o₁)		Social objective (o₂)		Environmental objective (o₃)	
0.2222	0.1795	0.2018	0.1805	0.1914	0.1786
0.1481	0.1778	0.1639	0.1770	0.1634	0.1769
0.2000	0.1603	0.1806	0.1587	0.1773	0.1599
0.1333	0.1586	0.1464	0.1552	0.1517	0.1582
0.1778	0.1627	0.1689	0.1661	0.1696	0.1641
0.1185	0.1610	0.1384	0.1625	0.1466	0.1623

the aggregation operator with a weighted cardinal fuzzy measure where the underlying relative weights vectors are given by Equation (38) for each decision maker are given by the following Equation (39)

$$\mu_{S_k}^0\left(u_i\right) = \frac{C_{\omega_k}^{wcfm}\left(S(u_i)\right)}{\sum_{j=1}^{6}\left\{C_{\omega_k}^{wcfm}\left(S(u_j)\right)\right\}}$$

and

$$\mu_{R_k}^0\left(u_i\right) = \frac{C_{\omega_k}^{wcfm}\left(R(u_i)\right)}{\sum_{j=1}^{6}\left\{C_{\omega_k}^{wcfm}\left(R(u_j)\right)\right\}}$$

(39)

and results presented on the following Table 3.

Now, let us suppose that the social influence structure between these three decision makers is summarized by the concordance and discordance weights resumed by the following matrices, see Equation (40)

$$\left[\omega_{ij}^c\right] = \begin{bmatrix} - & 0.5 & 0.5 \\ 0.7 & - & 0.3 \\ 0.2 & 0.8 & - \end{bmatrix} \text{ and } \left[\omega_{ij}^d\right] = \begin{bmatrix} - & 0.3 & 0.7 \\ 0.2 & - & 0.8 \\ 0.1 & 0.9 & - \end{bmatrix}$$

(40)

Table 3. Categorical satisfiability measures for each decision maker

	Economist (DM$_1$)		Socialist (DM$_2$)		Environmentalist (DM$_3$)	
	$\mu^0_{S_1}$	$\mu^0_{R_1}$	$\mu^0_{S_2}$	$\mu^0_{R_2}$	$\mu^0_{S_3}$	$\mu^0_{R_3}$
u_1	0.2103	0.1797	0.2035	0.1800	0.2019	0.1794
u_2	0.1555	0.1777	0.1607	0.1775	0.1598	0.1774
u_3	0.1910	0.1600	0.1846	0.1594	0.1854	0.1599
u_4	0.1400	0.1575	0.1443	0.1562	0.1446	0.1574
u_5	0.1776	0.1635	0.1736	0.1645	0.1751	0.1639
u_6	0.1257	0.1616	0.1332	0.1623	0.1332	0.1620

From these materials, and let us suppose that all the three decision makers are not too egoist nor too altruist that is their egoism degrees are given by $\left[\gamma_1 = \gamma_2 = \gamma_3 = 0.5\right]$ and similar selfishness indices δ_i, the ultimate satisfiability measures taking into account social influence as given by Equations (14)-(17) are shown on the following Table 4.

COMMUNITY RESULTS USING AGGREGATED SATISFIABILITY MEASURES APPROACH

From Equation (2) with $\alpha = 1$, the relative importance of each decision maker within the community is obtained as shown by Equation (41)

$$\theta = \begin{bmatrix} 0.38 & 0.34 & 0.28 \end{bmatrix} \tag{41}$$

so that the community satisfiability measures using Choquet integral are given on the following Table 5.

Without supplementary information, let us suppose that decision makers use maximum boldness ratio criterion, see Equation (27), as the selection criterion, then the selected alternative will be the alternative u_3. In fact, one can easily verify that using this selection criteria any decision maker be it at categorical level or taking into account the influence of other decision maker would have selected this alternative; thus there is some consensus around alternative u_3 making it a robust choice. One may notice that this alternative was the choice operated in the original study (Brauers *et al.*, 2008). There is no need here (unless one has information about caution indices) to search for solution using other presented approach as this will lead to the same result because of the existence of a consensus.

MODELING GAME PROBLEMS

Coordination scheme for game problems, as considered in this chapter, has been dominated by non cooperative game approach where it is supposed that each decision maker seeks the maximization

Table 4. Global satisfiability measures taking into account social influence

	Economist (DM$_1$)		Socialist (DM$_2$)		Environmentalist (DM$_3$)	
	μ_{S_1}	μ_{R_1}	μ_{S_2}	μ_{R_2}	μ_{S_3}	μ_{R_3}
u_1	0.2007	0.1854	0.1982	0.1860	0.1974	0.1861
u_2	0.1622	0.1733	0.1641	0.1728	0.1641	0.1730
u_3	0.1817	0.1662	0.1795	0.1666	0.1793	0.1665
u_4	0.1453	0.1541	0.1470	0.1533	0.1472	0.1536
u_5	0.1734	0.1664	0.1721	0.1674	0.1724	0.1668
u_6	0.1368	0.1547	0.1391	0.1541	0.1396	0.1541

Table 5. Aggregated satisfiability measures at group level

	u_1	u_2	u_3	u_4	u_5	u_6
μ_S	0.1987	0.1635	0.1802	0.1465	0.1729	0.1382
μ_R	0.1858	0.1731	0.1665	0.1536	0.1667	0.1543

of its own satisfaction regardless of other decision makers aspiration. But recent studies in different domains such as psychology, experimental economy, computer science, decision science, see (Stirling, 2003, 2012), show that human are not strictly selfish entity nor behave in the sense of any marginal increasing of satisfaction is better than none. For instance in the experiments where it is offered to an agent 1 to gain a certain amount of money if his proposition of the proportion of this amount to share with a second agent 2 is accepted, most of the time if the proportion proposed by agent 1 is too low, agent 2 will refuse the offer depriving agent 1 from gaining the money whereas according to classical satisfaction maximization concept, any offer greater than zero by agent 1

should be accepted by agent 2. Agent 2, here, is just *punishing* agent 1 from being too selfish.

To take into account issues raised in former lines and to remain in the spirit of bipolarity, we consider that each decision maker i begins to reason on an individual basis as in the case of collective decision to determine categorical measures $\mu_{s_i}^0(d_i^k)$ and $\mu_{R_i}^0(d_i^k)$ for each of its decision $d_i^k \in D_i$ and then considers the influence of the members of his vicinity $V(i)$. If decision makers of $V(i)$ fix their choice, for decision maker i, the analysis is similar to that of social or collective choice case. Normally the conditional selectability and rejectability measures elicitation for i should be done for any combination of the joint decision vectors of its vicinity members $V(i)$; but in practice this may be intractable if there are a great number of decision makers with large decision sets. To overcome this difficulty, we propose to reason on a bilateral basis and then obtain the approximated conditional measures by aggregation at vicinity level. So let us consider a decision maker $j \in V(i)$ of the vicinity of i, then i will elicit the parameters given by Equation (42)

$$\mu_{S_i/S_j}\left(d_i^k / d_j^l\right) \, and \, \mu_{R_i/S_j}\left(d_i^k / d_j^l\right) \, for \, d_i^k \in D_i$$
$$and \, d_j^l \in D_j \; \forall \; j \in V\left(i\right) \tag{42}$$

to be the degrees to which decision maker i is disposed to select (respect. to reject) his decision d_i^k if decision maker j who belongs to his vicinity does select his decision. d_j^l Elicitation process of these parameters may be carried up in a BOCR framework by identifying benefit, opportunity, cost and risk for option $d_i^k \in D_i$ by decision maker i given the fact that j has selected his option $d_j^l \in D_j$; we consider that it is more convenient to reason with regards to selectability of j as in the case of rejectability there remains many possibilities that may complicate elicitation process.

But decision maker j disposes of many options in terms of his decision set D_j so the overall attitude of i towards j will be measured by that represent the global selectability and rejectability degrees of decision d_i^k given the attitude of decision $\mu_{S_i/j}(d_i^k) \, and \, \mu_{R_i/j}(d_i^k)$ for any $j \in V(i)$ maker j towards all of his alternative decisions; these measures (similar to conditional probabilities) are therefore given by the following Equations (43) and (44)

$$\mu_{S_i/j}\left(d_i^k\right) = \sum_{d_j^l \in D_j} \left(\mu_{S_i/S_j}\left(d_i^k / d_j^l\right)\mu_{S_j}^0\left(d_j^l\right)\right) \tag{43}$$

and

$$\mu_{R_i/j}\left(d_i^k\right) = \sum_{d_j^l \in D_j} \left(\mu_{R_i/S_j}\left(d_i^k / d_j^l\right)\mu_{S_j}^0\left(d_j^l\right)\right) \tag{44}$$

Let us denote by Equation (45)

$$\mu_{S_i/V(i)}\left(d_i^k\right) = \left[\mu_{S_i/1}\left(d_i^k\right),\mu_{S_i/2}\left(d_i^k\right),\ldots,\mu_{S_i/V(i)}\left(d_i^k\right)\right] \tag{45}$$

and Equation (46)

$$\mu_{R_i/V(i)}\left(d_i^k\right) = \left[\mu_{R_i/1}\left(d_i^k\right),\mu_{R_i/2}\left(d_i^k\right),\ldots,\mu_{R_i/V(i)}\left(d_i^k\right)\right] \tag{46}$$

the vectors of global conditional selectability and rejectability measures for option $d_i^k \in D_i$ by decision maker i given the attitude of all members of his vicinity $V(i)$; given the relative importance vector θ_i assigned by i to the members of $V(i)$, the global selectability and rejectability degrees,, $\mu_{S_i/V(i)}\left(d_i^k\right) \; \mu_{R_i/V(i)}\left(d_i^k\right)$ of decision $\left(d_i^k\right)$ given the attitude of members of the vicinity of decision maker i are given by Equations (47) and (48)

$$\mu_{S_i/V(i)}\left(d_i^k\right) = \frac{C_{\theta_i}^{wcfm}\left(\mu_{S_i/V(i)}\left(d_i^k\right)\right)}{\sum_{d_i^p \in D_i}\left\{C_{\theta_i}^{wcfm}\left(\mu_{S_i/V(i)}\left(d_i^p\right)\right)\right\}} \tag{47}$$

and

$$\mu_{R_i/V(i)}\left(d_i^k\right) = \frac{C_{\theta_i}^{wcfm}\left(\mu_{R_i/V(i)}\left(d_i^k\right)\right)}{\sum_{d_i^p \in D_i}\left\{C_{\theta_i}^{wcfm}\left(\mu_{R_i/V(i)}\left(d_i^p\right)\right)\right\}} \tag{48}$$

Finally individual selectability and rejectability measures taking into account the influence of one's vicinity are given by Equations (49) and (50)

$$\mu_{S_i}\left(d_i^k\right) = \delta_i \mu_{S_i}^0\left(d_i^k\right) + \left(1-\delta_i\right)\mu_{S_i/V(i)}\left(d_i^k\right) \tag{49}$$

and

$$\mu_{R_i}\left(d_i^k\right) = \delta_i \mu_{R_i}^0\left(d_i^k\right) + \left(1-\delta_i\right)\mu_{R_i/V(i)}\left(d_i^k\right) \quad (50)$$

where $0 \leq \delta_i \leq 1$ is the selfishness degree of decision maker i. Let us denote by $d = (d_1, d_2, ...d_n) \in D = D_1 \times D_2 \times ... \times D_n$ t h e joint decision vectors of the n actors.

The joint selectability and rejectability are therefore given by Equation (51)

$$\mu_S\left(d\right) = \prod_{i=1}^n \left\{\mu_{S_i}\left(d_i\right)\right\} \text{ and } \mu_R\left(d\right) = \prod_{i=1}^n \left\{\mu_{R_i}\left(d_i\right)\right\}$$
$$(51)$$

Solution Procedures

For multi - person satisficing games, the analysis in terms of satisficing sets can be carried up in the point of view of the community or in the point of view of an individual actor. Each member i of the community comes with his own boldness index q_i and let us denote by $q = (q_1, q_2, ...q_n)$ the boldness indices vector and $q_l = \min(q_1, q_2, ...q_n)$ the least boldness index value then the following materials that can be used for negotiation are obtained. Let us denote by $\sum_{q_i}$ the satisficing set of member i given by the following Equation (52)

$$\Sigma_{q_i} = \left\{d_i \in D_i : \mu_{S_i}\left(d_i\right) \geq q_i \mu_{R_i}\left(d_i\right)\right\} \quad (52)$$

The joint satisficing set at an arbitrary boldness index q is given by the following by Equation (53)

$$\Sigma_q = \left\{d \in D : \mu_S\left(d\right) \geq q\mu_R\left(d\right)\right\} \quad (53)$$

For negotiation purpose it is important to characterize for each partner what can be consid- ered to be a compromise set, this is given by the following definition.

Definition 7: The set of all decision vectors d that are jointly satisficing at boldness index q_l where the component d_i is satisficing for decision maker i denoted C_i is called the compromise set of decision maker i and is given by the following Equation (54)

$$C_i = \left\{d \in \Sigma_{q_l} \text{ and } d_i \in \Sigma_{q_l}\right\} \quad (54)$$

It is known that the compromise set is always non empty, see (Stirling, 2003); the intersection of compromise set is known as the satisficing imputation set at the boldness index vector q and given by the following: a joint decisions vector is a satisficing imputation at boldness index vector if the following Equation (55) is valid

$$\mu_S\left(d\right) \geq q_l \mu_R\left(d\right) \text{ and } \mu_{S_i}\left(d_i\right) \geq q_i \mu_{R_i}\left(d_i\right) \quad (55)$$

Definition 8: The set of satisficing imputation set at boldness index vector q denoted N_q is given by Equation (56)

$$N_q = \bigcap_{i=1}^n C_i \quad (56)$$

The set N_q contains joint decision that provides benefit to the group while ensuring that each decision makers preferences are not compromised. If N_q is empty then no compromise is possible and some decision makers must lower their stan- dards in order to reach a compromise. The algo- rithm of finding an imputation set is as follows: each decision maker (i) supplies following pa- rameters to the analyst: categorical satisfiability measures $\mu_{S_i}^0\left(d_i^k\right) / \mu_{R_i}^0\left(d_i^k\right)$ for each of his alterna- tive decision; the set of his vicinity with the relative importance degrees of the members of this vicinity $V(i) / \theta_i$ where the considered decision maker is supposed to know possible decisions of the members of his vicinity; the conditional selectability/rejectability measures for each decision of each member of its vicinity $\mu_{S_i/S_j}(d_i^k / d_j^l)$ and $\mu_{R_i/S_j}(d_i^k / d_j^l)$ and finally his egoism degree δ_i and caution index q_i from this material, the analyst will compute the imputation set N_q; if this set is not empty then select final imputation joint decision within this set using some criterion; for instance that given by equation (57)

$$d^* = \arg\left\{\max_{d \in N_q}\left\{\frac{\mu_S(d)}{\mu_R(d)}\right\}\right\} \qquad (57)$$

otherwise reduce caution indices by some amount until a non empty imputation set is reached.

ILLUSTRATIVE APPLICATION

Problem

Let us consider the following situation: a company operating in environmental sensitive sector such as a chemical enterprise, would like to build a new plant in some region. To this end, this enterprise must negotiate with a local executive committee that is concerned by the development of its region in terms of jobs creation when preserving the health and quality of life of the population of that region; as well as a high level (national for instance) government that is in charge of fixing the tax that the enterprise must pay to compensate possible negative impact its activity will have on the environment. Thus this decision situation put together three decision makers:

- The company (decision maker 1) that must decide whether to invest (*decision* d_1^1 in a new operating unit in that region or not (*decision* d_1^2);
- Local executive committee (decision maker 2) that must decide whether to support the project of the new unit relatively to the national government (*decision* d_2^1) or not (*decision* d_2^2); and
- National government (decision maker 3) that have three alternatives decision in terms of high tax (*decision* d_3^1), moderate tax (*decision* d_3^2) or low tax (*decision* d_3^3).

Elicitation of Categorical Satisfiability Measures

The following scenario is considered at categorical level:

- The enterprise is very interested in the project of building a new operating unit in the considered region so that its selectability measures are given by $\mu_{S_1}^0(d_1^1) = 0.7$ and $\mu_{S_1}^0(d_1^2) = 0.3$; but because of some uncontrollable extra events, it considers that these two options are equally rejectable, that is $\mu_{R_1}^0(d_1^1) = \mu_{R_1}^0(d_1^2) = 0.5$;
- Local executive committee, because of its experience in relationship with the high level government and given forthcoming projects it must have to defend on one hand and the necessity to enhance economic development of its region, is very dubitative in front of its two alternative decisions so that it considers them to be equally selectable and equally rejectable that is its categorical satisfiability measures are given by $\mu_{S_2}^0(d_2^1) = \mu_{S_2}^0(d_2^2) = 0.5$ and $\mu_{R_2}^0(d_2^1) = \mu_{R_2}^0(d_2^2) = 0.5$

- National government is very sensible to environmental issues so that it tends to punish company whose activities have a negative impact on the environment but it is also sensible to socioeconomic issues in terms of jobs creation; its categorical satisfiability measures are therefore given by

$$\mu_{S_3}^0\left(d_3^1\right)=0.5; \mu_{S_3}^0\left(d_3^2\right)=0.3; \mu_{S_3}^0\left(d_3^3\right)=0.2$$

and

$$\mu_{R_3}^0\left(d_3^1\right)=0.1; \mu_{R_3}^0\left(d_3^2\right)=0.3; \mu_{R_3}^0\left(d_3^3\right)=0.6$$

Elicitation of Interaction Parameters

Let us suppose that an analysis leads to the conditional measures given by Tables 6 to 8.

Results

Let us suppose that the relative importance vectors assigned by each decision maker to others are given by Equation (58) where the first weight always represent that of decision maker with less index

$$\theta_1=\begin{bmatrix}0.7 & 0.3\end{bmatrix}; \theta_2=\begin{bmatrix}0.5 & 0.5\end{bmatrix}; \theta_3=\begin{bmatrix}0.4 & 0.6\end{bmatrix} \tag{58}$$

and that all decision makers have an egoism degree of *0.5*; then results of Equations (42)-(50) lead to following satisfiability measures when taking into account vicinity influence, Table 9.

Individual satisficing sets at a common caution index of *q = 1* are given by Equation (59)

$$\Sigma_1=\left\{d_1^1\right\}; \Sigma_2=\left\{d_2^1\right\}; \Sigma_3=\left\{d_3^1\right\} \tag{59}$$

The joint satisfiability measures, as defined by Equation (51), are given by Table 10.

The joint satisficing set at the caution index of *q=1* is given by Equation (60)

$$\Sigma=\left\{\begin{matrix}\left(d_1^1,d_2^1,d_3^1\right),\left(d_1^1,d_2^1,d_3^2\right),\left(d_1^2,d_2^1,d_3^1\right),\\\left(d_1^1,d_2^2,d_3^1\right),\left(d_1^2,d_2^2,d_3^1\right)\end{matrix}\right\} \tag{60}$$

The compromise sets are given by Equations (61)-(63)

$$C_1=\left\{\left(d_1^1,d_2^1,d_3^1\right),\left(d_1^1,d_2^1,d_3^2\right),\left(d_1^1,d_2^2,d_3^1\right)\right\} \tag{61}$$

$$C_2=\left\{\left(d_1^1,d_2^1,d_3^1\right),\left(d_1^1,d_2^1,d_3^2\right),\left(d_1^2,d_2^1,d_3^1\right)\right\} \tag{62}$$

$$C_3=\left\{\left(d_1^1,d_2^1,d_3^1\right),\left(d_1^2,d_2^1,d_3^1\right),\left(d_1^1,d_2^2,d_3^1\right),\left(d_1^2,d_2^2,d_3^1\right)\right\} \tag{63}$$

So the imputation set is given by Equation (64)

$$N=\left\{\left(d_1^1,d_2^1,d_3^1\right),\left(d_1^2,d_2^1,d_3^1\right)\right\} \tag{64}$$

as the imputation set is not empty, one can choose the final satisficing imputation alternative using Equation (57) that leads to $d^*=\left(d_1^1,d_2^1,d_3^1\right)$ meaning that the enterprise investing, the local executive committee supporting this project, and the national government highly taxing the activity is an acceptable situation for the tree decision makers.

FUTURE RESEARCH DIRECTIONS

Soft computing is a computing technique that exploits the tolerance for impression, uncertainty, partial truth, and approximation to achieve tractability, robustness, low solution cost and better rapport with reality in problems solving. Bipolar approach with the corresponding mathematical tools of satisficing or conditional games establishes a new framework to use soft computing paradigm in decision analysis. But there remain

Table 6. Conditional satisfiability measures of decision maker 1

		$\mu_{S_1/S_j}\left(d_i^k / d_j^l\right)$	$\mu_{R_1/S_j}\left(d_i^k / d_j^l\right)$
d_1^1	d_2^1	0.8	0.4
	d_2^2	0.2	0.6
d_1^2	d_2^1	0.5	0.7
	d_2^2	0.5	0.3
d_1^1	d_3^1	0.2	0.6
	d_3^2	0.3	0.2
	d_3^3	0.5	0.2
d_1^2	d_3^1	0.6	0.5
	d_3^2	0.2	0.3
	d_3^3	0.2	0.2

Table 7. Conditional satisfiability measures of decision maker 2

		$\mu_{S_2/S_j}\left(d_i^k / d_j^l\right)$	$\mu_{R_2/S_j}\left(d_i^k / d_j^l\right)$
d_2^1	d_1^1	0.7	0.5
	d_1^2	0.7	0.5
d_2^2	d_1^1	0.1	0.3
	d_1^2	0.9	0.7
d_2^1	d_3^1	0.6	0.2
	d_3^2	0.3	0.1
	d_3^3	0.1	0.7
d_2^2	d_3^1	0.2	0.4
	d_3^2	0.2	0.3
	d_3^3	0.6	0.3

a lot of things to achieve in terms of methodologies and modeling tools in order to reach practical usability of this framework in solving real world complex problems. The approach presented here greatly simplify the problem when it considers only relationships at decision makers level whereas the nature of relationships may depend on the context and/or decisions being considered by each partner. Among things that need to be addressed seriously there are:

- **Context**: For instance the attitude of a decision maker toward the members of his vicinity may depends on the context so that this issue must be taken into account to accurately address human attitude modeling process; though it may be not apparent through the text, the approach established in this paper is actually context dependent; indeed all presented components and parameters (vicinity, egoism degree, risk aversion degree, indecision attitude, etc.) will change from one context to another; but this changing mechanism needs a formal treatment;

- **Psychological parameters**: Definition and assessment of attributes as well as social relationships may depend on some psychological parameters such as emotion, fear, confidence, etc.;

- **Dynamics**: A same problem may be viewed differently by a same decision maker from an instant to another;

Table 8. Conditional satisfiability measures of decision maker 3

		$\mu_{S_3/S_j}\left(d_i^k/d_j^l\right)$	$\mu_{R_3/S_j}\left(d_i^k/d_j^l\right)$
d_3^1	d_1^1	0.7	0.6
	d_1^2	0.3	0.4
d_3^2	d_1^1	0.9	0.4
	d_1^2	0.1	0.6
d_3^3	d_1^1	0.5	0.7
	d_1^2	0.5	0.3
d_3^1	d_2^1	0.2	0.3
	d_2^2	0.8	0.7
d_3^2	d_2^1	0.5	0.4
	d_2^2	0.5	0.6
d_3^3	d_2^1	0.7	0.2
	d_2^2	0.3	0.8

Table 9. Individual satisfiability measures taking into account vicinity influence

	μ_{S_i}	μ_{R_i}
d_1^1	0.5776	0.5038
d_1^2	0.4224	0.4962
d_2^1	0.5527	0.4856
d_2^2	0.4473	0.5144
d_3^1	0.3821	0.2198
d_3^2	0.2862	0.3078
d_3^3	0.3317	0.4725

To dispose with a robust framework for decision analysis in a real world problem solving, a sensitivity analysis should be considered in order address how solution structure may vary according to some parameters such as attributes values, concordance/discordance degrees, egoism/selfishness/caution indices, etc.

CONCLUSION

In this chapter, a decision support framework that cope as much as possible with the reality of human decision making processes has been presented. Human attitude, behavior and judgment must be correctly addressed by the analyst when modeling decision making problem bringing together many decision makers, because of biases these attributes inherent to human beings may introduce in the final results. But, coping with human attitude and behavior in modeling decision analysis processes is a tremendous challenge, as one must deal with variability, context oriented behavior, instabil-

- **Implementation**: Implementing the approach established in this chapter into a practical decision support software needs clarifying different levels; at least two levels must be specified: a central level that will be in charge of aggregating parameters (vicinity, risk averse degree, egoism degree, etc.) specified at local level by decision makers; by so doing, the apparent great number of parameters to specify is distributed and this renders the decision process manageable.

Table 10. Joint satisfiability measures

			μ_S	μ_R
d_1^1	d_2^1	d_3^1	0.1220	0.0538
d_1^1	d_2^1	d_3^2	0.0914	0.0753
d_1^1	d_2^1	d_3^3	0.1059	0.1156
d_1^2	d_2^1	d_3^1	0.0892	0.0530
d_1^2	d_2^1	d_3^2	0.0668	0.0742
d_1^2	d_2^1	d_3^3	0.0774	0.1138
d_1^1	d_2^2	d_3^1	0.0987	0.0570
d_1^1	d_2^2	d_3^2	0.0739	0.0798
d_1^1	d_2^2	d_3^3	0.0857	0.1224
d_1^2	d_2^2	d_3^1	0.0722	0.0561
d_1^2	d_2^2	d_3^2	0.0541	0.0786
d_1^2	d_2^2	d_3^3	0.0627	0.1206

ity, or emotion, etc. In order to address correctly these issues in decision analysis to reach models that reflect as much as possible human behavior in front of a decision making problem, modeling process must rely on some cardinal concepts or notions. In this chapter, the concept of bipolarity has been the stepping stone that guides human attitude modeling process. This concept permits to take into account possible indecision of a decision maker between two alternatives by formulating the choice problem in the satisficing game theory framework; it permits also to efficiently address relationships between objectives and attributes through supporting and rejecting notions; and finally it is used in social influence modeling by considering concordance and discordance that may exist between two decision makers confronted to a decision analysis problem.

REFERENCES

Arrow, K. J. (1951). *Social choice and individual values*. New York: John Wiley..

Bouyssou, D., Marchant, T., Perny, P., Pirlot, M., Tsoukiàs, A., & Vincke, P. (2000). *Evaluation and decision models: A critical perspective*. Dordrecht, The Netherlands: Kluwer Academic. doi:10.1007/978-1-4615-1593-7.

Brans, J. P., Mareschal, B., & Vincke, P. (1986). PROMETHEE: A new family of outranking methods in multicriteria analysis. *Operations Research, 84*, 477–490.

Brans, J. P., Mareschal, B., & Vincke, P. (1986a). How to select and how to rank projects: The PROMETHEE method. *European Journal of Operational Research, 24*, 228–238. doi:10.1016/0377-2217(86)90044-5.

Brauers, W. K. M., Zavadskas, E. K., Peldschus, F., & Turskis, Z. (2008). Multi-objective decision-making for road design. *Transport, 23*(3), 183–193. doi:10.3846/1648-4142.2008.23.183-193.

Caciopo, J. T., & Berntson, G. G. (1994). Relationship between attitudes and evaluative space: A critical review, with emphasis on the separability of positive and negative substrates. *Psychological Bulletin, 115*, 401–423. doi:10.1037/0033-2909.115.3.401.

Dubois, D., & Fargier, H. (2006). *Qualitative decision making with bipolar information*. American Association for Artificial Intelligence. Retrieved from WWW.AAAI.ORG

Grabisch, M. (1996). The application of fuzzy integrals in multicriteria decision making. *European Journal of Operational Research*, *89*(3), 445–456. doi:10.1016/0377-2217(95)00176-X.

Greco, S., Matarazzo, B., & Slowinski, R. (2001). Rough sets theory for multicriteria decision analysis. *European Journal of Operational Research*, *129*(1), 1–47. doi:10.1016/S0377-2217(00)00167-3.

Hokkanen, J., & Salminen, P. (1997). Choosing a solid waste management system using multicriteria decision analysis. *European Journal of Operational Research*, *98*, 19–36. doi:10.1016/0377-2217(95)00325-8.

Osgood, C. E., Suci, G., & Tannenbaum, P. H. (1957). *The measurement of meaning*. Chicago, IL: Univ. of Illinois Press.

Saaty, T. (2005). *Theory and applications of the analytic network process: Decision making with benefits, opportunities, costs, and risks*. Pittsburgh, PA: RWS Publications..

Steuer, R. E. (1986). *Multicriteria optimization: Theory, computation, and application*. New York: Willey..

Stirling, W. C. (2003). *Satisficing games and decision making: With applications to engineering and computer science*. Cambridge, UK: Cambridge University Press. doi:10.1017/CBO9780511543456.

Stirling, W. C. (2012). *Theory of conditional games*. Cambridge, UK: Cambridge University Press..

Tchangani, A. P. (2006). A satisficing game theory approach for group evaluation of production units. *Decision Support Systems*, *42*, 778–788. doi:10.1016/j.dss.2005.05.010.

Tchangani, A. P. (2006a). SANPEV: A satisficing analytic network process framework for efficiency evaluation of alternatives. *Foundations of Computing and Decision Sciences*, *31*(3-4), 291–319.

Tchangani, A. P. (2009). Evaluation model for multi attributes - Multi agents decision making: Satisficing game approach. *International Journal of Information Technology and Decision Making*, *8*(1), 73–91. doi:10.1142/S0219622009003272.

Tchangani, A. P. (2009a). Modelling selecting and ranking alternatives characterized by multiple attributes to satisfy multiple objectives. *Journal of Information and Computing Science*, *4*(1), 3–16.

Tchangani, A. P. (2010). Considering bipolarity of attributes with regards to objectives in decisions evaluation. *Inzinerine Ekonomika*, *21*(5), 475–484.

Tchangani, A.P. (2013). Bipolar aggregation method for fuzzy nominal classification using weighted cardinal fuzzy measure (WCFM), *Journal of Uncertain Systems*.

Tchangani, A. P., Bouzarour-Amokrane, Y., & Pérès, F. (2012). Evaluation model in decision analysis: Bipolar approach. *INFORMATICA: An International Journal*, *23*(3), 461–485.

Tchangani, A. P., & Pérès, F. (2010). BOCR framework for decision analysis. In *Proceedings of 12th IFAC Symposium on Large Scale Systems: Theory and Applications*. IFAC.

Vincke, P. (1989). L'aide multicritere a la decision. Bruxelles, Belgium: Ed.s de l'Universite Libre de Bruxelles..

von Neumann, J., & Morgenstern, O. (1964). *Theory of games and economic behavior*. Hoboken, NJ: John Wiley..

Zadeh, L. A. (1994). Fuzzy logic, neural computing and soft computing. *Communications of the ACM*, *37*(3), 77–84. doi:10.1145/175247.175255.

ADDITIONAL READING

Bazerman, M. H. (2002). *Judgment in Managerial Decision Making*. New York, USA: John Wiley..

Bell, D. E., Raiffa, H., & Tversky, A. (1988). *Decision Making: Descriptive, normative, and prescriptive Interactions*. Cambridge, United Kingdom: Cambridge U. Press. doi:10.1017/CBO9780511598951.

Belton, V., & Gear, T. (1982). On a Shortcoming of Saaty's Method of Analytic Hierarchies. *Omega, 11*(3), 226–230.

Bouyssou, D., Dubois, D., Prade, H., & Pirlot, M. (2009) (Eds.). Decision Making Process: Concepts and Methods. New York, USA: Wiley-ISTE..

Coner, J. L., & Coner, P. D. (1995). Characteristics of decisions in Decision Analysis Practice. *The Journal of the Operational Research Society, 46*, 304–314.

Doron, G., & Sened, I. (2001). *Political Bargaining: Theory, Practice and Process*. London, United Kingdom: Sage Publications..

Driessen, T. (1988). *Cooperative Games, Solutions and Applications*. Dordrecht, The Netherlands: Kluwer Academic Publishers. doi:10.1007/978-94-015-7787-8.

Fischer, G. W., Carmon, Z., Ariely, D., & Zauberman, G. (1999). Goal-based Construction of Preferences: Task Goals and Prominence Effect. *Management Science, 45*(8), 1057–1075. doi:10.1287/mnsc.45.8.1057.

Fishburn, P. C. (1968). Utility Theory. *Management Science, 14*(5), 335–378. doi:10.1287/mnsc.14.5.335.

French, S. (1989). *Readings in Decision Analysis*. London, United Kingdom: Chapman and Hall..

Hanson, R. B. (1998). Consensus by Identifying Extremists. *Theory and Decision, 44*, 293–301. doi:10.1023/A:1004918905650.

Hogarth, R. M., & Kunreuther, H. (1992). Decision-Making under Uncertainty: The Effects of Role and Ambiguity. In F. Heller (Ed.), *Decision-Making and Leadership*. Cambridge, United Kingdom: Cambridge U. Press..

Howard, R. A. (1988). Decision Analysis: Practice and Promise. *Management Science, 34*(6), 679–695. doi:10.1287/mnsc.34.6.679.

Kahneman, D. (2003). Experienced Utility and Objective Happiness: A Moment-Based Approach. In I. Brocas, & J. D. CarrilloOxford University Press (Eds.), *The Psychology of Economic Decisions*..

Kahneman, D., & Tversky, A. (2000). *Choices, Values, and Frames*. Cambridge University Press..

Keeney, H., & Raiffa, R. A. (1999). *Decisions with Multiple Objectives: Preferences and Value Tradeoffs*. Cambridge University Press..

Keeney, R. E. (1994). Using Values in Operations Research. *Operations Research, 42*(5), 793–813. doi:10.1287/opre.42.5.793.

Leyton-Brown, K., & Shoham, Y. (2008). *Essentials of Game Theory: A Concise, Multidisciplinary Introduction*. San Rafael, CA: Morgan & Claypool Publishers. doi:10.2200/S00108ED-1V01Y200802AIM003.

Luce, R. D., & Raiffa, H. (1957). *Games and Decisions: An Introduction and Critical Survey*. New York, USA: Wiley & Sons..

McCord, M., & de Neufville, R. (1983). Fundamental Deficiency of Expected Utility Decision Analysis. In S. French, R. Hartley, L. C. Thomas, & D. J. London (Eds.), *Multi-Objective Decision Making*. United Kingdom: White. Academic Press..

McCord, M., & de Neufville, R. (1983b). Empirical Demonstration that Expected Utility Decision Analysis is not Operational. In S. Wenstop (Ed.), *Foundation of Utility and Risk Theory with Applications*. Reidel Publishing Company. doi:10.1007/978-94-017-1590-4_10.

Osborne, M. J., & Rubinstein, A. (1994). *A Course in Game Theory*. MIT Press..

Plous, S. (1993). *The Psychology of Judgment and Decision Making*. McGraw-Hill. Popper, M., R.

Raiffa, H. (1970). *Decision Analysis*. MA, USA: Addison-Wesley Publishing Company..

Raiffa, H., Richardson, H. J., & Metcalfe, D. (2002). *Negotiation Analysis: The Science and Art of Collaborative Decision Making*. The Belknap Press of Harvard University Press..

Richards, D., & Rowe, W. D. (1999). Decision Making with Heterogeneous Sources of Information. *Risk Analysis*, *19*(1), 69–81. doi:10.1111/j.1539-6924.1999.tb00390.x.

Saaty, T. (1986). Axiomatic Foundations of the Analytic Hierarchy Process. *Management Science*, *32*(7), 841–855. doi:10.1287/mnsc.32.7.841.

Savage, L. J. (1972). *The Foundations of Statistics*. New York, USA: Dover Publications, Inc.

Simon, H. (1991). Bounded Rationality and Organizational Learning. *Organization Science*, *2*(1), 125–134. doi:10.1287/orsc.2.1.125.

Simon, H. (1997). *Administrative Behavior: A Study of Decision-Making Processes in Administrative Organizations*. New York, USA: The Free Press..

Thomas, H., & Samson, D. (1986). Subjective Aspects of the Art of Decision Analysis: Exploring the Role of Decision Analysis in Decision Structuring, Decision Support and Policy Dialogue. *The Journal of the Operational Research Society*, *37*(3), 249–265.

Thorkildsen, T. A. (2005). *Fundamentals of Measurement in Applied Research*. Pearson Education Inc.

Tversky, A., & Kahneman, D. (1974). Judgment under Uncertainty: Heuristics and Biases. *Science*, *211*(4481), 453–458. doi:10.1126/science.7455683 PMID:17835457.

Tversky, A., & Kahneman, D. (2000). Rational Choice and the Framing of Decisions. In *Choices, Values, and Frames. Edited by Kahneman and Tversky*. Cambridge, United Kingdom: Cambridge University Press..

von Winterfeldt, D. (2001). Decisions with Multiple Stakeholders and Conflicting Objectives. In E. U. Weber, J. Baron, & G. Loomes (Eds.), *Conflict and Tradeoffs in Decision Making*. Cambridge, United Kingdom: Cambridge University Press..

Chapter 13
A Soft Computing–Based Idea Applied to the Truck and Trailer Routing Problem

Isis Torres Pérez
Instituto Superior Politécnico "José Antonio Echeverría," Cuba

Alejandro Rosete Suárez
Instituto Superior Politécnico "José Antonio Echeverría," Cuba

Carlos Cruz-Corona
Universidad de Granada, Spain

José L. Verdegay
Universidad de Granada, Spain

ABSTRACT

Techniques based on Soft Computing are useful to model and solve real-world problems where decision makers use subjective knowledge or linguistic information when making decisions, measuring parameters, objectives, and constraints, and even when modeling the problem. In many problems in transport and logistics, it is necessary to take into account that the available knowledge about some data and parameters of the problem model is imprecise or uncertain. Truck and Trailer Routing Problem, TTRP, is one of most recent and interesting problems in transport routing planning. TTRP is a combinatorial optimization problem, and it is computationally more difficult to solve than the known Vehicle Routing Problem, VRP. Most of models used in the literature assume that the data available is accurate; but this consideration does not correspond with reality. For this reason, it is appropriate to focus research toward defining TTRP models for incorporating the uncertainty present in their data. The aims of the present chapter are: a) to provide a study on the Truck and Trailer Routing Problem that serves as help to researchers interested on this topic and b) to present an approach using techniques of Soft Computing to solve this problem.

DOI: 10.4018/978-1-4666-4785-5.ch013

INTRODUCTION

Intelligent transport systems are advanced applications which, aim to provide innovative services relating to different modes of transport and traffic management and enable various users to be better informed and make safer, more coordinated, and 'smarter' use of transport networks. Vehicle Routing Problem, VRP, is a generic name given to a whole class of problems where it is needed to design a set of routes. In the VRP a fleet of vehicles has to be routed from one or several depots to serve a set of geographically dispersed cities or customers, subject to side constraints. The goal is to design vehicle routes originating from and terminating at the central depot to fulfill each customer's demand so that the total cost is minimized. The total demand on each route should not exceed the vehicle capacity and each customer can only be serviced once by exactly one vehicle (Toth & Vigo, 2002). There exists a wide variety of VRPs and a broad literature on this class of problems. The most important problems are: VRP with Time Windows (VRPTW), VRP with Backhauls (VRPB), VRP with Pick-Up and Delivery (VRPPD) and Capacitated VRP (CVRP).

Recently has been defined the Truck and Trailer Routing Problem (TTRP), an extension of the VRP that adds the use of trailers. In the standard TTRP, a set of customers with known demand is serviced by a fleet of vehicles (truck pulling a trailer) with known capacity. However, due to practical constraints, including government regulations, limited maneuvering space at customer site, road conditions, etc., some customers may only be serviced by a truck. All these characteristics generate different types of routes in a TTRP solution. These routes originating from and terminating at a central depot and they are limited by capacity of vehicle used.

TTRP is a combinatorial optimization problem and it is computationally more difficult to solve than VRP. It's worth noting, in the nature of the TTRP is patent the presence of vague, imprecise and inexact information such as the demand of customers, the distances between customers, the capacities of the vehicles or the windows time. For such a reason will be convenient to solve this problem using techniques of Soft Computing (Verdegay et al., 2008). The aims of the present paper are: a) to provide a study on the Truck and Trailer Routing Problem that serves as help to researchers interested on this topic; b) to present an approach using techniques of Soft Computing to solve this problem. The paper is organized as follow: Section Background gives a review of the related problems with TTRP and its definition. Also describes the formal definition of the TTRP, comments some variants and methods used to solve this problem, and a Soft Computing based approach is finally presented as general method to face the uncertainty in their data.

BACKGROUND

Related Problems

The term "Truck and Trailer Routing Problem" was first used in 2002 by Chao (Chao, 2002). However, previous works were developed to solve practical situation presents in real-life. The TTRP extends the basic VRP, which is one of the most studied combinatorial optimization problem. The VRP aims to find a set of routes of minimum total length to serve the demand of a set of customers using a homogeneous fleet of capacitated vehicles based at a main depot. Some variants of the VRP that had been studied can be viewed as closer approach to TTRP.

The first work related with TTRP was presented by Semet and Taillard in 1993 (Semet & Taillard, 1993). The problem occurred at a regional level of one of the major chain store in Switzerland. This Swiss chain store involves 45 grocery stores located in the cantons of Vaud and Valais. Each store may be place up two different orders. An order of a store cannot be split. To stock its shops, the company owns a heterogeneous fleet of vehicles consisting of 21 truck and 7 trailers. A truck pulling a trailer it is called road train. There are 9 stores that can receive deliveries by road train called trailer-store and others 36 stores that can be receive deliveries by truck only called truck store. The goal is to determine a transportation schedule using a heterogeneous fleet that minimizes the transportation costs. The authors studied a real-life VRP that deals with new features such as, the heterogeneous character of the fleet, in the sense that utilization costs are vehicle-dependent and the use of trailers under accessibility restrictions. Also, the customer's trailer-store cannot be serviced in a sub-tour. That paper proposed a heuristic method based on clustering methods and a standard Tabu search method for finding good solutions. The clustering methods used by these authors are variants or extensions of the generalized assignment heuristic developed by Fisher and Jaikumar (Fisher & Jaikumar, 1981).

Two years later is modeled the "Partial Accessibility Constrained Vehicle Routing Problem" (PACVRP) (Semet, 1995). PACVRP is an extension of the VRP and takes in account the partial accessibility constraint introduced in previous works (Semet & Taillard, 1993). In this problem are defined two categories of customers: trailer-customers and truck-customers due to access of road-trains to all customers unlikely. Therefore, the partial accessibility constraint consists of forbid same customers to be served by a truck and its trailer. Also, three types of routes can be designed in a solution: routes covered by truck alone or road-trains which include trailer-customers and truck-customers and routes covered by road-trains which include only trailer-customers. The route covered by road-trains to serve both customers is composed of two types of tours: one main tour and one or more sub-tours. It can be appreciated that PACVRP is very similar to the TTRP, but the main differences between them are:

1. The number of sub-tours to a parking place is restricted to a maximum of one;
2. The depot can be visited only once in a route;
3. All available trucks are used;
4. The number of trailers must be determined.

The author formulated the considered problem as an integer program and proposed a two-phase heuristic method. Also, to solve a combinatorial problem that has some similarities with the generalized assignment problem (GAP) proposes an enumerative procedure using Lagrangian relaxation.

Among the current variants of VRP, the Vehicle Routing Problem with Trailers (VRPT) is very similar to the TTRP. In this problem the combination of truck and trailer is called vehicle or complete vehicle. However, the use of a complete vehicle may be cause problem when serving customer with constraints. Time and trouble could be saved if these customers were served by the truck only. Also, an additional advantage will be the saving of fuel and drives faster. Gerdessen (Gerdessen, 1996) conducted a study on the VRPT and presented two real-world applications. The first one occurred in the distribution of dairy products by the Dutch dairy industry. In this case the truck-trailer combinations are used to distribute the products to customers that are located in crowded cities. Another application is the delivery of compound animal feed to be distributed among farmers. The distribution of compound animal feed was done with vehicles that consist of a truck and a trailer so-called double bottom. The trailer can be left behind at a parking place when the farmer is located in areas of difficult access. Gerdessen's model is simplified with a set the assumptions. The VRPT differs from TTRP mainly in:

- All customers have unit demand. It simplifies the problem because it is possible calculate the minimum number of vehicles beforehand.

- Each trailer is parked exactly once. This assumption is not corresponds with the reality where the number of times that a trailer is parked must be a free number.
- Each customer site can be used as a parking place.
- Each customer is assigned a maneuvering cost instead of customer type.

Various heuristics have been developed to find good solutions to the VRPT in reasonable time. These heuristics can be divided into two groups: construction heuristics that try to find a good feasible solution, and improvement heuristics that try to improve this feasible solution (Talbi, 2009).

The Site-Dependent Vehicle Routing Problem (SDVRP) is other problem related to the TTRP. In 1999, Chao et al. in (Chao, Golden, & Wasil, 1999) studied the SDVRP. In this case there is a fleet with several types of vehicles and compatibility relationship between the customer sites and the vehicle types. For example, some customers located in congested, urban areas can be serviced only by small-capacity vehicles, while some customers located in suburban areas can be serviced by any type of vehicle. Lastly in 2001 Cordeau and Laporte (Cordeau & Laporte, 2001) shows the SDVRP as a special case of Periodic Vehicle Routing Problem (PVRP) and solving with a Tabu search heuristic.

Summarizing, there were real-life applications related to this kind of problem before the formal definition of the TTRP. Each one is considered a variant of the classical VRP. However, all they present differences with the TTRP.

TRUCK AND TRAILER ROUTING PROBLEM

The TTRP is a combinatorial optimization problem and an extension of the well-known VRP. The main difference TTRP y VRP consist in the use of trailers; a commonly neglected feature in the VRP. The TTRP considers two forms of customer types: a customer who is accessible with or without a trailer (*vehicle customer*), and one who is only accessible without a trailer (*truck customer*). The access to a *truck customer* implied leaves the trailer in a parking place, called the root of sub-tour. The customers are geographically dispersed and have an associated demand.

The fleet of vehicles in a TTRP consists of trucks and trailers. Once a trailer is assigned to a truck; it may not be assigned to another truck. A truck with a trailer is called *complete vehicle*, while that a truck without a trailer is called *pure truck*. The use of truck alone is due to practical constraints such as government regulations, limited maneuvering space at customer site, road condition, etc. All trucks and all trailers have identical capacity. However it can be considered as a heterogeneous fleet capacity due to vehicle types that can be used: *complete vehicle* and *pure truck*.

There are three types of routes in a TTRP solution as illustrated in Figure 1. These types of routes originating from and terminating at a central depot and they are limited by capacity of vehicle used. The types of routes are:

- **Complete Vehicle Route (CVR):** Consisting of a main tour traveled by a complete vehicle, and at least one sub-tour traveled by the truck alone.
- **Pure Truck Route (PTR):** This type of route is traveled by a truck alone and are visited both customer type.
- **Pure Vehicle Route (PVR):** It is the tour traveled by a complete vehicle and contains only vehicle customer without any sub-tour.

The growing interest in TTRP is motivated by its practical relevance in many real world problems. Also, the broad range of actual applications that leads to the definition of many TTRP variants that presents real-world constraints.

Figure 1. Routes types in the TTRP. (Adapted from (Lin, Yu, & Chou, 2009).

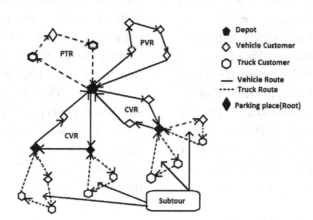

Problem Formulation

The TTRP can be formally defined on an undirected graph $G = (V; A)$, where $V = \{v_0, v_1, ..., v_n\}$ is a vertex set and $A = \{(v_i, v_j) / v_i, v_j \in V\ i \neq j\}$ is the set of edges. The vertexes represent customer, except the vertex v_0 that be corresponds to central depot. There is a vector of the customer demands d and each customer $i \in V\backslash\{v_0\}$ has a non-negative demand $d_i > 0$. The access constraints create a partition of V into two subsets: the subset of truck customer (V_c) accessible only by truck and the subset of vehicle customer (V_v) accessible either by truck or by truck with trailer.

C is a matrix of non-negative cost. Each edge $(i,j) \in V$ is associated with a cost c_{ij} that represents the travel time required on the edge or the travel distance between vertex i and vertex j. A heterogeneous fleet of m_c trucks and m_r trailers, where $m_r \leq m_c$. The capacities of the trucks and the trailers are q_c and q_r respectively. A route in the TTRP is composed of a partition of V: $R_1, R_2, ..., R_m$ and a permutation of δ_m specifying the order of the customers on route. Each route originating from and terminating at a central depot: $R_m = \{v_0, v_1, v_2, ..., v_{n+1}\}$, where $v_0 = v_{n+1}$ denotes the depot. Thus, the goal of the TTRP is to find a set of least cost vehicle routes that start and end at the central depot such that each customer is serviced exactly once and the total demand of any vehicle route

does not exceed the total capacity of the allocated vehicles used in that route; and the number of required trucks and trailers is not greater than m_c and m_r, respectively.

TTRP Variants

Few research efforts have been devoted to study the TTRP. However, there are some papers on several TTRP variants. Among variants more important are Truck and Trailer Routing Problem with Time Windows (TTRPTW) and Relaxed Truck and Trailer Routing Problem (RTTRP). Also, there are others as Multi-Depot Truck and Trailer Routing Problem (MDTTRP), Single Truck and Trailer Routing Problem with Satellite Depots (STTRPSD), Periodic Truck and Trailer Routing Problem (PTTRP), etc. Among extensions are considered Generalized Truck and Trailer Routing Problem (GTTRP) and Extended Truck and Trailer Routing Problem (ETTRP). The following section describes some of these variants:

Relaxed Truck and Trailer Routing Problem (RTTRP)

This variant relaxes the fleet size constraint for the TTRP. In the TTRP there are not fix costs associated with the vehicles although there are limitations on the number of available trucks and available trailers. Thus, it is possible to construct better vehicle routes by utilizing more vehicles or allowing vehicles to take on multiple trips. Further, if the reduction in costs resulting from such relaxation is significant, it may be worthwhile to acquire or lease extra vehicles provided that the acquisition or lease costs can be justified (Lin, Yu, & Chou, 2010). The resulting RTTRP can be also used to determine a better fleet mix. Therefore, it is reasonable to relax the fleet size constraint with the goal to further reduce the total routing cost.

Truck and Trailer Routing Problem with Time Windows (TTRPTW)

In many real-world routing applications the time windows constraints are present. Truck and Trailer Routing Problem with Time Windows (TTRPTW) can be regarded as a variant of the Vehicle Routing Problem with Time Windows (VRPTW). This model is an extension of the TTRP, thus that the problem definition is similar, only add in each vertex i a service time window $\left(et_i, lt_i\right)$ and a service time st_i. The parameter et_i and lt_i denote the earliest time and latest time that the service to customer i can start, respectively and st_i denotes the time required to service customer i. In this problem must be fulfilling that each customer is serviced within their specific time windows (Lin, Yu, & Lu, 2011).

Single Truck and Trailer Routing Problem with Satellite Depots (STTRPSD)

The Single Truck and Trailer Routing Problem with Satellite Depots (STTRPSD) is a generalization of the VRP. In the STTRPSD a vehicle composed of truck with a detachable trailer serves the demand of a set of customers reachable only by the truck without the trailer. There is a set of parking locations called trailer points or satellite depots, where it is possible to detach the trailer

and to transfer products between the truck and the trailer. Each customer is assigned to one trailer point in a feasible solution of the STTRPSD. Consequently, trailer points with assigned customers are said to be open. The tour is traveled in two levels. The first level trip departing from the main depot is performed by the truck with the trailer and visits the subset of open trailer points. The second level trip serves the demand of those customers reachable only by the truck without the trailer. The second level trip starts and ends at the allocated trailer point and the total load should not exceed the truck capacity. The goal of the STTRPSD is to minimize the total length of the trips (Villegas, Prins, Prodhon, Medaglia, & Velasco, 2010).

Generalized Truck and Trailer Routing Problem (GTTRP)

In (Drexl M., 2007) (Drexl M., 2011) the author presented GTTRP which is a rather complex generalization motivated by a real-world scenario. Here trucks and trailers can be either collection vehicles or support vehicles. Collection vehicles are used to collect the supplies of customers, while support vehicles are used as "mobile depots" that cannot visit customers. A trailer may be pulled by different trucks during the course of its tour, and the load of the truck may be transferred from any vehicle to any other vehicle during a tour. Also, any intermediate locations en-route can be used either for parking or for load transfer.

Extended Truck and Trailer Routing Problem (ETTRP)

ETTRP is an extended version of the TTRP, in which the main objective is to minimize the total length of all constructed routes. This thesis expands on the model initially defined by Chao by introducing several additional constraints, which mimic problems that could arise in a real-world application. Thus, both time window constraints as well as load constraints are considered (Zitz, 2010).

Solutions Applied to TTRP

Since TTRP itself is a very difficult combinatorial optimization problem are usually tackled by approximate algorithms because no exact algorithm can be guaranteed to find optimal tours within reasonable computing time when the number of customers is large. This is due to the NP-Hardness of the problem (Garey & Johnson, 1979). The only exact approach for the TTRP is due to Drexl (Drexl M. A., 2007). The author developed a branch and price algorithm for the TTRP, where the algorithm had only been tested on relatively small instances of the TTRP.

Otherwise, approximate algorithms are more and more popular to solve this type of problem. Approximate algorithms can further be decomposed into two classes: specific heuristics and metaheurístics. Specific heuristics are problem dependent; they are designed and applicable to a particular problem. The heuristic methods perform a relatively limited exploration of the search space and typically produce good quality solutions within modest computing times.

In the case of the VRP, most of these heuristics are used as construction heuristics, insertion heuristics or improvement heuristics inside the search methods more sophisticated as the metaheurístics. The metaheurístics represent more general approximate algorithms applicable to a large variety of optimization problems. In metaheuristics, the emphasis is on performing a deep exploration of the most promising regions of the solution space. The quality of solutions produced by these methods is much higher than that obtained by classical heuristics.

There exists a wide variety of metaheuristics proposed to solve TTRP. Each one have achieved satisfactory results for routing problems, between them are: Both Chao (Chao, 2002) and Scheuerer (Scheuerer, 2006) solved the TTRP by a 2-phase approach. In the first phase, construction heuristics were used to obtain an initial TTRP solution. The initial solution was then improved by a Tabu Search (TS) algorithm in the second phase.

Lin et al. in (Lin, Yu, & Chou, 2009) developed a very effective Simulated Annealing (SA) based heuristic to the TTRP and obtained results that are competitive with those obtained by Scheuerer. Also, applied a route combination procedure to reduce the number of required trucks and trailers.

In (Caramia & Guerriero, 2010) the authors designed a mathematical programming based heuristic that also employs the cluster-first route-second approach. Their method solves two subproblems sequentially. The first, called customer-route assignment problem (CAP) and the second, the route definition problem (RDP). The authors embedded these two models with in an iterative mechanism that adds new constraints to the CAP based on the information of the RDP solution. This restarting mechanism is intended to diversify the search, and includes a Tabu search mechanism that forbids (in the CAP) customers route assignments already explored in previous iterations of the algorithm.

Villegas et al. proposed in (Villegas J., Prins, Prodhon, Medaglia, & Velasco, 2011) solved the TTRP using a route-first, cluster-second procedure embedded within a hybrid metaheuristic based on a Greedy Randomized Adaptive Search Procedures(GRASP), Variable Neighborhood Search (VNS), and Path Relinking. Likewise, the same authors solved the STTRPSD with a multi start evolutionary local search and a hybrid GRASP/VND (Villegas J. G., Prins, Prodhon, Medaglia, & Velazco, 2011). These metaheurísticas use a route-first cluster-second procedure and a VND as building blocks.

Lastly, in (Derigs, Pullmann, & Vogel, 2013) is applied a heuristic approach to the TTRP which combines local search and large neighborhood search as well as standard metaheuristics control strategies. According to (Vogel, 2011) this approach can be applied to several variants of

VRPs. The author has developed a VRP-software framework based on this heuristic concept and shown how solvers for different VRPs in a rather simple and flexible manner.

Metaheuristics are present in each one of the proposals seen above. For their use is necessary to design common aspects, such as:

- The representation of solutions handled by algorithms and,
- The definition of the objective function that will guide the search.

In the next paragraphs are explained these aspects in the case of TTRP.

Solution Representation and Initial Solution

An encoding (representation) of a solution is a fundamental requirement in the development of metaheuristics. The encoding plays a major role in the efficiency and effectiveness of any metaheuristic and constitutes an essential step in designing a metaheuristic (Talbi, 2009). Several alternative representations may exist for a given problem. Some the representation used in the last years for the TTRP are:

In (Lin, Yu, & Chou, 2009) a solution is represented by a string of numbers consisting of permutation of n customers denoted by the set $\{0,1,2,..,n\}$ and N_{dummy} zeros followed by the service vehicle types of individual VCs. The N_{dummy} zeros are used to separate routes or terminate for such reason are called artificial depot or the root of a sub-tour. The parameter N_{dummy} is calculated by $\sum_i d_i / Q_k$, where d_i is the demand of customer i and Q_k is the capacity truck. The service vehicle type of a VC is either 0 or 1. If the VC is serviced by a complete vehicle, its service vehicle type is set to be 0. Otherwise, it is serviced by a truck alone, and its service ve-

hicle type is set to be 1. The TC does not need to be represented in the solution due to must be serviced by a truck alone. The service vehicle type of a VC determines the type of the vehicle used to service the VC so that each solution representation corresponds to exactly one TTRP solution. The simple way to start the procedure is generating randomly the initial solution. It is comprised of a randomly ordered sequence of the customers and the dummy zeros, and randomly set service vehicle types of individual VCs.

Others as (Villegas, Prins, Prodhon, Medaglia, & Velasco, 2011) use a route-first cluster second procedure for the randomized construction. The randomized route-first, cluster-second heuristic follows three steps. The fundamental idea is a randomized nearest neighbor heuristic with a restricted candidate list (RCL) of size k constructs a giant tour $T = (0, t_1, ..., t_i, ..., t_n, 0)$ that visits all the customers. Then, a solution of the TTRP is derived from T by means of a tour splitting procedure.

However others authors have used construction heuristics. In (Chao I.-M., 2002) is proposed a construction method that always finds a feasible solution. This construction approach consists of three steps: a relaxed generalized assignment, a route construction and a descent improvement. The construction step roughly allocated customers to routes and three types of routes are constructed by using a cheapest insertion heuristic. Later, two criteria are used to convert an infeasible solution to a feasible one.

In (Scheuerer, 2006) is extended the approach described in (Chao I.-M., 2002) and presented two new construction heuristics for the TTRP. Both heuristic follow the cluster-first route second principle, to find an initial solution. The first heuristic is T-Cluster, it can be considered as a cluster-based sequential insertion procedure. The routes are constructed one-by-one up to full vehicle utilization. A new route is initialized with the unrouted customer farthest away from the depot and the unused vehicle having maximum total capacity. Thereby, complete vehicles are always preferred over pure trucks. T-Sweep is another heuristic based on the classical sweep algorithm commonly attributed to Gillett and Miller (Gillet & Miler, 1974). It suits best to planar instances with a centrally located depot. The method constructs feasible routes by rotating a ray centered at the depot and gradually including customers in a vehicle route. A new route is initialized with the unused vehicle having maximum total vehicle capacity, whenever total vehicle capacity or route length constraint is attained. If no more unused vehicles are available, the last route is allowed to become infeasible. The experimental results indicate that the proposed heuristics are competitive to the existing approaches.

Lastly in (Caramia & Guerriero, 2010) the solution of this problem encodes the clusters of customers that each vehicle has to service, obeying demand and capacity constraints. Among the novelties of this approach is the fact that is not directly used a route construction heuristic, as generally happens in the state-of-the-art approaches.

Neighborhood Operators

The neighborhood $N(s)$ of a solution s is specified by all possible solutions that can be obtained by applying one transformation to s. For such reason a huge number of moves can be done to a solution and to obtain n neighbors of s.

Chao uses in (Chao I.-M., 2002) two types of movements to generate the neighborhood of a solution: a one-point tabu search movement (OPT) that tries to move a customer from one route to another route feasibly and a two-point tabu search exchange (TPT) that tries to exchange two customers between two different routes feasibly.

The shift move is used in (Scheuerer, 2006) to the shift of consecutive nodes to existing tours or new sub-tours. This move may reduce the number of tours in the solution. Also, it is used the swap of

two subsets of nodes simultaneously between two existing tours. Swap moves only appear between non empty tours and cannot reduce or increase the number tours. Lastly, the root refining of sub-tours evaluates a reconnection of an existing sub-tour to all other root candidates on its main-tour. The idea is to find a better root node for CVR sub-tours.

Other authors (Lin, Yu, & Chou, 2009; Lin, Yu, & Chou, 2010; Lin, Yu, & Lu, 2011) use a random neighborhood structure that features three types of moves to solve the TTRP:

- **Insertion:** Random selection the ith customer of solution X and inserting it into the position immediately preceding another randomly selected jth customer of X.
- **Swap:** Is performed by randomly selecting the ith and the jth customers of X, and then swapping the positions of these two customers.
- **Change of service vehicle type:** Is performed by randomly selecting a VC from X, and the changing its service vehicle type 1 to 0 or from 0 to 1.

In order to increase the chance of obtaining a better solution, besides randomly choosing one or two customers to undergo either one of the three operations, the *best-of-N-trials* moves are also performed, where N is a predetermined number of trails. The best solution among the N_{trial} solutions is chosen as the next solution. For swap and insertion, this number is set to be N_{trial}, calculated as:

$$\left(n + N_{dummy}\right)/3.$$

The probabilities of choosing the swap, insertion, or the change of service vehicle type of VCs moves are set to be 0.2, 0.2 and 0.1 respectively. Whiles the probability of performing the *best-of-*

N-trials moves is 0.5, making the total probability of performing these neighborhood moves is 1.

Solutions obtained from the GRASP construction phase in (Villegas, Prins, Prodhon, Medaglia, & Velasco, 2011) are improved by a variable neighborhood descent (VND). VND is a deterministic version of Variable Neighborhood Search, in which k_{max} neighborhoods are explored sequentially. Given the incumbent solution s_0, a subset of the solution space $N(s_0)$ is composed of the solutions reachable from s_0, when neighborhood k is applied to it. The procedure VND explores sequentially the following five neighborhoods of a given TTRP solution s using a best improvement strategy:

- **Modified Or-opt:** For a given chain of customers $(r_i,...,r_{i+l-1})$ of length l, check all possible reinsertions of the chain and its reverse $(r_{i+l-1},...,r_i)$ within the same route or sub-tour. The difference with classical Or-opt is the simultaneous evaluation of the reversal of the chain.
- **Node exchange (in single routes/sub-tours and between pairs of routes/sub-tours):** Given a pair of customers u and v served by routes (or sub-tours) R_u and R_v exchange their positions. If R_u a R_v, in addition to classical capacity constraints, it is necessary to verify the accessibility constraints of u in R_v and v in R_u. Moreover when R_u or R_v is a sub-tour the capacity of the associated vehicle route is also checked.
- **2-opt (in single routes/sub-tours, or pairs of routes (sub-tours) of the same type):** Remove a pair of arcs (u,v) and (w,y) and add two other arcs. For single routes add arcs (u,w) and (v,y); if the arcs belong to different routes we also consider the addition of arcs (u,y) and (w,v) and select the best of the two options.

Moreover, if the arcs belong to a pair of sub-tours they allocate the resulting sub-tours to the best root among those of the original sub-tours, provided the capacities of the associated vehicle routes are not exceeded.

- **Node relocation (in single routes/sub-tours and between pairs of routes/sub-tours):** Given a customer u served in route/sub-tour R_u and two consecutive nodes v, w in a route/sub-tour R', insert u between v and w. If $R_u \neq R'$ they check the conditions for a valid insertion of u in R'.
- **Root refining:** For each sub-tour they apply the root refining procedure described by (Chao I.-M., 2002), where they try to change the root of each sub-tour and simultaneously modify its routing.

Constraint Handling

The constraint handling in optimization problems is another important topic for the efficient design of metaheuristics. Indeed, many optimization problems present constraints and it is not trivial to deal with those constraints. According to (Talbi, 2009) the constraint handling strategies can be classified as reject strategies, penalizing strategies, repairing strategies, decoding strategies and preserving strategies. Other constraint handling approaches using search components. The constraint handling strategies applied to TTRP is commented in this subsection.

In the TTRP there is a set of constraints such as:

1. Each customer must be visited exactly once;
2. Each route starts and terminates at central depot;
3. The customers only accessible by the truck without trailer must be visited in a route PTR or a sub-tour of a route CVR;
4. The root of a sub-tour must be a vehicle customer;

5.   The maximum demand load of each type route to be less than or equal to the total capacity of the assigned vehicle;

6.   The number of vehicle used may not exceed the number of vehicles available.

A solution TTRP can be regarded infeasible if it does not satisfy some of the constraints mentioned previously. Thereby, most of revised articles in the literature used strategies for to deal with constraints. Mainly they act on the representation of solutions or the objective function.

In the case of (Chao I.-M., 2002), the used construction method tries to allocate customers to routes by solving a relaxed generalized assignment problem. The obtained solution can be infeasible due to that the total load on some routes exceed the capacity of the truck. The author use as repairing strategy the descent improvement steps that always converted an infeasible solution into a feasible one. Other that uses this strategy is Villegas et al. in (Villegas J. G., Prins, Prodhon, Medaglia, & Velazco, 2011). The authors used the mechanism VNS that acts as a reparation operator for infeasible solutions and as an improvement procedure for feasible ones.

Others as (Scheuerer, 2006) (Lin, Yu, & Chou, 2009) (Hoff & Lokketangen, 2007) apply penalizing approach. In the Tabu search heuristic proposed in (Scheuerer, 2006), the intermediate infeasible solutions are allowed during the search and infeasibility is controlled by a shifting penalty approach similar to (Gendreau, Hertz, & Laporte, 1994). Also, is allowed adding a second penalty term to the objective function. In (Hoff & Lokketangen, 2007), the authors to allow infeasible solutions in the search, a penalty function is introduced and a dynamic penalty factor is adjusted during the search to make it possible to oscillate between feasible and infeasible solutions.

Also, Lin et al. in (Lin, Yu, & Chou, 2009) apply this strategy when the resulting solution uses more vehicles than available. For each extra truck or trailer used, a penalty cost P is added to the objective function to make such solutions unattractive. This work and others as (Lin, Yu, & Chou, 2010) (Lin, Yu, & Lu, 2011) also used a preserving strategies. They incorporate search operators to generate only feasible solutions and then preserve the feasibility of solutions.

A SOFT COMPUTING - BASED APPROACH

Different sources of uncertainty in transport problems are present in real world contexts, and only approximate, vague and imprecise values are known. Therefore, often the decision maker cannot formulate all the data precisely. In general, users and decision makers diligently establish measurements based on observations and perceptions which determine the problem parameters and in the same way affect the evaluation of objectives and obtained solutions.

In 1974 Tanaka (Tanaka et al., 1974) defined the concept of fuzzy mathematical programming applying Soft Computing methodologies to decision problems based on the concept of Bellman and Zadeh (Bellman and Zadeh, 1970) for decision making under fuzzy conditions. Since then, Soft Computing methodologies have repeatedly proven their efficiency and effectiveness in modeling situations and solving complex problems on a wide variety of scenarios. Particularly relevant is the field of Fuzzy Linear Programming (FLP) that constitutes the basis for solving Fuzzy Optimization Problems. FLP and related problems have been extensively analyzed and many papers have been published displaying a variety of formulations and approaches, such as transportation, production planning, water supply planning and resource management, forest management, bank management, portfolio selection, pattern classification, and others (Lai and Hwang, 1992; Sahinidis, 2004).

The formulation of a linear programming problem under fuzzy environment depends on what and where the fuzziness is introduced. Uncertainties can be found in the relation, constants, decision variables or in all parameters of the problem, and therefore a variety of fuzzy linear programming problems have been defined:

- Linear programming problems with a fuzzy objective, i.e. with fuzzy numbers defining the costs of the objective function;
- Linear programming problems with a fuzzy goal, i.e. with some fuzzy value to be attained in the objective;
- Linear programming problems with fuzzy numbers defining the coefficients of the technological matrix; and
- With a fuzzy constraint set, i.e. with a feasible set defined by fuzzy constraints.

There are several approaches that solve fuzzy mathematical programming problems (Bector and Chandra, 2005; Lai and Hwang, 1992), which use some defuzzification index, represent the fuzzy coefficients by intervals or transform this fuzzy problem into a parametric mathematical programming problem. The main goal is to transform this imprecise problem into a classical problem and using classical techniques to solve the equivalent problem.

The TTRP is a problem which by its nature favors the presence of vagueness, imprecision and uncertainty in the information handled. Nevertheless, the models used in the literature assume that the data available are accurate; consideration does not correspond with reality. For this reason it would be appropriate to focus research toward defining TTRP models for incorporating the uncertainty present in the data.

The alternative presented proposes the application of Soft Computing techniques. Thus, one could obtain models that tolerate the uncertainty and tries to satisfy before to optimize. This proposal has been exploited in VRP variants; however the complexity of TTRP, as well as for the recent of topic has not been applied in this problem. Even

though, it's worth to say that the TTRP doesn't have a linear formulation like the VRP.

In this work, we will focus on a general parametric idea in order to transform fuzzy problems into many classical problems (Verdegay, 1982; Delgado et al, 1989, Silva et al. 2007). This parametric approach is divided into two parts (see Figure 2): transforming a fuzzy problem into a classical parametric problem with a parameter representing the maker´s satisfaction level (which belongs to the interval [0,1]); a mathematical formulation of the classical parametric problem that is equivalent to the original fuzzy problem. Also, this idea has been extended to solve fuzzy quadratic problems (Cruz et al., 2008; Cruz et al.2011; Cruz et al., 2013; Silva et al. 2010a; Silva et al. 2010b, Silva et al. 2013).

Thus, the fuzzy linear programming problem is parameterized at the end of the first phase, and it can be solved by solving an equivalent crisp parametric linear programming problem. Here, it may be noted that we have an optimal solution for each $\alpha \in [0, 1]$, so the solution with α grade of membership is actually fuzzy. In the second phase the parametric programming problem is solved for each of the different α values using conventional linear programming techniques. Since 1990, Delgado et al. (Delgado et al. 1990) showed that the set of solutions achieved by this approach contains the solutions reached by other

Figure 2. Fuzzy parametric approach

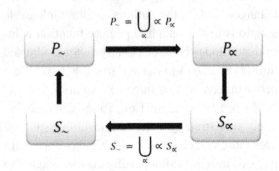

different approaches, which solve fuzzy linear programming problems too

An idea of application of this approach is considering that constraints of a problem are defined as having a fuzzy nature, that is, some violations in the accomplishment of such restrictions are permitted.

For example, in the case of TTRP the constraints associated to the availability of trucks and trailers imposes that the total of routes doesn't exceed the total of available vehicles in the fleet. This constraint can be represented by:

$$R_{vc} \leq m_r$$

$$R_{cp} \leq m_c + m_r$$

where R_{vc} is the number of routes of *complete vehicle*, R_{cp} is the number of routes of *pure truck*, m_c and m_r are the quantity of trucks and trailers respectively.

Our model allows considering as a fuzzy value the quantity of trucks and trailers in the problem and admits the violation of the constraint according with the value of the fuzzy element. Then, the constraint can be expressed as a fuzzy set and the membership function Gamma is defined for this fuzzy set. Lastly, to solve the model is used the Decomposition Theorem that permits us to represent a fuzzy set by means of its α-cuts, and to work, then, on these classical sets instead of the fuzzy ones.

CONCLUSION

Truck and Trailer Routing Problem, a variant of the Vehicle Routing Problem in which a subset of the vehicles is allowed pull trailers for the benefit of increased capacity, is one of the most interesting problems at this time in transport routing planning. Unfortunately to date, not much research has been done about this problem. Some of their most known variants and solutions applied to solve it were described here.

All these models assume that the data available are accurate; consideration does not correspond with reality where the vagueness appears in a natural way. For this reason it would be appropriate to focus research toward defining TTRP models for incorporating the uncertainty present in the data, and hence it makes perfect sense to think of Soft Computing techniques. This paper is only the beginning of future works about of how to solve the TTRP applying these techniques. Thus, a known fuzzy parametric approach is proposed as a general method to solve this problem when its elements are vague, imprecise and inexact. The authors aim to extend the line of research involving Fuzzy Programming problems in order to try to solve practical real-life problems by facilitating the building of Decision Support Systems.

REFERENCES

Bector, C. R., & Chandra, S. (2005). *Fuzzy mathematical programming and fuzzy matrix games*. Berlin: Springer..

Bellman, R. E., & Zadeh, L. A. (1970). Decision-making in a fuzzy environment. *Management Science. Application Series, 17*(4), B141–B164.

Caramia, M., & Guerriero, F. (2010). A heuristic approach for the truck and trailer routing problems. *Journalism, 61*, 1168–1180.

Chao, I.-M. (2002). A tabu search method for the truck and trailer routing problem. *Computers & Operations Research, 39*, 33–51. doi:10.1016/S0305-0548(00)00056-3.

Chao, I.-M., Golden, B., & Wasil, E. (1999). A computacional study of a new heuristic for the site-dependent vehicle routing problem. *Information Systems and Operational Research, 37*, 319–336.

Cruz, C., & Silva, R. C., Verdegay. (2013). Solving real-world fuzzy quadratic programming problems by a parametric method. *Communications in Computer and Information Science*, *299*, 102–111. doi:10.1007/978-3-642-31718-7_11.

Cruz, C., Silva, R. C., & Verdegay, J. L. (2011). Extending and relating different approaches for solving fuzzy quadratic problems. *Fuzzy Optimization and Decision Making*, *10*, 193–210. doi:10.1007/s10700-011-9104-7.

Cruz, C., Silva, R. C., Verdegay, J. L., & Yamakami, A. (2008). A survey of fuzzy quadratic programming. *Recent Patents on Computer Science*, *1*(3), 182–1930. doi:10.2174/2213275910801030182.

Drexl, M. A. (2007). *A branch and price algorithm for the truck and traier routing problem*. Aachen, Germany: RWTH Aachen University..

Fisher, M., & Jaikumar, R. (1981). A generalized assignment heuristic for vehicle routing. *Networks*, *11*(2), 109–124. doi:10.1002/net.3230110205.

Garey, M. R., & Johnson, D. S. (1979). *Computers and intractability: A guide to the theory of NP-completeness*. W. H. Freeman..

Gerdessen, J. C. (1996). Vehicle routing problem with trailer. *European Journal of Operational Research*, *93*(1), 135–147. doi:10.1016/0377-2217(95)00175-1.

Lai, Y. J., & Hwang, C. L. (1992). *Fuzzy mathematical programming: methods and applications*. Berlin: Springer. doi:10.1007/978-3-642-48753-8.

Lin, S., Yu, V., & Chou, S. (2009). Solving the truck and trailer routing problem based on a simulated annealing heuristic. *Computers & Operations Research*, *36*, 1638–1692. doi:10.1016/j.cor.2008.04.005.

Lin, S., Yu, V., & Chou, S. (2010). A note on a the truck and trailer routing problem. *Expert Systems with Applications*, *37*(1), 899–903. doi:10.1016/j.eswa.2009.06.077.

Lin, S., Yu, V., & Lu, C. (2011). A simulated annealing heuristic for the truck and trailer routing problem with time windows. *Expert Systems with Applications*, *38*(12), 15244–15252. doi:10.1016/j.eswa.2011.05.075.

Sahinidis, N. (2004). Optimization under uncertainty: State-of-the-art and opportunities. *Computers & Chemical Engineering*, *28*(6-7), 971–983. doi:10.1016/j.compchemeng.2003.09.017.

Scheuerer, S. (2006). A tabu search heuristic for the truck and trailer routing problem. *Computers & Operations Research*, *33*, 894–909. doi:10.1016/j.cor.2004.08.002.

Semet, F. (1995). A two-phase algorithm for the partial accessibility constrained vehicle routing problem. *Annals of Operations Research*, *61*, 45–65. doi:10.1007/BF02098281.

Semet, F., & Taillard, E. (1993). Solving real-life vehicle routing problems efficiently using tabu search. *Annals of Operations Research*, *41*(4), 469–488. doi:10.1007/BF02023006.

Silva, R. C., Cruz, C., & Verdegay, J. L. (2013). Fuzzy costs in quadratic programming problems. *Fuzzy Optimization and Decision Making*. doi:10.1007/s10700-013-9153-1.

Silva, R. C., Cruz, C., Verdegay, J. L., & Yamakami, A. (2010a). A survey of fuzzy convex programming models. In L. Weldon, & J. Kacprzyk (Eds.), *Fuzzy optimization: Studies in fuzziness and soft computing* (Vol. 254, pp. 127–143). Academic Press. doi:10.1007/978-3-642-13935-2_6.

Silva, R. C., Verdegay, J. L., & Yamakami, A. (2007). Two-phase method to solve fuzzy quadratic programming problems. In *Proceedings of IEEE International Conference on Fuzzy Systems*. IEEE.

Silva, R. C., Verdegay, J. L., & Yamakami, A. (2010b). A parametric convex programming approach applied in portfolio selection problem with fuzzy costs. In *Proceedings of the 2010 IEEE International Fuzzy Systems Conference*. IEEE.

Talbi, E.-G. (2009). *Metaheuristics from design to implementation*. Hoboken, NJ: John Wiley & Sons, Inc.

Tanaka, H., Okuda, T., & Asai, K. (1974). On fuzzy mathematical programming. *J. Cybernet., 3*, 37–46.

Toth & Vigo. (2002). *The vehicle routing problem*. Society for Industrial and Applied Mathematics..

Verdegay, J. L. (1982). Fuzzy mathematical programming. In M. M. Gupta, & E. Sanchez (Eds.), *Fuzzy Information and Decision Processes*. Amsterdam: North-Holland..

Verdegay, J. L., Yager, R. R., & Bonissone, P. P. (2008). On heuristics as a fundamental constituent of soft computing. *Fuzzy Sets and Systems, 159*(7), 846–855. doi:10.1016/j.fss.2007.08.014.

Villegas, J., Prins, C., Prodhon, C., Medaglia, A., & Velasco, N. (2010). GRASP/VND and multi-start evolutionary local search for the single truck and trailer routing problem with satellite depots. *Engineering Applications of Artificial Intelligence, 23*, 780–794. doi:10.1016/j.engappai.2010.01.013.

Villegas, J., Prins, C., Prodhon, C., Medaglia, A., & Velasco, N. (2011). A GRASP with evolutionary path relinking for the truck and trailer routing problem. *Computers & Operations Research, 38*, 1319–1334. doi:10.1016/j.cor.2010.11.011.

KEY TERMS AND DEFINITIONS

Fuzzy Optimization: Techniques for solving optimization problems whose objective function and constraint set are fuzzy.

Logistics Problem: Supply chain management and of the flow of resources between points of origin and points of destination in order to meet some requirements for the improvement of company efficiency (of customers and corporations).

Metaheuristic: A high-level strategy for solving a very general class of computational problems by combining user given black-box procedures — usually heuristics — in a hopefully efficient way.

Soft Computing: Series of techniques and methods so that real practical situations could be dealt with in the same way as humans deal with them, i.e. on the basis of intelligence, common sense, consideration of analogies, approaches, etc.

Chapter 14
Improving the Performance of Neuro-Fuzzy Function Point Backfiring Model with Additional Environmental Factors

Justin Wong
University of Western Ontario, Canada

Danny Ho
NFA Estimation Inc., Canada

Luiz Fernando Capretz
University of Western Ontario, Canada

ABSTRACT

Backfiring is a technique used for estimating the size of source code based on function points and programming. In this study, additional software environmental parameters such as Function Point count standard, development environment, problem domain, and size are applied to the Neuro-Fuzzy Function Point Backfiring (NFFPB) model. The neural network and fuzzy logic designs are introduced for both models. Both estimation models are compared against the same data source of software projects. It is found that the original NFFPB model outperforms the extended model. The results are investigated, and it is explained why the extended model performed worse.

DOI: 10.4018/978-1-4666-4785-5.ch014

INTRODUCTION

Software Estimation Background

Software estimation is important in software development. Project estimation is used to determine the necessary time and budget of projects. Many estimation techniques have been developed for software estimation such as: Constructive Cost Model (COCOMO), Putnam's Software Lifecycle Management (SLIM), and Function Point (Stutzke, 2005). Source lines of code (SLOC) and function points are two popular metrics used today.

SLOC metric is used to measure the amount of source code in software. SLOC can also be used to determine the cost and effort needed to develop a software application. SLOC can be referred to as physical SLOC or logical SLOC. Physical SLOC is the number of lines in an application. Problems with physical SLOC are that formatting and style affect the size of an application. Logical SLOC, on the other hand, is unaffected by formatting and style because it measures the number of statements. The SLOC metric still has shortcomings. It is sensitive to programming language and technology (Galorath & Evans, 2006). Despite these problems, SLOC is still a popular metric used in the software industry today.

Function point is a unit of measurement for determining the functional size of an information system introduced by Albrecht in the 1970s (Albrecht & Gaffney, 1983). In the 1990s, the popularity of function point grew. It became a major tool in software sizing. Function points are used today for sizing software in both industry and academia. As the usage of function points grew, the International Function Point User Group (IF-PUG) was formed (International Function Point Users Group, 2007).

Function point analysis is a process of classifying major system components as 'simple', 'average', or 'complex'. Unadjusted Function Points (UFP) is a measure obtained from identifying system components. The function components are Internal Logic Files (ILF), External Interface Files (EIF), External Inputs (EI), External Outputs (EO), and External Inquiries (EQ). The resulting function point count or Adjusted Function Points (AFP) is obtained by multiplying the UFP by the Value Adjustment Factor (VAF). There are 14 General System Characteristics (GSC) that defines VAF (International Function Point Users Group, 2005).

BACKFIRING TECHNIQUE

Backfiring is a technique used to size source code by converting function points to logical SLOC statements (Jones, 1995). Backfiring can be accomplished by multiplying the function point with the conversion ratios to obtain the SLOC. Similarly, backfiring can also be used for calculating function points by dividing the SLOC by the conversion ratios (Stutzke, 2005). Jones classified that the conversion ratios are defined based on the number of statements required to implement one function point based on the programming language (Jones, 1995). Based on these classifications, "high-level language" is defined as having less than 50 source lines-of-code per function point (SLOC/FP), while "low-level language" has over 100 SLOC/FP (Jones, 1995). Software Productivity Research (SPR) annually publishes the conversion ratios for many programming languages (Software Productivity Research Incorporated, 2006). Table 1 illustrates SPR's programming language's SLOC/FP and language levels.

The equation for converting function point to SLOC is defined in Equation 1. In Equation 1, FP is the function point input and conversion is the SLOC/FP. The SLOC equation can be rearranged to find the number of function points if the SLOC is known (Jones, 1995).

Table 1. SPR's programming language level and SLOC/FP

Language	Language Level	SLOC/FP		
		Low	Mean	High
Basic Assembly	1.0	213	320	427
C	2.5	21	128	235
Fortran	3.0	75	107	160
Cobol	3.0	65	107	170
C++	6.0	30	53	125
Java	9.0	20	36	51
SQL	25.0	8	13	17
Spreadsheet	50.0	1	8	18
MATHCAD	60.0	1	5	17

Equation 1: SLOC Equation.

SLOC = FP x Conversion

Problems with Backfiring Technique

Backfiring is a simple and quick method to convert between function point and SLOC because of its simplistic formula shown in Equation 1. However, there are major problems with backfiring.

Conversion ratios have a large range and it is difficult to determine the correct conversion ratios because of the large difference between the low and high SLOC/FP. For example, third generation languages have a range of 80 SLOC/FP (Software Productivity Research Incorporated, 2006). Selecting the wrong conversion ratio would result in a high error estimate. Furthermore, there are no instructions and method on choosing the correct conversion ratio.

Another problem is conversion ratios are generic, therefore it does not reflect accurately to specific organizations and environments. There are so many different types of organizations and different software practices, making conversion ratios unsuitable for most organizations. Furthermore, there is no documentation on what the mean conversion ratios represent.

Backfiring only uses function point count and programming language level as the input. It does not use any other inputs which can affect the conversion ratio value. Other factors such as business domain, type of development and team size can affect the size.

Backfiring fails to estimate enhancement projects because of reuse and changes in code. Furthermore, there is no consistent correlation between changed SLOC and changed function point because reusing code and program designs depend on the capabilities of the programming language.

Software implemented with an excessive amount of code may not mean it has a lot of functionality. Similarly, software implemented using less SLOC does not necessarily indicate that the software has less functionality.

Research Objective

A Neuro-Fuzzy Function Point Backfiring (NFFPB) model was developed to address the major problems of the backfiring technique (Wong & Ho & Capretz, 2008). The NFFPB model was shown to have a small improvement over the existing backfiring technique with its calibrated conversion ratios. However, the model only uses the function point count, conversion ratio and programming language level as inputs. It does not address other environmental factors that could affect software size.

In this study, an alternative extended NFFPB model is presented. The extended NFFPB model uses additional input parameters such as function point count standard, development environment, domain and team size. The extended NFFPB model is compared against the original NFFPB model to see if additional environmental input parameters would improve the software size estimates.

NEURO-FUZZY BACKFIRING MODEL DESIGN

The Neuro-Fuzzy Function Point Backfiring (NFFPB) model is a composite software size estimation model. It uses fuzzy logic, neural network, and a backfiring algorithmic model (Wong & Ho & Capretz, 2008).

Technical Overview

The NFFPB model is a method that calibrates the programming language level to improve backfiring estimations. Fuzzy logic is used to model the programming language level curve by grouping the programming language levels into fuzzy sets. The fuzzy sets are used for the input programming language level. A neural network is used to calibrate the fuzzy sets' conversion ratios. The calibrated SLOC/FP replaces the original backfiring conversion ratios (Wong & Ho & Capretz, 2008). Figure 1 shows a technical view of the NFFPB model.

Design

The objective of the NFFPB model is to improve the accuracy of the backfiring size estimates by calibrating the programming language's conversion ratio to a SPR's project dataset. Calibrated conversion ratios would produce more accurate estimates for specific organizations. The model consists of an input layer, processing layer, and output layer, which are shown in Figure 2.

The input layer is the preprocessing layer. In the preprocessing layer, each programming language from SPR are grouped into programming language levels. The group average SLOC/FP are then passed into the neural network in the processing layer. The input layer passes the historical function point data and SLOC project data from a dataset. Furthermore, the programming language levels and SLOC/FP from SPR are inputted into the Fuzzy Programming Language Levels System (FPLLS). The FPLLS converts the programming language into a fuzzy programming language. The FPLLS includes fuzzy programming language level sets, fuzzy membership functions, and fuzzy language rules.

The function point data are the inputs into the neural network and the SLOC data is used for training data for the neural network. Within the processing layer, the conversion ratios are calibrated by a neural network by learning from historical data. The neural network takes the inputs from the input layer and produces a size estimate, which is compared with the actual result. The error difference is then minimized by having conversion ratios calibrated. By calibrating the conversion ratios, the trained neural network can be reused in similar project environments, without requiring further training.

Figure 1. Technical view of the NFFPB Model

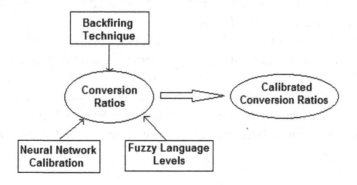

Figure 2. NFFPB layer model

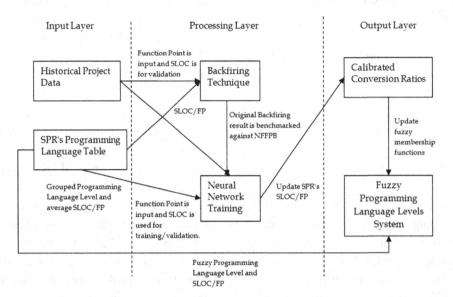

The calibrated conversion ratios are passed to the output layer. Afterwards, the calibrated conversion ratios are applied to the FPLLS. The fuzzy membership functions are adjusted according to the conversion ratios; thus, the FPLLS is tuned to the new conversion ratios. Furthermore, the FPLLS can be used for simulating new size estimates (Wong & Ho & Capretz, 2008).

Neural Network Training Data Source

A data source is used to train the neural network in order to obtain calibrated conversion ratios. Furthermore, it is used for validation and comparison against the original conversion ratios.

The International Software Benchmarking Standards Group (ISBSG) is a non-profit organization made up of a group of national software metrics associations. The goal of the ISBSG organization is to collect and maintain software project data for research. In addition, the ISBSG project data repository contains metrics on software development, enhancement, maintenance, and support (International Software Benchmarking Standards Group, 2004).

In the NFFPB model, the UFP, function points, programming language and SLOC are used from the ISBSG Release 9 (International Software Benchmarking Standards Group, 2004). In the Release 9 repository, there are 3,024 projects from twenty countries, with 70% of the project data being less than 6 years old. Furthermore, there are over 70 programming languages used in development environments and reported in the data repository. The data fields that are needed for the NFFPB model are lines of code, primary programming language and UFP. All project data missing any of those three fields are filtered out— a total of 260 projects were used out of 3,024.

Fuzzy Programming Language Levels System

The FPLLS is a fuzzy rule-based inference system which is used in the input and output layers of the NFFPB model. In the input layer, it converts the input programming language levels into fuzzy language levels which is used as inputs into the neural network. After calibrating the conversion ratios with the neural network, the conversion ratios are used to adjust the fuzzy membership functions of the output SLOC for each fuzzy programming level. The tuned conversion ratios for each fuzzy language levels are used as the output. The main components of the FPLLS are the fuzzy language level, input and output membership functions, fuzzy rules, and tuned fuzzy system (Wong & Ho & Capretz, 2008).

By using the FPLLS, the margin of size estimate error by the backfiring technique is minimized. The FPLLS calibrates the generic conversion ratios into specific conversion ratios that are geared towards a certain software environment to improve the accuracy of size estimates.

Fuzzy Language Level

Figure 3 shows the relationship between the language levels to the mean SLOC/FP based on SPR's project data (Software Productivity Research Incorporated, 2006) that was shown in Table 1. Furthermore, the equation of this relationship is defined in Equation 2, where *y* is the SLOC/FP and *x* is the language level.

The objective is to model project data from ISBSG into a curve similar to Figure 1. However, the project data from ISBSG does not contain sufficient data for certain programming languages; therefore, fuzzy language levels are proposed to solve this problem. A fuzzy language level is an abstract level which contains various programming languages that are similar in programming language level. The programming languages were broken into language levels, which translated to the number of SLOC/FP. For example, from Table 1, Fortran and Cobol both have programming language level of 3.0 so they are grouped as a fuzzy language level 3. In another example, in the ISBSG project data, there was a limited data for programming languages with language levels of 27 to 50, therefore these programming languages were grouped together shown in Table 2.

Equation 2: Inverse curve equation.

$$y = 319.4x^{-0.997}$$

Figure 3. Mean inverse curve of language levels versus SLOC/FP

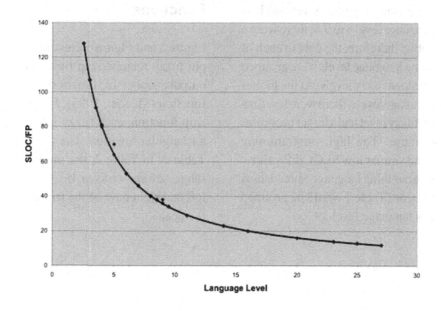

Table 2. Fuzzy input language level membership function

Fuzzy Programming Language Level (1-10)		Fuzzy Programming Language Level (11-19)	
Fuzzy Level	Programming Language Level Range	Fuzzy Level	Programming Language Level Range
1	[0, 2.5, 3]	11	[9, 9.5, 11]
2	[2.5, 3, 3.5]	12	[9.5, 11, 14]
3	[3, 3.5, 4]	13	[11, 14, 16]
4	[3.5, 4, 5]	14	[14, 16, 20]
5	[4, 5, 6]	15	[16, 20, 23]
6	[5, 6, 7]	16	[20, 23, 25]
7	[6, 7, 8]	17	[23, 25, 27]
8	[7, 8, 8.5]	18	[25, 27, 50]
9	[8, 8.5, 9]	19	[27, 50, 100]
10	[8.5, 9, 9.5]		

The inverse relationship is modeled by grouping the language levels based on similar SLOC/FP into various fuzzy levels which are fuzzy sets (Mendel, 1995). Table 2 shows the language levels being grouped into various fuzzy levels to model the curve. A programming language level belongs in more than one fuzzy level. Based on the ISBSG project data, there were 260 project's SLOC/FP data points distributed into 19 fuzzy sets which represent language levels from 0 to 50 ISBSG (International Software Benchmarking Standards Group, 2004). In certain language levels such as programming language level 8 to 9.5, there were a lot of data available; therefore, the data in each of those programming language levels were grouped into more fine-grained fuzzy levels. At the higher programming language levels, there were less data available so each fuzzy level had a larger programming language range. The high programming languages also had similar low SLOC/FP values. For example, programming language Spreadsheet and MATHCAD from Table 1 would be grouped together as fuzzy language level 19.

The average SLOC/FP was calculated by averaging all the backfiring conversion values within a fuzzy level shown in Table 3. Moreover, these average values were used as initial weights in the neural network and the initial peak of the fuzzy membership functions. Figure 4 illustrates how the two sample programming languages are processed into the neural network (Wong & Ho & Capretz, 2008).

Input and Output Membership Functions

Figure 5 and Figure 6 illustrate the input and output fuzzy membership functions. The input and output membership functions both use a triangular function (Mendel, 1995). For the input membership function, each fuzzy level is represented as a triangular function. The triangles are based on Table 2. In Table 2, the programming language ranges are shown as [a, b, c], a and c represent the left and right base of the triangle and b represent the peak.

Table 3. Fuzzy output SLOC/FP membership function

Fuzzy Programming Language Level (1-10)		Fuzzy Programming Language Level (11-19)	
Fuzzy Level	Average SLOC/FP	Fuzzy Level	Average SLOC/FP
1	[107, 128, 150]	11	[29, 34, 36]
2	[91, 107, 128]	12	[23, 29, 34]
3	[81, 91, 107]	13	[20, 23, 29]
4	[67, 81, 91]	14	[16, 20, 23]
5	[53, 67, 81]	15	[14, 16, 20]
6	[46, 53, 67]	16	[13, 14, 16]
7	[40, 46, 53]	17	[12, 13, 14]
8	[38, 40, 46]	18	[6, 12, 13]
9	[36, 38, 40]	19	[1, 6, 12]
10	[34, 36, 38]		

Figure 4. Processing programming language input

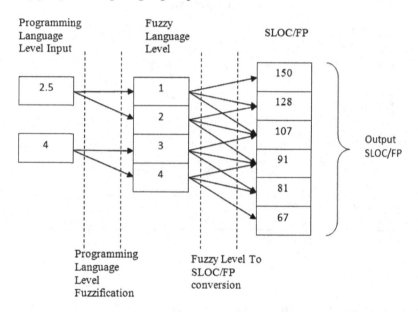

For the output membership functions, the peak of each membership function represents the average SLOC/FP per fuzzy level (Wong & Ho & Capretz, 2008). The output triangles from Figure 6 is based on Table 3. The average SLOC/FP range are represented as [a, b, c] notation. The a and c represent the left and right base of the triangle and b represent the peak.

Fuzzy Rules and Inference

Each fuzzy level was directly referenced to a fuzzy output. For example, f1 referenced o1, f2 referenced o2 and so on. Figure 7 shows the fuzzy rule block. For example, when programming language level 4 is the input, only RULE 3 and RULE4 are activated and have a membership value greater than 0. The fuzzy membership values are then used for defuzzification into SLOC/FP.

Figure 5. Fuzzy membership of the language levels

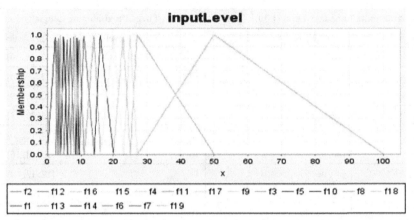

Figure 6. Fuzzy membership functions of the output SLOC/FP for each fuzzy level

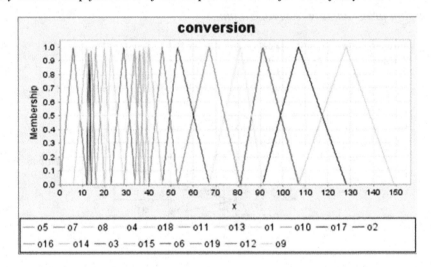

Figure 7. Fuzzy rule block

- **RULE 1:** IF inputLevel IS f1 THEN conversion IS o1;
- **RULE 2:** IF inputLevel IS f2 THEN conversion IS o2;
- **RULE 3:** IF inputLevel IS f3 THEN conversion IS o3;
- **RULE 18:** IF inputLevel IS f18 THEN conversion IS o18;
- **RULE 19:** IF inputLevel IS f19 THEN conversion IS o19;

For defuzzification, the maximum accumulation method and center of gravity method were used (Wong & Ho & Capretz, 2008).

CALIBRATING USING NEURAL NETWORK

The neural network is used to calibrate the generic conversion ratios within the processing layer. Afterwards, the newly calibrated conversion ratios are used by the fuzzy language levels in order to tune the FPLLS.

Neural Network Architecture

The neural network was used to calibrate the average source statements per function point for each fuzzy level. The SLOC, the UFP and the language level are the neural network inputs. The SLOC was used as the target during training and the UFP was used for both training and simulation. The language level inputs were initially processed into fuzzy language levels. These grouped language levels were fed into the network shown in Figure 8, which shows the network's design. The neural network was designed to be easily interpreted so that it avoids being a "black-box" model.

The L_1 to L_n were binary grouped language level inputs. When a language level was fed into the network, the input was in the form of a matrix and only contains one 1 entry. For example, for language level 4, it would be represented as [0 0 0 1 0 0 0 0 0 0 0 0 0 0 0 0] based on the proposed programming language level groups.

The result is obtained from the activation function by multiplying the UFP with the weight of the programming language level. The weight's initial values are from Table 1. During training, the output was obtained and compared with the target result. The error between the actual result and the predicted result was propagated back to the input layer. Additionally, the weights were then adjusted based on the error using back-propagation (Wong & Ho & Capretz, 2008).

Learning Process

A learning algorithm was used to minimize the difference between the size estimated and the actual SLOC during training. The error equation is defined in Equation 3, where E is the error signal.

Figure 8. Neural network design

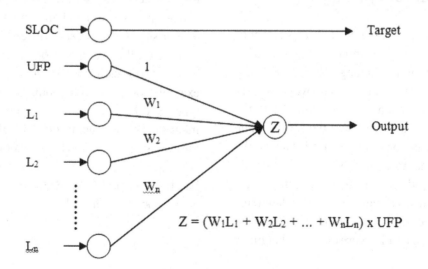

$$Z = (W_1L_1 + W_2L_2 + ... + W_nL_n) \times UFP$$

Equation 3: Error equation.

E = actual - prediction

The error was back-propagated from the output node to the input nodes of the neural network. In addition, the conversion weights were calibrated based on the error difference and the learning rate. The weight change equation is defined in Equation 4, where W_i is the ith initial conversion weight, W'_i is the ith modified conversion weight, n is the learning rate and E is the error signal.

Equation 4: Weight change equation.

$$W'_i = W_i + nE$$

During initial training, the weights were set to the original conversion ratio. The function point count and language level were inputted into the neural network. The size estimate was the output. Moreover, the estimate was compared with the actual SLOC to determine the error. Following the adjustment, the error was propagated back to the input nodes and the conversion weights were adjusted. This process continued until the specified epoch or error goal was reached.

Post-Tuned Fuzzy Programming Language Level System

The FPLLS is used in the input and output layer of the NFFPB model. In the input layer, it is used to convert programming language levels into a fuzzy language level. After the neural network calibrations of the conversion ratios are completed, the calibrated values are applied to the FPLLS. The calibrated conversion ratios are used to adjust the fuzzy output membership functions by adjusting the peak triangular functions based on the new conversion ratios. The new tuned fuzzy language levels are used in the output layer. The main components of the FPLLS are the fuzzy language level, input and output membership functions, fuzzy rules, and tuned fuzzy system.

The newly tuned FPLLS could then be used to perform size estimates more accurately. When more data becomes available, the neural network would be reused again to update the conversion values. The changes would then be applied back to the FPLLS (Wong & Ho & Capretz, 2008).

NEURO-FUZZY BACKFIRING MODEL WITH ENVIRONMENTAL FACTORS

In this research, external environmental factors were investigated because the backfiring technique only takes the function point count and programming language level as inputs. An extension was added to the NFFPB model to determine if the performance improves with additional inputs.

The extension to the NFFPB model uses similar environmental factors as Angelis et al.'s software cost estimation model based on ISBSG's environmental factor data (Angelis & Stamelos & Morisio, 2000). The new inputs used were development type, development platform, organization type, business area type, application type, maximum team size, function point standard, and architecture.

Similarly to Angelis et al.'s approach, the data for each factor were sorted into low and high levels and the averages were taken (Angelis & Stamelos & Morisio, 2000). For each different type of value in a factor, the average error between the actual SLOC and the estimated SLOC was observed. For example, for the environmental factor development type, the values were new development, redevelopment and enhancements. For each of these values, the average error, defined in Equation 3, was taken. If the average error is negative, that value would be classified as LOW. Moreover, if the average error is positive, the value is classified as HIGH.

Function Point Count Standard

The function point metrics used in this model are NESMA (NESMA, 2006) and IFPUG (International Function Point User Group, 2007). The older function point metrics were NESMA 1.0 and IFPUG 4.0. The up-to-date function point counts are NESMA 2.0 and IFPUG 4.1, which were very similar to one another (NESMA, 2006). However, when an error average test was performed, it was found that projects using the NESMA count had a negative error, while the IFPUG counts had a positive error; therefore, NESMA was grouped as HIGH and IFPUG was grouped as LOW. The high level indicates that when NESMA count is used, the SLOC is going to be overestimated. For the low level IFPUG, it indicates that the SLOC would be underestimated.

Development Environment

The development project type, development platform, and architecture categories were sorted as low and high based on each of the factors, where low represented low complexity and high represented high complexity. The result of the classifications was the same as Angelis et al. classification of ISBSG's categories (Angelis & Stamelos & Morisio, 2000).

New development, redevelopment and enhancement projects were investigated and classified. New development types were considered high complexity and redevelopment and enhancement were considered low complexity because of code reuse and previous knowledge of the project development. The error average test confirmed the high and low levels because new development had a positive error, while redevelopment and enhancement had a negative error.

For development platforms, the ISBSG repository contained three types of platforms, which were personal computer (PC), mainframe (MF), and mid-range (MR). PCs were considered to be low complexity because of their simplicity. MF

and MR were high complexity because they were more difficult in terms of development. These classifications were confirmed from the error average test because MF and MR had a positive error and PC had a negative error.

In the ISBSG architecture category, there were two types of architectures, which were client-server and standalone architecture. Client-server architecture was high because of its complexity, while standalone was low. The error average test confirmed that client-server had a large positive error and standalone had a negative error.

Domain

The domain categories were investigated to see how they affect size estimate. It was shown by Reifer that the size and cost of applications differ in different application domains (Reifer, 2002). Therefore, the organization type, business area type, and application type categories were investigated.

The organization types in the ISBSG repository were services, communications, finance, manufacturing, and operations. An error average test was performed for each organization type. Finance and communication were low complexity, while services, manufacturing, and operations were high complexity.

In the ISBSG project repository, the business area types were accounting, banking, engineering, insurance, inventory, manufacturing, marketing, sales and telecommunications. From the average error test, the low complexity business area types were accounting, banking, insurance, inventory, and sales. In addition, the business area types that were high complexity were engineering, manufacturing, marketing, and telecommunications.

The application types in the ISBSG repository were business, electronic data interchange, process control, network management, management information system, office information system, stock order/order processing system, workflow support/management, and transaction/production system. After conducting the average error test for the application types, the high complexity types found were business, management information system, transaction/production system, and process control. The low complexity types were electronic data exchange, network management, office information systems, stock order/order processing system, and workflow support/management.

Team Size

Maximum team size was used in Aggarwal et al.'s size estimation model (Aggarwal & Singh & Chandra & Puri, 2005) and Angelis et al.'s cost estimation model (Angelis & Stamelos & Morisio, 2000). The maximum team size was another input added to the extended NFFPB model. The team size could affect the software size because of large teams, source code management software and software programming standards.

Extended Model Design

The extended NFFPB model uses additional environmental inputs, which were organization type (OT), business area type (BT), application type (AT), development project type (DT), devel-

opment platform (DP), architecture (AR), function point standard count (count) and maximum team size (TEAM). The low complexity inputs were treated as -1 and high complexity is +1 in the neural network. For project data which had missing data fields, the neural network inputs are 0. Figure 9 illustrates the additional inputs being passed through an activation function. The environmental factor's weights were initially set to 1 and are adjusted during training. The activation function used was a sigmoid function because the input parameters were patterns. Furthermore, the results of the sigmoid function were used to calibrate the conversion ratio. This was done by multiplying the sigmoid function by difference of the maximum and minimum SLOC/FP for each programming language from SPR's conversion ratios. This difference is called the change value, which is defined in Equation 5 where *Change* is the change value, *max* is the maximum SLOC/FP, *min* is the minimum SLOC/FP, C_i is the *i*th programming language level conversion ratio range. The sigmoid function is used because it's output ranges from 0 to 1. The sigmoid function represents the adjustment between the minimum and maximum conversion ratio value of the programming language. For example, the sigmoid function can adjust the conversion ratio of the programming

Figure 9. Development environmental input parameters

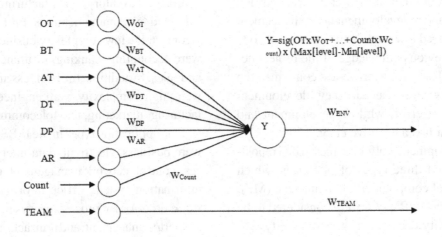

language Java between the minimum conversion ratio of 20 SLOC/FP to the maximum conversion ratio of 50 SLOC/FP, shown in Table 1.

Equation 5: Difference equation.

$$Change = max(C_i) - min(C_i)$$

Figure 10 shows the extended NFFPB model. The equation of the output node's activation is shown in Equation 6, where *Team* is the maximum team size, W_{Team} is the team weight, Y is the result of the sigmoid function multiplied by the *Change*,

W_{ENV} is the weight of the environment factors and Z is the result of the W_x multiplied by the UFP. The learning process was the same as the original model, except the error also propagates back to the environment inputs and team weights. Afterwards, the weights were adjusted.

Equation 6: Output Function.

$$Output = (Team \times W_{Team}) + (Y \times W_{ENV}) + Z$$

Figure 10. Extended NFFP model

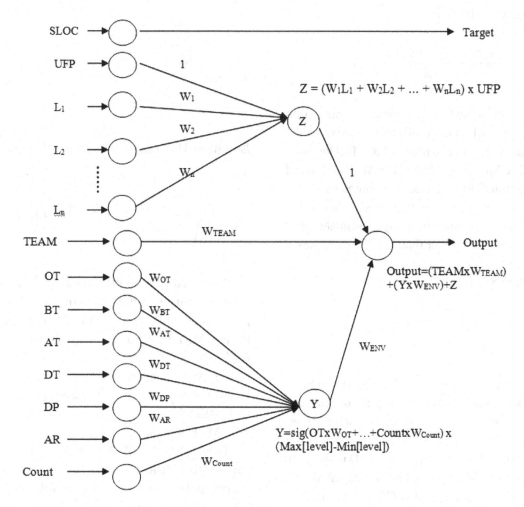

EVALUATING THE MODELS

Performance Evaluation Criteria

Magnitude of Relative Error (MRE) should not be used when evaluating and comparing prediction models because the results were misleading (Foss & Stensrud & Kitchenham & Myrtveit, 2003; Kitchenham & MacDonell & Pickad & Shepperd, 2001). MRE favored underestimation and performed worse in small sized projects. The equation for MRE is defined in Equation 7. Despite the misleading results, this method of evaluation is still commonly used in industry; thus, it was used to evaluate the experimental model.

Equation 7: MRE.

$$MRE = \frac{|\,actual - predicted\,|}{actual}$$

Another method used for comparing prediction models was Magnitude of error Relative to the Estimate (MER) (Kitchenham & MacDonell & Pickad & Shepperd, 2001). The MER is defined in Equation 8. MER has shortcomings similar to MRE. It favors overestimation because the estimation is a divisor; therefore larger estimates tend to perform much better than smaller estimates.

Equation 8: MER.

$$MER = \frac{|\,actual - predicted\,|}{predicted}$$

Standard Deviation (SD), Residual Error Standard Deviation (RSD) and Logarithmic Standard Deviation (LSD) were shown to be good and consistent criteria (Foss & Stensrud & Kitchenham & Myrtveit, 2003). The equation for SD is shown in Equation 9, where y_i represents the actual SLOC, $\hat{y}_i$ represents the predicted SLOC, and n is the total number of project points. Whereas in the RSD equation defined in Equation 10, y_i represents the

actual SLOC, $\hat{y}_i$ represents the predicted SLOC, x_i represents the number function points and n represents the total number of projects. The equation for LSD, shown in Equation 11, y_i represents the actual SLOC, $\hat{y}_i$ represents the predicted SLOC, n is the total number of projects, and the s^2 is the variance of $\ln y_i - \ln \hat{y}_i$. In addition to MRE and MER, SD, RSD and LSD were used for evaluation.

Equation 9: Standard Deviation.

$$SD = \sqrt{\frac{\sum \left(y_i - \hat{y}_i\right)^2}{n-1}}$$

Equation 10: Residual Error Standard Deviation.

$$RSD = \sqrt{\frac{\sum \left(\dfrac{y_i - \hat{y}_i}{x_i}\right)^2}{n-1}}$$

Equation 11: Logarithmic Standard Deviation.

$$LSD = \sqrt{\frac{\sum \left[\left(\ln y_i - \ln \hat{y}_i\right) - \left(-\dfrac{s^2}{2}\right)\right]^2}{n-1}}$$

Prediction at Level (PRED) was another criteria used to evaluate the prediction models. PRED(n) is the number of projects with a MRE lower than the n%. MRE less than 25% and 50% was utilized for PRED because other models have used these criteria for evaluation. PRED(25%) measures the number of projects with MRE less than 25% error and PRED(50%) measures the number of projects with MRE less than 50% error.

The goal of the NFFPB models is to achieve lower MRE, MER, SD, RSD and LSD values than the original conversion ratios. In the PRED criteria, the objective of the NFFPB models is to have a larger value than the original conversion ratios.

Experiment Methodology

The tuned NFFPB model's calibrated conversion ratios were benchmarked against the original conversion ratios from Software Productivity Research (SPR) (Software Productivity Research Incorporated, 2006). There were seven different experiments conducted for the original NFFPB and the extended NFFPB model. In each experiment, the MMRE, MMER, SD, LSD, and RSD were compared with the original and calibrated ratios.

The dataset was divided in half for training and evaluation in the first two experiments. The data points were randomly selected for each programming language level in each of the experiments.

In the next two experiments, the dataset was sorted based on the size of the projects. The effect on the performance was investigated when the NFFPB tool was trained with projects that have small function point counts and tested against projects with large function point counts. In the second size experiment, the opposite was performed. Large function point count projects were used for training and the small function point counts were used for simulation.

A larger training set was used to see if the performance improves. 75% of the dataset was used for training in two of the experiments. The data points were randomly selected for each programming level.

RESULTS

50% Random Test

In Experiment 1, the extended model was trained with the same data as the original experiment. The results were very similar to the results of the original model. Both models outperformed the original conversion ratios. Table 4 shows the comparison of the extended model against the original model's conversion ratios and the traditional backfiring conversion ratios.

In Experiment 2, the same experiment was conducted on both models except using a different dataset. The results were very similar to the calibrated conversion ratios shown in Table 5.

Size Test

In Experiment 3, the extended model demonstrated the same result as calibrated conversion ratio. Table 6 presents the result that the extended model produced the same improvement.

In Experiment 4, the extended model had a negative MMRE improvement. The evaluation results are shown in Table 7. The calibrated conversion ratios continue to outperform the original conversion ratio and the extended model.

Table 4. Experiment 1

Evaluation Criteria	Original Conversion Ratio	Calibrated Conversion Ratio	Extended Model
MMRE	1.26	**1.21**	**1.20**
MMER	1.30	**1.20**	**1.20**
PRED(MRE<25%)	31	31	31
PRED(MRE<50%)	55	56	56
SD	23618.33	23464.82	23465.77
LSD	1.07	1.04	1.04
RSD	70.54	69.51	69.53

Table 5. Experiment 2

Evaluation Criteria	Original Conversion Ratio	Calibrated Conversion Ratio	Extended Model
MMRE	4.40	4.36	4.38
MMER	1.16	1.02	1.02
PRED(MRE<25%)	39	40	39
PRED(MRE<50%)	60	60	59
SD	26133.26	26038.71	26052
LSD	1.12	1.08	1.08
RSD	85.97	85.99	85.99

Table 6. Experiment 3

Evaluation Criteria	Original Conversion Ratio	Calibrated Conversion Ratio	Extended Model
MMRE	0.92	**0.82**	**0.82**
MMER	1.07	**0.99**	**0.99**
PRED(MRE<25%)	36	36	37
PRED(MRE<50%)	54	58	58
SD	10347.88	10117.83	10120.42
LSD	0.92	0.87	0.87
RSD	70.85	69.11	69.13

Table 7. Experiment 4

Evaluation Criteria	Original Conversion Ratio	Calibrated Conversion Ratio	Extended Model
MMRE	**4.74**	**4.56**	**4.84**
MMER	1.32	1.28	1.27
PRED(MRE<25%)	35	34	36
PRED(MRE<50%)	62	63	62
SD	31947	32080.82	31964.92
LSD	1.22	1.21	1.21
RSD	68.87	68.81	68.76

75% Random Test

In the random test experiments, where more training data was provided, the extended model produced results similar to the calibrated conversion ratio. In Experiment 5 and experiment 6, different datasets were used. Table 8 and 9 illustrate the similarities. Both models outperformed the original conversion ratios.

DISCUSSIONS

NFFPB Models vs. Original Conversion Ratios

The results, from the experiments, have shown that the NFFPB models have small improvement over the SPR's backfiring conversion ratios. Despite the

Table 8. Experiment 5

Evaluation Criteria	Original Conversion Ratio	Calibrated Conversion Ratio	Extended Model
MMRE	1.07	**0.99**	**0.99**
MMER	1.30	**1.18**	**1.18**
PRED(MRE<25%)	17	17	17
PRED(MRE<50%)	31	30	30
SD	26134.51	24891.99	24920.66
LSD	1.04	0.99	0.99
RSD	75.48	73.83	73.84

Table 9. Experiment 6

Evaluation Criteria	Original Conversion Ratio	Calibrated Conversion Ratio	Extended Model
MMRE	1.25	1.14	1.13
MMER	0.77	0.72	0.73
PRED(MRE<25%)	19	21	21
PRED(MRE<50%)	30	31	31
SD	18107.94	17514.07	17513.33
LSD	0.94	0.90	0.90
RSD	51.10	48.25	48.01

small improvement, it was shown that with a larger dataset, a better improvement could be obtained.

The improvements were small in each experiment due to a limited number of data available. Because certain fuzzy language levels had insufficient data points, there was limited calibration for those language levels, which resulted in smaller improvements. However, regardless of the setback, in the 75% random test results, the improvements in MMRE and MMER were greater than in the 50% random test results. Another reason for the small improvements is that the model tried to satisfy the MMRE, MMER, PRED(MRE<25%) and PRED(MRE<50%) performance criteria, which resulted in only obtaining local minimum error points for each criteria.

NFFPB Model vs. Extended NFFPB Model

The extended model produced similar to worse results when compared to the original model due to various reasons. The dataset showed limited consistency for the categorical parameters. Moreover, while categorical parameters were shown to have impact on effort, it does not necessarily mean that they have a direct impact on size. More investigation in environmental variables that affect software size is needed.

Decreasing the size of a model and reducing the number of variables was shown to improve effort estimation (Chen & Menzies & Port & Boehm, 2005; Kirsopp & Shepperd, 2002; Miller, 2002). Based on the studies, the extended model would be worse than the original model. In addition, the results have shown that there was no improvement.

Threats to Validity

Certain language levels contained limited project data. If more data was available in those language levels, the results may have been different. However, other languages that had sufficient data points show improvement and have similar behavior.

Limited data in certain languages may have resulted in a less accurate model of the SLOC/FP versus language level curve.

Study has also shown that using different historical project data sets or experimental designs have different estimation accuracies when performed on the same model (Wen & Li & Lin & Hu & Huang, 2011). Even though different types of experimental designs and randomly selected project data were used, if a different project data set was used, there may be a possibility that the NFFPB model may have a much more different result.

Another threat to validity was that other environmental parameters may exist, which could have a direct effect on the programming language's SLOC/FP. For example, the general system characteristics for function point analysis may affect the estimate in lines of code. Studies have shown that the size and costs are affected by different application domains (Reifer, 2002). Angelis et al. showed a software cost estimation model based on attributes such as organization type, business type, development platform and development type; thus, these factors may have also affected the source lines of code per function point (Angelis & Stamelos & Morisio, 2000). Guyon et al. presented a variable selection method that could be used to identify which factors influence the size of the software (Guyon & Elisseeff, 2003). By using the variable selection method, the number of factors could be reduced which could improve the performance of the NFFPB model.

FUTURE RESEARCH DIRECTIONS

Research in Factors and Variables That Affect Software Size

The factors used in the extended model did not improve performance over the original calibrated model because they were proven to affect software effort but not size. Some other factors should be investigated such as reusability, security, system age (legacy and new), and system performance which may have more impact on software size.

Combine Calibrated Function Points with Calibrated Conversion Ratios

Xia developed a neuro-fuzzy function point technique which calibrates the function point complexity values (Xia & Ho & Capretz, 2008). In the study, the estimation model's size estimations showed improvements over the traditional complexity values. Others (Huang & Ho & Ren & Capretz, 2004; Du & Ho & Capretz, 2010) found improvements in estimation accuracy when a neuro-fuzzy approach is combined with an algorithmic model. Using the calibrated complexity values with the NFFPB model could potentially enhance the NFFPB model's size estimation.

CONCLUSION

The backfiring estimation technique had some major shortcomings such as the conversion ratios had a large range and were generic. Moreover, it only used the programming language and the function point count as inputs. Furthermore, this estimation technique did not work for enhancement projects.

The NFFPB was introduced to solve these problems by calibrating the conversion ratios. The NFFPB model used both fuzzy logic and neural network. Fuzzy logic was used to model the relationship between programming language level and source lines of code per function point (SLOC/FP). The neural network was used to calibrate the conversion ratios.

An extended NFFPB model was developed which used other inputs such as business area, organization type, development platform, function point count type, and team size. An investigation was conducted to determine if there was an improvement over the original NFFPB model.

The NFFPB models were benchmarked against SPR's conversion ratios. The ISBSG release 9 project data repository was used for training and evaluation. The extended model took additional input parameters such as environmental factors and team size.

The NFFPB models were shown to have an improvement in the Mean Magnitude of Relative Error (MMRE), Magnitude of error Relative to the Estimate (MER), Standard Deviation (SD), Logarithmic Standard Deviation (LSD), and Residual Standard Deviation (RSD). In the experiment where the training data set was smaller, the improvements were smaller. However, when a larger training set of data was used, the improvements increased.

The size of the data set available for training and evaluation weakened the conclusions being drawn because if more data became available, a greater improvement would show. Furthermore, there were only small improvements in the neural network because during training, the neural network was minimizing error based on both the MMRE and MMER criteria, which resulted in only obtaining local minimum error points (Angelis & Stamelos & Morisio, 2000).

The extended model was tested against the original NFFPB model and was shown to produce the same or worse results. A reason why there was no improvement over the original NFFPB model was that these additional factors have only been shown to affect software effort. There was no indication whether these factors would affect the size of a software system. Furthermore, it was shown that adding more variables into the model does not improve its performance estimation (Chen & Menzies & Port & Boehm, 2005; Kirsopp & Shepperd, 2002; Miller, 2002).

REFERENCES

Aggarwal, K. K., Singh, Y., Chandra, P., & Puri, M. (2005). Bayesian regularization in a neural network model to estimate lines of code using function points. *Journal of Computer Sciences*, *1*(4), 505–509.

Albrecht, A. J., & Gaffney, J. E. Jr. (1983). Software function, source lines of code, and development effort prediction: A software science validation. *IEEE Transactions on Software Engineering*, *9*(6), 639–648. doi:10.1109/TSE.1983.235271.

Angelis, L., Stamelos, I., & Morisio, M. (2000). Building a software cost estimation model based on categorical data. In *Proceedings Seventh International Software Metrics Symposium*, (pp. 4-15). IEEE.

Chen, Z., Menzies, T., Port, D., & Boehm, B. (2005). Finding the right data for software cost modeling. *IEEE Software*, *22*(6), 38–46. doi:10.1109/MS.2005.151.

Du, W. L., Ho, D., & Capretz, L. F. (2010). Improving software effort estimation using neuro-fuzzy model with SEER-SEM. *Global Journal of Computer Science and Technology*, *10*(12), 52–64.

Foss, T., Stensrud, E., Kitchenham, B., & Myrtveit, I. (2003). A simulation study of the model evaluation criterion MMRE. *IEEE Transactions on Software Engineering*, *29*(11), 985–995. doi:10.1109/TSE.2003.1245300.

Galorath, D., & Evans, M. (2006). *Software sizing, estimation, and risk management*. Boca Raton, FL: Auerbach Publications. doi:10.1201/9781420013122.

Guyon, I., & Elisseeff, A. (2003). An introduction to variable and feature selection. *Journal of Machine Learning Research*, (3): 1157–1182.

Huang, X., Ho, D., Ren, J., & Capretz, L. F. (2004). A neuro-fuzzy tool for software estimation. In *Proceedings of the 20th IEEE International Conference on Software Maintenance*. IEEE.

International Function Point User Group. (2007). *IFPUG*. Retrieved 2007 from http://www.ifpug.org

International Function Point Users Group. (2005). *Function point counting practices manual 4.2.1.* Retrieved January 2005 from http://www.ifpug.org

International Software Benchmarking Standards Group. (2004). *Data CD R9 demographics.* Retrieved 2004 from http://www.isbsg.org

Jones, C. (1995). Backfiring: Converting lines of code to function points. *Computer, 28*(11), 87–88. doi:10.1109/2.471193.

Kirsopp, C., & Shepperd, M. (2002). Case and feature subset selection in case-based software project effort prediction. In *Proceedings of the 22nd SGAI Int'l Conf. Knowledge-Based Systems and Applied Artificial Intelligence*. SGAI.

Kitchenham, B. A., MacDonell, S. G., Pickad, L. M., & Shepperd, M. J. (2001). What accuracy statistics really measure. *IEE Proceedings. Software, 148*(3), 81–85. doi:10.1049/ip-sen:20010506.

Mendel, J. M. (1995). Fuzzy logic systems for engineering: A tutorial. *Proceedings of the IEEE, 83*(2), 345–347. doi:10.1109/5.364485.

Miller, A. (2002). *Subset selection in regression.* Boca Raton, FL: Chapman & Hall. doi:10.1201/9781420035933.

NESMA. (2006). *NESMA: Section NESMA – All about NESMA.* Retrieved 2006 from http://www.nesma.nl

Reifer, D. J. (2002). Let the numbers do the talking. *CrossTalk*, 4-8.

Software Productivity Research Incorporated. (2006). *SPR programming languages table.* Retrieved from 2006 from http://www.spr.com

Stutzke, R. D. (2005). *Estimating software-intensive systems – Projects, products, and processes.* Westford, MA: Pearson Education, Inc.

Wen, J., Li, S., Lin, Z., Hu, Y., & Huang, C. (2012). Systematic literature review of machine learning based software development effort estimation models. *Information and Software Technology, 54*(1), 41–59. doi:10.1016/j.infsof.2011.09.002.

Wong, J., Ho, D., & Capretz, L. F. (2008). Calibrating function point backfiring conversion ratios using neuro-fuzzy technique. *International Journal of Uncertainty. Fuzziness and Knowledge-Based Systems, 16*(6), 847–862. doi:10.1142/S0218488508005650.

Xia, W., Capretz, L. F., & Ho, D. (2008). A neuro-fuzzy model for function point calibration. *Transactions on Information Science & Applications, 5*(1), 22–30.

Chapter 15
An Integrated Bi–Objective Reverse Logistics Network Design for Remanufacturing

Ali Zolghadr Shojai
Amirkabir University of Technology, Islamic Republic of Iran

Jamal Shahrabi
Amirkabir University of Technology, Islamic Republic of Iran

Masoud Jenabi
Amirkabir University of Technology, Islamic Republic of Iran

ABSTRACT

Growing environmental and economical concern has led to increasing attention towards management of product return flows. An effective and efficient reverse logistics network enables companies to gain more profit and customer satisfaction. Consequently, the reverse logistics network design problem has become a critical issue. After a brief introduction to the basic concepts of reverse logistics, the authors formulate a new integrated multi-stage, multi-period, multi-product reverse logistics model for a remanufacturing system where the inventory is considered. Two objectives, minimization of the costs and maximization of coverage, are addressed. Since such network design problems belong to a class of NP-hard problems, a multi-objective genetic algorithm and a multi-objective evolutionary strategy algorithm are developed in order to find the set of non-dominated solutions. Finally, the model is tested on test problems with different sizes, and the proposed algorithms are compared based on the number, quality, and distribution of non-dominated solutions that belong to the Pareto front.

DOI: 10.4018/978-1-4666-4785-5.ch015

1. INTRODUCTION

Reverse logistics can be defined as the process of moving goods and products from their usual destination to other locations and facilities in order to obtain value, or to manage safe disposal (Du & Evans, 2008). Environmental protection along with economic and service reasons has pushed a growing number of companies to consider product recovery and reverse flows within their logistics systems (Du & Evans, 2008; Lu & Bostel, 2007). Proper and effective implementation of reverse logistics can lead to savings in costs associated with inventory, transportation and waste disposal. It can also improve customer loyalty and future sales (Ko & Evans, 2007).

Product recovery options fall into different classes: refurbishing, cannibalization, repairing, recycling and remanufacturing (Thierry, Salomon, Van Nunen, & Van Waasenhove, 1995). Based on the condition and age of the returned product and economic considerations, the right option can be chosen (Guide, Jayaraman, Srivastava, & Benton, 2000). Common activities in product recovery systems can be grouped as follows (Aras & Aksen, 2008; Fleischmann, Krikke, Dekker, & Flapper, 2000):

- **Collection:**
  - Moving returned products physically from locations of product holders (customer zones) to some point for further treatment such as consolidation and storage.
- **Inspection/Separation:**
  - Determining if the returned products are in fact recoverable. Disassembly, testing, sorting and storage are some of the operations related to inspection/separation.
- **Reprocessing/Reconditioning:**
  - Transforming the returns into usable products once more. Repair, recycling and remanufacturing are common forms of reprocessing/reconditioning.

- **Disposal:**
  - Discarding products that cannot be reused due to economical and/or technological reasons. Landfilling and incineration are the usual steps of discarding the unrecoverable returns.
- **Redistribution:**
  - Directing and physically moving the reusable products to potential markets and future users. Sales and storage are the prevalent activities related to redistribution.

Remanufacturing is known as the main option of recovery in terms of its feasibility and benefits (Lu & Bostel, 2007). It can return the used product to 'as new' condition through disassembly and inspection of all modules. Parts or modules that cannot be salvaged are replaced and tested. Sometimes it is even necessary to include technological upgrades. Remanufacturing is usually performed in-house by manufacturers, since they own the specific product knowledge (Beamon & Fernandes, 2004). Over the past decade, some firms such as Dell, General Motors, HP, Kodak and Xerox have focused on remanufacturing activities and carried out related operations successfully (Pishvaee, Kianfar, & Karimi, 2010a; Üster, Easwaran, Akçali & Çetinkaya, 2007).

Obviously, the operational profitability of the underlying supply chain plays a key role in the financial success of product recovery practices. One of the main issues in this context is designing and establishing an effective and efficient infrastructure through optimal network design (Akçali, Çetinkaya, & Üster, 2009). The product return recovery usually entails the determination of the number and location/allocation of different facilities involved in the product recovery practice. Necessary decisions must be made in such a way that total reverse logistics costs (e.g., opening cost of facilities opened along with storage and transportation costs) are minimized and service level is maximized (Min & Ko, 2008).

The inventory control tries to reduce inventory cost (storage cost) by following the optimal control policy and satisfying some specific pattern of demand. In many cases, researchers impliedly assume that the existing supply chain entities have no storage function; so, the products just flow through the facilities. However, in real-world problems inventory control is tightly connected to logistics network design (Lin, Gen, & Wang, 2009).

Generally, each important real-world problem deals with more than one objective (Du & Evans, 2008). Consequently, considering several objectives concurrently can be an interesting option for decision makers. The level of logistics service has a major impact on customer satisfaction which in turn affects revenues and profit to a large extent (Du & Evans, 2008). The level of logistics service can be expressed through coverage. Coverage is one of classical objectives in the area of location modeling. This objective was formally introduced by Church and Revelle (1974) and can be applied to a wide variety of settings. The main interest in coverage problems is to ensure that every customer to be served by a set of facilities has a facility within a stated service distance (Berman, Drezner, & Krass, 2010). One of the major concerns of the companies involved in product recovery is the collection or acquisition of returns (Guide, Teunter, & Wassenhove, 2003). In fact, it is the first activity of product recovery and the efficiency with which returned products are collected directly affects the profitability of the remanufacturing operations (Üster et al., 2007).

A multi-stage, multi-period, multi-product reverse logistics network problem that covers remanufacturing activities is proposed in this chapter. Given that a company is focused on re-manufacturing initiatives, flows associated with returned products start from customer zones, go through collection and inspection centers, and then move to remanufacturing facilities, accompanied by the ability of collection and inspection centers to store received returns. The decisions involve: which locations to be chosen for installing different facilities, how to allocate physical flows among the facilities, how to implement the inventory control, and how to determine the best fleet size. In addition to the minimization of the total cost, maximization of coverage will be considered in this study as well. We seek to maximize the amount of returned products collected from customer zones attended by nearby collection centers (i.e., coverage).

The remainder of the chapter is organized as follows. In Section 2, we provide related works for reverse logistics network design. The problem definition and mathematical programming formulation are presented in Sections 3 and 4, respectively. The solution methodology is explained in Section 5 and the proposed multi-objective genetic algorithm and multi-objective evolutionary strategy algorithm are described. In Section 6 we compare the results obtained by the algorithms based on the number, quality and distribution of non-dominated solutions. Finally, Section 7 provides our conclusions and future research decisions.

2. RELATED LITERATURE

The general topic of network design for product recovery has received growing attention in recent years and its literature is rather extensive. For a comprehensive review of the works done in this area we refer the reader to Akçali et al. (2009), Fleischmann et al. (2000), Pishvaee, Zanjirani Farahani, and Dullaert (2010b) and Pokharel and Mutha (2009). The existing network design can be classified into two categories based on the underlying network structure. The first one is reverse supply chain network design where the focus is on reverse channel (reverse flows and activities) only. Collection, inspection, disposal and reprocessing are common reverse activities. The second category is closed-loop supply chain network design where both forward and reverse channels are studied simultaneously. Manufacturing and distribution operations are considered as forward activities (Akçali et al., 2009).

In order to present the literature review on reverse supply chain network design and closed-loop supply chain network design, we follow the approach introduced by Pishvaee et al. (2010b). A coding system is developed based on Table 1. Considering this system, available models in the literature are coded in Table 2 and Table 3.

As shown in Table 2 and Table 3, mixed integer programming models are common in this area. These models are usually aimed at minimization of the total cost or maximization of the profit, and range from single-period, single-product models (e.g., Lu & Bostel, 2007) to complex multi-period, multi-product models (e.g., Min & Ko, 2008). The number of multi-objective models (Dehghanian & Mansour, 2009; Du & Evans, 2008; Pishvaee & Torabi, 2010; Pishvaee et al., 2010b) is smaller compared to the number of single-objective models, and maximization of coverage has never been considered as an objective. In addition, few published papers (Kannan et al., 2010; Ko & Evans, 2007; Min & Ko, 2008; Salema et al., 2009; Salema et al., 2010) discuss multi-period and multi-product options simultaneously. Moreover, researchers who designed models with inventory level as a decision variable (El-Sayed et al., 2010; Salema et al., 2009; Salema et al., 2010), used commercial solvers to obtain solutions and did not present an algorithmic approach. Since the majority of logistics network design problems belong to NP-hard class, many powerful heuristics, metaheuristics, and Lagrangian-relaxation-based methods have been proposed to solve such models (Pishvaee et al., 2010b).

Motivated by the above facts, we shall design a multi-stage, multi-period, multi-product reverse supply chain network for remanufacturing with inventory decision (called integrated reverse logistics network). Considering multi-period and multi-product settings, our model is similar to the

ones proposed by Ko and Evans (2007), Min and Ko (2008) and Salema et al. (2009). In order to include inventory decision in our problem formulation, we reviewed the works done by Salema et al. (2009) and El-Sayed et al. (2010). To model this network, we will develop a bi-objective mixed integer programming formulation with one objective related to total cost and the other, which is a new objective in the literature of reverse logistics network design, related to coverage. Since our proposed network design problem belongs to NP-hard class, we will propose an algorithmic approach and use a multi-objective genetic algorithm and a multi-objective evolutionary strategy algorithm to find the set of non-dominated solutions.

3. PROBLEM DEFINITON

A company is considering using a reverse logistics supply chain network for remanufacturing. As shown in Figure 1, there are four participants along the network: customer zones, collection, inspection, and remanufacturing centers. In addition, the company owns a heterogeneous fleet of capacitated vehicles.

Reverse flow starts from customer zones. Vehicles of type 1 are dispatched (on direct routes) from the collection centers to the locations of product holders to fetch the returns. Shipped returns are stored in collection centers and, then, will be transported to inspection centers by vehicles of type 2 which are dispatched from the inspection centers. Returned products that are carried to the inspection centers will be classified and organized by the disposal and remanufacturing strategy. Returned products which are of good quality for remanufacturing will be stored and sent to the remanufacturing centers that are responsible for the process of remanufacturing. Products that do not meet quality standards for remanufacturing are redirected to a different supply chain which is not studied in this chapter.

Table 1. Classification of logistics network design problems

Characteristics	Abbreviation	Characteristics	Abbreviation
Objectives		**Outputs**	
Min Cost	C	Inventory	I
Max Profit	Pr	Number of vehicles	NV
Min Total tardiness of cycle time	TotTardCyc	Price of products	P
Max Responsiveness	Res	Demand satisfaction quantity	DS
Max Social impacts	SocImp	Transportation amount	TA
Min Negative environmental impacts	NegEnvImp	Location / allocation	LA
Min Total delivery tardiness	TotDeliTard	Facility capacity	FC
Modeling		**Logistics network entities**	
Mixed integer linear programming	MILP	Forward logistics entities	
Mixed integer non-linear programming	MINLP	Supply centers	SC
Stochastic mixed integer programming	SMIP	Production centers	PC
Fuzzy programming	FP	Distribution centers	DISC
Possibilistic programming	POP	Hybrid centers*	HC
Problem definition		Reverse logistics entities	
Planning horizon		Redistribution centers	RDISC
Single period	SP	Disposal centers	DC
Multi-period	MP	Collection / inspection centers	CIC
Number of facilities to be opened		Recycling / recovery centers	RCC
Determined	DET	Hybrid centers	HC
Undetermined	UNDET	*Hybrid centers are bidirectional facilities where both forward and reverse activities are performed.	
Product			
Single product	SPR		
Multi-product	MPR		
Flow capacity			
Capacitated flow	CF		
Uncapacitated flow	UCF		
Demand and supply			
Deterministic	D		
Stochastic / fuzzy	SF		
Facility capacity			
Capacitated	CAP		
Uncapacitated	UNCAP		

Remanufacturable returns are shipped to the remanufacturing centers by vehicles of type 2 which are dispatched from the inspection centers. It must be noted that all vehicles go to the designated destination and then come back to the center from which they were dispatched.

To specify the study scope, we use the following assumptions in the problem formulation:

- The model is multi-product. Moreover, some of the problem parameters such as the amount of returned products and unit

Table 2. Coding of reviewed models for reverse supply chain network design

Reference	Objective(s)	Modeling	Problem Definition	Logistics Network Entities	Outputs
Du and Evans (2008)	C, TotTardCyc	MILP	SP, UNDET, MPR, UCF, D, CAP	PC, DISC, RCC*	TA, LA, FC
Louwers, Kip, Peters, Souren, and Flapper (1999)	C	MILP	SP, UNDET, MPR, UCF, D, CAP	DC, CIC*	TA, LA
Barros, Dekker, and Scholten (1998)	C	MILP	SP, UNDET, MPR, UCF, D, CAP	CIC*, RCC*	TA, LA
Aras and Aksen (2008)	Pr	MINLP	SP, UNDET, SPR, UCF, D, UNCAP	CIC*	TA, LA, P
Aras, Aksen, and Tanuğur (2008)	Pr	MINLP	SP, DET, SPR, UCF, D, UNCAP	CIC*	TA, LA, NV, P
Lee, Gen, and Rhee (2009)	C	MILP	SP, UNDET, MPR, UCF, D, CAP	SC, PC, DISC, DC, CIC*, RCC*	TA, LA
Jayaraman, Patterson, and Rolland (2003)	C	MILP	SP, UNDET, SPR, UCF, D, CAP	CIC*, RCC*	TA, LA
Min, Ko and Ko (2006b)	C	MINLP	SP, UNDET, SPR, UCF, D, CAP	CIC*, RCC*	TA, LA
Min, Ko, and Ko (2006a)	C	MINLP	MP, UNDET, SPR, UCF, D, UNCAP	CIC*, RCC	TA, LA
Pishvaee et al. (2010a)	C	MILP	SP, UNDET, SPR, UCF, D, CAP	DC, CIC*, RCC	TA, LA
Mutha and Pokharel (2009)	C	MILP	SP, DET, MPR, UCF, D, CAP	SC, PC, DISC, DC, CIC, RCC, RDISC	TA, LA
Lieckens and Vandaele (2007)	Pr	MINLP	SP, UNDET, SPR, UCF, D, CAP	DC, CIC, RCC*	TA, LA, FC, DS
Chu, Shi, Lin, Sculli, and Ni (2009)	C	FP	SP, UNDET, SPR, UCF, D, CAP	DISC, HC, DC, CIC*, RCC*	TA, LA
Qin and Ji (2010)	C	FP	SP, UNDET, SPR, UCF, SF, CAP	PC, CIC*	TA, LA, DS
Dehghanian and Mansour (2009)	Pr, NegEnvImp, SocImp	MILP	SP, UNDET, MPR, UCF, D, CAP	DC, CIC, RCC*	TA, LA
Sasikumar, Kannan, and Noorul Haq (2010)	Pr	MINLP	MP, UNDET, SPR, UCF, D, CAP	DC, CIC*, RCC	TA, LA

*Facilities to be located in the network.

storage costs of returned products change drastically over time; so, our model is multi-period in order to support the dynamic nature of the problem;

- Collecting all potential returns is a requirement for the company due to environmental issues and governmental legislation. Moreover, all recoverable returns must be remanufactured;

- The potential locations of the collection and inspection centers are known;
- Collection and inspection centers have capacity limits for storage. Capacities of these centers are known in advance. Remanufacturing centers are uncapacitated;
- Numbers and locations of customer zones and remanufacturing centers are fixed and predefined;

Table 3. Coding of reviewed models for closed-loop supply chain network design

Reference	Objective(s)	Modeling	Problem Definition	Logistics Network Entities	Outputs
Lu and Bostel (2007)	C	MILP	SP, UNDET, SPR, UCF, D, UNCAP	PC*, DC, RCC*, CIC*	TA, LA
Ko and Evans (2007)	C	MINLP	MP, UNDET, MPR, UCF, D, CAP	PC, DISC*, HC, RCC, HC	TA, LA
Lee and Dong (2008)	C	MILP	SP, DET, SPR, CF, D, CAP	PC, HC*, HC*	TA, LA
Salema, Póvoa, and Novais (2006)	C	MILP	SP, UNDET, MPR, UCF, D, CAP	PC*, DISC*, DC, CIC*	TA, LA, DS
Salema, Póvoa, and Novais (2007)	C	SMIP	SP, UNDET, MPR, UCF, SF, CAP	PC*, DISC*, DC, CIC*	TA, LA, DS
Üster et al. (2007)	C	MILP	SP, UNDET, MPR, UCF, D, UNCAP	PC, DISC, CIC*, RCC*	TA, LA
Beamon and Fernanndes (2004)	C	MILP	MP, UNDET, SPR, UCF, D, CAP	PC, DISC*, HC*, CIC*, HC*	TA, LA
Min and Ko (2008)	C	MINLP	MP, UNDET, MPR, UCF, D, CAP	PC, DISC*, HC*, CIC*, HC*	TA, LA, FC
Marín and pelegrín (1998)	C	MILP	SP, UNDET, SPR, UCF, D, UNCAP	PC*	TA, LA
Wang and Hsu (2010)	C	MILP	SP, UNDET, SPR, UCF, D, CAP	SC*, PC*, DISC*, HC*, HC*	TA, LA
Kannan, Sasikumar, and Devika (2010)	C	MILP	MP, DET, MPR, UCF, D, CAP	SC, PC, DISC, DC, CIC, RCC	TA, LA
Demirel and Gökçen (2008)	C	MILP	SP, UNDET, MPR, UCF, D, CAP	PC, DISC*, CIC*, RCC*	TA, LA
Yongsheng and Shouyang (2008)	C	MILP	SP, UNDET, SPR, UCF, D, UNCAP	PC*, DISC*, HC, RCC*, HC	TA, LA, DS
Salema, Póvoa, and Novais (2010)	C	MILP	MP, UNDET, MPR, CF, D, CAP	PC*, DISC*, DC, CIC*	TA, LA, I, DS
Pishvaee et al. (2010b)	C, Res	MILP	SP, UNDET, SPR, UCF, D, CAP	PC*, DISC*, HC*, DC*, CIC*, HC*	TA, LA, FC
Salema, Póvoa, and Novais (2009)	C	MILP	MP, UNDET, MPR, CF, D, CAP	PC*, DISC*, DC, CIC*	TA, LA, I, DS
El-Sayed, Afia, and El-Kharbotly (2010)	Pr	SMIP	MP, UNDET, SPR, UCF, SF, CAP	SC*, PC*, DISC*, RDISK*, DC*, CIC*	TA, LA, I
Pishvaee and Torabi (2010)	C, TotDeliTard	POP	MP, UNDET, SPR, UCF, SF, CAP	DISC*, CIC*, RCC*	TA, LA

*Facilities to be located in the network.

- In every time period, the amount of returned products from each customer zone is deterministic and known in advance;
- Returned products from a customer zone can be sent to more than one collection center. Similarly, stored returns in each collection center can be shipped to more than one inspection center. Since remanufacturing centers do not have any capacity limits, recoverable returns in an inspection center will be transported to one remanufacturing center;
- The flow is only allowed to be transferred between two consecutive levels. It can be

Figure 1. Reverse logistics network for remanufacturing

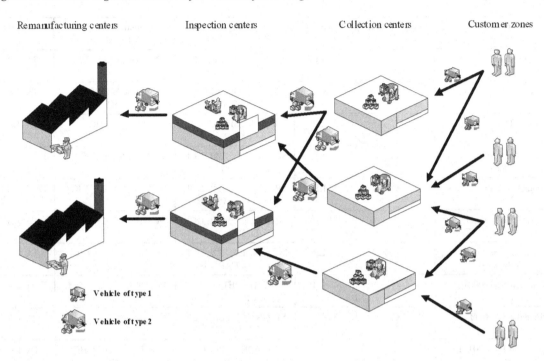

noted that there are no flows between the facilities at the same level. In addition, sending returns to the nearest collection or inspection center is of high priority;

- Stock levels at collection and inspection centers are assumed to be zero in the first and in the last time period;
- Transportation cost consists of two parts. The first one is the operating cost of a vehicle (rent, initial purchasing cost, driver wages, insurance and tax). The second part is traveling cost of the vehicle which is linearly proportional to the total distance, and is independent of the type of the returned product loaded on the vehicle (Aras et al., 2008). Furthermore, maximum carrying load associated with each type of vehicle is known;
- In every time period, costs parameters (fixed costs to set up collection and inspection centers, transportation costs and storage costs) are known for each type of facility and vehicle;

- Disposal fraction is a predefined value in the interval [0,1];
- The maximal covering distance is known in advance. Customer zones within this distance to an open collection center are considered well served.

One of the objectives of this study is to minimize the total cost of the multi-stage, multi-period, multi-product reverse logistics network by considering the decisions related to number and locations of facilities to open, fleet size, inventory level and allocation of corresponding returns flow. Moreover, another major consideration is the decision on coverage in order to achieve maximal customer satisfaction. In this research, the total coverage is used to measure the customers' satisfaction level of the collection operation. In other words, we seek to maximize the amount of product returns collected from customer zones attended by collection centers within the maximal covering distance. Notably, these two objectives are in conflict with each other (Villegas, Palacios, &

Medaglia, 2006; Zanjirani Farahani, SteadieSeifi, & Asgari, 2010). This means that an increase in one objective results in a decrease in another one. Thus, optimizing the network involves a trade-off between the two objectives.

The bi-objective mixed integer programming model which provides all of the aforementioned decisions is presented in the next section.

4. MATHEMATICAL PROGRAMMING FORMULATION

- **Indices:**
  - i: index for customer zones
  - j: index for collection centers
  - l: index for inspection centers
  - f: index for remanufacturing centers ($f=0$, imaginary remanufacturing center that allows unrecoverable returns to leave the reverse logistics network – disposal option)
  - p: index for returned products
  - t: index for time periods
- **Sets:**
  - I: set of fixed locations of customer zones
  - J: set of potential collection center locations
  - L: set of potential inspection center locations
  - F: set of fixed locations of remanufacturing centers (which can be extended to $F' = F \cup \{0\}$ in order to consider disposal option)
  - P: set of returned products
  - T: set of time periods
- **Parameters:**
  - γ: Disposal fraction; it takes values in the range [0,1]
  - r_{pit}: Amount of returned product p from customer zone i in time period t

- s^J_{pj0}: Initial stock of returned product p in collection center j
- s^L_{pl0}: Initial stock of returned product p in inspection center l
- fc^J_j: Fixed cost of opening collection center j
- fc^L_l: Fixed cost of opening inspection center l
- g^J_j: Maximum storage capacity of collection center j
- g^L_l: Maximum storage capacity of inspection center l
- cs^J_{pjt}: Unit storage cost of product p kept in collection center j in time period t
- cs^L_{plt}: Unit storage cost of product p kept in inspection center l in time period t
- d^{IJ}_{ij}: The distance between customer zone i and collection center j
- d^{JL}_{jl}: The distance between collection center j and inspection center l
- d^{LF}_{lf}: The distance between inspection center l and remanufacturing center f
- q_1: Maximum carrying load of vehicles of type 1
- q_2: Maximum carrying load of vehicles of type 2
- c_{11t}: Operating cost associated with vehicles of type 1 in time period t
- c_{12t}: Operating cost associated with vehicles of type 2 in time period t
- c_{21t}: Cost per unit distance traveled by vehicles of type 1 in time period t
- c_{22t}: Cost per unit distance traveled by vehicles of type 2 in time period t
- $D_{\max}$: Maximal covering distance

- **Decision variables:**

  ○ Y_{jt}^J
  $\begin{cases} 1, & \text{if collection center } j \text{ is opened in time period } t; \\ 0, & \text{otherwise} \end{cases}$

  ○ Y_{lt}^L
  $\begin{cases} 1, & \text{if inspection center } l \text{ is opened in time period } t; \\ 0, & \text{otherwise} \end{cases}$

  ○ X_{pijt}^{IJ} : Quantity of returned product p shipped to collection center j from customer zone i in time period t

  ○ X_{pjlt}^{JL} : Quantity of returned product p shipped to inspection center l from collection center j in time period t

  ○ $X_{plft}^{LF'}$: Quantity of remanufacturable returned product p shipped to remanufacturing center f from inspection center l in time period t

  ○ S_{pjt}^J : Amount of product p stocked in collection center j, over time period t

  ○ S_{plt}^L : Amount of product p stocked in inspection center l, over time period t

  ○ N_{1ijt}^{IJ} : Number of vehicles of type 1 required to transport returned products from customer zone i to collection center j in time period t

  ○ N_{2jlt}^{JL} : Number of vehicles of type 2 required to transport returned products from collection center j to inspection center l in time period t

  ○ N_{2lft}^{LF} : Number of vehicles of type 2 required to transport remanufacturable returned products from inspection center l to remanufacturing center f in time period t

Based on the above notations, the multi-stage, multi-period, multi-product reverse logistics network can be formulated are shown Box 1.

The equations in Box 1 are subjected to:

$$\sum_{j \in J} X_{pijt}^{IJ} = r_{pit}, \qquad \forall p \in P, \qquad \forall i \in I, \qquad \forall t \in T \tag{3}$$

$$\gamma \sum_{j \in J} X_{pjlt}^{JL} = X_{pl0t}^{LF'}, \qquad \forall p \in P, \qquad \forall l \in L, \qquad \forall t \in T \tag{4}$$

$$\sum_{i \in I} X_{pijt}^{IJ} + S_{pj(t-1)}^J = \sum_{l \in L} X_{pjlt}^{JL} + S_{pjt}^J, \\ \forall p \in P, \qquad \forall j \in J, \qquad \forall t \in T \tag{5}$$

Box 1.

$$\begin{aligned}
\text{Min} \quad Z_1 &= \sum_{j \in J} \sum_{t \in T, t=1} fc_j^J Y_{jt}^J + \sum_{j \in J} \sum_{t \in T, t \geq 2} fc_j^J Y_{jt}^J - \sum_{j \in J} \sum_{t \in T, t \geq 2} fc_j^J Y_{jt}^J Y_{j(t-1)}^J \\
&+ \sum_{l \in L} \sum_{t \in T, t=1} fc_l^L Y_{lt}^L + \sum_{l \in L} \sum_{t \in T, t \geq 2} fc_l^L Y_{lt}^L - \sum_{l \in L} \sum_{t \in T, t \geq 2} fc_l^L Y_{lt}^L Y_{l(t-1)}^L \\
&+ \sum_{p \in P} \sum_{j \in J} \sum_{t \in T} cs_{pjt}^J S_{pjt}^J + \sum_{p \in P} \sum_{l \in L} \sum_{t \in T} cs_{plt}^L S_{plt}^L \\
&+ \sum_{i \in I} \sum_{j \in J} \sum_{t \in T} \left(c_{11t} + 2c_{21t} d_{ij}^{IJ} \right) N_{1ijt}^{IJ} + \sum_{j \in J} \sum_{l \in L} \sum_{t \in T} \left(c_{12t} + 2c_{22t} d_{jl}^{JL} \right) N_{2jlt}^{JL} \\
&+ \sum_{l \in L} \sum_{f \in F} \sum_{t \in T} \left(c_{12t} + 2c_{22t} d_{lf}^{LF} \right) N_{2lft}^{LF}
\end{aligned} \tag{1}$$

$$\text{Max} \quad Z_2 = \sum_{p \in P} \sum_{i \in I} \sum_{j \in Q_i} \sum_{t \in T} X_{pijt}^{IJ} \tag{2}$$

$$\sum_{j\in J} X_{pjlt}^{JL} + S_{pl(t-1)}^{L} = \sum_{f\in F} X_{plft}^{LF'} + X_{pl0t}^{LF'} + S_{plt}^{L},$$
$$\forall p \in P, \qquad \forall l \in L, \qquad \forall t \in T \tag{6}$$

$$\sum_{p\in P} S_{pjt}^{J} \leq g_{j}^{J} Y_{jt}^{J}, \qquad \forall j \in J, \qquad \forall t \in T \tag{7}$$

$$\sum_{p\in P} S_{plt}^{L} \leq g_{l}^{L} Y_{lt}^{L}, \qquad \forall l \in L, \qquad \forall t \in T \tag{8}$$

$$\sum_{p\in P} X_{pijt}^{IJ} \leq q_{1} N_{1ijt}^{IJ}, \qquad \forall i \in I, \qquad \forall j \in J, \qquad \forall t \in T \tag{9}$$

$$\sum_{p\in P} X_{pjlt}^{JL} \leq q_{2} N_{2jlt}^{JL}, \qquad \forall j \in J, \qquad \forall l \in L, \qquad \forall t \in T \tag{10}$$

$$\sum_{p\in P} X_{plft}^{LF'} \leq q_{2} N_{2lft}^{LF}, \qquad \forall l \in L, \qquad \forall f \in F, \qquad \forall t \in T \tag{11}$$

$$Y_{jt}^{J} \in \{0,1\}, Y_{lt}^{L} \in \{0,1\}, \qquad \forall j \in J, \qquad \forall l \in L, \qquad \forall t \in T \tag{12}$$

$$X_{pijt}^{IJ} \geq 0, X_{pjlt}^{JL} \geq 0, X_{plft}^{LF'} \geq 0,$$
$$\forall p \in P, \quad \forall i \in I, \quad \forall j \in J, \quad \forall f \in F', \quad \forall t \in T \tag{13}$$

$$S_{pjt}^{J} \geq 0, S_{plt}^{L} \geq 0,$$
$$\forall p \in P, \qquad \forall j \in J, \qquad \forall l \in L, \qquad \forall t \in T \tag{14}$$

$$N_{1ijt}^{IJ} \in \mathbb{Z}^{+}, N_{2jlt}^{JL} \in \mathbb{Z}^{+}, N_{2lft}^{LF} \in \mathbb{Z}^{+},$$
$$\forall i \in I, \forall j \in J, \forall l \in L, \forall f \in F, \forall t \in T \tag{15}$$

Objective function (1) minimizes the total cost that consists of investment costs related to the opening/usage of collection and inspection centers in each possible location, storage costs, and transportation costs. If a facility is open over two

consecutive time periods, the corresponding investment cost will be considered once. The objective function (2) measures coverage as the sum of returned products from customer zones collected by collection centers within the maximal coverage distance (Let $Q_{i} = \left\{ j \in J \big| d_{ij}^{IJ} \leq D_{max} \right\}$ be the set of collection centers that could collect returned products from customer zone i within the maximal covering distance D_{max}). Constraints (3) guarantee that all returned products are collected and shipped to collection centers. Constraints (4) ensure that a part of the inbound flows of inspection center l can be sent to an imaginary remanufacturing center ($f=0$) that represents any facility outside the reverse logistics network. Constraints (5) and (6) assure the flow balance at collection and inspection centers where the inbound flow plus existing stock equals the outbound flow plus the remaining stock. Constraints (7) and (8) impose the capacity limitations on collection and inspection centers across the time period. Constraints (9) – (11) determine the number of vehicles required to transport the returns among network entities. $\left\lceil \sum_{p\in P} X_{pijt}^{IJ} / q_{1} \right\rceil$, $\left\lceil \sum_{p\in P} X_{pjlt}^{JL} / q_{2} \right\rceil$ and $\left\lceil \sum_{p\in P} X_{plft}^{LF'} / q_{2} \right\rceil$ give the number of vehicles where $\lceil w \rceil$ denotes the smallest integer greater than or equal to w for $w \succ 0$. Finally, Constraints (12) – (15) define the scope of each set of variables.

In multi-objective optimization, if all objective functions, Z_{1} and Z_{2}, are to be minimized (a maximization type objective can be converted to a minimization type by multiplying negative one), a feasible solution x is said to dominate another feasible solution y ($x \prec y$), if and only if, $Z_{i'}(x) \leq Z_{i'}(y)$ for $i' = 1,2$ and $Z_{j'}(x) \prec Z_{j'}(y)$ for at least one objective function j'. A solution is Pareto optimal if it is not dominated by any other solutions in the solution space. Pareto optimal set consists of all feasible non-dominated solutions in the solution space. For a given Pareto optimal set, the corresponding values of objective functions are called the Pareto front. A practical approach to multi-objective optimization is to obtain a set of solutions (the best-known Pareto set) that represents the Pareto optimal set as well as possible (Konak, Coit, & Smith, 2006).

5. SOLUTION METHODOLGY

The reverse logistics network model considered in this chapter can be viewed as a capacitated plant location problem and a flow optimization problem. Since the capacitated plant location problem belongs to NP-complete class (Davis & Ray, 1969), the proposed model in this study is NP-hard. Moreover, the inclusion of inventory decision makes it much harder to tackle the problem. Using traditional mixed integer programming tools and software programs to solve the proposed model is computationally intractable due to the complexity of the problem. This becomes severe as we encounter large-scaled problems with large number of variables and constraints. Consequently, an approach based on evolutionary computation techniques can be a practical method for the problem solution. One of the classic components of soft computing and possibly the newest yet likely most up-to-date is that of evolutionary algorithms, and related to these are four significant areas: evolutionary strategies, evolutionary programming, genetic algorithms and genetic programming. Evolutionary algorithms employ a structured but randomized way to use genetic information in finding new research directions.

Depending on this consideration, we use a multi-objective genetic algorithm and a multi-objective evolutionary strategy algorithm to solve the reverse logistics network design problem based on an extended priority-based encoding and decoding method.

5.1 Extended Priority-Based Encoding and Decoding

A chromosome contains the necessary gene information for solving the problem. The performance of evolutionary algorithms is greatly influenced by chromosome representation. With respect to different problems, different data structures have been developed (Altiparmak, Gen, Lin, & Karaoglan, 2009). Tree-based representation is one of the ways to represent network models. In this method, a gene in chromosome contains two types of information: the position of the gene within the structure of a chromosome that represents the type of the facility, and the value taken by the gene which is used to identify the priority of the facility for constructing a tree among other candidates (Lee et al., 2009). Gen, Altiparmak, and Lin (2006) proposed a new representation based on priority-based encoding to solve a two-stage, single-period, single-product transportation problem. Their proposed representation does not need any repair mechanisms. Based on the improvements made by Lin et al. (2009) and Altiparmak et al. (2009), we extend the priority-based encoding and decoding of transportation trees to a multi-stage, multi-period, multi-product case. The most desirable characteristic of this encoding is that unlike conventional methods such as Prüfer number, it provides feasible solutions to the problem without the need for defining any feasibility criteria or designing any special operators for crossover and mutation.

When a single-product transportation problem is dealt with through priority-based encoding, a chromosome consists of sources ($m \in M$) and depots ($n \in N$) to obtain a transportation tree and its length equals to the total number of sources ($|M|$) and depots ($|N|$), that is $|M| + |N|$. In the multi-product setting, shipping lines and capacitated facilities have joint capacities and this characteristic must be included in the traditional priority-based encoding. Let P be the set of returned products. The chromosome based on the priority-based encoding consists of $|P|$ parts and the length of each part is $|M| + |N|$. A gene value comes from the interval $\left[1, |P|\left(|M| + |N|\right)\right]$. To obtain a transportation tree for each type of returned product, the corresponding part of the chromosome is used (Altiparmak et al., 2009).

Since the proposed reverse logistics network in this chapter has three stages (Stage 1: Collecting returned products and transporting them to collection centers; Stage 2: Transporting returned products to inspection centers for checking; Stage 3: Shipping recoverable returned products to remanufacturing centers for further treatment), a chromosome consists of three segments. Each segment is used to obtain a transportation tree of a stage on the reverse supply chain network (Altiparmak et al., 2009). A feasible chromosome for the reverse logistics network design problem with four customer zones, three collection centers, two inspection centers, two remanufacturing centers, and two types of returned products is depicted in Figure 2.

Decoding is the process of mapping from chromosomes to candidate solutions. At each step of the decoding procedure, the highest priority in the chromosome is identified. The corresponding position reveals not only the type of the returned product but also the type of the network entity (source or depot) (Altiparmak et al., 2009). Considering the minimum distance, a depot (source)

is determined with respect to the chosen source (depot). The decoding procedures of 1st, 2nd and 3rd stages are given in Figures 3-5, respectively.

As an example of the decoding procedure, Figure 6 depicts a transportation tree for the first stage of the network with three customer zones and two collection centers along with the corresponding priority-based encoding. The data for the single-period problem with two types of returned products can be found in Tables 4-7.

As it is seen in Figure 6, the highest priority in the chromosome (i.e., 10) belongs to the returned product 2 and collection center 2. Customer zone 1 is the closest customer zone to collection center 2; so, $i^* = 1$. With respect to the step 5 of Procedure 1 (see Figure 3) available amount of returned product 2 is assigned ($X_{2121}^{IJ} = 163$) and availabilities on customer zone 1 and collection center 2 are updated: $r_{211} = 0$, $g_2^J = 127$. Considering the step 6 of Procedure 1, the value of $v_1(6)$ is set to 0. This process repeats until all returned products are collected. The number of vehicles of type 1 and the total transportation cost can be easily calculated ($TC_1 = 1907$). The value of $D_{\max}$ is 6.5; thus, $Z_2 = 676$. The trace table is given in Table 8.

5.2 Wagner and Whitin Algorithm

Considering the transportation costs and storage costs of returned products kept in collection and

---

Figure 2. An example of representation for the multi-stage, multi-product reverse logistics network

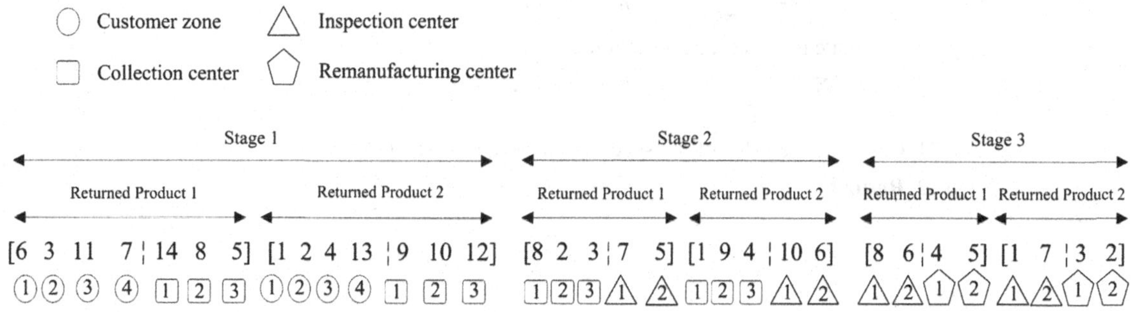

Figure 3. Decoding procedure for the 1st segment of the chromosome

Procedure 1: 1st stage decoding

Input: problem data

$v_1\left(p(i+j)\right)$: the first segment of the chromosome

Output: X_{pijt}^{IJ}; N_{1ijt}^{IJ}, $\forall p \in P$, $\forall i \in I$, $\forall j \in J$, $\forall t \in T$

TC_1: total transportation cost for the first stage

Z_2: value of the second objective function (coverage)

Follow the steps 1-8 for all $t \in T$

step 1. Consider intitial gene values; $X_{pijt}^{IJ} \leftarrow 0$, $\forall p \in P$, $\forall i \in I$, $\forall j \in J$

step 2. $h \leftarrow \arg\max\left\{v_1(e),\ e \in |P|(|I|+|J|)\right\}$; select a returned product

step 3. $p^* = \left\lceil h/(|I|+|J|)\right\rceil$; determine the type of the returned product

step 4. *If* $h \in I$ for the returned product p^*

then $i^* \leftarrow h$; select a customer zone

$$j^* \leftarrow \arg\min\left\{d_{i^*j}^{IJ}\middle| v_1\left((p^*-1).(|I|+|J|)+|I|+j\right) \neq 0, j \in J\right\};$$

select a collection center with the minimum distance

else $j^* \leftarrow h$; select a collection center

$$i^* \leftarrow \arg\min\left\{d_{ij^*}^{IJ}\middle| v_1\left((p^*-1).(|I|+|J|)+i\right) \neq 0, i \in I\right\};$$

select a customer zone with the minimum distance

step 5. $X_{p^*i^*j^*t}^{IJ} = \min\left\{r_{p^*i^*t}, g_{j^*}^{J}\right\}$; assign available amount of returned products

Update availabilities on customer zone (i^*) and collection center (j^*)

$$g_{j^*}^{J} = g_{j^*}^{J} - X_{p^*i^*j^*t}^{IJ};\quad r_{p^*i^*t} = r_{p^*i^*t} - X_{p^*i^*j^*t}^{IJ}$$

step 6. *If* $r_{p^*i^*t} = 0$ then $v_1\left((p^*-1).(|I|+|J|)+i^*\right) = 0$

If $g_{j^*}^{J} = 0$ then $v_1\left((p-1).(|I|+|J|)+|I|+j^*\right) = 0$, $\forall p \in P$

step 7. *If* $\exists \hat{p} \in P$ so that $r_{\hat{p}it} = 0$ for all $i \in I$

then $v_1\left((\hat{p}-1).(|I|+|J|)+|I|+j\right) = 0$, $\forall j \in J$

step 8. *If* $v_1\left((p-1).(|I|+|J|)+i+j\right) = 0$ for all $p \in P$, $i \in I$, $j \in J$

then goto step 9

else goto step 2

step 9. Determine the number of vehicles of type 1

$$N_{1ijt}^{IJ} = \left\lceil \sum_{p \in P} X_{pijt}^{IJ}/q_1\right\rceil,\ \forall i \in I,\ \forall j \in J$$

step 10. Calculate the total transportation cost for the first stage

$$TC_1 = \sum_{i \in I}\sum_{j \in J}\sum_{t \in T}\left(c_{11t} + 2c_{21t}d_{ij}^{IJ}\right)N_{1ijt}^{IJ}$$

step 11. Calculate the value of the second objective function (coverage)

step 12. **Return**

Figure 4. Decoding procedure for the 2nd segment of the chromosome

Procedure 2: 2nd stage decoding

Input: problem data

$v_2\big(p(j+l)\big)$: the second segment of the chromosome

r'_{pjt} : amount of returned product p that must be shipped from

collection center j in time period t, $\forall p \in P$, $\forall j \in J$, $\forall t \in T$

Output: X^{JL}_{pjlt}; N^{JL}_{2jlt}, $\forall p \in P$, $\forall j \in J$, $\forall l \in L$, $\forall t \in T$

TC_2: total transportation cost for the second stage

Follow the steps 1-8 for all $t \in T$

step 1. Consider intitial gene values; $X^{JL}_{pjlt} \leftarrow 0$, $\forall p \in P$, $\forall j \in J$, $\forall l \in L$

step 2. $h \leftarrow \arg\max\big\{v_2(e),\ e \in |P|\big(|J|+|L|\big)\big\}$; select a returned product

step 3. $p^* = \big\lceil h/\big(|J|+|L|\big)\big\rceil$; determine the type of the returned product

step 4. *If* $h \in J$ for the returned product p^*

then $j^* \leftarrow h$; select a collection center

$l^* \leftarrow \arg\min\Big\{d^{JL}_{j^*l}\Big|v_2\big((p^*-1).(|J|+|L|)+|J|+l\big)\neq 0, l \in L\Big\}$;

select an inspection center with the minimum distance

else $l^* \leftarrow h$; select an inspection center

$j^* \leftarrow \arg\min\Big\{d^{JL}_{jl^*}\Big|v_2\big((p^*-1).(|J|+|L|)+j\big)\neq 0, j \in J\Big\}$;

select a collection center with the minimum distance

step 5. $X^{JL}_{p^*j^*l^*t} = \min\big\{r'_{p^*j^*t}, g^L_{l^*}\big\}$; assign available amount of returned products

Update availabilities on collection center (j^*) and inspection center (l^*)

$g^L_{l^*} = g^L_{l^*} - X^{JL}_{p^*j^*l^*t}$;　$r'_{p^*j^*t} = r'_{p^*j^*t} - X^{JL}_{p^*j^*l^*t}$

step 6. *If* $r'_{p^*j^*t} = 0$ *then* $v_2\big((p^*-1).(|J|+|L|)+j^*\big) = 0$

If $g^L_{l^*} = 0$ *then* $v_2\big((p-1).(|J|+|L|)+|J|+l^*\big) = 0$, $\forall p \in P$

step 7. *If* $\exists \hat{p} \in P$ so that $r'_{\hat{p}jt} = 0$ for all $j \in J$

then $v_2\big((\hat{p}-1).(|J|+|L|)+|J|+l\big) = 0$, $\forall l \in L$

step 8. *If* $v_2\big((p-1).(|J|+|L|)+j+l\big)=0$ for all $p \in P$, $j \in J$, $l \in L$

then goto step 9

else goto step 2

step 9. Determine the number of vehicles of type 2

$N^{JL}_{2jlt} = \Big\lceil \sum_{p\in P} X^{JL}_{pjlt}/q_2\Big\rceil$, $\forall j \in J$, $\forall l \in L$

step 10. Calculate the total transportation cost for the second stage

$TC_2 = \sum_{j\in J}\sum_{l\in L}\sum_{t\in T}\big(c_{12t}+2c_{22t}d^{JL}_{jl}\big)N^{JL}_{2jlt}$

step 11. **Return**

Figure 5. Decoding procedure for the 3rd segment of the chromosome

Procedure 3: 3rd stage decoding

Input: problem data

$v_3\left(p(l+f)\right)$: the third segment of the chromosome

r''_{plt} : amount of remanufacturable returned product p that must be

shipped from inspection center l in time period t, $\forall p \in P$, $\forall l \in L$, $\forall t \in T$

Output: $X^{LF'}_{plft}$; N^{LF}_{2lft}, $\forall p \in P$, $\forall l \in L$, $\forall f \in F$, $\forall t \in T$

TC_3: total transportation cost for the third stage

Follow the steps 1-8 for all $t \in T$

step 1. Consider intitial gene values; $X^{LF'}_{plft} \leftarrow 0$, $\forall p \in P$, $\forall l \in L$, $\forall f \in F$

step 2. $h \leftarrow \arg\max\left\{v_3\left(e\right), \ e \in |P|\left(|L|+|F|\right)\right\}$; select a returned product

step 3. $p^* = \left\lceil h/\left(|L|+|F|\right)\right\rceil$; determine the type of the returned product

step 4. *If $h \in L$ for the returned product p^**

then $l^* \leftarrow h$; select an inspection center

$$f^* \leftarrow \arg\min\left\{d^{LF}_{l^*f}\Big|v_3\left(\left(p^*-1\right).\left(|L|+|F|\right)+|L|+f\right)\neq 0, f \in F\right\};$$

select a remanufacturing center with the minimum distance

else $f^* \leftarrow h$; select a remanufacturing center

$$l^* \leftarrow \arg\min\left\{d^{LF}_{lf^*}\Big|v_3\left(\left(p^*-1\right).\left(|L|+|F|\right)+l\right)\neq 0, l \in L\right\};$$

select an inspection with the minimum distance

step 5. $X^{LF'}_{p^*l^*f^*t} = r''_{p^*l^*t}$; assign available amount of returned products

Update availabilities on inspection center (l^*)

$$r''_{p^*l^*t} = r''_{p^*l^*t} - X^{LF'}_{p^*l^*f^*t}$$

step 6. *If $r''_{p^*l^*t} = 0$ then* $v_3\left(\left(p^*-1\right).\left(|L|+|F|\right)+l^*\right) = 0$

step 7. *If $\exists \hat{p} \in P$ so that $r''_{\hat{p}lt} = 0$ for all $l \in L$*

then $v_3\left(\left(\hat{p}-1\right).\left(|L|+|F|\right)+|L|+f\right) = 0$, $\forall f \in F$

step 8. *If $v_3\left(\left(p-1\right).\left(|L|+|F|\right)+l+f\right)=0$ for all $p \in P, l \in L, f \in F$*

then goto step 9

else goto step 2

step 9. Determine the number of vehicles of type 2

$$N^{LF}_{2lft} = \left\lceil \sum_{p\in P} X^{LF'}_{plft}/q_2 \right\rceil, \ \forall l \in L, \ \forall f \in F$$

step 10. Calculate the total transportation cost for the third stage

$$TC_3 = \sum_{l\in L}\sum_{f\in F}\sum_{t\in T}\left(c_{12t} + 2c_{22t}d^{LF}_{lf}\right)N^{LF}_{2lft}$$

step 11. **Return**

Figure 6. An example of the transportation tree and its encoding

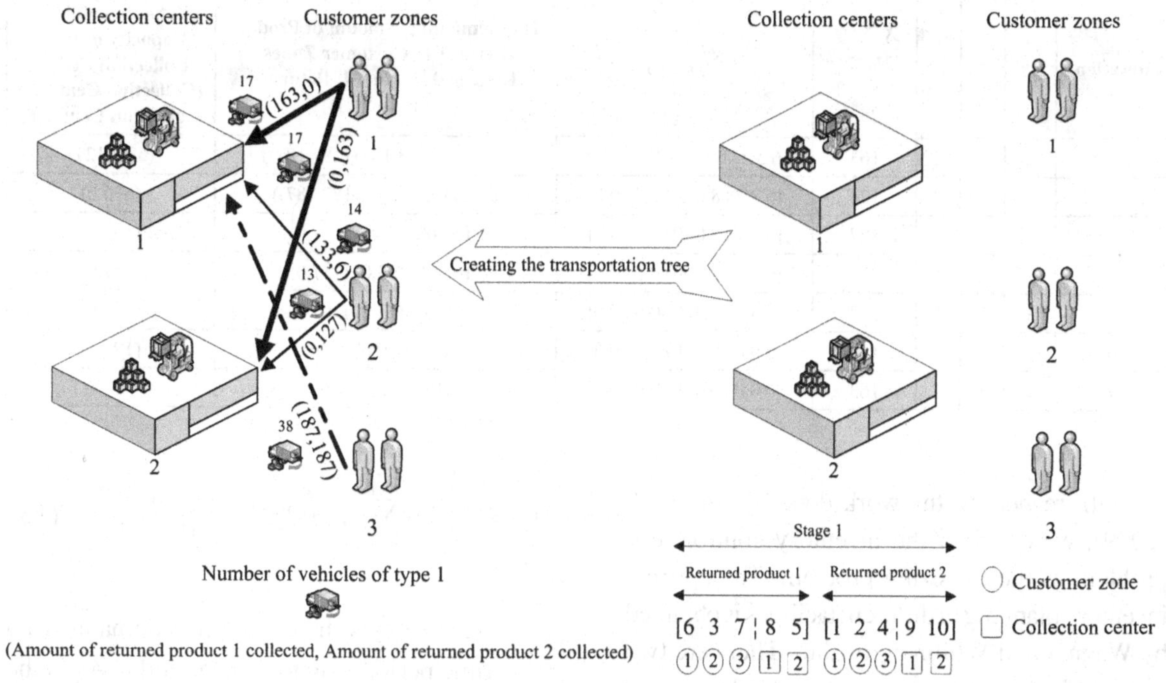

Table 4. The amount of returned products from customer zones

	Customer Zone 1	Customer Zone 2	Customer Zone 3
Returned product 1	163	133	187
Returned product 2	163	133	187

Table 6. The distance between customer zones and collection centers

	Collection Center 1	Collection Center 2
Customer zone 1	5	8
Customer zone 2	4	9
Customer zone 3	3	10

Table 5. The maximum storage capacity of collection centers

	Maximum Storage Capacity
Collection center 1	690
Collection center 2	290

Table 7. The rest of the problem data

	q_1	c_{111}	c_{211}	D_{max}
Value	10	9	1	6.5

inspection centers, it is economically necessary to calculate the optimal amount of stored product returns. Thus, we employ Wagner and Whitin algorithm to obtain appropriate amount of product returns that need to be stored with respect to the

related costs and maximum capacity of collection and inspection centers. In this section, we will describe the Wagner and Whitin algorithm. In Section 5.3, we will explain how this algorithm is incorporated into our proposed solution methodology.

Table 8. Trace table of the first stage decoding

Iteration	p^*	i^*	j^*	$X^{IJ}_{p^* i^* j^* 1}$	$v_1(p(i+j))$	The Remaining Amount of Product Returns in Customer Zones (Returned Product 1, Returned Product 2)	The Remaining Capacity of Each Collection Center (Collection Center 1, Collection Center 2)
1	2	1	2	163	[6 3 7 ¦ 8 5] [0 2 4 ¦ 9 10]	((163,0),(133,133),(187,187))	(690, 127)
2	2	2	2	127	[6 3 7 ¦ 8 0] [0 2 4 ¦ 9 0]	((163,0),(133,6),(187,187))	(690,0)
3	2	3	1	187	[6 3 7 ¦ 8 0] [0 2 0 ¦ 9 0]	((163,0),(133,6),(187,0))	(503,0)
4	2	2	1	6	[6 3 7 ¦ 8 0] [0 0 0 ¦ 0 0]	((163,0),(133,0),(187,0))	(497,0)
5	1	3	1	187	[6 3 0 ¦ 8 0] [0 0 0 ¦ 0 0]	((163,0),(133,0),(0,0))	(310,0)
6	1	2	1	133	[6 0 0 ¦ 8 0] [0 0 0 ¦ 0 0]	((163,0),(0,0),(0,0))	(177,0)
7	1	1	1	163	[0 0 0 ¦ 0 0] [0 0 0 ¦ 0 0]	((0,0),(0,0),(0,0))	(14,0)

With respect to the work done by Lin et al. (2009), we consider the inventory control sub-problem as the lot sizing problem. The optimal inventory planning of different facilities is obtained by Wagner and Whitin algorithm. There are two main differences between our work and the study carried out by Lin et al. (2009). The first difference is that we consider a multi-product case and not a single-product setting. And, the second difference is that after applying Wagner and Whitin algorithm, capacity limits of facilities will not be violated in this study. Thus, no repair mechanism is needed in order to obtain feasible solutions.

Wagner and Whitin algorithm was developed based on dynamic programming to tackle determinate time-varying demand problem (Lin et al., 2009). The algorithm may be generally stated as:

- Calculating varying ordering cost for all possible order quantities over a N-period planning horizon. This cost consists of storage and transportation costs. Let W_{ce} be the varying cost from time period c up to time period e incurred by an order placed in time period c to meet cumulative demand from time period c up to time period e. We can write:

$$W_{ce} = A_{ce} + \sum_{i''=c}^{e-1} H_{i''} \left(Q'_{ce} - Q'_{(i''+1),e} \right) \quad (16)$$

where Q'_{ce} is the cumulative demand from time period c up to time period e. A_{ce} is the cost incurred by transportation, and $H_{i''}$ is the unit storage cost from time period i'' up to time period $i'' + 1$. Let $g'_{ji''}$ be the remaining capacity of facility j in time period i''. To prevent the violation of capacity limits, we calculate (16) for any values of c and e, only if the following inequality is satisfied:

$$Q'_{ci''} \le g'_{ji''}, \quad i'' = c, (c+1), \dots, (e-1) \quad (17)$$

It must be noted that, in this study we assume that returned product p' is stored before returned product p'' if $p' \prec p''$ (e.g., returned product 1 is stored before returned product 2).

- Calculating f_e that is the minimum cost associated with the first time period up to time period e. We have $f_0 = 0$ and can write:

$$f_e = \min \left(W_{ce} + f_{c-1} \right), \quad c = 1, 2, \dots, e \quad (18)$$

f_N is the optimal ordering cost.

- Associated decisions can be found by backtracking. The last order is placed in time period N'. Backtracking can be given by:

$$f_N = W_{N'N} + f_{(N'-1)}$$
$$f_{(N'-1)} = W_{v',(N'-1)} + f_{(v'-1)}$$
$$\vdots \qquad\qquad (19)$$
$$f_{(u'-1)} = W_{1,(u'-1)} + f_0$$

5.3 Integrated Multi-Stage, Multi-Period, Multi-Product Decoding

The extended priority-based decoding method introduced in Section 5.1 and Wagner and Whitin algorithm are integrated in this section to obtain the allocation and inventory planning of facilities in a multi-stage, multi-period, multi-product setting. The decoding procedure is given in Figure 7.

5.4 A Multi-Objective Genetic Algorithm to Solve the Reverse Logistics Network Model

Genetic algorithms, as one of the evolutionary computation techniques, have been successfully used to solve many combinational optimization

Figure 7. The procedure of integrated multi-stage, multi-period, multi-product decoding

Procedure 4: Integrated multi-stage, multi-period, multi-product decoding

Input: problem data and the three-segment chromosome

Output: network configuration, inventory planning of facilities

step 1. **Call Procedure 1** to allocate customer zones and calculate the value of the second objective function

step 2. Obtain inventory planning of collection centers using Wagner and Whitin algorithm

step 3. **Call Procedure 2** to allocate collection centers

step 4. Consider the amount of returned products that are not remanufacturable;
Obtain inventory planning of inspection centers using Wagner and Whitin algorithm

step 5. **Call Procedure 3** to allocate inspection centers

step 6. Calculate the value of the first objective function (i.e., total cost)

step 7. **Return**

problems (Lee et al., 2009). Since a genetic algorithm is a population-based approach, it can be modified to find a set of non-dominated solutions in a single run and solve multi-objective optimization problems. The crossover operator of genetic algorithm can exploit structures of good solutions with respect to different objectives to create new non-dominated solutions in unexplored parts of the Pareto front (Konak et al., 2006).

In this chapter, we use NSGA-II (Deb, Agrawal, Pratap, & Meyarivan, 2002) which is one of the multi-objective genetic algorithms. The following sections describe the implementation of NSGA-II. It must be noted that we will not make any major changes to the standard NSGA-II. For more detailed information on NSGA-II, we refer the reader to Deb et al. (2002) and Konak et al. (2006).

5.4.1 Fitness Evaluation

In NSGA-II algorithm, the population is classified into non-dominated fronts $(F_1, F_2, \ldots)$ utilizing the concept of Pareto dominance in evaluating fitness. Then, a dummy fitness value is assigned to each front in a way that the worst fitness value assigned to F_i is better than the best fitness value assigned to F_{i+1}. F_1 is the Pareto front of population. In order to form non-dominated fronts, NSGA-II employs an efficient algorithm called fast non-dominated sorting algorithm (Konak et al., 2006).

5.4.2 Selection Mechanism

To build new population, NSGA-II algorithm starts from the first front and selects solutions until the number of selected solutions equals the population size. If the number of solutions in the first front is less than the population size, the algorithm goes through other fronts, respectively (Dehghanian & Mansour, 2009). In NSGA-II, a measure called crowding distance is used as tie-breaker in a selection technique named tournament selection operator: Two solutions are randomly selected; if

the solutions belong to the same non-dominated front, the solution with a higher crowding distance is the winner. Otherwise, the solution with the lower rank is selected (when all objective functions are minimization type) (Konak et al., 2006).

5.4.3 Crossover and Mutation

The crossover is performed to explore new solution space. We use a segment-based crossover operator (Altiparmak et al., 2009; Altiparmak, Gen, Lin, & Paksoy, 2006). In this operator, each segment of offspring is randomly selected with equal chance among the corresponding segments of parents. This crossover operator utilizes a binary mask. Its length is equal to the number of the stages in the reverse logistics network. "0" means that the first parent will transfer its genetic materials to the offspring, and "1" means that the second parent will transfer its genetic information to the offspring. Figure 8 provides an illustration of segment-based crossover operator.

Mutation is done to prevent the premature convergence and explore new solution space (Lin et al., 2009). As in the crossover operator, we use a segment-based mutation. In this operator, firstly, a decision about which segments will be mutated is made through the use of a binary mask with probability of 0.5. Then, selected segments are mutated. Swap operator is used for all the segments. This operator selects two genes from the corresponding segment and exchanges their places (Altiparmak et al., 2009, Altiparmak et al., 2006). Segment-based mutation operator is shown in Figure 9.

5.4.4 Overall Procedure of Proposed NSGA-II for Solving the Model

The overall pseudo-code procedure of the proposed NSGA-II for the reverse logistics network design problem is given in Figure 10.

Figure 8. An illustration of crossover operator

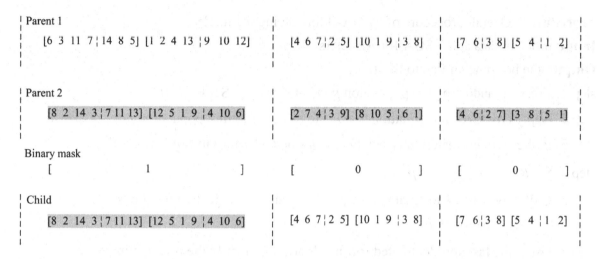

Figure 9. An illustration of mutation operator

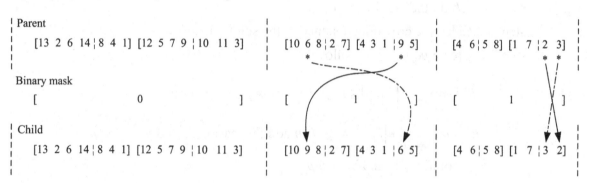

5.5 A Multi-Objective Evolutionary Strategy Algorithm to Solve the Reverse Logistics Network Model

Evolution strategies (*ES*) belong to the class of evolutionary solution algorithms. As the name suggests, these algorithms mimic features of natural evolution such as adapting to the environment and passing on genetic information to future generations (Master, Bräysy, & Dullaert, 2007). Mutation is the main evolutionary operation. Each offspring is created by the random Gaussian mutation of each gene, according to a vector of mutation variances which evolves over time (Bäck & Schwefel, 1993). Changes due to mutation are only accepted in the case of success. Selection of parents for reproduction is usually random. At each generation, λ offspring are generated from μ parents. One of the main strategies in this case is $(\lambda + \mu) - ES$. In this strategy, the combined parents and offspring ($1 \leq \mu \leq \lambda \prec \infty$) compete to find a place among the best μ individual used as parents for the next generation (Mayer, Belward, Widell, & Burrage, 1999).

Let $pop_{n_{gen}} = \left\{ X_{1,n_{gen}}, X_{2,n_{gen}}, ..., X_{\mu,n_{gen}} \right\}$ be a population at generation n_{gen} in which $X_{k,n_{gen}} = \left\{ x_{k,1,n_{gen}}, x_{k,2,n_{gen}}, ..., x_{k,D,n_{gen}} \right\}$, $k = 1, 2, ..., \mu$ is a solution vector in a continuous search space. Offspring population $pop'_{n_{gen}}$ consists of $Y_{i,n_{gen}} = \left\{ y_{i,1,n_{gen}}, y_{i,2,n_{gen}}, ..., y_{i,D,n_{gen}} \right\}$, $i = 1, 2, ..., \lambda$, where:

Figure 10. Overall procedure of proposed NSGA-II for the reverse logistics network design problem

Procedure 5: Overall procedure of NSGA-II for solving the model

Input: problem data and NSGA-II parameters

Output: the best-known Pareto front

step 1. Create a random parent population pop_0 of size n_{pop}; Set $n_{gen} = 0$

step 2. Apply crossover and mutation to pop_0 to create offspring population pop'_0 of size n_{pop}

step 3. *If* the stopping criterion is satisfied *then* stop and return to $pop_{n_{gen}}$

step 4. Set $R_{n_{gen}} = pop_{n_{gen}} \cup pop'_{n_{gen}}$

step 5. **Call Procedure 4** to obtain corresponding values of objective functions for each solution in $R_{n_{gen}}$

step 6. Using the fast non-dominated sorting algorithm, identify the non-dominated fronts $F_1, F_2, \ldots, F_k$ in $R_{n_{gen}}$

step 7. *For* $i''' = 1, \ldots, k$ do the the following steps:

step 7.1. Calculate crowding distance of the solutions in $F_{i''}$

step 7.2. Create $pop_{(n_{gen}+1)}$ as follows:

$$\text{If } \left| pop_{(n_{gen}+1)} \right| + \left| F_{i''} \right| \leq n_{pop} \text{ then set } pop_{(n_{gen}+1)} = pop_{(n_{gen}+1)} \cup F_{i''}$$

$$\text{If } \left| pop_{(n_{gen}+1)} \right| + \left| F_{i''} \right| \succ n_{pop} \text{ then add the least crowded } n_{pop} - \left| pop_{(n_{gen}+1)} \right|$$

$$\text{solutions from } F_{i''} \text{ to } pop_{(n_{gen}+1)}$$

step 8. Use binary tournament selection based on the crowding distance to select parents from $pop_{(n_{gen}+1)}$; Apply crossover and mutation to $pop_{(n_{gen}+1)}$ to create offspring population $pop'_{(n_{gen}+1)}$ of size n_{pop}

step 9. Set $n_{gen} = n_{gen} + 1$ and goto Step 3

$$y_{i,d,n_{gen}} = x_{i,d,n_{gen}} + z_d = x_{i,d,n_{gen}} + \sigma_{n_{gen}} N_d(0,1), \quad i = 1, 2, \ldots, \lambda, \quad d = 1, 2, \ldots, D \tag{20}$$

In (20), $N_d(0,1)$ is a random number from standardized normal distribution and is associated with dimension d. $\sigma_{n_{gen}}$ is called strategy parameter or mutation strength. It determines the expected distance of an offspring from the parent (Husseinzadeh Kashan, Jenabi, & Husseinzadeh Kashan, 2009).

The strategy parameter must be adapted during the search. 1/5 success rule is one of the schemes for this adaptation and is given by (Husseinzadeh Kashan et al., 2009):

$$\sigma_{n_{gen}} = \begin{cases} \sigma_{n_{gen}}/\alpha & if \quad n_{success} \succ 1/5 \\ \alpha.\sigma_{n_{gen}} & if \quad n_{success} \prec 1/5 \\ \sigma_{n_{gen}} & if \quad n_{success} = 1/5 \end{cases} \quad (21)$$

where, $n_{success}$ is the relative frequency of successful mutations over a certain period (n_{period}). For α, we usually have $0.8 \leq \alpha \leq 1$. An offspring generated from a successful mutation has a better fitness than the parent.

Since evolutionary strategy algorithm is a population-based approach, it can be modified to solve multi-objective optimization problems. Knowles and Corne (1999) and Costa and Oliveira (2002) have successfully implemented multi-objective evolutionary strategy algorithm (MO-*ES*) and acknowledged its good performance in solving combinatorial optimization problems. Motivated by this and the fact that MO-*ES* has never been used by researchers in the field of reverse logistics network design, we developed a MO-*ES* which is similar to the one proposed by Costa and Oliveira (2002). The main difference between MO-*ES* in this study and the one given by Costa and Oliveira (2002) is that we use clustering technique in the process of generating populations. Fitness evaluation is similar to that given in Section 5.4.1. Moreover, crowding distance measure is still used as tie-breaker in binary tournament selection. The following sections discuss important aspects of MO-*ES*.

5.5.1 Mutation Operator

In MO-*ES*, mutation operator works based on (20). If the mutated gene has a value less than 1, we set its value to 1 in order to maintain the feasibility of the solution.

To evaluate the improvements achieved through mutation, we compare the quality of corresponding Pareto fronts of two consecutive populations (i.e., $F_{1,n_{gen}}$ and $F_{1,(n_{gen}+1)}$) using a measure developed by Hyun, Kim, & Kim (1998).

Let $S_{n_{gen}}$ and $S_{n_{gen}+1}$ be the set of Pareto-solutions from two consecutive populations. Suppose S' is the set of non-dominated solutions obtained after combining $S_{n_{gen}}$ and $S_{n_{gen}+1}$. The quality measure is defined as $\left|\left(S_{n_{gen}+1} \cap S'\right)\right|/\left|S'\right|$ or $\left|\left(S_{n_{gen}} \cap S'\right)\right|/\left|S'\right|$ where $|X|$ denotes the cardinality of the set X. This measure calculates the contribution of $S_{n_{gen}}$ and $S_{n_{gen}+1}$ in construction of the final Pareto front. Thus, higher values of this measure are preferable.

5.5.2 MO-ES Implementation

MO-*ES* uses a fixed population size ($n_{pop} = \mu$). In generation n_{gen}, an offspring population $pop'_{n_{gen}}$ of size λ is created from parent population $pop_{n_{gen}}$. These two populations are combined into a bigger population. This combined population is sorted into non-dominated fronts. The next population $pop_{(n_{gen}+1)}$ is filled starting from solutions in F_1, then F_2, and so on as follows. Let k be the index of a non-dominated front F_k that $\left|F_1 \cup F_2 \cup ... \cup F_k\right| \leq n_{pop}$ and $\left|F_1 \cup F_2 \cup ... \cup F_k \cup F_{k+1}\right| \succ n_{pop}$. First, all solutions in fronts $F_1, F_2, ..., F_k$ are copied to $pop_{(n_{gen}+1)}$. Then, solutions in the last permissible front are clustered. Let $n_{remaining}$ be the number of remaining population slots to be filled. Suppose that $\left|F_{k+1}\right| = n_{F_{k+1}}$. By definition, we can claim that $n_{F_{k+1}} \geq n_{remaining}$. To choose $n_{remaining}$ solutions from $n_{F_{k+1}}$, $n_{remaining}$ clusters are formed from $n_{F_{k+1}}$ solutions and a representative solution is selected from each cluster. The reason to use clustering approach in MO-*ES* is similar to that given for clustering approach of SPEA algorithm (Zitzler & Thiele, 1999) that is, obtaining solutions with good (uniform) distribution. The main difference between clustering approach in this study and the one given for SPEA algorithm is that we perform the clustering based on four attributes: corresponding values of objective functions and corresponding values of crowding distance measures associated with each objective function. Indeed, we combine clustering and crowding distance mechanisms. Although this requires a larger computational time, we expect to obtain a better distributed set of Pareto-optimal solutions. In this research, we apply hierarchical clustering method with Euclidean distance and complete linkage. Detailed explanation on hierarchical clustering can be found in Han & Kamber (2006).

5.5.3 Overall Procedure of Proposed MO-ES for Solving the Model

The overall pseudo-code procedure of proposed MO-*ES* for the reverse supply chain network design problem is given in Figure 11.

6. COMPUTATIONAL RESULTS

In this section we compare the proposed multi-objective algorithms introduced in Section 5. Both algorithms were coded in Matlab R2007a and the computational experiments were carried out in a PC with 1.80-GHz Intel dual CPU and 3.25 GB of RAM.

6.1 Metrics for Comparing Non-Dominated Sets

To compare non-dominated sets, their desirable aspects must be identified. Zitzler, Deb, and Thiele (2000) discuss three goals that can be identified and measured:

- The distance of the resulting non-dominated set to the true Pareto front should be minimized;
- Solutions must have a good distribution (in most cases, uniform);
- For each objective function, a wide range of values should be covered by non-dominated solutions.

With these goals in mind, we employ five metrics. The first metric is the C metric which was introduced by Zitzler and Thiele (1999). Let A and B be two Pareto fronts. The function C maps the ordered pair (A, B) into the interval $[0,1]$. $C(A, B)$ is defined as:

$$C(A, B) = \frac{\left|\left\{b \in B \mid \exists a \in A : a \prec b\right\}\right|}{|B|} \qquad (22)$$

In (22), "$a \prec b$" means that the solution b is dominated by the solution a. $C(A, B)$ is not necessarily equal to $1 - C(B, A)$, and front A is better than front B if $C(A, B) \succ C(B, A)$.

The second and third metrics are D_{av} and D_{max}, respectively. These metrics were introduced in Arroyo and Armentano (2005). Let $ND_{NSGA-II}$ and ND_{MO-ES} be the set of non-dominated solutions from NSGA-II and MO-*ES* algorithms, respectively. Since the Pareto optimal set is not known, we define the reference set R as the non-dominated solutions of $ND_{NSGA-II} \cup ND_{MO-ES}$. The definitions of D_{av} and D_{max} are given below:

$$D_{av}(ND) = \frac{1}{|ND|} \sum_{x \in ND} \min_{x^* \in R} d(x, x^*) \qquad (23)$$

$$D_{max}(ND) = \max_{x \in ND} \left\{ \min_{x^* \in R} d(x, x^*) \right\} \qquad (24)$$

Figure 11. Overall procedure of proposed MO-ES for the reverse supply chain network design problem

Procedure 6: Overall procedure of MO-*ES* for solving the model

Input: problem data and MO-*ES* parameters

Output: the best-known Pareto front

step 1. Create a random parent population pop_0 of size $n_{pop} = \mu$; Set $n_{gen} = 0$

step 2. Apply crossover and mutation to pop_0 to create offspring population pop'_0 of size λ;
    Set $n_{success} = 0$, $n_{iteration} = 0$

step 3. *If* the stopping criterion is satisfied *then* stop and return to $pop_{n_{gen}}$

step 4. Set $R_{n_{gen}} = pop_{n_{gen}} \cup pop'_{n_{gen}}$

step 5. **Call Procedure 4** to obtain corresponding values of objective functions
    for each solution in $R_{n_{gen}}$

step 6. Using the fast non-dominated sorting algorithm, identify the non-dominated
    fronts $F_1, F_2, \ldots, F_k$ in $R_{n_{gen}}$

step 7. Save the non-dominated solutions that belong to F_1

step 8. *If* $n_{gen} \geq 1$ *then* compare the quality of corresponding Pareto fronts of two
    consecutive populations $pop_{n_{gen}}$ and $pop_{(n_{gen}-1)}$

    If the quality of the Pareto front at generation n_{gen} is better than the

        quality of the Pareto front at generation $(n_{gen}-1)$ *then* Set $n_{success} = n_{success} + 1$

step 9. *If* $n_{iteration} = n_{period}$ *then* update the strategy parameter; Set $n_{success} = 0$, $n_{iteration} = 0$

step 10. *For* $i''' = 1, \ldots, k$ do the the following steps:

    step 10.1. Calculate crowding distance of the solutions in $F_{i''}$

    step 10.2. Create $pop_{(n_{gen}+1)}$ as follows:

$$If \; \left|pop_{(n_{gen}+1)}\right| + \left|F_{i''}\right| \leq \mu \; then \; set \; pop_{(n_{gen}+1)} = pop_{(n_{gen}+1)} \cup F_{i''}$$

$$If \; \left|pop_{(n_{gen}+1)}\right| + \left|F_{i''}\right| \succ \mu \; then \; form \; \left(\mu - \left|pop_{(n_{gen}+1)}\right|\right) \; clusters$$

        from solutions in $F_{i''}$ and copy one representative solution
        from each cluster to $pop_{(n_{gen}+1)}$

step 11. Use binary tournament selection based on the crowding distance to select parents
    from $pop_{(n_{gen}+1)}$; Apply crossover and mutation to $pop_{(n_{gen}+1)}$ to create offspring
    population $pop'_{(n_{gen}+1)}$ of size λ

step 12. Set $n_{gen} = n_{gen} + 1$, $n_{iteration} = n_{iteration} + 1$ and goto Step 3 where, d is defined by:

$$d\left(\mathrm{x},\mathrm{x}^*\right) = \max_{k=1,\ldots,r}\left\{\frac{1}{\Delta_k}\left(x_k - x_k^*\right)\right\},$$
$$\mathrm{x} = \left(x_1, x_2, \ldots, x_r\right) \in \mathrm{ND},\ \mathrm{x}^* = \left(x_1^*, x_2^*, \cdots x_r^*\right) \in R$$

$$(25)$$

where, Δ_k is the range of the objective function f_k among all reference and heuristic solutions. D_{av}(ND) is the average distance from a solution $\mathrm{x}^* \in R$ to its closest solution in ND, and D_{max}(ND) is the maximum of the minimum distance from a solution $\mathrm{x}^* \in R$ to any solution in ND. Lower values of D_{av} and D_{max} are preferable (Dayou, Pu, & Ji, 2009).

The next metric is Schott's Spacing metric (*SS*) (Schott, 1995). The aim of this metric is to measure how evenly the solutions are distributed. For a bi-objective problem, this metric is given by:

$$SS = \sqrt{\frac{1}{n-1}\sum_{i=1}^{n}\left(d_i - \bar{d}\right)^2}$$

$$(26)$$

where

$$d_i = \min_{j}\left(\left|z_1^i\left(\mathrm{x}\right) - z_1^j\left(\mathrm{x}\right)\right| + \left|z_2^i\left(\mathrm{x}\right) - z_2^j\left(\mathrm{x}\right)\right|\right),$$
$$i, j = 1, 2, \ldots, n$$

$$(27)$$

$\bar{d}$ is the mean of all d_i and n is the size of the known Pareto front. The lower values of *SS* are preferable.

The last metric is the *N* metric which gives the number of non-dominated solutions that belong to the Pareto front (Hyun et al., 1998). Higher values of this metric are desirable.

6.2 Experiments Design

Fifteen test problems with different sizes were generated to evaluate the performance of proposed algorithms. The sizes and number of time periods were selected in the range of test problems in the recent literature (Ko & Evans, 2007; Lin et al., 2009; Pishvaee et al., 2010a; Pishvaee et al., 2010b). The sizes of the test problems and the number of time periods are listed in Table 9. It must be noted that two types of returned products were considered for computational experiments.

In small-size test problems, the locations of network entities were generated from a uniform distribution with minimum and maximum distances of 0 and 20, respectively on the x and y coordinate system. Similarly, for medium-size test problems the minimum and maximum distances were 0 and 40, respectively. Finally, in large-size test problems the locations of facilities and customer zones were generated from a uniform distribution with minimum and maximum distances 0 and 60, respectively on the x and y coordinate system.

Since all returned products must be collected in each time period, the total capacity of collection centers is calculated as $1.5 \times \max_{t \in T}\left\{\sum_{p \in P}\sum_{i \in I} r_{pit}\right\}$ and, then, is shared among all collection centers. Furthermore, it is possible that all collection centers collect and store returned products only, before the last time period and send the returned products to inspection centers in the last time period. Thus, the total capacity of inspection centers is calculated as $\sum_{p \in P}\sum_{i \in I}\sum_{t \in T} r_{pit}$ and, then, is shared among all inspection centers.

The range and values of other parameters are given in Table 10.

6.3 Parameter Setting for the Evolutionary Algorithms

The performance of evolutionary algorithms is generally influenced by the setting of the parameters affecting the behavior and the quality of convergence. Basically, we explored a wide

Table 9. Test problems' sizes and the number of time periods

Size of the Test Problem	Test Problem no.	No. of Customer Zones	No. of Potential Collection Centers	No. of Potential Inspection Centers	No. of Remanufacturing Centers	No. of Time Periods
Small	1	5	5	3	1	3
	2	7	12	5	1	3
	3	10	14	7	1	3
	4	13	17	8	1	3
	5	15	20	10	1	3
Medium	6	20	25	12	2	8
	7	30	40	18	2	8
	8	40	55	27	2	8
	9	45	64	28	2	8
	10	50	70	30	2	8
Large	11	60	80	40	3	15
	12	65	85	41	3	15
	13	70	90	43	3	15
	14	75	95	47	3	15
	15	80	100	50	3	15

Table 10. The range and values of parameters used in the test problems

Parameter	Range/Value	Parameter	Range/Value
γ	= 0.2	q_1	= 10
r_{pit}	$\approx \left(\text{Uniform}\left(80, 250\right) \times \text{Uniform}\left(0.75, 0.9\right)\right)$	q_2	= 12
s^J_{pj0}	= 0	c_{11t}	= 150 (for every time period)
s^L_{pl0}	= 0	c_{12t}	= 300 (for every time period)
fc^J_j	$\approx \text{Uniform}\left(200000, 450000\right)$	c_{21t}	= 50 (for every time period)
fc^L_l	$\approx \text{Uniform}\left(250000, 500000\right)$	c_{22t}	= 100 (for every time period)
cs^J_{pjt}	$\approx \text{Uniform}\left(1, 6\right)$	$D_{\max}$	= $\bar{d}^{IJ}_{ij}/2$ ($\bar{d}^{IJ}_{ij}$ is the mean of all d^{IJ}_{ij})
cs^L_{plt}	$\approx \text{Uniform}\left(7, 11\right)$		

range of parameter settings to obtain high quality solutions.

For NSGA-II, we consider the population size to be equal to 250. Different values are considered for the crossover rate: 0.7, 0.8 and 0.9. For the mutation rate three different values are considered too: 0.1, 0.2 and 0.3.

For MO-*ES*, we set μ and λ to 250. We consider n_{period} to be equal to 5. Different values are examined for the strategy parameter: 0.5, 1 and 1.5. For α we consider three values: 0.8, 0.9 and 0.98.

Moreover, both NSGA-II and MO-*ES* are stopped after the same execution time. In order to determine the execution time for each test problem, we conducted preliminary experiments. In these experiments and for each test problem, the execution of each algorithm went on until the number of non-dominated solutions in the Pareto front stopped varying. It must be noted that for each test problem and multi-objective algorithm, all possible combinations of parameter values (3^2 combinations for NSGA-II and 3^2 combinations for MO-*ES*) were tested too. Based on the results obtained from these experiments, an appropriate execution time was selected for solving each test problem. The average execution time for small, medium and large test problems is 1 hour and 15 minutes, 2 hours and 35 minutes and 4 hours and 30 minutes, respectively.

6.4 Results and Statistical Analysis

In order to obtain non-dominated solutions through the implementation of each proposed evolutionary algorithm, the following 2-step procedure was repeated 10 times:

1. Solving the test problem for all possible combinations of parameter values (i.e., 9 combinations) and saving the Pareto front in each case;

2. Combining the Pareto fronts obtained in step 1 to form the final Pareto front.

Considering the above 2-step procedure, 20 Pareto fronts were obtained for each test problem (10 Pareto fronts found by NSGA-II and 10 Pareto fronts found by MO-*ES*).

Five performance measures were used to compare the algorithms. Furthermore, for each performance measure, we have considered applying Friedman and Iman-Davenport tests in order to see whether there are global differences in the obtained results. If the *p*-values of these two tests are smaller than the level of significance, the null-hypothesis which states that the obtained results are equivalent is rejected. Then, we proceed with two post-hoc tests, namely Wilcoxon paired signed-rank test and Nemenyi test, to identify concrete differences between the proposed algorithms (the null-hypothesis is that both algorithms perform equally well). It must be noted that all these statistical tests are non-parametric and the level of significance is 0.05 for all statistical tests. Moreover, average values of performance measures are considered for the implementation of the statistical tests. Finally, for detailed information on the aforementioned statistical tests, we refer the reader to Sheskin (2003), Devore (2012), García, Molina, Lozano and Herrera (2009) and Nemenyi (1963).

Table 11 shows the best and average values of the *N* metric. Table 12 summarizes the results of statistical tests applied to the obtained data from Table 11. Based on Tables 11 and 12, we can say that MO-*ES* has a better performance than NSGA-II.

Best and average values of the *SS* metric are illustrated in Table 13. The results of statistical tests applied to the obtained data from Table 13 are shown in Table 14. Based on Tables 13 and 14, it can be said that for this performance measure MO-*ES* outperforms NSGA-II.

Best and average values of the *C* metric are given in Table 15. The results of statistical tests

Table 11. Best and average values of the N metric

Test Problem no.	NSGA-II		MO-*ES*	
	Best	Average	Best	Average
1	19	15.7	19	16.7
2	11	9.9	12	10.1
3	9	7.7	13	12.3
4	15	14.2	17	15.3
5	19	12.7	46	33.3
6	18	16	30	27.3
7	14	9.8	29	18.9
8	12	8.3	20	17.7
9	15	12.7	31	20.7
10	16	8.7	35	23
11	9	6	22	20
12	12	7.3	19	14.2
13	13	8.7	18	15.3
14	10	5.8	10	4.1
15	6	4.7	10	6

Table 12. Results of statistical tests applied to the obtained data from Table 11

Friedman test		Iman-Davenport test	
Statistic value	*p*-value	Statistic value	*p*-value
11.27	0.0008	42.3	0.0001
	Post-hoc tests		
Wilcoxon paired signed-rank test	Nemenyi test		
p-value	Statistic value	ψ^*	
0.000061035	0.5096	0.86	
	*Absolute value of the difference of the average ranks: $$\psi = \left| \bar{R}_{\text{NSGA-II}} - \bar{R}_{\text{MO}-ES} \right|$$ If $\psi \geq$ statistic value, the null-hypothesis is rejected.		

applied to the obtained data from Table 15 are summarized in Table 16. Based on Tables 15 and 16, we can say that NSGA-II performs better than MO-*ES*.

Table 17 gives the best and average values of the D_{av} metric. Table 18 summarizes the results of statistical tests applied to the obtained data from Table 17. Based on Tables 17 and 18, we can say that NSGA-II has a better performance than MO-*ES*.

Best and average values of the D_{max} metric are illustrated in Table 19. The results of statistical tests applied to the obtained data from Table 19 are shown in Table 20. Based on Tables 19 and 20, it can be said that for this performance measure NSGA-II outperforms MO-*ES*.

From our experiments, we have observed that for the *N* and *SS* metrics MO-*ES* outperforms NSGA-II and for the C, D_{av} and D_{max} metrics NSGA-II provides better performance than MO-*ES*. Applying MO-*ES* leads to well-spread solutions and larger number of solutions in the Pareto front. One of the reasons for obtaining more non-dominated solutions in the Pareto front can be the better mechanism of neighborhood exploration. Moreover, combination of clustering and crowding distance mechanisms has resulted in better distribution and diversity of obtained solutions. On the other hand, NSGA-II obtains a better approximation of the true Pareto front. Perhaps, the reason behind the inferior performance of MO-*ES* is its simple search strategy.

7. CONCLUSION AND FUTURE RESEARCH DECISIONS

The number of scientific publications in the field of reverse logistics has been steadily growing due to increasing environmental and economical concern. After providing a brief introduction to the basic concepts of reverse logistics, we addressed reverse logistics network design problem for treating a remanufacturing problem that is faced by a company engaged in product recovery operations. The problem can be viewed as a location allocation problem combined with lot sizing problem.

Table 13. Best and average values of the SS metric

Test Problem no.	NSGA-II		MO-ES	
	Best	Average	Best	Average
1	0.0156	0.0360	0.0112	0.0203
2	0.0102	0.0308	0.0093	0.0227
3	0.0035	0.0119	0.0209	0.0312
4	0.0116	0.0275	0.0108	0.0197
5	0.0112	0.0200	0.0086	0.0121
6	0.0128	0.0185	0.0096	0.0121
7	0.0119	0.0165	0.0050	0.0094
8	0.0114	0.0138	0.0041	0.0087
9	0.0126	0.0176	0.0164	0.0184
10	0.0121	0.0157	0.0073	0.0119
11	0.0046	0.0132	0.0065	0.0132
12	0.0061	0.0147	0.0081	0.0134
13	0.0075	0.0253	0.0157	0.0312
14	0.0070	0.0245	0.0135	0.0173
15	0.0075	0.0267	0.0077	0.0186

Table 15. Best and average values of the C metric

Test Problem no.	NSGA-II		MO-ES	
	Best	Average	Best	Average
1	0.6667	0.4137	0.8571	0.4440
2	07235	0.6472	0.4813	0.0890
3	0.6923	0.4499	0.8889	0.2610
4	0.9629	0.8993	0.7299	0.4263
5	0.9688	0.9097	0.1000	0.0170
6	0.7586	0.5129	0.4615	0.2166
7	0.8031	0.5382	0.8713	0.1656
8	0.7500	0.5649	0.5000	0.0926
9	0.7787	0.5154	0.4922	0.1851
10	0.8286	0.5860	0.6000	0.1819
11	0.9500	0.7398	0.0000	0.0000
12	0.8432	0.4315	0.8611	0.5284
13	0.8333	0.4059	0.8571	0.3101
14	0.8966	0.6982	0.7283	0.4093
15	1.0000	0.5296	0.4000	0.1222

Table 14. Results of statistical tests applied to the obtained data from Table 13

Friedman Test		Iman-Davenport Test	
Statistic value	p-value	Statistic value	p-value
4.57	0.0325	6.13	0.0267
Post-hoc tests			
Wilcoxon paired signed-rank test	Nemenyi test		
p-value	Statistic value		ψ^*
0.0419	0.5096		0.54
	*Absolute value of the difference of the average ranks: $$\psi = \left| \bar{R}_{\text{NSGA-II}} - \bar{R}_{\text{MO}-ES} \right|$$ If $\psi \geq$ statistic value, the null-hypothesis is rejected.		

Table 16. Results of statistical tests applied to the obtained data from Table 15

Friedman Test		Iman-Davenport Test	
Statistic value	p-value	Statistic value	p-value
8.07	0.0045	16.30	0.0012
Post-hoc tests			
Wilcoxon paired signed-rank test	Nemenyi test		
p-value	Statistic value		ψ^*
0.00042725	0.5096		0.74
	*Absolute value of the difference of the average ranks: $$\psi = \left| \bar{R}_{\text{NSGA-II}} - \bar{R}_{\text{MO}-ES} \right|$$ If $\psi \geq$ statistic value, the null-hypothesis is rejected.		

Table 17. Best and average values of the D_{av} metric

Test Problem no.	NSGA-II		MO-ES	
	Best	Average	Best	Average
1	0.0450	0.0579	0.0264	0.0447
2	0.0449	0.0685	0.0547	0.0788
3	0.0348	0.0764	0.0808	0.1352
4	0.0315	0.0516	0.0627	0.1160
5	0.0234	0.0448	0.0960	0.1399
6	0.0286	0.0378	0.0433	0.0673
7	0.0372	0.0619	0.0477	0.0742
8	0.0485	0.0902	0.0444	0.1330
9	0.0449	0.0781	0.0457	0.0952
10	0.0229	0.0737	0.0500	0.1092
11	0.0337	0.0818	0.0995	0.1564
12	0.0414	0.0949	0.0766	0.1820
13	0.0238	0.0661	0.0490	0.0978
14	0.1019	0.2023	0.0840	0.2014
15	0.1288	0.2154	0.0340	0.2666

Table 19. Best and average values of the D_{max}

Test Problem no.	NSGA-II		MO-ES	
	Best	Average	Best	Average
1	0.1199	0.2114	0.1101	0.1555
2	0.0618	0.1793	0.1362	0.3844
3	0.0585	0.1489	0.2749	0.4753
4	0.1174	0.2000	0.2841	0.4156
5	0.0812	0.1527	0.3542	0.5265
6	0.0740	0.1393	0.1046	0.2517
7	0.0776	0.1571	0.1453	0.3659
8	0.0915	0.2544	0.1078	0.3027
9	0.0875	0.2174	0.1636	0.2683
10	0.0677	0.2360	0.1674	0.4395
11	0.0765	0.1379	0.3533	0.5436
12	0.1677	0.2870	0.0941	0.4467
13	0.0489	0.1831	0.2341	0.3929
14	0.2015	0.3063	0.1808	0.3008
15	0.2166	0.3322	0.0893	0.4278

Table 18. Results of statistical tests applied to the obtained data from Table 17

Friedman Test		Iman-Davenport Test	
Statistic value	p-value	Statistic value	p-value
8.07	0.0045	16.30	0.0012
	Post-hoc tests		
Wilcoxon paired signed-rank test	Nemenyi test		
p-value	Statistic value	ψ^*	
0.00061035	0.5096	0.74	
	*Absolute value of the difference of the average ranks: $$\psi = \left| \bar{R}_{\text{NSGA-II}} - \bar{R}_{\text{MO-}ES} \right|$$ If $\psi \geq$ statistic value, the null-hypothesis is rejected.		

Table 20. Results of statistical tests applied to the obtained data from Table 19

Friedman Test		Iman-Davenport Test	
Statistic value	p-value	Statistic value	p-value
8.07	0.0045	16.30	0.0012
	Post-hoc tests		
Wilcoxon paired signed-rank test	Nemenyi test		
p-value	Statistic value	ψ^*	
0.00061035	0.5096	0.74	
	*Absolute value of the difference of the average ranks: $$\psi = \left| \bar{R}_{\text{NSGA-II}} - \bar{R}_{\text{MO-}ES} \right|$$ If $\psi \geq$ statistic value, the null-hypothesis is rejected.		

This chapter presented a bi-objective mixed integer programming model for the multi-stage, multi-period, multi-product reverse supply chain network, with one objective related to total cost and the other related to coverage and customer satisfaction.

Basically, location allocation problem is NP-hard, and the combination with inventory control problem makes the search space of the problem much larger and more complex. To solve the proposed model and find the non-dominated set of solutions, two multi-objective evolutionary algorithms (NSGA-II and MO-*ES*) were designed based on an extended priority-based encoding and decoding approach. In this approach, the decoding method and Wagner and Whitin algorithm are integrated into one procedure which is able to solve the subproblems of location allocation and inventory control at the same time. Moreover, we implemented Wagner and Whitin algorithm in way that the resulting solutions are all feasible.

Computational results were generated from a set of fifteen test problems and the proposed algorithms were compared based on the number, quality and distribution of non-dominated solutions that belong to the Pareto front. According to the five performance measures, applying MO-*ES* leads to well-spread solutions and larger number of solutions in the Pareto front; but, results in poor approximation of the true Pareto front compared to NSGA-II. In addition to the combination of clustering and crowding distance mechanisms which was included in MO-*ES*, it is necessary to develop more sophisticated strategies that could improve the true Pareto approximation by MO-*ES*.

For the future research, the model can be expanded to include the element of risk and uncertainty involved in the reverse logistics network design problem. Furthermore, priority-based encoding method can be used in other multi-objective algorithms such as multi-objective tabu search or multi-objective scatter search, which in turn may offer promising avenues for developing richer reverse logistics networks.

REFERENCES

Akçali, E., Çetinkaya, S., & Üster, H. (2009). Network design for reverse and closed-loop supply chains: An annotated bibliography of models and solution approaches. *Networks*. doi:10.1002/net.20267.

Altiparmak, F., Gen, M., Lin, L., & Karaoglan, I. (2009). A steady-state genetic algorithm for multi-product supply chain network design. *Computers & Industrial Engineering*, *56*, 521–537. doi:10.1016/j.cie.2007.05.012.

Altiparmak, F., Gen, M., Lin, L., & Paksoy, T. (2006). A genetic algorithm approach for multi-objective optimization of supply chain networks. *Computers & Industrial Engineering*, *51*, 196–215. doi:10.1016/j.cie.2006.07.011.

Aras, N., & Aksen, D. (2008). Locating collection centers for distance-and-incentive-dependent returns. *International Journal of Production Economics*, *111*, 316–333. doi:10.1016/j.ijpe.2007.01.015.

Aras, N., Aksen, D., & Tanuğur, A. G. (2008). Locating collection centers for incentive-dependent returns under a pick-up policy with capacitated vehicles. *European Journal of Operational Research*, *191*, 1223–1240. doi:10.1016/j.ejor.2007.08.002.

Arroyo, J. E. C., & Armentano, V. A. (2005). Genetic local search for multi-objective flowshop scheduling problems. *European Journal of Operational Research*, *167*, 717–738. doi:10.1016/j.ejor.2004.07.017.

Bäck, T., & Schwefel, H. P. (1993). An overview of evolutionary algorithms for parameter optimization. *Evolutionary Computation*, *1*, 1–23. doi:10.1162/evco.1993.1.1.1.

Barros, A. I., Dekker, R., & Scholten, V. (1998). A two-level network for recycling sand: A case study. *European Journal of Operational Research*, *110*, 199–214. doi:10.1016/S0377-2217(98)00093-9.

Beamon, B. M., & Fernandes, C. (2004). Supply-chain network configuration for product recovery. *Production Planning and Control, 15*, 270–281. doi:10.1080/09537280410001697701.

Berman, O., Drezner, Z., & Krass, D. (2010). Generalized coverage: New developments in covering location models. *Computers & Operations Research, 37*, 1675–1687. doi:10.1016/j.cor.2009.11.003.

Chu, L. K., Shi, Y., Lin, S., Sculli, D., & Ni, J. (2009). Fuzzy chance-constrained programming model for a multi- echelon reverse logistics network for household appliances. *The Journal of the Operational Research Society*. doi: doi:10.1057/jors.2008.162.

Church, R., & Revelle, C. (1974). The maximal covering location problem. *Papers / Regional Science Association. Regional Science Association. Meeting, 32*, 101–118. doi:10.1007/BF01942293.

Costa, L., & Oliveira, P. (2002). An evolution strategy for multiobjective optimization. In *The IEEE Congress: Evolutionary computation* (pp. 97-102). IEEE.

Davis, P. S., & Ray, T. L. (1969). A branch-and-bound algorithm for the capacitated facilities location problem. *Naval Research Logistics Quarterly, 16*, 331–344.

Dayou, L., Pu, Y., & Ji, Y. (2009). Development of a multiobjective GA for advanced planning and scheduling problem. *International Journal of Advanced Manufacturing Technology, 42*, 974–992. doi:10.1007/s00170-008-1653-8.

Deb, K., Agrawal, S., Pratap, A., & Meyarivan, T. (2002). A fast elitist non-dominated sorting genetic algorithm for multi-objective optimization: NSGA-II. *IEEE Transactions on Evolutionary Computation, 6*, 182–197. doi:10.1109/4235.996017.

Dehghanian, F., & Mansour, S. (2009). Designing sustainable recovery network of end-of-life products using genetic algorithm. *Resources, Conservation and Recycling, 53*, 559–570. doi:10.1016/j.resconrec.2009.04.007.

Demirel, N. Ö., & Gökçen, H. (2008). A mixed integer programming model for remanufacturing in reverse logistics environment. *International Journal of Advanced Manufacturing Technology, 39*, 1197–1206. doi:10.1007/s00170-007-1290-7.

Devore, J. L. (2012). *Probability and statistics for engineering and the sciences* (8th ed.). Boston, MA: Brooks/Cole Cengage Learning..

Du, F., & Evans, G. W. (2008). A bi-objective reverse logistics network analysis for post-sale service. *Computers & Operations Research, 35*, 2617–2634. doi:10.1016/j.cor.2006.12.020.

El-Sayed, M., Afia, N., & El-Kharbotly, A. (2010). A stochastic model for forward–reverse logistics network design under risk. *Computers & Industrial Engineering, 58*, 423–431. doi:10.1016/j.cie.2008.09.040.

Fleischmann, M., Krikke, H. R., Dekker, R., & Flapper, S. D. P. (2000). A characterisation of logistics networks for product recovery. *Omega, 28*, 653–666. doi:10.1016/S0305-0483(00)00022-0.

García, S., Molina, D., Lozano, M., & Herrera, F. (2009). A study on the use of non-parametric tests for analyzing the evolutionary algorithms' behavior: A case study on the CEC'2005 special session on real parameter optimization. *Journal of Heuristics, 15*, 617–644. doi:10.1007/s10732-008-9080-4.

Gen, M., Altiparmak, F., & Lin, L. (2006). A genetic algorithm for two-stage transportation problem using priority-based encoding. *OR-Spektrum, 28*, 337–354. doi:10.1007/s00291-005-0029-9.

Guide, V. D. Jr, Jayaraman, V., Srivastava, R., & Benton, W. C. (2000). Supply chain management for recoverable manufacturing systems. *Interfaces, 30,* 125–142. doi:10.1287/inte.30.3.125.11656.

Guide, V. D. R., Teunter, R., & Wassenhove, L. N. (2003). Matching demand and supply to maximize profits from remanufacturing. *Manufacturing and Service Operations Management, 5,* 303–316. doi:10.1287/msom.5.4.303.24883.

Han, J., & Kamber, M. (2006). *Data mining: Concepts and techniques.* San Francisco: Morgan Kaufmann Publishers..

Husseinzadeh Kashan, A., Jenabi, M., & Husseinzadeh Kashan, M. (2009). *A new solution approach for grouping problems based on evolution strategies.* Paper presented at International Conference of Soft Computing and Pattern Recognition. doi: 10.1109/SoCPaR.2009.29

Hyun, C. J., Kim, Y., & Kim, Y. K. (1998). A genetic algorithm for multiple objective sequencing problem in mixed model assembly lines. *Computers & Operations Research, 25,* 675–690. doi:10.1016/S0305-0548(98)00026-4.

Jayaraman, V., Patterson, R. A., & Rolland, E. (2003). The design of reverse distribution networks: Models and solution procedures. *European Journal of Operational Research, 150,* 128–149. doi:10.1016/S0377-2217(02)00497-6.

Kannan, G., Sasikumar, P., & Devika, K. (2010). A genetic algorithm approach for solving a closed loop supply chain model: A case of battery recycling. *Applied Mathematical Modelling, 34,* 655–670. doi:10.1016/j.apm.2009.06.021.

Knowles, J. D., & Corne, D. W. (1999). The pareto archived evolution strategy: A new baseline algorithm for Pareto multiobjective optimization. In *The IEEE congress: Evolutionary computation* (pp. 98–105). IEEE..

Ko, H. J., & Evans, G. W. (2007). A genetic algorithm-based heuristic for the dynamic integrated forward/reverse logistics network for 3PLs. *Computers & Operations Research, 34,* 346–366. doi:10.1016/j.cor.2005.03.004.

Konak, A., Coit, D. W., & Smith, A. E. (2006). Multi-objective optimization using genetic algorithms: A tutorial. *Reliability Engineering & System Safety, 91,* 992–1007. doi:10.1016/j.ress.2005.11.018.

Lee, D. H., & Dong, M. (2008). A heuristic approach to logistics network design for end-of-lease computer products recovery. *Transportation Research Part E, Logistics and Transportation Review, 44,* 455–474. doi:10.1016/j.tre.2006.11.003.

Lee, J. E., Gen, M., & Rhee, K. G. (2009). Network model and optimization of reverse logistics by hybrid genetic algorithm. *Computers & Industrial Engineering, 56,* 951–964. doi:10.1016/j.cie.2008.09.021.

Lieckens, K., & Vandaele, N. (2007). Reverse logistics network design with stochastic lead times. *Computers & Operations Research, 34,* 395–416. doi:10.1016/j.cor.2005.03.006.

Lin, L., Gen, M., & Wang, X. (2009). Integrated multistage logistics network design by using hybrid evolutionary algorithm. *Computers & Industrial Engineering, 56,* 854–873. doi:10.1016/j.cie.2008.09.037.

Louwers, D., Kip, B. J., Peters, E., Souren, F., & Flapper, S. D. P. (1999). A facility location allocation model for reusing carpet materials. *Computers & Industrial Engineering, 36,* 855–869. doi:10.1016/S0360-8352(99)00168-0.

Lu, Z., & Bostel, N. (2007). A facility location model for logistics systems including reverse flows: The case of remanufacturing activities. *Computers & Operations Research, 34,* 299–323. doi:10.1016/j.cor.2005.03.002.

Marín, A., & Pelegrín, B. (1998). The return plant location problem: modelling and resolution. *European Journal of Operational Research, 104,* 375–392. doi:10.1016/S0377-2217(97)00192-6.

Master, D., Bräysy, O., & Dullaert, W. (2007). A multi-parametric evolution strategies algorithm for vehicle routing problems. *Expert Systems with Applications, 32,* 508–517. doi:10.1016/j.eswa.2005.12.014.

Mayer, D. G., Belward, J. A., Widell, H., & Burrage, K. (1999). Survival of the fittest - Genetic algorithms versus evolution strategies in the optimization of systems models. *Agricultural Systems, 60,* 113–122. doi:10.1016/S0308-521X(99)00022-0.

Min, H., Ko, C. S., & Ko, H. J. (2006a). The spatial and temporal consolidation of returned products in a closed-loop supply chain network. *Computers & Industrial Engineering, 51,* 309–320. doi:10.1016/j.cie.2006.02.010.

Min, H., & Ko, H. J. (2008). The dynamic design of a reverse logistics network from the perspective of third-party logistics service providers. *International Journal of Production Economics, 113,* 176–192. doi:10.1016/j.ijpe.2007.01.017.

Min, H., Ko, H. J., & Ko, C. S. (2006b). A genetic algorithm approach to developing the multi-echelon reverse logistics network for product returns. *Omega, 34,* 56–69. doi:10.1016/j.omega.2004.07.025.

Mutha, A., & Pokharel, S. (2009). Strategic network design for reverse logistics and remanufacturing using new and old product modules. *Computers & Industrial Engineering, 56,* 334–346. doi:10.1016/j.cie.2008.06.006.

Nemenyi, P. B. (1963). *Distribution-free multiple comparisons*. (Doctoral dissertation). Princeton University, Princeton, NJ.

Pishvaee, M. S., Kianfar, K., & Karimi, B. (2010a). Reverse logistics network design using simulated annealing. *International Journal of Advanced Manufacturing Technology, 47,* 269–281. doi:10.1007/s00170-009-2194-5.

Pishvaee, M. S., & Torabi, S. A. (2010). A possibilistic programming approach for closed-loop supply chain network design under uncertainty. *Fuzzy Sets and Systems, 161,* 2668–2683. doi:10.1016/j.fss.2010.04.010.

Pishvaee, M. S., Zanjirani Farahani, R., & Dullaert, W. (2010b). A memetic algorithm for bi-objective integrated forward/reverse logistics network design. *Computers & Operations Research, 37,* 1100–1112. doi:10.1016/j.cor.2009.09.018.

Pokharel, S., & Mutha, A. (2009). Perspectives in reverse logistics: A review. *Resources, Conservation and Recycling, 53,* 175–182. doi:10.1016/j.resconrec.2008.11.006.

Qin, Z., & Ji, X. (2010). Logistics network design for product recovery in fuzzy environment. *European Journal of Operational Research, 202,* 479–490. doi:10.1016/j.ejor.2009.05.036.

Salema, M. I. G., Póvoa, A. P. B., & Novais, A. Q. (2006). A warehouse-based design model for reverse logistics. *The Journal of the Operational Research Society, 57,* 615–629. doi:10.1057/palgrave.jors.2602035.

Salema, M. I. G., Póvoa, A. P. B., & Novais, A. Q. (2007). An optimization model for the design of a capacitated multi-product reverse logistics network with uncertainty. *European Journal of Operational Research, 179,* 1063–1077. doi:10.1016/j.ejor.2005.05.032.

Salema, M. I. G., Póvoa, A. P. B., & Novais, A. Q. (2009). A strategic and tactical model for closed-loop supply chains. *OR-Spektrum, 31,* 573–599. doi:10.1007/s00291-008-0160-5.

Salema, M. I. G., Póvoa, A. P. B., & Novais, A. Q. (2010). Simultaneous design and planning of supply chains with reverse flows: A generic modelling framework. *European Journal of Operational Research*, *203*, 336–349. doi:10.1016/j. ejor.2009.08.002.

Sasikumar, P., Kannan, G., & Noorul Haq, A. (2010). A multi-echelon reverse logistics network design for product recovery - A case of truck tire remanufacturing. *International Journal of Advanced Manufacturing Technology*, *49*, 1223–1234. doi:10.1007/s00170-009-2470-4.

Schott, J. R. (1995). *Fault tolerant design using single and multicriteria genetic algorithm optimization*. (Master's thesis). Massachusetts Institute of Technology, Cambridge, MA.

Sheskin, D. J. (2003). *Handbook of parametric and non-parametric statistical procedures* (3rd ed.). Boca Raton, FL: Chapman & Hall/CRC. doi:10.1201/9781420036268.

Thierry, M., Salomon, M., Van Nunen, J., & Van Waasenhove, L. (1995). Strategic issues in product recovery management. *California Management Review*, *37*, 114–135. doi:10.2307/41165792.

Üster, H., Easwaran, G., Akçali, E., & Çetinkaya, S. (2007). *Benders decomposition with alternative multiple cuts for a multi-product closed-loop supply chain network design model*. Naval Research Logistics..

Villegas, J. G., Palacios, F., & Medaglia, A. L. (2006). Solution methods for the bi-objective (cost-coverage) unconstrained facility location problem with an illustrative example. *Annals of Operations Research*, *147*, 109–141. doi:10.1007/ s10479-006-0061-4.

Wang, H. F., & Hsu, H. W. (2010). A closed-loop logistic model with a spanning-tree based genetic algorithm. *Computers & Operations Research*, *37*, 376–389. doi:10.1016/j.cor.2009.06.001.

Yongsheng, Z., & Shouyang, W. (2008). Generic model of reverse logistics network design. *International Journal of Transportation Systems Engineering and Information Technology*, *8*, 71–78. doi:10.1016/S1570-6672(08)60025-2.

Zanjirani Farahani, R., SteadieSeifi, M., & Asgari, N. (2010). Multiple criteria facility location problems: A survey. *Applied Mathematical Modelling*, *34*, 1689–1709. doi:10.1016/j.apm.2009.10.005.

Zitzler, E., Deb, K., & Thiele, L. (2000). Comparison of multiobjective evolutionary algorithms: Empirical results. *Evolutionary Computation*, *8*, 173–195. doi:10.1162/106365600568202 PMID:10843520.

Zitzler, E., & Thiele, L. (1999). Multiobjective evolutionary algorithms: A comparative case study and the strength Pareto approach. *IEEE Transactions on Evolutionary Computation*, *3*, 257–271. doi:10.1109/4235.797969.

Compilation of References

Aggarwal, K. K., Singh, Y., Chandra, P., & Puri, M. (2005). Bayesian regularization in a neural network model to estimate lines of code using function points. *Journal of Computer Sciences*, *1*(4), 505–509.

Ahern, D. M., Clouse, A., & Turner, R. (2008). *CMMI distilled: A practical introduction to integrated process improvement* (3rd ed.). Boston, MA: Pearson Education Inc.

Akçali, E., Çetinkaya, S., & Üster, H. (2009). Network design for reverse and closed-loop supply chains: An annotated bibliography of models and solution approaches. *Networks*. doi:10.1002/net.20267.

Al Harbi, K. M. A. (2001). Application of the AHP in project management. *International Journal of Project Management*, *19*(1), 19–27. doi:10.1016/S0263-7863(99)00038-1.

Albrecht, A. J., & Gaffney, J. E. Jr. (1983). Software function, source lines of code, and development effort prediction: A software science validation. *IEEE Transactions on Software Engineering*, *9*(6), 639–648. doi:10.1109/TSE.1983.235271.

Alkahtani, A. M. S., Woodward, M. E., & Al-Begain, K. (2006). Prioritised best effort routing with four quality of service metrics applying the concept of the analytic hierarchy process. *Computers & Operations Research*, *33*(3), 559–580. doi:10.1016/j.cor.2004.07.008.

Almuallim, H., & Dietterich, T. G. (1991). Learning with many irrelevant features. In *Proceedings of the 9th National Conference on Artificial Intelligence* (pp. 547-552). Cambridge, MA: MIT Press.

Alonso, J. A., & Lamata, M. T. (2006). Consistency in the analytic hierarchy process: New approach. *International Journal of Uncertainty. Fuzziness and Knowledge-Based Systems*, *14*(4), 445–459. doi:10.1142/S0218488506004114.

Altiparmak, F., Gen, M., Lin, L., & Karaoglan, I. (2009). A steady-state genetic algorithm for multi-product supply chain network design. *Computers & Industrial Engineering*, *56*, 521–537. doi:10.1016/j.cie.2007.05.012.

Altiparmak, F., Gen, M., Lin, L., & Paksoy, T. (2006). A genetic algorithm approach for multi-objective optimization of supply chain networks. *Computers & Industrial Engineering*, *51*, 196–215. doi:10.1016/j.cie.2006.07.011.

Al-Yahyai, S., Charabi, Y., Gastli, A., & Al-Badi, A. (2012). Wind farm land suitability indexing using multi-criteria analysis. *Renewable Energy*, *44*, 80–87. doi:10.1016/j.renene.2012.01.004.

Angelis, L., Stamelos, I., & Morisio, M. (2000). Building a software cost estimation model based on categorical data. In *Proceedings Seventh International Software Metrics Symposium*, (pp. 4-15). IEEE.

Arán-Carrión, J., Espín-Estrella, A., Aznar-Dols, F., Zamorano-Toro, M., Rodríguez, M., & Ramos-Ridao, A. (2008). Environmental decision-support systems for evaluating the carrying capacity of land areas: Optimal site selection for grid-connected photovoltaic power plants. *Renewable & Sustainable Energy Reviews*, *12*, 2358–2380. doi:10.1016/j.rser.2007.06.011.

Aras, N., & Aksen, D. (2008). Locating collection centers for distance-and-incentive-dependent returns. *International Journal of Production Economics*, *111*, 316–333. doi:10.1016/j.ijpe.2007.01.015.

Aras, N., Aksen, D., & Tanuğur, A. G. (2008). Locating collection centers for incentive-dependent returns under a pick-up policy with capacitated vehicles. *European Journal of Operational Research, 191*, 1223–1240. doi:10.1016/j.ejor.2007.08.002.

Armstrong, J. S. (1984). Forecasting by extrapolation: Conclusions from 25 years of research. *Interfaces, 14*(6), 52–66. doi:10.1287/inte.14.6.52.

Arrhenius, S. (1896). On the influence of carbonic acid in the air upon the temperature of the ground. *Philosophical Magazine and Journal of Science, 5*(41), 237–276. doi:10.1080/14786449608620846.

Arrow, K. J. (1951). *Social choice and individual values*. New York: John Wiley..

Arroyo, J. E. C., & Armentano, V. A. (2005). Genetic local search for multi-objective flowshop scheduling problems. *European Journal of Operational Research, 167*, 717–738. doi:10.1016/j.ejor.2004.07.017.

Attarzadeh, I., & Ow, S. H. (2010). Proposing a new software cost estimation model based on artificial neural networks.In *Proceedings of 2nd International Conference on Computer Engineering and Technology* (ICCET). Chengdu, China: ICCET.

Awad, R., & Chinneck, J. (1998). Proctor assignment at Carleton University.*Interfaces,28*(2),58–71.doi:10.1287/inte.28.2.58.

Aydin, N. Y., Kentel, E., & Duzgun, S. (2010). GIS-based environmental assessment of wind energy systems for spatial planning: A case study from Western Turkey. *Renewable & Sustainable Energy Reviews, 14*, 364–373. doi:10.1016/j.rser.2009.07.023.

Azadeh, A., Moghaddam, M., Khakzad, M., & Ebrahimipour, V. (2012). A flexible neural network-fuzzy mathematical programming algorithm for improvement of oil price estimation and forecasting. *Computers & Industrial Engineering, 62*(2), 421–430. doi:10.1016/j.cie.2011.06.019.

Azmat, C. S., & Widmer, T. M. (2004). A case study of single shift planning and scheduling under annualized hours: A simple three-step approach. *European Journal of Operational Research, 153*, 148–175. doi:10.1016/S0377-2217(03)00105-X.

Bachou, R. B., Guinet, A., & Hjri-Gabouj, S. (2009). A model for scheduling drug deliveries in a French homecare. In *Proceedings of International Conference on Industrial Engineering and Systems Management.* Montreal, Canada: IEEE.

Bachou, R. B., Guinet, A., & Hjri-Gabouj, S. (2010). An optimization model for task assignment in home health care. In *Proceedings of IEEE Conference on Health Care Management*. IEEE.

Bäck, T., & Schwefel, H. P. (1993). An overview of evolutionary algorithms for parameter optimization. *Evolutionary Computation, 1*, 1–23. doi:10.1162/evco.1993.1.1.1.

Badeau, P., Gendreau, M., Guertin, F., Potvin, J. Y., & Taillard, E. D. (1997). A parallel tabu search heuristic for the vehicle routing problem with time windows. *Transportation Research Part C, Emerging Technologies, 5*, 109–122. doi:10.1016/S0968-090X(97)00005-3.

Bana e Costa, C. A., & Oliveira, M. D. (2012). A multicriteria decision analysis model for faculty evaluation. *Omega, 40*, 424–436. doi:10.1016/j.omega.2011.08.006.

Barndorff-Nielsen, O. (1977). Exponentially decreasing distributions for the logarithm of particle size. *Proc. Roy. Soc.*, 401–419.

Barros, A. I., Dekker, R., & Scholten, V. (1998). A two-level network for recycling sand: A case study. *European Journal of Operational Research, 110*, 199–214. doi:10.1016/S0377-2217(98)00093-9.

Beal, M. (2003). *Variational algorithms for approximate bayesian inference.* (Unpublished doctoral dissertation). Gatsby Computational Neuroscience Unit, University College London, London, UK.

Beamon, B. M., & Fernandes, C. (2004). Supply-chain network configuration for product recovery. *Production Planning and Control, 15*, 270–281. doi:10.1080/09537280410001697701.

Beasley, J. E., & Jörnsten, K. (1992). Enhancing an algorithm for set covering problems. *European Journal of Operational Research, 58*, 293–300. doi:10.1016/0377-2217(92)90215-U.

Beccali, M., Cellura, M., & Ardente, D. (1998). Decision making in energy planning: The ELECTRE multicriteria analysis approach compared to a fuzzy-sets methodology. *Energy Conversion and Management, 39*(16-18), 1869–1881. doi:10.1016/S0196-8904(98)00053-3.

Bector, C. R., & Chandra, S. (2005). *Fuzzy mathematical programming and fuzzy matrix games*. Berlin: Springer..

Bellabas, A., Lahoud, S., & Molnár, M. (2012). Performance evaluation of efficient solutions for the QoS unicast routing. *Journal of Networks, 7*(1), 73–80. doi:10.4304/jnw.7.1.73-80.

Bella, J. E., & McMullen, P. R. (2004). Ant colony optimization techniques for the vehicle routing problem. *Advanced Engineering Informatics, 18*, 41–48. doi:10.1016/j.aei.2004.07.001.

Bellman, R. E., & Zadeh, L. A. (1970). Decision making in a fuzzy environment. *Management Science, 17*(4), 141–164. doi:10.1287/mnsc.17.4.B141.

Benitez, J. M., Martin, J. C., & Roman, C. (2007). Using fuzzy number for measuring quality of service in the hotel industry. *Tourism Management, 28*(2), 544–555. doi:10.1016/j.tourman.2006.04.018.

Bent, R., & Van Hentenryck, P. (2006). A two-stage hybrid algorithm for pickup and delivery vehicle routing problems with time windows. *Computers & Operations Research, 33*, 875–893. doi:10.1016/j.cor.2004.08.001.

Berkley, B. J., & Gupta, A. (1994). Improving service quality with information technology. *International Journal of Information Management, 14*(1), 109–121. doi:10.1016/0268-4012(94)90030-2.

Berman, O., Drezner, Z., & Krass, D. (2010). Generalized coverage: New developments in covering location models. *Computers & Operations Research, 37*, 1675–1687. doi:10.1016/j.cor.2009.11.003.

Bermúdez, J. D., Segura, J. V., & Vercher, E. (2006). A decision support system methodology for forecasting of time series based on soft computing. *Computational Statistics & Data Analysis, 51*(1), 177–191. doi:10.1016/j.csda.2006.02.010.

Bezdek, J. C. (1993). Editorial: Fuzzy models-what are they and why? *IEEE Transactions on Fuzzy Systems, 1*(1), 1–6. doi:10.1109/TFUZZ.1993.6027269.

Bilsel, R. U., Buyukozkan, G., & Ruan, D. (2006). A fuzzy preference-ranking model for a quality evaluation of hospital web sites. *International Journal of Intelligent Systems, 21*(11), 1181–1197. doi:10.1002/int.20177.

Blackstone, J. H. (Ed.). (2010). *APICS dictionary* (13th ed.). APICS The Association for Operations Management..

Blockley, D. I. (1979). The role of fuzzy sets in civil engineering. *Fuzzy Sets and Systems, 2*(4), 267–278. doi:10.1016/0165-0114(79)90001-0.

Boehm, B. W. (1981). *Software engineering economics*. Englewood Cliffs, NJ: Prentice Hall..

Boehm, B. W. (1991). Software risk management: Principles and practices. *IEEE Software, 8*(1), 32–41. doi:10.1109/52.62930.

Boros, E., Hammer, P. L., Ibaraki, T., Kogan, A., Mayoraz, E., & Muchnik, I. (2000). An implementation of logical analysis of data. *IEEE Transactions on Knowledge and Data Engineering, 12*(2), 292–306. doi:10.1109/69.842268.

Bouyssou, D., Marchant, T., Perny, P., Pirlot, M., Tsoukiàs, A., & Vincke, P. (2000). *Evaluation and decision models: A critical perspective*. Dordrecht, The Netherlands: Kluwer Academic. doi:10.1007/978-1-4615-1593-7.

Bowerman, B. L., & O'Connell, R. T. (1993). Forecasting and time series: An applied approach. Belmont.

Box, G. E. P., & Jenkins, G. M. (1976). *Time series analysis: Forecasting and control*. San Francisco: Holden-Day..

Brandao, J. (2011). A tabu search algorithm for the heterogeneous fixed fleet vehicle routing problem. *Computers & Operations Research, 38*(1), 140–151. doi:10.1016/j.cor.2010.04.008.

Branke, J. (2002). *Evolutionary optimization in dynamic environments*. Boston: Kluwer Academic Publishers. doi:10.1007/978-1-4615-0911-0.

Brans, J. P., Mareschal, B., & Vincke, P. (1986). PROMETHEE: A new family of outranking methods in multicriteria analysis. *Operations Research, 84*, 477–490.

Brans, J. P., Mareschal, B., & Vincke, P. (1986a). How to select and how to rank projects: The PROMETHEE method. *European Journal of Operational Research, 24*, 228–238. doi:10.1016/0377-2217(86)90044-5.

Brauers, W. K. M., Zavadskas, E. K., Peldschus, F., & Turskis, Z. (2008). Multi-objective decision-making for road design. *Transport, 23*(3), 183–193. doi:10.3846/1648-4142.2008.23.183-193.

British Hydropower Association. (2005). *A guide to UK mini-hydro developments*. Retrieved from britishhydro.org

Broderick, A. J., & Vachirapornpuk, S. (2002). Service quality in internet banking: The importance of customer role. *Marketing Intelligence & Planning, 20*(6), 327–335. doi:10.1108/02634500210445383.

Buffa, E. S., & Miller, J. G. (1979). *Production-inventory systems: Planning and control*. Richard D. Irwin..

Burke, E., Causmaecker, P., Berghe, V. G., & Landeghem, H. (2004). The state of the art of nurse rostering. *Journal of Scheduling, 7*, 441–499. doi:10.1023/B:JOSH.0000046076.75950.0b.

Büyüközkan, G., Arsenyan, J., & Ertek, G. (2010). Evaluation of e-learning web sites using fuzzy axiomatic design based approach. *International Journal of Computational Intelligence Systems, 3*(1), 28–42.

Büyüközkan, G., & Çifçi, G. (2012). A combined fuzzy AHP and fuzzy TOPSIS based strategic analysis of electronic service quality in healthcare industry. *Expert Systems with Applications, 39*(3), 2341–2354. doi:10.1016/j.eswa.2011.08.061.

Byns, N., Leunis, K., Peeters, K., & Tonnet, L. (2011). *The use of hydropower in water supply*. K.U. Leuven..

Cables, E. H., & Lamata, M. T. (2009). OWA weights determination by means of linear functions. *Mathware & Soft Computing, 16*(2), 107–122.

Cabrerizo, F. J., Martínez, M. A., López–Gijón, J., Esteban, B., & Herrera–Viedma, E. (2011). A new quality evaluation model generating recommendations to improve the digital services provided by the academic digital libraries. In *Proceedings of International Fuzzy Systems Association World Congress & Asian Fuzzy Systems Society* (IFSA 2011). IFSA.

Caciopo, J. T., & Berntson, G. G. (1994). Relationship between attitudes and evaluative space: A critical review, with emphasis on the separability of positive and negative substrates. *Psychological Bulletin, 115*, 401–423. doi:10.1037/0033-2909.115.3.401.

Cadenas, J. M., Canós, M. J., Garrido, M. C., Ivorra, C., & Liern, V. (2011). Soft-computing based heuristics for location on networks: The p-median problem. *Applied Soft Computing, 11*, 1540–1547. doi:10.1016/j.asoc.2008.03.015.

Cadenas, J. M., Carrillo, J. V., Garrido, M. C., Ivorra, C., & Liern, V. (2012). Exact and heuristic procedures for solving the fuzzy portfolio selection problem. *Fuzzy Optimization and Decision Making, 11*, 29–46. doi:10.1007/s10700-011-9114-5.

Cadenas, J. M., Garrido, M. C., & Muñoz, E. (2008). Using machine learning in a cooperative hybrid parallel strategy of metaheuristics. *Information Sciences: An International Journal, 179*, 3255–3267. doi:10.1016/j.ins.2009.05.014.

Callegaro, A. (2010). Forecasting methods for spare parts demand. Universita' Degli Studi Di Padova, Italy..

Calvo, C., Ivorra, C., & Liern, V. (2011). The geometry of the efficient frontier of the portfolio selection problem. *Journal of Financial Decision Making, 7*, 27–36.

Calvo, C., Ivorra, C., & Liern, V. (2012a). On the computation of the efficient frontier of the portfolio selection problem. *Journal of Applied Mathematics*. doi:10.1155/2012/105616.

Calvo, C., Ivorra, C., & Liern, V. (2012b). Fuzzy portfolio selection under integer conditions. *European Journal of Operational Research*.

Canós, M. J., Ivorra, C., & Liern, V. (1999). An exact algorithm for the fuzzy p-median problem. *European Journal of Operational Research, 116*, 80–86. doi:10.1016/S0377-2217(98)00330-0.

Canós, M. J., Ivorra, C., & Liern, V. (2001). The fuzzy p-median problem: A global analysis of the solutions. *European Journal of Operational Research, 130*, 430–436. doi:10.1016/S0377-2217(99)00500-7.

Canós, M. J., Ivorra, C., & Liern, V. (2003). Finding satisfactory near-optimal solutions in location problems. In J. L. Verdegay (Ed.), *Fuzzy Sets Based Heuristics for Optimization*. Heidelberg, Germany: Physica-Verlag. doi:10.1007/978-3-540-36461-0_17.

Canós, M. J., Ivorra, C., & Liern, V. (2004). The fuzzy *p*-median problem. *International Journal of Technology. Policy and Management, 4*, 365–381.

Canós, M. J., Ivorra, C., & Liern, V. (2008). Marginal analysis for the fuzzy *p*-median problem. *European Journal of Operational Research, 191*, 264–271. doi:10.1016/j.ejor.2007.08.011.

Cao, H., & Chen, G. (1983). Some applications of fuzzy sets to meteorological forecasting. *Fuzzy Sets and Systems, 9*(1–3), 1–12. doi:10.1016/S0165-0114(83)80001-3.

Caramia, M., & Guerriero, F. (2010). A heuristic approach for the truck and trailer routing problems. *Journalism, 61*, 1168–1180.

Carlsson, C., & Fuller, R. (2000). Soft computing and the bullwhip effect. *Ecological Complexity, 2*, 1–26.

Carlsson, C., & Fuller, R. (2001). On possibilistic mean value and variance of fuzzy numbers. *Fuzzy Sets and Systems, 22*, 315–326. doi:10.1016/S0165-0114(00)00043-9.

Carr, M., et al. (1993). *Taxonomy–based risk identification* (Report SEI-93-TR-006). Pittsburgh, PA: Software Engineering Institute.

Casdagli, M., & Eubank, S. (1992). *Nonlinear modeling and forecasting*. Westview Press..

Cavique, L., Rego, C., & Themido, I. (1999). Subgraph ejection chains and tabu search for the crew scheduling problem. *The Journal of the Operational Research Society, 50*(6), 608–616.

Celso Penche. (1997). *Layman's guide on how to develop a small hydro site*. Directorate-General for Energy by European Small Hydropower Association. ESHA..

Chan, F. T. S., Chan, M. H., & Tang, N. K. H. (2000a). Evaluation methodologies for technology selection. *Journal of Materials Processing Technology, 107*, 330–337. doi:10.1016/S0924-0136(00)00679-8.

Chan, F. T. S., Jiang, B., & Tang, N. K. H. (2000b). The development of intelligent decision support tools to aid the design flexible manufacturing systems. *International Journal of Production Economics, 65*(1), 73–84. doi:10.1016/S0925-5273(99)00091-2.

Chang, C. W., Wu, C. R., & Lin, H. L. (2008). Integrating fuzzy theory and hierarchy concepts to evaluate software quality. *Software Quality Journal, 16*(2), 263–276. doi:10.1007/s11219-007-9035-2.

Chang, C. W., Wu, C. R., & Lin, H. L. (2009). Applying fuzzy hierarchy multiple attributes to construct an expert decision making process. *Expert Systems with Applications, 36*(4), 7363–7368. doi:10.1016/j.eswa.2008.09.026.

Chang, Y.-H., & Yeh, C.-H. (2002). A survey analysis of service quality for domestic airlines. *European Journal of Operational Research, 139*(1), 166–177. doi:10.1016/S0377-2217(01)00148-5.

Chao, I.-M. (2002). A tabu search method for the truck and trailer routing problem. *Computers & Operations Research, 39*, 33–51. doi:10.1016/S0305-0548(00)00056-3.

Chao, I.-M., Golden, B., & Wasil, E. (1999). A computacional study of a new heuristic for the site-dependent vehicle routing problem. *Information Systems and Operational Research, 37*, 319–336.

Chen, C. T. (2001). Applying linguistic decision-making method to deal with service quality evaluation problems. *International Journal of Uncertainty Fuzziness and Knowledge-Based Systems, 9*, 103–114. doi:10.1142/S0218488501001022.

Chen, G., Xie, Q., & Shieh, L. (1998). Fuzzy Kalman filtering. *Journal of Information Science*, 197–209.

Cheng, C. H., Chang, J. R., Ho, T. H., & Chen, A. P. (2005). Evaluating the airline service quality by fuzzy OWA operators. In V. N. Y. M. S. Torra (Ed.), *Modeling Decisions for Artificial Intelligence* (Vol. 3558, pp. 77–88). Berlin: Springer. doi:10.1007/11526018_9.

Cheng, C.-H., & Chang, J.-R. (2006). MCDM aggregation model using situational ME-OWA and ME-OWGA operators. *International Journal of Uncertainty Fuzziness and Knowledge-Based Systems, 14*(4), 421–443. doi:10.1142/S0218488506004102.

Cheng, C.-H., Yang, K.-L., & Hwang, C.-L. (1999). Evaluating attack helicopters by AHP based on linguistic variable weight. *European Journal of Operational Research*, *116*(2), 423–435. doi:10.1016/S0377-2217(98)00156-8.

Chen, T., & Wang, M. J. J. (1999). Forecasting methods using fuzzy concepts. *Fuzzy Sets and Systems*, *105*(3), 339–352. doi:10.1016/S0165-0114(97)00265-0.

Chen, Z., Menzies, T., Port, D., & Boehm, B. (2005). Finding the right data for software cost modeling. *IEEE Software*, *22*(6), 38–46. doi:10.1109/MS.2005.151.

Chifu, H., & Litzenberg, R. H. (1988). *Foundations for finalcial economics*. Amsterdam: North Holland..

Chikalov, I., Lozin, V., Lozina, I., Moshkov, M., Nguyen, H. S., Skowron, A., & Zielosko, B. (2013). *Three approaches to data analysis: Test theory, rough sets and logical analysis of data*. Berlin: Springer. doi:10.1007/978-3-642-28667-4.

Chu, C. W., & Zhang, G. P. (2003). A comparative study of linear and nonlinear models for aggregate retail sales forecasting. *International Journal of Production Economics*, *86*(3), 217–231. doi:10.1016/S0925-5273(03)00068-9.

Chu, L. K., Shi, Y., Lin, S., Sculli, D., & Ni, J. (2009). Fuzzy chance-constrained programming model for a multi- echelon reverse logistics network for household appliances. *The Journal of the Operational Research Society*. doi: doi:10.1057/jors.2008.162.

Church, R., & Revelle, C. (1974). The maximal covering location problem. *Papers / Regional Science Association. Regional Science Association. Meeting*, *32*, 101–118. doi:10.1007/BF01942293.

Chvatal, V. (1979). A greedy heuristic for the set-covering problem. *Mathematics of Operations Research*, *4*, 233–235. doi:10.1287/moor.4.3.233.

Cohen, J. (1960). A coefficient of agreement for nominal scales. *Educational and Psychological Measurement*, *20*, 37–46. doi:10.1177/001316446002000104.

Comisión de las Comunidades Europeas. (1996). *Energía para el futuro: Fuentes de energía renovables: Libro verde para una estrategia comunitaria. Bruselas*. Author..

Comisión Europea. (1997). *Energía para el futuro: Fuentes de energía renovables: Libro blanco para una estrategia y un plan de acción comunitarios. Bruselas*. Author..

Computerworld. (2002, May 20). *Five reasons why software projects fail*. Retrieved January 20, 2012 from http://www.computerworld.com/s/article/71209/Why_Projects_Fail

Corduneanu, A., & Bishop, C. (2001). *Variational Bayesian model selection for mixture distribution*. Artificial Intelligence and Statistics..

Costa, L., & Oliveira, P. (2002). An evolution strategy for multiobjective optimization. In *The IEEE Congress: Evolutionary computation* (pp. 97-102). IEEE.

Crainic, T. G., Ricciardi, N., & Storchi, G. (2009). Models for evaluating and planning city logistics systems. *Transportation Science*, *43*(4), 432–454. doi:10.1287/trsc.1090.0279.

Crama, Y., Hammer, P. L., & Ibaraki, T. (1988). Cause-effect relationships and partially defined boolean functions. *Annals of Operations Research*, *16*, 299–326. doi:10.1007/BF02283750.

Croston, J. D. (1972). Forecasting and stock control for intermittent demands. *Operational Research Quarterly*, *23*(3), 289.

Cruz, C., & Silva, R. C., Verdegay. (2013). Solving real-world fuzzy quadratic programming problems by a parametric method. *Communications in Computer and Information Science*, *299*, 102–111. doi:10.1007/978-3-642-31718-7_11.

Cruz, C., Silva, R. C., & Verdegay, J. L. (2011). Extending and relating different approaches for solving fuzzy quadratic problems. *Fuzzy Optimization and Decision Making*, *10*, 193–210. doi:10.1007/s10700-011-9104-7.

Cruz, C., Silva, R. C., Verdegay, J. L., & Yamakami, A. (2008). A survey of fuzzy quadratic programming. *Recent Patents on Computer Science*, *1*(3), 182–1930. doi:10.2174/2213275910801030182.

Daskin, M. S. (1995). *Network and discrete location: Models, algorithms and application*. New York: Wiley & Sons. doi:10.1002/9781118032343.

Davis, P. S., & Ray, T. L. (1969). A branch-and-bound algorithm for the capacitated facilities location problem. *Naval Research Logistics Quarterly, 16,* 331–344.

Dayou, L., Pu, Y., & Ji, Y. (2009). Development of a multiobjective GA for advanced planning and scheduling problem. *International Journal of Advanced Manufacturing Technology, 42,* 974–992. doi:10.1007/s00170-008-1653-8.

Deb, K., Agrawal, S., Pratap, A., & Meyarivan, T. (2002). A fast elitist non-dominated sorting genetic algorithm for multi-objective optimization: NSGA-II. *IEEE Transactions on Evolutionary Computation, 6,* 182–197. doi:10.1109/4235.996017.

Dehghanian, F., & Mansour, S. (2009). Designing sustainable recovery network of end-of-life products using genetic algorithm. *Resources, Conservation and Recycling, 53,* 559–570. doi:10.1016/j.resconrec.2009.04.007.

Delgado, M., Verdegay, J. L., & Vila, M. A. (1994). Fuzzy linear programming: from classical methods to new applications. In M. Delgado, J. Kacprzyk, J. L. Verdegay, & M. A. Vila (Eds.), *Fuzzy optimization: Recent advances.* Heidelberg, Germany: Physica-Verlag..

Demirbas, A. (2005). Potential applications of renewable energy sources, biomass combustion problems in boiler power systems and combustion related environmental issues. *Progress in Energy and Combustion Science, 31*(2), 171–192. doi:10.1016/j.pecs.2005.02.002.

Demirel, N. Ö., & Gökçen, H. (2008). A mixed integer programming model for remanufacturing in reverse logistics environment. *International Journal of Advanced Manufacturing Technology, 39,* 1197–1206. doi:10.1007/s00170-007-1290-7.

Devore, J. L. (2012). *Probability and statistics for engineering and the sciences* (8th ed.). Boston, MA: Brooks/Cole Cengage Learning..

Domínguez-Bravo, J., García-Casals, X., & Pinedo Pascua, I. (2007). GIS approach to the definition of capacity and generation ceilings of renewable energy technologies. *Energy Policy, 35,* 4879–4892. doi:10.1016/j.enpol.2007.04.025.

Donati, A. V., Montemanni, R., Casagrande, N., Rizzoli, A. E., & Gambardella, L. M. (2008). Time dependent vehicle routing problem with a multi ant colony system. *European Journal of Operational Research, 185*(3), 1174–1191. doi:10.1016/j.ejor.2006.06.047.

Dorigo, M., Maniezzo, V., & Colorni, A. (1996). Ant system: Optimization by a colony of cooperating agents. *IEEE Transactions on Systems, Man, and Cybernetics - Part B, 26*(1), 29–41. doi:10.1109/3477.484436 PMID:18263004.

Dorigo, M., & Stützle, T. (2003). Ant colony optimization metaheuristic. In F. Glover, & G. A. Kochenberger (Eds.), *Handbook of Metaheuristics* (pp. 251–286). London: Kluwer Academic Publisher..

Doucet, A., & Johansen, A. (2009). A tutorial on particle filtering and smoothing: Fifteen years later. In *Handbook of Nonlinear Filtering* (pp. 656–704). Academic Press..

Doucet, A., & Tadic, V. (2003). Parameter estimation in general state-space models using particle methods. *Annals of the Institute of Statistical Mathematics,* 409–422. doi:10.1007/BF02530508.

Drexl, M. A. (2007). *A branch and price algorithm for the truck and traier routing problem.* Aachen, Germany: RWTH Aachen University..

Drud, A. S. (1994). CONOPT: A large scale GRG code. *ORSA Journal on Computing, 6,* 207–216. doi:10.1287/ijoc.6.2.207.

Du, W. L. (2009). *A neuro-fuzzy model with SEER-SEM for software effort estimation.* (Unpublished MESc Thesis). University of Western Ontario, Ontario, Canada.

Dubois, D., & Fargier, H. (2006). *Qualitative decision making with bipolar information.* American Association for Artificial Intelligence. Retrieved from WWW.AAAI.ORG

Dubois, D., & Prade, H. M. (1980). *Fuzzy sets and systems: Theory and applications.* Academic Press..

Du, F., & Evans, G. W. (2008). A bi-objective reverse logistics network analysis for post-sale service. *Computers & Operations Research, 35,* 2617–2634. doi:10.1016/j.cor.2006.12.020.

Du, W. L., Ho, D., & Capretz, L. F. (2010). Improving software effort estimation using neuro-fuzzy model with SEER-SEM. *Global Journal of Computer Science and Technology, 10*(12), 52–64.

El-Sayed, M., Afia, N., & El-Kharbotly, A. (2010). A stochastic model for forward–reverse logistics network design under risk. *Computers & Industrial Engineering, 58*, 423–431. doi:10.1016/j.cie.2008.09.040.

Ernst, A. T., Jiang, H., Krishnamoorthy, M., Owens, B., & Sier, D. (2004a). An annotated bibliography of personnel scheduling and rostering. *Annals of Operations Research, 127*, 21–144. doi:10.1023/B:ANOR.0000019087.46656.e2.

Ernst, A. T., Jiang, H., Krishnamoorthy, M., & Sier, D. (2004b). Staff scheduling and rostering: A review of applications, methods and models. *European Journal of Operational Research, 153*, 3–27. doi:10.1016/S0377-2217(03)00095-X.

Falkenauer, E. (1992). The grouping genetic algorithms - Widening the scope of the GAs. *Belgian Journal of Operations Research. Statistics and Computer Science, 33*, 79–102.

Fawcett, T. (2006). An introduction to ROC analysis. *Pattern Recognition Letters, 27*, 861–874. doi:10.1016/j.patrec.2005.10.010.

Figliozzi, M. A. (2009). Planning approximations to the average length of vehicle routing problems with time window constraints. *Transportation Research Part B: Methodological, 43*, 438–447. doi:10.1016/j.trb.2008.08.004.

Filho, E. V. G., & Tiberti, A. J. (2006). A group genetic algorithm for the machine cell formation problem. *International Journal of Production Economics, 102*, 1–21. doi:10.1016/j.ijpe.2004.12.029.

Fisher, M., & Jaikumar, R. (1981). A generalized assignment heuristic for vehicle routing. *Networks, 11*(2), 109–124. doi:10.1002/net.3230110205.

Fleischmann, M., Krikke, H. R., Dekker, R., & Flapper, S. D. P. (2000). A characterisation of logistics networks for product recovery. *Omega, 28*, 653–666. doi:10.1016/S0305-0483(00)00022-0.

Foss, T., Stensrud, E., Kitchenham, B., & Myrtveit, I. (2003). A simulation study of the model evaluation criterion MMRE. *IEEE Transactions on Software Engineering, 29*(11), 985–995. doi:10.1109/TSE.2003.1245300.

Frantti, T., & Mähönen, P. (2001). Fuzzy logic-based forecasting model. *Engineering Applications of Artificial Intelligence, 14*(2), 189–201. doi:10.1016/S0952-1976(00)00076-2.

Fuellerera, G., Doernera, K. F., Hartla, R. F., & Iorib, M. (2009). Ant colony optimization for the two-dimensional loading vehicle routing problem. *Computers & Operations Research, 36*, 655–673. doi:10.1016/j.cor.2007.10.021.

Funk, G., & Funk, M. (2001a). *Pérolas da sabedoria popular: Os provérbios Açoreanos nos EUA.* Lisboa: Salamandra..

Funk, G., & Funk, M. (2001b). *Pérolas da sabedoria popular: Os provérbios de S. Miguel.* Lisboa: Salamandra..

Funk, G., & Funk, M. (2003). *Pérolas da sabedoria popular: Provérbios das Ilhas do Grupo Central dos Açores (Faial, Graciosa, Pico, São Jorge e Terceira).* Lisboa: Salamandra..

Gajpal, Y., & Abad, P. L. (2009). Multi-ant colony system (MACS) for a vehicle routing problem with backhauls. *European Journal of Operational Research, 196*, 102–117. doi:10.1016/j.ejor.2008.02.025.

Galorath, D. D., & Evans, M. W. (2006). *Software sizing, estimation, and risk management.* Boca Raton, FL: Auerbach Publication. doi:10.1201/9781420013122.

Ganoulis, J., & Skoulikaris, C. (2011). Impact of climate change on hydropower generation and irrigation: A case study from Greece. In *Climate Change and its Effects on Water Resources* (pp. 87–95). Berlin: Springer. doi:10.1007/978-94-007-1143-3_10.

García-Cáscales, M. S., & Lamata, M. T. (2010). ¿Cómo clasificar titulaciones de ingeniería por su calidad?. *Dyna, 85*(8).

García-Cáscales, M. S., Lamata, M. T., & Sánchez-Lozano, J. M. (2012). Evaluation of photovoltaic cells in a multi-criteria decision making process. *Annals of Operations Research, 199*, 373–391. doi:10.1007/s10479-011-1009-x.

García, S., Molina, D., Lozano, M., & Herrera, F. (2009). A study on the use of non-parametric tests for analyzing the evolutionary algorithms' behavior: A case study on the CEC'2005 special session on real parameter optimization. *Journal of Heuristics*, *15*, 617–644. doi:10.1007/s10732-008-9080-4.

Garey, M. R., & Johnson, D. S. (1979). *Computers and intractability: A guide to the theory of NP-completeness.* W. H. Freeman..

Geem, Z., Kim, J., & Loganathan, G. (2001). A new heuristic optimization algorithm: Harmony search. *Simulation*, *76*(2), 60–68. doi:10.1177/003754970107600201.

Gendreau, M., Laporte, G., Musaraganyi, C., & Taillard, E. D. (1999). A tabu search heuristic for the heterogeneous fleet vehicle routing problem. *Computers & Operations Research*, *26*, 1153–1173. doi:10.1016/S0305-0548(98)00100-2.

Gen, M., Altiparmak, F., & Lin, L. (2006). A genetic algorithm for two-stage transportation problem using priority-based encoding. *OR-Spektrum*, *28*, 337–354. doi:10.1007/s00291-005-0029-9.

Gerdessen, J. C. (1996). Vehicle routing problem with trailer. *European Journal of Operational Research*, *93*(1), 135–147. doi:10.1016/0377-2217(95)00175-1.

Ghobbar, A. A., & Friend, C. H. (2002). Sources of intermittent demand for aircraft spare parts within airline operations. *Journal of Air Transport Management*, *8*, 221–231. doi:10.1016/S0969-6997(01)00054-0.

Ghobbar, A. A., & Friend, C. H. (2003). Evaluation of forecasting methods for intermittent parts demand in the field of aviation: A predictive model. *Computers & Operations Research*, *30*(14), 2097–2114. doi:10.1016/S0305-0548(02)00125-9.

Goldberg, D. E. (1989). *Genetic algorithm in search, optimization, and machine learning.* Reading, MA: Addison-Wesley..

Gomes, M., Cavique, L., & Themido, I. (2006). The crew time tabling problem: An extension of the crew scheduling problem. *Annals of Operations Research. Optimization in Transportation*, *144*(1), 111–132.

Grabisch, M. (1996). The application of fuzzy integrals in multicriteria decision making. *European Journal of Operational Research*, *89*(3), 445–456. doi:10.1016/0377-2217(95)00176-X.

Granger, C. W. J., Clive, W. J., & Terasvita, T. (1993). *Modelling nonlinear economic relationships.* Oxford, UK: Oxford University Press..

Greco, S., Matarazzo, B., & Slowinski, R. (2001). Rough sets theory for multicriteria decision analysis. *European Journal of Operational Research*, *129*(1), 1–47. doi:10.1016/S0377-2217(00)00167-3.

Green Paper. (2001). *Opinion of the economic and social committee on the green paper: Towards a European strategy for the security of energy supply.* European Economic and Social Committee, Office for Official Publications of the European Communities..

Grewal, M., & Andrews, A. (2008). *Kalman filtering: Theory and practice using MATLAB.* Hoboken, NJ: John Wiley and Sons. doi:10.1002/9780470377819.

Grossman, T., Samuelson, D., Oh, S., & Rohleder, T. (1999). *Call centres.* Calgary, Canada: University of Calgary..

Guérin, R. A., & Orda, A. (1999). QoS routing in networks with inaccurate information: Theory and algorithms. *IEEE/ACM Transactions on Networking*, *7*(3), 350–364. doi:10.1109/90.779203.

Guide, V. D. R., Teunter, R., & Wassenhove, L. N. (2003). Matching demand and supply to maximize profits from remanufacturing. *Manufacturing and Service Operations Management*, *5*, 303–316. doi:10.1287/msom.5.4.303.24883.

Guide, V. D. Jr, Jayaraman, V., Srivastava, R., & Benton, W. C. (2000). Supply chain management for recoverable manufacturing systems. *Interfaces*, *30*, 125–142. doi:10.1287/inte.30.3.125.11656.

Guiffrida, A. L., & Nagi, R. (1998). Fuzzy set theory applications in production management research: A literature survey. *Journal of Intelligent Manufacturing*, *9*(1), 39–56. doi:10.1023/A:1008847308326.

Gupta, D., & Sadiq, M. (2008). Software risk assessment and estimation model. In *Proceeding International Conference on Computer Science and Information Technology* (pp. 963-967). Singapore: IEEE.

Guyon, I., & Elisseeff, A. (2003). An introduction to variable and feature selection. *Journal of Machine Learning Research*, (3): 1157–1182.

Hakimi, S. L. (1964). Optimum locations of switching centers and the absolute centers and medians of a graph. *Operations Research*, *12*, 450–459. doi:10.1287/opre.12.3.450.

Hakimi, S. L. (1965). Optimum distribution of switching centers in a communication network and some related graph theoretic problems. *Operations Research*, *13*, 462–475. doi:10.1287/opre.13.3.462.

Hakimi, S. L., & Maheshwari, S. N. (1972). Optimum locations of centers in networks. *Operations Research*, *20*, 967–973. doi:10.1287/opre.20.5.967.

Hall, E. M. (1998). *Managing risk: Methods for software systems development*. Reading, MA: Addison Wesley Longman, Inc.

Hallerbach, W., Ning, H., Soppe, A., & Spronk, J. A. (2004). A framework for managing a portfolio of socially responsible investments. *European Journal of Operational Research*, *153*, 517–529. doi:10.1016/S0377-2217(03)00172-3.

Han, J., & Kamber, M. (2006). *Data mining: Concepts and techniques*. San Francisco: Morgan Kaufmann Publishers..

Hax, A. C., & Candea, D. (1984). *Production and inventory management*. Upper Saddle River, NJ: Prentice-Hall..

Heldman, K., & Heldman, W. (2010). *CompTIA project+: Study guide*. Indianapolis, IN: Wiley Publishing Inc.

Hoff, A., Anderson, H., Christiansen, M., Hasle, G., & Lokketangen, A. (2010). Industrial aspects and literature survey: Fleet composition and routing. *Computers & Operations Research*, *37*, 2041–2061. doi:10.1016/j.cor.2010.03.015.

Hokkanen, J., & Salminen, P. (1997). Choosing a solid waste management system using multicriteria decision analysis. *European Journal of Operational Research*, *98*, 19–36. doi:10.1016/0377-2217(95)00325-8.

Holt, C. (1957). *Forecasting trends and seasonals by exponentially weighted averages*. Pittsburgh, PA: Carnegie Institute of Technology..

Huang, X., Ho, D., Ren, J., & Capretz, L. F. (2004). A neuro-fuzzy tool for software estimation. In *Proceedings of the 20th IEEE International Conference on Software Maintenance*. IEEE.

Huang, S. J., Lin, C. Y., & Chiu, N. H. (2006). Fuzzy decision tree approach for embedding risk assessment information into software estimation model. *Journal of Information Science and Engineering*, *22*, 297–313.

Huang, X., Ho, D., Ren, J., & Capretz, L. F. (2007). Improving the COCOMO model using a neuro fuzzy approach. *Applied Soft Computing Journal*, *7*, 29–40. doi:10.1016/j.asoc.2005.06.007.

Husseinzadeh Kashan, A., Jenabi, M., & Husseinzadeh Kashan, M. (2009). *A new solution approach for grouping problems based on evolution strategies*. Paper presented at International Conference of Soft Computing and Pattern Recognition. doi: 10.1109/SoCPaR.2009.29

Hu, Y. C. (2009). Fuzzy multiple-criteria decision making in the determination of critical criteria for assessing service quality of travel websites. *Expert Systems with Applications*, *36*(3), 6439–6445. doi:10.1016/j.eswa.2008.07.046.

Hu, Y.-C., & Liao, P.-C. (2011). Finding critical criteria of evaluating electronic service quality of internet banking using fuzzy multiple-criteria decision making. *Applied Soft Computing*, *11*(4), 3764–3770. doi:10.1016/j.asoc.2011.02.008.

Hyun, C. J., Kim, Y., & Kim, Y. K. (1998). A genetic algorithm for multiple objective sequencing problem in mixed model assembly lines. *Computers & Operations Research*, *25*, 675–690. doi:10.1016/S0305-0548(98)00026-4.

IEEE Spectrum. (2005, September). *Why software fails*. Retrieved January 20, 2012 from http://spectrum.ieee.org/computing/software/why-software-fails/3

Ijumba, N. M., & Hunsley, J. P. (1999). Improved load forecasting techniques for the newly electrified areas. In Proceedings of 1999 IEEE Africon, (Vol. 2, pp. 989-994). IEEE..

Instituto para la Diversificación y Ahorro de la Energía IDAE. (2005). *Plan de energías renovables en españa (PER) 2005-2010*. Madrid: Ministerio de Industria, Turismo y Comercio..

Instituto para la Diversificación y Ahorro de la Energía IDAE. (2010). *Plan de acción nacional de energías renovables de españa (PANER) 2011 – 2020*. Madrid: Ministerio de Industria, Turismo y Comercio..

International Function Point User Group. (2007). *IFPUG*. Retrieved 2007 from http://www.ifpug.org

International Function Point Users Group. (2005). *Function point counting practices manual 4.2.1*. Retrieved January 2005 from http://www.ifpug.org

International Software Benchmarking Standards Group. (2004). *Data CD R9 demographics*. Retrieved 2004 from http://www.isbsg.org

Inuiguchi, M., & Ramik, J. (2000). Possibilistic linear programming: A brief review of fuzzy mathematical programming and a comparison with stochastic programming in portfolio selection problem. *Fuzzy Sets and Systems*, *111*(1), 3–28. doi:10.1016/S0165-0114(98)00449-7.

Inuiguchi, M., Sakawa, M., & Kume, Y. (1994). The usefulness of possibilistic programming in production planning problems. *International Journal of Production Economics*, *33*, 45–52. doi:10.1016/0925-5273(94)90117-1.

Inuiguchi, M., & Tanino, T. (2000). Portfolio selection under independent possibilistic information. *Fuzzy Sets and Systems*, *115*, 83–92. doi:10.1016/S0165-0114(99)00026-3.

Iranmanesh, S. H., et al. (2009). Risk assessment of software project using fuzzy inference system. In *Proceeding International Conference on Computers & Industrial Engineering* (pp.1149-1154). IEEE.

Iversen, J. H., Mathiassen, L., & Nielsen, P. A. (2004). Managing risk in software process improvement: An action research approach. *Management Information Systems Quarterly*, *28*(3), 395–433.

Janke, J. R. (2010). Multicriteria GIS modeling of wind and solar farms in Colorado. *Renewable Energy*, *35*, 2228–2234. doi:10.1016/j.renene.2010.03.014.

Jayaraman, V., Patterson, R. A., & Rolland, E. (2003). The design of reverse distribution networks: Models and solution procedures. *European Journal of Operational Research*, *150*, 128–149. doi:10.1016/S0377-2217(02)00497-6.

John, G. H., Kohavi, R., & Pfleger, K. (1994). Irrelevant features and the subset selection problem. In *Proceedings of the 11th International Conference on Machine Learning*, (pp. 121-129). ICML.

Johnston, F. R., & Boylan, J. E. (1996). Forecasting for items with intermittent demand. *The Journal of the Operational Research Society*, *47*(1), 113.

Jones, C. (1995). Backfiring: Converting lines of code to function points. *Computer*, *28*(11), 87–88. doi:10.1109/2.471193.

Jones, C. (2012). *Early sizing and early risk analysis of software project*. New York: Jones & Associates, LLC..

Julier, S., & Uhlmann, J. (1997). New extension of the Kalman filter to nonlinear systems. In *Proceedings of SPIE* (pp. 182–193). SPIE. doi:10.1117/12.280797.

Kablan, M. M. (2004). Decision support for energy conservation promotion: An analytic hierarchy process approach. *Energy Policy*, *32*(10), 1151–1158. doi:10.1016/S0301-4215(03)00078-8.

Kahraman, C., Cebeci, U., & Ruan, D. (2004). Multi-attribute comparison of catering service companies using fuzzy AHP: The case of Turkey. *International Journal of Production Economics*, *87*(2), 171–184. doi:10.1016/S0925-5273(03)00099-9.

Kahraman, C., Kaya, I., & Cebi, S. (2009). A comparative analysis for multiattribute selection among renewable energy alternatives using fuzzy axiomatic design and fuzzy analytic hierarchy process. *Energy*, *34*, 1603–1616. doi:10.1016/j.energy.2009.07.008.

Kaldellis, J. K. (2007). The contribution of small hydro power stations to the electricity generation in Greece: Technical and economic considerations. *Energy Policy*, *35*(4), 2187–2196. doi:10.1016/j.enpol.2006.06.021.

Kaleva, O. (1994). Interpolation of fuzzy data. *Fuzzy Sets and Systems*, *61*(1), 63–70. doi:10.1016/0165-0114(94)90285-2.

Kaminaris, S. D., Tsoutsos, T. D., Agoris, D., & Machias, A. V. (2006). Assessing renewables-to-electricity systems: A fuzzy expert system model. *Energy Policy, 34,* 1357–1366. doi:10.1016/j.enpol.2004.08.054.

Kandil, M., El-Debeiky, S., & Hasanien, N. (2001). Overview and comparison of long-term forecasting techniques for a fast developing utility: Part I. *Electric Power Systems Research, 58*(1), 11–17. doi:10.1016/S0378-7796(01)00097-9.

Kannan, G., Sasikumar, P., & Devika, K. (2010). A genetic algorithm approach for solving a closed loop supply chain model: A case of battery recycling. *Applied Mathematical Modelling, 34,* 655–670. doi:10.1016/j.apm.2009.06.021.

Kansala, K. (1997). Integrating risk assessment with cost estimation. *IEEE Software, 14*(3), 61–67. doi:10.1109/52.589236.

Kawanaka, H., Yamamoto, K., Yoshikawa, T., Shinogi, T., & Tsuruoka, S. (2001). Genetic algorithm with the constraints for nurse scheduling problem. *IEEE Conference on Evolutionary Computation, 2,* 1123-1130.

Kaya, T. (2010). Multi-attribute evaluation of website quality in e-business using an integrated fuzzy AHP TOPSIS methodology. *International Journal of Computational Intelligence Systems, 3*(3), 301–314.

Kenworthy, J. R. (2006). The eco-city: Ten key transport and planning dimensions for sustainable city development. *Environment and Urbanization, 18*(1), 67–85. doi:10.1177/0956247806063947.

Kim, Y., Sul, S., & Park, M. (1994). Speed sensorless vector control of induction motor using extended kalman filter. *IEEE Transactions on Industry Applications, 30*(5), 1225–1233. doi:10.1109/28.315233.

Kira, K., & Rendell, L. A. (1992). The feature selection problem: Traditional methods and a new algorithm. In *Proceedings of Ninth National Conference on Artificial Intelligence* (pp. 129-134). NCAI.

Kirsopp, C., & Shepperd, M. (2002). Case and feature subset selection in case-based software project effort prediction. In *Proceedings of the 22nd SGAI Int'l Conf. Knowledge-Based Systems and Applied Artificial Intelligence.* SGAI.

Kitchenham, B. A., MacDonell, S. G., Pickad, L. M., & Shepperd, M. J. (2001). What accuracy statistics really measure. *IEE Proceedings. Software, 148*(3), 81–85. doi:10.1049/ip-sen:20010506.

Knowles, J. D., & Corne, D. W. (1999). The pareto archived evolution strategy: A new baseline algorithm for Pareto multiobjective optimization. In *The IEEE congress: Evolutionary computation* (pp. 98–105). IEEE..

Ko, H. J., & Evans, G. W. (2007). A genetic algorithm-based heuristic for the dynamic integrated forward/reverse logistics network for 3PLs. *Computers & Operations Research, 34,* 346–366. doi:10.1016/j.cor.2005.03.004.

Konak, A., Coit, D. W., & Smith, A. E. (2006). Multi-objective optimization using genetic algorithms: A tutorial. *Reliability Engineering & System Safety, 91,* 992–1007. doi:10.1016/j.ress.2005.11.018.

Kotecha, J., & Djuric, P. (2003). Gaussian particle filtering. *IEEE Transactions on Signal Processing,* 2592–2601. doi:10.1109/TSP.2003.816758.

Kougias, I., & Theodossiou, N. (2010). A new music-inspired, harmony based optimization algorithm: Theory and applications. In *Proceedings of 10ᵗʰ International Conference on Protection and Restoration of the Environment.* Athens, Greece: Academic Press.

Kougias, I., & Theodossiou, N. (2012). Application of the harmony search optimization algorithm for the solution of the multiple dam system scheduling. *Optimization and Engineering.*

Kreinovich, V., Quintana, C., & Reznik, L. (1992). Gaussian membership functions are most adequate in representing uncertainty in measurements. In *Proceeding NAFIPS: North America Fuzzy Information Processing Society Conference,* (pp.618–624). NAFIPS.

Krishnamoorthy, M., & Ernst, A. T. (2001). The personnel task scheduling problem. In *Optimisation Methods and Applications.* Dordrecht, The Netherlands: Kluwer Academic Publishers. doi:10.1007/978-1-4757-3333-4_20.

Kucukali, S. (2011). Water supply lines as a source of small hydropower in Turkey: A case study in Edremit. In *Proceedings of World Renewable Energy Congress 2011.* Stockholm: Academic Press.

Kucukali, S. (2010a). Municipal water supply dams as a source of small hydropower in Turkey. *Renewable Energy*, *35*, 2001–2007. doi:10.1016/j.renene.2010.01.032.

Kucukali, S. (2010b). Hydropower potential of municipal water supply dams in Turkey: A case study in Ulutan Dam. *Energy Policy*, *38*, 6534–6539. doi:10.1016/j.enpol.2010.06.021.

Kuo, M. S. (2011). A novel interval-valued fuzzy MCDM method for improving airlines' service quality in Chinese cross-strait airlines. *Transportation Research Part E, Logistics and Transportation Review*, *47*(6), 1177–1193. doi:10.1016/j.tre.2011.05.007.

Kuo, M.-S., & Liang, G.-S. (2011). Combining VIKOR with GRA techniques to evaluate service quality of airports under fuzzy environment. *Expert Systems with Applications*, *38*(3), 1304–1312. doi:10.1016/j.eswa.2010.07.003.

Kuo, M.-S., Wu, J.-W., & Pei, L. (2007). A soft computing method for selecting evaluation criteria of service quality. *Applied Mathematics and Computation*, *189*(1), 241–254. doi:10.1016/j.amc.2006.11.084.

Lacagnina, V., & Pecorella, A. (2006). A stochastic soft constraints fuzzy model for a portfolio selection problem. *Fuzzy Sets and Systems*, *157*, 1317–1327. doi:10.1016/j.fss.2005.10.002.

Ladhari, R. (2008). Alternative measures of service quality: A review. *Managing Service Quality*, *18*(1), 65–86. doi:10.1108/09604520810842849.

Lai, Y. J., & Hwang, C. L. (1992). *Fuzzy mathematical programming: methods and applications*. Berlin: Springer. doi:10.1007/978-3-642-48753-8.

Lamata, M. T., & Cables, E. (2012). Obtaining OWA operators starting from a linear order and preference quantifiers. *International Journal of Intelligent Systems*, *27*, 242–258. doi:10.1002/int.21520.

Lee, D. H., & Dong, M. (2008). A heuristic approach to logistics network design for end-of-lease computer products recovery. *Transportation Research Part E, Logistics and Transportation Review*, *44*, 455–474. doi:10.1016/j.tre.2006.11.003.

Lee, J. E., Gen, M., & Rhee, K. G. (2009). Network model and optimization of reverse logistics by hybrid genetic algorithm. *Computers & Industrial Engineering*, *56*, 951–964. doi:10.1016/j.cie.2008.09.021.

Li, R. J. (1990). *Multiple objective decision-making in a fuzzy environment*. (Ph.D. Thesis). Department of Industrial Engineering, Kansas State University, Manhattan, KS.

Lieckens, K., & Vandaele, N. (2007). Reverse logistics network design with stochastic lead times. *Computers & Operations Research*, *34*, 395–416. doi:10.1016/j.cor.2005.03.006.

Li, F., Golden, B., & Wasil, E. (2007). A record-to-record travel algorithm for solving the heterogeneous fleet vehicle routing problem. *Computers & Operations Research*, *34*, 2734–2742. doi:10.1016/j.cor.2005.10.015.

Lin, L., Gen, M., & Wang, X. (2009). Integrated multistage logistics network design by using hybrid evolutionary algorithm. *Computers & Industrial Engineering*, *56*, 854–873. doi:10.1016/j.cie.2008.09.037.

Lin, S., Yu, V., & Chou, S. (2009). Solving the truck and trailer routing problem based on a simulated annealing heuristic. *Computers & Operations Research*, *36*, 1638–1692. doi:10.1016/j.cor.2008.04.005.

Lin, S., Yu, V., & Chou, S. (2010). A note on a the truck and trailer routing problem. *Expert Systems with Applications*, *37*(1), 899–903. doi:10.1016/j.eswa.2009.06.077.

Lin, S., Yu, V., & Lu, C. (2011). A simulated annealing heuristic for the truck and trailer routing problem with time windows. *Expert Systems with Applications*, *38*(12), 15244–15252. doi:10.1016/j.eswa.2011.05.075.

Ljung, L. (1979). Asymptotic behavior of the extended Kalman filter as a parameter estimator for linear systems. *IEEE Trans. on Automatic Control*, 36–50.

Louwers, D., Kip, B. J., Peters, E., Souren, F., & Flapper, S. D. P. (1999). A facility location allocation model for re-using carpet materials. *Computers & Industrial Engineering*, *36*, 855–869. doi:10.1016/S0360-8352(99)00168-0.

Lu, Z., & Bostel, N. (2007). A facility location model for logistics systems including reverse flows: The case of remanufacturing activities. *Computers & Operations Research*, *34*, 299–323. doi:10.1016/j.cor.2005.03.002.

Madachy, R. (1997). Heuristic risk assessment using cost factors. *IEEE Software*, *14*(3), 51–59. doi:10.1109/52.589234.

Maenhout, B., & Vanhoucke, M. (2011). An evolutionary approach for the nurse re-rostering problem. *Computers & Operations Research*, *38*, 1400–1411. doi:10.1016/j.cor.2010.12.012.

Makowski, D., Hillier, D., Wallach, D., Andrieu, B., & Jeuffroy, M.-H. (2006). Parameter estimation for crop models. In *Working with Dynamic Crop Models*. London: Elsevier..

Makridakis, S. G., Wheelwright, S. C., & Hyndman, R. J. (1998). *Forecasting: Methods and applications*. Hoboken, NJ: Wiley..

Manalif, E., Capretz, L. F., & Ho, D. (2012). Fuzzy-ExCOM software project risk assessment. In *Proceedings of 11th IEEE Conference on Machine Learning and Application*. Boca Raton, FL: IEEE.

Mansouri, M., Dumont, B., & Destain, M.-F. (2011). Bayesian methods for predicting LAI and soil Moisture. In *Proceedings of the 12th International Conference on Precision Agriculture* (ICPA). Indianapolis, IN: ICPA.

Mansouri, M., Dumont, B., & Destain, M.-F. (2013). Modeling and prediction of nonlinear environmental system using bayesian methods. *Computers and Electronics in Agriculture*, *92*, 16–31. doi:10.1016/j.compag.2012.12.013.

Marchewka, J. T. (2009). *Information technology project management* (3rd ed.). Hoboken, NJ: John Wiley & Sons, Inc.

Marín, A., & Pelegrín, B. (1998). The return plant location problem: modelling and resolution. *European Journal of Operational Research*, *104*, 375–392. doi:10.1016/S0377-2217(97)00192-6.

Markowitz, H. M. (1952). Portfolio selection. *The Journal of Finance*, *7*, 79–91.

Markowitz, H. M. (1959). *Portfolio selection: Efficient diversification of investments*. New York: John Willey..

Master, D., Bräysy, O., & Dullaert, W. (2007). A multi-parametric evolution strategies algorithm for vehicle routing problems. *Expert Systems with Applications*, *32*, 508–517. doi:10.1016/j.eswa.2005.12.014.

Mavrovouniotis, M., & Yang, S. (2011). A memetic ant colony optimization algorithm for the dynamic travelling salesman problem. *Soft Computing*, *15*(7), 1405–1425. doi:10.1007/s00500-010-0680-1.

Mayer, D. G., Belward, J. A., Widell, H., & Burrage, K. (1999). Survival of the fittest - Genetic algorithms versus evolution strategies in the optimization of systems models. *Agricultural Systems*, *60*, 113–122. doi:10.1016/S0308-521X(99)00022-0.

McKenzie, E. (1984). General exponential smoothing and the equivalent ARMA process. *Journal of Forecasting*, *3*(3), 333–344. doi:10.1002/for.3980030312.

Mendel, J. M. (1995). Fuzzy logic systems for engineering: A tutorial. *Proceedings of the IEEE*, *83*(2), 345–347. doi:10.1109/5.364485.

Mendes, A. B., Funk, M., & Cavique, L. (2010). Knowledge discovery in the virtual social network due to common knowledge of proverbs. In *Proceedings of DMIN'10, the 6th International Conference on Data Mining*, (pp. 213-219). DMIN.

Mendes, A., Funk, G., & Funk, M. (2009). Extrair conhecimento de provérbios. In M. F. Salgueiro (Ed.), *Temas em Métodos Quantitativos* (pp. 89–107). Lisboa: Sílabo..

Mentzer, J. T., & Bienstock, C. C. (1998). *Sales forecasting management*. Thousand Oaks, CA: SAGE..

Miller, A. (2002). *Subset selection in regression*. Boca Raton, FL: Chapman & Hall. doi:10.1201/9781420035933.

Min, H., Ko, C. S., & Ko, H. J. (2006a). The spatial and temporal consolidation of returned products in a closed-loop supply chain network. *Computers & Industrial Engineering*, *51*, 309–320. doi:10.1016/j.cie.2006.02.010.

Min, H., & Ko, H. J. (2008). The dynamic design of a reverse logistics network from the perspective of third-party logistics service providers. *International Journal of Production Economics*, *113*, 176–192. doi:10.1016/j.ijpe.2007.01.017.

Min, H., Ko, H. J., & Ko, C. S. (2006b). A genetic algorithm approach to developing the multi-echelon reverse logistics network for product returns. *Omega*, *34*, 56–69. doi:10.1016/j.omega.2004.07.025.

Moghadam, B. F., & Seyedhosseini, S. M. (2010). A particle swarm approach to solve vehicle routing problem with uncertain demand: A drug distribution case study. *International Journal of Industrial Engineering Computations, 1*, 55–66. doi:10.5267/j.ijiec.2010.01.005.

Montemanni, R., Gambardella, L. M., Rizzoli, A. E., & Donati, A. V. (2005). Ant colony system for a dynamic vehicle routing problem. *Journal of Combinatorial Optimization, 10*, 327–343. doi:10.1007/s10878-005-4922-6.

Mould, G. (1996). Case study of manpower planning for clerical operations. *The Journal of the Operational Research Society, 47*(3), 358–368.

Moz, M., & Pato, M. V. (2007). A genetic algorithm approach to a nurse rerostering problem. *Computers & Operations Research, 34*, 667–691. doi:10.1016/j.cor.2005.03.019.

Mula, J., Poler, R., García-Sabater, J. P., & Lario, F. C. (2006). Models for production planning under uncertainty: A review. *International Journal of Production Economics, 103*(1), 271–285. doi:10.1016/j.ijpe.2005.09.001.

Mutha, A., & Pokharel, S. (2009). Strategic network design for reverse logistics and remanufacturing using new and old product modules. *Computers & Industrial Engineering, 56*, 334–346. doi:10.1016/j.cie.2008.06.006.

Mutingi, M., & Mbohwa, C. (2012). Enhanced group genetic algorithm for the heterogeneous fixed fleet vehicle routing problem. In *Proceedings of IEEE Conference on Industrial Engineering and Engineering Management*. Hong Kong: IEEE.

Mutingi, M., & Mbohwa, C. (2013). A satisficing approach to home healthcare worker scheduling. In *Proceedings of International Conference on Law, Entrepreneurship and Industrial Engineering* (ICLEIE'2013). Johannesburg, South Africa: ICLEIE.

Nejati, M., & Shafaei, A. (2009). Ranking airlines' service quality factors using a fuzzy approach: Study of the Iranian society. *International Journal of Quality & Reliability Management, 26*(3), 247–260. doi:10.1108/02656710910936726.

Nemenyi, P. B. (1963). *Distribution-free multiple comparisons*. (Doctoral dissertation). Princeton University, Princeton, NJ.

NESMA. (2006). *NESMA: Section NESMA – All about NESMA*. Retrieved 2006 from http://www.nesma.nl

Nuortioa, T., Kytöjokib, J., Niskaa, H., & Bräysyb, O. (2006). Improved route planning and scheduling of waste collection and transport. *Expert Systems with Applications, 30*, 223–232. doi:10.1016/j.eswa.2005.07.009.

Odzaly, E. E., Greer, D., & Sage, P. (2009). Software risk management barriers: En empirical study. In *Proceeding 3rd International Symposium on Empirical Software Engineering and Measurement* (pp.418-421). IEEE.

Okur, A., Nasibov, E. N., Kiliç, M., & Yavuz, M. (2009). Using OWA aggregation technique in QFD: A case study in education in a textile engineering department. *Quality & Quantity, 43*(6), 999–1009. doi:10.1007/s11135-008-9170-2.

Osgood, C. E., Suci, G., & Tannenbaum, P. H. (1957). *The measurement of meaning*. Chicago, IL: Univ. of Illinois Press.

Paraskevopoulos, D., Repoussis, P., Tarantilis, C., Ioannou, G., & Prastacos, G. (2008). A reactive variable neighbourhood tabu search for the heterogeneous fleet vehicle routing problem with time windows. *Journal of Heuristics, 14*, 425–455. doi:10.1007/s10732-007-9045-z.

Parasuraman, A., Zeithaml, V. A., & Berry, L. L. (1985). A conceptual models of service quality and its implications for future research. *Journal of Marketing, 29*(4), 41–50. doi:10.2307/1251430.

Parasuraman, A., Zeithaml, V. A., & Berry, L. L. (1988). SERVQUAL: A multiple-item scale for measuring consumers perceptions of service quality. *Journal of Retailing, 64*(1), 12–40.

Parasuraman, A., Zeithaml, V. A., & Malhotra, A. (2005). E-S-QUAL: A multiple-item scale for assessing electronic service quality. *Journal of Service Research, 7*(3), 213–233. doi:10.1177/1094670504271156.

Parlamento Europeo. (2009). *Directiva 2009/28/EC del parlamento europeo y del consejo relativa al fomento del uso de energía procedente de fuentes renovables*. Bruselas. Author..

Pavan, M., & Todeschini, R. (2008). Total-order ranking methods. *Data Handling in Science and Technology, 27*, 51–70. doi:10.1016/S0922-3487(08)10002-8.

Pawlak, Z. (1982). Rough sets. *International Journal of Computer and Information Science, 11*, 341–356. doi:10.1007/BF01001956.

Pawlak, Z. (1991). *Rough sets: Theoretical aspects of reasoning about data.* Boston: Kluwer Academic Publishers..

Peidro, D., Mula, J., Poler, R., & Lario, F. C. (2009). Quantitative models for supply chain planning under uncertainty: A review. *International Journal of Advanced Manufacturing Technology, 43*(3-4), 400–420. doi:10.1007/s00170-008-1715-y.

Perron, O. (1907). Zur theorie der matrizen. *Math. Ann., 64.*

Peters, J. F., & Skowron, A. (2010). *Transactions on rough sets XI.* Berlin: Springer. doi:10.1007/978-3-642-11479-3.

Pishvaee, M. S., Kianfar, K., & Karimi, B. (2010a). Reverse logistics network design using simulated annealing. *International Journal of Advanced Manufacturing Technology, 47*, 269–281. doi:10.1007/s00170-009-2194-5.

Pishvaee, M. S., & Torabi, S. A. (2010). A possibilistic programming approach for closed-loop supply chain network design under uncertainty. *Fuzzy Sets and Systems, 161*, 2668–2683. doi:10.1016/j.fss.2010.04.010.

Pishvaee, M. S., Zanjirani Farahani, R., & Dullaert, W. (2010b). A memetic algorithm for bi-objective integrated forward/reverse logistics network design. *Computers & Operations Research, 37*, 1100–1112. doi:10.1016/j.cor.2009.09.018.

Pokharel, S., & Mutha, A. (2009). Perspectives in reverse logistics: A review. *Resources, Conservation and Recycling, 53*, 175–182. doi:10.1016/j.resconrec.2008.11.006.

Poler, R., & Mula, J. (2011). Forecasting model selection through out-of-sample rolling horizon weighted errors. *Expert Systems with Applications, 38*(12), 14778–14785. doi:10.1016/j.eswa.2011.05.072.

Polkowski, L. (2002). *Rough sets, mathematical foundations.* Berlin: Physica-Verlag Heidelberg. doi:10.1007/978-3-7908-1776-8.

Potvin, J., & Bengio, S. (1996). The vehicle routing problem with time windows –Part II: Genetic search. *INFORMS Journal on Computing, 8*, 165–172. doi:10.1287/ijoc.8.2.165.

Poyiadjis, G., Doucet, A., & Singh, S. (2005). Maximum likelihood parameter estimation in general state-space models using particle methods. In *Proceedings of the American Stat. Assoc.* ASA.

Pressman, R. S. (2005). *Software engineering - Practitioner's Approach* (6th ed.). New York: McGraw Hill..

Puris, A., Bello, R., Martinez, Y., & Nowe, A. (2007). Twostage ant colony optimization for solving the traveling salesman problem. In J. Mira, & J. R. Álvarez (Eds.), *Nature Inspired Problem-Solving Methods in Knowledge Engineering* (pp. 307–316). Berlin: Springer. doi:10.1007/978-3-540-73055-2_33.

Putnam, L. H., & Myers, W. (1992). *Measures for excellence.* Englewood Cliffs, NJ: Prentice Hall..

Qin, Z., & Ji, X. (2010). Logistics network design for product recovery in fuzzy environment. *European Journal of Operational Research, 202*, 479–490. doi:10.1016/j.ejor.2009.05.036.

Ramírez-Rosado, I. J., García-Garrido, E. G., Fernández-Jiménez, L. A., Zorzano-Santamaría, P. J., Monteiro, C., & Miranda, V. (2008). Promotion of new wind farms based on a decision support system. *Renewable Energy, 33*, 558–566. doi:10.1016/j.renene.2007.03.028.

Reifer, D. J. (2002). Let the numbers do the talking. *CrossTalk*, 4-8.

Report of Shapes FP6 Project. (2010). *Energy recovery in existing infrastructures with small hydropower plants: Multipurpose schemes – Overview and examples.* Retrieved from www.esha.be

ReVelle, C.S., & Swain, R.W. (1972). Central facilities location. *Geographical Analysis, 2*, 30–42.

Rizzoli, A. E., Montemanni, R., Lucibello, E., & Gambardella, L. M. (2007). Ant colony optimisation for real world vehicle routing problems: From theory to applications. *Swarm Intelligence, 1*(2), 135–151. doi:10.1007/s11721-007-0005-x.

Rochat, Y., & Taillard, E. D. (1995). Probabilistic diversification and intensification in local search for vehicle routing. *Journal of Heuristics, 1*, 147–167. doi:10.1007/BF02430370.

Saaty, T. (2005). *Theory and applications of the analytic network process: Decision making with benefits, opportunities, costs, and risks.* Pittsburgh, PA: RWS Publications..

Saaty, T. L. (1980). *The analytic hierarchy process.* New York: McGraw-Hill..

Saaty, T. L. (1989). *Group decision making and the AHP.* New York: Springer Verlag..

Sahinidis, N. (2004). Optimization under uncertainty: State-of-the-art and opportunities. *Computers & Chemical Engineering, 28*(6-7), 971–983. doi:10.1016/j.compchemeng.2003.09.017.

Sakawa, M. (1993). *Fuzzy sets and interactive multi-objective optimization.* New York: Plenum Press. doi:10.1007/978-1-4899-1633-4.

Salema, M. I. G., Póvoa, A. P. B., & Novais, A. Q. (2006). A warehouse-based design model for reverse logistics. *The Journal of the Operational Research Society, 57*, 615–629. doi:10.1057/palgrave.jors.2602035.

Salema, M. I. G., Póvoa, A. P. B., & Novais, A. Q. (2007). An optimization model for the design of a capacitated multi-product reverse logistics network with uncertainty. *European Journal of Operational Research, 179*, 1063–1077. doi:10.1016/j.ejor.2005.05.032.

Salema, M. I. G., Póvoa, A. P. B., & Novais, A. Q. (2009). A strategic and tactical model for closed-loop supply chains. *OR-Spektrum, 31*, 573–599. doi:10.1007/s00291-008-0160-5.

Salema, M. I. G., Póvoa, A. P. B., & Novais, A. Q. (2010). Simultaneous design and planning of supply chains with reverse flows: A generic modelling framework. *European Journal of Operational Research, 203*, 336–349. doi:10.1016/j.ejor.2009.08.002.

Santos, J. (2003). E-service quality: A model of virtual service quality dimensions. *Managing Service Quality, 13*(3), 233–246. doi:10.1108/09604520310476490.

Sarkka, S. (2007). On unscented kalman filtering for state estimation of continuous-time nonlinear systems. *IEEE Trans. Automatic Control*, 1631–1641.

Sasikumar, P., Kannan, G., & Noorul Haq, A. (2010). A multi-echelon reverse logistics network design for product recovery - A case of truck tire remanufacturing. *International Journal of Advanced Manufacturing Technology, 49*, 1223–1234. doi:10.1007/s00170-009-2470-4.

Scheuerer, S. (2006). A tabu search heuristic for the truck and trailer routing problem. *Computers & Operations Research, 33*, 894–909. doi:10.1016/j.cor.2004.08.002.

Schott, J. R. (1995). *Fault tolerant design using single and multicriteria genetic algorithm optimization.* (Master's thesis). Massachusetts Institute of Technology, Cambridge, MA.

Segura, J. V., & Vercher, E. (2001). A spreadsheet modeling approach to the Holt–Winters optimal forecasting. *European Journal of Operational Research, 131*(2), 375–388. doi:10.1016/S0377-2217(00)00062-X.

Semet, F. (1995). A two-phase algorithm for the partial accessibility constrained vehicle routing problem. *Annals of Operations Research, 61*, 45–65. doi:10.1007/BF02098281.

Semet, F., & Taillard, E. (1993). Solving real-life vehicle routing problems efficiently using tabu search. *Annals of Operations Research, 41*(4), 469–488. doi:10.1007/BF02023006.

Seth, N., & Deshmukh, S. G. (2005). Service quality models: A review. *International Journal of Quality & Reliability Management, 22*(9), 913–949. doi:10.1108/02656710510625211.

Sheskin, D. J. (2003). *Handbook of parametric and nonparametric statistical procedures* (3rd ed.). Boca Raton, FL: Chapman & Hall/CRC. doi:10.1201/9781420036268.

Silva, R. C., Verdegay, J. L., & Yamakami, A. (2007). Two-phase method to solve fuzzy quadratic programming problems. In *Proceedings of IEEE International Conference on Fuzzy Systems.* IEEE.

Silva, R. C., Verdegay, J. L., & Yamakami, A. (2010b). A parametric convex programming approach applied in portfolio selection problem with fuzzy costs. In *Proceedings of the 2010 IEEE International Fuzzy Systems Conference.* IEEE.

Silva, C. A., Sousa, J. M. C., & Runkler, T. A. (2008). Rescheduling and optimization of logistic processes using GA and ACO. *Engineering Applications of Artificial Intelligence, 21*(3), 343–352. doi:10.1016/j.engappai.2007.08.006.

Silva, R. C., Cruz, C., & Verdegay, J. L. (2013). Fuzzy costs in quadratic programming problems. *Fuzzy Optimization and Decision Making.* doi:10.1007/s10700-013-9153-1.

Silva, R. C., Cruz, C., Verdegay, J. L., & Yamakami, A. (2010a). A survey of fuzzy convex programming models. In L. Weldon, & J. Kacprzyk (Eds.), *Fuzzy optimization: Studies in fuzziness and soft computing* (Vol. 254, pp. 127–143). Academic Press. doi:10.1007/978-3-642-13935-2_6.

Silver, E. A., Pyke, D. F., & Peterson, R. (1998). *Inventory management and production planning and scheduling.* Hoboken, NJ: John Wiley & Sons..

Simon, D. (2003). Kalman filtering of fuzzy discrete time dynamic systems. *Applied Soft Computing,* 191–207. doi:10.1016/S1568-4946(03)00034-6.

Simon, D. (2006). *Optimal state estimation: Kalman, H1, and nonlinear approaches.* Hoboken, NJ: John Wiley and Sons. doi:10.1002/0470045345.

Skikos, G. D., & Machias, A. V. (1992). Fuzzy multi criteria decision making for evaluation of wind sites. *Wind Energy (Chichester, England), 6*(4), 213–228.

Smidl, V., & Quinn, A. (2005). *The variational Bayes method in signal processing.* New York: Springer-Verlag..

Snyder, R. (2002). Forecasting sales of slow and fast moving inventories. *European Journal of Operational Research, 140*(3), 684–699. doi:10.1016/S0377-2217(01)00231-4.

Soffia, C., Miotto, F., Poggi, D., & Claps, P. (2010). Hydropower potential from the drinking water systems of the Piemonte region (Italy). In *Proceedings of SEEP 2010 Conference.* SEEP.

Software Productivity Research Incorporated. (2006). *SPR programming languages table.* Retrieved from 2006 from http://www.spr.com

Sommerville, I. (2007). *Software engineering* (8th ed.). Essex, UK: Addison-Wesley Published Ltd.

Standish Group. (n.d.). *Chaos report2009.* Retrieved January 16, 2012, from http://www1.standishgroup.com/newsroom/chaos_2009.php

Stellman, A., & Greene, J. (2006). *Applied software project management.* Sebastopol, CA: O'Reilly Media, Inc.

Steuer, R. E. (1986). *Multicriteria optimization: Theory, computation, and application.* New York: Willey..

Stirling, W. C. (2003). *Satisficing games and decision making: With applications to engineering and computer science.* Cambridge, UK: Cambridge University Press. doi:10.1017/CBO9780511543456.

Stirling, W. C. (2012). *Theory of conditional games.* Cambridge, UK: Cambridge University Press..

Stutzke, R. D. (2005). *Estimating software-intensive systems – Projects, products, and processes.* Westford, MA: Pearson Education, Inc.

Stützle, T., & Hoos, H.H. (1996). *Improving the ant system: A detailed report on the max-min ant system* (Technical Report AIDA- 96-12). Darmstadt, Germany: FG Intellektik, FB Informatik, TU Darmstadt.

Stützle, T., & Hoos, H. H. (2000). Max-min ant system. *Future Generation Computer Systems, 16*(8), 889–914. doi:10.1016/S0167-739X(00)00043-1.

Syntetos, A. A. (2001). *Forecasting of intermittent demand.* (Ph.D. thesis). Buckinghamshire Business School, Brunel University, UK.

Taillard, E. D. (1999). A heuristic column generation method for the heterogeneous fleet VRP. *RAIRO, 33,* 1–34. doi:10.1051/ro:1999101.

Talbi, E.-G. (2009). *Metaheuristics from design to implementation.* Hoboken, NJ: John Wiley & Sons, Inc.

Tanaka, H., & Guo, P. (1999). Portfolio selection based on upper and lower exponential possibility distributions. *European Journal of Operational Research, 114,* 115–126. doi:10.1016/S0377-2217(98)00033-2.

Tanaka, H., Guo, P., & Türksen, L. B. (2000). Portfolio selection based on fuzzy possibility distributions. *Fuzzy Sets and Systems, 111,* 387–397. doi:10.1016/S0165-0114(98)00041-4.

Tanaka, H., Okuda, T., & Asai, K. (1974). On fuzzy mathematical programming. *J. Cybernet., 3,* 37–46.

Tarantilis, C. D., Kiranoudis, C. T., & Vassiliadis, V. S. A. (2003). A list based threshold accepting metaheuristic for the heterogeneous fixes fleet vehicle routing problem. *The Journal of the Operational Research Society, 54*(1), 65–71. doi:10.1057/palgrave.jors.2601443.

Tarantilis, C. D., Kiranoudis, C. T., & Vassiliadis, V. S. A. (2004). A threshold accepting metaheuristic for the heterogeneous fixed fleet vehicle routing problem. *European Journal of Operational Research, 152,* 148–158. doi:10.1016/S0377-2217(02)00669-0.

Tchangani, A. P., & Pérès, F. (2010). BOCR framework for decision analysis. In *Proceedings of 12th IFAC Symposium on Large Scale Systems: Theory and Applications.* IFAC.

Tchangani, A.P. (2013). Bipolar aggregation method for fuzzy nominal classification using weighted cardinal fuzzy measure (WCFM), *Journal of Uncertain Systems.*

Tchangani, A. P. (2006). A satisficing game theory approach for group evaluation of production units. *Decision Support Systems, 42,* 778–788. doi:10.1016/j.dss.2005.05.010.

Tchangani, A. P. (2006a). SANPEV: A satisficing analytic network process framework for efficiency evaluation of alternatives. *Foundations of Computing and Decision Sciences, 31*(3-4), 291–319.

Tchangani, A. P. (2009). Evaluation model for multi attributes - Multi agents decision making: Satisficing game approach. *International Journal of Information Technology and Decision Making, 8*(1), 73–91. doi:10.1142/S0219622009003272.

Tchangani, A. P. (2009a). Modelling selecting and ranking alternatives characterized by multiple attributes to satisfy multiple objectives. *Journal of Information and Computing Science, 4*(1), 3–16.

Tchangani, A. P. (2010). Considering bipolarity of attributes with regards to objectives in decisions evaluation. *Inzinerine Ekonomika, 21*(5), 475–484.

Tchangani, A. P., Bouzarour-Amokrane, Y., & Pérès, F. (2012). Evaluation model in decision analysis: Bipolar approach. *INFORMATICA: An International Journal, 23*(3), 461–485.

Teodorovic, D., & Lucic, P. (1998). A fuzzy set theory approach to the aircrew rostering problem. *Fuzzy Sets and Systems, 95,* 261–271. doi:10.1016/S0165-0114(96)00277-1.

Teunter, R. H., Syntetos, A. A., & Babai, M. Z. (2010). Determining order-up-to levels under periodic review for compound binomial (intermittent) demand. *European Journal of Operational Research, 16,* 619–624. doi:10.1016/j.ejor.2009.09.013.

Thierry, M., Salomon, M., Van Nunen, J., & Van Waasenhove, L. (1995). Strategic issues in product recovery management. *California Management Review, 37,* 114–135. doi:10.2307/41165792.

Tiryaki, F. (2006). Interactive compensatory fuzzy programming for decentralized multi-level linear programming (DMLLP) problems. *Fuzzy Sets and Systems, 157,* 3072–3090. doi:10.1016/j.fss.2006.04.001.

Tong, H. (1983). *Threshold models in non-linear time series analysis.* Berlin: Springer-Verlag. doi:10.1007/978-1-4684-7888-4.

Topaloglu, S., & Ozkarahan, I. (2004). An implicit goal programming model for the tour scheduling problem considering the employee work preferences. *Annals of Operations Research, 128,* 135–158. doi:10.1023/B:ANOR.0000019102.68222.df.

Topaloglu, S., & Selim, H. (2010). Nurse scheduling using fuzzy modelling approach. *Fuzzy Sets and Systems, 161*(11), 1543–1563. doi:10.1016/j.fss.2009.10.003.

Toth & Vigo. (2002). *The vehicle routing problem.* Society for Industrial and Applied Mathematics..

Tremblay, M., & Wallach, D. (2004). Comparison of parameter estimation methods for crop models. *Agronomie, 24*(6-7), 351–365. doi:10.1051/agro:2004033.

Tsai, W.-H., Chou, W.-C., & Leu, J.-D. (2011). An effectiveness evaluation model for the web-based marketing of the airline industry. *Expert Systems with Applications, 38*(12), 15499–15516.

Tsai, W.-H., Hsu, W., & Chou, W.-C. (2011). A gap analysis model for improving airport service quality. *Total Quality Management & Business Excellence, 22*(10), 1025–1040. doi:10.1080/14783363.2011.611326.

Tsaur, S. H., Chang, T. Y., & Yen, C. H. (2002). The evaluation of airline service quality by fuzzy MCDM. *Tourism Management*, *23*(2), 107–115. doi:10.1016/S0261-5177(01)00050-4.

Tseng, F. M., & Tzeng, G.-H. (2002). A fuzzy seasonal ARIMA model for forecasting. *Fuzzy Sets and Systems*, *126*(3), 367–376. doi:10.1016/S0165-0114(01)00047-1.

Tseng, F. M., Tzeng, G.-H., Yu, H.-C., & Yuan, B. J. C. (2001). Fuzzy ARIMA model for forecasting the foreign exchange market. *Fuzzy Sets and Systems*, *118*(1), 9–19. doi:10.1016/S0165-0114(98)00286-3.

Tseng, M.-L. (2009). A causal and effect decision making model of service quality expectation using grey-fuzzy DEMATEL approach. *Expert Systems with Applications*, *36*(4), 7738–7748. doi:10.1016/j.eswa.2008.09.011.

Tseng, M.-L. (2011). Using hybrid MCDM to evaluate the service quality expectation in linguistic preference. *Applied Soft Computing*, *11*(8), 4551–4562. doi:10.1016/j.asoc.2011.08.011.

Tutuncu, G. Y. (2010). An interactive algorithm for the heterogeneous fixed fleet vehicle routing problem with and without backhauls. *European Journal of Operational Research*, *201*(2), 593–600. doi:10.1016/j.ejor.2009.03.044.

Tzeng, G.-H., Cheng, H.-J., & Huang, T. D. (2007). Multiobjective optimal planning for designing relief delivery systems. *Transportation Research Part E, Logistics and Transportation Review*, *43*, 673–686. doi:10.1016/j.tre.2006.10.012.

United Nations Environment Programme/ World Meteorological Organization. (1992). *Climate change: The IPCC 1990 and 1992 assessments*. Intergovernmental Panel on Climate Change..

United Nations Framework Convention on Climate Change. (2013). *Message to parties: Early submission of information and views*. United Nations Climate Change Secretariat..

United Nations. (1992). *Conference on environment and development: Rio declaration on environment and development*. Rio de Janeiro, Brazil: UN.

United Nations. (1997). *Framework convention on climatic change: Report of the conference of the parties on its third session*. Kyoto, Japan: UN.

Üster, H., Easwaran, G., Akçali, E., & Çetinkaya, S. (2007). *Benders decomposition with alternative multiple cuts for a multi-product closed-loop supply chain network design model*. Naval Research Logistics..

Van Der Merwe, R., & Wan, E. (2001). The square-root unscented kalman filter for state and parameter-estimation. In *Proceedings of IEEE International Conference on Acoustics, Speech, and Signal Processing*, (pp. 3461–3464). IEEE.

Van Haren, R., & Fthenakis, V. (2011). GIS-based wind farm site selection using spatial multi-criteria analysis (SMCA): Evaluating the case for New York State. *Renewable & Sustainable Energy Reviews*, *15*, 3332–3340. doi:10.1016/j.rser.2011.04.010.

Van Mieghem, P., & Kuipers, F. A. (2004). Concepts of exact QoS routing algorithms. *IEEE/ACM Transactions on Networking*, *12*(5), 851–864. doi:10.1109/TNET.2004.836112.

Varghese, V., & Rossetti, M. (2008). A classification approach for selecting forecasting techniques for intermittent demand. In *Proceedings of the 2008 Industrial Engineering Research Conference*. IEEE.

Verdegay, J. L. (1982). Fuzzy mathematical programming. In M. M. Gupta, & E. Sanchez (Eds.), *Fuzzy Information and Decision Processes*. Amsterdam: North-Holland..

Verdegay, J. L., Yager, R. R., & Bonissone, P. P. (2008). On heuristics as a fundamental constituent of soft computing. *Fuzzy Sets and Systems*, *159*(7), 846–855. doi:10.1016/j.fss.2007.08.014.

Vermaak, J., Lawrence, N., & Perez, P. (2003). Variational inference for visual tracking. In *Proceedings of Computer Vision and Pattern Recognition*. IEEE..

Vila, M. A., & Delgado, M. (1983). On medical diagnosis using possibility measures. *Fuzzy Sets and Systems*, *10*(1–3), 211–222. doi:10.1016/S0165-0114(83)80116-X.

Villegas, J. G., Palacios, F., & Medaglia, A. L. (2006). Solution methods for the bi-objective (cost-coverage) unconstrained facility location problem with an illustrative example. *Annals of Operations Research*, *147*, 109–141. doi:10.1007/s10479-006-0061-4.

Villegas, J., Prins, C., Prodhon, C., Medaglia, A., & Velasco, N. (2010). GRASP/VND and multi-start evolutionary local search for the single truck and trailer routing problem with satellite depots. *Engineering Applications of Artificial Intelligence, 23*, 780–794. doi:10.1016/j.engappai.2010.01.013.

Villegas, J., Prins, C., Prodhon, C., Medaglia, A., & Velasco, N. (2011). A GRASP with evolutionary path relinking for the truck and trailer routing problem. *Computers & Operations Research, 38*, 1319–1334. doi:10.1016/j.cor.2010.11.011.

Vincke, P. (1989). L'aide multicritere a la decision. Bruxelles, Belgium: Ed.s de l'Universite Libre de Bruxelles..

von Neumann, J., & Morgenstern, O. (1964). *Theory of games and economic behavior*. Hoboken, NJ: John Wiley..

Wan, E., & Van Der Merwe, R. (2000). The unscented Kalman filter for nonlinear estimation. In *Adaptive Systems for Signal Processing, Communications, and Control Symposium*, (pp. 153–158). Academic Press.

Wang, P., Chao, K. M., Lo, C. C., Huang, C. L., & Li, Y. (2006). A fuzzy model for selection of QoS-aware web services. In *Proceedings - IEEE International Conference on e-Business Engineering*, (pp. 585-592). IEEE.

Wang, R., Shu, L., Hsu, Lin, Y. H., & Tseng, M.-L. (2011). Evaluation of customer perceptions on airline service quality in uncertainty. *Procedia - Social and Behavioral Sciences, 25*, 419-437.

Wang, H. F., & Hsu, H. W. (2010). A closed-loop logistic model with a spanning-tree based genetic algorithm. *Computers & Operations Research, 37*, 376–389. doi:10.1016/j.cor.2009.06.001.

Watada, J. (1997). Fuzzy portfolio selection and its application to decision making. *Tratra Mountains Mathematical Publication, 13*, 219–248.

Wendell, R. E., & Hurter, A. P. (1973). Location theory, dominance and convexity. *Operations Research, 21*, 314–320. doi:10.1287/opre.21.1.314.

Wen, J., Li, S., Lin, Z., Hu, Y., & Huang, C. (2012). Systematic literature review of machine learning based software development effort estimation models. *Information and Software Technology, 54*(1), 41–59. doi:10.1016/j.infsof.2011.09.002.

Willemain, T. R., Smart, C. N., & Schwarz, H. F. (2004). A new approach to forecasting intermittent demand for service parts inventories. *International Journal of Forecasting, 20*(3), 375–387. doi:10.1016/S0169-2070(03)00013-X.

Willemain, T. R., Smart, C. N., Shockor, J. H., & DeSautels, P. A. (1994). Forecasting intermittent demand in manufacturing: A comparative evaluation of Croston's method. *International Journal of Forecasting, 10*(4), 529–538. doi:10.1016/0169-2070(94)90021-3.

Williams, R. et al. (1997). Putting risk management into practice. *IEEE Software, 14*(3), 75–82. doi:10.1109/52.589240.

Williams, T. M. (1984). Stock control with sporadic and slow-moving demand. *The Journal of the Operational Research Society, 35*(10), 939–948.

Winters, P. R. (1960). Forecasting sales by exponentially weighted moving averages. *Management Science, 6*(3), 324–342. doi:10.1287/mnsc.6.3.324.

Wong, J., Ho, D., & Capretz, L. F. (2008). Calibrating function point backfiring conversion ratios using neuro-fuzzy technique. *International Journal of Uncertainty. Fuzziness and Knowledge-Based Systems, 16*(6), 847–862. doi:10.1142/S0218488508005650.

Working Group I. (1990). *Climate change: The IPCC scientific assessment*. Cambridge, UK: Cambridge University Press..

Working Group II. (1990). *Climate change: The IPCC impacts assessment*. Canberra, Australia: Australian Government Publishing Service..

Working Group III. (1990). *Climate change: The IPCC response strategies*. World Meteorological Organization/United Nations Environment Program.

World Bank. (2007). *Technical and economic assessment of off-grid, mini-grid and grid electrification technologies*. Washington, DC: World Bank..

Wu, S. I., & Lu, R. P. (1993). Combining artificial neural networks and statistics for stock-market forecasting. In *Proceedings of the 1993 ACM conference on Computer Science* (pp. 257–264). New York, NY: ACM.

Wu, J. J., Shih, S. F., Wang, H., Liu, P., & Wang, C. M. (2012). QoS-aware replica placement for grid computing. *Concurrency and Computation, 24*(3), 193–213. doi:10.1002/cpe.1817.

Xia, W., Capretz, L. F., & Ho, D. (2008). A neuro-fuzzy model for function point calibration. *Transactions on Information Science & Applications, 5*(1), 22–30.

Xia, W., Ho, D., & Capretz, L. F. (2008). A neuro-fuzzy model for function point calibration. *WSEAS Transactions on Information Science and Applications, 5*(1), 22–30.

Yao, Y. Y. (2007). Neighborhood systems and approximate retrieval. *Information Sciences, 176*, 3431–3452. doi:10.1016/j.ins.2006.02.002.

Yeh, C.-H., & Kuo, Y.-L. (2003). Evaluating passenger services of Asia-Pacific international airports. *Transportation Research Part E, Logistics and Transportation Review, 39*(1), 35–48. doi:10.1016/S1366-5545(02)00017-0.

Yongsheng, Z., & Shouyang, W. (2008). Generic model of reverse logistics network design. *International Journal of Transportation Systems Engineering and Information Technology, 8*, 71–78. doi:10.1016/S1570-6672(08)60025-2.

Zadeh, L. A. (1965). Fuzzy sets. *Information and Control, 8*, 338–353. doi:10.1016/S0019-9958(65)90241-X.

Zadeh, L. A. (1978). Fuzzy sets as a basis for a theory of possibility. *Fuzzy Sets and Systems, 1*, 3–28. doi:10.1016/0165-0114(78)90029-5.

Zadeh, L. A. (1994). Fuzzy logic, neural networks, and soft computing. *Communications of the ACM, 37*(3), 77–84. doi:10.1145/175247.175255.

Zanjirani Farahani, R., SteadieSeifi, M., & Asgari, N. (2010). Multiple criteria facility location problems: A survey. *Applied Mathematical Modelling, 34*, 1689–1709. doi:10.1016/j.apm.2009.10.005.

Zhu, F. X., Wymer, W. J., & Chen, I. (2002). IT-based services and service quality in consumer banking. *International Journal of Service Industry Management, 13*(1), 69–90. doi:10.1108/09564230210421164.

Zimmerman, H. J. (1993). *Fuzzy set theory and its applications* (2nd ed.). Boston: Kluwer Academic Publishers..

Zimmermann, H. J. (1978). Fuzzy programming and linear programming with several objective functions. *Fuzzy Sets and Systems, 1*, 45–55. doi:10.1016/0165-0114(78)90031-3.

Zimmermann, H. J. (1997). Fuzzy mathematical programming. In T. Gal, & H. J. Greenberg (Eds.), *Advances in sensitivity analysis and parametric programming*. Dordrecht, The Netherlands: Kluwer Academic Press. doi:10.1007/978-1-4615-6103-3_15.

Zitzler, E., Deb, K., & Thiele, L. (2000). Comparison of multiobjective evolutionary algorithms: Empirical results. *Evolutionary Computation, 8*, 173–195. doi:10.1162/106365600568202 PMID:10843520.

Zitzler, E., & Thiele, L. (1999). Multiobjective evolutionary algorithms: A comparative case study and the strength Pareto approach. *IEEE Transactions on Evolutionary Computation, 3*, 257–271. doi:10.1109/4235.797969.

About the Contributors

Antonio D. Masegosa received the degree in Computer Engineering in 2005 and the PhD degree in Computer Sciences in 2010 from the School of Computer and Telecommunications Engineering, University of Granada, Spain. From 2010, he has been working as a post-doc researcher in the Center for Research on ICT of the University of Granada. He has published three books and more than 20 papers in leading scientific journals, international and national conferences. He has participated in a wide variety of research projects and he is currently involved in two: "Applicability of the Soft Computing in Advance Technology Environments: Sustainability" and "Intelligent Software Platform for Unification of Police Services." He has attended numerous national and international conferences and he has been member of the organizing committee of the VI Nature Inspired Cooperative Strategies for Optimization Conference (NICSO2013). His research interests include Intelligent Systems, Soft Computing, Metaheuristics, Cooperative Strategies for Optimization and Technology Foresight, among others.

Pablo J. Villacorta received his M.S. degree in Informatics in 2009, his M.S. in Statistics in 2012 and his M.S. in Soft Computing and Intelligent Systems in 2010 from the University of Granada, Spain. He is currently pursuing his PhD degree within the Models of Decision and Optimization Research Group, in the Department of Computer Science and Artificial Intelligence, University of Granada. He has published over a dozen of papers in national and international conferences and international journals. Recently, his PhD thesis proposal was awarded the GENIL Prize to the most promising thesis proposal in the 2011 Conference of the Spanish Association for Artificial Intelligence (CAEPIA). His research interests include soft computing, metaheuristics, adversarial decision-making, and game theory.

Carlos Cruz-Corona received the MS degree in Electronic Engineering in 1986 from the Central University of Las Villas, Cuba, and the PhD degree in Computer Sciences from the University of Granada, Granada, Spain, in 2005. He is a Lecturer at Department of Computer Science and Artificial Intelligence (DECSAI), University of Granada, Spain. He has published several scientific and technical papers in leading scientific journals. He has served on many international program committees and has attended numerous national and international conferences, congresses, and workshops. He has participated in a variety of national and international research and educational projects. His current scientific interests are soft computing, fuzzy sets and systems, decision support systems, metaheuristic algorithms, and nature inspired systems.

M. Socorro Garcia-Cascales received the M.S. degree in Industrial Engineering and the Ph.D. degree in Industrial Engineering from the Technical University of Cartagena, Murcia, Spain, in 2009. She received the Technical University of Cartagena's doctorate award in 2010. She is a Professor in the Department of Electronic Computer Architecture and Project Engineering (DETCP) of the Technical University of Cartagena, and a member of the Models of Decision and Optimization (MODO) Research Group of the University of Granada, Spain. She has published twelve papers in scientific journals of impact and ten chapters of books. She has more than forty publications in national and international congresses. She is currently involved in a research project on "Applicability of Soft Computing in Advanced Technology Environments: Sustainability." Her current scientific interests are soft computing, fuzzy sets and systems, decision support systems, applications in engineering projects and renewable energy.

María T. Lamata received the M.S. degree in mathematics and the Ph.D. degree in sciences from the University of Granada, Spain, in 1975 and 1986, respectively. He is a full Professor at Department of Computer Science and Artificial Intelligence (DECSAI), University of Granada, Spain, and director of the Models of Decision and Optimization (MODO) Research Group. She has published more than 150 scientific and technical papers in leading scientific journals, and has been Advisor of 4 Ph.D. dissertations. He has served on many international program committees and has attended numerous national and international conferences, congresses, and workshops. She has been Principal Investigator in a variety of national and international research and educational projects. She currently lead two research projects on "Quality Solution Evaluation Using Soft Computing Techniques: Applications" and on "Viability of the Applications of Soft Computing to Sustainable Areas." Apart from this, she is currently involved in a research project on "Applicability of the Soft Computing in Advanced Technology Environments: Sustainability." She also is a member of the Editorial Board of the International Journal of Uncertainty, Fuzziness, and Knowledge-Based Systems. Her current scientific interests are soft computing, fuzzy sets and systems, OWA operators, decision support systems, and linguistic labels.

José L. Verdegay received the MS degree in mathematics and the PhD degree in sciences from the University of Granada, Granada, Spain, in 1975 and 1981, respectively. He is a full Professor at Department of Computer Science and Artificial Intelligence (DECSAI),University of Granada, Spain, Director of the Models of Decision and Optimization (MODO) Research Group, Coordinator of the Master on Soft Computing between University of Granada and Universidad Central Marta Abreu de las Villas (Cuba) and Delegate of the Rector for ICT in University of Granada. He has published 14 books and more than 250 scientific and technical papers in leading scientific journals, and has been Advisor of 17 PhD dissertations. He has served on many international program committees and has attended numerous national and international conferences, congresses, and workshops. He has been Principal Researcher in a variety of national and international research and educational projects. He has much experience in the evaluation of the quality of academic institutions. He has been member and President of a number of committees with the European Training Foundation and the Spanish Ministry of Education. He also is a member of the Editorial Board of several international leading journals. He has been Chairman of DECSAI (1990–1994), President of the Spanish Association for Fuzzy Logic and Technologies (1990–1996), Advisor for Intelligent Technologies of the Spanish Science Inter-Ministry Commission (1995–1996), and Director of International Affairs at the University of Granada (1996–2000). His current scientific interests are Soft Computing, fuzzy sets and systems, decision support systems, metaheuristic algorithms, nature inspired systems, and bioinformatics.

* * *

Enrique Muñoz Ballester obtained his degree in Computer Science Engineering at the University of Murcia in 2006. In 2007, he received a master's degree on Advanced Information Technologies and Telematics. In 2010, he finished his PhD (Artificial Intelligence) at the University of Murcia, obtaining the "Best Doctoral Dissertation Award" in Computer Science. He has written several publications (papers in journals, conferences, book chapters, etc.), he is member of the editorial board of the Soft Computing journal, and has been TPC member in several journals and international conferences. He has participated into several research projects. His research interests include multi-agent systems, machine learning, and optimization strategies.

José M. Cadenas received the Ph.D. degree in Sciences from Granada University, Spain, in 1993. He is currently a Professor in Computer Science in the Department of Information Engineering and Communications at the Murcia University, Spain. He has published extensively in the areas of Fuzzy Systems, Heuristics Algorithms in Uncertain Environments, Soft Computing applied to Optimization Problems, DatabMining and Learning, including over 140 refereed research papers in journals, books and in conference proceedings. Dr. Cadenas is member of international associations (European Society for Fuzzy Logic and Technology, and IEEE Computational Intelligence Society) and is also member of different thematic research networks.

Clara Calvo is an Associate Professor at the Bussines Mathematics Department of the Faculty of Economics of University of Valencia since 2011. She graduated in Mathematical Sciences in 2002 and received her Ph.D. in Mathematics in 2007. In 2008, she obtained a position as lecturer at the Faculty of Economics and then she began her research on fuzzy optimization together with Dr. Carlos Ivorra and Dr. Vicente Liern.

Luiz Fernando Capretz is a Professor of Software Engineering and Assistant Dean (IT and e-Learning) at The University of Western Ontario, Canada. His present research interests include Software Engineering (SE), human factors in SE, software estimation, e-learning technologies, and software engineering education. He is an IEEE senior member, ACM distinguished member, MBTI certified practitioner, and Professional Engineer in Ontario (Canada). He holds a Ph.D. degree from University of Newcastle (UK), M.Sc. from Space Research Institute (INPE, Brazil), and B.Sc. from State University of Campinas (UNICAMP, Brazil) – all degrees in computer science.

Luís Cavique is an Assistant Professor of the Computer Science Section in the Department of Sciences and Technology at Universidade Aberta and Research member in LabMAg from Universidade de Lisboa. He worked in the Polytechnic Education System from 1991 to 2008, namely as Adjunct Professor in the Setubal and in the Lisbon Polytechnic Institute. He received the degree in Computer Science Engineering from the New University of Lisbon (FCT-UNL) in 1988, the M.Sc. degree in Operational Research and Systems Engineering from the Technical Lisbon University (IST-UTL) in 1994 and the Ph.D. degree in Systems Engineering from the Technical Lisbon University (IST-UTL) in 2002. His research areas are in the intersection of Computer Science and Systems Engineering, namely the Heuristic Optimization and the Data Mining.

María del Carmen Garrido received the MS degree in Computer Sciences from the University of Granada, Spain, in 1991, and PhD degree in Computer Sciences from the University of Murcia, Spain, in 1999. She is an Associate Professor in the Department of Information and Communications Engineering at the University of Murcia (Spain). She has published in the areas (research areas of interest) of Heuristics Algorithms in Uncertain Environments and Soft Computing applied to Hybrid Systems and Intelligent Data Analysis.

Marie-France Destain has a PhD in Agricultural Engineering. She is teaching Precision Agriculture in a Master of Environmental Science and Technology at University of Liege (Gembloux Agro-Bio Tech, Belgium). She is involved with the development of sensors, models and decision support systems aimed at managing crop inputs in an environmentally sensible manner. She is responsible of several national and international research projects related to engineering in the field of agro-biosystems. She is member of several European networks (ManuFuture-AET, ICT-Agri ERANET, MACSur).

Manuel Díaz-Madroñero is a Teaching Assistant in the Department of Business Management and a researcher at the Research Centre on Production Management and Engineering (CIGIP) at the Universitat Politècnica de València (Spain). He obtained a Masters Degree in Advanced Production Engineering, Logistics, and Supply Chain at the Universitat Politècnica de València in 2009. Mr. Díaz-Madroñero is currently doing his PhD dissertation on the integration of transport planning and MRP systems and extensions. His research interests lie in production planning, transport planning, supply chain management, and mathematical programming models under uncertainty.

Benjamin Dumont has an MSc in Environmental Science and Technology. He is working in the Department of Environmental Science and Technology at University of Liege (Gembloux Agro-Bio Tech, Belgium). He is responsible of a research project aimed to improve the fertilizers amount by modelling the crop growth, taking into account the real time information provided by networks of microsensors.

Raquel Martínez España graduated from Computer Engineering at the University of Murcia (Spain) in 2009. She received the master's degree in Information Technologies from University of Murcia in 2010. Currently, she is developing her PhD and she is a grant holder in Department of Information and Communications Engineering at the University of Murcia (Spain). Her current research areas include Heuristics Algorithms in Uncertain Environments and Soft Computing applied to Hybrid Systems and Intelligent Data Analysis.

Matthias Günther Andreas Funk graduated in 1988 from the University of Mannheim, Germany, in Mathematics and Computing. At the same university, he concluded in 1992 his Masters in Computer and a Ph.D. in Mathematics (Number Theory) in 2002. Since 1993, he teaches at the Department of Mathematics at the University of the Azores several units in the Informatics and Mathematics. He works in the scientific area of Artificial Intelligence, Game Theory, and the Theory of Numbers. He also researches topics of Portuguese Paremiology and Paremiografy since 1998, when he began to develop the database "Knowledge of Azorean Proverbs" with a thousand Azorean interviewees and more than twenty thousand Portuguese proverbs, whence resulted in several scientific publications. He participated in the organization of several international scientific meetings in IT and Popular Culture.

Jacques Ganoulis is a Professor of Hydraulics and Environmental Engineering at the Aristotle University of Thessaloniki, Greece, the Director of the University's Laboratory of Environmental Engineering and Planning and the Coordinator of the UNESCO Chair and Network INWEB (International Network of Water/Environment Centres for the Balkans) on "sustainable management of water and conflict resolution" www.inWeb.gr. He holds a PhD (Doctorat d'État) from the University of Toulouse (France) and has been a Visiting Professor at the Universities of Erlangen (Germany), McGill (Canada), Melbourne (Australia), and Paris VI (France). He has more than 25 years experience in Greece, Europe, and overseas on water resources management, environmental impact assessment and engineering risk analysis. He cooperates closely with UNESCO and has initiated several UNESCO projects in the Balkans, such as ISARM-Balkans and PCCP-Balkans. His research interests include risk-based water quality and flood management, multicriteria decision making, and fuzzy logic modeling. He has published more than 200 papers in scientific journals and conference proceedings, is the editor of 10 books.

Carlos Sierra Garriga received the M.S. degree in Industrial Engineering in 1992 and the Ph.D. degree in Project Engineering from the Technical University of Catalonia, Spain in 2002. He is a Professor in the Department of Project Engineering of the Technical University of Catalonia teaching Engineering Projects, Lighting, Basic design, energy auditing, and modeling techniques and visualization. Responsible Lighting Laboratory of the Technical University of Catalonia. Besides teaching, within the university, developing research and technology transfer to industry and administration, computer issues, lighting, environmental, electrical, energy, and design. He has been developing research projects, development, and transfer of technology for over 20 years, both nationally and internationally, with the government clients and private customers. He has collaborated in European projects in the design of lighting systems, new product development and designing master plans for lighting pilot installations and energy audits related to lighting fixtures He is a member of the Engineering Research Group Project: Design, sustainability and communication of the Technical University of Catalonia. His current scientific interests are Lighting, Efficiency Energy, Renewable Energy, Product Design, and Life Cycle Analysis.

Danny Ho is an independent management consultant and advisor for two startup companies. Prior to this, he held senior management and technical positions with Motorola Canada Limited, Nortel Networks Corporation, and IBM Canada Limited. He is also appointed as an Adjunct Research Professor at the Department of Software Engineering, Faculty of Engineering, the University of Western Ontario. His areas of special interest include software estimation, project management, object-oriented software development, and complexity analysis. He is currently a member of the Professional Engineers Ontario (PEO) and a Project Management Professional (PMP).

Carlos Ivorra is a professor of Mathematics at the Business Mathematics Department of the Faculty of Economics of University of Valencia since 2008. He graduated in Mathematical Sciences in 1991, and he began his teaching career the same year. In 1995, he received the Ph. D. in Mathematics from University of Valencia. His research interests are related to optimization on uncertain or vague environments.

Masoud Jenabi received his Bachelors of Science degree with honors in Industrial Engineering from Islamic Azad University of Qazvin in Islamic Republic of Iran in 2002. He, then, completed his Master of Science studies in Industrial Engineering at Amirkabir University of Technology in Islamic Republic of Iran in 2005. Now, he is pursuing the Doctor of Philosophy degree in Industrial Engineering at Amirkabir University of Technology. He has authored a book on Production Planning and Inventory Control. His research interests include Optimization Theory and its Applications in Production Planning and Control, Scheduling, Supply Chain Management, and Power Systems.

Mariano Jiménez is a Professor at the University of the Basque Country, Spain, where he teaches mathematics, operational research and fuzzy logic for business, finance and management. His principal research topics are fuzzy sets, fuzzy and standard goal programming and the applications of multicriteria analysis to support the decision making process in finance and management problems. He has published more than 30 articles in relevant international peer-review journals and in books of the most important international publishing companies.

Ioannis Kougias is a Civil Engineer currently working as a Researcher at the Division of Hydraulics and Environmental Engineering of the Department of Civil Engineering of the Aristotle University of Thessaloniki (A.U.Th.). He holds a PhD from the same University (2012), after implementing research on Water Engineering and Management with the use of Metaheuristic Optimization Algorithms. His PhD research has been funded by the Research Committee and praised with the "PhD Distinction Prize" of the A.U.Th. Among others, his scientific interests focus in the field of Hydrology (hydrological modeling, environmental flow regimes) and energy production (hydropower, hybrid energy production systems). Dr. Kougias has been content to follow a series of workshops, seminars, summer courses and international conferences and has published about 15 papers in journals, conference proceedings, and book chapters. Moreover, he acts as a reviewer in several scientific journals.

Vicente Liern is a professor in the Department of Mathematics for Economics and Business. He holds a degree in Mathematics and a PhD in Theoretical Physics from the University of Valencia. His research interests are Mathematical Physics, Optimization under Uncertainty Conditions and Mathematics Divulgation. He is currently editor of the journals Rect@ and Anales de ASEPUMA.

Juan Miguel Sánchez Lozano has been an Industrial Engineering from the Technical University of Cartagena since 2004 and has the Master in Renewable Energies title, Murcia 2010 and the European Doctorate in Renewable Energy from the Technical University of Cartagena, Murcia 2013. Currently he develops his work as a well-known professional in the field of engineering projects and he is also an Associate Professor in the Area of Graphic Expression in Engineering in the Graphic Expression Department at the Polytechnic University of Cartagena. He is a member of the Official College of Industrial Engineers of the Region of Murcia. He has published papers in scientific journals and he has more than ten publications in national and international conferences. His research is currently focused on decision making in Renewable Energy, Geographic Information Systems (GIS) and Cartography, multi criteria decision methods in engineering projects and fuzzy logic applied to multi criteria decision-making.

Ekananta Manalif is a management system and technology professional and independent researcher with more than ten years working experiences in the IT and Management Consulting field with focus on information system and strategic management system development. He obtained a Master of Engineering Science degree in Software Engineering from Western University Canada and Master of Science degree in Computer Science (Information System) from University of Indonesia. His research interest areas are information system development and software engineering, which includes the topics in software effort estimation, soft computing, and project management.

Majdi Mansouri has over five years of research and practical experiences in the area of systems engineering and signal processing. His work focuses on the utilization of applied mathematics and statistics concepts to develop data-driven techniques and algorithms for modeling, estimation and control, which can help improve process operations. In academia, he worked extensively on the utilization and development of Bayesian inference to improve filtering, modeling, and state estimation. Dr. Mansouri is the author of over 50 papers (20 international journals, 5 book chapters, and 25 international conferences).

Charles Mbohwa is an Associate Professor at the University of Johannesburg. He has previously been a senior lecturer in mechanical engineering at the University of Zimbabwe and a mechanical engineer at the National Railways of Zimbabwe. He has a Doctor of Engineering from Tokyo Metropolitan Institute of Technology, masters in operations management and manufacturing systems from the University of Nottingham and a bachelor of science (honours) in mechanical engineering from the University of Zimbabwe. He has been a British Council Scholar, Japan Foundation Fellow, a Heiwa Nakajima Fellow, a Kubota Foundation Fellow and a Fulbright Fellow. His research interests are in operations management, engineering management, energy systems and in sustainability assessment. He has published a book, 2 book chapters, and more than 120 academic papers.

Armando B. Mendes is an Assistant Professor in the Mathematical Department of the Azores University, Portugal, and belongs to the CEEAplA – Atlantic Center for Applied Economic Studies. In 2005, he had received a Ph.D. degree with a thesis titled "New Food Store Turnover Modeling" by the Lisbon Technical University (UTL – IST) in the domain of Systems Engineering; in 1997, he had prepared and discussed the master thesis titled "Modeling the Price Effect for High Consumption Products." He has been working and publishing in the fields of Operational Research and Systems Engineering. More recently, the research work has been focused in decision support systems and data mining.

Josefa Mula is a Senior Lecturer in operations management at the Universitat Politècnica de València. She is member of the scientific committee of the Research Centre on Production Management and Engineering (CIGIP). Her key research topics include production planning and control, supply chain management and uncertainty modelling. She has published (in collaboration) more than forty research papers in a number of leading journals. She is editor of the *Journal of Industrial Engineering and Management* and the *International Journal of Production Management and Engineering* and member of the editorial board of the *Journal of Industrial Engineering*.

Michael Mutingi is a Lecturer with the Faculty of Engineering and Technology at the University of Botswana, Botswana. He has professional experience as a Research Associate at the National University of Singapore, and a Lecturer in Industrial Engineering at the National University of Science and Technology, Zimbabwe. He obtained his MEng and BEng in Industrial Engineering from the National University of Science and Technology, Zimbabwe. Michael Mutingi is a PhD candidate at the University of Johannesburg, South Africa. His research interests are in supply chain management, manufacturing systems, and healthcare operations management. He also researches in naturally inspired meta-heuristics, system dynamics, and operations research. Michael Mutingi is a member of the Southern African Institution of Industrial Engineers (SA), and the System Dynamics Society (USA). He has published in various international journals, including *Computers & Industrial Engineering, Production Planning & Control, Journal of Intelligent Manufacturing, International Journal of Production Research*, and the *Journal of Industrial Engineering Computations*. In addition, he has published a couple of chapters in edited books.

Thomas Patsialis is a Rural and Survey Engineer of the Aristotle University of Thessaloniki (A.U.Th.) and a PhD Candidate at the Division of Hydraulics and Environmental Engineering of the Department of Civil Engineering, A.U.Th. His research interests include simulation and integrated water management in basin scale, reservoir management – flood protection and hydroelectric project design. His PhD research deals with the integrated investigation of the viability of small-scale hydroelectric projects and their installation in water basins and reservoirs in the area of Greece. Additionally, he is a member of the UNESCO Chair/International Network of Water-Environment Centers for the Balkans (INWEB). Mr. Patsialis works at "ESTIA Consulting and Engineering S.A.," a company active in the planning, development and management of energy projects and investments. He is Director of ESTIA's Laboratory, which specializes in stream-flow measurements and energy yield study/optimization of small-scale hydropower plants. In addition, he is very experienced in the environmental impact assessment of such plants and their licensing procedure, according to European Union's legislation.

Isis Torres Pérez graduated in Computer Engineering in High Polytecnic Institute (CUJAE) of Habana in 2008. She acts as Instructor in the Department of Software Engineering of the Faculty of Computer Engineering at this university. She obtained a master's degree in Applied Informatics in 2010. She is a member of the Research Group in Decision Models and Optimization (MODO) of the University of Granada and the Research Group on Artificial Intelligence (GRIAL) of the Faculty Computer Engineering in the CUJAE.

Raul Poler is Professor in Operations Management and Operations Research at the Universitat Politècnica de València. He received his PhD in Industrial Engineering in 1998. He is Director of the Research Centre on Production Management and Engineering (CIGIP). He has published a hundred of research papers in a number of leading journals and in several international conferences. He is member of several research associations as EurOMA, POMS, INTEROP-VLab, IFIP WG 5.8 Enterprise Interoperability and ADINGOR among other. His key research topics include Enterprise Modelling, Knowledge Management, Production Planning, and Control and Supply Chain Management.

Jorge Manuel Azevedo Santos is currently Assistant Professor at Departamento de Matemática da Universidade de Évora and a researcher at Research Centre in Mathematics and Applications. His main research interests are mathematical programming, graphs/networks and efficiency analysis. He is published several chapters in books in leading publishing companies as Springer and World Scientific. He has publications in international journals as the *International Journal of Services Technology and Management*. He is one of the three editors of *Efficiency Measures in the Agricultural Sector with Applications*, Springer. He is a referee for several journals: *Journal of The Operational Research Society, International Journal of Management & Decision Making, Multi-Criteria Decision Analysis, Investigação Operacional, International Journal of Business Performance Management, European Journal of Operations Research, Group Decision and Negotiation, American Journal of Applied Mathematics and Statistics*. He is also referee in McGraw-Hill and Springer.

Jamal Shahrabi received his Bachelors of Science degree with honors in Mechanical Engineering from Amirkabir University of Technology in Islamic Republic of Iran in 1990. He received his Master of Science degree in Industrial Engineering from the same university in 1993. In 2004, he earned his Doctor of Philosophy degree in Industrial Engineering from Dalhousie University, Canada. His doctoral dissertation focused on Risk-Based Spatial Analysis and was carried out under the guidance and supervision of Prof. Ronald Pelot. He is currently a faculty member in the Industrial Engineering Department at Amirkabir University of Technology. Dr. Shahrabi has authored 13 books and 14 papers in ISI-indexed journals. He is particularly interested in Data Mining and its Applications, Information Technology, Supply Chain Management, and Quality Control and Management.

Ali Zolghadr Shojai received his Bachelors of Science degree with honors in Applied Mathematics from Shahed University in Islamic Republic of Iran in 2005. Afterwards, he completed his Master of Science studies in Industrial Engineering at Amirkabir University of Technology in Islamic Republic of Iran in 2010. His Thesis work focused on Reverse Logistics Network Design. He has authored a book on Data Mining. His research interests include Supply Chain Management, Data Mining, Project Management, Knowledge Management, and Organizational Management.

Alejandro Rosete Suárez graduated as Systems Engineer in High Polytecnic Institute (CUJAE) of Habana in 1993, Ph.D. in Technical Sciences – Informatics in 2000. He is a Professor of the Facultad de Ingeniería Informática of CUJAE since 1993, and Titular Professor since 2007. He is Head of the Department of Artificial Intelligence and Computer Systems (DIAISI) of CUJAE since 2009. He has been invited professor in several universities such as Tec nológico de Monterrey in México, Universidad Peruana de CienciasAplicadas in Peru, Universidad Gabriel René Moreno in Bolivia, etc. He is a reviewer of some journals such as Computación y Sistemas (México); DYNA and Revista de Ingeniería de la Universidad de Antoioquia (Colombia); Revistas de Ingeniería Industrial, Revista Investigación Operacional and Revistas Cubana de Ciencias Informáticas (Cuba). He has also been reviewer of international conferences such Genetic and Evolutionary Computation Conferene (GECCO) in 1999 and 2000.

Ayeley Philippe Tchangani received ingenieur degree (1995) from Ecole Centrale de Lille, France, an MSc degree (1995) and a PhD degree (1999) from Université des Sciences et Technologies de Lille, France, in control and automation. After a postdoctoral fellowship at French South Africa Technical Institute in electronics (Pretoria, South Africa), he joined Université Toulouse III – IUT de Tarbes in 2001 where he is currently an associate professor. He holds a research position at Laboratoire Génie de Production (LGP) of Ecole Nationale d'Ingenieurs de Tarbes (ENIT) since 2003. Dr. Tchangani's current research interests are in decision analysis, uncertainty modeling and risk assessment and management. Results of his researches appeared in a number of international refereed journals; a list of his publications is available at http://publicationslist.org/tchangani. He regularly serves as Internal Program Committee (IPC) member of international conferences. Dr. Tchangani is a member of IEEE and MCDM societies.

Nicolaos Theodossiou, associate professor at the Division of Hydraulics and Environmental Engineering of the Department of Civil Engineering of the Aristotle University of Thessaloniki. His research activities include simulation and optimization in water resources management as well as protection and restoration of groundwater aquifers. He has been involved in the development of groundwater simulation models and he has applied a series of commercial and scientific models. He has also participated in a number of technical studies concerning water related works and their environmental impacts. He is a member of various important Greek national and international organisations concerning water resources, while he has been involved in the evaluation of research projects submitted under FP7. At the same time, he acts as a reviewer in the most significant journals and conferences. His published work includes about 50 papers and their scientific value is evaluated by more than 100 references. He has also participated in 20 research projects.

Daymi Morales Vega graduated in Computer Engineering in High Polytechnic Institute (CUJAE) of Habana in 2008 and received the master degree in Applied Informatics in 2010. Acts as Instructor teacher in Department of Software Engineering of the Faculty of Computer Engineering of the CUJAE. She is a Member of the Research Group in Decision Models and Optimization (MODO) of the University of Granada and the Research Group on Artificial Intelligence (GRIAL) of the Faculty of Computer Engineering of the CUJAE. Her research interest includes Soft Computing, Multicriteria Decision Making, and Metaheuristic, among others.

Justin Wong is a software developer at SAP Business Objects. He holds a Masters in Engineering Science (MESc) from the University of Western Ontario in software engineering and a Bachelor of Science in computer engineering from Queen's University. His areas of research include software estimation and soft computing.

Index

A

actors 217, 222, 224, 226, 236
AHP 80-81, 84-86, 199, 202-206, 212-214, 219, 222
alternatives 2, 37, 60, 63-64, 77, 80, 82-84, 142, 202-204, 214, 216-221, 223, 225, 227, 229-231, 237, 241-242
Ant Colony 1, 3-4, 8-10, 13, 16-18
Ant Colony Optimization 1, 3-4, 8-10, 17-18
attributes 40, 42-48, 50, 53, 55-56, 79-80, 85, 95, 217-220, 223-225, 230-232, 239-242, 278, 304

B

backfiring 260-263, 265-266, 270, 275-276, 278, 280
bipolarity 216, 219-222, 224, 234, 241-242
BOCR analysis 216, 220, 223, 225
Break Pressure Tank 59-60, 63, 71, 75

C

choquet integral 220-221, 223-224, 226, 231, 233
combinatorial optimization problem 42, 45, 245-246, 248, 251
complex decision 203, 216
contingency 88-89, 98-100, 105-110
Coverage 13, 139, 152-153, 281, 283-284, 288, 291, 312-313
Crisp Set 142, 159

D

data mining 38, 58, 314
Days-Off 139, 144, 159
decision-maker 19-21, 23, 31-33, 80, 203-205
decision making 13, 34-35, 37, 81, 84-87, 156, 162, 185, 201-203, 207, 213-214, 216-221, 230, 240-244, 255, 258

Decision Support 37, 90, 138, 156, 175-176, 195, 202, 213-214, 217, 220, 240, 242, 244, 257
Dynamic Problem 18

E

Ecological dynamic logistics 1-5
Ecological Logistics Problem 18
Ecological Vehicle 18
Efficient Frontier 23, 26-27, 29-31, 34, 37
Efficient Portfolio 27, 29-30, 37
Energy Sources 59, 61, 72, 199, 201
Environmental Data 60, 64, 112, 137
environmental factor 270, 272
Extended Kalman Filter (EKF) 112-113, 131, 137

F

feature selection 38, 40-41, 50, 55-57, 279
Fleet Composition 162-163, 177, 179-180
Forecasting 150, 181-198
function point 111, 260-263, 269-272, 275, 278-280
Fuzzy Arithmetic Operations 181, 183, 189, 198
Fuzzy Constraint Set 20, 23, 25, 256
Fuzzy Decision Variables 181, 183
Fuzzy Goal Set 20, 25
Fuzzy Linear Programming 35-36, 255-257
Fuzzy Logic 97, 111, 138, 140, 142, 160, 186, 242, 260, 263, 278, 280
fuzzy mathematical programming 35-36, 157, 185, 255-259
Fuzzy Model 25-27, 32, 35, 87, 147, 150, 152-155, 181, 183, 186, 192-193, 195
Fuzzy Nonlinear Programming 181, 183, 185-186, 188, 191, 193-195
fuzzy numbers 81-82, 181, 183, 186, 188-189, 195-196, 198-199, 209, 256
Fuzzy Optimization 19-21, 34-35, 37, 194, 255, 258-259

fuzzy rule 88, 267-268
Fuzzy Set Theory 19-20, 27, 33, 138, 140, 142, 156-158, 185, 196
fuzzy technique 88-89, 98
Fuzzy Triangular Numbers 181, 198-199

G

game theory 216-217, 219-222, 225, 241-244
Genetic Algorithm 73-74, 157, 161-163, 172, 176-180, 281, 283-284, 292, 299-300, 312-316
Global Satisfaction Level 21
greenhouse gases 199-201
Group Genetic Algorithm 161-163, 172, 176-178, 180

H

Harmony Search Algorithm 59-60, 64, 67-70, 72, 74-75
Heterogeneous Fleet 162-163, 176-180, 247-249, 284
heuristic information 1, 9, 11
Hydroelectricity 59-61, 75

I

Intermittent Demand 181-184, 186, 188, 194, 196-198
Inventory control 281, 283, 298, 312

K

Kyoto 199-201, 214

L

Leaf Area Index 112, 119-120, 131, 137
Linguistic Variables 77, 84, 142, 160
logical analysis of data 38, 40, 42, 44, 56-57
logical analysis of inconsistent data 38, 41, 46
Logistics Problem 5, 18, 259

M

Manpower 138-140, 143-145, 150, 154, 156-157, 159-160
Manpower Scheduling 138-140, 143-145, 156, 160
Max-Min ant system 9, 18
Mean Value of Fuzzy Values 198

Membership Functions 19, 24-27, 33, 111, 138, 140, 142, 147-148, 152-153, 155, 159, 263-268, 270
Metaheuristics 3, 8, 17, 75, 251-252, 254, 259, 284
Mini Hydroelectric Plants 75
Mixed-Integer Programming 37, 150, 153, 155
Multicriteria Decision Methods 76, 82
Multicriteria Decision Problem 76
Multi-objective evolutionary strategy algorithm 281, 283-284, 292, 301, 303
Multi-objective genetic algorithm 281, 283-284, 292, 299

N

neural network 97-98, 260, 263-264, 266, 269-270, 272, 278-279
Neuro-Fuzzy Function Point Backfiring Model 260
Nonlinear Programming 181, 183-186, 188, 190-195, 198

O

Optimal location 199, 202, 207

P

pareto optimality 83
Particle Filter (PF) 112-113, 131, 137
Pheromone 9-11, 18
P-Median Problem 19, 21-24, 28, 31-34, 36-37
Portfolio Selection Problem 19-20, 22-23, 25-29, 34-37, 157, 259
Possibility Theory 140
Product returns 281, 288, 297, 315
programming language level 262-263, 265-267, 269-270, 272, 275, 278
proverbs 38-41, 50, 52-56, 58

R

ranking 76-77, 80-84, 86, 204, 210, 216-217, 242
Remanufacturing 281-291, 293, 309, 313-316
renewable energy sources 59, 61, 72, 200
Reverse logistics network design 281, 283-284, 292-293, 300, 302-303, 309, 312-316
risk assessment 88-90, 92, 94, 97-100, 102, 104, 109-111
risk management 88-94, 97, 109-111, 162, 279
rough sets 38, 40-44, 46-47, 56-58, 242

S

satisficing game 219-222, 225, 241-242
Semicontinuous variable constraints 19
SERVQUAL 77-80, 83, 86
set covering problem 41, 45, 47-49
Social choice 216-217, 221, 228, 241
social influence 219-220, 222, 232-234, 241
software estimation 106, 110, 260-261, 280
software project 88-92, 94-95, 97-100, 104-105, 109-111, 264, 280
Soil Moisture 112, 114, 119, 131, 136-137
States and Parameters Estimation 137
Syntetos and Boylan 181, 186

T

Time Series 182-185, 191-195, 197-198
transition rule 9, 11
Truck and Trailer Routing Problem 245-246, 248-250, 257-259
Types of Turbines 65, 75

U

Unscented Kalman Filter (UKF) 112-113, 131, 137

V

Variational Filter (VF) 137
Vehicle Routing 1, 3, 5-8, 12, 17-18, 161, 163, 175-180, 245-248, 250, 257-259, 315
Vehicle Routing Problem 3, 17, 161, 163, 175-180, 245-248, 250, 257-259

W

water engineering 59, 70
water supply network 59, 62-63, 71-72
Water Turbine 59, 75
Wind farms 199, 201-203, 207, 209-211, 214